17th SIGMORPHON Workshop on Computational Research in Phonetics Phonology, and Morphology (SIGMORPHON 2020)

Online
10 July 2020

ISBN: 978-1-7138-1390-3

17th SIGMORPHON Workshop on Computational Research in Phonetics Phonology, and Morphology (SIGMORPHON 2020)

Online
10 July 2020

SIGMORPHON 2020

The 17th SIGMORPHON Workshop on Computational Research in Phonetics Phonology, and Morphology

Proceedings of the Workshop

July 10, 2020

Google

Preface

Welcome to the 17th SIGMORPHON Workshop on Computational Research in Phonetics, Phonology, and Morphology, to be held on July 10, 2020 as part of a virtual ACL. The workshop aims to bring together researchers interested in applying computational techniques to problems in morphology, phonology, and phonetics. Our program this year highlights the ongoing and important interaction between work in computational linguistics and work in theoretical linguistics. This year, work in both theoretical phonology and computational morphology were strongly represented in the workshop submissions. We received 14 submissions, and after a competitive reviewing process, we accepted 8. The workshop is privileged to present four invited talks this year, all from very respected members of the SIGMORPHON community.

This year also marks the fifth iteration of the SIGMORPHON Shared Task. Unlike previous years, this year, we hosted three distinct tasks:

Task 0: SIGMORPHON's fifth installment of its inflection generation shared task focuses on languages that are typologically diverse from languages in our previous tasks. Many of these languages are extremely low-resource. In this edition, we are specifically interested in inflection generation systems' ability to generalize to new languages, including languages that are typologically distinct. For example, if you have a neural network architecture that works well for a sample of Indo-European languages, should you expect the same architecture to also work well for Tupi–Guarani languages (where nouns are "declined" for tense)?

Task 1: This new task, the first of its kind at SIGMORPHON, focuses on grapheme-to-phoneme conversion. This technology is a key component of speech recognition and synthesis engines, but much of the existing published research is either limited to a small number of closely related languages/scripts, or uses proprietary data sets, limiting replicability. The training and development data consists of words and corresponding IPA pronunciations extracted from Wiktionary, a free online encyclopedia, in 15 languages and scripts. 9 teams submitted a total of 23 different systems.

Task 2: Task 2 fills the gap between recent SIGMORPHON shared tasks on morphological inflection learned from limited training data and completely unsupervised morphological generation by proposing the task of unsupervised morphological paradigm completion. The goal is to generate complete inflection tables exclusively from raw text and a lemma list for a known part of speech. 3 teams submitted a total of 7 different systems to tackle this new task.

We are grateful to the program committee for their careful and thoughtful reviews of the papers submitted this year. Likewise, we are thankful to the shared task organizers for their hard work in preparing the shared tasks. We are looking forward to a workshop covering a wide range of topics, and we hope for lively discussions.

Garrett Nicolai
Kyle Gorman
Ryan Cotterell

Organizers:

Garrett Nicolai (University of British Columbia, Canada)
Kyle Gorman (The Graduate Center, City University of New York, USA)
Ryan Cotterell (ETH Zürich, Switzerland)

Program Committee:

Çağrı Çöltekin (University of Tübingen, Germany)
Daniel Dakota (Indiana University, USA)
Ewan Dunbar (Université Paris Diderot, France)
Micha Elsner (The Ohio State University, USA)
Jeffrey Heinz (Stony Brook University, USA)
Mans Hulden (University of Colorado, USA)
Adam Jardine (Rutgers University, USA)
Christo Kirov (Google AI, USA)
Greg Kondrak (University of Alberta, Canada)
Sandra Kübler (Indiana University, USA)
Andrew Lamont (University of Massachusetts Amherst, USA)
Fred Mailhot (Dialpad, Inc., Canada)
Arya D. McCarthy (Johns Hopkins University, USA)
Kemal Oflazer (CMU Qatar, Qatar)
Jeff Parker (Brigham Young University, USA)
Gerald Penn (University of Toronto, Canada)
Jelena Prokic (Ludwig Maximilian University of Munich, Germany)
Mohamad Salameh (Huawei, Canada)
Miikka Silfverberg (University of British Columbia, Canada)
Kairit Sirts (University of Tartu, Estonia)
Kenneth Steimel (Indiana University, USA)
Francis Tyers (Indiana University, USA)
Ivan Vulić (University of Cambridge, United Kingdom)
Ekaterina Vylomova (University of Melbourne, Australia)
Anssi Yli-Jyrä (University of Helsinki, Finland)
Kristine Yu (University of Massachusetts Amherst, USA)

Shared Task Organizers:

Task 0:
Adina Williams (Facebook AI Research NYC, USA)
Antonios Anastasopoulos (Carnegie Mellon University, USA)
Christo Kirov (Google Research NYC, USA)
Ekaterina Vylomova (University of Melbourne, Australia)
Eleanor Chodroff (University of York, UK)
Elizabeth Salesky (Johns Hopkins University, USA)
Garrett Nicolai (University of British Columbia, Canada)
Mans Hulden (University of Colorado Boulder, USA)
Miikka Silfverberg (University of British Columbia, Canada)
Ryan Cotterell (ETH Zürich, Switzerland)
Sabrina Mielke (Johns Hopkins University, USA)
Shijie Wu (Johns Hopkins University, USA)
Andrej Krizhanovsky (Karelian Research Centre, Russia)
Edoardo Ponti (University of Cambridge, UK)
Elena Klyachko (National Research University Higher School of Economics, Russia)
Francis Tyers (Indiana University, US)
Hilaria Cruz (University of Louisville, US)
Ilya Yegorov (Lomonosov Moscow State University, Russia)
Irene Nikkarinen (University of Cambridge, UK)
Jennifer White (University of Cambridge, UK)
Josef Valvoda (University of Cambridge, UK)
Lucas Torroba Hennigen (University of Cambridge, UK)
Natalia Krizhanovsky (Karelian Research Centre, Russia)
Paula Czarnowska (University of Cambridge, UK)
Ran Zmigrod (University of Cambridge, UK)
Rowan Hall Maudslay (University of Cambridge, UK)
Svetlana Toldova (National Research University Higher School of Economics, Russia)
Tiago Pimentel (University of Cambridge, UK)

Task 1:
Kyle Gorman (Graduate Center, City University of New York, USA)
Lucas F. E. Ashby (Graduate Center, City University of New York, USA)
Aaron Goyzueta (Graduate Center, City University of New York, USA)
Arya D. McCarthy (Johns Hopkins University, USA)
Shijie Wu (Johns Hopkins University, USA)
Daniel You (Jericho High School, USA)

Task 2:
Arya McCarthy (Johns Hopkins University, USA)
Katharina Kann (University of Colorado Boulder, USA)
Garrett Nicolai (University of British Columbia, Canada)
Mans Hulden (University of Colorado Boulder, USA)
Chen Xia (Carnegie Mellon University, USA)
Huiming Jin (Carnegie Mellon University, USA)
Liwei Cai (Carnegie Mellon University, USA)
Yihui Peng (Carnegie Mellon University, USA)

Invited Speakers:

Jane Chandlee, (Haverford College, USA)
Bruce Hayes, (University of California, Los Angeles, USA)
Rob Malouf, (San Diego State University, USA)
Clara Vania (New York University, USA)

Table of Contents

Conference Program

July 10, 2020

08:30–10:30   **Morning Session**

08:30–09:30   *Invited Talk: On Understanding Character-level Models for Representing Morphology*
Clara Vania, NYU

09:30–10:30   *Invited Talk: Recursive Schemes for Phonological Analysis*
Jane Chandlee, Haverford College

10:30–10:45   **Break**

10:45–12:30   **Shared Task**

10:45–11:00   *SIGMORPHON 2020 Shared Task 0: Typologically Diverse Morphological Inflection*
Ekaterina Vylomova, Jennifer White, Elizabeth Salesky, Sabrina J. Mielke, Shijie Wu, Edoardo Maria Ponti, Rowan Hall Maudslay, Ran Zmigrod, Josef Valvoda, Svetlana Toldova, Francis Tyers, Elena Klyachko, Ilya Yegorov, Natalia Krizhanovsky, Paula Czarnowska, Irene Nikkarinen, Andrew Krizhanovsky, Tiago Pimentel, Lucas Torroba Hennigen, Christo Kirov, Garrett Nicolai, Adina Williams, Antonios Anastasopoulos, Hilaria Cruz, Eleanor Chodroff, Ryan Cotterell, Miikka Silfverberg and Mans Hulden

11:00–11:15   *The SIGMORPHON 2020 Shared Task on Multilingual Grapheme-to-Phoneme Conversion*
Kyle Gorman, Lucas F.E. Ashby, Aaron Goyzueta, Arya McCarthy, Shijie Wu and Daniel You

11:15–11:30   *The SIGMORPHON 2020 Shared Task on Unsupervised Morphological Paradigm Completion*
Katharina Kann, Arya D. McCarthy, Garrett Nicolai and Mans Hulden

11:30–12:30   *Shared Task Poster Session*
Multiple

    One-Size-Fits-All Multilingual Models
Ben Peters and André F. T. Martins

    Ensemble Self-Training for Low-Resource Languages: Grapheme-to-Phoneme Conversion and Morphological Inflection
Xiang Yu, Ngoc Thang Vu and Jonas Kuhn

    The CMU-LTI submission to the SIGMORPHON 2020 Shared Task 0: Language-Specific Cross-Lingual Transfer
Nikitha Murikinati and Antonios Anastasopoulos

CLUZH at SIGMORPHON 2020 Shared Task on Multilingual Grapheme-to-Phoneme Conversion
Peter Makarov and Simon Clematide

The UniMelb Submission to the SIGMORPHON 2020 Shared Task 0: Typologically Diverse Morphological Inflection
Andreas Scherbakov

Data Augmentation for Transformer-based G2P
Zach Ryan and Mans Hulden

12:30–14:00   Lunch

14:00–15:06   Paper Session

14:00–14:10   *Transliteration for Cross-Lingual Morphological Inflection*
Nikitha Murikinati, Antonios Anastasopoulos and Graham Neubig

14:11–14:21   *Evaluating Neural Morphological Taggers for Sanskrit*
Ashim Gupta, Amrith Krishna, Pawan Goyal and Oliver Hellwig

14:22–14:32   *Getting the ##life out of living: How Adequate Are Word-Pieces for Modelling Complex Morphology?*
Stav Klein and Reut Tsarfaty

14:33–14:43   *Induced Inflection-Set Keyword Search in Speech*
Oliver Adams, Matthew Wiesner, Jan Trmal, Garrett Nicolai and David Yarowsky

14:44–14:54   *Representation Learning for Discovering Phonemic Tone Contours*
Bai Li, Jing Yi Xie and Frank Rudzicz

14:55–15:05   *Joint learning of constraint weights and gradient inputs in Gradient Symbolic Computation with constrained optimization*
Max Nelson

15:06–15:30   Best Paper Session

15:06–15:18   *In search of isoglosses: continuous and discrete language embeddings in Slavic historical phonology*
Chundra Cathcart and Florian Wandl

15:18–15:30   *Multi-Tiered Strictly Local Functions*
Phillip Burness and Kevin McMullin

15:30–16:00   Break

16:00–18:00   Afternoon Session

16:00–17:00   *Invited Talk: Inflectional data science and human/computer-aided linguistic analysis*
Robert Malouf, San Diego State University

Invited Talk: Modeling failure in morphophonological learning
Bruce Hayes, UCLA

SIGMORPHON 2020 Shared Task 0: Typologically Diverse Morphological Inflection

Ekaterina Vylomova[ə] Jennifer White[ſ] Elizabeth Salesky[3] Sabrina J. Mielke[3] Shijie Wu[3]
Edoardo Ponti[ſ] Rowan Hall Maudslay[ſ] Ran Zmigrod[ſ] Josef Valvoda[ſ] Svetlana Toldova[ε]
Francis Tyers[I,ε] Elena Klyachko[ε] Ilya Yegorov[ɱ] Natalia Krizhanovsky[ʁ] Paula Czarnowska[ſ]
Irene Nikkarinen[ſ] Andrew Krizhanovsky[ʁ] Tiago Pimentel[ſ] Lucas Torroba Hennigen[ſ]
Christo Kirov[ʁ] Garrett Nicolai[6] Adina Williams[Φ] Antonios Anastasopoulos[ǂ]
Hilaria Cruz[Λ] Eleanor Chodroff[ϒ] Ryan Cotterell[ſ,ð] Miikka Silfverberg[6] Mans Hulden[χ]

[ə]University of Melbourne [ſ]University of Cambridge [3]Johns Hopkins University
[ε]Higher School of Economics [ɱ]Moscow State University [ʁ]Karelian Research Centre
[ʁ]Google AI [6]University of British Columbia [Φ]Facebook AI Research
[ǂ]Carnegie Mellon University [I]Indiana University [Λ]University of Louisville
[ϒ]University of York [ð]ETH Zürich [χ]University of Colorado Boulder

ekaterina.vylomova@unimelb.edu.au   ryan.cotterell@ethz.inf.ch

Abstract

A broad goal in natural language processing (NLP) is to develop a system that has the capacity to process any natural language. Most systems, however, are developed using data from just one language such as English. The SIGMORPHON 2020 shared task on morphological reinflection aims to investigate systems' ability to generalize across typologically distinct languages, many of which are low resource. Systems were developed using data from 45 languages and just 5 language families, fine-tuned with data from an additional 45 languages and 10 language families (13 in total), and evaluated on all 90 languages. A total of 22 systems (19 neural) from 10 teams were submitted to the task. All four winning systems were neural (two monolingual transformers and two massively multilingual RNN-based models with gated attention). Most teams demonstrate utility of data hallucination and augmentation, ensembles, and multilingual training for low-resource languages. Non-neural learners and manually designed grammars showed competitive and even superior performance on some languages (such as Ingrian, Tajik, Tagalog, Zarma, Lingala), especially with very limited data. Some language families (Afro-Asiatic, Niger-Congo, Turkic) were relatively easy for most systems and achieved over 90% mean accuracy while others were more challenging.

1 Introduction

Human language is marked by considerable diversity around the world. Though the world's languages share many basic attributes (e.g., Swadesh, 1950 and more recently, List et al., 2016), grammatical features, and even abstract implications (proposed in Greenberg, 1963), each language nevertheless has a unique evolutionary trajectory that is affected by geographic, social, cultural, and other factors. As a result, the surface form of languages varies substantially. The morphology of languages can differ in many ways: Some exhibit rich grammatical case systems (e.g., 12 in Erzya and 24 in Veps) and mark possessiveness, others might have complex verbal morphology (e.g., Oto-Manguean languages; Palancar and Léonard, 2016) or even "decline" nouns for tense (e.g., Tupi–Guarani languages). Linguistic typology is the discipline that studies these variations by means of a systematic comparison of languages (Croft, 2002; Comrie, 1989). Typologists have defined several dimensions of morphological variation to classify and quantify the degree of cross-linguistic variation. This comparison can be challenging as the categories are based on studies of known languages and are progressively refined with documentation of new languages (Haspelmath, 2007). Nevertheless, to understand the potential range of morphological variation, we take a closer look at three dimensions here: fusion, inflectional synthesis, and position of case affixes (Dryer and Haspelmath, 2013).

Fusion, our first dimension of variation, refers to the degree to which morphemes bind to one another in a phonological word (Bickel and Nichols, 2013b). Languages range from strictly isolating (i.e., each morpheme is its own phonological word) to concatenative (i.e., morphemes

1

Proceedings of the Seventeenth SIGMORPHON Workshop on Computational Research in Phonetics, Phonology, and Morphology, pages 1–39
Online, July 10, 2020. ©2020 Association for Computational Linguistics
https://doi.org/10.18653/v1/P17

bind together within a phonological word); non-linearities such as ablaut or tonal morphology can also be present. From a geographic perspective, isolating languages are found in the Sahel Belt in West Africa, Southeast Asia and the Pacific. Ablaut–concatenative morphology and tonal morphology can be found in African languages. Tonal–concatenative morphology can be found in Mesoamerican languages (e.g., Oto-Manguean). Concatenative morphology is the most common system and can be found around the world. Inflectional synthesis, the second dimension considered, refers to whether grammatical categories like tense, voice or agreement are expressed as affixes (synthetic) or individual words (analytic) (Bickel and Nichols, 2013c). Analytic expressions are common in Eurasia (except the Pacific Rim, and the Himalaya and Caucasus mountain ranges), whereas synthetic expressions are used to a high degree in the Americas. Finally, affixes can variably surface as prefixes, suffixes, infixes, or circumfixes (Dryer, 2013). Most Eurasian and Australian languages strongly favor suffixation, and the same holds true, but to a lesser extent, for South American and New Guinean languages (Dryer, 2013). In Mesoamerican languages and African languages spoken below the Sahara, prefixation is dominant instead.

These are just three dimensions of variation in morphology, and the cross-linguistic variation is already considerable. Such cross-lingual variation makes the development of natural language processing (NLP) applications challenging. As Bender (2009, 2016) notes, many current architectures and training and tuning algorithms still present language-specific biases. The most commonly used language for developing NLP applications is English. Along the above dimensions, English is productively concatenative, a mixture of analytic and synthetic, and largely suffixing in its inflectional morphology. With respect to languages that exhibit inflectional morphology, English is relatively impoverished.[1] Importantly, English is just one morphological system among many. A larger goal of natural language processing is that the system work for *any* presented language. If an NLP system is trained on just one language, it could be missing important flexibility in its ability to account for cross-linguistic morphological variation.

In this year's iteration of the SIGMORPHON shared task on morphological reinflection, we specifically focus on typological diversity and aim to investigate systems' ability to generalize across typologically distinct languages many of which are low-resource. For example, if a neural network architecture works well for a sample of Indo-European languages, should the same architecture also work well for Tupi–Guarani languages (where nouns are "declined" for tense) or Austronesian languages (where verbal morphology is frequently prefixing)?

2   Task Description

The 2020 iteration of our task is similar to CoNLL-SIGMORPHON 2017 (Cotterell et al., 2017) and 2018 (Cotterell et al., 2018) in that participants are required to design a model that learns to generate inflected forms from a lemma and a set of morphosyntactic features that derive the desired target form. For each language we provide a separate training, development, and test set. More historically, all of these tasks resemble the classic "wug"-test that Berko (1958) developed to test child and human knowledge of English nominal morphology.

Unlike the task from earlier years, this year's task proceeds in three phases: a Development Phase, a Generalization Phase, and an Evaluation Phase, in which each phase introduces previously unseen data. The task starts with the **Development Phase**, which was an elongated period of time (about two months), during which participants *develop* a model of morphological inflection. In this phase, we provide training and development splits for 45 languages representing the Austronesian, Niger-Congo, Oto-Manguean, Uralic and Indo-European language families. Table 1 provides details on the languages. The **Generalization Phase** is a short period of time (it started about a week before the Evaluation Phase) during which participants fine-tune their models on new data. At the start of the phase, we provide training and development splits for 45 new languages where approximately half are genetically related (belong to the same family) and half are genetically unrelated (are isolates or belong to a different family) to the languages presented in the Development Phase. More specifically, we introduce (surprise) languages from Afro-Asiatic, Algic, Dravidian, Indo-European, Niger-Congo, Sino-Tibetan,

---

[1] Note that many languages exhibit no inflectional morphology e.g., Mandarin Chinese, Yoruba, etc.: Bickel and Nichols (2013a).

Siouan, Songhay, Southern Daly, Tungusic, Turkic, Uralic, and Uto-Aztecan families. See Table 2 for more details.

Finally, test splits for all 90 languages are released in the **Evaluation Phase**. During this phase, the models are evaluated on held-out forms. Importantly, the languages from both previous phases are evaluated simultaneously. This way, we evaluate the extent to which models (especially those with shared parameters) overfit to the development data: a model based on the morphological patterning of the Indo-European languages may end up with a bias towards suffixing and will struggle to learn prefixing or infixation.

3 Meet our Languages

In the 2020 shared task we cover 15 language families: Afro-Asiatic, Algic, Austronesian, Dravidian, Indo-European, Niger-Congo, Oto-Manguean, Sino-Tibetan, Siouan, Songhay, Southern Daly, Tungusic, Turkic, Uralic, and Uto-Aztecan.[2] Five language families were used for the Development phase while ten were held out for the Generalization phase. Tab. 1 and Tab. 2 provide information on the languages, their families, and sources of data. In the following section, we provide an overview of each language family's morphological system.

3.1 Afro-Asiatic

The Afro-Asiatic language family, consisting of six branches and over 300 languages, is among the largest language families in the world. It is mainly spoken in Northern, Western and Central Africa as well as West Asia and spans large modern languages such as Arabic, in addition to ancient languages like Biblical Hebrew. Similarly, some of its languages have a long tradition of written form, while others have yet to incorporate a writing system. The six branches differ most notably in typology and syntax, with the Chadic language being the main source of differences, which has sparked discussion of the division of the family (Frajzyngier, 2018). For example, in the Egyptian and Semitic branches, the root of a verb may not contain vowels, while this is allowed in Chadic. Although only four of the six branches, excluding Chadic and Omotic, use a prefix and suffix in conjugation when adding a subject to a verb, it is con-

sidered an important characteristic of the family. In addition, some of the families in the phylum use tone to encode tense, modality and number among others. However, all branches use objective and passive suffixes. Markers of tense are generally simple, whereas aspect is typically distinguished with more elaborate systems.

3.2 Algic

The Algic family embraces languages native to North America—more specifically the United States and Canada—and contain three branches. Of these, our sample contains Cree, the language from the largest genus, Algonquian, from which most languages are now extinct. The Algonquian genus is characterized by its concatenative morphology. Cree morphology is also concatenative and suffixing. It distinguishes between impersonal and non-impersonal verbs and presents four apparent declension classes among non-impersonal verbs.

3.3 Austronesian

The Austronesian family of languages is largely comprised of languages from the Greater Central Philippine and Oceanic regions. They are characterized by limited morphology, mostly prefixing in nature. Additionally, tense–aspect affixes are predominantly seen as prefixes, though some suffixes are used. In the general case, verbs do not mark number, person, or gender. In Māori, verbs may be suffixed with a marker indicating the passive voice. This marker takes the form of one of twelve endings. These endings are difficult to predict as the language has undergone a loss of word-final consonants and there is no clear link between a stem and the passive suffix that it employs (Harlow, 2007).

3.4 Dravidian

The family of Dravidian languages comprises several languages which are primarily spoken across Southern India and Northern Sri Lanka, with over 200 million speakers. The shared task includes Kannada and Telugu. Dravidian languages primarily use the SOV word order. They are agglutinative, and primarily use suffixes. A Dravidian verb indicates voice, number, tense, aspect, mood and person, through the affixation of multiple suffixes. Nouns indicate number, gender and case.

---

[2]The data splits are available at `https://github.com/sigmorphon2020/task0-data/`

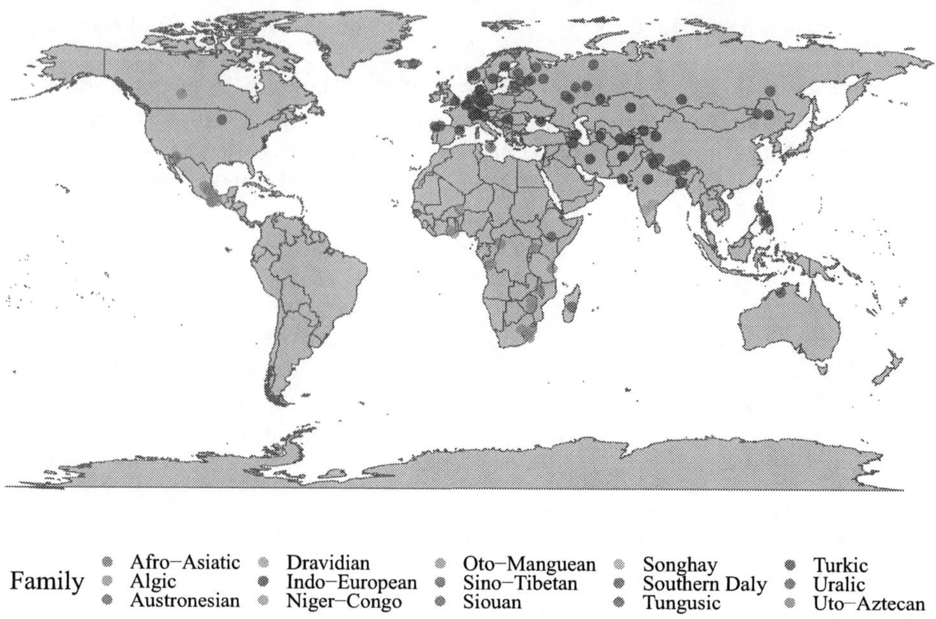

Figure 1: Languages in our sample colored by family.

3.5 Indo-European

Languages in the Indo-European family are native to most of Europe and a large part of Asia—with our sample including languages from the genera: Germanic, Indic, Iranian, and Romance. This is (arguably) the most well studied language family, containing a few of the highest-resource languages in the world.

Romance The Romance genus comprises of a set of fusional languages evolved from Latin. They traditionally originated in Southern and Southeastern Europe, though they are presently spoken in other continents such Africa and the Americas. Romance languages mark tense, person, number and mood in verbs, and gender and number in nouns. Inflection is primarily achieved through suffixes, with some verbal person syncretism and suppletion for high-frequency verbs. There is some morphological variation within the genus, such as French, which exhibits comparatively less inflection, and Romanian has comparatively more—it still marks case.

Germanic The Germanic genus comprises several languages which originated in Northern and Northwestern Europe, and today are spoken in many parts of the world. Verbs in Germanic languages mark tense and mood, in many languages person and number are also marked, predominantly through suffixation. Some Germanic languages exhibit widespread Indo-European ablaut. The gendering of nouns differs between Germanic languages: German nouns can be masculine, feminine or neuter, while English nouns are not marked for gender. In Danish and Swedish, historically masculine and feminine nouns have merged to form one common gender, so nouns are either common or neuter. Marking of case also differs between the languages: German nouns have one of four cases and this case is marked in articles and adjectives as well as nouns and pronouns, while English does not mark noun case (although Old English, which also appears in our language sample, does).

Indo-Iranian The Indo-Iranian genus contains languages spoken in Iran and across the Indian subcontinent. Over 1.5 billion people worldwide speak an Indo-Iranian language. Within the Indo-European family, Indo-Iranian languages belong to the Satem group of languages. Verbs in Indo-Iranian languages indicate tense, aspect, mood, number and person. In languages such as Hindi verbs can also express levels of formality. Noun gender is present in some Indo-Iranian languages, such as Hindi, but absent in languages such as Persian. Nouns generally are marked for case.

Development Family	Genus	ISO 639-3	Language	Source of Data
Austronesian	Barito	mlg (plt)	Malagasy	Kasahorow (2015a)
	Greater Central Philippine	ceb	Cebuano	Reyes (2015)
	Greater Central Philippine	hil	Hiligaynon	Santos (2018)
	Greater Central Philippine	tgl	Tagalog	NIU (2017)
	Oceanic	mao (mri)	Māori	Moorfield (2019)
Indo-European	Germanic	ang	Old English	UniMorph
	Germanic	dan	Danish	UniMorph
	Germanic	deu	German	UniMorph
	Germanic	eng	English	UniMorph
	Germanic	frr	North Frisian	UniMorph
	Germanic	gmh	Middle High German	UniMorph
	Germanic	isl	Icelandic	UniMorph
	Germanic	nld	Dutch	UniMorph
	Germanic	nob	Norwegian Bokmål	UniMorph
	Germanic	swe	Swedish	UniMorph
Niger-Congo	Bantoid	kon (kng)	Kongo	Kasahorow (2016)
	Bantoid	lin	Lingala	Kasahorow (2014a)
	Bantoid	lug	Luganda	Namono (2018)
	Bantoid	nya	Chewa	Kasahorow (2019a)
	Bantoid	sot	Sotho	Kasahorow (2020)
	Bantoid	swa (swh)	Swahili	Kasahorow (2012b)
	Bantoid	zul	Zulu	Kasahorow (2015b)
	Kwa	aka	Akan	Imbeah (2012)
	Kwa	gaa	Gã	Kasahorow (2012a)
Oto-Manguean	Amuzgoan	azg	San Pedro Amuzgos Amuzgo	Feist and Palancar (2015)
	Chichimec	pei	Chichimeca-Jonaz	Feist and Palancar (2015)
	Chinantecan	cpa	Tlatepuzco Chinantec	Feist and Palancar (2015)
	Mixtecan	xty	Yoloxóchitl Mixtec	Feist and Palancar (2015)
	Otomian	ote	Mezquital Otomi	Feist and Palancar (2015)
	Otomian	otm	Sierra Otomi	Feist and Palancar (2015)
	Zapotecan	cly	Eastern Chatino of San Juan Quiahije	Cruz et al. (2020)
	Zapotecan	ctp	Eastern Chatino of Yaitepec	Feist and Palancar (2015)
	Zapotecan	czn	Zenzontepec Chatino	Feist and Palancar (2015)
	Zapotecan	zpv	Chichicapan Zapotec	Feist and Palancar (2015)
Uralic	Finnic	est	Estonian	UniMorph
	Finnic	fin	Finnish	UniMorph
	Finnic	izh	Ingrian	UniMorph
	Finnic	krl	Karelian	Zaytseva et al. (2017)
	Finnic	liv	Livonian	UniMorph
	Finnic	vep	Veps	Zaytseva et al. (2017)
	Finnic	vot	Votic	UniMorph
	Mari	mhr	Meadow Mari	Arkhangelskiy et al. (2012)
	Mordvin	mdf	Moksha	Arkhangelskiy et al. (2012)
	Mordvin	myv	Erzya	Arkhangelskiy et al. (2012)
	Saami	sme	Northern Sami	UniMorph

Table 1: Development languages used in the shared task.

3.6 Niger–Congo

Our language sample includes two genera from the Niger–Congo family, namely Bantoid and Kwa languages. These have mostly exclusively concatenative fusion, and single exponence in verbal tense–aspect–mood. The inflectional synthesis of verbs is moderately high, e.g. with 4-5 classes per word in Swahili and Zulu. The locus of marking is inconsistent (it falls on both heads and dependents), and most languages are are predominantly prefixing. Full and partial reduplication is attested in most languages. Verbal person–number markers tend to be syncretic.

As for nominal classes, Bantoid languages are characterized by a large amount of grammatical genders (often more than 5) assigned based on both semantic and formal rules, whereas some Akan languages (like Ewe) lack a gender system. Plural tends to be always expressed by affixes or other morphological means. Case marking is generally absent or minimal. As for verbal classes, aspect is grammaticalized in Akhan (Kwa) and Zulu (Bantoid), but not in Luganda and Swahili (Bantoid). Both past and future tenses are inflectional in Bantoid languages. 2-3 degrees of remoteness can be distinguished in Zulu and Luganda, but not in Swahili. On the other hand, Akan (Kwa) has no opposition between past and non-past. There are

Generalization (Surprise)

Family	Genus	ISO 639-3	Language	Source of Data
Afro-Asiatic	Semitic	mlt	Maltese	UniMorph
	Lowland East Cushitic	orm	Oromo	Kasahorow (2017)
	Semitic	syc	Syriac	UniMorph
Algic	Algonquian	cre	Plains Cree	Hunter (1923)
Tungusic	Tungusic	evn	Evenki	Klyachko et al. (2020)
Turkic	Turkic	aze (azb)	Azerbaijani	UniMorph
	Turkic	bak	Bashkir	UniMorph
	Turkic	crh	Crimean Tatar	UniMorph
	Turkic	kaz	Kazakh	Nabiyev (2015); Turkicum (2019a)
	Turkic	kir	Kyrgyz	Aytnatova (2016)
	Turkic	kjh	Khakas	UniMorph
	Turkic	tuk	Turkmen	Abdulin (2016); US Embassy (2018)
	Turkic	uig	Uyghur	Kadeer (2016)
	Turkic	uzb	Uzbek	Abdullaev (2016); Turkicum (2019b)
Dravidian	Southern Dravidian	kan	Kannada	UniMorph
	South-Central Dravidian	tel	Telugu	UniMorph
Indo-European	Indic	ben	Bengali	UniMorph
	Indic	hin	Hindi	UniMorph
	Indic	san	Sanskrit	UniMorph
	Indic	urd	Urdu	UniMorph
	Iranian	fas (pes)	Persian	UniMorph
	Iranian	pus (pst)	Pashto	UniMorph
	Iranian	tgk	Tajik	UniMorph
	Romance	ast	Asturian	UniMorph
	Romance	cat	Catalan	UniMorph
	Romance	frm	Middle French	UniMorph
	Romance	fur	Friulian	UniMorph
	Romance	glg	Galician	UniMorph
	Romance	lld	Ladin	UniMorph
	Romance	vec	Venetian	UniMorph
	Romance	xno	Anglo-Norman	UniMorph
	West Germanic	gml	Middle Low German	UniMorph
	West Germanic	gsw	Swiss German	Egli-Wildi (2007)
	North Germanic	nno	Norwegian Nynorsk	UniMorph
Niger-Congo	Bantoid	sna	Shona	Kasahorow (2014b); Nandoro (2018)
Sino-Tibetan	Bodic	bod	Tibetan	Di et al. (2019)
Siouan	Core Siouan	dak	Dakota	LaFontaine and McKay (2005)
Songhay	Songhay	dje	Zarma	Kasahorow (2019b)
Southern Daly	Murrinh-Patha	mwf	Murrinh-Patha	Mansfield (2019)
Uralic	Permic	kpv	Komi-Zyrian	Arkhangelskiy et al. (2012)
	Finnic	lud	Ludic	Zaytseva et al. (2017)
	Finnic	olo	Livvi	Zaytseva et al. (2017)
	Permic	udm	Udmurt	Arkhangelskiy et al. (2012)
	Finnic	vro	Võro	Iva (2007)
Uto-Aztecan	Tepiman	ood	O'odham	Zepeda (2003)

Table 2: Surprise languages used in the shared task.

no grammatical evidentials.

3.7 Oto-Manguean

The Oto-Manguean languages are a diverse family of tonal languages spoken in central and southern Mexico. Even though all of these languages are tonal, the tonal system within each language varies widely. Some have an inventory of two tones (e.g., Chichimec and Pame) others have ten tones (e.g., the Eastern Chatino languages of the Zapotecan branch, Palancar and Léonard (2016)).

Oto-Manguean languages are also rich in tonal morphology. The inflectional system marks person–number and aspect in verbs and person–number in adjectives and noun possessions, relying heavily on tonal contrasts. Other interesting aspects of Oto-Manguean languages include the fact that pronominal inflections use a system of enclitics, and first and second person plural has a distinction between exclusive and inclusive (Campbell, 2016). Tone marking schemes in the writing systems also vary greatly. Some writing systems do not represent tone, others use diacritics, and others represent tones with numbers. In languages that use numbers, single digits represent level tones and double digits represent contour tones. For example, in San Juan Quiahije of Eastern Chatino number 1 represents high tone, number 4 represents low tone, and numbers 14 represent a descending tone contour and numbers 42 represent an ascending tone contour Cruz (2014).

3.8 Sino-Tibetan

The Sino-Tibetan family is represented by the Tibetan language. Tibetan uses an abugida script and contains complex syllabic components in which vowel marks can be added above and below the base consonant. Tibetan verbs are inflected for tense and mood. Previous studies on Tibetan morphology (Di et al., 2019) indicate that the majority of mispredictions produced by neural models are due to allomorphy. This is followed by generation of nonce words (impossible combinations of vowel and consonant components).

3.9 Siouan

The Siouan languages are located in North America, predominantly along the Mississippi and Missouri Rivers and in the Ohio Valley. The family is represented in our task by Dakota, a critically endangered language spoken in North and South Dakota, Minnesota, and Saskatchewan. The Dakota language is largely agglutinating in its derivational morphology and fusional in its inflectional morphology with a mixed affixation system (Rankin et al., 2003). The present task includes verbs, which are marked for first and second person, number, and duality. All three affixation types are found: person was generally marked by an infix, but could also appear as a prefix, and plurality was marked by a suffix. Morphophonological processes of fortition and vowel lowering are also present.

3.10 Songhay

The Songhay family consists of around eleven or twelve languages spoken in Mali, Niger, Benin, Burkina Faso and Nigeria. In the shared task we use Zarma, the most widely spoken Songhay language. Most of the Songhay languages are predominantly SOV with medium-sized consonant inventories (with implosives), five phonemic vowels, vowel length distinctions, and word level tones, which also are used to distinguish nouns, verbs, and adjectives (Heath, 2014).

3.11 Southern Daly

The Southern Daly is a small language family of the Northern Territory in Australia that consists of two distantly related languages. In the current task we only have one of the languages, Murrinh-patha (which was initially thought to be a language isolate). Murrinh-patha is classified as polysynthetic with highly complex verbal morphology. Verbal roots are surrounded by prefixes and suffixes that indicate tense, mood, object, subject. As Mansfield (2019) notes, Murrinh-patha verbs have 39 conjugation classes.

3.12 Tungusic

Tungusic languages are spoken principally in Russia, China and Mongolia. In Russia they are concentrated in north and eastern Siberia and in China in the east, in Manchuria. The largest languages in the family are Xibe, Evenki and Even; we use Evenki in the shared task. The languages are of the agglutinating morphological type with a moderate number of cases, 7 for Xibe and 13 for Evenki. In addition to case markers, Evenki marks possession in nominals (including reflexive possession) and distinguishes between alienable and inalienable possession. In terms of morphophonological processes, the languages exhibit vowel harmony, consonant alternations and phonological vowel length.

3.13 Turkic

Languages of the Turkic family are primarily spoken in Central Asia. The family is morphologically concatenative, fusional, and suffixing. Turkic languages generally exhibit back vowel harmony, with the notable exception of Uzbek. In addition to harmony in backness, several languages also have labial vowel harmony (e.g., Kyrgyz, Turkmen, among others). In addition, most of the languages have dorsal consonant allophony that accompanies back vowel harmony. Additional morphophonological processes include vowel epenthesis and voicing assimilation. Selection of the inflectional allomorph can frequently be determined from the infinitive morpheme (which frequently reveals vowel backness and roundedness) and also the final segment of the stem.

3.14 Uralic

The Uralic languages are spoken in Russia from the north of Siberia to Scandinavia and Hungary in Europe. They are agglutinating with some subgroups displaying fusional characteristics (e.g., the Sámi languages). Many of the languages have vowel harmony. The languages have almost complete suffixal morphology and a medium-sized case inventory, ranging from 5–6 cases to numbers in the high teens. Many of the larger case paradigms are made up of spatial cases, sometimes with distinctions for direction and position. Most of the languages have possessive suffixes, which can express possession, or agreement in non-finite clauses. The paradigms are largely regular, with few, if any, irregular forms. Many exhibit complex patterns of consonant gradation—consonant mutations that occur in specific morphological forms in some stems. Which gradation category a stem belongs to in often unpredictable. The languages spoken in Russia are typically SOV, while those in Europe have SVO order.

3.15 Uto-Aztecan

The Uto-Aztecan family is represented by the Tohono O'odham (Papago–Pima) language spoken along the US–Mexico border in southern Arizona and northern Sonora. O'odham is agglutinative with a mixed prefixing and suffixing system. Nominal and verbal pluralization is frequently realized by partial reduplication of the initial consonant and/or vowel, and occasionally by final consonant deletion or null affixation. Processes targeting vowel length (shortening or lengthening) are also present. A small number of verbs exhibit suppletion in the past tense.

4 Data Preparation

4.1 Data Format

Similar to previous years, training and development sets contain triples consisting of a lemma, a target form, and morphosyntactic descriptions (MSDs, or morphological tags).[3] Test sets only contain two fields, i.e., target forms are omitted. All data follows UTF-8 encoding.

4.2 Conversion and Canonicalization

A significant amount of data for this task was extracted from corresponding (language-specific) grammars. In order to allow cross-lingual comparison, we manually converted their features (tags) into the UniMorph format (Sylak-Glassman, 2016). We then canonicalized the converted language data[4] to make sure all tags are consistently ordered and no category (e.g., "Number") is assigned two tags (e.g., singular and plural).[5]

4.3 Splitting

We use only noun, verb, and adjective forms to construct training, development, and evaluation sets. We de-duplicate annotations such that there are no multiple examples of exact lemma-form-tag matches. To create splits, we randomly sample 70%, 10%, and 20% for train, development, and test, respectively. We cap the training set size to 100k examples for each language; where languages exceed this (e.g., Finnish), we subsample to this point, balancing lemmas such that all forms for a given lemma are either included or discarded. Some languages such as Zarma (dje), Tajik (tgk), Lingala (lin), Ludian* (lud), Māori (mao), Sotho (sot), Võro (vro), Anglo-Norman (xno), and Zulu (zul) contain less than 400 training samples and are extremely low-resource.[6] Tab. 6 and Tab. 7 in the Appendix provide the number of samples for every language in each split, the number of samples per lemma, and statistics on inconsistencies in the data.

5 Baseline Systems

The organizers provided two types of pre-trained baselines. Their use was optional.

5.1 Non-neural

The first baseline was a non-neural system that had been used as a baseline in earlier shared tasks on morphological reinflection (Cotterell et al., 2017, 2018). The system first heuristically extracts lemma-to-form transformations; it assumes that these transformations are suffix- or prefix-based.

---

[3] Each MSD is a set of features separated by semicolons.

[4] Using the UniMorph schema canonicalization script `https://github.com/unimorph/um-canonicalize`

[5] Conversion schemes and canonicalization scripts are available at `https://github.com/sigmorphon2020/task0-data`

[6] We also note that Ludian contained inconsistencies in data due to merge of various dialects.

A simple majority classifier is used to apply the most frequent suitable transformation to an input lemma, given the morphological tag, yielding the output form. See Cotterell et al. (2017) for further details.

5.2 Neural

Neural baselines were based on a neural transducer (Wu and Cotterell, 2019), which is essentially a hard monotonic attention model (`mono-*`). The second baseline is a transformer (Vaswani et al., 2017) adopted for character-level tasks that currently holds the state-of-the-art on the 2017 SIG-MORPHON shared task data (Wu et al., 2020, `trm-*`). Both models take the lemma and morphological tags as input and output the target inflection. The baseline is further expanded to include the data augmentation technique used by Anastasopoulos and Neubig (2019, `-aug-`) (conceptually similar to the one proposed by Silfverberg et al. (2017)). Relying on a simple character-level alignment between lemma and form, this technique replaces shared substrings of length > 3 with random characters from the language's alphabet, producing hallucinated lemma–tag–form triples. Both neural baselines were trained in mono- (`*-single`) and multilingual (shared parameters among the same family, `*-shared`) settings.

6 Competing Systems

As Tab. 3 shows, 10 teams submitted 22 systems in total, out of which 19 were neural. Some teams such as **ETH Zurich** and **UIUC** built their models on top of the proposed baselines. In particular, **ETH Zurich** enriched each of the (multilingual) neural baseline models with exact decoding strategy that uses Dijkstra's search algorithm. **UIUC** enriched the transformer model with synchronous bidirectional decoding technique (Zhou et al., 2019) in order to condition the prediction of an affix character on its environment from both sides. (The authors demonstrate positive effects in Oto-Manguean, Turkic, and some Austronesian languages.)

A few teams further improved models that were among top performers in previous shared tasks. **IMS** and **Flexica** re-used the hard monotonic attention model from (Aharoni and Goldberg, 2017). **IMS** developed an ensemble of two models (with left-to-right and right-to-left generation or-

der) with a genetic algorithm for ensemble search (Haque et al., 2016) and iteratively provided hallucinated data. **Flexica** submitted two neural systems. The first model (`flexica-02-1`) was multilingual (family-wise) hard monotonic attention model with improved alignment strategy. This model is further improved (`flexica-03-1`) by introducing a data hallucination technique which is based on phonotactic modelling of extremely low-resource languages (Shcherbakov et al., 2016). **LTI** focused on their earlier model (Anastasopoulos and Neubig, 2019), a neural multi-source encoder–decoder with two-step attention architecture, training it with hallucinated data, cross-lingual transfer, and romanization of scripts to improve performance on low-resource languages. **DeepSpin** reimplemented gated sparse two-headed attention model from Peters and Martins (2019) and trained it on all languages at once (massively multilingual). The team experimented with two modifications of the softmax function: sparsemax (Martins and Astudillo, 2016, `deepspin-02-1`) and 1.5-entmax (Peters et al., 2019, `deepspin-01-1`).

Many teams based their models on the transformer architecture. **NYU-CUBoulder** experimented with a vanilla transformer model (`NYU-CUBoulder-04-0`), a pointer-generator transformer that allows for a copy mechanism (`NYU-CUBoulder-02-0`), and ensembles of three (`NYU-CUBoulder-01-0`) and five (`NYU-CUBoulder-03-0`) pointer-generator transformers. For languages with less than 1,000 training samples, they also generate hallucinated data. **CULing** developed an ensemble of three (monolingual) transformers with identical architecture but different input data format. The first model was trained on the initial data format (lemma, target tags, target form). For the other two models the team used the idea of lexeme's principal parts (Finkel and Stump, 2007) and augmented the initial input (that only used the lemma as a source form) with entries corresponding to other (non-lemma) slots available for the lexeme. The **CMU Tartan** team compared performance of models with transformer-based and LSTM-based encoders and decoders. The team also compared monolingual to multilingual training in which they used several (related and unrelated) high-resource languages for low-resource language training.

Although the majority of submitted systems

Team	Description	System	Neural	Ensemble	Multilingual	Hallucination
					Model Features	
Baseline	Wu and Cotterell (2019)	`mono-single`	✓			
		`mono-aug-single`	✓			✓
		`mono-shared`	✓		✓	
		`mono-aug-shared`	✓		✓	✓
	Wu et al. (2020)	`trm-single`	✓			
		`trm-aug-single`	✓			✓
		`trm-shared`	✓		✓	
		`trm-aug-shared`	✓		✓	✓
CMU Tartan	Jayarao et al. (2020)	`cmu_tartan_00-0`	✓			✓
		`cmu_tartan_00-1`	✓		✓	✓
		`cmu_tartan_01-0`	✓			✓
		`cmu_tartan_01-1`	✓		✓	✓
		`cmu_tartan_02-1`	✓		✓	✓
CU7565	Beemer et al. (2020)	`CU7565-01-0`				
		`CU7565-02-0`				
CULing	Liu and Hulden (2020)	`CULing-01-0`	✓	✓		
DeepSpin	Peters and Martins (2020)	`deepspin-01-1`	✓		✓	
		`deepspin-02-1`	✓		✓	
ETH Zurich	Forster and Meister (2020)	`ETHZ00-1`	✓		✓	
		`ETHZ02-1`	✓		✓	
Flexica	Scherbakov (2020)	`flexica-01-0`				
		`flexica-02-1`	✓		✓	
		`flexica-03-1`	✓		✓	✓
IMS	Yu et al. (2020)	`IMS-00-0`	✓	✓		✓
LTI	Murikinati and Anastasopoulos (2020)	`LTI-00-1`	✓		✓	✓
NYU-CUBoulder	Singer and Kann (2020)	`NYU-CUBoulder-01-0`	✓	✓		✓
		`NYU-CUBoulder-02-0`	✓			✓
		`NYU-CUBoulder-03-0`	✓	✓		✓
		`NYU-CUBoulder-04-0`	✓			✓
UIUC	Canby et al. (2020)	`uiuc-01-0`	✓			

Table 3: The list of systems submitted to the shared task.

were neural, some teams experimented with non-neural approaches showing that in certain scenarios they might surpass neural systems. A large group of researchers from **CU7565** manually developed finite-state grammars for 25 languages (`CU7565-01-0`). They additionally developed a non-neural learner for all languages (`CU7565-02-0`) that uses hierarchical paradigm clustering (based on similarity of string transformation rules between inflectional slots). Another team, **Flexica**, proposed a model (`flexica-01-0`) conceptually similar to Hulden et al. (2014), although they did not attempt to reconstruct the paradigm itself and treated transformation rules independently assigning each of them a score based on its frequency and specificity as well as diversity of the characters surrounding the pattern.[7]

---

[7]English plural noun formation rule "$* \rightarrow *s$" has high diversity whereas past tense rule such as "$*a* \rightarrow *oo*$" as in *(understand, understood)* has low diversity.

7 Evaluation

This year, we instituted a slightly different evaluation regimen than in previous years, which takes into account the statistical significance of differences between systems and allows for an informed comparison across languages and families better than a simple macro-average.

The process works as follows:

1. For each language, we rank the systems according to their accuracy (or Levenshtein distance). To do so, we use paired bootstrap resampling (Koehn, 2004)[8] to only take statistically significant differences into account. That way, any system which is the same (as assessed via statistical significance) as the best performing one is also ranked 1st for that language.

2. For the set of languages where we want collective results (e.g. languages within a linguistic genus), we aggregate the systems' ranks and

---

[8]We use 10,000 samples with 50% ratio, and $p < 0.005$.

Individual Language Rankings								Final Ranking		
cly		ctp		czn		zpv			avg	#1 #3 #4 #6
uiuc	(1)	CULing	(1)	deepspin	(1)	NYU-CUB	(1)	uiuc	1	4
trm-single	(1)	uiuc	(1)	uiuc	(1)	CULing	(1)	trm-single	1	4
CULing	(3)	trm-single	(1)	IMS	(1)	deepspin	(1)	CULing	1.5	3 1
deepspin	(3)	IMS	(4)	NYU-CUB	(1)	uiuc	(1)	deepspin	2.25	2 1 1
NYU-CUB	(3)	deepspin	(4)	CULing	(1)	trm-single	(1)	NYU-CUB	2.25	2 1 1
IMS	(6)	NYU-CUB	(4)	trm-single	(1)	IMS	(1)	IMS	3	2 0 1 1

Table 4: Illustration of our ranking method, over the four Zapotecan languages. Note: The final ranking is based on the actual counts (#1,#2, etc), not on the system's average rank.

re-rank them based on the amount of times they ranked 1st, 2nd, 3rd, etc.

Table 4 illustrates an example of this process using four Zapotecan languages and six systems.

8 Results

This year we had four winning systems (i.e., ones that outperform the best baseline): CULing-01-0, deepspin-02-1, uiuc-01-0, and deepspin-01-1, all neural. As Tab. 5 shows, they achieve over 90% accuracy. Although CULing-01-0 and uiuc-01-0 are both monolingual transformers that do not use any hallucinated data, they follow different strategies to improve performance. The strategy proposed by CULing-01-0 of enriching the input data with extra entries that included non-lemma forms and their tags as a source form, enabled their system to be among top performers on all language families; uiuc-01-0, on the other hand, did not modify the data but rather changed the decoder to be bidirectional and made family-wise fine-tuning of each (monolingual) model. The system is also among the top performers on all language families except Iranian. The third team, **DeepSpin**, trained and fine-tuned their models on all language data. Both models are ranked high (although the sparsemax model, deepspin-02-1, performs better overall) on most language groups with exception of Algic. Sparsemax was also found useful by **CMU-Tartan**. The neural ensemble model with data augmentation from **IMS** team shows superior performance on languages with smaller data sizes (under 10,000 samples). **LTI** and **Flexica** teams also observed positive effects of multilingual training and data hallucination on low-resource languages. The latter was also found useful in the ablation study made by **NYU-CUBoulder** team. Several teams aimed to address particular research questions; we will further summarize their results.

System	Rank	Acc
uiuc-01-0	**2.4**	**90.5**
deepspin-02-1	2.9	**90.9**
BASE: trm-single	2.8	90.1
CULing-01-0	3.2	**91.2**
deepspin-01-1	3.8	**90.5**
BASE: trm-aug-single	3.7	90.3
NYU-CUBoulder-04-0	7.1	88.8
NYU-CUBoulder-03-0	8.9	88.8
NYU-CUBoulder-02-0	8.9	88.7
IMS-00-0	10.6	89.2
NYU-CUBoulder-01-0	9.6	88.6
BASE: trm-shared	10.3	85.9
BASE: mono-aug-single	7.5	88.8
cmu_tartan_00-0	8.7	87.1
BASE: mono-single	7.9	85.8
cmu_tartan_01-1	9.0	87.1
BASE: trm-aug-shared	12.5	86.5
BASE: mono-shared	10.8	86.0
cmu_tartan_00-1	9.4	86.5
LTI-00-1	12.0	86.6
BASE: mono-aug-shared	12.8	86.8
cmu_tartan_02-1	10.6	86.1
cmu_tartan_01-0	10.9	86.6
flexica-03-1	16.7	79.6
ETHZ-00-1	20.1	75.6
CU7565-01-0	*24.1*	*90.7*
flexica-02-1	17.1	78.5
CU7565-02-0	*19.2*	*83.6*
ETHZ-02-1	17.0	80.9
flexica-01-0	24.4	70.8
Oracle (Baselines)		96.1
Oracle (Submissions)		97.7
Oracle (All)		97.9

Table 5: Aggregate results on all languages. **Bolded** results are the ones which beat the best baseline. ∗ and *italics* denote systems that did not submit outputs in all languages (their accuracy is a partial average).

11

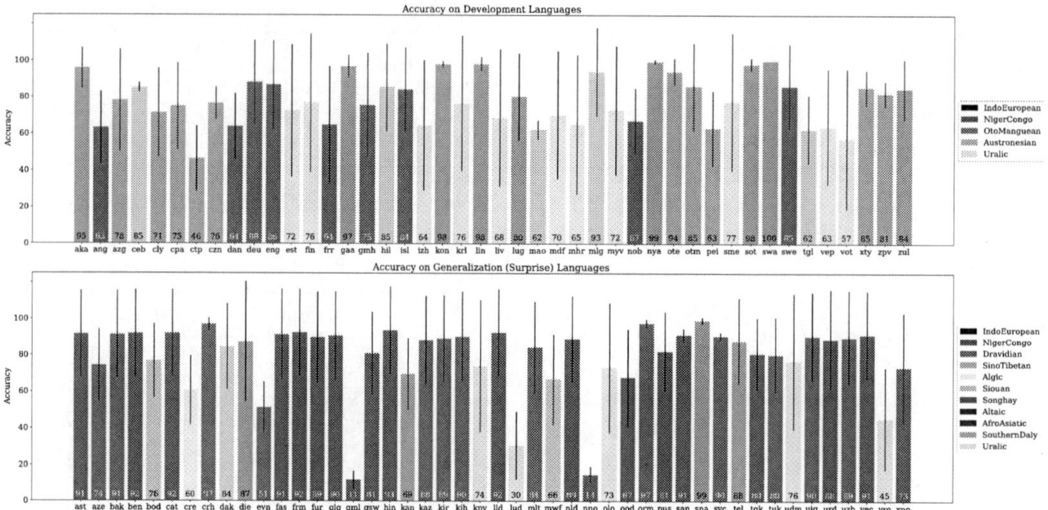

Figure 2: Accuracy by language averaged across all the final submitted systems with their standard deviations. Language families are demarcated by color, with accuracy on development languages (top), and generalization languages (bottom).

Is developing morphological grammars manually worthwhile? This was the main question asked by **CU7565** who manually designed finite-state grammars for 25 languages. Paradigms of some languages were relatively easy to describe but neural networks also performed quite well on them even with a limited amount of data. For low-resource languages such as Ingrian and Tagalog the grammars demonstrate superior performance but this comes at the expense of a significant amount of person-hours.

What is the best training strategy for low-resource languages? Teams that generated hallucinated data highlighted its utility for low-resource languages. Augmenting the data with tuples where lemmas are replaced with non-lemma forms and their tags is another technique that was found useful. In addition, multilingual training and ensembles yield extra gain in terms of accuracy.

Are the systems complementary? To address this question, we evaluate oracle scores for baseline systems, submitted systems, and all of them together. Typically, as Tables 8–21 in the Appendix demonstrate, the baselines and the submissions are complementary - adding them together increases the oracle score. Furthermore, while the full systems tend to dominate the partial systems (that were designed for a subset of languages, such as CU7565-01-0), there are a number of cases where the partial systems find the solution when the full systems don't - and these languages often then get even bigger gains when combined with the baselines. This even happens when the accuracy of the baseline is very high - Finnish has baseline oracle of 99.89; full systems oracle of 99.91; submission oracle of 99.94 and complete oracle of 99.96, so an ensemble might be able to improve on the results. The largest gaps in oracle systems are observed in Algic, Oto-Manguean, Sino-Tibetan, Southern Daly, Tungusic, and Uto-Aztecan families.[9]

Has morphological inflection become a solved problem in certain scenarios? The results shown in Fig. 2 suggest that for some of the development language families, such as Austronesian and Niger-Congo, the task was relatively easy, with most systems achieving high accuracy, whereas the task was more difficult for Uralic and Oto-Manguean languages, which showed greater variability in level of performance across submitted systems. Languages such as Ludic (lud), Norwegian Nynorsk (nno), Middle Low German

---

[9] Please see the results per language here:
https://docs.google.com/spreadsheets/
d/1ODFRnHuwN-mvGtzXAlsNdCi-jNqZjiE-
i9jRxZCK0kg/edit?usp=sharing

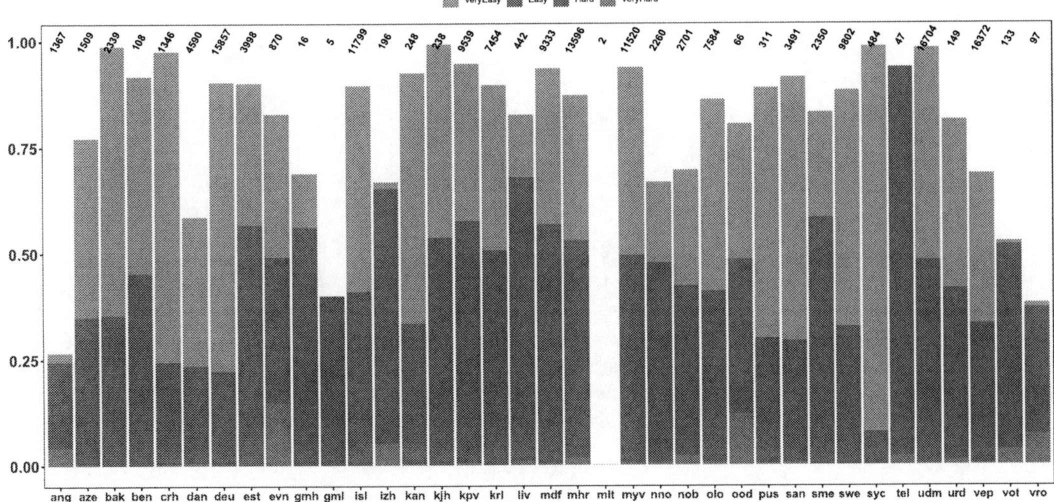

Figure 3: Difficulty of Nouns: Percentage of test samples falling into each category. The total number of test samples for each language is outlined on the top of the plot.

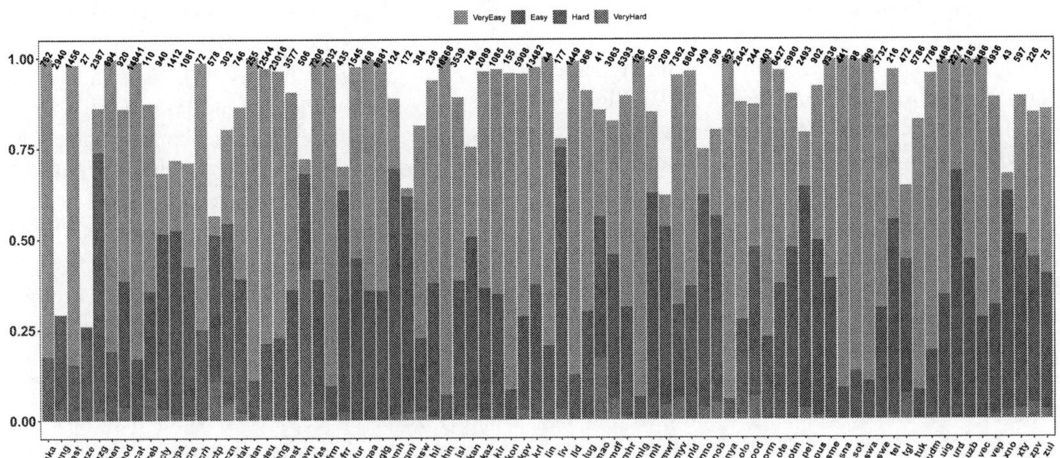

Figure 4: Difficulty of Verbs: Percentage of test samples falling into each category. The total number of test samples for each language is outlined on the top of the plot.

(gml), Evenki (evn), and O'odham (ood) seem to be the most challenging languages based on simple accuracy. For a more fine-grained study, we have classified test examples into four categories: "very easy", "easy", "hard", and "very hard". "Very easy" examples are ones that all submitted systems got correct, while "very hard" examples are ones that no submitted system got correct. "Easy" examples were predicted correctly for 80% of systems, and "hard" were only correct in 20% of systems. Fig. 3, Fig. 4, and Fig. 5 represent percentage of noun, verb, and adjective samples that

fall into each category and illustrate that most language samples are correctly predicted by majority of the systems. For noun declension, Old English (ang), Middle Low German (gml), Evenki (evn), O'odham (ood), Võro (vro) are the most difficult (some of this difficulty comes from language data inconsistency, as described in the following section). For adjective declension, Classic Syriac presents the highest difficulty (likely due to its limited data).

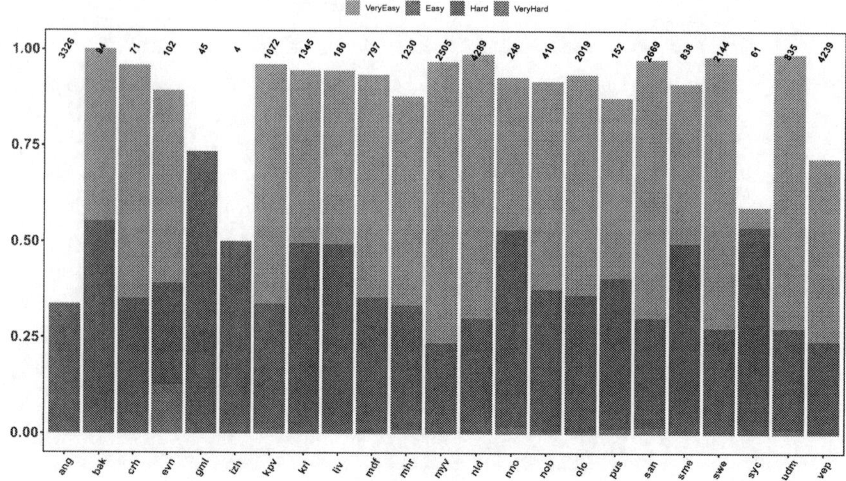

Figure 5: Difficulty of Adjectives: Percentage of test samples falling into each category. The total number of test samples for each language is outlined on the top of the plot.

9 Error Analysis

In our error analysis we follow the error type taxonomy proposed in Gorman et al. (2019). First, we evaluate systematic errors due to inconsistencies in the data, followed by an analysis of whether having seen the language or its family improved accuracy. We then proceed with an overview of accuracy for each of the language families. For a select number of families, we provide a more detailed analysis of the error patterns.

Tab. 6 and Tab. 7 provide the number of samples in the training, development, and test sets, percentage of inconsistent entries (the same lemma–tag pair has multiple infected forms) in them, percentage of contradicting entries (same lemma–tag pair occurring in train and development or test sets but assigned to different inflected forms), and percentage of entries in the development or test sets containing a lemma observed in the training set. The train, development and test sets contain 2%, 0.3%, and 0.6% inconsistent entries, respectively. Azerbaijani (aze), Old English (ang), Cree (cre), Danish (dan), Middle Low German (gml), Kannada (kan), Norwegian Bokmål (nob), Chichimec (pei), and Veps (vep) had the highest rates of inconsistency. These languages also exhibit the highest percentage of contradicting entries. The inconsistencies in some Finno-Ugric languages (such as Veps and Ludic) are due to dialectal variations.

The overall accuracy of system and language pairings appeared to improve with an increase in the size of the dataset (Fig. 6; see also Fig. 7 for accuracy trends by language family and Fig. 8 for accuracy trends by system). Overall, the variance was considerable regardless of whether the language family or even the language itself had been observed during the Development Phase. A linear mixed-effects regression was used to assess variation in accuracy using fixed effects of language category, the size of the training dataset (log count), and their interactions, as well as random intercepts for system and language family accuracy.[10] Language category was sum-coded with three levels: development language–development family, surprise language–development family, or surprise language–surprise family.

A significant effect of dataset size was observed, such that a one unit increase in log count corresponded to a 2% increase in accuracy ($\beta = 0.019$, $p < 0.001$). Language category type also significantly influenced accuracy: both development languages and surprise languages from development families were less accurate on average ($\beta_{dev-dev} = -0.145$, $\beta_{sur-dev} = -0.167$, each $p < 0.001$). These main effects were, however, significantly modulated by interactions with dataset size: on top of the main effect of dataset size, accuracy for development languages increased an additional $\approx 1.7\%$ ($\beta_{dev-dev\times size} = 0.017$, $p < 0.001$) and accuracy for surprise languages from development families

---

[10]Accuracy should ideally be assessed at the trial level using a logistic regression as opposed to a linear regression. By-trial accuracy was however not available at analysis time.

increased an additional $\approx 2.9\%$ ($\beta_{sur-dev \times size} = 0.029$, $p < 0.001$).

Afro-Asiatic: This family was represented by three languages. Mean accuracy across systems was above average at 91.7%. Relative to other families, variance in accuracy was low, but nevertheless ranged from 41.1% to 99.0%.

Algic: This family was represented by one language, Cree. Mean accuracy across systems was below average at 65.1%. Relative to other families, variance in accuracy was low, ranging from 41.5% to 73%. All systems appeared to struggle with the choice of preverbal auxiliary. Some auxiliaries were overloaded: 'kitta' could refer to future, imperfective, or imperative. The morphological features for mood and tense were also frequently combined, such as SBJV+OPT (subjunctive plus optative mood). While the paradigms were very large, there were very few lemmas (28 impersonal verbs and 14 transitive verbs), which may have contributed to the lower accuracy. Interestingly, the inflections could largely be generated by rules.[11]

Austronesian: This family was represented by five languages. Mean accuracy across systems was around average at 80.5%. Relative to other families, variance in accuracy was high, with accuracy ranging from 39.5% to 100%. One may notice a discrepancy among the difficulty in processing different Austronesian languages. For instance, we see a difference of over 10% in the baseline performance of Cebuano (84%) and Hiligaynon (96%).[12] This could come from the fact that Cebuano only has partial reduplication while Hiligaynon has full reduplication. Furthermore, the prefix choice for Cebuano is more irregular, making it more difficult to predict the correct conjugation of the verb.

Dravidian: This family was represented by two languages: Kannada and Telugu. Mean accuracy across systems was around average at 82.2%. Relative to other families, variance in accuracy was high: system accuracy ranged from 44.6% to 96.0%. Accuracy for Telugu was systematically higher than accuracy for Kannada.

Indo-European: This family was represented by 29 languages and four main branches. Mean accuracy across systems was slightly above average at 86.9%. Relative to other families, variance in accuracy was very high: system accuracy ranged from 0.02% to 100%. For Indo-Aryan, mean accuracy was high (96.0%) with low variance; for Germanic, mean accuracy was slightly below average (79.0%) but with very high variance (ranging from 0.02% to 99.5%), for Romance, mean accuracy was high (93.4%) but also had a high variance (ranging from 23.5% to 99.8%), and for Iranian, mean accuracy was high (89.2%), but again with a high variance (ranging from 25.0% to 100%). Languages from the Germanic branch of the Indo-European family were included in the Development Phase.

Niger–Congo: This family was represented by ten languages. Mean accuracy across systems was very good at 96.4%. Relative to other families, variance in accuracy was low, with accuracy ranging from 62.8% to 100%. Most languages in this family are considered low resource, and the resources used for data gathering may have been biased towards the languages' regular forms, as such this high accuracy may not be representative of the "easiness" of the task in this family. Languages from the Niger–Congo family was included in the Development Phase.

Oto-Manguean: This family was represented by nine languages. Mean accuracy across systems was slightly below average at 78.5%. Relative to other families, variance in accuracy was high, with accuracy ranging from 18.7% to 99.1%. Languages from the Oto-Manguean family were included in the Development Phase.

Sino-Tibetan: This family was represented by one language, Bodic. Mean accuracy across systems was average at 82.1%, and variance across systems was also very low. Accuracy ranged from 67.9% to 85.1%. The results are similar to those in Di et al. (2019) where majority of errors relate to allomorphy and impossible combinations of Tibetan unit components.

Siouan: This family was represented by one language, Dakota. Mean accuracy across systems was

---

[11] Minor issues with the encoding of diacritics were identified, and will be corrected for release.

[12] We also note that some Hiligaynon entries contained multiple lemma forms ("bati/batian/pamatian") for a single entry. We decided to leave it since we could not find any more information on which of the lemmas should be selected as the main. A similar issue was observed in Chichicapan Zapotec.

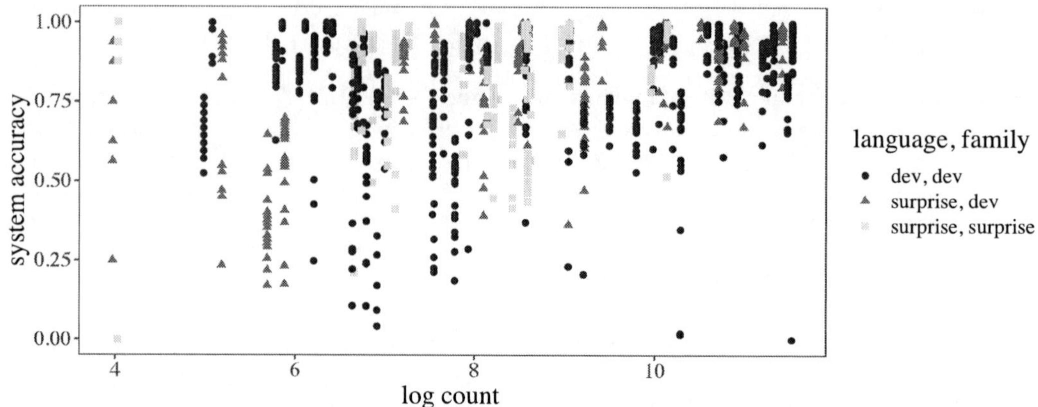

Figure 6: Accuracy for each system and language by the log size of the dataset. Points are color-coded according to language type: development language – development family, surprise language – development family, surprise language – surprise family.

above average at 89.4%, and variance across systems was also low, despite the range from 0% to 95.7%. Dakota presented variable prefixing and infixing of person morphemes, along some complexities related to fortition processes. Determining the factor(s) that governed variation in affix position was difficult from a linguist's perspective, though many systems were largely successful. Success varied in the choice of the first or second person singular allomorphs which had increasing degrees of consonant strengthening (e.g., /wa/, /ma/, /mi/ /bde/, /bdu/ for the first person singular and /ya/, /na/, /ni/, /de/, or /du/ for the second person singular). In some cases, these fortition processes were overapplied, and in some cases, entirely missed.

Songhay: This family was represented by one language, Zarma. Mean accuracy across systems was above average at 88.6%, and variance across systems was relatively high. Accuracy ranged from 0% to 100%.

Southern Daly: This family was represented by one language, Murrinh-Patha. Mean accuracy across systems was below average at 73.2%, and variance across systems was relatively high. Accuracy ranged from 21.2% to 91.9%.

Tungusic: This family was represented by one language, Evenki. The overall accuracy was the lowest across families. Mean accuracy was 53.8% with very low variance across systems. Accuracy ranged from 43.5% to 59.0%. The low accuracy is due to several factors. Firstly and primarily, the dataset was created from oral speech samples

in various dialects of the language. The Evenki language is known to have rich dialectal variation. Moreover, there was little attempt at any standardization in the oral speech transcription. These peculiarities led to a high number of errors. For instance, some of the systems synthesized a wrong plural form for a noun ending in /-n/. Depending on the dialect, it can be /-r/ or /-l/, and there is a trend to have /-hVl/ for borrowed nouns. Deducing such a rule as well as the fact that the noun is a loanword is a hard task. Other suffixes may also have variable forms (such as /-kVllu/ vs /-kVldu/ depending on the dialect for the 2PL imperative. Some verbs have irregular past tense forms depending on the dialect and the meaning of the verb (e. g. /o:-/ 'to make' and 'to become'). Next, various dialects exhibit various vowel and consonant changes in suffixes. For example, some dialects (but not all of them) change /w/ to /b/ after /l/, and the systems sometimes synthesized a wrong form. The vowel harmony is complex: not all suffixes obey it, and it is also dialect-dependent. Some suffixes have variants (e. g., /-sin/ and /-s/ for SEMEL (semelfactive)), and the choice between them might be hard to understand. Finally, some of the mistakes are due to the markup scheme scarcity. For example, various past tense forms are all annotated as PST, or there are several comitative suffixes all annotated as COM. Moreover, some features are present in the word form but they receive no annotation at all. It is worth mentioning that some of the predictions could theoretically be possible. To sum up, the Evenki case presents the challenges of oral non-standardized speech.

Turkic: This family was represented by nine languages. Mean accuracy across systems was relatively high at 93%, and relative to other families, variance across systems was low. Accuracy ranged from 51.5% to 100%. Accuracy was lower for Azerbaijani and Turkmen, which after closer inspection revealed some slight contamination in the 'gold' files. There was very marginal variation in the accuracy for these languages across systems. Besides these two, accuracies were predominantly above 98%. A few systems struggled with the choice and inflection of the postverbal auxiliary in various languages (e.g., Kyrgyz, Kazakh, and Uzbek).

Uralic: This family was represented by 16 languages. Mean accuracy across systems was average at 81.5%, but the variance across systems and languages was very high. Accuracy ranged from 0% to 99.8%. Languages from the Uralic family were included in the Development Phase.

Uto-Aztecan: This family was represented by one language, O'odham. Mean accuracy across systems was slightly below average at 76.4%, but the variance across systems and languages was fairly low. Accuracy ranged from 54.8% to 82.5%. The systems with higher accuracy may have benefited from better recall of suppletive forms relative to lower accuracy systems.

10   Conclusion

This years's shared task on morphological reinflection focused on building models that could generalize across an extremely typologically diverse set of languages, many from understudied language families and with limited available text resources. As in previous years, neural models performed well, even in relatively low-resource cases. Submissions were able to make productive use of multilingual training to take advantage of commonalities across languages in the dataset. Data augmentation techniques such as hallucination helped fill in the gaps and allowed networks to generalize to unseen inputs. These techniques, combined with architecture tweaks like sparsemax, resulted in excellent overall performance on many languages (over 90% accuracy on average). However, the task's focus on typological diversity revealed that some morphology types and language families (Tungusic, Oto-Manguean, South-

ern Daly) remain a challenge for even the best systems. These families are extremely low-resource, represented in this dataset by few or a single language. This makes cross-linguistic transfer of similarities by multilanguage training less viable. They may also have morphological properties and rules (e.g., Evenki is agglutinating with many possible forms for each lemma) that are particularly difficult for machine learners to induce automatically from sparse data. For some languages (Ingrian, Tajik, Tagalog, Zarma, and Lingala), optimal performance was only achieved in this shared task by hand-encoding linguist knowledge in finite state grammars. It is up to future research to imbue models with the right kinds of linguistic inductive biases to overcome these challenges.

Acknowledgements

We would like to thank each of the participants for their time and effort in developing their task systems. We also thank Jason Eisner for organization and guidance. We thank Vitalij Chernyavskij for his help with Võro and Umida Boltaeva and Bahriddin Abdiev for their contribution in Uzbek data annotation.

References

Murat Abdulin. 2016. *Turkmen Verbs: 100 Turkmen Verbs Conjugated in All Tenses*. CreateSpace Independent Publishing Platform, Online.

Daniyar Abdullaev. 2016. *Uzbek language: 100 Uzbek verbs conjugated in common tenses*. CreateSpace Independent Publishing Platform, Online.

Roee Aharoni and Yoav Goldberg. 2017. Morphological inflection generation with hard monotonic attention. In *Proceedings of the 55th Annual Meeting of the Association for Computational Linguistics (Volume 1: Long Papers)*, pages 2004–2015, Vancouver, Canada. Association for Computational Linguistics.

Antonios Anastasopoulos and Graham Neubig. 2019. Pushing the limits of low-resource morphological inflection. In *Proceedings of the 2019 Conference on Empirical Methods in Natural Language Processing and the 9th International Joint Conference on Natural Language Processing (EMNLP-IJCNLP)*, pages 983–995.

Timofey Arkhangelskiy, Oleg Belyaev, and Arseniy Vydrin. 2012. The creation of large-scale annotated corpora of minority languages using UniParser and the EANC platform. In *Proceedings of COLING 2012: Posters*, pages 83–92, Mumbai, India. The COLING 2012 Organizing Committee.

Alima Aytnatova. 2016. *Kyrgyz Language: 100 Kyrgyz Verbs Fully Conjugated in All Tenses*. CreateSpace Independent Publishing Platform, Online.

Sarah Beemer, Zak Boston, April Bukoski, Daniel Chen, Princess Dickens, Andrew Gerlach, Torin Hopkins, Parth Anand Jawale, Chris Koski, Akanksha Malhotra, Piyush Mishra, Saliha Muradoğlu, Lan Sang, Tyler Short, Sagarika Shreevastava, Elizabeth Spaulding, Tetsumichi Umada, Beilei Xiang, Changbing Yang, and Mans Hulden. 2020. Linguist vs. machine: Rapid development of finite-state morphological grammars. In *Proceedings of the 17th SIGMORPHON Workshop on Computational Research in Phonetics, Phonology, and Morphology*.

Emily M. Bender. 2009. Linguistically naïve!= language independent: Why NLP needs linguistic typology. In *Proceedings of the EACL 2009 Workshop on the Interaction between Linguistics and Computational Linguistics: Virtuous, Vicious or Vacuous?*, pages 26–32.

Emily M. Bender. 2016. Linguistic typology in natural language processing. *Linguistic Typology*, 20(3):645–660.

Jean Berko. 1958. The child's learning of english morphology. *Word*, 14(2-3):150–177.

Balthasar Bickel and Johanna Nichols. 2013a. Exponence of selected inflectional formatives. In Matthew S. Dryer and Martin Haspelmath, editors, *The World Atlas of Language Structures Online*. Max Planck Institute for Evolutionary Anthropology, Leipzig.

Balthasar Bickel and Johanna Nichols. 2013b. Fusion of selected inflectional formatives. In Matthew S. Dryer and Martin Haspelmath, editors, *The World Atlas of Language Structures Online*. Max Planck Institute for Evolutionary Anthropology, Leipzig.

Balthasar Bickel and Johanna Nichols. 2013c. Inflectional synthesis of the verb. In Matthew S. Dryer and Martin Haspelmath, editors, *The World Atlas of Language Structures Online*. Max Planck Institute for Evolutionary Anthropology, Leipzig.

Eric Campbell. 2016. Tone and inflection in zenzontepec chatino. *Tone and inflection*, pages 141–162.

Marc Canby, Aidana Karipbayeva, Bryan Lunt, Sahand Mozaffari, Charlotte Yoder, and Julia Hockenmaier. 2020. University of illinois submission to the SIGMORPHON 2020 shared task 0: Typologically diverse morphological inflection. In *Proceedings of the 17th SIGMORPHON Workshop on Computational Research in Phonetics, Phonology, and Morphology*.

Bernard Comrie. 1989. *Language Universals and Linguistic Typology: Syntax and Morphology*. University of Chicago Press.

Ryan Cotterell, Christo Kirov, John Sylak-Glassman, Géraldine Walther, Ekaterina Vylomova, Arya D McCarthy, Katharina Kann, Sebastian J Mielke, Garrett Nicolai, Miikka Silfverberg, et al. 2018. The conll–sigmorphon 2018 shared task: Universal morphological reinflection. In *Proceedings of the CoNLL–SIGMORPHON 2018 Shared Task: Universal Morphological Reinflection*, pages 1–27.

Ryan Cotterell, Christo Kirov, John Sylak-Glassman, Géraldine Walther, Ekaterina Vylomova, Patrick Xia, Manaal Faruqui, Sandra Kübler, David Yarowsky, Jason Eisner, and Mans Hulden. 2017. CoNLL-SIGMORPHON 2017 shared task: Universal morphological reinflection in 52 languages. In *Proceedings of the CoNLL SIGMORPHON 2017 Shared Task: Universal Morphological Reinflection*, pages 1–30, Vancouver. Association for Computational Linguistics.

William Croft. 2002. *Typology and Universals*. Cambridge University Press.

Hilaria Cruz. 2014. *Linguistic Poetic and Rhetoric of Eastern Chatino of San Juan Quiahije*. Ph.D. thesis.

Hilaria Cruz, Antonios Anastasopoulos, and Gregory Stump. 2020. A resource for studying chatino verbal morphology. In *Proceedings of The 12th Language Resources and Evaluation Conference*, pages 2820–2824, Marseille, France. European Language Resources Association.

Qianji Di, Ekaterina Vylomova, and Timothy Baldwin. 2019. Modelling Tibetan verbal morphology. In *Proceedings of the The 17th Annual Workshop of the Australasian Language Technology Association*, pages 35–40.

Matthew S. Dryer. 2013. Position of case affixes. In Matthew S. Dryer and Martin Haspelmath, editors, *The World Atlas of Language Structures Online*. Max Planck Institute for Evolutionary Anthropology, Leipzig.

Matthew S. Dryer and Martin Haspelmath, editors. 2013. *WALS Online*. Max Planck Institute for Evolutionary Anthropology, Leipzig.

Renate Egli-Wildi. 2007. *Züritüütsch verstaa - Züritüütsch rede*. Küsnacht.

Timothy Feist and Enrique L. Palancar. 2015. *Oto-Manguean Inflectional Class Database*. University of Surrey, Online.

Raphael Finkel and Gregory Stump. 2007. Principal parts and morphological typology. *Morphology*, 17(1):39–75.

Martina Forster and Clara Meister. 2020. SIGMORPHON 2020 task 0 system description: ETH Zürich team. In *Proceedings of the 17th SIGMORPHON Workshop on Computational Research in Phonetics, Phonology, and Morphology*.

Zygmunt Frajzyngier. 2018. Afroasiatic Languages. In *Oxford Research Encyclopedia of Linguistics*.

Kyle Gorman, Arya D. McCarthy, Ryan Cotterell, Ekaterina Vylomova, Miikka Silfverberg, and Magdalena Markowska. 2019. Weird inflects but ok: Making sense of morphological generation errors. In *Proceedings of the 23rd Conference on Computational Natural Language Learning (CoNLL)*, pages 140–151.

Joseph Harold Greenberg. 1963. Universals of language.

Mohammad Nazmul Haque, Nasimul Noman, Regina Berretta, and Pablo Moscato. 2016. Heterogeneous ensemble combination search using genetic algorithm for class imbalanced data classification. *PloS one*, 11(1).

Ray Harlow. 2007. *Maori: A Linguistic Introduction*. Cambridge University Press.

Martin Haspelmath. 2007. Pre-established categories don't exist: Consequences for language description and typology. *Linguistic Typology*, 11(1):119–132.

Jeffrey Heath. 2014. Grammar of humburi senni (songhay of hombori, mali).

Mans Hulden, Markus Forsberg, and Malin Ahlberg. 2014. Semi-supervised learning of morphological paradigms and lexicons. In *Proceedings of the 14th Conference of the European Chapter of the Association for Computational Linguistics*, pages 569–578.

James Hunter. 1923. *A Lecture on the Grammatical Construction of the Cree Language. Also Paradigms of the Cree Verb (Original work published 1875*. The Society for Promoting Christian Knowledge, London.

Paa Kwesi Imbeah. 2012. *102 Akan Verbs*. CreateSpace Independent Publishing Platform, Online.

Sulev Iva. 2007. *Võru kirjakeele sõnamuutmissüsteem*. Ph.D. thesis.

Pratik Jayarao, Siddhanth Pillay, Pranav Thombre, and Aditi Chaudhary. 2020. Exploring neural architectures and techniques for typologically diverse morphological inflection. In *Proceedings of the 17th SIGMORPHON Workshop on Computational Research in Phonetics, Phonology, and Morphology*.

Alim Kadeer. 2016. *Uyghur language: 94 Uyghur verbs in common tenses*. CreateSpace Independent Publishing Platform, Online.

Kasahorow. 2012a. *102 Ga Verbs*. CreateSpace Independent Publishing Platform, Online.

Kasahorow. 2012b. *102 Swahili Verbs*. CreateSpace Independent Publishing Platform, Online.

Kasahorow. 2014a. *102 Lingala Verbs: Master the Simple Tenses of the Lingala*. CreateSpace Independent Publishing Platform, Online.

Kasahorow. 2014b. *102 Shona Verbs: Master the simple tenses of the Shona language*. CreateSpace Independent Publishing Platform, Online.

Kasahorow. 2015a. *Modern Malagasy Verbs: Master the Simple Tenses of the Malagasy Language*. CreateSpace Independent Publishing Platform, Online.

Kasahorow. 2015b. *Modern Zulu Verbs: Master the simple tenses of the Zulu language*. CreateSpace Independent Publishing Platform, Online.

Kasahorow. 2016. *Modern Kongo Verbs: Master the Simple Tenses of the Kongo Language*. CreateSpace Independent Publishing Platform, Online.

Kasahorow. 2017. *Modern Oromo Dictionary: Oromo-English, English-Oromo*. CreateSpace Independent Publishing Platform, Online.

Kasahorow. 2019a. *Modern Chewa Verbs: Master the basic tenses of Chewa*. CreateSpace Independent Publishing Platform, Online.

Kasahorow. 2019b. *Modern Zarma Verbs: Master the basic tenses of Zarma*. CreateSpace Independent Publishing Platform, Online.

Kasahorow. 2020. *Modern Sotho Verbs: Master the basic tenses of Sotho (Sotho dictionary*. CreateSpace Independent Publishing Platform, Online.

Elena Klyachko, Alexey Sorokin, Natalia Krizhanovskaya, Andrew Krizhanovsky, and Galina Ryazanskaya. 2020. LowResourceEval-2019: a shared task on morphological analysis for low-resource languages. *arXiv preprint arXiv:2001.11285*.

Philipp Koehn. 2004. Statistical significance tests for machine translation evaluation. In *Proceedings of the 2004 Conference on Empirical Methods in Natural Language Processing*, pages 388–395, Barcelona, Spain. Association for Computational Linguistics.

Harlan LaFontaine and Neil McKay. 2005. *550 Dakota Verbs*. Minnesota Historical Society Press, Online.

Johann-Mattis List, Michael Cysouw, and Robert Forkel. 2016. Concepticon: A resource for the linking of concept lists. In *Proceedings of the Tenth International Conference on Language Resources and Evaluation (LREC'16)*, pages 2393–2400.

Ling Liu and Mans Hulden. 2020. Leveraging principal parts for morphological inflection. In *Proceedings of the 17th SIGMORPHON Workshop on Computational Research in Phonetics, Phonology, and Morphology*.

John Mansfield. 2019. *Murrinhpatha Morphology and Phonology*, volume 653. Walter de Gruyter.

André Martins and Ramon Astudillo. 2016. From softmax to sparsemax: A sparse model of attention and multi-label classification. In *International Conference on Machine Learning*, pages 1614–1623.

John C. Moorfield. 2019. *Te Aka Online Māori Dictionary*. Online.

Nikitha Murikinati and Antonios Anastasopoulos. 2020. The CMU-LTI submission to the SIGMORPHON 2020 shared task 0: Language-specific cross-lingual transfer. In *Proceedings of the 17th SIGMORPHON Workshop on Computational Research in Phonetics, Phonology, and Morphology*.

Temir Nabiyev. 2015. *Kazakh Language: 101 Kazakh Verbs*. Preceptor Language Guides, Online.

Mirembe Namono. 2018. *Luganda Language: 101 Luganda Verbs*. CreateSpace Independent Publishing Platform, Online.

Idai Nandoro. 2018. *Shona Language: 101 Shona Verbs*. CreateSpace Independent Publishing Platform, Online.

Center for Southeast Asian Studies NIU. 2017. *Table of Tagalog Verbs*. CreateSpace Independent Publishing Platform, Online.

Enrique L Palancar and Jean Léo Léonard. 2016. *Tone and inflection: New facts and new perspectives*, volume 296. Walter de Gruyter GmbH & Co KG.

Ben Peters and André F. T Martins. 2020. One-size-fits-all multilingual models. In *Proceedings of the 17th SIGMORPHON Workshop on Computational Research in Phonetics, Phonology, and Morphology*.

Ben Peters and André FT Martins. 2019. It–ist at the sigmorphon 2019 shared task: Sparse two-headed models for inflection. In *Proceedings of the 16th Workshop on Computational Research in Phonetics, Phonology, and Morphology*, pages 50–56.

Ben Peters, Vlad Niculae, and André FT Martins. 2019. Sparse sequence-to-sequence models. In *Proceedings of the 57th Annual Meeting of the Association for Computational Linguistics*, pages 1504–1519.

Robert L Rankin, John Boyle, Randolph Graczyk, and John E Koontz. 2003. Synchronic and diachronic perspective on'word'in siouan. *Word: a cross-linguistic typology*, pages 180–204.

Dakila Reyes. 2015. *Cebuano Language: 101 Cebuano Verbs*. CreateSpace Independent Publishing Platform, Online.

Anj Santos. 2018. *Hiligaynon Language. 101 Hiligaynon Verbs*. CreateSpace Independent Publishing Platform, Online.

Andei Scherbakov. 2020. The UniMelb submission to the SIGMORPHON 2020 shared task 0: Typologically diverse morphological inflection. In *Proceedings of the 17th SIGMORPHON Workshop on Computational Research in Phonetics, Phonology, and Morphology*.

Andrei Shcherbakov, Ekaterina Vylomova, and Nick Thieberger. 2016. Phonotactic modeling of extremely low resource languages. In *Proceedings of the Australasian Language Technology Association Workshop 2016*, pages 84–93.

Miikka Silfverberg, Adam Wiemerslage, Ling Liu, and Lingshuang Jack Mao. 2017. Data augmentation for morphological reinflection. In *Proceedings of the CoNLL SIGMORPHON 2017 Shared Task: Universal Morphological Reinflection*, pages 90–99, Vancouver. Association for Computational Linguistics.

Assaf Singer and Katharina Kann. 2020. The NYU-CUBoulder systems for SIGMORPHON 2020 task 0 and task 2. In *Proceedings of the 17th SIGMORPHON Workshop on Computational Research in Phonetics, Phonology, and Morphology*.

Morris Swadesh. 1950. Salish internal relationships. *International Journal of American Linguistics*, 16(4):157–167.

John Sylak-Glassman. 2016. The composition and use of the universal morphological feature schema (unimorph schema). *Johns Hopkins University*.

Turkicum. 2019a. *The Kazakh Verbs: Review Guide*. Preceptor Language Guides, Online.

Turkicum. 2019b. *The Uzbek Verbs: Review Guide*. CreateSpace Independent Publishing Platform, Online.

Turkmenistan US Embassy. 2018. *501 Turkmen verbs*. Peace Corps, Online.

Ashish Vaswani, Noam Shazeer, Niki Parmar, Jakob Uszkoreit, Llion Jones, Aidan N Gomez, Łukasz Kaiser, and Illia Polosukhin. 2017. Attention is all you need. In *Advances in neural information processing systems*, pages 5998–6008.

Shijie Wu and Ryan Cotterell. 2019. Exact hard monotonic attention for character-level transduction. In *Proceedings of the 57th Annual Meeting of the Association for Computational Linguistics*, pages 1530–1537.

Shijie Wu, Ryan Cotterell, and Mans Hulden. 2020. Applying the transformer to character-level transduction.

Xiang Yu, Ngoc Thang Vu, and Jonas Kuhns. 2020. Ensemble self-training for low-resource languages:grapheme-to-phoneme conversion and morphological inflection. In *Proceedings of the 17th SIGMORPHON Workshop on Computational Research in Phonetics, Phonology, and Morphology*.

Nina Zaytseva, Andrew Krizhanovsky, Natalia Krizhanovsky, Natalia Pellinen, and Aleksndra Rodionova. 2017. Open corpus of Veps and Karelian languages (VepKar): preliminary data collection and dictionaries. In *Corpus Linguistics-2017*, pages 172–177.

Ofelia Zepeda. 2003. *A Tohono O'odham grammar (Original work published 1983)*. University of Arizona Press, Online.

Long Zhou, Jiajun Zhang, and Chengqing Zong. 2019. Synchronous bidirectional neural machine translation. *Transactions of the Association for Computational Linguistics*, 7:91–105.

A Language data statistics

Lang	Total			Inconsistency (%)			Contradiction (%)		In Vocabulary (%)	
	Train	Dev	Test	Train	Dev	Test	Dev	Test	Dev	Test
aka	2793	380	763	0.0	0.0	0.0	0.0	0.0	24.7	12.5
ang	29270	4122	8197	11.8	1.8	3.4	21.6	21.9	35.1	21.3
ast	5096	728	1457	0.0	0.0	0.0	0.0	0.0	23.9	12.4
aze	5602	801	1601	11.9	1.9	4.0	22.3	20.9	31.5	20.2
azg	8482	1188	2396	0.8	0.0	0.0	1.3	1.1	26.9	13.8
bak	8517	1217	2434	0.0	0.0	0.0	0.0	0.0	59.8	40.1
ben	2816	402	805	0.0	0.0	0.0	0.0	0.0	29.9	16.0
bod	3428	466	936	1.0	0.2	0.3	2.4	1.9	80.0	73.4
cat	51944	7421	14842	0.0	0.0	0.0	0.0	0.0	20.8	10.4
ceb	420	58	111	1.0	0.0	0.0	0.0	2.7	72.4	62.2
cly	3301	471	944	0.0	0.0	0.0	0.0	0.0	37.4	19.3
cpa	5298	727	1431	3.4	0.6	0.8	6.6	4.3	60.2	39.8
cre	4571	584	1174	18.5	2.1	4.9	29.8	29.6	5.5	2.7
crh	5215	745	1490	0.0	0.0	0.0	0.0	0.0	77.4	60.7
ctp	2397	313	598	15.9	1.6	3.0	22.0	21.7	52.7	34.1
czn	1088	154	305	0.2	0.0	0.0	1.3	0.0	86.4	74.8
dak	2636	376	750	0.0	0.0	0.0	0.0	0.0	75.5	55.7
dan	17852	2550	5101	16.5	2.5	5.0	34.5	32.9	71.4	51.8
deu	99405	14201	28402	0.0	0.0	0.0	0.0	0.0	55.8	37.8
dje	56	9	16	0.0	0.0	0.0	0.0	0.0	100.0	87.5
eng	80865	11553	23105	1.1	0.2	0.4	2.1	1.9	80.3	66.2
est	26728	3820	7637	2.7	0.4	0.8	6.1	5.1	22.4	11.6
evn	5413	774	1547	9.6	2.8	4.3	8.9	10.0	38.9	32.5
fas	25225	3603	7208	0.0	0.0	0.0	0.0	0.0	7.6	3.8
fin	99403	14201	28401	0.0	0.0	0.0	0.0	0.0	32.6	17.2
frm	24612	3516	7033	0.0	0.0	0.0	0.0	0.0	17.1	8.6
frr	1902	224	477	4.0	0.0	1.7	9.8	6.1	22.8	10.7
fur	5408	772	1546	0.0	0.0	0.0	0.0	0.0	21.6	10.9
gaa	607	79	169	0.0	0.0	0.0	0.0	0.0	74.7	47.3
glg	24087	3441	6882	0.0	0.0	0.0	0.0	0.0	14.1	7.1
gmh	496	71	141	1.2	0.0	0.0	5.6	2.8	38.0	20.6
gml	890	127	255	17.3	3.1	5.5	22.8	27.8	39.4	20.4
gsw	1345	192	385	0.0	0.0	0.0	0.0	0.0	55.7	35.6
hil	859	116	238	0.0	0.0	0.0	0.0	0.0	59.5	36.6
hin	36300	5186	10372	0.0	0.0	0.0	0.0	0.0	5.0	2.5
isl	53841	7690	15384	1.0	0.1	0.3	1.9	2.0	48.8	29.5
izh	763	112	224	0.0	0.0	0.0	0.0	0.0	42.9	22.3
kan	3670	524	1049	13.2	2.7	4.7	18.7	20.7	21.9	14.0
kaz	7852	1063	2113	1.1	0.2	0.4	1.9	1.8	10.6	5.3
kir	3855	547	1089	0.0	0.0	0.0	0.0	0.0	17.9	9.0
kjh	840	120	240	0.0	0.0	0.0	0.0	0.0	50.8	30.4
kon	568	76	156	0.0	0.0	0.0	0.0	0.0	78.9	71.8
kpv	57919	8263	16526	0.0	0.0	0.0	0.0	0.0	48.8	35.0
krl	80216	11225	22290	0.2	0.0	0.0	0.3	0.3	19.7	10.3
lin	159	23	46	0.0	0.0	0.0	0.0	0.0	100.0	73.9
liv	2787	398	802	0.0	0.0	0.0	0.0	0.0	40.7	24.1

Table 6: Number of samples in training, development, test sets, as well as statistics on systematic errors (inconsistency) and percentage of samples with lemmata observed in the training set.

Lang	Total			Inconsistency (%)			Contradiction (%)		In Vocabulary (%)	
	Train	Dev	Test	Train	Dev	Test	Dev	Test	Dev	Test
lld	5073	725	1450	0.0	0.0	0.0	0.0	0.0	24.3	12.3
lud	294	41	82	7.8	0.0	3.7	9.8	11.0	31.7	20.7
lug	3420	489	977	4.0	0.6	0.8	5.1	7.6	18.2	9.1
mao	145	21	42	0.0	0.0	0.0	0.0	0.0	61.9	81.0
mdf	46362	6633	13255	1.6	0.2	0.5	3.1	3.3	49.0	35.1
mhr	71143	10081	20233	0.3	0.0	0.0	0.4	0.5	48.8	34.3
mlg	447	62	127	0.0	0.0	0.0	0.0	0.0	90.3	74.0
mlt	1233	176	353	0.1	0.0	0.0	0.6	0.0	52.3	30.6
mwf	777	111	222	2.6	0.0	0.9	2.7	4.5	25.2	13.1
myv	74928	10738	21498	1.7	0.3	0.5	3.1	3.1	45.5	32.7
nld	38826	5547	11094	0.0	0.0	0.0	0.0	0.0	58.2	38.4
nno	10101	1443	2887	3.4	0.4	1.0	6.0	6.8	80.0	70.2
nob	13263	1929	3830	10.5	1.8	3.1	18.5	19.7	80.5	70.5
nya	3031	429	853	0.0	0.0	0.0	0.0	0.0	46.4	26.5
olo	43936	6260	12515	1.4	0.3	0.5	3.3	2.9	83.0	70.8
ood	1123	160	314	0.4	0.0	0.0	1.9	1.0	70.0	58.0
orm	1424	203	405	0.2	0.0	0.2	0.5	0.7	41.9	22.7
ote	22962	3231	6437	0.4	0.1	0.1	0.5	0.8	48.4	29.5
otm	21533	3020	5997	0.9	0.1	0.3	1.8	1.7	49.4	29.4
pei	10017	1349	2636	15.8	2.6	4.9	21.5	21.4	9.1	4.7
pus	4861	695	1389	3.9	0.6	1.6	9.9	7.7	34.2	23.0
san	22968	3188	6272	3.1	0.5	0.9	4.5	5.5	26.9	14.6
sme	43877	6273	12527	0.0	0.0	0.0	0.0	0.0	28.2	16.3
sna	1897	246	456	0.0	0.0	0.0	0.0	0.0	31.3	18.0
sot	345	50	99	0.0	0.0	0.0	0.0	0.0	48.0	25.3
swa	3374	469	910	0.0	0.0	0.0	0.0	0.0	20.7	10.5
swe	54888	7840	15683	0.0	0.0	0.0	0.0	0.0	70.6	51.9
syc	1917	275	548	3.5	1.5	0.4	7.6	8.6	47.3	28.1
tel	952	136	273	1.4	0.0	1.1	0.7	2.6	62.5	39.6
tgk	53	8	16	0.0	0.0	0.0	0.0	0.0	0.0	0.0
tgl	1870	236	478	7.6	1.3	1.0	11.9	10.0	74.2	55.6
tuk	20963	2992	5979	9.5	1.5	3.2	16.8	16.0	16.7	8.3
udm	88774	12665	25333	0.0	0.0	0.0	0.0	0.0	38.1	24.8
uig	5372	750	1476	0.3	0.0	0.0	0.3	0.5	12.0	6.1
urd	8486	1213	2425	0.0	0.0	0.0	0.0	0.0	9.4	6.0
uzb	25199	3596	7191	0.0	0.0	0.0	0.0	0.0	11.9	6.0
vec	12203	1743	3487	0.0	0.0	0.0	0.0	0.0	20.8	10.6
vep	94395	13320	26422	10.9	1.8	3.3	19.3	19.8	25.1	12.9
vot	1003	146	281	0.0	0.0	0.0	0.0	0.0	35.6	19.6
vro	357	51	103	1.1	0.0	0.0	2.0	1.0	70.6	50.5
xno	178	26	51	0.0	0.0	0.0	0.0	0.0	19.2	9.8
xty	2110	299	600	0.1	0.3	0.0	0.3	1.3	78.6	65.8
zpv	805	113	228	0.0	0.0	0.4	2.7	0.9	78.8	78.9
zul	322	42	78	1.9	0.0	0.0	2.4	0.0	83.3	66.7
TOTAL	1574004	223649	446580	2.0	0.3	0.6	3.6	3.6	41.1	27.9

Table 7: Number of samples in training, development, test sets, as well as statistics on systematic errors (inconsistency) and percentage of samples with lemmata observed in the training set.

B Accuracy trends

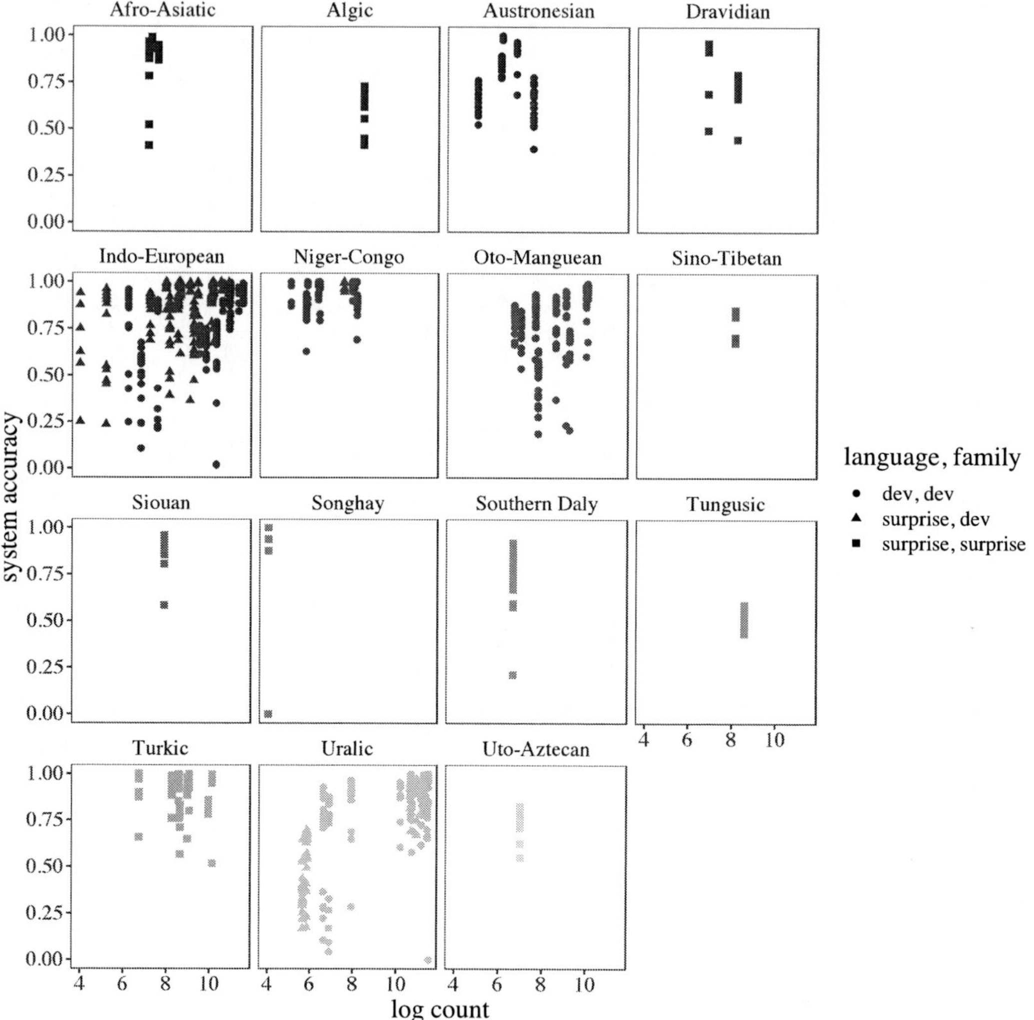

Figure 7: Accuracy for each system and language by the log size of the dataset, **grouped by language family**. Points are color-coded according to language family, and shape-coded according to language type: development language – development family, surprise language – development family, surprise language – surprise family.

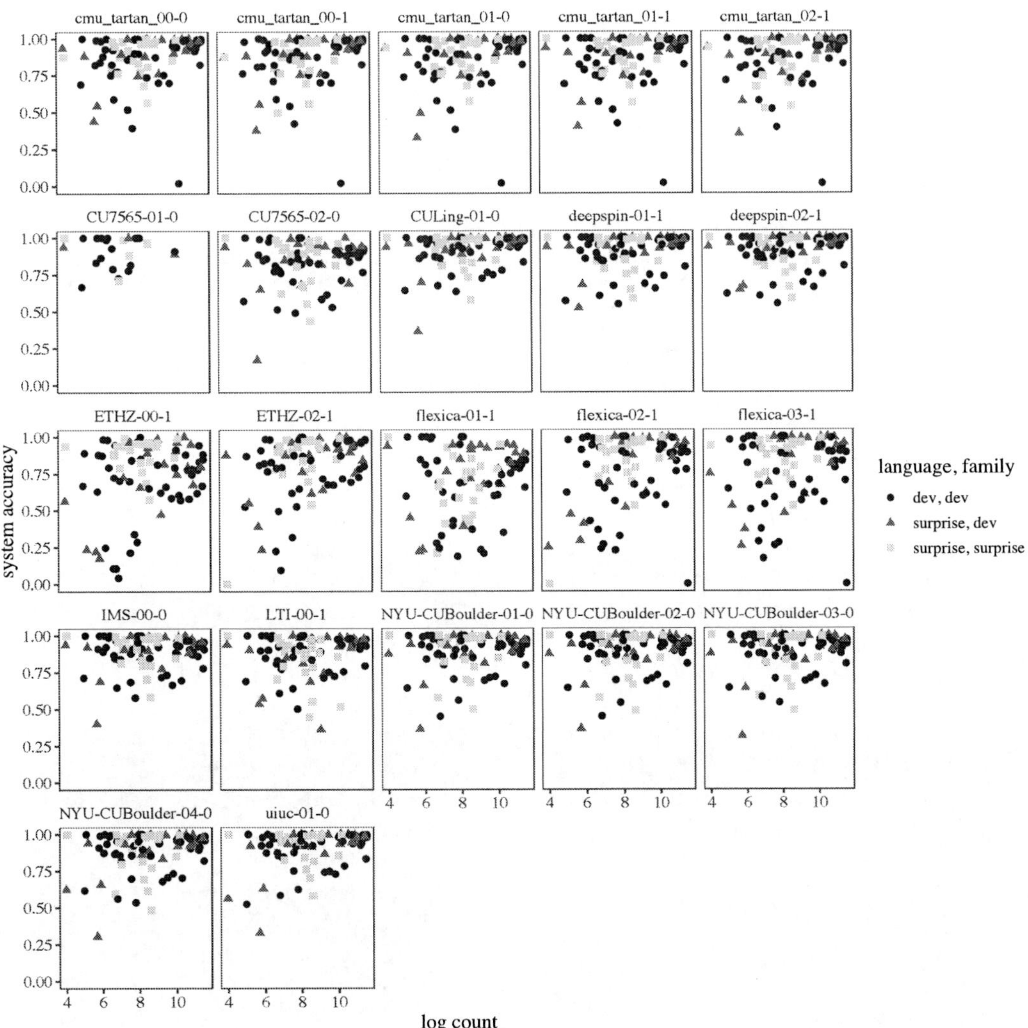

Figure 8: Accuracy for each language by the log size of the dataset, **grouped by submitted system**. Points are color- and shape-coded according to language type: development language – development family, surprise language – development family, surprise language – surprise family.

Table 8: **Results per Language Family: Afro-Asiatic and Algic**

System	Rank	Acc
uiuc-01-0	1.0	96.4
CULing-01-0	1.0	96.3
deepspin-02-1	3.7	95.2
BASE: trm-single	4.0	95.5
BASE: trm-aug-single	4.0	95.0
deepspin-01-1	4.0	94.7
NYU-CUBoulder-01-0	4.0	94.4
NYU-CUBoulder-02-0	4.0	94.4
NYU-CUBoulder-04-0	9.7	94.3
BASE: mono-single	6.3	92.8
cmu_tartan_00-0	6.3	92.7
cmu_tartan_01-0	9.3	89.6
cmu_tartan_01-1	9.3	89.4
cmu_tartan_02-1	10.0	80.9
ETHZ-00-1	6.7	94.7
BASE: trm-shared	6.7	94.2
BASE: trm-aug-shared	6.7	94.0
IMS-00-0	6.7	93.6
BASE: mono-aug-single	6.7	93.5
NYU-CUBoulder-03-0	12.3	93.7
flexica-02-1	9.3	92.9
ETHZ-02-1	9.3	92.3
flexica-03-1	9.3	92.1
BASE: mono-shared	9.3	91.5
CU7565-01-0	*19.3*	*93.7*
BASE: mono-aug-shared	16.0	89.8
CU7565-02-0	15.0	91.6
cmu_tartan_00-1	17.7	91.7
LTI-00-1	17.7	91.3
flexica-01-1	28.3	73.4
Oracle (Baselines)		98.7
Oracle (Submissions)		99.7
Oracle (All)		99.8

(a) Results on the Afro-Asiatic family (3 languages)

System	Rank	Acc
CULing-01-0	1.0	73.0
flexica-03-1	1.0	70.4
IMS-00-0	1.0	70.3
uiuc-01-0	1.0	70.3
ETHZ-02-1	1.0	69.4
cmu_tartan_02-1	1.0	69.4
flexica-02-1	1.0	69.4
cmu_tartan_00-1	8.0	69.2
BASE: mono-aug-shared	8.0	68.5
BASE: mono-aug-single	8.0	68.5
ETHZ-00-1	8.0	68.4
BASE: trm-aug-shared	8.0	68.0
BASE: trm-aug-single	8.0	68.0
cmu_tartan_01-1	8.0	68.0
NYU-CUBoulder-01-0	8.0	67.9
BASE: trm-shared	8.0	67.7
BASE: trm-single	8.0	67.7
cmu_tartan_00-0	8.0	67.6
cmu_tartan_01-0	8.0	67.6
BASE: mono-shared	8.0	66.8
BASE: mono-single	8.0	66.8
NYU-CUBoulder-02-0	8.0	66.5
deepspin-02-1	8.0	66.5
deepspin-01-1	24.0	65.1
NYU-CUBoulder-03-0	24.0	64.7
NYU-CUBoulder-04-0	26.0	61.8
CU7565-02-0	27.0	55.5
LTI-00-1	28.0	44.9
flexica-01-1	28.0	41.5
CU7565-01-0	*30.0*	*0.0*
Oracle (Baselines)		86.9
Oracle (Submissions)		98.7
Oracle (All)		98.8

(b) Results on the Algic family (1 language)

Table 9: **Results per Language Family: Austronesian and Dravidian**

System	Rank	Acc
CULing-01-0	1.0	84.4
IMS-00-0	1.6	85.1
NYU-CUBoulder-03-0	1.6	83.6
ETHZ-00-1	1.6	83.4
NYU-CUBoulder-01-0	1.6	82.9
NYU-CUBoulder-04-0	1.6	82.9
BASE: trm-shared	1.6	82.8
NYU-CUBoulder-02-0	1.6	82.7
deepspin-02-1	3.2	82.4
BASE: trm-aug-single	3.2	81.6
CU7565-01-0	*6.8*	*82.7*
uiuc-01-0	5.4	82.3
BASE: trm-single	6.0	81.2
BASE: mono-aug-shared	6.0	82.9
LTI-00-1	6.0	82.0
BASE: mono-aug-single	7.8	81.3
deepspin-01-1	7.6	81.0
BASE: trm-aug-shared	7.6	79.8
flexica-03-1	7.6	79.3
cmu_tartan_00-0	8.2	79.1
BASE: mono-shared	10.4	79.2
BASE: mono-single	10.4	77.6
cmu_tartan_00-1	12.8	80.3
cmu_tartan_02-1	12.8	78.9
cmu_tartan_01-0	12.8	78.6
flexica-02-1	12.8	78.3
cmu_tartan_01-1	12.8	78.2
ETHZ-02-1	12.0	77.4
CU7565-02-0	*22.4*	*73.7*
flexica-01-1	21.2	69.7
Oracle (Baselines)		89.1
Oracle (Submissions)		93.5
Oracle (All)		93.7

(a) Results on the Austronesian family (5 languages)

System	Rank	Acc
IMS-00-0	1.0	87.6
CULing-01-0	1.0	87.0
BASE: trm-aug-shared	1.0	86.8
cmu_tartan_00-0	1.0	86.3
cmu_tartan_01-1	1.0	86.3
BASE: trm-aug-single	1.0	85.9
BASE: trm-shared	1.0	85.8
ETHZ-02-1	1.0	85.5
cmu_tartan_01-0	5.0	85.7
deepspin-02-1	5.0	85.6
cmu_tartan_02-1	5.0	85.5
BASE: trm-single	5.0	85.4
uiuc-01-0	5.0	85.3
deepspin-01-1	5.0	85.2
LTI-00-1	5.0	85.0
ETHZ-00-1	5.0	84.9
BASE: mono-single	5.0	84.8
BASE: mono-aug-single	5.0	84.1
NYU-CUBoulder-02-0	12.0	82.2
NYU-CUBoulder-01-0	12.0	82.2
NYU-CUBoulder-03-0	12.0	82.1
NYU-CUBoulder-04-0	12.0	81.9
CU7565-02-0	14.5	81.4
flexica-02-1	16.5	83.7
BASE: mono-shared	16.5	83.7
flexica-03-1	16.5	83.0
cmu_tartan_00-1	19.0	62.6
BASE: mono-aug-shared	23.5	79.7
flexica-01-1	28.5	56.9
CU7565-01-0	*30.0*	*0.0*
Oracle (Baselines)		95.9
Oracle (Submissions)		98.2
Oracle (All)		98.6

(b) Results on the Dravidian family (2 languages)

Table 10: Results per Language Family: Indo-European and Niger-Congo

System	Rank	Acc
deepspin-02-1	2.3	92.9
uiuc-01-0	3.1	91.6
deepspin-01-1	2.9	92.9
BASE: trm-single	2.9	91.7
CULing-01-0	3.9	93.5
BASE: trm-aug-single	3.4	92.9
NYU-CUBoulder-04-0	7.3	90.7
BASE: trm-shared	12.0	86.9
cmu_tartan_00-1	8.1	88.6
BASE: mono-shared	8.9	90.3
NYU-CUBoulder-03-0	10.0	91.2
cmu_tartan_00-0	8.9	88.5
NYU-CUBoulder-02-0	11.4	90.6
BASE: mono-aug-shared	12.9	90.5
NYU-CUBoulder-01-0	12.4	90.4
BASE: mono-single	8.1	88.0
BASE: mono-aug-single	7.9	91.9
cmu_tartan_01-0	10.5	88.6
cmu_tartan_01-1	9.9	88.5
IMS-00-0	15.9	90.4
cmu_tartan_02-1	10.7	88.4
BASE: trm-aug-shared	15.0	88.6
LTI-00-1	15.8	87.5
CU7565-02-0	20.3	86.3
flexica-03-1	19.4	80.7
ETHZ-02-1	18.1	83.8
ETHZ-00-1	23.5	73.7
flexica-02-1	21.8	77.5
CU7565-01-0	*28.8*	*91.4*
flexica-01-1	26.0	76.7
Oracle (Baselines)		98.0
Oracle (Submissions)		98.8
Oracle (All)		99.1

(a) Results on the Indo-European family (28 languages)

System	Rank	Acc
IMS-00-0	1.0	98.1
uiuc-01-0	1.0	97.9
NYU-CUBoulder-01-0	1.3	98.1
NYU-CUBoulder-02-0	1.3	98.1
deepspin-02-1	1.3	98.0
NYU-CUBoulder-03-0	1.3	98.0
BASE: mono-aug-single	1.3	97.9
deepspin-01-1	1.3	97.9
NYU-CUBoulder-04-0	1.3	97.8
LTI-00-1	1.3	97.7
BASE: trm-shared	1.3	97.7
BASE: trm-single	1.3	97.7
BASE: mono-single	1.3	97.7
BASE: mono-shared	1.3	97.6
BASE: trm-aug-single	1.3	97.5
BASE: trm-aug-shared	1.3	97.4
BASE: mono-aug-shared	1.3	97.2
CU7565-01-0	*3.9*	*98.0*
CULing-01-0	3.4	97.1
flexica-03-1	3.1	96.9
flexica-02-1	3.1	96.9
cmu_tartan_01-1	3.6	96.4
cmu_tartan_00-0	3.6	96.3
cmu_tartan_01-0	3.6	96.3
CU7565-02-0	6.5	95.6
cmu_tartan_00-1	7.8	95.4
flexica-01-1	9.2	94.2
cmu_tartan_02-1	11.2	94.4
ETHZ-02-1	18.9	91.7
ETHZ-00-1	20.3	89.3
Oracle (Baselines)		99.2
Oracle (Submissions)		99.4
Oracle (All)		99.6

(b) Results on the Niger-Congo family (10 languages)

Table 11: Results per Language Family: Oto-Manguean and Sino-Tibetan

System	Rank	Acc
uiuc-01-0	1.0	87.5
BASE: trm-single	2.0	86.2
CULing-01-0	3.1	86.7
deepspin-02-1	3.4	85.4
deepspin-01-1	3.4	85.3
NYU-CUBoulder-04-0	6.4	84.2
BASE: mono-single	7.9	82.4
NYU-CUBoulder-03-0	8.4	83.5
BASE: mono-aug-single	6.1	83.5
BASE: mono-shared	8.2	82.9
NYU-CUBoulder-02-0	9.1	83.5
IMS-00-0	10.3	83.3
LTI-00-1	9.4	82.4
NYU-CUBoulder-01-0	9.4	83.6
BASE: mono-aug-shared	9.8	82.0
cmu_tartan_00-0	13.9	78.5
cmu_tartan_01-1	14.9	78.5
cmu_tartan_02-1	15.2	78.2
BASE: trm-shared	14.5	80.2
BASE: trm-aug-shared	20.3	73.8
flexica-01-1	26.3	47.2
BASE: trm-aug-single	7.4	84.3
cmu_tartan_00-1	14.1	79.0
ETHZ-02-1	14.0	81.4
CU7565-02-0	20.9	75.1
cmu_tartan_01-0	18.3	76.5
CU7565-01-0	*27.8*	*81.0*
ETHZ-00-1	25.4	70.5
flexica-02-1	25.6	67.0
flexica-03-1	26.1	64.2
Oracle (Baselines)		94.1
Oracle (Submissions)		96.2
Oracle (All)		96.7

(a) Results on the Oto-Manguean family (10 languages)

System	Rank	Acc
deepspin-01-1	1.0	85.1
deepspin-02-1	1.0	85.0
LTI-00-1	1.0	84.7
uiuc-01-0	1.0	84.4
BASE: trm-single	1.0	84.4
BASE: trm-shared	1.0	84.4
CULing-01-0	1.0	84.1
ETHZ-02-1	1.0	83.8
flexica-02-1	1.0	83.7
cmu_tartan_01-1	1.0	83.4
BASE: mono-aug-shared	1.0	83.4
BASE: mono-aug-single	1.0	83.4
NYU-CUBoulder-01-0	1.0	83.4
IMS-00-0	1.0	83.3
BASE: trm-aug-single	1.0	83.3
BASE: trm-aug-shared	1.0	83.3
BASE: mono-shared	1.0	83.2
BASE: mono-single	1.0	83.2
cmu_tartan_00-0	1.0	83.1
cmu_tartan_02-1	1.0	83.1
cmu_tartan_00-1	1.0	83.0
NYU-CUBoulder-03-0	22.0	82.8
ETHZ-00-1	22.0	82.8
cmu_tartan_01-0	22.0	82.7
NYU-CUBoulder-02-0	22.0	82.6
flexica-03-1	22.0	82.5
NYU-CUBoulder-04-0	22.0	81.7
flexica-01-1	28.0	70.6
CU7565-02-0	28.0	67.9
CU7565-01-0	*30.0*	*0.0*
Oracle (Baselines)		91.3
Oracle (Submissions)		96.0
Oracle (All)		96.2

(b) Results on the Sino-Tibetan family (1 language)

Table 12: **Results per Language Family: Siouan and Songhay**

System	Rank	Acc
NYU-CUBoulder-01-0	1.0	95.7
BASE: trm-single	1.0	95.6
CULing-01-0	1.0	95.6
BASE: trm-shared	1.0	95.6
ETHZ-00-1	1.0	95.5
uiuc-01-0	1.0	94.9
deepspin-01-1	1.0	94.8
NYU-CUBoulder-02-0	1.0	94.8
NYU-CUBoulder-03-0	1.0	94.7
deepspin-02-1	1.0	94.5
BASE: mono-aug-shared	1.0	94.4
BASE: mono-aug-single	1.0	94.4
NYU-CUBoulder-04-0	1.0	94.3
ETHZ-02-1	14.0	93.3
BASE: mono-single	14.0	92.9
BASE: mono-shared	14.0	92.9
BASE: trm-aug-single	14.0	92.5
BASE: trm-aug-shared	14.0	92.5
flexica-02-1	14.0	91.5
IMS-00-0	14.0	90.9
LTI-00-1	21.0	89.7
flexica-03-1	21.0	89.3
cmu_tartan_01-0	23.0	85.7
cmu_tartan_01-1	23.0	85.7
cmu_tartan_02-1	23.0	85.7
cmu_tartan_00-0	23.0	85.5
cmu_tartan_00-1	23.0	85.5
CU7565-02-0	28.0	80.5
flexica-01-1	29.0	58.4
CU7565-01-0	30.0	0.0
Oracle (Baselines)		97.3
Oracle (Submissions)		98.1
Oracle (All)		98.1

(a) Results on the Siouan family (1 language)

System	Rank	Acc
BASE: mono-aug-single	1.0	100.0
BASE: trm-aug-single	1.0	100.0
CU7565-02-0	1.0	100.0
CU7565-01-0	1.0	100.0
uiuc-01-0	1.0	100.0
NYU-CUBoulder-02-0	1.0	100.0
NYU-CUBoulder-03-0	1.0	100.0
BASE: mono-aug-shared	1.0	100.0
NYU-CUBoulder-01-0	1.0	100.0
LTI-00-1	1.0	100.0
IMS-00-0	1.0	100.0
flexica-01-1	1.0	100.0
deepspin-02-1	1.0	100.0
deepspin-01-1	1.0	100.0
CULing-01-0	1.0	100.0
cmu_tartan_01-1	1.0	100.0
NYU-CUBoulder-04-0	1.0	100.0
BASE: trm-aug-shared	1.0	100.0
flexica-03-1	1.0	93.8
ETHZ-00-1	1.0	93.8
cmu_tartan_02-1	1.0	93.8
cmu_tartan_01-0	1.0	93.8
cmu_tartan_00-0	1.0	87.5
cmu_tartan_00-1	1.0	87.5
BASE: trm-shared	1.0	87.5
BASE: trm-single	1.0	87.5
flexica-02-1	27.0	0.0
BASE: mono-shared	27.0	0.0
BASE: mono-single	27.0	0.0
ETHZ-02-1	27.0	0.0
Oracle (Baselines)		100.0
Oracle (Submissions)		100.0
Oracle (All)		100.0

(b) Results on the Songhay family/genus (1 language)

Table 13: Results per Language Family: Southern Daly and Tungusic

System	Rank	Acc
CULing-01-0	1.0	91.9
BASE: trm-single	1.0	89.6
BASE: trm-shared	1.0	89.6
ETHZ-00-1	1.0	88.7
uiuc-01-0	1.0	87.8
BASE: trm-aug-single	1.0	86.9
BASE: trm-aug-shared	1.0	86.9
IMS-00-0	1.0	86.0
deepspin-01-1	9.0	83.8
deepspin-02-1	9.0	83.3
cmu_tartan_01-1	9.0	81.1
cmu_tartan_01-0	9.0	81.1
cmu_tartan_00-0	9.0	80.2
cmu_tartan_00-1	9.0	80.2
ETHZ-02-1	15.0	77.9
CU7565-02-0	15.0	77.5
flexica-03-1	15.0	73.4
flexica-02-1	15.0	72.5
LTI-00-1	15.0	70.3
cmu_tartan_02-1	20.0	67.1
BASE: mono-shared	20.0	60.8
BASE: mono-single	20.0	60.8
NYU-CUBoulder-04-0	20.0	59.5
NYU-CUBoulder-03-0	20.0	59.0
NYU-CUBoulder-02-0	20.0	57.7
NYU-CUBoulder-01-0	20.0	57.7
BASE: mono-aug-single	27.0	44.6
BASE: mono-aug-shared	27.0	44.6
flexica-01-1	29.0	21.2
CU7565-01-0	*30.0*	*0.0*
Oracle (Baselines)		91.4
Oracle (Submissions)		96.4
Oracle (All)		96.4

(a) Results on the Southern Daly family (1 language)

System	Rank	Acc
deepspin-02-1	1.0	59.0
deepspin-01-1	1.0	58.8
uiuc-01-0	1.0	58.3
IMS-00-0	1.0	58.2
CULing-01-0	1.0	58.0
BASE: trm-aug-single	1.0	57.7
BASE: trm-aug-shared	1.0	57.7
ETHZ-00-1	1.0	57.2
BASE: trm-single	1.0	57.1
cmu_tartan_01-0	1.0	57.1
BASE: trm-shared	1.0	57.1
cmu_tartan_00-0	12.0	56.8
cmu_tartan_01-1	12.0	56.5
cmu_tartan_00-1	12.0	55.9
LTI-00-1	12.0	55.0
cmu_tartan_02-1	16.0	54.1
BASE: mono-single	16.0	54.0
BASE: mono-shared	16.0	54.0
ETHZ-02-1	16.0	53.6
BASE: mono-aug-single	16.0	53.5
BASE: mono-aug-shared	16.0	53.5
flexica-02-1	16.0	53.1
flexica-03-1	16.0	52.7
NYU-CUBoulder-01-0	24.0	50.0
NYU-CUBoulder-03-0	24.0	48.8
NYU-CUBoulder-02-0	24.0	48.6
NYU-CUBoulder-04-0	24.0	48.2
flexica-01-1	28.0	46.5
CU7565-02-0	29.0	43.5
CU7565-01-0	*30.0*	*0.0*
Oracle (Baselines)		67.7
Oracle (Submissions)		75.9
Oracle (All)		76.3

(b) Results on the Tungusic family (1 language)

Table 14: Results per Language Family: Turkic and Uralic

System	Rank	Acc
BASE: trm-single	1.0	91.8
BASE: trm-aug-single	1.0	91.8
uiuc-01-0	1.8	92.0
CULing-01-0	3.5	91.9
deepspin-02-1	6.7	91.3
deepspin-01-1	6.7	91.1
NYU-CUBoulder-04-0	5.5	90.4
BASE: mono-single	5.1	90.9
NYU-CUBoulder-02-0	6.8	90.6
NYU-CUBoulder-03-0	6.8	90.5
cmu_tartan_01-1	7.2	91.0
cmu_tartan_00-1	6.6	90.8
BASE: mono-aug-single	7.3	90.7
BASE: trm-shared	7.7	91.3
cmu_tartan_02-1	7.4	90.8
NYU-CUBoulder-01-0	8.9	90.5
BASE: trm-aug-shared	9.3	91.1
cmu_tartan_00-0	9.7	90.9
cmu_tartan_01-0	11.8	90.7
ETHZ-00-1	16.6	88.9
IMS-00-0	11.2	91.0
BASE: mono-shared	15.1	88.9
flexica-02-1	13.1	89.7
LTI-00-1	17.1	83.3
flexica-03-1	17.0	88.6
BASE: mono-aug-shared	19.5	86.3
CU7565-02-0	21.6	85.9
ETHZ-02-1	17.5	88.6
CU7565-01-0	*29.1*	*96.4*
flexica-01-1	28.9	72.4
Oracle (Baselines)		95.8
Oracle (Submissions)		97.4
Oracle (All)		97.5

(a) Results on the Turkic family (10 languages)

System	Rank	Acc
deepspin-02-1	1.8	90.7
deepspin-01-1	3.1	89.7
uiuc-01-0	2.8	88.2
CULing-01-0	3.9	88.9
BASE: trm-single	3.8	88.1
BASE: trm-aug-single	4.3	88.5
NYU-CUBoulder-04-0	10.6	86.8
NYU-CUBoulder-02-0	13.4	86.4
NYU-CUBoulder-03-0	13.4	86.0
IMS-00-0	14.8	86.1
NYU-CUBoulder-01-0	15.4	85.9
cmu_tartan_00-1	7.7	85.8
cmu_tartan_02-1	9.8	84.8
LTI-00-1	12.3	86.7
cmu_tartan_01-1	7.6	86.0
cmu_tartan_00-0	8.7	86.2
BASE: trm-aug-shared	18.8	82.6
CU7565-02-0	*22.2*	*79.4*
CU7565-01-0	*28.2*	*92.9*
BASE: mono-single	10.8	83.0
cmu_tartan_01-0	10.6	84.8
BASE: mono-shared	17.6	81.1
BASE: mono-aug-shared	19.4	81.9
BASE: trm-shared	19.5	76.8
ETHZ-02-1	22.6	67.9
BASE: mono-aug-single	11.4	85.9
flexica-02-1	19.5	70.7
flexica-03-1	20.5	67.8
flexica-01-1	26.8	66.0
ETHZ-00-1	28.3	54.9
Oracle (Baselines)		95.5
Oracle (Submissions)		96.8
Oracle (All)		97.2

(b) Results on the Uralic family (16 languages)

Table 15: **Results per Language Family (Uto-Aztecan) and Semitic Genus (Afro-Asiatic Family)**

System	Rank	Acc
uiuc-01-0	1.0	82.5
NYU-CUBoulder-01-0	1.0	82.2
NYU-CUBoulder-02-0	1.0	81.8
NYU-CUBoulder-03-0	1.0	81.5
IMS-00-0	1.0	81.5
BASE: trm-single	1.0	80.9
CULing-01-0	1.0	80.9
BASE: trm-shared	1.0	80.9
deepspin-02-1	1.0	80.6
NYU-CUBoulder-04-0	1.0	79.6
ETHZ-00-1	1.0	79.3
LTI-00-1	1.0	79.0
deepspin-01-1	1.0	79.0
BASE: trm-aug-single	14.0	78.0
BASE: trm-aug-shared	14.0	78.0
flexica-02-1	14.0	77.7
BASE: mono-aug-single	14.0	77.4
BASE: mono-aug-shared	14.0	77.4
cmu_tartan_00-0	14.0	76.1
cmu_tartan_00-1	14.0	76.1
cmu_tartan_01-0	14.0	75.8
cmu_tartan_01-1	14.0	75.8
BASE: mono-shared	14.0	75.8
BASE: mono-single	14.0	75.8
flexica-03-1	14.0	75.5
ETHZ-02-1	14.0	74.5
cmu_tartan_02-1	14.0	74.2
CU7565-01-0	28.0	71.0
CU7565-02-0	29.0	62.4
flexica-01-1	30.0	54.8
Oracle (Baselines)		87.2
Oracle (Submissions)		92.0
Oracle (All)		92.3

(a) Results on the Uto-Aztecan family (1 language)

System	Rank	Acc
uiuc-01-0	1.0	95.6
CULing-01-0	1.0	94.9
deepspin-02-1	5.0	93.3
BASE: trm-single	5.5	93.9
BASE: trm-aug-single	5.5	93.1
deepspin-01-1	5.5	92.5
NYU-CUBoulder-01-0	5.5	92.4
NYU-CUBoulder-02-0	5.5	92.3
NYU-CUBoulder-04-0	14.0	92.0
BASE: mono-aug-shared	9.0	91.3
BASE: mono-single	9.0	90.2
cmu_tartan_00-0	9.0	90.0
cmu_tartan_01-1	13.5	85.4
cmu_tartan_01-0	13.5	85.2
cmu_tartan_02-1	14.5	72.3
ETHZ-00-1	9.5	92.5
BASE: trm-aug-shared	9.5	91.8
BASE: trm-shared	9.5	91.7
IMS-00-0	9.5	91.7
BASE: mono-aug-single	9.5	90.9
CU7565-02-0	9.5	90.6
NYU-CUBoulder-03-0	18.0	91.2
LTI-00-1	13.5	90.1
flexica-02-1	13.5	90.1
ETHZ-02-1	13.5	89.5
flexica-03-1	13.5	89.2
cmu_tartan_00-1	13.5	89.0
BASE: mono-shared	13.5	88.5
CU7565-01-0	*28.5*	*88.3*
flexica-01-1	28.0	63.9
Oracle (Baselines)		98.4
Oracle (Submissions)		99.6
Oracle (All)		99.7

(b) Results on the Semitic genus (2 languages)

Table 16: **Results per Language Genus (in Indo-European family)**

System	Rank	Acc
deepspin-02-1	3.4	87.1
deepspin-01-1	4.6	87.0
uiuc-01-0	3.5	87.4
BASE: trm-single	3.1	87.5
CULing-01-0	3.5	88.3
BASE: trm-aug-single	4.9	87.4
IMS-00-0	15.1	83.1
BASE: mono-single	5.3	86.3
BASE: mono-aug-single	6.8	86.3
NYU-CUBoulder-04-0	10.2	85.2
NYU-CUBoulder-02-0	13.1	83.3
NYU-CUBoulder-03-0	12.0	84.4
LTI-00-1	11.1	84.3
cmu_tartan_00-1	9.8	79.5
NYU-CUBoulder-01-0	14.5	83.0
BASE: mono-aug-shared	13.2	84.4
cmu_tartan_01-0	11.1	78.9
cmu_tartan_01-1	11.1	78.8
cmu_tartan_00-0	10.8	79.3
BASE: trm-shared	19.5	77.7
BASE: trm-aug-shared	19.5	79.1
BASE: mono-shared	11.7	83.7
cmu_tartan_02-1	13.2	78.5
CU7565-02-0	19.4	78.6
ETHZ-02-1	18.9	76.4
flexica-01-1	26.2	66.6
flexica-03-1	25.5	66.5
flexica-02-1	25.9	64.2
ETHZ-00-1	27.1	60.1
CU7565-01-0	*30.0*	*0.0*
Oracle (Baselines)		97.0
Oracle (Submissions)		98.4
Oracle (All)		98.9

(a) Results on the Germanic genus (13 languages)

System	Rank	Acc
uiuc-01-0	1.0	98.2
deepspin-02-1	1.5	98.1
deepspin-01-1	1.5	98.0
BASE: trm-single	1.5	97.9
BASE: trm-aug-single	1.5	97.8
BASE: trm-shared	2.8	97.9
CULing-01-0	7.5	98.0
BASE: mono-single	6.0	97.6
NYU-CUBoulder-04-0	5.0	97.7
cmu_tartan_02-1	7.8	97.4
cmu_tartan_00-1	7.0	97.4
BASE: mono-shared	7.0	97.3
cmu_tartan_01-1	7.8	97.3
cmu_tartan_00-0	8.8	97.1
NYU-CUBoulder-03-0	8.5	97.4
NYU-CUBoulder-02-0	9.2	97.4
NYU-CUBoulder-01-0	9.2	97.3
BASE: trm-aug-shared	11.0	97.7
BASE: mono-aug-single	9.5	97.2
flexica-03-1	9.5	97.1
flexica-02-1	11.0	96.8
ETHZ-02-1	11.5	97.4
ETHZ-00-1	13.8	96.4
BASE: mono-aug-shared	15.8	94.2
cmu_tartan_01-0	17.2	96.9
IMS-00-0	17.0	96.6
CU7565-02-0	19.8	94.8
LTI-00-1	19.8	81.5
CU7565-01-0	*29.0*	*89.0*
flexica-01-1	28.8	88.1
Oracle (Baselines)		99.2
Oracle (Submissions)		99.6
Oracle (All)		99.7

(b) Results on the Indic genus (4 languages)

Table 17: **Results per Language Genus (in Indo-European family)**

System	Rank	Acc
CULing-01-0	1.0	95.3
deepspin-01-1	2.0	94.6
deepspin-02-1	2.0	94.6
BASE: trm-aug-shared	2.0	94.5
BASE: trm-aug-single	2.0	94.5
BASE: trm-shared	2.0	86.2
cmu_tartan_02-1	4.3	94.0
BASE: mono-aug-single	4.3	93.8
BASE: mono-shared	4.3	92.0
NYU-CUBoulder-03-0	4.3	91.8
cmu_tartan_00-1	4.3	91.8
ETHZ-02-1	4.3	91.8
NYU-CUBoulder-04-0	4.3	83.7
uiuc-01-0	9.3	82.5
BASE: trm-single	9.3	82.2
IMS-00-0	9.3	94.3
ETHZ-00-1	10.3	81.7
cmu_tartan_01-0	10.0	94.0
cmu_tartan_01-1	10.0	93.8
cmu_tartan_00-0	13.0	91.9
NYU-CUBoulder-02-0	10.0	91.8
flexica-03-1	11.7	87.2
BASE: mono-single	14.0	62.7
CU7565-01-0	*20.3*	*93.8*
BASE: mono-aug-shared	14.7	93.3
NYU-CUBoulder-01-0	14.7	91.4
CU7565-02-0	17.7	90.9
LTI-00-1	18.3	86.2
flexica-01-1	19.3	77.5
flexica-02-1	20.0	70.6
Oracle (Baselines)		97.3
Oracle (Submissions)		97.5
Oracle (All)		97.7

(a) Results on the Iranian genus (3 languages)

System	Rank	Acc
deepspin-02-1	1.0	99.3
BASE: trm-single	1.0	99.2
deepspin-01-1	1.0	99.1
uiuc-01-0	1.0	98.7
BASE: trm-aug-single	2.5	98.7
CULing-01-0	3.8	99.1
cmu_tartan_00-0	4.4	98.0
BASE: mono-shared	7.1	97.0
NYU-CUBoulder-04-0	4.9	98.8
cmu_tartan_01-0	6.4	98.2
BASE: trm-shared	8.0	96.6
BASE: mono-aug-shared	10.4	97.6
cmu_tartan_00-1	7.4	97.9
cmu_tartan_01-1	9.0	98.1
NYU-CUBoulder-03-0	9.8	98.9
NYU-CUBoulder-01-0	9.8	98.6
NYU-CUBoulder-02-0	10.2	98.5
BASE: mono-aug-single	10.2	97.5
BASE: mono-single	11.5	95.5
cmu_tartan_02-1	10.5	97.8
BASE: trm-aug-shared	14.5	97.2
flexica-03-1	17.2	93.1
IMS-00-0	19.0	97.6
LTI-00-1	20.4	96.3
CU7565-02-0	23.1	92.9
flexica-02-1	21.2	92.0
flexica-01-1	26.9	87.1
ETHZ-02-1	25.1	86.1
ETHZ-00-1	27.5	81.4
CU7565-01-0	*30.0*	*0.0*
Oracle (Baselines)		99.4
Oracle (Submissions)		99.7
Oracle (All)		99.7

(b) Results on the Romance genus (8 languages)

Table 18: **Results per Language Genus (in Niger-Congo family)**

System	Rank	Acc
uiuc-01-0	1.0	97.7
IMS-00-0	1.0	97.6
CULing-01-0	1.0	96.9
NYU-CUBoulder-01-0	1.4	97.9
NYU-CUBoulder-02-0	1.4	97.9
NYU-CUBoulder-03-0	1.4	97.9
deepspin-02-1	1.4	97.6
BASE: mono-aug-single	1.4	97.5
BASE: trm-single	1.4	97.4
deepspin-01-1	1.4	97.3
NYU-CUBoulder-04-0	1.4	97.3
LTI-00-1	1.4	97.3
BASE: trm-shared	1.4	97.2
BASE: mono-single	1.4	97.1
BASE: trm-aug-single	1.4	97.0
BASE: mono-shared	1.4	97.0
BASE: trm-aug-shared	1.4	96.7
BASE: mono-aug-shared	1.4	96.6
CU7565-01-0	*4.6*	*97.4*
flexica-02-1	3.6	96.2
flexica-03-1	3.6	96.2
CU7565-02-0	4.2	95.8
cmu_tartan_01-1	4.2	95.6
cmu_tartan_01-0	4.2	95.5
cmu_tartan_00-0	4.2	95.5
cmu_tartan_00-1	6.5	94.9
flexica-01-1	7.9	93.4
cmu_tartan_02-1	13.8	93.3
ETHZ-02-1	16.9	92.0
ETHZ-00-1	18.2	89.6
Oracle (Baselines)		98.9
Oracle (Submissions)		99.3
Oracle (All)		99.5

(a) Results on the Bantoid genus (8 languages)

System	Rank	Acc
BASE: mono-shared	1.0	100.0
BASE: mono-single	1.0	100.0
CU7565-01-0	1.0	100.0
IMS-00-0	1.0	100.0
deepspin-02-1	1.0	100.0
deepspin-01-1	1.0	100.0
flexica-03-1	1.0	99.9
BASE: trm-shared	1.0	99.9
BASE: mono-aug-single	1.0	99.9
cmu_tartan_00-0	1.0	99.9
BASE: trm-aug-shared	1.0	99.9
BASE: trm-aug-single	1.0	99.7
cmu_tartan_01-1	1.0	99.7
BASE: mono-aug-shared	1.0	99.6
NYU-CUBoulder-04-0	1.0	99.6
LTI-00-1	1.0	99.5
flexica-02-1	1.0	99.3
cmu_tartan_01-0	1.0	99.3
BASE: trm-single	1.0	98.8
NYU-CUBoulder-01-0	1.0	98.8
NYU-CUBoulder-02-0	1.0	98.8
NYU-CUBoulder-03-0	1.0	98.7
cmu_tartan_02-1	1.0	98.7
uiuc-01-0	1.0	98.5
CULing-01-0	13.0	98.0
cmu_tartan_00-1	13.0	97.7
flexica-01-1	14.5	97.4
CU7565-02-0	15.5	94.9
ETHZ-02-1	27.0	90.4
ETHZ-00-1	28.5	87.9
Oracle (Baselines)		100.0
Oracle (Submissions)		100.0
Oracle (All)		100.0

(b) Results on the Kwa genus (2 languages)

Table 19: **Results per Language Genus (in Oto-Manguean Family)**

System	Rank	Acc
CULing-01-0	1.0	93.9
uiuc-01-0	1.0	93.5
BASE: trm-single	1.0	92.8
deepspin-01-1	2.5	93.1
NYU-CUBoulder-04-0	2.5	93.1
deepspin-02-1	2.5	92.6
NYU-CUBoulder-03-0	2.5	92.5
NYU-CUBoulder-02-0	6.0	92.3
BASE: mono-single	6.0	92.1
NYU-CUBoulder-01-0	6.0	92.0
BASE: mono-aug-single	6.0	91.6
BASE: trm-aug-single	6.0	91.4
IMS-00-0	10.5	91.4
BASE: mono-aug-shared	10.5	90.0
BASE: mono-shared	10.5	89.9
LTI-00-1	13.0	89.6
cmu_tartan_00-1	13.0	87.9
ETHZ-02-1	15.5	89.7
BASE: trm-shared	15.5	89.5
cmu_tartan_02-1	18.0	87.3
cmu_tartan_00-0	18.0	87.1
cmu_tartan_01-1	20.5	86.7
cmu_tartan_01-0	18.0	86.3
BASE: trm-aug-shared	21.0	84.2
ETHZ-00-1	22.0	82.7
CU7565-01-0	*28.0*	*81.7*
CU7565-02-0	26.5	76.3
flexica-02-1	26.5	69.2
flexica-03-1	28.0	66.1
flexica-01-1	29.5	40.9
Oracle (Baselines)		96.4
Oracle (Submissions)		97.1
Oracle (All)		97.4

(a) Results on the Amuzgo-Mixtecan genus (2 languages)

System	Rank	Acc
uiuc-01-0	1.0	81.1
CULing-01-0	1.5	80.3
BASE: trm-single	3.5	78.9
deepspin-02-1	2.2	78.7
deepspin-01-1	2.2	78.3
NYU-CUBoulder-04-0	2.2	77.2
IMS-00-0	3.8	78.0
NYU-CUBoulder-02-0	3.8	77.1
NYU-CUBoulder-03-0	3.8	77.0
LTI-00-1	6.8	73.9
NYU-CUBoulder-01-0	4.8	77.5
BASE: mono-aug-single	8.2	73.8
BASE: mono-aug-shared	9.2	72.9
cmu_tartan_01-1	12.0	69.2
cmu_tartan_00-0	13.0	68.5
cmu_tartan_02-1	13.0	68.5
BASE: trm-aug-shared	15.2	65.9
BASE: mono-shared	11.2	73.5
flexica-01-1	21.8	51.0
BASE: trm-aug-single	9.2	75.7
ETHZ-02-1	15.0	71.7
CU7565-02-0	16.5	68.5
BASE: trm-shared	15.2	71.0
BASE: mono-single	15.2	70.4
cmu_tartan_00-1	16.5	68.9
cmu_tartan_01-0	17.5	66.5
CU7565-01-0	*26.2*	*75.7*
ETHZ-00-1	26.2	60.5
flexica-02-1	27.0	54.3
flexica-03-1	28.2	49.0
Oracle (Baselines)		89.9
Oracle (Submissions)		93.7
Oracle (All)		94.3

(b) Results on the Zapotecan genus (4 languages)

Table 20: **Results per Language Genus (in Oto-Manguean and Uralic Families)**

System	Rank	Acc
BASE: mono-shared	1.0	98.6
uiuc-01-0	1.0	98.6
deepspin-02-1	1.0	98.5
BASE: trm-single	1.0	98.4
BASE: mono-single	1.0	98.4
BASE: mono-aug-single	1.0	98.4
deepspin-01-1	1.0	98.4
BASE: mono-aug-shared	8.0	98.2
BASE: trm-aug-single	8.0	98.1
CULing-01-0	9.5	97.7
LTI-00-1	11.5	97.2
cmu_tartan_01-1	12.0	96.2
cmu_tartan_00-1	12.0	96.8
cmu_tartan_00-0	12.0	96.7
NYU-CUBoulder-04-0	13.5	96.5
cmu_tartan_02-1	14.0	96.3
ETHZ-02-1	15.5	95.9
BASE: trm-shared	16.5	94.2
NYU-CUBoulder-03-0	18.5	94.1
NYU-CUBoulder-02-0	18.5	94.1
NYU-CUBoulder-01-0	20.0	93.7
flexica-03-1	21.0	93.1
flexica-02-1	22.5	93.1
cmu_tartan_01-0	20.5	91.9
CU7565-02-0	25.0	91.1
IMS-00-0	24.5	91.0
CU7565-01-0	28.5	90.9
BASE: trm-aug-shared	25.5	87.3
ETHZ-00-1	27.5	85.3
flexica-01-1	29.5	64.2
Oracle (Baselines)		99.7
Oracle (Submissions)		99.9
Oracle (All)		99.9

(a) Results on the Otomian genus (2 languages)

System	Rank	Acc
deepspin-02-1	2.2	87.4
uiuc-01-0	2.6	83.5
deepspin-01-1	3.8	85.8
BASE: trm-aug-single	4.0	84.1
BASE: trm-single	4.3	83.4
CULing-01-0	5.2	84.6
NYU-CUBoulder-04-0	7.0	83.0
NYU-CUBoulder-02-0	10.0	82.8
NYU-CUBoulder-03-0	9.8	82.2
IMS-00-0	12.3	82.2
NYU-CUBoulder-01-0	12.0	82.4
cmu_tartan_00-1	8.3	80.0
cmu_tartan_02-1	8.3	80.2
LTI-00-1	12.3	81.9
cmu_tartan_01-1	8.0	80.3
cmu_tartan_00-0	9.4	80.8
BASE: trm-aug-shared	18.9	76.9
CU7565-02-0	20.3	74.0
CU7565-01-0	27.1	92.9
BASE: mono-single	12.6	75.5
cmu_tartan_01-0	11.7	78.6
BASE: mono-shared	15.8	74.8
BASE: mono-aug-shared	16.9	77.4
BASE: trm-shared	21.2	67.3
ETHZ-02-1	20.6	61.0
BASE: mono-aug-single	11.2	80.7
flexica-02-1	21.2	57.3
flexica-03-1	23.0	52.5
flexica-01-1	26.6	56.1
ETHZ-00-1	28.2	45.7
Oracle (Baselines)		93.9
Oracle (Submissions)		95.8
Oracle (All)		96.3

(b) Results on the Finnic genus (10 languages)

Table 21: **Results per Language Genus (in Uralic Family)**

System	Rank	Acc
deepspin-01-1	1.0	97.9
deepspin-02-1	1.0	97.9
CULing-01-0	2.0	97.8
BASE: trm-single	3.0	97.7
cmu_tartan_00-1	5.0	97.4
uiuc-01-0	5.0	97.6
BASE: trm-aug-single	5.0	97.6
cmu_tartan_00-0	6.0	97.4
cmu_tartan_01-1	6.0	97.3
cmu_tartan_02-1	12.5	95.6
cmu_tartan_01-0	9.0	97.1
BASE: mono-single	9.5	97.0
BASE: mono-aug-single	11.0	96.7
NYU-CUBoulder-04-0	14.0	95.6
LTI-00-1	13.5	96.7
BASE: trm-shared	14.5	95.7
BASE: trm-aug-shared	17.0	95.6
flexica-02-1	18.5	95.0
NYU-CUBoulder-02-0	18.5	94.8
IMS-00-0	19.0	94.8
NYU-CUBoulder-03-0	18.5	94.8
NYU-CUBoulder-01-0	18.5	94.7
flexica-03-1	19.0	94.6
BASE: mono-shared	21.0	94.5
CU7565-02-0	23.5	93.3
BASE: mono-aug-shared	26.0	91.5
flexica-01-1	27.0	88.7
ETHZ-02-1	28.0	79.4
ETHZ-00-1	29.0	73.4
CU7565-01-0	*30.0*	*0.0*
Oracle (Baselines)		98.6
Oracle (Submissions)		99.0
Oracle (All)		99.2

(a) Results on the Permic genus (2 languages)

System	Rank	Acc
deepspin-02-1	1.0	94.0
CULing-01-0	1.0	93.9
BASE: trm-single	1.0	93.9
uiuc-01-0	1.0	93.8
BASE: trm-aug-single	3.5	93.7
deepspin-01-1	3.5	93.6
cmu_tartan_02-1	6.5	93.3
cmu_tartan_00-1	6.5	93.2
cmu_tartan_01-1	6.5	93.2
cmu_tartan_01-0	6.5	93.2
cmu_tartan_00-0	6.5	93.2
BASE: mono-single	9.5	93.0
LTI-00-1	9.5	92.8
BASE: trm-shared	13.5	92.0
BASE: mono-aug-single	14.5	92.3
BASE: trm-aug-shared	15.0	91.9
IMS-00-0	17.0	91.5
NYU-CUBoulder-04-0	18.5	90.8
flexica-03-1	18.5	90.5
flexica-02-1	18.5	90.5
NYU-CUBoulder-03-0	19.5	90.2
NYU-CUBoulder-02-0	19.5	90.2
NYU-CUBoulder-01-0	23.5	89.5
BASE: mono-shared	21.5	88.9
BASE: mono-aug-shared	24.5	87.2
CU7565-02-0	25.5	85.2
flexica-01-1	27.0	82.1
ETHZ-02-1	28.0	73.7
ETHZ-00-1	28.5	67.9
CU7565-01-0	*30.0*	*0.0*
Oracle (Baselines)		97.0
Oracle (Submissions)		97.6
Oracle (All)		98.0

(b) Results on the Mordvin genus (2 languages)

The SIGMORPHON 2020 Shared Task on Multilingual Grapheme-to-Phoneme Conversion

Kyle Gorman[*], **Lucas F.E. Ashby**[*], **Aaron Goyzueta**[*],
Arya D. McCarthy[†], **Shijie Wu**[†], **Daniel You**[‡]
[*]The Graduate Center, City University of New York
[†]Johns Hopkins University
[‡]Jericho High School

Abstract

We describe the design and findings of the SIGMORPHON 2020 shared task on multilingual grapheme-to-phoneme conversion. Participants were asked to submit systems which consume a sequence of graphemes then emit output a sequence of phonemes representing the pronunciation of that grapheme sequence in one of fifteen languages. Nine teams submitted a total of 23 systems, at best achieving an 18% relative reduction in word error rate (macro-averaged over languages), versus strong neural sequence-to-sequence baselines. To facilitate error analysis, we publicly release the complete outputs for all systems—a first for the SIGMORPHON workshop.

1 Introduction

Speech technologies such as automatic speech recognition and text-to-speech synthesis require mappings between written words and their pronunciations. Even recent attempts to do away with explicit pronunciation models via "end-to-end" systems (e.g., Watts et al. 2013, Chan et al. 2016, Sotelo et al. 2017, Chiu et al. 2018, Pino et al. 2019, McCarthy et al. 2020) must induce an implicit mapping of this sort. For open-vocabulary applications, these mappings must generalize to unseen words, and so must be expressed as mappings between sequences of *graphemes*—i.e., glyphs— and *phonemes* or *phones*—i.e., sounds.[1]

For some languages, this mapping is sufficiently consistent that a literate, linguistically-sophisticated speaker can simply enumerate the necessary rules; this sequence of rules can then

be compiled into a finite-state transducer (e.g., Sproat 1996, Black et al. 1998). However, rule-based systems require linguistic expertise to develop and maintain, and may be brittle or inaccurate. Therefore, modern speech engines usually treat grapheme-to-phoneme conversion as a machine learning problem, either using generative models expressed as weighted finite-state transducers (e.g., Taylor 2005, Bisani and Ney 2008, Wu et al. 2014, Novak et al. 2016) or discriminative models based on conditional random fields (Lehnen et al. 2013), recurrent neural networks (e.g., Rao et al. 2015, Yao and Zweig 2015, van Esch et al. 2016, Lee et al. 2020) or transformers (Yolchuyeva et al. 2019).

While the grapheme-to-phoneme conversion (or G2P) task is crucial to speech technology, the vast majority of published research focuses on English or a few other highly-resourced, globally hegemonic languages for which free pronunciation dictionaries are available. One exception, a recent study by van Esch et al. (2016), compares naïve rule-based systems and neural network-based sequence-to-sequence models for 20 languages; unfortunately, the data used in this study is proprietary. Like many other types of language resources, pronunciation dictionaries are expensive to create and maintain, and until recently, free high-quality dictionaries were only available for a small number of languages.

This limitation to a handful of languages is unfortunate because, as we discuss below, writing systems are almost as diverse as languages themselves. Therefore, we present a *multilingual grapheme-to-phoneme conversion task* with data sets, evaluation metrics, and strong baselines. In this we are aided by the recent release of WikiPron (Lee et al. 2020), a freely available collection of pronunciation dictionaries. The resulting task, the

---

[1]We note that the term *phoneme* is a well-defined object in linguistic theory, and that referring to the elements of transcriptions as *phonemes* makes strong ontological commitments which may not be appropriate for a given pronunciation dictionary (cf. Lee et al. 2020, fn. 4). Therefore, in what follows we use the term *phone*, in a pre-theoretical sense, to refer to transcriptions symbols.

Proceedings of the Seventeenth SIGMORPHON Workshop on Computational Research in Phonetics, Phonology, and Morphology, pages 40–50
Online, July 10, 2020. ©2020 Association for Computational Linguistics
https://doi.org/10.18653/v1/P17

first of its kind, included data from fifteen languages and scripts, and received 23 submissions from nine teams.

2 Data

Fifteen language/script pairs were chosen to cover a wide variety of script types. Ten of the scripts are alphabetic systems known to descend from Phoenician (and ultimately from Egyptian hieroglyphs); of these, seven are variants of the Latin script. Two others, the Armenian *aybuben* and the Georgian *mkhedruli*, are alphabetic scripts of unknown origin, but may ultimately be modeled on Greek (Sanjian 1996). The *devanāgarī* script used to write Hindi, is an *alphasyllabary*, in which most glyphs—known traditionally as *akṣara*—denote consonant and consonant-vowel sequences. Vowels (or their absence) are primarily indicated with diacritics. It too is thought to ultimately descend from Phoenician. *Hiragana*, one of several scripts used to write Japanese, is a *syllabary*, in which most glyphs denote entire syllables The glyphs themselves are derived from Chinese characters. Like hiragana, the Korean *hangul* script is also a syllabary It may have been have been inspired by *'phags-pa*, a Tibetan alphabet which is itself a distant cousin of devanāgarī (Ledyard 1966).

It is important to note that languages—and the scripts used to write them—differ enormously in their affordances for grapheme-to-phoneme conversion. Writing systems are, at their core, linguistic analyses, albeit sometimes quite naïve, and (as argued in DeFrancis 1989) explicitly encode details of the phonological and phonetic structure of the language they are used to write. Still, the exact details of these mappings can vary greatly between even closely related languages and/or scripts. Whereas related languages may retain telltale grammatical features across millennia, dozens of languages have abruptly switched from one script to another in just the last century, usually in response to political—rather than linguistic—concerns. It is thus unsurprising that Bjerva and Augenstein (2018) find grapheme embeddings induced by training G2P systems are poorly correlated with gross phonological typology, and experiments with "polyglot" G2P models (e.g., Peters et al. 2017) have produced equivocal results.

While we did not pay particular attention to language families when selecting language family, we note that nine of the languages are Indo-

European (though no two are closely related) and none of the remaining six—Adyghe, Georgian, Hungarian, Japanese, Korean, and Vietnamese—are known to be genetically related to each other.

3 Methods

The primary data for the shared task is derived from WikiPron (Lee et al. 2020), a massively multilingual resource of grapheme–phoneme pairs extracted from Wiktionary, an online multilingual dictionary. Depending on language and script, these pronunciations may be manually entered by human volunteers—usually working from language-specific pronunciation guidelines—or generated using server-side scripting routines; some languages (e.g., Bulgarian and French) use a mixture of the two approaches. WikiPron is configured to apply case-folding where appropriate. It removes stress and syllable boundary markers and segments pronunciation strings—encoded in the International Phonetic Alphabet—using the segments library (Moran and Cysouw 2018).

For this task, words with multiple pronunciations—both homographs and free pronunciation variants—were excluded, since pronunciations for such words are often selected by a rather different procedure: they are chosen from a small, predetermined set of possible pronunciations using classifiers conditioned on local context (e.g., Gorman et al. 2018).

Training and development data for ten languages—the "development" languages—was released at the start of the task; equivalent data for the five "surprise" languages was released one week before the start the evaluation phase. Table 1 provides sample training data pairs for the development and surprise languages.

As there is considerable variation in the number of available examples for any given language, each languages' data was downsampled to 4,500 examples. We regard as a "medium-resource" setting for this task; these data sets are, for instance, several orders of magnitude smaller than the proprietary G2P data used by van Esch et al. (2016). Following similar procedures in other shared tasks (e.g., Cotterell et al. 2017), words were sampled according to their frequency in the largest available Wortschatz (Goldhahn et al. 2012) corpus for that language. These frequencies were smoothed by adding a 0.3 pseudo-count to the frequency of all WikiPron entries. Wortschatz frequency data

Language	ISO 639-2	Example training data pair	
Armenian	arm	մեծաքանակ	m ɛ t͡s ɑ kʰ ɑ n ɑ k
Bulgarian	bul	североизток	s ɛ v ɛ r o i s t o k
French	fre	hébergement	e b ɛ ʁ ʒ ə m ã
Georgian	geo	ფორმიანი	pʰ ɔ r m ɪ ɑ n ɪ
Modern Greek	gre	καθισμένες	k a θ i z m e n e s
Hindi	hin	कैलकुलेटर	k ɛː l k ʊ l eː ʈ ə ɾ
Hungarian	hun	csendőrök	t͡ʃ ɛ n d øː r ø k
Icelandic	hin	þýskaland	θ i s k a l a n t
Korean	kor	말레이시아	m a̠ l l e̞ i ɕʰ i a̠
Lithuanian	lit	galinčiais	g aː lʲ ɪ nʲ tʲ ʃʲ ɛ j s
Adyghe	ady	бзыукъолэн	b z ə w qʷ a l a n
Dutch	dut	aanduiding	aː n d œ y̆ d ɪ ŋ
Japanese hiragana	jpn	どちらさま	d o̞ t͡ɕ i r a̠ s a̠ m a̠
Romanian	rum	bineînțeles	b i n e ɨ n t s e l e s
Vietnamese	vie	duyên phận	z w i ə n ˩˩ f ə n ˧˩ ʔ

Table 1: Languages, language codes, and example training data pairs for the shared task.

was not available for Adyghe, so uniform sampling was used for this language.

The downsampled data was then randomly split into training (80%; 3,600 examples), development (10%; 450 examples), and testing (10%; 450 examples) shards. For some languages, Wiktionary contains pronunciations for both lemmas (i.e., headwords, citations forms) and inflection variants; for others, pronunciations are only available for lemmas. We hypothesized that cases where one inflectional variant of a lemma is present in the training data and another in the test data—as might occur if the data was split totally at random—would make the overall task somewhat easier. To forestall this possibility, the splitting procedure was constrained so that all inflectional variants of any given lemma—according to the UniMorph 2 (Kirov et al. 2018) paradigm tables, also extracted from Wiktionary—are limited to a single shard. For example, since the French word *acteur* 'actor' occurs in the training shard, so must its plural form *acteurs*. This additional constraint was applied to all languages but Japanese and Vietnamese, for which no UniMorph data was available. We note that Wiktionary does not generally provide pronunciations for inflectional variants in Japanese, and that Vietnamese is a highly isolating language with no discernable system of inflection (Noyer 1998), so this is unlikely to have introduced bias.

4 Evaluation

The primary metric for this task was word error rate (WER); we also report phone error rate (PER).

WER This is the percentage of words for which the hypothesized transcription sequence is not identical to the gold reference transcription; lower WER indicates better performance. Following common practice in speech research, we multiply the WER by 100 and display it as a percentage. We choose this as the primary metric for the shared task because we hypothesize that *any* G2P error, no matter how small, will result in a substantial degradation in subjective quality for downstream speech applications.

PER This is a more forgiving measure measuring the normalized distance (i.e., in number of insertions, deletions, and substitutions) between the predicted and reference transcriptions. It is computed by summing the minimum edit distance—computed with the Wagner and Fischer (1974) algorithm—between prediction and reference transcriptions, and dividing by the sum of the reference transcription lengths. That is,

$$\text{PER} := 100 \times \frac{\sum_i^n \text{edits}(p, r)}{\sum_i^n |r|}$$

where p is the predicted pronunciation sequence, r is the reference sequence, and $\text{edits}(p, r)$ is the

Levenshtein distance between the two. Once again, we multiply it by 100, though strictly speaking it is not a true percentage because it can hypothetically exceed 100. As with WER, lower PER indicates better performance.

Participants were provided with two evaluation scripts: one which computes the two metrics for a single language, and another which macro-averages the metrics across all languages.

5 Baselines

Three baselines were made available at the start of the task. To aid reproducibility, participants were also provided with a Conda "environment", a schematic that allows users to reconstruct the exact software environment used to train and evaluate the baselines. Several submissions made use of the baselines for data augmentation or ensemble construction. We make these baseline implementations available under the `task1/baselines` subdirectory of the shared task repository.[2]

Pair n-gram model The first baseline consists of a pair n-gram model, which be can thought of as a finite-state approximation of a hidden Markov model with states representing graphemes and emissions representing output phones. The model is quite similar to the Phonetisaurus toolkit (Novak et al. 2016), but here is implemented using the OpenGrm toolkit (Roark et al. 2012, Gorman 2016); see Lee et al. 2020 for a full description. The sole hyperparameter for this model, Markov model order, is tuned separately for each language using the development set.

Encoder-decoder LSTM The second baseline is a neural network sequence-to-sequence model consisting of a single-layer bidirectional LSTM encoder and a single-layer unidirectional LSTM decoder connected using an attention mechanism (Luong et al. 2015). It is implemented using the `fairseq` library (Ott et al. 2019). LSTM-based encoder-decoder models have been claimed to outperform pair n-gram G2P models, both in monolingual (e.g., Rao et al. 2015, Yao and Zweig 2015) and multilingual (e.g., van Esch et al. 2016, Lee et al. 2020) evaluations, though these prior studies use substantially more training data than is available in this task. During training, we perform 4,000 updates to minimize label-smoothed cross-entropy (Szegedy et al. 2016) with a smoothing

rate of .1. We use the Adam optimizer (Kingma and Ba 2015) with a learning rate of $\alpha = .001$ and weight decay coefficients of $\beta = (.9, .98)$, and clip norms exceeding 1.0. We use the development set to tune—for each language—batch size (256, 512, 1024), dropout (.1, .2, .3), and the size of the encoder and decoder modules. A module is said to be "small" when it has a 128-dimension embedding layer and a 512-unit hidden layer, and "large" when it has a 256-dimension embedding layer and a 1024-unit hidden layer. In both cases, the decoder shares a single embedding layer for both inputs and outputs. Altogether, this defines a 36-element hyperparameter grid. During tuning, we employ a form of *early stopping*; we save a checkpoint every 5 epochs, and then use the checkpoint that achieves the lowest WER on the development set. We use a beam of size 5 for decoding.

Encoder-decoder transformer The third baseline is a transformer, a neural sequence-to-sequence models that replaces hidden layer recurrence with layers of multi-head self-attention (Vaswani et al. 2017). Once again, it is implemented using `fairseq`. Here the model consists of four encoder layers and four decoder layers, both with pre-layer normalization, tuned for character-level tasks (Wu et al. 2020). The hyperparameter grid, tuning procedures, and beam size are the same as for the LSTM model above, except that learning rate is decayed on an inverse square-root schedule after a 1,000-update linear warm-up period. While most participants chose to compare their results to the transformer and not the LSTM in system description papers, the transformer was outperformed by the LSTM baseline in most setting with the hyperparameter exploration budget.

6 System descriptions

Below we provide brief descriptions of submissions to the shared task.

CLUZH The Institute of Computational Linguistics at the University of Zurich submitted a single system (Makarov and Clematide 2020) extending earlier work (Makarov and Clematide 2018) on imitation learning-based transducers that output a sequence of edit actions rather than a target string itself. To adapt to the G2P task, where input (grapheme) and output (phone) vocabularies are largely disjoint, they add a substitution action. The costs of each edit action are drawn from a weighted

<hr>

[2]`https://github.com/sigmorphon/2020`

finite state transducer (WFST). The authors suggest that external lexical information such as part of speech, etymology (borrowing particularly) and morphological segmentation would improve systems. During preprocessing, they decompose Korean hangul characters into their constituent *jamo*, each corresponding roughly to a single phoneme.

CU   One team from the University of Colorado Boulder (Prabhu and Kann 2020) ensembled several transformer models created with different random seeds using majority voting. They also experiment with a form of multi-task learning: they train a "bidirectional" model to do both grapheme-to-phoneme and phoneme-to-grapheme prediction.

CUZ   A second team from the University of Colorado Boulder (Ryan and Hulden 2020) uses a "slice-and-shuffle" data augmentation strategy. First, they perform character-level one-to-one alignment between graphemes and phonemes. Then they concatenate frequent subsequence pairs to each other to create nonce training examples. Their submission is an LSTM model with a bidirectional encoder trained on this augmented data. While they also developed transformer models, these did not finish training in time for submission. Results for their transformer system, not reported here, are included in their system description.

DeepSPIN   Researchers at the Instituto Superior Técnico and Unbabel produced four submissions (Peters and Martins 2020) based on sparse attention models. Each submission consists of a single multilingual neural model in which separate learned "language embeddings" are concatenated to all encoder and decoder states, rather than prepending a language-identification token to the input sequence. Their submissions either use LSTM- or transformer-based encoder-decoder sequence-to-sequence models with different values of a hyperparameter enforcing sparsity in the final layer (Peters et al. 2019). Like CLUZH, they preprocess Korean hangul characters, decomposing them into constituent *jamo*, each corresponding roughly to a single phoneme.

IMS   A single submission from the Institut für Maschinelle Sprachverarbeitung at the University of Stuttgart (Yu et al. 2020) uses *self-training* (Yarowsky 1995) and ensembles of the baseline models. The components of the ensemble are selected using a genetic algorithm. They report

that their data augmentation does not affect performance substantially, except in a simulated low-resource setting with 200 training examples. They romanize Japanese and Korean texts as a preprocessing step, and they use external word frequency lists.

NSU   The Novosibirsk State University team did not provide a system description.

UA   The submissions from the University of Alberta (Hauer et al. 2020) either use a non-neural discriminative string transduction model (DTLM; Nicolai et al. 2018), or tranformers. They leverage both grapheme-to-phoneme and phoneme-to-grapheme models to filter candidates for data augmentation, enforcing a cyclic consistency constraint. They further show strong performance in a simulated low-resource scenario with 100 training examples. They note that the DTLM system is much faster to train than transformer models. Their six submissions vary the amount of training data and use either DTLM, a transformer, or a transformer with data augmentation.

UBCNLP   The University of British Columbia submitted two systems (Vesik et al. 2020). One is a multilingual model akin to Peters et al. (2017), in which a language-identification token is prepended to the input sequence. They also ensemble multiple checkpoints. Their second submission adds self-training on Wikipedia text; they report that this data augmentation strategy does not improve scores.

UZH   For all three of their submissions, the team from the Department of Informatics at the University of Zurich (ElSaadany and Suter 2020) used a single set of encoder-decoder parameters shared across all languages. UZH-1 is a large transformer model with large embedding, hidden layers, and batches, with a high dropout probability. UZH-2 augments this model with WikiPron data for six other languages. UZH-3 is an ensemble of the previous two models which selects from the predictions of the two component models using whichever model's prediction has a higher posterior probability. The ensemble outperformed the component models for most languages. During preprocessing they also decompose Korean hangul characters into their constituent jamo; they report this results in a 46% relative word error reduction.

7 Results

We now review baseline and submission results.

7.1 Baseline results

Baseline results are shown in Table 2. The encoder-decoder LSTM (Lee et al. 2020) performed best for nine out of fifteen languages; the transformer was the strongest for four languages, and for the remaining two—Modern Greek and Hungarian—there was a virtual tie between the two neural network baselines. The pair n-gram model was outperformed by the neural baselines on all languages, and by 10 or more points WER in Bulgarian, Georgian, and Korean. This suggest that this model is no longer competitive with powerful discriminative neural methods, at least in this medium-resource G2P task.

While this task was not designed explicitly to compare LSTM and transformer sequence-to-sequence models, it does suggest an advantage for LSTM models. However, we speculate that additional training data, or a more generous hyperparameter tuning budget, might favor transformer models. Indeed, anticipating the results below, the one team that directly compared transformer and LSTM systems, DeepSPIN, achieved the third best submission overall using a transformer.

We also note that for four languages, the baseline system that achieves the best WER does not achieve the best PER, though the two metrics produce the same one-best ranking for the remaining eleven languages.

7.2 Submission results

Table 3 shows, for each language, the system or systems that achieved the best WER, as well as the best baseline WER. For all fifteen languages, at least one team outperformed the baselines, sometimes quite substantially. Six of the nine teams achieved the best WER on at least one language. More detailed per-language, per-submission results are available online.[3]

Table 4 gives the macro-averaged WER and PER for the three baselines, and for the best overall submission from each team. As expected, the strongest baseline is the LSTM model. Across all submissions, the IMS team achieves both the lowest average WER, a 3% absolute (18% relative)

word error reduction over the LSTM baseline, and the lowest overall PER, a 1% absolute (31% relative) phone error reduction over the LSTM baseline. The CLUZH and DeepSPIN-3 submissions achieve second and third place, respectively; the CU, UCBNLP, and UZH teams also submitted systems that outperform the LSTM baseline's WER.

8 Discussion

When this task was initially proposed, there was some concern that the submissions—if not the baselines themselves—would easily achieve perfect or near-perfect performance on some languages. This was not the case. Even on the "easiest" language, the best submission has .89% WER, and for three languages, no submission achieves an error rate below 20%.

At the same time, we observe a large range of error rates across languages. It is tempting to speculate that word and/or phone error rates actually represent differences in difficulty. Insofar as this is correct, we can begin to ask what makes a language "hard to pronounce", much like how Mielke et al. (2019) ask what makes a language "hard to language-model".

One thing that may make a language hard to pronounce is data sparsity. Consider the case of Korean, which has by far the highest baseline error rate of all fifteen languages. Three features of Korean and of hangul conspire to make this task particularly challenging. First, hangul is a syllabary, and therefore necessarily has a much larger graphemic inventory than an alphabet or alphasyllabary. A whopping 889 unique hangul characters appear across the 4,500 words used for this task.[4] Secondly, hangul is a relatively *deep* or *abstract* orthography (in the sense of Rogers 2005); it operates at a roughly-morphophonemic level whereas Lithuanian and Hungarian, for example, are is roughly phonemic. Third, Korean has many phonological processes that operate across syllable boundaries. Since the effect of these processes is not indicated by the highly abstract, morphophonemic orthography, they can only be learned by observing the targeted syllable bigrams during training. Lee et al. (2020) perform a manual error analysis of a Korean G2P system similar

---

[3]https://docs.google.com/spreadsheets/d/
1gOHyGeVzFrNt2pvNuu8LlvoFFQY-OCwjTxGA3VXXNGI/
edit?usp=sharing

[4]Few syllabaries are so large. For instance, there are only 79 unique hiragana symbols in the Japanese data, but this relative size difference is not surprising given that Korean has a more permissive syllable structure than Japanese.

	Pair n-gram		LSTM		Transformer	
	WER	PER	WER	PER	WER	PER
arm	18.00	3.90	14.67	3.49	**14.22**	**3.29**
bul	41.33	9.05	**31.11**	**5.94**	34.00	7.89
fre	13.56	3.12	**6.22**	**1.32**	6.89	1.72
geo	37.78	6.48	**26.44**	**5.14**	28.00	5.43
gre	21.78	4.05	**18.89**	3.30	**18.89**	**3.06**
hin	12.67	2.82	**6.67**	**1.47**	9.56	2.40
hun	6.67	1.51	**5.33**	**1.18**	**5.33**	1.28
ice	17.56	3.62	**10.00**	2.36	10.22	**2.21**
kor	52.22	15.88	46.89	**16.78**	**43.78**	17.50
lit	23.11	4.43	**19.11**	**3.55**	20.67	3.65
ady	32.00	7.56	**28.00**	6.53	28.44	**6.49**
dut	23.78	3.97	16.44	2.94	**15.78**	**2.89**
jap	9.56	2.07	7.56	**1.79**	**7.33**	1.86
rum	11.56	3.55	**10.67**	**2.53**	12.00	2.62
vie	8.44	1.79	**4.67**	**1.52**	7.56	2.27

Table 2: Results for the three baseline systems.

to the LSTM baseline and observe errors caused by underapplication of these coda-onset cluster rules. It is unsurprising then that several submissions achieved substantial gains by either romanizing hangul or decomposing it into its constituent jamo during preprocessing, since both techniques reduce the size of the input vocabulary.

The results suggest that G2P technologies are not yet language-agnostic (in the sense of Bender 2009). However, some caution is in order here: inter-language differences in word error rate may also reflect inconsistencies in the WikiPron data itself. During the task, participants reported apparent transcription inconsistencies in the Bulgarian, Georgian, and Lithuanian Wiktionary data. If these inconsistencies are due to overly-narrow allophonic transcriptions, one might suspect that they can be learned by sufficiently sophisticated sequence-to-sequence models. However, if they represent free variation, inconsistent application of the transcription guidelines, or even typographical errors, they inflate error rates and increase the risk of overfitting. In response to this, we have begun development of quality assurance software for WikiPron, including a phone-based whitelisting approach. We anticipate that manual error analysis will reveal errors in the Wiktionary data, similar to the large number of test data errors identified by Gorman et al. (2019) for the 2017 CoNLL–SIGMORPHON morphological inflection task. To encourage this sort of error analysis, for the first time in the history of the SIGMORPHON workshop, we publicly release the predictions made by all 23 submissions.[5] Finally, we plan to apply large-scale consistency-enforcing edits upstream, i.e., to Wiktionary itself.

While the baselines are somewhat naïve and lack the sophisticated data augmentation and ensembling techniques used by the top submissions, we were pleasantly surprised by the substantial reductions in error achieved by the participating teams. As mentioned above, the best submissions handily outperforms the baselines for all languages. Interestingly, this is true for the most challenging languages—like Korean, where the best submission achieves a 45% relative word error reduction over the baseline—but also for Vietnamese, the language with the lowest baseline WER; there, the best submission achieves an impressive 81% relative word error reduction.

As mentioned above, top submissions make use of techniques such as preprocessing, data augmentation, ensembling, multi-task learning (e.g., phoneme-to-grapheme conversion), and self-

[5]https://drive.google.com/drive/folders/
1kdawyeI17iGC0jlY_2dZQpK75hpShY_H?usp=sharing

	Best baseline			Best submission	
arm	14.22	transformer	**12.22**	CLUZH	
bul	31.11	LSTM	**22.22**	IMS	
fre	6.22	LSTM	**5.11**	DeepSPIN-3	
geo	26.44	LSTM	**24.89**	IMS	
gre	18.89	LSTM, transformer	**14.44**	CU-2, CUZ	
hin	6.67	LSTM	**5.11**	CLUZH, IMS	
hun	5.33	LSTM, transformer	**4.00**	CLUZH	
ice	10.00	LSTM	**9.11**	CLUZH, UBCNLP-2	
kor	43.78	transformer	**24.00**	DeepSPIN-1, DeepSPIN-2	
lit	19.11	LSTM	**18.67**	CLUZH	
ady	28.00	LSTM	**24.67**	DeepSPIN-4	
dut	16.44	transformer	**13.56**	IMS	
jap	7.33	transformer	**4.89**	DeepSPIN-4	
rum	10.67	LSTM	**9.78**	DeepSPIN-3	
vie	4.67	LSTM	**0.89**	DeepSPIN-2	

Table 3: The best baseline(s) and submission(s) WERs for each language.

	WER	PER
Pair n-gram	22.00	4.92
LSTM	16.84	3.99
Transformer	17.51	4.30
CLUZH	14.13	2.82
CU-1	14.52	3.24
CUZ	20.87	5.23
DeepSPIN-3	14.15	2.92
IMS	**13.81**	**2.76**
NSU-1	63.56	20.76
UA-2	17.47	4.26
UBCNLP-1	14.99	3.30
UZH-3	16.34	3.27

Table 4: Macro-averaged results for the baselines and the best submission from each team.

training. These techniques are commonly used in shared tasks and are essentially task-agnostic. However, we were surprised that few teams made use of task-specific resources such as the PHOIBLE phonemic inventories and feature specifications (Moran and McCloy 2019) or rule-based G2P systems like Epitran (Mortensen et al. 2018). Nor do any of the submissions make use of morphological analyzers or lexicons, which were found to be helpful in earlier work (e.g., Coker et al. 1990, Demberg et al. 2007). We speculate that such resources might further improve performance. Finally we note that submissions make use of unsupervised tokenization techniques such as byte-pair encoding (Schuster and Nakajima 2012).

Finally, we note that several participants expressed interest in a low-resource version of this challenge, and two teams simulated a low-resource setting. We leave the design of a low-resource task for future work.

9 Conclusion

SIGMORPHON, under whose auspices this task was conducted, was once known as SIGPHON and was primarily focused on computational phonetics and phonology. The shared task on multilingual grapheme-to-phoneme conversion, a uniquely phonological problem, thus represents something of a return to the roots of this special interest group. In this task, nine teams submitted 23 G2P systems for fifteen languages and achieved substantial improvements over the provided baselines. The results suggest many directions for improving G2P systems and the pronunciation dictionaries used to train them.

Acknowledgements

We thank the contributors to WikiPron—especially Jackson Lee—and to Wiktionary itself. We also thank all those who met for lunch at Florence's *mercato centrale* to plan this task.

References

Emily M. Bender. 2009. Linguistically naïve != language independent: why NLP needs linguistic typology. In *Proceedings of the EACL 2009 Workshop on the Interaction between Linguistics and Computational Linguistics: Virtuous, Vicious or Vacuous?*, pages 26–32, Athens.

Maximilian Bisani and Hermann Ney. 2008. Joint-sequence models for grapheme-to-phoneme conversion. *Speech Communication*, 50(5):434–451.

Johannes Bjerva and Isabella Augenstein. 2018. From phonology to syntax: unsupervised linguistic typology at different levels with language embeddings. In *Proceedings of the 2018 Conference of the North American Chapter of the Association for Computational Linguistics: Human Language Technologies, Volume 1 (Long Papers)*, pages 907–916, New Orleans.

Alan W. Black, Kevin Lenzo, and Vincent Pagel. 1998. Issues in building general letter to sound rules. In *Third ESCA/COCOSDA Workshop on Speech Synthesis*, pages 77–80, Jenolan, Australia.

William Chan, Navdeep Jaitly, Quoc Le, and Oriol Vinyals. 2016. Listen, attend and spell: a neural network for large vocabulary conversational speech recognition. In *2016 IEEE International Conference on Acoustics, Speech and Signal Processing*, pages 4960–4964, Shanghai.

Chung-Cheng Chiu, Tara N. Sainath, Yonghei Wu, Rohit Prabhavalkar, Patrick Nyugen, Zhifeng Chen, Anjuli Kannan, Ron J. Weiss, Kanishka Rao, Ekaterina Gonina, Navdeep Jaitly, Bo Li, Chorowski, and Michiel Bacchiani. 2018. State-of-the-art speech recognition with sequence-to-sequence models. In *2018 IEEE International Conference on Acoustics, Speech and Signal Processing*, pages 4774–4778, Calgary.

Cecil H. Coker, Kenneth W. Church, and Mark Y. Liberman. 1990. Morphology and rhyming: two powerful alternatives to letter-to-sound rules for speech synthesis. In *ESCA Workshop on Speech Synthesis*, pages 83–86, Autrans, France.

Ryan Cotterell, Christo Kirov, John Sylak-Glassman, Géraldine Walther, Ekaterina Vylomova, Patrick Xia, Manaal Faruqui, Sandra Kübler, David Yarowsky, Jason Eisner, and Mans Hulden. 2017. CoNLL–SIGMORPHON 2017 shared task: universal morphological reinflection in 52 languages. In *Proceedings of the CoNLL SIGMORPHON 2017 Shared Task: Universal Morphological Reinflection*, pages 1–30, Vancouver.

John DeFrancis. 1989. *Visible speech: the diverse oneness of writing systems*. University of Hawaii Press.

Vera Demberg, Helmut Schmid, and Gregor Möhler. 2007. Phonological constraints and morphological preprocessing for grapheme-to-phoneme conversion. In *Proceedings of the 45th Annual Meeting of the Association of Computational Linguistics*, pages 96–103, Prague.

Omnia ElSaadany and Benjamin Suter. 2020. Grapheme-to-phoneme conversion with a multilingual transformer model: a contribution to the SIGMORPHON 2020 Shared Task 1. In *Proceedings of the 17th SIGMORPHON Workshop on Computational Research in Phonetics, Phonology, and Morphology*, Seattle.

Daan van Esch, Mason Chua, and Kanishka Rao. 2016. Predicting pronunciations with syllabification and stress with recurrent neural networks. In *INTERSPEECH 2016: 17th Annual Conference of the International Speech Communication Association*, pages 2841–2845, San Francisco.

Dirk Goldhahn, Thomas Eckart, and Uwe Quasthoff. 2012. Building large monolingual dictionaries at the Leipzig Corpora Collection: from 100 to 200 languages. In *Proceedings of the Eighth International Conference on Language Resources and Evaluation*, pages 759–765, Istanbul.

Kyle Gorman. 2016. Pynini: a Python library for weighted finite-state grammar compilation. In *Proceedings of the SIGFSM Workshop on Statistical NLP and Weighted Automata*, pages 75–80, Berlin.

Kyle Gorman, Gleb Mazovetskiy, and Vitaly Nikolaev. 2018. Improving homograph disambiguation with supervised machine learning. In *Proceedings of the Eleventh International Conference on Language Resources and Evaluation*, pages 1349–1352, Miyazaki, Japan.

Kyle Gorman, Arya D. McCarthy, Ryan Cotterell, Ekaterina Vylomova, Miikka Silfverberg, and Magdalena Markowska. 2019. Weird inflects but OK: making sense of morphological generation errors. In *Proceedings of the 23rd Conference on Computational Natural Language Learning (CoNLL)*, pages 140–151, Hong Kong.

Bradley Hauer, Amir Ahmad Habibi, Yixing Luan, Arnob Mallik, and Grzegorz Kondrak. 2020. Low-resource G2P and P2G conversion with synthetic training data. In *Proceedings of the 17th SIGMORPHON Workshop on Computational Research in Phonetics, Phonology, and Morphology*, Seattle.

Diederik P. Kingma and Jimmy Ba. 2015. Adam: a method for stochastic optimization. In *3rd International Conference on Learning Representations: Conference Track Proceedings*, San Diego.

Christo Kirov, Ryan Cotterell, John Sylak-Glassman, Géraldine Walther, Ekaterina Vylomova, Patrick Xia, Manaal Faruqui, Arya D. McCarthy, Sandra Kübler, David Yarowsky, Jason Eisner, and Mans Hulden. 2018. UniMorph 2.0: universal morphology. In *Proceedings of the 11th Language Resources and Evaluation Conference*, pages 1868–1873, Miyazaki, Japan.

Gari K. Ledyard. 1966. *The Korean language reform of 1446: the origin, background, and early history of the Korean alphabet*. Ph.D. thesis, University of California, Berkeley.

Jackson L. Lee, Lucas F.E. Ashby, M. Elizabeth Garza, Yeonju Lee-Sikka, Sean Miller, Alan Wong, Arya D. McCarthy, and Kyle Gorman. 2020. Massively multilingual pronunciation mining with WikiPron. In *Proceedings of the 12th Language Resources and Evaluation Conference*, pages 4216–4221, Marseille.

Patrick Lehnen, Alexandre Allauzen, Thomas Lavergne, François Yvon, Stefan Hahn, and Hermann Ney. 2013. Structure learning in hidden conditional random fields for grapheme-to-phoneme conversion. In *INTERSPEECH 2013: 14th Annual Conference of the International Speech Communication Association*, pages 2326–2330, Lyon.

Minh-Thang Luong, Hieu Pham, and Christopher D. Manning. 2015. Effective approaches to attention-based neural machine translation. In *Proceedings of the 2015 Conference on Empirical Methods in Natural Language Processing*, pages 1412–1421, Lisbon.

Peter Makarov and Simon Clematide. 2018. Imitation learning for neural morphological string transduction. In *Proceedings of the 2018 Conference on Empirical Methods in Natural Language Processing*, pages 2877–2882, Brussels.

Peter Makarov and Simon Clematide. 2020. CLUZH at SIGMORPHON 2020 shared task on multilingual grapheme-to-phoneme conversion. In *Proceedings of the 17th SIGMORPHON Workshop on Computational Research in Phonetics, Phonology, and Morphology*, Seattle.

Arya D. McCarthy, Liezl Puzon, and Juan Pino. 2020. SkinAugment: auto-encoding speaker conversions for automatic speech translation. In *IEEE International Conference on Acoustics, Speech and Signal Processing*, pages 7924–7928, Barcelona.

Sabrina J. Mielke, Ryan Cotterell, Kyle Gorman, Brian Roark, and Jason Eisner. 2019. What kind of language is hard to language-model? In *Proceedings of the 57th Annual Meeting of the Association for Computational Linguistics*, pages 4975–4989, Florence.

Steven Moran and Michael Cysouw. 2018. *The Unicode cookbook for linguists: managing writing systems using orthography profiles*. Language Science Press.

Steven Moran and Daniel McCloy. 2019. *PHOIBLE 2.0*. Max Planck Institute for the Science of Human History.

David R. Mortensen, Siddharth Dalmia, and Patrick Littell. 2018. Epitran: precision G2P for many languages. In *Proceedings of the Eleventh International Conference on Language Resources and Evaluation*, pages 2710–2714, Miyazaki, Japan.

Garrett Nicolai, Saeed Najafi, and Grzegorz Kondrak. 2018. String transduction with target language models and insertion handling. In *Proceedings of the Fifteenth Workshop on Computational Research in Phonetics, Phonology, and Morphology*, pages 43–53, Brussels.

Josef R. Novak, Nobuaki Minematsu, and Keikichi Hirose. 2016. Phonetisaurus: exploring grapheme-to-phoneme conversion with joint n-gram models in the WFST framework. *Natural Language Engineering*, 22(6):907–938.

Rolf Noyer. 1998. Vietnamese 'morphology' and the definition of word. *University of Pennsylvania Working Papers in Linguistics*, 5(2):65–89.

Myle Ott, Sergey Edunov, Alexei Baevski, Angela Fan, Sam Gross, Nathan Ng, David Grangier, and Michael Auli. 2019. Fairseq: a fast, extensible toolkit for sequence modeling. In *Proceedings of the 2019 Conference of the North American Chapter of the Association for Computational Linguistics (Demonstrations)*, pages 48–53, Minneapolis.

Ben Peters, Jon Dehdari, and Josef van Genabith. 2017. Massively multilingual neural grapheme-to-phoneme conversion. In *Proceedings of the First Workshop on Building Linguistically Generalizable NLP Systems*, pages 19–26, Copenhagen.

Ben Peters and André F. T. Martins. 2020. One-size-fits-all multilingual models. In *Proceedings of the 17th SIGMORPHON Workshop on Computational Research in Phonetics, Phonology, and Morphology*, Seattle.

Ben Peters, Vlad Niculae, and André F.T. Martins. 2019. Sparse sequence-to-sequence models. In *Proceedings of the 57th Annual Meeting of the Association for Computational Linguistics*, pages 1504–1519, Florence.

Juan Pino, Liezl Puzon, Jiatao Gu, Xutai Ma, Arya D. McCarthy, and Deepak Gopinath. 2019. Harnessing indirect training data for end-to-end automatic speech translation: tricks of the trade. In *16th International Workshop on Spoken Language Translation*.

Nikhil Prabhu and Katharina Kann. 2020. Frustratingly easy multilingual grapheme-to-phoneme conversion. In *Proceedings of the 17th SIGMORPHON Workshop on Computational Research in Phonetics, Phonology, and Morphology*, Seattle.

Kanishka Rao, Fuchun Peng, Haşim Sak, and Françoise Beaufays. 2015. Grapheme-to-phoneme conversion using long short-term memory recurrent neural networks. In *2015 IEEE International Conference on Acoustics, Speech and Signal Processing*, pages 4225–4229, Brisbane.

Brian Roark, Richard Sproat, Cyril Allauzen, Michael Riley, Jeffrey Sorensen, and Terry Tai. 2012. The OpenGrm open-source finite-state grammar software libraries. In *Proceedings of the ACL 2012 System Demonstrations*, pages 61–66, Jeju Island, Korea.

Henry Rogers. 2005. *Writing systems: a linguistic approach*. Blackwell.

Zach Ryan and Mans Hulden. 2020. Data augmentation for transformer-based G2P. In *Proceedings of the 17th SIGMORPHON Workshop on Computational Research in Phonetics, Phonology, and Morphology*, Seattle.

Avedis Sanjian. 1996. The Armenian alphabet. In Peter T. Daniels and Williams Bright, editors, *The World's Writing Systems*, pages 356–357. Oxford University Press.

Michael Schuster and Kaisuke Nakajima. 2012. Japanese and Korean voice search. In *IEEE International Conference on Acoustics, Speech and Signal Processing*, pages 5149–5152, Kyoto.

Jose Sotelo, Soroush Mehri, Kundan Kumar, João Felipe Santos, Kyle Kastner, Aaron C. Courville, and Yoshua Bengio. 2017. Char2Wav: end-to-end speech synthesis. In *5th International Conference on Learning Representations: Workshop Track Proceedings*, Toulon.

Richard Sproat. 1996. Multilingual text analysis for text-to-speech synthesis. *Natural Language Engineering*, 2(4):369–380.

Christian Szegedy, Vincent Vanhoucke, Sergey Ioffe, Jon Shlens, and Zbigniew Wojna. 2016. Rethinking the inception architecture for computer vision. In *Proceedings of IEEE Computer Society Conference on Computer Vision and Pattern Recognition*, pages 2818–2826, Las Vegas.

Paul Taylor. 2005. Hidden Markov models for grapheme to phoneme conversion. In *INTERSPEECH 2005–EUROSPEECH 2005: 9th European Conference on Speech Communication and Technology*, pages 1973–1976, Lisbon.

Ashish Vaswani, Noam Shazeer, Niki Parmar, Jakob Uzskoreit, Llion Jones, Aidan N. Gomez, Łukasz Kaiser, and Illia Polosukhin. 2017. Attention is all you need. In *Advances in Neural Information Processing Systems 30*, pages 5998–6008, Long Beach.

Kaili Vesik, Muhammad Abdul-Mageed, and Miikka Silfverberg. 2020. One model to pronounce them all: multilingual grapheme-to-phoneme conversion with a transformer ensemble. In *Proceedings of the 17th SIGMORPHON Workshop on Computational Research in Phonetics, Phonology, and Morphology*, Seattle.

Robert A. Wagner and Michael J. Fischer. 1974. The string-to-string correction problem. *Journal of the ACM*, 21(1):168–173.

Oliver Watts, Adriana Stan, Robert Clark, Yoshitaka Mamiya, Mircea Giurgiu, Junichi Yamagishi, and Simon King. 2013. Unsupervised and lightly-supervised learning for rapid construction of TTS systems in multiple languages from 'found' data: evaluation and analysis. In *Eighth ISCA Workshop on Speech Synthesis*, pages 101–106, Barcelona.

Ke Wu, Cyril Allauzen, Keith Hall, Michael Riley, and Brian Roark. 2014. Encoding linear models as weighted finite-state transducers. In *INTERSPEECH 2014: 15th Annual Conference of the International Speech Communication Association*, pages 1258–1262, Singapore.

Shijie Wu, Ryan Cotterell, and Mans Hulden. 2020. Applying the transformer to character-level transduction. arXiv:2005.10213.

Kaisheng Yao and Geoffrey Zweig. 2015. Sequence-to-sequence neural net models for grapheme-to-phoneme conversion. In *INTERSPEECH 2015: 16th Annual Conference of the International Speech Communication Association*, pages 3330–3334, Dresden.

David Yarowsky. 1995. Unsupervised word sense disambiguation rivaling supervised methods. In *33rd Annual Meeting of the Association for Computational Linguistics*, pages 189–196, Cambridge, MA.

Sevinj Yolchuyeva, Géza Németh, and Bálint Gyires-Tóth. 2019. Transformer based grapheme-to-phoneme conversion. In *INTERSPEECH 2019: 20th Annual Conference of the International Speech Communication Association*, pages 2095–2099, Graz, Austria.

Xiang Yu, Ngoc Thang Vu, and Jonas Kuhn. 2020. Ensemble self-training for low-resource languages: grapheme-to-phoneme conversion and morphological inflection. In *Proceedings of the 17th SIGMORPHON Workshop on Computational Research in Phonetics, Phonology, and Morphology*, Seattle.

The SIGMORPHON 2020 Shared Task on
Unsupervised Morphological Paradigm Completion

Katharina Kann[*]
University of Colorado Boulder
katharina.kann@colorado.edu

Arya D. McCarthy[*]
Johns Hopkins University
arya@jhu.edu

Garrett Nicolai
University of British Columbia
garrett.nicolai@ubc.ca

Mans Hulden
University of Colorado Boulder
mans.hulden@colorado.edu

Abstract

In this paper, we describe the findings of the SIGMORPHON 2020 shared task on unsupervised morphological paradigm completion (SIGMORPHON 2020 Task 2), a novel task in the field of inflectional morphology. Participants were asked to submit systems which take raw text and a list of lemmas as input, and output all inflected forms, i.e., the entire morphological paradigm, of each lemma. In order to simulate a realistic use case, we first released data for 5 development languages. However, systems were officially evaluated on 9 surprise languages, which were only revealed a few days before the submission deadline. We provided a modular baseline system, which is a pipeline of 4 components. 3 teams submitted a total of 7 systems, but, surprisingly, none of the submitted systems was able to improve over the baseline on average over all 9 test languages. Only on 3 languages did a submitted system obtain the best results. This shows that unsupervised morphological paradigm completion is still largely unsolved. We present an analysis here, so that this shared task will ground further research on the topic.

1 Introduction

In morphologically rich languages, words *inflect*: grammatical information like person, number, tense, and case are incorporated into the word itself, rather than expressed via function words. Not all languages mark the same properties: German nouns, for instance, have more inflected forms than their English counterparts.

When acquiring a language, humans usually learn to inflect words without explicit instruction. Thus, most native speakers are capable of generating inflected forms even of artificial lemmas (Berko, 1958). However, models that can generate paradigms without explicit morphological train-

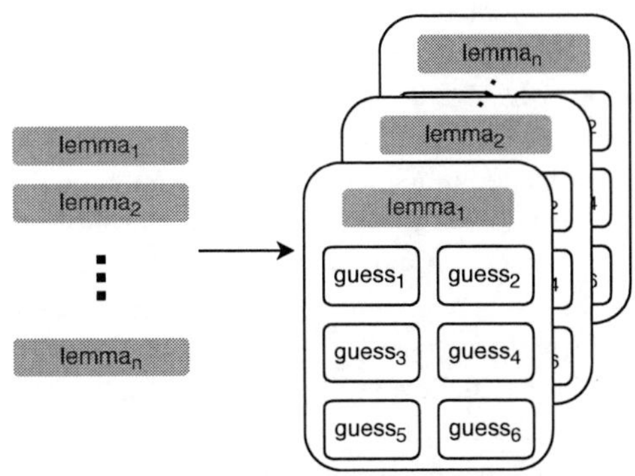

Figure 1: The task of *unsupervised morphological paradigm completion* (Jin et al., 2020) consists of generating complete inflectional paradigms for given lemmas, with the only additional available information being a corpus without annotations.

ing have not yet been developed. We anticipate that such systems will be extremely useful, as they will open the possibility of rapid development of first-pass inflectional paradigms in a large set of languages. These can be utilized both *in se* for generation and as a starting point for elicitation (Sylak-Glassman et al., 2016), thus aiding the development of low-resource human language technologies (Christianson et al., 2018).

In this paper, we present the SIGMORPHON 2020 shared task on unsupervised morphological paradigm completion (SIGMORPHON 2020 Task 2). We asked participants to produce systems that can learn to inflect *in an unsupervised fashion*: given a small corpus (the Bible) together with a list of lemmas for each language, systems for the shared task should output all corresponding inflected forms. In their output, systems had to mark which forms expressed the same morphosyntactic features, e.g., demonstrate knowledge of the fact that *walks* is to *walk* as *listens* is to *listen*, despite not recognizing the morphological features explic-

---

[*]Equal contribution.

Proceedings of the Seventeenth SIGMORPHON Workshop on Computational Research in Phonetics, Phonology, and Morphology, pages 51–62
Online, July 10, 2020. ©2020 Association for Computational Linguistics
https://doi.org/10.18653/v1/P17

itly. We show a visualization of our shared task setup in Figure 1.

Unsupervised morphological paradigm completion requires solving multiple subproblems either explicitly or implicitly. First, a system needs to figure out which words in the corpus belong to the same paradigm. This can, for instance, be done via string similarity: *walks* is similar to *walk*, but less so to *listen*. Second, it needs to figure out the shape of the paradigm. This requires detecting which forms of different lemmas express the same morphosyntactic features, even if they are not constructed from their respective lemmas in the exact same way. Third, a system needs to generate all forms not attested in the provided corpus. Using the collected inflected forms as training data, this can be reduced to the supervised morphological inflection task (Cotterell et al., 2016).

This year's submitted systems can be split into two categories: those that built on the baseline (**Retrieval+X**) and those that did not (**Segment+Conquer**). The baseline system is set up as a pipeline which performs the following steps: edit tree retrieval, additional lemma retrieval, paradigm size discovery, and inflection generation (Jin et al., 2020). As it is highly modular, we provided two versions that employ different inflection models.[1] All systems built on the baseline substituted the morphological inflection component.

No system outperformed the baseline overall. However, two **Retrieval+X** models slightly improved over the baseline on three individual languages. We conclude that the task of unsupervised morphological paradigm completion is still an open challenge, and we hope that this shared task will inspire future research in this area.

2 Task and Evaluation

2.1 Unsupervised Morphological Paradigm Completion

Informal description. The task of unsupervised morphological paradigm completion mimics a setting where the only resources available in a language are a corpus and a short list of dictionary forms, i.e., lemmas. The latter could, for instance, be obtained via basic word-to-word translation. The goal is to generate all inflected forms of the given lemmas.

For an English example, assume the following lemma list to be given:

$$walk$$

$$listen$$

With the help of raw text, systems should then produce an output like this:

$$
\begin{array}{ll}
walk\ walk\ 1 \\
walk\ walks\ 2 \\
walk\ walked\ 3 \\
walk\ walking\ 4 \\
walk\ walked\ 5 \\
listen\ listens\ 2 \\
listen\ listened\ 5 \\
listen\ listened\ 3 \\
listen\ listening\ 4 \\
listen\ listen\ 1
\end{array}
\tag{1}
$$

The numbers serve as unique identifiers for paradigm slots: in above example, "4" corresponds to the *present participle*. The inflections *walking* and *talking* therefore belong to the same paradigm slot. For the task, participants are not provided any knowledge of the grammatical content of the slots.

Formal definition. We denote the paradigm $\pi(\ell)$ of a lemma ℓ as

$$\pi(\ell) = \langle f(\ell, \vec{t}_\gamma) \rangle_{\gamma \in \Gamma(\ell)}, \tag{2}$$

with $f : \Sigma^* \times \mathcal{T} \to \Sigma^*$ being a function that maps a lemma and a vector of morphological features $\vec{t}_\gamma \in \mathcal{T}$ expressed by paradigm slot γ to the corresponding inflected form. $\Gamma(\ell)$ is the set of slots in lemma ℓ's paradigm.

We then formally describe the task of unsupervised morphological paradigm completion as follows. Given a corpus $\mathcal{D} = w_1, \ldots, w_{|\mathcal{D}|}$ together with a list $\mathcal{L} = \{\ell_j\}$ of $|\mathcal{L}|$ lemmas belonging to the same part of speech,[2] unsupervised morphological paradigm completion consists of generating the paradigms $\{\pi(\ell)\}$ of all lemmas $\ell \in \mathcal{L}$.

Remarks. It is impossible for unsupervised systems to predict the names of the features expressed by paradigm slots, an arbitrary decision made by human annotators. This is why, for the shared task,

---

[1] In this report, we use the words *baseline* and *baselines* interchangeably.

[2] This edition of the shared task was only concerned with verbs, though we are considering extending the task to other parts of speech in the future.

we asked systems to mark which forms belong to the same slot by numbering them, e.g., to predict that *walked* is the form for slot 3, while *listens* corresponds to slot 2.

2.2 Macro-averaged Best-Match Accuracy

The official evaluation metric was macro-averaged best-match accuracy (BMAcc; Jin et al., 2020).

In contrast to supervised morphological inflection (Cotterell et al., 2016), our task cannot be evaluated with word-level accuracy. For the former, one can compare the prediction for each lemma and morphological feature vector to the ground truth. However, for unsupervised paradigm completion, this requires a mapping from predicted slots to the gold standard's paradigm slots.

BMAcc, thus, first computes the word-level accuracy each predicted slot would obtain against each true slot. It then constructs a complete bipartite graph, with those accuracies as edge weights. This enables computing of the maximum-weight full matching with the algorithm of Karp (1980). BMAcc then corresponds to the sum of all accuracies for the best matching, divided by the maximum of the number of gold and predicted slots.

BMAcc penalizes systems for predicting a wrong number of paradigm slots. However, detecting the correct number of *identical* slots – something we encounter in some languages due to syncretism – is extremely challenging. Thus, we merge slots with identical forms for all lemmas in both the predictions and the ground truth before evaluating.

Example. Assume our gold standard is (1) (the complete, 5-slot English paradigms for the verbs *walk* and *listen*) and a system outputs the following, including an error in the fourth row:

$$\begin{array}{ll} walk & walks \; 1 \\ walk & walking \; 2 \\ listen & listens \; 1 \\ listen & listenen \; 2 \end{array}$$

First, we merge slots 3 and 5 in the gold standard, since they are identical for both lemmas. Ignoring slot 5, we then compute the BMAcc as follows. Slot 1 yields an accuracy of 100% as compared to gold slot 2, and 0% otherwise. Similarly, slot 2 reaches an accuracy of 50% for gold slot 4, and 0% otherwise. Additionally, given the best mapping of those two slots, we obtain 0% accuracy for gold

slots 1 and 3. Thus, the BMAcc is

$$\text{BMAcc} = \frac{1 + 0.5 + 0 + 0}{4} = 0.375 \qquad (3)$$

3 Shared Task Data

3.1 Provided Resources

We provided data for 5 development and 9 test languages. The development languages were available for system development and hyperparameter tuning, while the test languages were released shortly before the shared task deadline. For the test languages, no ground truth data was available before system submission. This setup emulated a real-world scenario with the goal to create a system for languages about which we have no information.

For the raw text corpora, we leveraged the JHU Bible Corpus (McCarthy et al., 2020). This resource covers 1600 languages, which will enable future work to quickly produce systems for a large set of languages. Additionally, using the Bible allowed for a fair comparison of models across languages without potential confounds such as domain mismatch. 7 of the languages have only the New Testament available (approximately 8k sentences), and 7 have both the New and Old Testaments (approximately 31k sentences).

All morphological information was taken from UniMorph (Sylak-Glassman et al., 2015; Kirov et al., 2018), a resource which contains paradigms for more than 100 languages. However, this information was only accessible to the participants for the development languages. UniMorph paradigms were further used internally for evaluation on the test languages—this data was then released after the conclusion of the shared task.

3.2 Languages

During the development phase of the shared task, we released 5 languages to allow participants to investigate various design decisions: Maltese (MLT), Persian (FAS), Portuguese (POR), Russian (RUS), and Swedish (SWE). These languages are typologically and genetically varied, representing a number of verbal inflectional phenomena. Swedish and Portuguese are typical of Western European languages, and mostly exhibit fusional, suffixing verbal inflection. Russian, as an exemplar of Slavic languages, is still mostly suffixing, but does observe regular ablaut, and has considerable phonologically-conditioned allomorphy. Maltese is a Semitic language with a heavy Romance influence, and verbs

		MLT	FAS	POR	RUS	SWE
1	# Tokens in corpus	193257	227584	828861	727630	871707
2	# Types in corpus	16017	11877	31446	46202	25913
3	# Lemmas	20	100	100	100	100
4	# Lemmas in corpus	10	22	50	50	50
5	# Inflections	640	13600	7600	1600	1100
6	# Inflections in corpus	252	545	1037	306	276
7	Paradigm size	16	136	76	16	11
8	Paradigm size (merged)	15	132	59	16	11

Table 1: Dataset statistics: **development** languages. # Inflections=number of inflected forms in the gold file, token-based; # Inflections in corpus=number of inflections from the gold file which can be found in the corpus, token-based; Paradigm size=number of different morphological feature vectors in the dataset for the language; Paradigm size (merged)=paradigm size, but counting slots with all forms being identical only once.

		EUS	BUL	ENG	FIN	DEU	KAN	NAV	SPA	TUR
1	# Tokens in corpus	195459	801657	236465	685699	826119	193213	104631	251581	616418
2	# Types in corpus	18367	37048	7144	54635	22584	28561	18799	9755	59458
3	# Lemmas	20	100	100	100	100	20	100	100	100
4	# Lemmas in corpus	4	50	50	50	50	10	9	50	50
5	# Inflections	10446	5600	500	14100	2900	2612	3000	7000	12000
6	# Inflections in corpus	97	915	127	497	631	1040	54	630	986
7	Paradigm size	1659	56	5	141	29	85	30	70	120
8	Paradigm size (merged)	1658	54	5	141	20	59	30	70	120

Table 2: Dataset statistics: **test** languages. # Inflections=number of inflected forms in the gold file, token-based; # Inflections in corpus=number of inflections from the gold file which can be found in the corpus, token-based; Paradigm size=number of different morphological feature vectors in the dataset for the language; Paradigm size (merged)=paradigm size, but counting slots with all forms being identical only once.

combine templatic and suffixing inflection. Persian is mostly suffixing, but does allow for verbal inflectional prefixation, such as negation and marking subjunctive mood. Since the development languages were used for system tuning, their scores did not count towards the final ranking.

After a suitable period for system development and tuning, we released nine test languages: Basque (EUS), Bulgarian (BUL), English (ENG), Finnish (FIN), German (DEU), Kannada (KAN), Navajo (NAV), Spanish (SPA), and Turkish (TUR). Although these languages observe many features common to the development languages, such as fusional inflection, suffixation, and ablaut, they also cover inflectional categories absent in the development languages. Navajo, unlike any of the development languages, is strongly prefixing. Basque, Finnish, and Turkish are largely agglutinative, with long, complex affix chains that are difficult to identify through longest suffix matching. Furthermore, Finnish and Turkish feature vowel harmony and consonant gradation, which both require a method to identify allomorphs correctly to be able to merge different variants of the same paradigm slot.

3.3 Statistics

Statistics of the resources provided for all languages are shown in Table 1 for the development languages and in Table 2 for the test languages.

The token count (line 1) and, thus, the size of the provided Bible corpora, differs between 104,631 (Kannada) and 871,707 (Swedish). This number depends both on the typology of a language and on the completeness of the provided Bible translation. The number of types (line 2) is between 7,144 (English) and 59,458 (Turkish). It is strongly influenced by how morphologically rich a language is, i.e., how large the paradigms are, which is often approximated with the *type–token ratio*. The verbal paradigm size is listed in line 7: English has with a size of 5 the smallest paradigms, and, correspondingly, the lowest type count. Turkish, which has the highest number of types, in contrast, has large paradigms (120). The last line serves as an indicator of syncretism: subtracting line 8 from line 7 results in the number of paradigm slots that have been merged as a language evolved to use identical forms for different inflectional categories.

Lines 3 and 4 show the number of lemmas in the lemma lists for all languages, as well as the

Institution	Systems	Rank	Description Paper
KU-CST	KU-CST-1	7	Agirrezabal and Wedekind (2020)
KU-CST	KU-CST-2	6	Agirrezabal and Wedekind (2020)
IMS-CUBoulder	IMS-CUBoulder-1	5	Mager and Kann (2020)
IMS-CUBoulder	IMS-CUBoulder-2	1	Mager and Kann (2020)
NYU-CUBoulder	NYU-CUBoulder-1	4	Singer and Kann (2020)
NYU-CUBoulder	NYU-CUBoulder-2	2	Singer and Kann (2020)
NYU-CUBoulder	NYU-CUBoulder-3	3	Singer and Kann (2020)

Table 3: All submitted systems by institution, together with a reference to their description paper. The rank is relative to all other submitted systems and does not take the baselines into account.

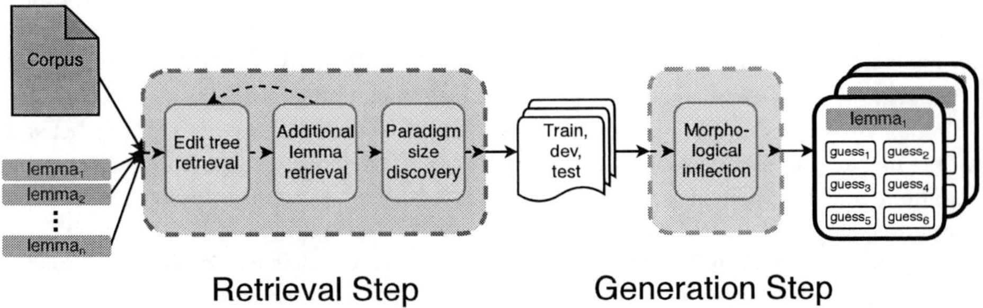

Figure 2: Our baseline system: the retrieval component bootstraps lemma–form–slot triplets, which are then used by the generation component to generate unobserved inflections in the paradigm of each input lemma.

number of lemmas which can be found in the corpus. For the majority of languages, 100 lemmas are provided, out of which 50 appear in the Bible. Exceptions are Maltese (20, 10), Persian (100, 22), Basque (20, 4), Kannada (20, 10), and Navajo (100, 9). These are due to limited UniMorph coverage.

In line 5, we list the number of total inflections, counting each one in the case of identical forms, i.e., this corresponds to the number of lines in our gold inflection file. English, due to its small verbal paradigm size, has only 500 inflections in our data. Conversely, Finnish has with 14,100 the largest number of inflections. Line 6 describes how many of the forms from line 5 appear in the corpus. As before, all forms are counted, even if they are identical. For all languages, a large majority of forms cannot be found in the corpus. This makes the task of unsupervised morphological paradigm completion with our provided data a challenging one.

4 Systems

In this section, we first review the baseline before describing the submitted systems. An additional overview of the submissions is shown in Table 3.

4.1 Baseline

We compared all submissions to the baseline system of Jin et al. (2020), graphically summarized in Figure 2. It is a pipeline system, which consists of 4 separate modules, which, in turn, can be grouped into two major components: *retrieval* and *generation*. The *retrieval component* discovers and returns inflected forms – and, less importantly, additional lemmas – from the provided Bible corpus. The *generation component* produces new inflected forms which cannot be found in the raw text.

The **retrieval component** performs three steps: First, it extracts the most common edit trees (Chrupała, 2008), i.e., it detects regularities with regards to word formation, based on the lemma list. If, for instance, both *walk* and *listen* are the lemmas provided and both *walked* and *listened* are encountered in the corpus, the system notes that appending *-ed* is a common transformation, which might correspond to an inflectional strategy.

Second, it retrieves new lemmas, with the goal to gather additional evidence for our collected edit trees. If, for instance, it has already identified the suffix *-ed* as an inflectional marker, finding both *pray* and *prayed* in the Bible is an indication that *pray* might be a lemma. New lemmas can then, in turn, be used to detect new regularities, e.g., in the case that *listen* and *listens* as well as *pray* and *prays* are attested in the corpus, but *walks* is not. Due to their complementary nature, components one and two can, as a unit, be applied iteratively to bootstrap a larger list of lemmas and transformations. For the baseline, we apply each of them only once.

Finally, the baseline's retrieval component predicts the paradigm size by analyzing which edit trees might be representing the same inflection. For instance, the suffixes *-d* and *-ed* both represent the past tense in English. The output of the retrieval component is a list of inflected forms with their lemmas, annotated with a paradigm slot number.

The **generation component** receives this output and prepares the data to train an inflectional generator. First, identified inflections are divided into a training and development split, and missing paradigm slots are identified. The generator is trained on the discovered inflections, and new forms are predicted for each missing slot.

We used two morphological inflection systems for the two variants of our baseline: the non-neural baseline from Cotterell et al. (2017) and the model proposed by Makarov and Clematide (2018). Both are highly suitable for the low-resource setting.

4.2 Submitted Systems: Retrieval+X

We now describe the first category of shared task submissions: Retrieval+X. Systems in this category leverage the retrieval component of the baseline, while substituting the morphological inflection component with a custom inflection system.

The **IMS–CUBoulder team** relied on LSTM (Hochreiter and Schmidhuber, 1997) sequence-to-sequence models for inflection. In IMS-CUB-1, the generation component is based on the architecture by Bahdanau et al. (2015), but with fewer parameters, as suggested by Kann and Schütze (2016). This model – as well as all other inflection components used for systems in this category – receives the sequence of the lemma's characters and the paradigm slot number as input and produces a sequence of output characters.

Their second system, IMS-CUB-2, uses an LSTM pointer-generator network (See et al., 2017) instead. This architecture has originally been proposed for low-resource morphological inflection by Sharma et al. (2018).

The **NYU–CUBoulder team** also substituted the baseline's generation component. Their morphological inflection models are ensembles of different combinations of transformer sequence-to-sequence models (Vaswani et al., 2017) and pointer-generator transformers, a model they introduced for the task.

NYU-CUB-1 is an ensemble of 6 pointer-generator transformers, while NYU-CUB-2 is an ensemble of 6 vanilla transformers. Their last system, NYU-CUB-3, is an ensemble of all 12 models.

4.3 Submitted Systems: Segment+Conquer

The **KU–CST team** did not modify the baseline directly, but, nevertheless, was heavily inspired by it. Their system first employs a character-segmentation algorithm to identify stem–suffix splits in both the provided lemma list and the corpus, thus identifying potential suffix-replacement rules. Next, k-means is used to cluster the extracted suffixes into allomorphic groups. These suffixes are then concatenated with the most frequent stems obtained from the lemma list, and scored by a language model, in order to arrive at plausible inflectional candidates. This approach is KU-CST-2.

However, KU-CST-2 often produces very small inflectional paradigms; unsurprisingly, given that the provided corpora are small as well, and, thus, any particular lemma is only inflected in limited ways – if at all. Therefore, KU-CST-1 expands the lemma list with a logistic-regression classifier that identifies novel verbs to be added.

5 Results and Analysis

5.1 Results on Development Languages

To encourage reproducibility, we first report the performance of all systems on the development languages in the upper part of Table 4. Although participants were not evaluated on these languages, the results provide insight and enable future researchers to benchmark their progress, while maintaining the held-out status of the test languages.

5.2 Official Shared Task Results

We show the official test results in the lower part of Table 4. Baseline-2 obtained the highest BMAcc on average, followed in order by Baseline-1, IMS-CUB-2, and NU-CUB-2. Overall, systems built on top of the baseline, i.e., systems from Retrieval+X, performed better than systems from Segment+Conquer: the best Segment+Conquer system only reached 4.66% BMAcc on average. This shows the effectiveness of the baseline. However, it also shows that we still have substantial room

	Baseline				KU-CST				IMS-CUB				NYU-CUB					
	1		2		1		2		1		2		1		2		3	
MLT	9.12	(17)	**20.00**	(17)	0.22	(254)	1.30	(2)	14.41	(17)	17.35	(17)	15.29	(17)	15.59	(17)	15.88	(17)
FAS	**6.67**	(31)	6.54	(31)	1.55	(11)	0.74	(2)	2.52	(31)	2.70	(31)	2.76	(31)	2.73	(31)	2.74	(31)
POR	**40.39**	(34)	39.56	(34)	1.09	(1104)	12.75	(70)	38.69	(34)	39.17	(34)	39.93	(34)	39.95	(34)	40.07	(34)
RUS	40.68	(19)	**41.68**	(19)	0.35	(387)	7.06	(10)	38.63	(19)	41.11	(19)	39.26	(19)	40.00	(19)	39.74	(19)
SWE	**45.07**	(15)	40.93	(15)	0.93	(588)	22.82	(17)	37.60	(15)	39.93	(15)	39.80	(15)	39.93	(15)	40.13	(15)
avg.	28.39		**29.74**		0.83		8.93		26.37		28.05		27.41		27.64		27.71	
EUS	0.06	(30)	0.06	(27)	0.02	(30)	0.01	(2)	0.04	(30)	0.06	(30)	0.05	(30)	0.05	(30)	**0.07**	(30)
BUL	28.30	(35)	31.69	(34)	2.99	(138)	4.15	(13)	27.22	(35)	**32.11**	(35)	27.69	(35)	28.94	(35)	27.89	(35)
ENG	65.60	(4)	**66.20**	(4)	3.53	(51)	17.29	(7)	47.80	(4)	61.00	(4)	50.20	(4)	52.80	(4)	51.20	(4)
FIN	5.33	(21)	**5.50**	(21)	0.39	(1169)	2.08	(108)	4.90	(21)	5.38	(21)	5.36	(21)	5.47	(21)	5.35	(21)
DEU	28.35	(9)	**29.00**	(9)	0.70	(425)	4.98	(40)	24.60	(9)	28.35	(9)	27.30	(9)	27.35	(9)	27.35	(9)
KAN	15.49	(172)	15.12	(172)	4.27	(44)	1.69	(1)	10.50	(172)	**15.65**	(172)	11.10	(172)	11.16	(172)	11.10	(172)
NAV	3.23	(3)	**3.27**	(3)	0.13	(38)	0.20	(2)	0.33	(3)	1.17	(3)	0.40	(3)	0.43	(3)	0.43	(3)
SPA	22.96	(29)	**23.67**	(29)	3.52	(225)	10.84	(40)	19.50	(29)	22.34	(29)	20.39	(29)	20.56	(29)	20.30	(29)
TUR	14.21	(104)	**15.53**	(104)	0.11	(1772)	0.71	(502)	13.54	(104)	14.73	(104)	14.88	(104)	15.39	(104)	15.13	(104)
avg.	20.39		**21.12**		1.74		4.66		16.49		20.09		17.49		18.02		17.65	

Table 4: BMAcc in percentages and the number of predicted paradigm slots after merging for all submitted systems and the baselines on all development (top) and test languages (bottom). Best scores are in bold.

for improvement on unsupervised morphological paradigm completion.

Looking at individual languages, `Baseline-2` performed best for all languages except for EUS, where `NYU-CUB-3` obtained the highest BMAcc, and BUL and KAN, where `IMS-CUB-2` was best.

5.3 Analysis: Seen and Unseen Lemmas

We further look separately at the results for lemmas which appear in the corpus and those that do not. While seeing a lemma in context might help some systems, we additionally assume that inflections of attested lemmas are also more likely to appear in the corpus. Thus, we expect the performance for seen lemmas to be higher on average.

Examining the performance with respect to observed *inflected forms* might give cleaner results. However, we instead perform this analysis on a per-lemma basis, since the lemmas are part of a system's *input*, while the inflected forms are not.

Table 5 shows the performance of all systems for seen and unseen lemmas. Surprisingly, both versions of the baseline show similar BMAcc for both settings with a maximum difference of 0.12% on average. However, the baseline is the only system that performs equally well for unseen lemmas; `IMS-CUB-1` observes the largest difference, with an absolute drop of 7.85% BMAcc when generating the paradigms of unseen lemmas. Investigating the cause for `IMS-CUB-1`'s low BMAcc, we manually inspected the English output files, and found that, for unseen lemmas, many generations are nonsensi-

cal (e.g., *demoates* as an inflected form of *demodulate*). This does not happen in the case of seen lemmas. A similar effect has been found by Kann and Schütze (2018), who concluded that this might be caused by the LSTM sequence-to-sequence model not having seen similar character sequences during training. The fact that `IMS-CUB-2`, which uses another inflection model, performs better for unseen lemmas confirms this suspicion. Thus, additional training of the inflection component of `IMS-CUB-1` on words from the corpus might improve generation. Conversely, the baseline – which benefits from inflection models specifically catered to low-resource settings – is better suited to inflecting unseen lemmas. Overall, we conclude that there is little evidence that the difficulty of the task increases for unseen lemmas. Rather, inflection systems need to compensate for the low contextual variety in their training data.

6 Where from and Where to?

6.1 Previous Work

Prior to this shared task, most research on unsupervised systems for morphology was concerned with developing approaches to segment words into morphemes, i.e., their smallest meaning-bearing units (Goldsmith, 2001; Creutz, 2003; Creutz and Lagus, 2007; Snyder and Barzilay, 2008; Goldwater et al., 2009; Kurimo et al., 2010; Kudo and Richardson, 2018). These methods were built around the observation that inflectional morphemes are very common across word types, and leveraged probabil-

	Baseline		KU-CST		IMS-CUB		NYU-CUB		
	1	2	1	2	1	2	1	2	3
EUS	0.11 (30)	0.11 (19)	0.03 (30)	0.03 (2)	0.11 (28)	**0.19** (30)	0.11 (30)	0.11 (30)	0.11 (30)
BUL	25.48 (35)	28.93 (34)	5.62 (138)	6.33 (13)	27.85 (35)	29.70 (34)	29.30 (35)	**29.78** (35)	29.52 (35)
ENG	70.80 (4)	**71.20** (4)	3.02 (51)	18.86 (7)	69.60 (4)	70.40 (4)	69.20 (4)	70.00 (4)	70.00 (4)
FIN	6.17 (21)	6.38 (21)	0.70 (1169)	3.60 (108)	6.11 (21)	**6.65** (21)	6.55 (21)	6.58 (21)	6.57 (21)
DEU	26.70 (9)	27.00 (9)	1.14 (425)	8.75 (40)	27.40 (9)	27.30 (9)	27.50 (9)	**27.60** (9)	27.40 (9)
KAN	16.35 (171)	15.61 (172)	6.61 (44)	1.69 (1)	13.99 (172)	**16.49** (172)	14.63 (172)	14.68 (172)	14.63 (172)
NAV	**2.96** (3)	**2.96** (3)	1.46 (38)	2.22 (2)	**2.96** (3)	**2.96** (3)	**2.96** (3)	**2.96** (3)	**2.96** (3)
SPA	20.97 (29)	**21.60** (29)	4.43 (225)	16.37 (40)	20.40 (29)	21.14 (29)	21.17 (29)	21.09 (29)	21.14 (29)
TUR	14.68 (104)	16.38 (104)	0.23 (1772)	1.42 (502)	16.98 (104)	18.02 (104)	18.30 (104)	**18.70** (104)	18.50 (104)
avg.	20.47	21.13	2.58	6.59	20.60	**21.43**	21.08	21.28	21.20
EUS	0.06 (30)	0.06 (30)	0.03 (30)	0.00 (2)	0.03 (30)	0.04 (30)	0.05 (30)	0.05 (30)	**0.07** (30)
BUL	31.11 (35)	34.44 (34)	0.83 (138)	2.04 (13)	26.59 (35)	**34.52** (35)	26.07 (35)	28.11 (35)	26.26 (35)
ENG	60.40 (4)	**61.20** (4)	4.12 (51)	15.71 (7)	26.00 (4)	51.60 (4)	31.20 (4)	35.60 (4)	32.40 (4)
FIN	4.52 (21)	**4.62** (21)	0.12 (1169)	0.98 (108)	3.69 (21)	4.11 (21)	4.17 (21)	4.37 (21)	4.13 (21)
DEU	30.84 (9)	**32.63** (9)	0.55 (425)	3.05 (40)	22.95 (9)	30.95 (9)	28.74 (9)	28.63 (9)	28.95 (9)
KAN	14.64 (172)	14.55 (172)	1.88 (24)	1.69 (1)	6.72 (172)	**14.72** (172)	7.27 (172)	7.33 (172)	7.28 (172)
NAV	3.26 (3)	**3.30** (3)	0.00 (38)	0.00 (2)	0.07 (3)	0.99 (3)	0.15 (3)	0.18 (3)	0.18 (3)
SPA	24.94 (29)	**25.74** (29)	3.86 (225)	8.94 (40)	18.60 (29)	23.54 (29)	19.60 (29)	20.03 (29)	19.46 (29)
TUR	13.73 (104)	**14.70** (104)	0.00 (1757)	0.00 (500)	10.12 (104)	11.47 (104)	11.48 (104)	12.08 (104)	11.77 (104)
avg.	20.39	**21.25**	1.27	3.60	12.75	19.10	14.30	15.15	14.50

Table 5: BMAcc in percentages and the number of predicted paradigm slots after merging for all submitted systems and the baselines on all test languages; listed separately for lemmas which appear in the corpus (top) and lemmas which do not (bottom). Best scores are in bold.

ity estimates such as maximum likelihood (MLE) or maximum a posteriori (MAP) estimations to determine segmentation points, or minimum description length (MDL)-based approaches. However, they tended to make assumptions regarding how morphemes are combined, and worked best for purely concatenative morphology. Furthermore, these methods had no productive method of handling allomorphy—morphemic variance was simply treated as separate morphemes.

The task of unsupervised morphological paradigm completion concerns more than just segmentation: besides capturing how morphology is reflected in the word form, it also requires correctly clustering transformations into paradigm slots and, finally, generation of unobserved forms.

While Xu et al. (2018) did discover something similar to paradigms, those paradigms were a means to a segmentation end and the shape or size of the paradigms was not a subject of their research. Moon et al. (2009) similarly uses segmentation and clustering of affixes to group words into *conflation sets*, groups of morphologically related words, in an unsupervised way. Their work assumes prefixing and suffixing morphology. In a more task-driven line of research, Soricut and Och (2015) develop an approach to learn morphological transformation rules from observing how consis-

tently word embeddings change between related word forms, with the goal of providing useful word embeddings for unseen words.

Our task further differs from traditional paradigm completion (e.g., Dreyer and Eisner, 2011; Ahlberg et al., 2015) in that *no* seed paradigms are observed. Thus, no information is being provided regarding the paradigm size, inflectional features, or relationships between lemmas and inflected forms. Other recent work (Nicolai and Yarowsky, 2019; Nicolai et al., 2020) learned fine-grained morphosyntactic tools from the Bible, though they leveraged supervision projected from higher-resource languages (Yarowsky et al., 2001; Täckström et al., 2013).

Past shared tasks. This task extends a tradition of SIGMORPHON shared tasks concentrating on inflectional morphology.

The first such task (Cotterell et al., 2016) encouraged participants to create inflectional tools in a typologically diverse group of 10 languages. The task was fully-supervised, requiring systems to learn inflectional morphology from a large annotated database. This task is similar to human learners needing to generate inflections of previously unencountered word forms, after having studied thousands of other types.

The second task (Cotterell et al., 2017) extended

the first task from 10 to 52 languages and started to encourage the development of tools for the low-resource setting. While the first shared task approximated an adult learner with experience with thousands of word forms, low-resource inflection was closer to the language learner that has only studied a small number of inflections—however, it was closer to L2 learning than L1, as it still required training sets with lemma–inflection–slot triplets. The 2017 edition of the shared task also introduced a paradigm-completion subtask: participants were given partially observed paradigms and asked to generate missing forms, based on complete paradigms observed during training. This could be described as the supervised version of our unsupervised task, and notably did not require participants to identify inflected forms from raw text—a crucial step in L1 learning.

The third year of the shared task (Cotterell et al., 2018) saw a further extension to more than 100 languages and another step away from supervised learning, in the form of a contextual prediction task. This task stripped away inflectional annotations, requiring participants to generate an inflection solely utilizing a provided lemma and sentential cues. This task further imitated language learners, but extended beyond morphological learning to morphosyntactic incorporation. Furthermore, removing the requirement of an inflectional feature vector more closely approximated the generation step in our task. However, it was still supervised in that participants were provided with lemma–inflection pairs in context during training. We, in contrast, made no assumption of the existence of such pairs.

Finally, the fourth iteration of the task (McCarthy et al., 2019) again concentrated on less-supervised inflection. Cross-lingual training allowed low-resource inflectors to leverage information from high-resource languages, while a contextual analysis task flipped the previous year's contextual task on its head—tagging a sentence with inflectional information. This process is very similar to the retrieval portion of our task. We extended this effort to not only identify the paradigm slot of particular word, but to combine learned information from each class to extend and complete existing paradigms. Furthermore, we lifted the requirement of named inflectional features, more closely approximating the problem as approached by L1 language learners.

6.2 Future Shared Tasks

Future editions of the shared task could extend this year's Task 2 to a larger variety of languages or parts of speech. Another possible direction is to focus on derivational morphology instead of or in addition to inflectional morphology. We are also considering merging Task 2 with the traditional morphological inflection task: participants could then choose to work on the overall task or on either of the retrieval or generation subproblem.

Finally, we are looking into extending the shared task to use speech data as input. This is closer to how L1 learners acquire morphological knowledge, and, while this could make the task harder in some aspects, it could make it easier in others.

7 Conclusion

We presented the findings of the SIGMORPHON 2020 shared task on unsupervised morphological paradigm completion (SIGMORPHON 2020 Task 2), in which participants were asked to generate paradigms without explicit supervision.

Surprisingly, no team was able to outperform the provided baseline, a pipeline system, on average over all test languages. Even though 2 submitted systems were better on 3 individual languages, this highlights that the task is still an open challenge for the NLP community. We argue that it is an important one: systems obtaining high performance will be able to aid the development of human language technologies for low-resource languages.

All teams that participated in the shared task devised modular approaches. Thus, it will be easy to include improved components in the future as, for instance, systems for morphological inflection improve. We released all data, the baseline, the evaluation script, and the system outputs in the official repository,[3] in the hope that this shared task will lay the foundation for future research on unsupervised morphological paradigm completion.

Acknowledgments

First and foremost, we would like to thank all of our shared task participants. We further thank the passionate morphologists who joined for lunch in Florence's *mercato centrale* on the last day of ACL 2019 to plan the 2020 shared task, as well as the SIGMORPHON Exec, who made this shared task possible.

---

[3] `https://github.com/sigmorphon/2020/tree/master/task2`

References

Manex Agirrezabal and Jürgen Wedekind. 2020. KU-CST at the SIGMORPHON 2020 task 2 on unsupervised morphological paradigm completion. In *Proceedings of the 17th Workshop on Computational Research in Phonetics, Phonology, and Morphology*. Association for Computational Linguistics.

Malin Ahlberg, Markus Forsberg, and Mans Hulden. 2015. Paradigm classification in supervised learning of morphology. In *Proceedings of the 2015 Conference of the North American Chapter of the Association for Computational Linguistics: Human Language Technologies*, pages 1024–1029, Denver, Colorado. Association for Computational Linguistics.

Dzmitry Bahdanau, Kyunghyun Cho, and Yoshua Bengio. 2015. Neural machine translation by jointly learning to align and translate. In *3rd International Conference on Learning Representations, ICLR 2015, San Diego, CA, USA, May 7-9, 2015, Conference Track Proceedings*.

Jean Berko. 1958. The child's learning of english morphology. *Word*, 14(2-3):150–177.

Caitlin Christianson, Jason Duncan, and Boyan Onyshkevych. 2018. Overview of the DARPA LORELEI program. *Machine Translation*, 32(1):3–9.

Grzegorz Chrupała. 2008. *Towards a machine-learning architecture for lexical functional grammar parsing*. Ph.D. thesis, Dublin City University.

Ryan Cotterell, Christo Kirov, John Sylak-Glassman, Géraldine Walther, Ekaterina Vylomova, Arya D. McCarthy, Katharina Kann, Sebastian Mielke, Garrett Nicolai, Miikka Silfverberg, David Yarowsky, Jason Eisner, and Mans Hulden. 2018. The CoNLL–SIGMORPHON 2018 shared task: Universal morphological reinflection. In *Proceedings of the CoNLL–SIGMORPHON 2018 Shared Task: Universal Morphological Reinflection*, pages 1–27, Brussels. Association for Computational Linguistics.

Ryan Cotterell, Christo Kirov, John Sylak-Glassman, Géraldine Walther, Ekaterina Vylomova, Patrick Xia, Manaal Faruqui, Sandra Kübler, David Yarowsky, Jason Eisner, and Mans Hulden. 2017. CoNLL-SIGMORPHON 2017 shared task: Universal morphological reinflection in 52 languages. In *Proceedings of the CoNLL SIGMORPHON 2017 Shared Task: Universal Morphological Reinflection*, pages 1–30, Vancouver. Association for Computational Linguistics.

Ryan Cotterell, Christo Kirov, John Sylak-Glassman, David Yarowsky, Jason Eisner, and Mans Hulden. 2016. The SIGMORPHON 2016 shared Task—Morphological reinflection. In *Proceedings of the 14th SIGMORPHON Workshop on Computational Research in Phonetics, Phonology, and Morphology*, pages 10–22, Berlin, Germany. Association for Computational Linguistics.

Mathias Creutz. 2003. Unsupervised segmentation of words using prior distributions of morph length and frequency. In *Proceedings of the 41st Annual Meeting of the Association for Computational Linguistics*, pages 280–287, Sapporo, Japan. Association for Computational Linguistics.

Mathias Creutz and Krista Lagus. 2007. Unsupervised models for morpheme segmentation and morphology learning. *ACM Trans. Speech Lang. Process.*, 4(1).

Markus Dreyer and Jason Eisner. 2011. Discovering morphological paradigms from plain text using a Dirichlet process mixture model. In *Proceedings of the 2011 Conference on Empirical Methods in Natural Language Processing*, pages 616–627, Edinburgh, Scotland, UK. Association for Computational Linguistics.

John Goldsmith. 2001. Unsupervised learning of the morphology of a natural language. *Computational Linguistics*, 27(2):153–198.

Sharon Goldwater, Thomas L. Griffiths, and Mark Johnson. 2009. A Bayesian framework for word segmentation: Exploring the effects of context. *Cognition*, 112(1):21 – 54.

Sepp Hochreiter and Jürgen Schmidhuber. 1997. Long short-term memory. *Neural Computation*, 9(8):1735–1780.

Huiming Jin, Liwei Cai, Yihui Peng, Chen Xia, Arya D. McCarthy, and Katharina Kann. 2020. Unsupervised morphological paradigm completion. In *Proceedings of the 58th Annual Meeting of the Association for Computational Linguistics*. Association for Computational Linguistics.

Katharina Kann and Hinrich Schütze. 2016. Single-model encoder-decoder with explicit morphological representation for reinflection. In *Proceedings of the 54th Annual Meeting of the Association for Computational Linguistics (Volume 2: Short Papers)*, pages 555–560, Berlin, Germany. Association for Computational Linguistics.

Katharina Kann and Hinrich Schütze. 2018. Neural transductive learning and beyond: Morphological generation in the minimal-resource setting. In *Proceedings of the 2018 Conference on Empirical Methods in Natural Language Processing*, pages 3254–3264, Brussels, Belgium. Association for Computational Linguistics.

Richard M. Karp. 1980. An algorithm to solve the $m \times n$ assignment problem in expected time $O(mn \log n)$. *Networks*, 10(2):143–152.

Christo Kirov, Ryan Cotterell, John Sylak-Glassman, Géraldine Walther, Ekaterina Vylomova, Patrick Xia, Manaal Faruqui, Sebastian Mielke, Arya McCarthy, Sandra Kübler, David Yarowsky, Jason Eisner, and Mans Hulden. 2018. UniMorph 2.0: Universal morphology. In *Proceedings of the Eleventh*

International Conference on Language Resources and Evaluation (LREC-2018), Miyazaki, Japan. European Languages Resources Association (ELRA).

Taku Kudo and John Richardson. 2018. SentencePiece: A simple and language independent subword tokenizer and detokenizer for neural text processing. In *Proceedings of the 2018 Conference on Empirical Methods in Natural Language Processing: System Demonstrations*, pages 66–71, Brussels, Belgium. Association for Computational Linguistics.

Mikko Kurimo, Sami Virpioja, Ville Turunen, and Krista Lagus. 2010. Morpho challenge 2005-2010: Evaluations and results. In *Proceedings of the 11th Meeting of the ACL Special Interest Group on Computational Morphology and Phonology*, pages 87–95, Uppsala, Sweden. Association for Computational Linguistics.

Manuel Mager and Katharina Kann. 2020. The IMS–CUBoulder system for the SIGMORPHON 2020 shared task on unsupervised morphological paradigm completion. In *Proceedings of the 17th Workshop on Computational Research in Phonetics, Phonology, and Morphology*. Association for Computational Linguistics.

Peter Makarov and Simon Clematide. 2018. Imitation learning for neural morphological string transduction. In *Proceedings of the 2018 Conference on Empirical Methods in Natural Language Processing*, pages 2877–2882, Brussels, Belgium. Association for Computational Linguistics.

Arya D. McCarthy, Ekaterina Vylomova, Shijie Wu, Chaitanya Malaviya, Lawrence Wolf-Sonkin, Garrett Nicolai, Christo Kirov, Miikka Silfverberg, Sebastian J. Mielke, Jeffrey Heinz, Ryan Cotterell, and Mans Hulden. 2019. The SIGMORPHON 2019 shared task: Morphological analysis in context and cross-lingual transfer for inflection. In *Proceedings of the 16th Workshop on Computational Research in Phonetics, Phonology, and Morphology*, pages 229–244, Florence, Italy. Association for Computational Linguistics.

Arya D. McCarthy, Rachel Wicks, Dylan Lewis, Aaron Mueller, Winston Wu, Oliver Adams, Garrett Nicolai, Matt Post, and David Yarowsky. 2020. The Johns Hopkins University Bible Corpus: 1600+ tongues for typological exploration. In *Proceedings of the Twelfth International Conference on Language Resources and Evaluation (LREC 2020)*. European Language Resources Association (ELRA).

Taesun Moon, Katrin Erk, and Jason Baldridge. 2009. Unsupervised morphological segmentation and clustering with document boundaries. In *Proceedings of the 2009 Conference on Empirical Methods in Natural Language Processing*, pages 668–677, Singapore. Association for Computational Linguistics.

Garrett Nicolai, Dylan Lewis, Arya D. McCarthy, Aaron Mueller, Winston Wu, and David Yarowsky.

2020. Fine-grained morphosyntactic analysis and generation tools for more than one thousand languages. In *Proceedings of The 12th Language Resources and Evaluation Conference*, pages 3963–3972, Marseille, France. European Language Resources Association.

Garrett Nicolai and David Yarowsky. 2019. Learning morphosyntactic analyzers from the Bible via iterative annotation projection across 26 languages. In *Proceedings of the 57th Annual Meeting of the Association for Computational Linguistics*, pages 1765–1774, Florence, Italy. Association for Computational Linguistics.

Abigail See, Peter J. Liu, and Christopher D. Manning. 2017. Get to the point: Summarization with pointer-generator networks. In *Proceedings of the 55th Annual Meeting of the Association for Computational Linguistics (Volume 1: Long Papers)*, pages 1073–1083, Vancouver, Canada. Association for Computational Linguistics.

Abhishek Sharma, Ganesh Katrapati, and Dipti Misra Sharma. 2018. IIT(BHU)–IIITH at CoNLL–SIGMORPHON 2018 shared task on universal morphological reinflection. In *Proceedings of the CoNLL–SIGMORPHON 2018 Shared Task: Universal Morphological Reinflection*, pages 105–111, Brussels. Association for Computational Linguistics.

Assaf Singer and Katharina Kann. 2020. The NYU–CUBoulder systems for SIGMORPHON 2020 Task 0 and Task 2. In *Proceedings of the 17th Workshop on Computational Research in Phonetics, Phonology, and Morphology*. Association for Computational Linguistics.

Benjamin Snyder and Regina Barzilay. 2008. Unsupervised multilingual learning for morphological segmentation. In *Proceedings of ACL-08: HLT*, pages 737–745, Columbus, Ohio. Association for Computational Linguistics.

Radu Soricut and Franz Och. 2015. Unsupervised morphology induction using word embeddings. In *Proceedings of the 2015 Conference of the North American Chapter of the Association for Computational Linguistics: Human Language Technologies*, pages 1627–1637, Denver, Colorado. Association for Computational Linguistics.

John Sylak-Glassman, Christo Kirov, and David Yarowsky. 2016. Remote elicitation of inflectional paradigms to seed morphological analysis in low-resource languages. In *Proceedings of the Tenth International Conference on Language Resources and Evaluation (LREC 2016)*, pages 3116–3120, Portorož, Slovenia. European Language Resources Association (ELRA).

John Sylak-Glassman, Christo Kirov, David Yarowsky, and Roger Que. 2015. A language-independent feature schema for inflectional morphology. In *Pro-*

ceedings of the 53rd Annual Meeting of the Association for Computational Linguistics and the 7th International Joint Conference on Natural Language Processing (Volume 2: Short Papers), pages 674–680, Beijing, China. Association for Computational Linguistics.

Oscar Täckström, Dipanjan Das, Slav Petrov, Ryan McDonald, and Joakim Nivre. 2013. Token and type constraints for cross-lingual part-of-speech tagging. *Transactions of the Association for Computational Linguistics*, 1:1–12.

Ashish Vaswani, Noam Shazeer, Niki Parmar, Jakob Uszkoreit, Llion Jones, Aidan N. Gomez, Lukasz Kaiser, and Illia Polosukhin. 2017. Attention is all you need. In *Advances in Neural Information Processing Systems 30: Annual Conference on Neural Information Processing Systems 2017, 4-9 December 2017, Long Beach, CA, USA*, pages 5998–6008.

Hongzhi Xu, Mitchell Marcus, Charles Yang, and Lyle Ungar. 2018. Unsupervised morphology learning with statistical paradigms. In *Proceedings of the 27th International Conference on Computational Linguistics*, pages 44–54, Santa Fe, New Mexico, USA. Association for Computational Linguistics.

David Yarowsky, Grace Ngai, and Richard Wicentowski. 2001. Inducing multilingual text analysis tools via robust projection across aligned corpora. In *Proceedings of the First International Conference on Human Language Technology Research*.

DeepSPIN at SIGMORPHON 2020:
One-Size-Fits-All Multilingual Models

Ben Peters[†] and **André F. T. Martins**[†‡]
[†]Instituto de Telecomunicações, Lisbon, Portugal
[‡]Unbabel, Lisbon, Portugal
benzurdopeters@gmail.com, andre.t.martins@tecnico.ulisboa.pt

Abstract

This paper presents DeepSPIN's submissions to Tasks 0 and 1 of the SIGMORPHON 2020 Shared Task. For both tasks, we present multilingual models, training jointly on data in all languages. We perform no language-specific hyperparameter tuning – each of our submissions uses the same model for all languages. Our basic architecture is the sparse sequence-to-sequence model with entmax attention and loss, which allows our models to learn sparse, local alignments while still being trainable with gradient-based techniques. For Task 1, we achieve strong performance with both RNN- and transformer-based sparse models. For Task 0, we extend our RNN-based model to a multi-encoder set-up in which separate modules encode the lemma and inflection sequences. Despite our models' lack of language-specific tuning, they tie for first in Task 0 and place third in Task 1.

1 Introduction

Character transduction tasks such as grapheme-to-phoneme conversion (g2p) and morphological inflection are important in many practical real-world applications. However, it is often difficult to train models for these tasks with deep learning techniques, due to the scarcity of labeled data for most of the world's languages. In these circumstances, it is common to use a non-neural method with a stronger inductive bias (Novak et al., 2016) or to generate synthetic data that hopefully ameliorates the data scarcity problem. We find both of these choices unsatisfying. First, older non-neural techniques have a higher floor but also a lower ceiling – previous SIGMORPHON shared tasks have shown that neural methods outpace them in the presence of even moderate quantities of data (Cotterell et al., 2017). Second, although data augmentation has proven helpful for morphological inflection (Anas-

tasopoulos and Neubig, 2019), any data augmentation procedure makes implicit assumptions about language structure: techniques that work for Western languages may fail when confronted with reduplication, vowel harmony, or non-concatenative morphology. The kinds of languages for which labeled data are scarce are precisely the languages for which NLP practitioners' assumptions are most suspect. Therefore, our submissions to this shared task make use of a third alternative: multilingual training. Similarly to hallucinated data, multilingual training improves results in low resource settings by acting as a regularizer. However, the models it yields are more versatile, as they are capable of good performance on several languages at the same time. We show that our technique is competitive with state-of-the-art monolingually trained models regardless of training data size for both g2p and morphological inflection. This is despite our approach having a significant disadvantage from a tuning perspective – while conventional monolingual models can tune their hyperparameters separately for each language, we use exactly the same model for each language within a submission.

Our contributions are as follows:

- We reimplement gated sparse two-headed attention (Peters and Martins, 2019) and apply it to a massively multilingual setting. We submit versions of this model using 1.5-entmax (Peters et al., 2019) and sparsemax (Martins and Astudillo, 2016) as softmax alternatives. We tie for first place in Task 0 (Vylomova et al., 2020). Among the winners, ours are the only multilingual models.

- We show that sparse *seq2seq* techniques, previously used for morphological inflection and machine translation (Peters et al., 2019), are also effective for multilingual g2p. We make four submissions to Task 1 (Gorman et al.,

Proceedings of the Seventeenth SIGMORPHON Workshop on Computational Research
in Phonetics, Phonology, and Morphology, pages 63–69
Online, July 10, 2020. ©2020 Association for Computational Linguistics
https://doi.org/10.18653/v1/P17

2020), which differ based on their choice of softmax replacement (1.5-entmax or sparsemax) and their architecture (RNN or transformer). Our strongest models finish third in word error rate (WER) and second in phoneme error rate (PER). Our submissions record the top result on at least one metric for 7 out of 15 languages, including 4 out of 5 surprise languages.

2 Models

The common theme of the models we submit is their use of **sparse functions** for attention weights and output distributions, in place of the better-known softmax (Bridle, 1990). Sparse functions have the following motivations:

- Sparse attention has previously shown success on morphological inflection (Peters and Martins, 2019). It allows the decoder to attend to a small number of source positions at each time step, unlike the dense softmax. While hard attention has previously performed well for character transduction (Aharoni and Goldberg, 2017; Makarov et al., 2017; Wu et al., 2018; Wu and Cotterell, 2019), it usually requires an elaborate and slow training procedure. On the other hand, sparse attention does not require any training techniques beyond those used for standard *seq2seq* models.

- Sparse output distributions allow probability mass to be concentrated in a small number of hypotheses. In practice, this happens frequently for morphological inflection (Peters et al., 2019), sometimes making beam search exact.

2.1 Entmax and its loss

Our tool for achieving sparsity is the entmax activation function (Peters et al., 2019), which is parameterized by a scalar $\alpha \geq 1$ and maps a vector $z \in \mathbb{R}^n$ onto the n–dimensional probability simplex $\triangle^n := \{p \in \mathbb{R}^n : p \geq 0, \mathbf{1}^\top p = 1\}$:

$$\alpha\text{-entmax}(z) := \underset{p \in \triangle^n}{\arg\max}\, p^\top z + \mathsf{H}_\alpha(p), \quad (1)$$

where

$$\mathsf{H}_\alpha(p) := \begin{cases} \frac{1}{\alpha(\alpha-1)} \sum_j \left(p_j - p_j^\alpha \right), & \alpha \neq 1, \\ -\sum_j p_j \log p_j, & \alpha = 1 \end{cases} \quad (2)$$

is the Tsallis α-entropy (Tsallis, 1988). For purposes of the shared task, the key point is that α **controls the sparsity** of the distribution. $\alpha = 1$ recovers softmax, while any value greater than 1 can result in a sparse probability distribution. Sparsemax (Martins and Astudillo, 2016) is equivalent to entmax with $\alpha = 2$.

An important note about models with sparse output layers is that they cannot be trained with cross entropy loss, as the cross entropy loss becomes infinite when the model assigns zero probability to the gold label. Fortunately, for each value α, there is a corresponding loss function, which is given by

$$\mathsf{L}_\alpha(y, z) := (p^\star - e_y)^\top z + \mathsf{H}_\alpha(p^\star), \quad (3)$$

where $p^\star := \alpha\text{-entmax}(z)$. This is an instance of a Fenchel-Young loss (Blondel et al., 2020).

2.2 Task 0 Architecture

For morphological inflection, we use an RNN-based two-encoder model with gated attention (Peters and Martins, 2019). In this model, two separate bidirectional LSTMs (Graves and Schmidhuber, 2005) encode the lemma character sequence and the set of inflectional tags. A unidirectional LSTM (Hochreiter and Schmidhuber, 1997) decoder then generates the target sequence. The decoder is similar to a conventional RNN decoder with input feeding, except that separate attention mechanisms compute context vectors independently for each encoder. A gate function then interpolates the two context vectors. Like Peters and Martins (2019), we use a sparse gate, which allows the model to completely ignore one encoder or the other at each time step. Each individual attention head uses bilinear attention (Luong et al., 2015).

2.3 Task 1 Architecture

We experiment with both RNN-based (Bahdanau et al., 2015) and transformer-based (Vaswani et al., 2017) models for g2p. As in Task 0, our RNNs use input feeding and bilinear attention.

2.4 Handling Multilinguality

Multilingual NLP tasks are intrinsically more difficult than their monolingual counterparts, as the correct way to process a sample depends on what sample the language is in. A simple approach to multilingual NLP is to append a token to each input sequence identifying the language of the sample; this has proven effective for both g2p (Peters et al., 2017) and morphological inflection (Peters et al., 2019), and is similar to techniques for multilingual neural machine translation (Johnson et al., 2017). However, this technique has drawbacks: it forces the true characters and the language token to "compete" for attention, and it requires the learned language embedding to have the same size as the character embeddings.

Therefore, we use the alternative technique of concatenating a language embedding to the encoder and decoder input at each time step. Within an example, the language embedding is the same across all time steps. We do not tie language embeddings between the encoder (or encoders) and decoder, allowing each model to learn different language representations for different purposes.

3 Experiments

3.1 Preprocessing

Task 0 We used character-level tokenization for lemma and inflected forms. Each inflectional tag was treated as a separate token.

Task 1 Prior to training, we decomposed compound characters in the grapheme sequences in all languages. For most languages, this simply amounts to splitting diacritics and their base characters into separate tokens. For Korean, however, it makes a major difference due to the unique structure of the Hangul alphabet. Individual letters in Hangul, called *jamo*, are composed into blocks representing syllables. Modern Hangul contains 40 *jamo*, but the number of possible syllables licensed by Korean phonotactics is much larger. Consequently, a naïve tokenization of the Korean training data gives a vocabulary size of 834 types, of which more than 30% occur only once. We suspect that the lack of *jamo* tokenization is the reason for the baselines' poor performance on Korean.

3.2 Experimental Set-up

We ran experiments with three sparse *seq2seq* architectures: RNNs for inflection, RNNs for g2p, and transformers for g2p. For entmax, we used two α values: 1.5 and 2 (i.e. sparsemax). We used the same α value in both the attention mechanism and loss function. Combining the architectures and entmax functions gives six model configurations. For each, we trained three[1] model runs with the

Hyperparameters	RNN	Transformer
Embedding size	108	236
Language embedding size	20	20
Hidden size	512	256
Positionwise feedforward size	-	1024
Layers (all enc. and dec.)	2	4
Dropout	0.3	0.3
Batch size	128 words	1600 char.

Table 1: Hyperparameters for all models.

Model	Acc. ↑	Lev. Dist. ↓
INFLECTION-ENTMAX-1.5	90.5	0.217
INFLECTION-SPARSEMAX	90.9	0.211
Baseline (Wu et al., 2020)	90.6	0.215

Table 2: Macro-averaged test results for Task 0.

same hyperparameters. At test time, we ensembled the models by averaging their probabilities.

3.3 Training

We implemented our models with JoeyNMT (Kreutzer et al., 2019).[2] Our hyperparameters are shown in Table 1. Each model was trained with early stopping for a maximum of 100 epochs. We used greedy decoding at validation time, saving the model if it had the best character error rate so far. We used the Adam optimizer (Kingma and Ba, 2015). For RNNs, we set the initial learning rate to 0.001, reducing it by half whenever the model failed to improve for two consecutive validations. Validation was performed every 10,000 steps for Task 0 and every 500 steps for Task 1. Transformers were trained with a linear learning rate warm up for 4,000 steps, after which the learning rate was decayed by an inverse square root schedule.

3.4 Results

At test time, we decoded with a beam size of 5. Task 0 results are shown in Table 2 and Task 1 results are in Table 3. For Task 0, our sparsemax model outperforms a very strong baseline, with entmax not far behind. For Task 1, all of our models outperform all three baselines. In both tasks, the baselines were trained monolingually, so they were able to use language-specific hyperparameter tuning that is unavailable for multilingual models.

---

[1]Due to time constraints, the TRANSFORMER-SPARSEMAX ensemble used only two models.

[2]Our code and configuration files are available at https://github.com/deep-spin/sigmorphon-seq2seq.

Model	WER $\downarrow$	PER $\downarrow$
RNN-ENTMAX-1.5	14.47	2.85
RNN-SPARSEMAX	14.19	2.78
TRANSFORMER-ENTMAX-1.5	14.15	2.92
TRANSFORMER-SPARSEMAX	14.53	2.92
FST Baseline	22.00	4.92
RNN Baseline	16.84	3.99
Transformer Baseline	17.51	4.30

Table 3: Macro-averaged test results for Task 1.

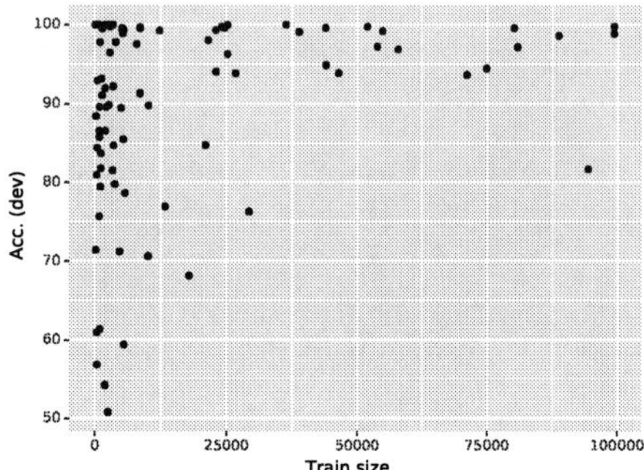

Figure 1: Single-language development set accuracies for INFLECTION-SPARSEMAX.

4 Analysis

Next we consider a few questions that multilingual models raise.

4.1 How much data does inflection need?

All other things being equal, we expect the performance of a model to improve as the amount of training data is increased. And indeed, this is generally the case, as Figure 1 shows that accuracy is usually above 90% for languages with more than 10,000 training samples. However, there is much more *diversity* of performance at smaller training sizes. Per-family development set results are shown in Table 4. While families like Niger-Congo record very strong results with modest resources, Germanic and Uralic struggle despite their large training sets. It is likely that certain morphological patterns are easier to learn than others, but we hesitate to make strong statements. Often results are very different between closely related languages, such as Danish (68.20% on dev) and Swedish (99.20%). More research is needed to identify other factors besides morphological typology that influence results.

Family	#languages	Train size (avg.)	Acc.
Afro-Asiatic	3	1524.67	94.90
Algic	1	4571.00	71.23
Australian	1	777.00	75.68
Austronesian	5	748.20	79.96
Dravidian	2	2311.00	88.78
Germanic	13	30995.69	87.30
Indo-Aryan	4	17642.50	98.37
Iranian	3	10046.33	96.49
Niger-Congo	10	1651.60	97.32
Nilo-Saharan	1	56.00	100.00
Oto-Manguean	10	7799.30	83.45
Romance	8	16075.12	98.15
Sino-Tibetan	1	3428.00	84.76
Siouan	1	2636.00	89.89
Tungusic	1	5413.00	59.43
Turkic	9	9268.33	94.76
Uralic	16	45805.31	89.21
Uto-Aztecan	1	1123.00	83.75

Table 4: Task 0 dev accuracy by language family for INFLECTION-SPARSEMAX.

4.2 Crosslingual Character Embeddings

Learning good word representations has been a prominent subject in NLP for several years (Mikolov et al., 2013; Peters et al., 2018). Although many models operate at the character level, relatively little attention has been paid to the character embeddings themselves. Characters lack semantic meaning, so character embeddings learned for "semantic" tasks are unlikely to learn any particular structure. However, Figure 2 shows that multilingual g2p may be useful for learning **phonologically grounded** character representations: graphemes from different scripts cluster together if they represent similar phonemes. We suspect that the multilingual training with phonological supervision is a necessary ingredient for this to work – characters from different scripts are never mixed within a single sample, so the grapheme contexts in which they occur are completely disjoint.

This idea differs from work on *phoneme* embeddings (Silfverberg et al., 2018; Sofroniev and Çöltekin, 2018) in that the focus is explicitly on the *graphemes*. Grapheme embeddings learned for phonological tasks may prove useful for transliteration, or for processing informally romanized text (Irvine et al., 2012) jointly with data from the official orthography.

5 Related Work

Multi-encoder models Several previous works have considered ways to integrate information from

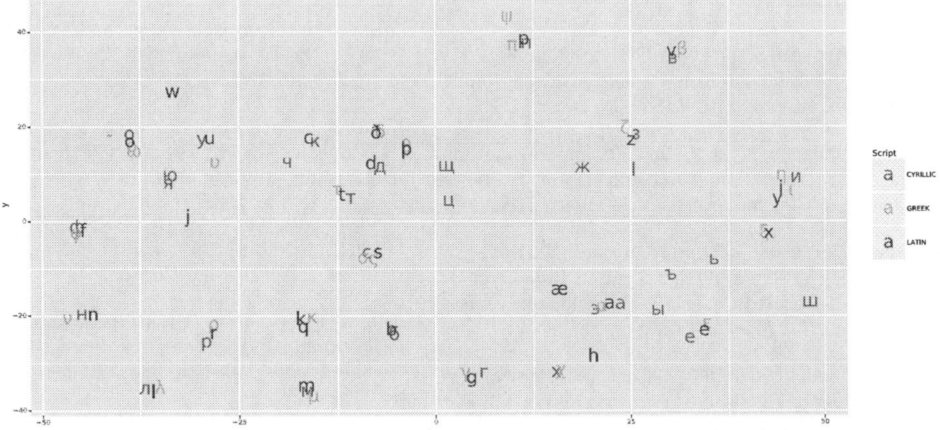

Figure 2: t-SNE projection (Maaten and Hinton, 2008) of the grapheme embeddings learned by TRANSFORMER-1.5. For improved readability, we include only Cyrillic, Greek, and Latin graphemes. Graphemes that tend to represent similar phonemes are clustered together.

multiple sources in a neural *seq2seq* model. Although initially proposed as a way to leverage multiparallel data in machine translation (Zoph and Knight, 2016), it has also been used for handling multimodal data, and Ács (2018) applied it to morphological inflection: our architecture is essentially a sparsified version of this model. Past works have also considered the effect of different strategies for merging the attention from the various encoders (Libovický and Helcl, 2017; Libovický et al., 2018). This is worth exploring for morphological inflection, as Peters and Martins (2019) showed that the behavior of the attention gating mechanism varies between language families. The optimal strategy is probably different for different languages.

Phonemes and multilinguality Multilingual methods have previously been used for low resource g2p in conjunction with both non-neural (Deri and Knight, 2016) and neural (Peters et al., 2017; Route et al., 2019) architectures. Our model is essentially identical to Peters et al. (2017)'s, but with a different mechanism for identifying the language, inspired by a technique for learning language embeddings from multilingual language modeling (Östling and Tiedemann, 2017). A natural connection is to work that makes use of typological information in multilingual NLP (Tsvetkov et al., 2016). However, care needs to be taken when applying this to g2p: Bjerva and Augenstein (2018)

showed that language representations learned from multilingual g2p generally do not encode typological features because orthographic similarity does not correlate with typological similarity.

6 Conclusion

We showed that massively multilingual models are competitive with the individually-tuned state of the art for morphological inflection and g2p. We presented the first result applying entmax-based sparse attention and losses to g2p, showing that it performed with both RNN and transformer models. We release our code to facilitate further research.

Acknowledgments

This work was supported by the European Research Council (ERC StG DeepSPIN 758969), and by the Fundação para a Ciência e Tecnologia through contracts UID/EEA/50008/2019 and CMUPERI/TIC/0046/2014 (GoLocal). We thank the anonymous reviewers for their helpful feedback.

References

Judit Ács. 2018. BME-HAS system for CoNLL–SIGMORPHON 2018 shared task: Universal morphological reinflection. In *Proc. CoNLL–SIGMORPHON*.

Roee Aharoni and Yoav Goldberg. 2017. Morphological inflection generation with hard monotonic attention. In *Proc. ACL*.

Antonios Anastasopoulos and Graham Neubig. 2019. Pushing the Limits of Low-Resource Morphological Inflection. In *Proc. EMNLP–IJCNLP*.

Dzmitry Bahdanau, Kyunghyun Cho, and Yoshua Bengio. 2015. Neural machine translation by jointly learning to align and translate. In *Proc. ICLR*.

Johannes Bjerva and Isabelle Augenstein. 2018. From Phonology to Syntax: Unsupervised Linguistic Typology at Different Levels with Language Embeddings. In *Proc. NAACL–HLT*.

Mathieu Blondel, André FT Martins, and Vlad Niculae. 2020. Learning with fenchel-young losses. *Journal of Machine Learning Research*, 21(35):1–69.

John S Bridle. 1990. Probabilistic interpretation of feedforward classification network outputs, with relationships to statistical pattern recognition. In *Neurocomputing*, pages 227–236. Springer.

Ryan Cotterell, Christo Kirov, John Sylak-Glassman, Géraldine Walther, Ekaterina Vylomova, Patrick Xia, Manaal Faruqui, Sandra Kübler, David Yarowsky, Jason Eisner, and Mans Hulden. 2017. CoNLL-SIGMORPHON 2017 shared task: Universal morphological reinflection in 52 languages. In *Proc. CoNLL–SIGMORPHON*.

Aliya Deri and Kevin Knight. 2016. Grapheme-to-phoneme models for (almost) any language. In *Proc. ACL*.

Kyle Gorman, Lucas F.E. Ashby, Aaron Goyzueta, Arya D. McCarthy, Shijie Wu, and Daniel You. 2020. The sigmorphon 2020 shared task on multilingual grapheme-to-phoneme conversion. In *Proc. SIGMORPHON*.

Alex Graves and Jürgen Schmidhuber. 2005. Framewise phoneme classification with bidirectional LSTM and other neural network architectures. *Neural Networks*, 18(5-6):602–610.

Sepp Hochreiter and Jürgen Schmidhuber. 1997. Long short-term memory. *Neural Computation*, 9(8):1735–1780.

Ann Irvine, Jonathan Weese, and Chris Callison-Burch. 2012. Processing Informal, Romanized Pakistani Text Messages. In *Proceedings of the Second Workshop on Language in Social Media*.

Melvin Johnson, Mike Schuster, Quoc V Le, Maxim Krikun, Yonghui Wu, Zhifeng Chen, Nikhil Thorat, Fernanda Viégas, Martin Wattenberg, Greg Corrado, et al. 2017. Google's multilingual neural machine translation system: Enabling zero-shot translation. *Transactions of the Association for Computational Linguistics*, 5:339–351.

Diederik Kingma and Jimmy Ba. 2015. Adam: A method for stochastic optimization. In *Proc. ICLR*.

Julia Kreutzer, Joost Bastings, and Stefan Riezler. 2019. Joey NMT: A minimalist NMT toolkit for novices. In *Proc. EMNLP–IJCNLP*.

Jindřich Libovický and Jindřich Helcl. 2017. Attention Strategies for Multi-Source Sequence-to-Sequence Learning. In *Proc. ACL*.

Jindřich Libovický, Jindřich Helcl, and David Mareček. 2018. Input Combination Strategies for Multi-Source Transformer Decoder. In *Proc. WMT*.

Minh-Thang Luong, Hieu Pham, and Christopher D Manning. 2015. Effective approaches to attention-based neural machine translation. In *Proc. EMNLP*.

Laurens van der Maaten and Geoffrey Hinton. 2008. Visualizing data using t-sne. *Journal of machine learning research*, 9(Nov):2579–2605.

Peter Makarov, Tatiana Ruzsics, and Simon Clematide. 2017. "Align and Copy: UZH at SIGMORPHON 2017 Shared Task for Morphological Reinflection". In *Proc. CoNLL–SIGMORPHON*.

André FT Martins and Ramón Fernandez Astudillo. 2016. From softmax to sparsemax: A sparse model of attention and multi-label classification. In *Proc. ICML*.

Tomas Mikolov, Ilya Sutskever, Kai Chen, Greg S Corrado, and Jeff Dean. 2013. Distributed representations of words and phrases and their compositionality. In *Proc. NeurIPS*.

Josef Robert Novak, Nobuaki Minematsu, and Keikichi Hirose. 2016. Phonetisaurus: Exploring grapheme-to-phoneme conversion with joint n-gram models in the wfst framework. *Natural Language Engineering*, 22(6):907–938.

Robert Östling and Jörg Tiedemann. 2017. Continuous multilinguality with language vectors. In *Proc. EACL*.

Ben Peters, Jon Dehdari, and Josef van Genabith. 2017. Massively multilingual neural grapheme-to-phoneme conversion. In *Proc. Workshop on Building Linguistically Generalizable NLP Systems*.

Ben Peters and André F. T. Martins. 2019. IT–IST at the SIGMORPHON 2019 shared task: Sparse two-headed models for inflection. In *Proc. SIGMORPHON*.

Ben Peters, Vlad Niculae, and André FT Martins. 2019. Sparse Sequence-to-Sequence Models. In *Proc. ACL*.

Matthew Peters, Mark Neumann, Mohit Iyyer, Matt Gardner, Christopher Clark, Kenton Lee, and Luke Zettlemoyer. 2018. Deep Contextualized Word Representations. In *Proc. NAACL–HLT*.

James Route, Steven Hillis, Isak Czeresnia Etinger, Han Zhang, and Alan W Black. 2019. Multimodal, Multilingual Grapheme-to-Phoneme Conversion for Low-Resource Languages. In *Proc. 2nd Workshop on Deep Learning Approaches for Low-Resource NLP (DeepLo 2019)*.

Miikka P. Silfverberg, Lingshuang Mao, and Mans Hulden. 2018. Sound analogies with phoneme embeddings. In *Proc. SCiL*.

Pavel Sofroniev and Çağrı Çöltekin. 2018. Phonetic vector representations for sound sequence alignment. In *Proc. SIGMORPHON*.

Constantino Tsallis. 1988. Possible generalization of Boltzmann-Gibbs statistics. *Journal of Statistical Physics*, 52:479–487.

Yulia Tsvetkov, Sunayana Sitaram, Manaal Faruqui, Guillaume Lample, Patrick Littell, David Mortensen, Alan W Black, Lori Levin, and Chris Dyer. 2016. Polyglot neural language models: A case study in cross-lingual phonetic representation learning. In *Proc. NAACL–HLT*.

Ashish Vaswani, Noam Shazeer, Niki Parmar, Jakob Uszkoreit, Llion Jones, Aidan N Gomez, Łukasz Kaiser, and Illia Polosukhin. 2017. Attention is all you need. In *Proc. NeurIPS*.

Ekaterina Vylomova, Jennifer White, Elizabeth Salesky, Sabrina J. Mielke, Shijie Wu, Edoardo Ponti, Rowan Hall Maudslay, Ran Zmigrod, Joseph Valvoda, Svetlana Toldova, Francis Tyers, Elena Klyachko, Ilya Yegorov, Natalia Krizhanovsky, Paula Czarnowska, Irene Nikkarinen, Andrej Krizhanovsky, Tiago Pimentel, Lucas Torroba Hennigen, Christo Kirov, Garrett Nicolai, Adina Williams, Antonios Anastasopoulos, Hilaria Cruz, Eleanor Chodroff, Ryan Cotterell, Miikka Silfverberg, and Mans Hulden. 2020. The SIGMORPHON 2020 Shared Task 0: Typologically diverse morphological inflection. In *Proc. SIGMORPHON*.

Shijie Wu and Ryan Cotterell. 2019. Exact Hard Monotonic Attention for Character-Level Transduction. *Proc. ACL*.

Shijie Wu, Ryan Cotterell, and Mans Hulden. 2020. Applying the transformer to character-level transduction.

Shijie Wu, Pamela Shapiro, and Ryan Cotterell. 2018. Hard non-monotonic attention for character-level transduction. In *Proc. EMNLP*.

Barret Zoph and Kevin Knight. 2016. Multi-source neural translation. In *Proc. NAACL–HLT*.

Ensemble Self-Training for Low-Resource Languages: Grapheme-to-Phoneme Conversion and Morphological Inflection

Xiang Yu, Ngoc Thang Vu, Jonas Kuhn
Institut für Maschinelle Sprachverarbeitung
University of Stuttgart, Germany
`firstname.lastname@ims.uni-stuttgart.de`

Abstract

We present an iterative data augmentation framework, which trains and searches for an optimal ensemble and simultaneously annotates new training data in a self-training style. We apply this framework on two SIGMORPHON 2020 shared tasks: grapheme-to-phoneme conversion and morphological inflection. With very simple base models in the ensemble, we rank the first and the fourth in these two tasks. We show in the analysis that our system works especially well on low-resource languages. The system is available at `https://www.ims.uni-stuttgart.de/en/institute/team/Yu-00010/`.

1 Introduction

The vast majority of languages in the world have very few annotated dataset available for training natural language processing models, if at all. Dealing with the low-resource languages has sparked much interest in the NLP community (Garrette et al., 2013; Agić et al., 2016; Zoph et al., 2016).

When annotation is difficult to obtain, data augmentation is a common practice to increase training data size with reasonable quality to feed to powerful models (Ragni et al., 2014; Bergmanis et al., 2017; Silfverberg et al., 2017). For example, the data hallucination method by Anastasopoulos and Neubig (2019) automatically creates non-existing "words" to augment morphological inflection data, which alleviates the label bias problem in the generation model. However, the data created by such method can only help regularize the model, but cannot be viewed as valid words of a language.

Orthogonal to the data augmentation approach, another commonly used method to boost model performance without changing the architecture is ensembling, i.e., by training several models of the same kind and selecting the output by majority voting. It has been shown that a key to the success of ensembling is the diversity of the base models (Surdeanu and Manning, 2010), since models with different inductive biases are less likely to make the same mistake.

In this work, we pursue a combination of both directions, by developing a framework to search for the optimal ensemble and simultaneously annotate unlabeled data. The proposed method is an iterative process, which uses an ensemble of heterogeneous models to select and annotate unlabeled data based on the agreement of the ensemble, and use the annotated data to train new models, which are in turn potential members of the new ensemble. The ensemble is a subset of all trained models that maximizes the accuracy on the development set, and we use a genetic algorithm to find such combination of models.

This approach can be viewed as a type of self-training (Yarowsky, 1995; Clark et al., 2003), but instead of using the confidence of one model, we use the agreement of many models to annotate new data. The key difference is that the model diversity in the ensemble can alleviate the confirmation bias of typical self-training approaches.

We apply the framework on two of the SIGMORPHON 2020 Shared Tasks: grapheme-to-phoneme conversion (Gorman et al., 2020) and morphological inflection (Vylomova et al., 2020). Our system rank the first in the former and the fourth in the latter.

While analyzing the contribution of each component of our framework, we found that the data augmentation method does not significantly improve the results for languages with medium or large training data in the shared tasks, i.e., the advantage of our system mainly comes from the massive ensemble of a variety of base models. However, when we simulate the low-resource scenario or consider only the low-resource languages, the benefit of data augmentation becomes prominent.

Proceedings of the Seventeenth SIGMORPHON Workshop on Computational Research in Phonetics, Phonology, and Morphology, pages 70–78
Online, July 10, 2020. ©2020 Association for Computational Linguistics
https://doi.org/10.18653/v1/P17

2 Ensemble Self-Training Framework

2.1 General Workflow

In this section we describe the details of our framework. It is largely agnostic to the type of supervised learning task, while in this work we apply it on two sequence generation tasks: morphological inflection and grapheme-to-phoneme conversion. The required component includes one or more types of base models and large amount of unlabeled data. Ideally, the base models should be simple and fast to train with reasonable performance, and as diverse as possible, i.e., models with different architectures are better than the same architecture with different random seeds.

The workflow is described in Algorithm 1. Initially, we have the original training data L_0, unlabeled data U, and several base model types $T^{1...k}$. In each iteration n, there are two major steps: (1) ensemble training and (2) data augmentation. In the ensemble training step, we train each base model type on the current training data L_n to obtain the models $m_n^{1...k}$, and add them into the model pool (line 4-8). We then search for an optimal subset of the models from the pool as the current ensemble, based on its performance on the development set (line 9). In the data augmentation step, we sample a batch of unlabeled data (line 10), then use the ensemble to predict and select a subset of the instances based on the agreement among the models (line 11). The selected data are then aggregated into the training set for later iterations (line 12-13).

2.2 Ensemble Search

Simply using all the models as the ensemble would be not only slow but also inaccurate, since too many inferior models might even mislead the ensemble, therefore searching for the optimal combination is needed. However, an exact search is not feasible, since the number of combinations grows exponentially. We use the genetic algorithm for heterogeneous ensemble search largely following Haque et al. (2016). In the preliminary experiments, the genetic algorithm consistently finds better ensembles than random sampling or using all models.

We use a binary encoding such as 0100101011 to represent an ensemble combination (denoted as an individual in genetic algorithms), where each bit encodes whether to use one particular model.

As we aim to maximizing the prediction accuracy of the ensemble, we define the fitness score of an individual as the accuracy on the development

---

Algorithm 1 Ensemble Self-Training (EST)

1: **function** EST(L, U, T)
Require: labeled data L
Require: unlabeled data U
Require: tools T
  2:      Initial data $L_0 = L$
  3:      Model pool $M = \emptyset$
  4:      **for** $n : 0...N$ **do**
  5:          **for** $t^k \in T$ **do**
  6:             $m_n^k = \text{TRAIN}(t^k, L_n)$
  7:             $M = M \cup \{m_n^k\}$
  8:          **end for**
  9:      $E = \text{SEARCHENSEMBLE}(M)$
10:      Sample $u \sim U$
11:      $l = \text{SELECTDATA}(E, u)$
12:      $L_{n+1} = \text{AGGREGATEDATA}(L_n, l)$
13:      $U = U - l$
14:      **end for**
15:      **return** E, L_k
16: **end function**

---

set by the ensemble represented by the individual.

Initially, we generate 100 random individuals into a pool, which is maintained at the size of 100. Whenever a new individual enters the pool, the individual with the lowest fitness score will be removed.

Each new individual is created through three steps: parent selection, crossover, and mutation. Both parents are selected in a tournament style, in which we sample 10 individuals from the pool, and take the one with the highest fitness score. In the crossover process, we take each bit randomly from one parent with a rate of 60%, and 40% from the other. In the mutation process, we flip each bit of the child with a probability of 1%. To ensure the efficiency of the ensemble, we also limit the number of models in the combination to 20: if a newly evolved combination exceeds 20 models, we randomly reduce the number to 20 before evaluating the fitness.

In each search, we evolve 100,000 individuals, and return the one with the highest fitness score. Since the data size is relatively small, the ensemble search procedure typically only takes a few seconds.

2.3 Data Selection and Aggregation

In each iteration, we use the current optimal ensemble to predict a batch of new data, and select a subset as additional data to train models in the next iteration.

There are various heuristics to select new data, with two major principles to consider: (1) one should prefer the instances with higher agreement among the models, since they are more likely to be correct; (2) instances with unanimous agreement might be too trivial and does not provide much new information to train the models.

To strike a balance between the two considerations, we first rank the data by the agreement, but only take at most half of the instances with unanimous agreement as new annotated data. Concretely, we sample 20,000 instances to predict, and use at most 3,600 instances as new data if their predictions have over 80% agreement, among which, at most 1,800 instances have 100% agreement. Note that we chose the data size of 3,600 because it is the training data size in the grapheme-to-phoneme conversion task, and we used the same setting for the morphological inflection task without tuning.

There are also different ways to aggregate the new data. One could simply accumulate all the selected data, resulting in much larger training data in the later iterations, which might slow down the training process and dilute the original data too much. Alternatively, one could append only the selected data from the current iteration to the original data, which might limit the potential of the models.

Again, we took the middle path, in which we keep half of all additional data from the previous iteration together with the selected data in the current iteration. For example, there are 3600 additional instances produced in iteration 0, $3600/2 + 3600 = 5400$ in iteration 1, $5400/2 + 3600 = 6300$ in iteration 2, and the size eventually converges to $3600 \times 2 = 7200$.

3 Grapheme-to-Phoneme Conversion

3.1 Task and Data

We first apply our framework on the grapheme-to-phoneme conversion task (Gorman et al., 2020), which includes 15 languages from the WikiPron project (Lee et al., 2020) with a diverse typological spectrum: Armenian (arm), Bulgarian (bul), French (fre), Georgian (geo), Hindi (hin), Hungarian (hun), Icelandic (ice), Korean (kor), Lithuanian (lit), Modern Greek (gre), Adyghe (ady), Dutch (dut), Japanese hiragana (jpn), Romanian (rum), and Vietnamese (vie).

As preprocessing, we romanize the scripts of

Japanese and Korean,[12] which show improvements in preliminary experiments. The reason is that the Japanese Hiragana and Korean Hangul characters are both syllabic, in which one grapheme typically corresponds to multiple phonemes, and by romanizing them (1) the alphabet size is reduced, and (2) the length ratio of the source and target sequences are much closer to 1:1, which empirically improve the quality of the alignment.

As unlabeled data, we use word frequency lists,[3] which are mostly extracted from OpenSubtitles (Lison and Tiedemann, 2016). For the two languages we did not find in OpenSubtitles, Adyghe is obtained from the corpus by Arkhangelskiy and Lander (2016),[4] and Georgian is obtained from several text corpora.[56]

Since the word lists are automatically extracted from various sources with different methods and quality, we filter them by the alphabet of the training set of each language, and keep at most 100,000 most frequent words.

3.2 Models

As the framework desires the models to be as diverse as possible to maximize its benefit, we employ four different types of base models with different inductive biases.

The first type is the Finite-State-Transducer (FST) baseline by Lee et al. (2020), based on the pair n-gram model (Novak et al., 2016).

The other three types are all variants of Seq2Seq models, where we use the same BiLSTM encoder to encode the input grapheme sequence. The first one is a vanilla Seq2Seq model with attention (`attn`), similar to Luong et al. (2015), where the decoder applies attention on the encoded input and use the attended input vector to predict the output phonemes.

The second one is a hard monotonic attention model (`mono`), similar to Aharoni and Goldberg (2017), where the decoder uses a pointer to select the input vector to make a prediction: either produc-

---

[1] `https://pypi.org/project/pykakasi/`
[2] `https://pypi.org/project/hangul-romanize/`
[3] `https://github.com/hermitdave/FrequencyWords/`
[4] `https://github.com/timarkh/uniparser-grammar-adyghe`
[5] `https://github.com/akalongman/geo-words`
[6] Georgian is actually in OpenSubtitles, but we accidentally missed it because of a confusion with the language code.

ing a phoneme, or moving the pointer to the next position. The monotonic alignment of the input and output is obtained with the Chinese Restaurant Process following Sudoh et al. (2013), which is provided in the baseline model of the SIGMORPHON 2016 Shared Task (Cotterell et al., 2016).

The third one is essentially a hybrid of hard monotonic attention model and tagging model (`tag`), i.e., for each grapheme we predict a short sequence of phonemes that is aligned to it. It relies on the same monotonic alignment for training. This model is different from the previous one in that it can potentially alleviate the error propagation problem, since the short sequences are non-autoregressive and independent of each other, much like tagging.

For each of the three models, we further create a reversed variant, where we reverse the input sequence and subsequently the output sequence. On average, the best model types are the tagging models of both directions.

Since we need to train many base models, we keep their sizes at a minimal level: the LSTM encoder and decoder both have one layer, all dimensions are 128, and no beam search is used. As a result, each base model has about 0.3M parameters and takes less than 10 minutes to train on a single CPU core.

3.3 Experiments

With the ensemble self-training framework, we train 14 base models at each iteration: FST models with 3-grams and 7-grams (`fst-3`, `fst-7`), two instances for each direction of the attention model (`attn-l2r`, `attn-r2l`), hard monotonic model (`mono-l2r`, `mono-r2l`), and tagging model (`tag-l2r`, `tag-r2l`).

Table 1 shows the number of iterations when the optimal ensemble is found and the number of models it contains, as well as the Word Error Rate (WER) and Phone Error Rate (PER) on the test set, in comparison to the Seq2Seq baseline provided by the organizer. Generally, our system outperforms the strong baseline in 13 out of 15 languages, and the gap for Korean is especially large, due to the romanization in our preprocessing. For three languages (Hungarian, Japanese, and Lithuanian), the best ensemble is in the 0-th iteration, which means the augmented data for them is not helpful at all.

Our ensemble system rank the first in terms of both WER and PER on the test set, with an average

	#iter	#model	IMS		Seq2Seq	
			WER	PER	WER	PER
ady	4	20	**25.33**	**5.79**	28.00	6.53
arm	5	20	**12.67**	**2.94**	14.67	3.49
bul	4	10	**22.22**	**4.85**	31.11	5.94
dut	2	13	**13.56**	**2.36**	16.44	2.94
fre	1	17	6.89	1.60	**6.22**	**1.32**
geo	6	20	**24.89**	**4.57**	26.44	5.14
gre	1	12	**18.67**	**2.97**	18.89	3.30
hin	1	20	**5.11**	**1.20**	6.67	1.47
hun	0	5	**5.11**	**1.12**	5.33	1.18
ice	5	20	**9.33**	**2.04**	10.00	2.36
jpn	0	6	**5.33**	**1.26**	7.56	1.79
kor	4	8	**26.22**	**4.38**	46.89	16.78
lit	0	5	20.00	3.63	**19.11**	**3.55**
rum	1	8	**10.22**	**2.23**	10.67	2.53
vie	5	20	**1.56**	**0.48**	4.67	1.52
AVG	3	14	13.81	2.76	16.84	3.99

Table 1: Evaluation on the test set of the grapheme-to-phoneme conversion task, comparing our system with the best performing seq2seq baseline. The first two columns are the number of iterations when the best ensemble is found and the number of base models in the ensemble.

WER of 13.8 and PER of 2.76. However, a large ensemble of simple models is not exactly comparable with other single-model systems, and it is thus difficult to derive a conclusion from the evaluation alone. We are more interested in understanding how much of the improvement comes from the ensemble and its model diversity and how much from the data augmentation process.

For this purpose, we run our framework in two additional scenarios. In the first scenario, we reduce the diversity of the models (denoted as -diversity), where we only use the base model `tag-l2r` and `tag-r2l`, which performs the best among others, but keep the same number of models trained in each iteration as before. In the second scenario, we do not perform data augmentation (denoted as -augmentation), i.e., all models are trained on the same original training data in each iteration.

Table 2 shows the WER on the development set of the default scenario and the two experimental scenarios. For each scenario, we show the average WER of all models and the WER of the ensemble from the initial iteration and the best iteration.

We can observe three trends in the table. (1) In all scenarios, there is a large gap between the aver-

	default				-diversity				-augment			
	average		ensemble		average		ensemble		average		ensemble	
	init	best	init	best	init	best	init	best	init	best	init	best
ady	28.9	27.7	22.4	21.6	26.6	27.2	22.9	22.2	28.7	28.1	22.7	20.9
arm	18.8	17.4	13.1	11.3	16.1	15.4	12.2	11.8	18.7	18.1	12.2	10.7
bul	36.8	36.2	25.3	20.0	35.5	35.5	27.6	23.8	37.3	36.1	24.2	18.7
dut	19.5	18.8	11.8	10.4	18.5	18.8	12.2	10.9	19.7	19.6	11.6	9.8
fre	15.1	15.7	6.0	5.6	13.2	13.6	6.7	6.2	15.6	15.2	7.1	5.1
geo	26.9	26.7	20.2	17.8	26.6	25.1	20.7	18.4	27.0	26.8	19.6	16.7
gre	20.1	18.4	13.8	12.7	17.3	16.8	12.7	11.3	19.9	19.8	12.9	11.8
hin	9.7	9.0	4.0	3.6	8.1	6.9	4.2	4.0	9.7	9.3	4.0	3.6
hun	4.5	4.5	2.0	2.0	4.0	3.9	2.4	2.2	4.7	4.7	2.4	2.4
ice	15.3	14.1	6.4	5.6	11.9	11.4	5.6	5.3	14.8	14.6	6.2	5.6
jpn	8.0	8.0	6.0	6.0	7.7	7.7	6.2	6.2	8.0	8.0	5.8	5.8
kor	25.9	23.4	16.2	14.4	20.9	20.7	16.9	16.0	25.9	25.6	16.4	14.2
lit	24.5	24.5	18.4	18.4	22.7	22.7	18.2	18.2	24.4	24.9	18.2	16.7
rum	14.6	13.7	10.2	9.8	12.2	12.2	10.0	9.3	14.4	14.5	9.8	8.7
vie	6.0	5.8	1.1	0.9	5.3	5.3	2.0	2.0	6.0	6.2	1.3	0.7
AVG	18.3	17.6	11.8	10.7	16.4	16.2	12.0	11.2	18.3	18.1	11.6	10.1

Table 2: WER on the development set in the three scenarios (default, reduced diversity, and without data augmentation). In each scenario, we show the average model performance and the ensemble performance in the first iteration and the best iteration.

age model performance and the ensemble performance, which clearly demonstrates the benefit of the ensemble. (2) In the -diversity scenario, the average model performance is better than the default scenario, but the ensemble performance is worse than the default scenario, which demonstrates the importance of the model diversity. (3) The average model performance in the default scenario has clear improvement as opposed to the random fluctuation in the -augmentation scenario, which means that the data augmentation can indeed benefit some individual models. However, to our surprise and disappointment, the ensemble performance of the -augmentation scenario is even slightly better than the default scenario, which casts a shadow over the data augmentation method in this framework.

As our framework is designed for low-resource languages, and the data size of 3,600 in the task is already beyond low-resource, we therefore experiment in a simulated low-resource scenario.[7] For each language, we randomly sample 200 instances as the new training data, while ensuring that all graphemes and phonemes in the training

data appear at least once.

Table 3 shows the WER of the default and -augment scenario in the low-resource experiment. Similar to the previous experiment, the ensemble greatly reduces errors of individual models. More importantly, the individual models benefit significantly from the augmented data (from 54.2 to 35.5), and the final ensemble further reduces the error rate to 25.2. The WER in the default scenario is much better than the -augment scenario (25.2 vs 29.2), which means that the data augmentation is indeed beneficial when the training data is scarce.

4 Morphological Inflection

4.1 Task and Data

We also apply our framework on the morphological inflection task (Vylomova et al., 2020), where the input is a combination of lemmata and morphological tags according to the UniMorph schema (Sylak-Glassman et al., 2015), and the output is the inflected word forms. There are 90 languages with various data sizes, ranging from around 100 to 100,000.

As unlabeled data for the augmentation process, we simply recombine the lemmata and morphological tags of the same category in the training set (i.e.,

[7]Consider the Swadesh list (Swadesh, 1950) with only 100-200 basic concepts/words, which could be thought of as a typical low-resource scenario. In the WikiPron collection, more than 20% of the 165 languages have less than 200 words.

	default				-augment			
	average		ensemble		average		ensemble	
	init	best	init	best	init	best	init	best
ady	62.3	41.3	44.4	30.0	63.0	62.1	44.4	37.8
arm	42.6	30.2	28.0	22.9	42.5	41.9	28.9	23.3
bul	68.8	58.0	53.6	48.4	67.4	66.8	53.3	47.3
dut	64.9	37.8	45.6	27.6	64.7	63.2	43.1	32.4
fre	62.0	34.0	34.9	18.9	61.8	61.3	35.1	29.3
geo	40.5	34.4	29.8	26.0	40.6	39.6	30.4	24.7
gre	56.8	37.7	37.3	28.0	57.4	55.8	39.3	31.3
hin	53.8	22.2	32.2	12.7	53.5	52.8	33.8	24.4
hun	42.2	19.7	21.8	12.7	42.8	41.6	21.6	16.7
ice	71.1	51.1	53.8	42.9	73.6	70.4	55.8	49.8
jpn	41.4	16.5	19.8	11.1	42.1	40.4	21.3	15.6
kor	53.4	39.4	36.9	30.4	54.6	53.1	38.2	32.9
lit	66.3	51.8	49.1	38.4	67.4	65.9	48.7	39.8
rum	37.5	24.7	22.9	16.4	38.1	37.1	23.1	18.2
vie	50.3	33.4	23.8	11.1	50.6	49.3	21.6	14.4
AVG	54.2	35.5	35.6	25.2	54.7	53.4	35.9	29.2

Table 3: WER on the development set for the simulated low-resource experiment in the scenarios with and without data augmentation. In each scenario, we show the average model performance and the ensemble performance in the first iteration and the best iteration.

a verb lemma only combines with all morphological tags for verbs), with a maximum size of 100,000 for each language. For many languages, however, the recombination is as scarce as the original data since they are from (almost) complete inflection paradigms of a few lemmata. In total, we obtained 1,422,617 instances, which is slightly smaller than the training set with 1,574,004 instances. Since the additional data come directly from the original training data, we consider it the restricted setting, where no external data sources or cross-lingual methods are used.

4.2 Models

Due to our late start in this task, we only implemented two types of base models, paired with left-to-right and right-to-left generation order. The first type is a Seq2Seq model with soft attention, very similar to the one in the grapheme-to-phoneme conversion task, except that an additional BiLSTM is used to encode the morphological tags. The second type is a hard monotonic attention model, also similar as before, but instead of using the alignment with the Chinese Restaurant Process, we use Levenshtein edit scripts to obtain the target sequence,

Model	Accuracy
CULing-01-0	0.912
deepspin-02-1	0.909
uiuc-01-0	0.905
IMS-00-0	0.892
mono	0.858
trm	0.901
mono-aug	0.888
trm-aug	0.903

Table 4: Evaluation on the test set of the morphological inflection task, comparing our system to three winning systems and four baselines.

since the input and the output share the same alphabet. At each step, the model either outputs a character from the alphabet, or copies the currently pointed input character, or advances the input pointer to the next position. In total, we train 8 models per iteration, i.e., two models with different random seeds for each variant. The hyperparameters are largely the same as in the previous task, and each model has about 0.5M parameters.

4.3 Experiments

Table 4 compares the average test accuracy between our system (IMS-00-0) and the systems of the winning teams as well as the baselines. The baselines include a hard monotonic attention model with latent alignment (Wu and Cotterell, 2019) and a carefully tuned transformer (Vaswani et al., 2017; Wu et al., 2020), noted as mono and trm. They are additionally trained with augmented data by Anastasopoulos and Neubig (2019), noted as mono-aug and trm-aug.

On average, our system ranks the fourth among the participating teams and the third in the restricted setting (without external data source or cross-lingual methods). It outperforms the hard monotonic attention baseline, but not the transformer baseline. More details on the systems and their comparisons are described in Vylomova et al. (2020). Compared to the previous task, we used fewer base models, in terms of both number and diversity, which partly explains the relatively lower ranking.

In this task, the data size ranges across several magnitude for different languages. We thus analyze the performance difference of our system against the two baselines with their own data augmentation

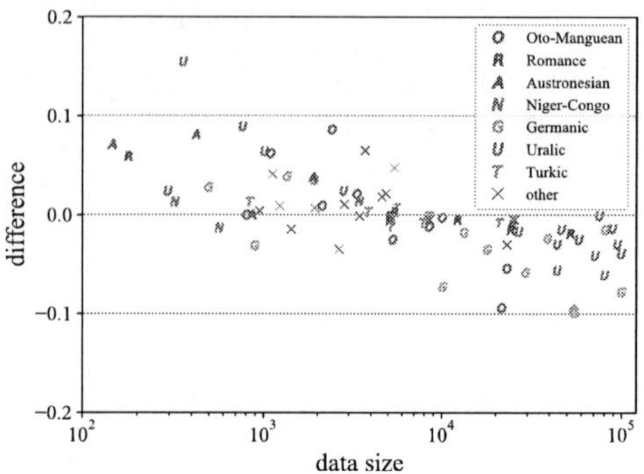

(a) Hard Monotonic Attention

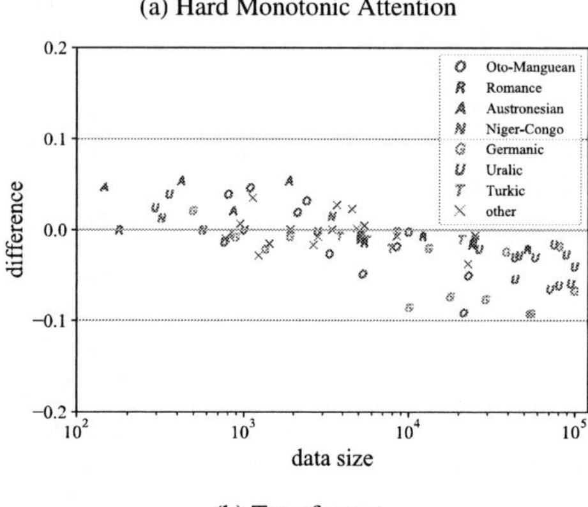

(b) Transformer

Figure 1: Performance difference between our system and the two baselines with data augmentation, with respect to the training data size.

(`mono-aug` and `trm-aug`) with respect to the original training data size, as illustrated in Figure 1. We removed the trivial cases in which both models achieved 100% accuracy.

Clearly, our system performs better for languages with smaller training data size, while losing to the powerful baseline models when the data size is large. This again demonstrates the benefit of our framework for low-resource languages.

We also mark the major language families to see whether they play a role in the performance difference, since different inductive biases might work differently on particular language families. For example, the right-to-left generation order might work better on languages with inflectional prefixes. However, we could not find any convincing patterns regarding language families in the plot, i.e., there is not a language family in the data set where our model always performs better or worse than the baseline. The only exception is the Austronesian family, where our system generally outperforms the baselines, but they all have relatively small data size, which is a more probable explanation.

Note that our augmentation method is theoretically orthogonal to the hallucination method (Anastasopoulos and Neubig, 2019), and could be combined to further improve the performance of the baseline models for low-resource languages.

5 Conclusion

We present an ensemble self-training framework and apply it on two sequence-to-sequence generation tasks: grapheme-to-phoneme conversion and morphological inflection. Our framework includes an improved self-training method by optimizing and utilizing the ensemble to obtain more reliable training data, which shows clear advantage on low-resource languages. The optimal ensemble search method with the genetic algorithm easily accommodates the inductive biases of different model architectures for different languages.

As a potential future direction, we could incorporate the framework into the scenario of active learning to reduce annotator workload, i.e., by suggesting plausible predictions to minimize the need of correction.

Acknowledgements

This work was in part supported by funding from the Ministry of Science, Research and the Arts of the State of Baden-Württemberg (MWK), within the CLARIN-D research project.

References

Željko Agić, Anders Johannsen, Barbara Plank, Héctor Martínez Alonso, Natalie Schluter, and Anders Søgaard. 2016. Multilingual projection for parsing truly low-resource languages. *Transactions of the Association for Computational Linguistics*, 4:301–312.

Roee Aharoni and Yoav Goldberg. 2017. Morphological inflection generation with hard monotonic attention. In *Proceedings of the 55th Annual Meeting of the Association for Computational Linguistics (Volume 1: Long Papers)*, pages 2004–2015, Vancouver, Canada. Association for Computational Linguistics.

Antonios Anastasopoulos and Graham Neubig. 2019. Pushing the limits of low-resource morphological inflection. In *Proceedings of the 2019 Conference on Empirical Methods in Natural Language Processing and the 9th International Joint Conference on Natural Language Processing (EMNLP-IJCNLP)*, pages 984–996, Hong Kong, China. Association for Computational Linguistics.

Timofey Arkhangelskiy and Yury Lander. 2016. Developing a Polysynthetic Language Corpus: Problems and Solutions. In *Computational Linguistics and Intellectual Technologies: Proceedings of the International Conference "Dialogue 2016"*, pages 40–49.

Toms Bergmanis, Katharina Kann, Hinrich Schütze, and Sharon Goldwater. 2017. Training data augmentation for low-resource morphological inflection. In *Proceedings of the CoNLL SIGMORPHON 2017 Shared Task: Universal Morphological Reinflection*, pages 31–39.

Stephen Clark, James Curran, and Miles Osborne. 2003. Bootstrapping POS-taggers using unlabelled data. In *Proceedings of the Seventh Conference on Natural Language Learning at HLT-NAACL 2003*, pages 49–55.

Ryan Cotterell, Christo Kirov, John Sylak-Glassman, David Yarowsky, Jason Eisner, and Mans Hulden. 2016. The SIGMORPHON 2016 shared Task—Morphological reinflection. In *Proceedings of the 14th SIGMORPHON Workshop on Computational Research in Phonetics, Phonology, and Morphology*, pages 10–22, Berlin, Germany. Association for Computational Linguistics.

Dan Garrette, Jason Mielens, and Jason Baldridge. 2013. Real-world semi-supervised learning of postaggers for low-resource languages. In *Proceedings of the 51st Annual Meeting of the Association for Computational Linguistics (Volume 1: Long Papers)*, pages 583–592.

Kyle Gorman, Lucas F.E. Ashby, Aaron Goyzueta, Shijie Wu, and Daniel You. 2020. The SIGMOR-PHON 2020 shared task on multilingual grapheme-to-phoneme conversion. In *SIGMORPHON*.

Mohammad Nazmul Haque, Nasimul Noman, Regina Berretta, and Pablo Moscato. 2016. Heterogeneous Ensemble Combination Search Using Genetic Algorithm for Class Imbalanced Data Classification. *PloS one*, 11(1):e0146116.

Jackson L. Lee, Lucas F.E. Ashby, M. Elizabeth Garza, Yeonju Lee-Sikka, Sean Miller, Alan Wong, Arya D. McCarthy, and Kyle Gorman. 2020. Massively multilingual pronunciation mining with WikiPron. In *Proceedings of the 12th Language Resources and Evaluation Conference*, pages 4216–4221, Marseille.

Pierre Lison and Jörg Tiedemann. 2016. OpenSubtitles2016: Extracting Large Parallel Corpora from Movie and TV Subtitles. In *Proceedings of the Tenth International Conference on Language Resources and Evaluation (LREC'16)*, pages 923–929.

Thang Luong, Hieu Pham, and Christopher D. Manning. 2015. Effective approaches to attention-based neural machine translation. In *Proceedings of the 2015 Conference on Empirical Methods in Natural Language Processing*, pages 1412–1421, Lisbon, Portugal. Association for Computational Linguistics.

Josef R. Novak, Nobuaki Minematsu, and Keikichi Hirose. 2016. Phonetisaurus: exploring grapheme-to-phoneme conversion with joint n-gram models in the WFST framework. *Natural Language Engineering*, 22(6):907–938.

Anton Ragni, Kate M Knill, Shakti P Rath, and Mark JF Gales. 2014. Data augmentation for low resource languages. In *Fifteenth Annual Conference of the International Speech Communication Association*.

Miikka Silfverberg, Adam Wiemerslage, Ling Liu, and Lingshuang Jack Mao. 2017. Data augmentation for morphological reinflection. In *Proceedings of the CoNLL SIGMORPHON 2017 Shared Task: Universal Morphological Reinflection*, pages 90–99.

Katsuhito Sudoh, Shinsuke Mori, and Masaaki Nagata. 2013. Noise-aware character alignment for bootstrapping statistical machine transliteration from bilingual corpora. In *Proceedings of the 2013 Conference on Empirical Methods in Natural Language Processing*, pages 204–209, Seattle, Washington, USA. Association for Computational Linguistics.

Mihai Surdeanu and Christopher D. Manning. 2010. Ensemble models for dependency parsing: Cheap and good? In *Human Language Technologies: The 2010 Annual Conference of the North American Chapter of the Association for Computational Linguistics*, pages 649–652, Los Angeles, California. Association for Computational Linguistics.

Morris Swadesh. 1950. Salish internal relationships. *International Journal of American Linguistics*, 16(4):157–167.

John Sylak-Glassman, Christo Kirov, David Yarowsky, and Roger Que. 2015. A language-independent feature schema for inflectional morphology. In *Proceedings of the 53rd Annual Meeting of the Association for Computational Linguistics and the 7th International Joint Conference on Natural Language Processing (Volume 2: Short Papers)*, pages 674–680, Beijing, China. Association for Computational Linguistics.

Ashish Vaswani, Noam Shazeer, Niki Parmar, Jakob Uszkoreit, Llion Jones, Aidan N Gomez, Łukasz Kaiser, and Illia Polosukhin. 2017. Attention is all you need. In *Advances in neural information processing systems*, pages 5998–6008.

Ekaterina Vylomova, Jennifer White, Elizabeth Salesky, Sabrina J. Mielke, Shijie Wu, Edoardo Ponti, Rowan Hall Maudslay, Ran Zmigrod, Joseph Valvoda, Svetlana Toldova, Francis Tyers, Elena Klyachko, Ilya Yegorov, Natalia Krizhanovsky, Paula Czarnowska, Irene Nikkarinen, Andrej Krizhanovsky, Tiago Pimentel, Lucas Torroba Hennigen, Christo Kirov, Garrett Nicolai, Adina Williams, Antonios Anastasopoulos, Hilaria Cruz, Eleanor Chodroff, Ryan Cotterell, Miikka Silfverberg, and Mans Hulden. 2020. The SIG-MORPHON 2020 Shared Task 0: Typologically diverse morphological inflection. In *Proceedings of the 17th SIGMORPHON Workshop on Computational Research in Phonetics, Phonology, and Morphology*.

Shijie Wu and Ryan Cotterell. 2019. Exact hard monotonic attention for character-level transduction. In *Proceedings of the 57th Annual Meeting of the Association for Computational Linguistics*, pages 1530–1537, Florence, Italy. Association for Computational Linguistics.

Shijie Wu, Ryan Cotterell, and Mans Hulden. 2020. Applying the transformer to character-level transduction.

David Yarowsky. 1995. Unsupervised word sense disambiguation rivaling supervised methods. In *33rd annual meeting of the association for computational linguistics*, pages 189–196.

Barret Zoph, Deniz Yuret, Jonathan May, and Kevin Knight. 2016. Transfer learning for low-resource neural machine translation. In *Proceedings of the 2016 Conference on Empirical Methods in Natural Language Processing*, pages 1568–1575.

The CMU-LTI submission to the SIGMORPHON 2020
Shared Task 0: Language-Specific Cross-Lingual Transfer

Nikitha Murikinati and Antonios Anastasopoulos

Language Technologies Institute

Carnegie Mellon University

nmurikin@andrew.cmu.edu, aanastas@cs.cmu.edu

Abstract

This paper describes the CMU-LTI submission to the SIGMORPHON 2020 Shared Task 0 on typologically diverse morphological inflection. The (unrestricted) submission uses the cross-lingual approach of our last year's winning submission (Anastasopoulos and Neubig, 2019), but adapted to use specific transfer languages for each test language. Our system, with fixed non-tuned hyperparameters, achieved a macro-averaged accuracy of 80.65 ranking 20th among 31 systems, but it was still tied for best system in 25 of the 90 total languages.

1 Introduction

Morphological inflection is the process that creates grammatical forms (typically guided by sentence structure) of a lexeme/lemma. As a computational task it is framed as mapping from the lemma and a set of morphological tags to the desired form, which simplifies the task by removing the necessity to infer the form from context. For an example from Asturian, given the lemma `aguar` and tags `V;PRS;2;PL;IND`, the task is to create the indicative voice, present tense, 2nd person plural form `aguà`.

Let $\mathbf{X} = x_1 \ldots x_N$ be a character sequence of the lemma, $\mathbf{T} = t_1 \ldots t_M$ a set of morphological tags, and $\mathbf{Y} = y_1 \ldots y_K$ be an inflection target character sequence. The goal is to model $P(\mathbf{Y} \mid \mathbf{X}, \mathbf{T})$. The problem has been studied in various settings through the SIGMORPHON shared tasks (Cotterell et al., 2016, 2017, 2018; McCarthy et al., 2019), with the 2019 edition focusing in particularly challenging low-resource scenarios. The 2020 edition (Vylomova et al., 2020) focused on generalization of systems across typologically diverse languages, regardless of data size.

In our submission we built upon our previous work (Anastasopoulos and Neubig, 2019), utilizing cross-lingual transfer from related languages, data hallucination, and a series of training techniques and regularizers. The defining change was that we attempted to create language-specific regimes for each test language, depending on the particular characteristics of the language, on the data availability for the particular test language and the availability of other related language data. As a result, for some high-resource languages we submitted systems without cross-lingual transfer, for some we used a single related high resource language, and for some we used multiple related languages. Last, for a few test languages we augmented our datasets with romanized versions of the training data, an approach that has shown promising results in concurrent work (Murikinati et al., 2020).

Our submissions are very competitive in 25 of the 90 test languages, with performance statistically significant similar to the best performing system, but fall behind in many other languages. We suspect that this is due to our not tuning of the system's hyperparameters towards higher-resource settings.

Proceedings of the Seventeenth SIGMORPHON Workshop on Computational Research in Phonetics, Phonology, and Morphology, pages 79–84
Online, July 10, 2020. ©2020 Association for Computational Linguistics
https://doi.org/10.18653/v1/P17

Language	Accuracy	Language	Accuracy	Language	Accuracy	Language	Accuracy
aka	**99.1**	fas	96.2	lld	97.7	sna	**100.0**
ang	75.4	fin	97.3	lud	**53.7**	sot	**100.0**
ast	91.4	frm	98.8	lug	90.6	swa	**100.0**
aze	78.5	frr	85.5	mao	**69.0**	swe	95.4
azg	89.0	fur	98.3	mdf	92.7	syc	91.6
bak	97.4	gaa	**100.0**	mhr	90.8	tel	**94.9**
ben	98.6	glg	97.4	mlg	**100.0**	tgk	**93.8**
bod	**84.7**	gmh	90.1	mlt	88.7	tgl	64.0
cat	97.5	gml	**60.8**	mwf	70.3	tuk	85.4
ceb	**84.7**	gsw	84.9	myv	93.0	udm	97.5
cly	81.0	hil	92.4	nld	97.5	uig	91.9
cpa	83.5	hin	98.4	nno	74.2	urd	36.3
cre	44.9	isl	95.3	nob	**75.1**	uzb	51.5
crh	97.2	izh	80.8	nya	**100.0**	vec	98.8
ctp	50.2	kan	75.1	olo	91.5	vep	79.3
czn	**81.3**	kaz	88.5	ood	**79.0**	vot	77.2
dak	89.7	kir	88.4	orm	93.6	vro	**57.3**
dan	72.3	kjh	**98.8**	ote	97.0	xno	**90.2**
deu	92.8	kon	**98.1**	otm	97.4	xty	90.2
dje	**100.0**	kpv	95.9	pei	71.2	zpv	**82.9**
eng	96.5	krl	95.0	pus	68.6	zul	**89.7**
est	93.5	lin	**100.0**	san	92.6		
evn	55.0	liv	93.1	sme	97.9		

Table 1: Accuracy of our system on every language. We **highlight** the languages where our system was statistically equal to the best system (with $p < 0.005$).

2 System Description

Our system is the same as the one of Anastasopoulos and Neubig (2019): a neural multi-source encoder-decoder (which reads in the lemma and the tag sequences in a disentangled manner using two separate encoders) with a task-specific attention mechanism. We skip providing further redundant information and we direct the interested reader to (Anastasopoulos and Neubig, 2019) for all details. It is important to note, however, that we did not tune any model hyperparameters for our submissions (which we suspect contributed to the poor performance of our system in some languages); we used the default parameters from the system's distribution [1] which are tuned towards extremely low-resource settings.

Here, we provide an exhaustive list of modifications to the general pipeline that we devised for specific languages and language families.

Data Hallucination for tonal languages The data hallucination process of Anastasopoulos and Neubig (2019), inspired by Silfverberg et al. (2017), samples random characters from the language's alphabet to replace characters in *stem-like* regions discovered from the training examples through a simple alignment-based heuristic.

Tonal languages like Eastern Highland Chatino (cly), importantly, often denote the syllable's tone through superscript diacritics: take the Eastern Highland Chatino lemma sqwe[14] and its second person singular number habitual mood inflected form nsqwe[20]. The data hallucination technique would identify the substring sqwe as a stem-like region, and replace its characters with random ones. A completely random substitution, however, could lead to the creation of nonsensical syllables, if tone diacritics are inserted instead of letter characters e.g. if we hallucinated a s[3]ae[14] lemma for the above example. Similarly, if a stem-like region includes a tone diacritic, we would not want to randomly replace it with non-diacritic characters,

---

[1] https://github.com/antonisa/inflection

lest we end up with badly formed syllables without tone information.

To avoid these issues, we restrict the random substitutions for Oto-Manguean languages with tone diacritics, so that we only sample tone diacritics if we are substituting a tone diacritic (and similarly for letter characters). We have found this approach to significantly improve results in previous work on morphological inflection for Eastern Highland Chatino (Cruz et al., 2020).

Single-Language Systems for High Resource Languages For languages with more than 20,000 training examples, we decided to not use cross-lingual transfer nor data hallucination, as systems in previous SIGMORPHON shared tasks achieved very competitive performance on such high-resource settings without these additions. For languages with less than 20,000 but more than 10,000 training examples, we used our data hallucination process to create 10,000 additional training examples to be used for training.

Cross-Lingual Transfer from a Single Language For some languages we decided to use a single, high-resource related language to combine into our training to perform cross-lingual transfer, along with data hallucination. We based most these decisions in previous results (mainly from (Anastasopoulos and Neubig, 2019)), but some where our semi-arbitrary experimenter's intuitions. We provide a complete list of these settings:

- for Middle High German (gmh) we used German (deu),
- for Middle Low German (gml) we used German (deu) also bypassing data hallucination,
- for Swiss German (gsw) we used German (deu),
- for North Frisian (frr) we used Dutch (nld),
- for Kannada (kan) we used Telugu (tel),
- for Telugu (tel) we used Kannada (kan),
- for Asturian (ast) we used Galician (glg),
- for Friulian (fur) we used French (fra),
- for Ladin (lad) we used Friulian (fur),
- for Venetian (vec) we used Italian (vec),
- for Anglo-Norman (xno) we used Middle French (frm),
- for Azerbaijani (aze) we used Turkish (tur),
- for Khakas (kjh) we used Turkish (tur), but not including data hallucination, and
- for Võro (vro) we used Estonian (est).

Family	Sub-family	Acc.
Afro-Asiatic		91.3
	Semitic	90.1
Algic		44.9
Turkic		83.3
Austronesian		82.0
	Gr. Ctr. Philippines	80.4
Dravidian		85.0
IndoEuropean		87.5
	Germanic	84.3
	Romance	96.3
	Iranian	86.2
	Indic	81.5
Niger-Congo		97.7
	Bantoid	97.3
	Kwa	99.5
Oto-Manguean		82.4
	Zapotecan	73.9
	Otomian	97.2
Sino-Tibetan		84.7
Siouan		89.7
Songhay		100.0
Southern Daly		70.3
Uralic		86.7
	Mordvin	92.8
	Finnic	81.9
	Permic	96.7
Uto-Aztecan		79.0
Tungusic		55.0

Table 2: Results per language Family/Genus.

Multiple-Language Cross-Lingual Transfer We submitted systems with unique transfer language combinations for extremely low-resource languages for which several very related languages were available (all systems also included hallucinated data in the test language). Specifically:

- for Ingrian (izh) we used Estonian (est), Votic (vot), and a random sample (20,000 instances) from Finnish (fin) data,
- for Votic (vot) we used Estonian (est), Ingrian (izh), and a random sample (20,000 instances) from Finnish (fin) data,
- for Urdu (urd) we used Hindi (hin) and Bengali (ben),

- for Bashkir (bad) we used Turkish (tur), Kazakh (kaz), and Kyrgyz (kir),
- for Crimean Tatar (crh) we used Turkish (tur), Kazakh (kaz), and Kyrgyz (kir),
- for Kazakh (kaz) we used Turkish (tur), Bashkir (bad), and Kyrgyz (kir),
- for Kyrgyz (kir) we used Turkish (tur), Bashkir (bad), and Kazakh (kaz),
- for Uighur (uig) we used Turkish (tur) and Uzbek (uzb), and
- for Ludian (lud) we used 20,000 random samples from Karelian (krl) and Veps (vep).

Romanization for Different Scripts Last, we experimented with cross-lingual transfer *and* transliteration of related languages written in different script. The motivation lies in the observation made by Anastasopoulos and Neubig (2019) that often cross-lingual transfer results in smaller improvements if the transfer and the test language do not share the same script, even if the languages are related. They bring Arabic–Maltese and Kurmanji–Sorani as possible examples. In concurrent work (Murikinati et al., 2020) we experimented with transliterating the transfer language into the test language's script, with encouraging results in low-resource settings. Alternatively, if the training languages use the latin script but the test language does not, we found that that by romanizing the test language training data and concatenating them as another language (along with the data in the original script) also helped. We applied these strategies on the following language pairs.

Transliterating a transfer language into the test language's script:

1. for Maltese (mlt) we used Italian (ita) and romanized Hebrew (heb),
2. for Oromo (orm) we used romanized Arabic (ara) and romanized Hebrew (heb), and
3. for Bengali (ben) we used Sanskrit (san), Hindi (hin), and Sanskrit transliterated into the Bengali script using the Indic NLP library[2] (Kunchukuttan, 2020).

Romanizing the test language training data and training with both romanized and original, along with more romanized, related languages:

1. for Classical Syriac (syc) we used romanized Arabic (ara) and romanized Hebrew (heb), as

---

[2] https://github.com/anoopkunchukuttan/indic_nlp_library

well as romanized Classical Syriac (Classical Syriac originally uses a distinct script),
2. for Pashto (pus) we used romanized Farsi (fas) and romanized Pashto, while
3. for Tajik (tgk) we used romanized Farsi (fas) and romanized Tajik.

3 Results

Table 1 lists the accuracy of our submitted system in every language. We also report results per language family and genus in Table 2, to further facilitate an equitable evaluation across language families. Our system achieves a macro-averaged accuracy of 86.6% with a standard deviation of 14.3. Even though it does not use self-attention and we did not tune any hyper-parameters, our system still achieved competitive performance, tying for first in 25 of the 90 total languages (it still however does not outperform the best baseline system (Wu et al., 2020)).

These include languages that were generally easy for all systems, such as the Austronesian and the Niger-Congo ones. However, they also include the extremely low-resource languages like Ludian (lud), Võro (vro), and Middle Low German (gml), where we suspect that our system performed en par with the more sophisticated (and we suspect, tuned) systems due to our informed selection of languages for cross-lingual transfer.

The two languages where our system performs the worst are Algic (Cree) and Tungusic (Evenki). We suspect this is due to the fact that the data hallucination technique, which is crucial for such low resource settings, is not appropriate for capturing the vowel harmony of Evenki along with its agglutinating morphological patterns – the hallucinated data do not follow these patterns and hence do not guide the model towards learning them. As for Cree, we suspect that the problem lies again in the data hallucination process: the polysynthetic *and* fusional nature of Cree verb inflected forms is too complicated to be modeled by the simple character-level alignment model which is the first step for hallucination.

4 Conclusion and Future Work

The performance of our system in the 2020 SIG-MORPHON Shared Task leaves many questions unanswered and several avenues to explore in future work. Regarding the choice of languages to use for cross-lingual transfer, we will further investigate the use of automatic suggestion systems such as the one of Lin et al. (2019). With regards to modeling, we will update our model to use sparsemax (Martins and Astudillo, 2016), which can facilitate exact search and hopefully lead to better results (Peters and Martins, 2019).

As we anticipate and hope the shared task and the whole community will become more multilingual in the future, in the future we will employ the language/task selection method of Xia et al. (2020), which will allow us to tune the systems in a small subset of languages that will generalize well in all others. Similarly, we will employ more sophisticated techniques for learning in multilingual settings, such as differential data selection (Wang et al., 2019, 2020) which will allow us to optimize a single model to multiple model objectives (namely, each target language).

Acknowledgments

This material is based upon work generously supported by the National Science Foundation under grant 1761548.

References

Antonios Anastasopoulos and Graham Neubig. 2019. Pushing the limits of low-resource morphological inflection. In *Proc. EMNLP*, Hong Kong.

Ryan Cotterell, Christo Kirov, John Sylak-Glassman, Géraldine Walther, Ekaterina Vylomova, Arya D. McCarthy, Katharina Kann, Sebastian Mielke, Garrett Nicolai, Miikka Silfverberg, David Yarowsky, Jason Eisner, and Mans Hulden. 2018. The CoNLL–SIGMORPHON 2018 shared task: Universal morphological reinflection. In *Proc. CoNLL–SIGMORPHON*.

Ryan Cotterell, Christo Kirov, John Sylak-Glassman, Géraldine Walther, Ekaterina Vylomova, Patrick Xia, Manaal Faruqui, Sandra Kübler, David Yarowsky, Jason Eisner, and Mans Hulden. 2017. CoNLL-SIGMORPHON 2017 shared task: Universal morphological reinflection in 52 languages. In *Proc. CoNLL SIGMORPHON*.

Ryan Cotterell, Christo Kirov, John Sylak-Glassman, David Yarowsky, Jason Eisner, and Mans Hulden. 2016. The SIGMORPHON 2016 shared task— morphological reinflection. In *Proc. SIGMORPHON*.

Hilaria Cruz, Antonios Anastasopoulos, and Gregory Stump. 2020. A resource for studying chatino verbal morphology. In *Proc. LREC*. To appear.

Anoop Kunchukuttan. 2020. The indicnlp library.

Yu-Hsiang Lin, Chian-Yu Chen, Jean Lee, Zirui Li, Yuyan Zhang, Mengzhou Xia, Shruti Rijhwani, Junxian He, Zhisong Zhang, Xuezhe Ma, Antonios Anastasopoulos, Patrick Littell, and Graham Neubig. 2019. Choosing transfer languages for cross-lingual learning. In *Proceedings of the 57th Annual Meeting of the Association for Computational Linguistics*, pages 3125–3135, Florence, Italy. Association for Computational Linguistics.

Andre Martins and Ramon Astudillo. 2016. From softmax to sparsemax: A sparse model of attention and multi-label classification. In *Proc. ICML*, pages 1614–1623.

Arya D. McCarthy, Ekaterina Vylomova, Shijie Wu, Chaitanya Malaviya, Lawrence Wolf-Sonkin, Garrett Nicolai, Miikka Silfverberg, Sebastian J. Mielke, Jeffrey Heinz, Ryan Cotterell, and Mans Hulden. 2019. The SIGMORPHON 2019 shared task: Morphological analysis in context and cross-lingual transfer for inflection. In *Proceedings of the 16th Workshop on Computational Research in Phonetics, Phonology, and Morphology*, pages 229–244, Florence, Italy.

Nikitha Murikinati, Antonios Anastasopoulos, and Graham Neubig. 2020. Transliteration for cross-lingual morphological inflection. In *Proc. SIGMORPHON*. To appear.

Ben Peters and André FT Martins. 2019. It–ist at the sigmorphon 2019 shared task: Sparse two-headed models for inflection. In *Proceedings of the 16th Workshop on Computational Research in Phonetics, Phonology, and Morphology*, pages 50–56.

Miikka Silfverberg, Adam Wiemerslage, Ling Liu, and Lingshuang Jack Mao. 2017. Data augmentation for morphological reinflection. *Proc. SIGMORPHON*.

Ekaterina Vylomova, Jennifer White, Elizabeth Salesky, Sabrina J. Mielke, Shijie Wu, Edoardo Ponti, Rowan Hall Maudslay, Ran Zmigrod, Joseph Valvoda, Svetlana Toldova, Francis Tyers, Elena Klyachko, Ilya Yegorov, Natalia Krizhanovsky, Paula Czarnowska, Irene Nikkarinen, Andrej Krizhanovsky, Tiago Pimentel, Lucas Torroba Hennigen, Christo Kirov, Garrett Nicolai, Adina Williams, Antonios Anastasopoulos, Hilaria Cruz, Eleanor Chodroff, Ryan Cotterell, Miikka Silfverberg, and Mans Hulden. 2020. The SIGMORPHON 2020 Shared Task 0: Typologically diverse morphological inflection. In *Proceedings of the 17th SIGMORPHON Workshop on Computational Research in Phonetics, Phonology, and Morphology*.

Xinyi Wang, Hieu Pham, Paul Michel, Antonios Anastasopoulos, Graham Neubig, and Jaime Carbonell. 2019. Optimizing data usage via differentiable rewards. arXiv:1911.10088.

Xinyi Wang, Yulia Tsvetkov, and Graham Neubig. 2020. Balancing training for multilingual neural machine translation. In *Annual Conference of the Association for Computational Linguistics (ACL)*.

Shijie Wu, Ryan Cotterell, and Mans Hulden. 2020. Applying the transformer to character-level transduction.

Mengzhou Xia, Antonios Anastasopoulos, Ruochen Xu, Yiming Yang, and Graham Neubig. 2020. Predicting performance for natural language processing tasks. In *Proc. ACL*. To appear.

Grapheme-to-Phoneme Conversion
with a Multilingual Transformer Model

Omnia ElSaadany
Department of Informatics
University of Zurich, Switzerland
omnia.elsaadany@uzh.ch

Benjamin Suter
Department of Informatics
University of Zurich, Switzerland
benjamin.suter@uzh.ch

Abstract

In this paper, we describe our three submissions to the SIGMORPHON 2020 shared task 1 on grapheme-to-phoneme conversion for 15 languages. We experimented with a single multilingual Transformer model. We observed that the multilingual model achieves results on par with our separately trained monolingual models and is even able to avoid a few of the errors made by the monolingual models.

1 Introduction

Grapheme-to-phoneme conversion is the task of predicting the phonemic representation for a given orthographic word, where a phoneme is the smallest unit of sound which can distinguish one word from another. In many languages, some phonemes have different realizations depending on their context, and these variants are called allophones. While the task is about predicting phonemes and not allophones, in fact most datasets (e.g., the datasets for Hungarian, Bulgarian, and Armenian) also contain allophones. However, since the distribution of allophones conditioned on the context is learnable, this is not an issue.

The shared task training data consists of 15 languages which have diverse phonologies, ranging from tonal languages to languages with glottalized consonants, and they are written in eight different writing systems. The data comes from the English version of Wiktionary. Each training set contains 3600 words, and each development and test set contains 450 words. The official metrics for the task are Word Error Rate (WER) and Phoneme Error Rate (PER).

A multilingual approach for grapheme-to-phoneme conversion has been explored by Milde et al. (2017). They propose a sequence-to-sequence multilingual model that benefits from

training on additional phonetic representations for the same language (which was not permitted in our shared task).

The Transformer (Vaswani et al. 2017) with its attention mechanism has been applied very successfully to machine translation tasks, and it was also used for grapheme-to-phoneme conversion. Yolchuyeva et al. (2019) suggested using a Transformer-based approach for grapheme-to-phoneme conversion and Yu et al. (2020) proposed a multilingual Transformer model for languages with different writing systems by employing byte-level input representation.

In our submission to the shared task, we explore the performance of a multilingual Transformer model with augmented input representation which can transduce a word from any language present in the training data into its IPA representation.

2 Linguistic Background

2.1 IPA

The phonemic representation in this task uses the International Phonetic Alphabet (IPA). Interestingly, there is an issue with IPA which is lack of "orthography". This might seem surprising given that the IPA aims at representing the pronunciation of words with more rigor than typical orthographies. However, different levels of depth of analysis are possible with IPA, and this makes inconsistent use of symbols among annotators unavoidable. To give an example, Bulgarian exhibits a voiceless coronal plosive /t/~/t̪/. The phoneme is articulated as a dental plosive in Bulgarian. Somewhat randomly, the IPA provides an atomic symbol for the voiceless alveolar plosive (/t/), but only a composed symbol for the voiceless dental plosive (/t̪/). In principle, /t̪/ would be the correct representation for the phoneme in question, but since there is no phonemic contrast between den-

Proceedings of the Seventeenth SIGMORPHON Workshop on Computational Research
in Phonetics, Phonology, and Morphology, pages 85–89
Online, July 10, 2020. ©2020 Association for Computational Linguistics
https://doi.org/10.18653/v1/P17

tal and alveolar articulation in Bulgarian, a simple /t/ suffices to represent the voiceless coronal plosive phoneme in Bulgarian. Hence, as is expected, the phoneme is not transcribed consistently in the training data; while /t̪/ is used 1588 times, /t/ is applied 681 times. Similar issues are found frequently for other phonemes, and for other languages.

2.2 Languages

In our monolingual baseline models trained with the Transformer baseline published by the task organizers, the WER (PER) ranged from only 3.78 (0.66) for Hungarian up to 40.00 (16.38) for Korean. Seeing these huge differences in performance, it seemed worth analyzing the difficulties faced by the model for the three languages with the worst WER, viz. Korean (40.00), Bulgarian (30.67), and Georgian (28.44).

2.2.1 Georgian

We were particularly surprised to see Georgian among the seemingly most difficult languages. Georgian has a fully phonemic alphabet; each character represents exactly one phoneme, and each phoneme is represented by exactly one character (Hewitt 1995). Grapheme-to-phoneme conversion (and phoneme-to-grapheme conversion) for Georgian is thus a trivial task and can be done in principle with 100% accuracy using a simple 1-to-1 look-up table.

We actually implemented this look-up table, and this allowed us to identify and quantify the issues in the Georgian dataset. We found that there are three phonemes that are each inconsistently represented by two IPA symbols (and distributed roughly 50/50): i~ɪ; x~χ; ɣ~ʁ. The difference between these symbols is neither phonemic nor allophonic. Rather, it is caused by different annotators using different representation for a given phoneme, in line with the orthographic weakness of the IPA outlined above in Section 2.1.

We reported these data inconsistencies,[1] and we prepared a consistent dataset produced with our look-up table. Together with the organizers, we planned to update the Georgian data directly on Wiktionary and then re-retrieve the training data from there. Unfortunately, bulk uploading to Wiktionary is not trivial, and it was not possible for us to update the data before the task deadline. For the current task, it means that the WER cannot be substantially reduced for Georgian due to these inconsistencies.

2.2.2 Bulgarian

Bulgarian exhibits vowel reduction in unstressed syllables (similar phenomena are found, for instance, in English, German, and Russian), which leads to many allophones for vowels in unstressed positions (Leafgren 2020). These allophones should not be present in a purely phonemic transcription, however they are in the given training set. Furthermore, the pronunciation of a vowel in Bulgarian depends on the position of stress, yet Bulgarian word stress can fall on any syllable and is not completely predictable. We experimented with a self-written tool which predicts the stress position in Bulgarian based on heuristics, however the WER could only be decreased marginally using a stress-annotated training set, which is why we abandoned this approach. Similar issues like the ones discussed above for Georgian are present in the Bulgarian training data, and these were also discussed on GitHub.[2] However, these issues are somewhat more difficult to solve automatically compared to Georgian.

2.2.3 Korean

Korean uses an alphabet that provides a symbol for each consonant and for each vowel, yet it groups symbols into square syllable blocks, which makes it look somewhat close to Chinese and Japanese writing, although it is much simpler. By default, Unicode encodes Korean in syllable blocks and not as single sounds, which results in a character set comprising thousands of characters. Luckily, Unicode also provides code points for the single-sound characters (called Jamo), and syllable characters can easily be decomposed to single-sound characters.[3] We used `hangul-jamo`[4] for this decomposition. To give an example of the decomposition, 가감 /k a̠ g a̠ m/, is decomposed to ㄱ ㅏ ㄱ ㅏ ㅁ . With this approach, we were able to decrease the WER and PER of our Korean baseline Transformer model considerably: the WER was reduced from 40.00 to 21.50, and the PER from 16.38 to 3.86. We use this preprocessing step for Korean for all our submitted models.

---

[1] `https://github.com/sigmorphon/2020/issues/8`

[2] `https://github.com/sigmorphon/2020/issues/9`
[3] `http://www.unicode.org/versions/Unicode8.0.0/ch03.pdf`
[4] `https://github.com/jonghwanhyeon/hangul-jamo`

3   Approach

We trained a multilingual model which can transduce a word in any of the 15 source languages into its IPA representation. Multilingual models can be of the types many-to-one, one-to-many, or many-to-many. In our case, there are obviously multiple languages on the source side. On the target side, there is usually exactly one desired phoneme sequence for a given source word. Superficially, we thus have a many-to-one problem. However, many character sequences exist in more than one language. For instance, the character sequence <transformation> without further context can be read as an English word or as a French word, and its pronunciation depends on the choice of language (/tɹæns.fɔɹ.meɪ.ʃən/ vs. /tʁɑ̃s.fɔʁ.ma.sjɔ̃/). This makes it a many-to-many problem for a subset of the data.

The possibility of multiple desired sequences on the target side for a given source word makes it necessary to annotate the source words with the desired language. In our approach, we prefix each source word with its two-letter ISO language code, followed by an underscore, e.g. 'fr_maison', or 'ka_აგᲗომი'. This is similar to the approach in Johnson et al. (2017).

A side effect of our multilingual approach is that the size of the training data is increased from 3600 to 54000 (15 x 3600) samples. Ideally, a model might profit from this enlarged dataset, and languages can learn from each other. Given the various source-side writing systems and differences in phoneme sets across languages, we expect cross-language learning to be somewhat limited.

The multilingual approach proposed here allows for language-specific preprocessing where needed. In our case, we only used a preprocessing step for Korean, as outlined above in Section 2.2.3.

3.1   Model UZH-1

For our first submission, we used the Transformer baseline[5] provided by the organizers and experimented with different hyperparameters. The Transformer (Vaswani et al. 2017) is implemented in Fairseq (Ott et al. 2019) and uses Adam (Kingma and Ba 2015) for optimization and ReLU as an activation function. It has 4 encoder and decoder layers with 4 attention heads each.

---

[5]`https://github.com/sigmorphon/2020/tree/`
`master/task1/baselines/transformer`

In our hyperparameter tuning, we experimented with the following values: embedding dimension {128, 256} and hidden size {512, 1024} for both the encoder and the decoder, batch size {256, 512, 1024}, and dropout probability {0.1, 0.2, 0.3}. The number of epochs is limited to 400.

Our submitted model has the largest possible values for all tuned hyperparameters: embedding dimensions of 256, hidden sizes of 1024, a batch size of 1024, and a dropout probability of 0.3. Due to limitations in available computation power, further tuning with even larger hyperparameter values was not feasible for us.

3.2   Model UZH-2

For our second submission, we added extra language data from 6 languages not addressed in the task, viz. English, Italian, Portuguese, Czech, Danish, and Macedonian. Some of these languages have rather small data sets available on Wiktionary, therefore we added only 2400 training samples per language, and 300 development samples each, which is two thirds of the data for the other languages.

We selected the additional languages based on our intuition regarding whether a language might be useful for one or more of the 15 languages in the task. An additional restriction was the fact that large enough data sets are available mainly for European languages. Of the selected additional languages, some are closely related to another one from the official training set (e.g., Macedonian to Bulgarian, or, to a lesser degree, Danish to Dutch). Others have similar phonologies (e.g., Spanish and Greek, or Czech and Hungarian). In addition, some training sets (e.g., the one for French) contain English loanwords whose irregular pronunciation might be learned from additional English data.

The data was retrieved from Wiktionary using WikiPron (Lee et al. 2020) and sampled randomly. We used the same model architecture and the same hyperparameter search space for this experiment as in UZH-1, and the final model has the same hyperparameter values as UZH-1.

3.3   Model UZH-3

Our third submission is an ensemble model. It uses the predictions of UZH-1 and UZH-2, and for each word it takes the higher probability prediction from the two models.

4 Results

	UZH-1		UZH-2		UZH-3	
	WER	PER	WER	PER	WER	PER
arm	15.56	3.29	15.78	3.52	**14.89**	**3.17**
bul	32.89	6.48	**30.00**	**5.59**	30.22	5.77
fre	7.78	1.88	8.00	1.80	**6.89**	**1.64**
geo	26.44	5.00	28.00	5.11	**26.22**	**4.97**
gre	**18.00**	**2.97**	21.33	3.41	18.89	3.03
hin	6.89	1.58	7.78	2.16	**6.00**	**1.43**
hun	**5.78**	**1.15**	7.11	1.54	6.00	1.18
ice	**11.78**	**2.39**	12.89	2.78	**11.78**	2.46
kor	28.67	4.99	29.11	4.99	**28.44**	**4.88**
lit	27.33	4.69	28.44	4.84	**27.11**	**4.61**
ady	26.00	6.05	28.00	6.35	**25.78**	**5.94**
dut	**17.78**	**3.27**	21.56	3.94	18.67	3.42
jpn	9.33	2.46	**6.00**	1.58	**6.00**	**1.54**
rum	13.33	2.96	13.78	3.11	**12.00**	**2.59**
vie	8.44	2.91	6.67	2.62	**6.22**	**2.46**
macro avg	17.07	3.47	17.63	3.56	**16.34**	**3.27**

Table 1: WER and PER of our 3 models for each language and as macro-average on the official test set.

As can be seen from Table 1, our basic multilingual system (UZH-1) achieved a macro-average WER of 17.07 and a PER of 3.47 on the official test set.

For the multilingual model with additional data from six extra languages (UZH-2), we achieved a macro-average WER of 17.63 and a PER of 3.56. While performance did not increase with this approach, it also did not decrease dramatically, which indicates that it would be possible to have an even larger multilingual model for more than 15 languages without major performance loss.

More interestingly, even though the performance of UZH-2 was slightly worse, the model was able to resolve some of the errors made by UZH-1, while at the same time introducing others. We assume that there is indeed a cross-language interference which can influence the result both positively and negatively. We observed similar behavior on the development set during our experiments, which brought us to the idea of combining the results of both systems to get the best of both. Indeed, our ensemble model (UZH-3), which takes the prediction with the higher probability from UZH-1 and UZH-2, was the best-performing model among our submissions with a macro-average WER of 16.34 and PER of 3.27.

5 Conclusion

While other submissions outperformed our models, our PER for UZH-3 is only 0.51 points higher than that of the winning model (IMS). The difference in WER is slightly higher, with an increase of 2.53 points compared to the winning model. Overall, this shows that a single multilingual model can achieve competitive results even in a setting with highly unrelated languages, by simply prefixing each word with its language code. In future work, we like to explore further how cross-language interference in a multilingual model influences performance both positively and negatively.

References

Brian G. Hewitt. 1995. Georgian: A Structural Reference Grammar. John Benjamins Publishing, Amsterdam, Netherlands.

Melvin Johnson, Mike Schuster, Quoc V. Le, Maxim Krikun, Yonghui Wu, Zhifeng Chen, Nikhil Thorat, Fernanda Viégas, Martin Wattenberg, Greg Corrado, Macduff Hughesa, and Jeffrey Dean. 2017. Google's multilingual neural machine translation system: Enabling zero-shot translation. In Transactions of the Association for Computational Linguistics, Volume 5, page 339–351.

Diederik P. Kingma and Jimmy Ba. 2015. Adam: A method for stochastic optimization. In Proceedings of the 3rd International Conference on Learning Representations.

John Leafgren. 2020. A Concise Bulgarian Grammar. (to be published).

Jackson L. Lee, Lucas F.E. Ashby, M. Elizabeth Garza, Yeonju Lee-Sikka, Sean Miller, Alan Wong, Arya D. McCarthy, and Kyle Gorman. 2020. Massively multilingual pronunciation mining with WikiPron. In Proceedings of the 12th Language Resources and Evaluation Conference, page 4216–4221.

Benjamin Milde, Christoph Schmidt, and Joachim Köhler. 2017. Multitask sequence-to-sequence models for grapheme-to-phoneme conversion. In Proceedings of Interspeech 2017, page 2536–2540.

Myle Ott, Sergey Edunov, Alexei Baevski, Angela Fan, Sam Gross, Nathan Ng, David Grangier, and Michael Auli. 2019. fairseq: A fast, extensible toolkit for sequence modeling. In Proceedings of NAACL-HLT 2019: Demonstrations.

Ashish Vaswani, Noam Shazeer, Niki Parmar, Jakob Uszkoreit, Llion Jones, Aidan N. Gomez, Lukasz Kaiser, and Illia Polosukhin. 2017. Attention is all you need. In Proceedings of the 31st International Conference on Neural Information Processing Systems, page 6000–6010.

Sevinj Yolchuyeva, Géza Németh, and Bálint Gyires-
Tóth. 2019. Transformer based grapheme-to-
phoneme conversion. In Proceedings of Interspeech
2019.

Mingzhi Yu, Hieu Duy Nguyen, Alex Sokolov, Jack
Lepird, Kanthashree Mysore Sathyendra, Sam-
ridhi Choudhary, Athanasios Mouchtaris, and
Siegfried Kunzmann. 2020. Multilingual grapheme-
to-phoneme conversion with byte representation.
In IEEE International Conference on Acoustics,
Speech and Signal Processing (ICASSP), page
8234–8238.

The NYU-CUBoulder Systems for SIGMORPHON 2020 Task 0 and Task 2

Assaf Singer
New York University
USA
as12152@nyu.edu

Katharina Kann
University of Colorado Boulder
USA
katharina.kann@colorado.edu

Abstract

We describe the NYU-CUBoulder systems for the SIGMORPHON 2020 Task 0 on typologically diverse morphological inflection and Task 2 on unsupervised morphological paradigm completion. The former consists of generating morphological inflections from a lemma and a set of morphosyntactic features describing the target form. The latter requires generating entire paradigms for a set of given lemmas from raw text alone. We model morphological inflection as a sequence-to-sequence problem, where the input is the sequence of the lemma's characters with morphological tags, and the output is the sequence of the inflected form's characters. First, we apply a transformer model to the task. Second, as inflected forms share most characters with the lemma, we further propose a pointer-generator transformer model to allow easy copying of input characters. Our best performing system for Task 0 is placed 6th out of 23 systems. We further use our inflection systems as subcomponents of approaches for Task 2. Our best performing system for Task 2 is the 2nd best out of 7 submissions.

1 Introduction

In morphologically rich languages, a word's surface form reflects syntactic and semantic properties that are expressed by the word. For example, most English nouns have both singular and plural forms (e.g., *robot/robots*, *process/processes*), which are known as the inflected forms of the noun. Some languages display little inflection. In contrast, others have many inflections per base form or lemma: a Polish verb has nearly 100 inflected forms (Janecki, 2000) and an Archi verb has around 1.5 million (Kibrik, 1998).

Morphological inflection is the task of, given an input word – a lemma – together with morphosyntactic features defining the target form, gen-

Lemma	Features	Inflected form
hug	V;PST	hugged
seel	V;3;SG;PRS	seels

Figure 1: Morphological inflection examples in English. A lemma and features are mapped to an inflected form.

erating the indicated inflected form, cf. Figure 1. Morphological inflection is a useful tool for many natural language processing tasks (Seeker and Çetinoglu, 2015; Cotterell et al., 2016b), especially in morphologically rich languages where handling inflected forms can reduce data sparsity (Minkov et al., 2007).

The SIGMORPHON 2020 Shared Task consists of three separate tasks. We participate in Task 0 on typologically diverse morphological inflection (Vylomova et al., 2020) and Task 2 on unsupervised morphological paradigm completion (Kann et al., 2020). **Task 0** consists of generating morphological inflections from a lemma and a set of morphosyntactic features describing the target form. For this task, we implement a pointer-generator transformer model, based on the vanilla transformer model (Vaswani et al., 2017) and the pointer-generator model (See et al., 2017). After adding a copy mechanism to the transformer, it produces a final probability distribution as a combination of generating elements from its output vocabulary and copying elements – characters in our case – from the input. As most inflected forms derive their characters from the source lemma, the use of a mechanism for copying characters directly from the lemma has proven to be effective for morphological inflection generation, especially in the low resource setting (Aharoni and Goldberg, 2017; Makarov et al., 2017).

For our submissions, we further increase the size of all training sets by performing multi-task train-

90

*Proceedings of the Seventeenth SIGMORPHON Workshop on Computational Research
in Phonetics, Phonology, and Morphology*, pages 90–98
Online, July 10, 2020. ©2020 Association for Computational Linguistics
https://doi.org/10.18653/v1/P17

ing on morphological inflection and morphological reinflection, i.e., the task of generating inflected forms from forms *different from the lemma*. For languages with small training sets, we also perform hallucination pretraining (Anastasopoulos and Neubig, 2019), where we generate pseudo training instances for the task, based on suffixation and prefixation rules collected from the original dataset.

For **Task 2**, participants are given raw text and a source file with lemmas. The objective is to generate the complete paradigms for all lemmas. Our systems for this task consist of a combination of the official baseline system (Jin et al., 2020) and our systems for Task 0. The baseline system finds inflected forms in the text, decides on the number of inflected forms per lemma, and produces pseudo training files for morphological inflection. Our inflection model then learns from these and, subsequently, generates all missing forms.

2 Related Work

SIGMORPHON and CoNLL–SIGMORPHON shared tasks. In recent years, the SIGMORPHON and CoNLL–SIGMORPHON shared tasks have promoted research on computational morphology, with a strong focus on morphological inflection. Research related to those shared tasks includes Kann and Schütze (2016b), who used an LSTM (Hochreiter and Schmidhuber, 1997) sequence-to-sequence model with soft attention (Bahdanau et al., 2015) and achieved the best result in the SIGMORPHON 2016 shared task (Kann and Schütze, 2016a; Cotterell et al., 2016a). Due to the often monotonic alignment between input and output, Aharoni and Goldberg (2017) proposed a model with hard monotonic attention. Based on this, Makarov et al. (2017) implemented a neural state-transition system which also used hard monotonic attention and achieved the best results for Task 1 of the SIGMORPHON 2017 shared task. In 2018, the best results were achieved by a revised version of the neural transducer, trained with imitation learning (Makarov and Clematide, 2018). That model learned an alignment instead of maximizing the likelihood of gold action sequences given by a separate aligner.

Transformers. Transformers have produced state-of-the-art results on various tasks such as machine translation (Vaswani et al., 2017) language modeling (Al-Rfou et al., 2019), question answering (Devlin et al., 2019) and language understanding (Devlin et al., 2019). There has been very little work on transformers for morphological inflection, with, to the best of our knowledge, Erdmann et al. (2020) being the only published paper. However, the widespread success of transformers in NLP leads us to believe that a transformer model could perform well on morphological inflection.

Pointer-generators. In addition to the transformer, the architecture of our model is also inspired by See et al. (2017), who used a pointer-generator network for abstractive summarization. Their model could choose between generating a new element and copying an element from the input directly to the output. This copying of words from the source text via pointing (Vinyals et al., 2015), improved the handling of out-of-vocabulary words. Copy mechanisms have also been used for other tasks, including morphological inflection (Sharma et al., 2018). *Transformers* with copy mechanisms have been used for word-level tasks (Zhao et al., 2019), but, as far as we know, never before on the character level.

3 SIGMORPHON 2020 Shared Task

The SIGMORPHON 2020 Shared Task is composed of three tasks: Task 0 on typologically diverse morphological inflection (Vylomova et al., 2020), Task 1 on multilingual grapheme-to-phoneme conversion (Gorman et al., 2020), and Task 2 on unsupervised morphological paradigm completion (Kann et al., 2020). We submit systems to Tasks 0 and 2.

3.1 Task 0: Typologically Diverse Morphological Inflection

SIGMORPHON 2020 Task 0 focuses on morphological inflection in a set of typologically diverse languages. Different languages inflect differently, so it is not trivially clear that systems that work on some languages also perform well on others. For Task 0, systems need to generalize well to a large group of languages, including languages unseen during model development.

The task features 90 languages in total. 45 of them are development languages, coming from five families: Austronesian, Niger–Congo, Uralic, Oto-Manguean, and Indo-European. The remaining 45 are surprise languages, and many of those are from language families different from the development languages. Some languages have very small training sets, which makes them hard to model. For those cases, the organizers recommend a family-based multilingual approach to exploit similarities between related languages. While this might be effective, we believe that using multitask training in combination with hallucination pretraining can give the model enough information to learn the task well, while staying true to the specific structure of each individual language.

3.2 Task 2: Unsupervised Morphological Paradigm Completion

Task 2 is a novel task, designed to encourage work on unsupervised methods for computational morphology. As morphological annotations are limited for many of the world's languages, the study of morphological generation in the low-resource setting is of great interest (Cotterell et al., 2018). However, a different way to tackle the problem is by creating systems that are able to use data without annotations.

For Task 2, a tokenized Bible in each language is given to the participants, along with a list of lemmas. Participants should then produce complete paradigms for each lemma. As slots in the paradigm are not labeled with gold data paradigm slot descriptions, an evaluation metric called best-match accuracy was designed for this task. First, this metric matches predicted paradigm slots with gold slots in the way which leads to the highest overall accuracy. It then evaluates the correctness of individual inflected forms.

4 Methods

In this section, we introduce our models for Tasks 0 and 2 and describe all approaches we use, such as multitask training, hallucination pretraining and ensembling. The code for our models is available online.[1]

4.1 Transformer

Our model is built on top of the transformer architecture (Vaswani et al., 2017). It consists of an encoder and a decoder, each composed of a stack of layers. Each encoder layer consists, in turn, of a self-attention layer, followed by a fully connected layer. Decoder layers contain an additional inter-attention layer between the two.

With inputs $(x_1, \cdots, x_T)$ being a lemma's characters followed by tags representing the mor-

---

[1] https://github.com/AssafSinger94/sigmorphon-2020-inflection

phosyntactic features of the target form, the encoder processes the input sequence and outputs hidden states $(h_1, \cdots, h_T)$. At generation step t, the decoder reads the previously generated sequence $(y_1, \cdots, y_{t-1})$ to produce states $(s_1, \cdots, s_{t-1})$. The last decoder state s_{t-1} is then passed through a linear layer followed by a softmax, to generate a probability distribution over the output vocabulary:

$$P_{\text{vocab}} = \text{softmax}(V s_{t-1} + b) \tag{1}$$

During training, the entire target sequence $(y_1, \cdots, y_{T_y})$ is input to the decoder at once, along with a sequential mask to prevent positions from attending to subsequent positions.

4.2 Pointer-Generator Transformer

The pointer-generator transformer allows for both generating characters from a fixed vocabulary, as well as copying from the source sequence via pointing (Vinyals et al., 2015). This is managed by p_{gen} – the probability of generating as opposed to copying – which acts as a soft switch between the two actions. p_{gen} is computed by passing a concatenation of the decoder state s_t, the previously generated output y_{t-1}, and a context vector c_t through a linear layer, followed by the sigmoid function.

$$p_{\text{gen}} = \sigma(w[s_t; c_t; y_{t-1}] + b) \tag{2}$$

The context vector is computed as the weighted sum of the encoder hidden states

$$c_t = \sum_{i=1}^{T} a_i^t h_i \tag{3}$$

with attention weights $(a_1^t, \cdots, a_T^t)$. For each inflection example, let the extended vocabulary denote the union of the output vocabulary, and all characters appearing in the source lemma. We then use $p_{\text{gen}}, P_{\text{vocab}}$ produced by the transformer, and the attention weights of the last decoder layer $(a_1^t, \cdots, a_T^t)$ to compute a distribution over the extended vocabulary:

$$P(c) = p_{\text{gen}} P_{\text{vocab}}(c) + (1 - p_{\text{gen}}) P_{\text{copy}}(c), \tag{4}$$

with

$$P_{\text{copy}}(c) = \sum_{i:x_i=c} a_i^t \tag{5}$$

The copy distribution $P_{\text{copy}}(c)$ for each character c is the sum of attention weights over all source positions where $x_i = c$. Note that if c is an out-of-vocabulary (OOV) character, then $P_{\text{vocab}}(c)$ is zero; similarly, if c does not appear in the source lemma,

raw	grip	grips	V;SG;3;PRS
	grip	gripped	V;PST
generated	grips	grip	V;LEMMA
	grips	gripped	V;PST
	gripped	grip	V;LEMMA

Figure 2: English multitask training example (Task 0).

then $\sum_{i:x_i=c} a_i^t$ is zero. The ability to produce OOV characters is one of the primary advantages of pointer-generator models; by contrast models such as our vanilla transformer are restricted to their pre-set vocabulary.

4.3 Multitask Training

Some languages in Task 0 have small training sets, which makes them hard to model. In order to handle that, we perform multitask training, and, thereby, increase the amount of examples available for training.

Morphological reinflection. Morphological re-inflection is a generalized version of the morphological inflection task, which consists of producing an inflected form for any given source form – i.e., not necessarily the lemma –, and target tag. For example:

$$(\text{hugging; V;PST}) \rightarrow \text{hugged.} \tag{6}$$

This is a more complex task, since a model needs to infer the underlying lemma of the source form in order to inflect it correctly to the desired form.

Many morphological inflection datasets contain lemmas that are converted to several inflected forms. Treating separate instances for the same source lemma as independent is missing an opportunity to utilize the connection between the different inflected forms. We approach this by converting our morphological inflection training set into one for morphological reinflection as described in the following.

From inflection to reinflection. Inflected forms of the same lemma are grouped together to sets of one or more (inflected form, morphological features) pairs. Then, for each set, we create new training instances by inflecting all forms to one another, as shown in Figure 2. We also let the model inflect forms back to the lemma by adding the lemma as one of the inflected forms, marked with the synthetically generated LEMMA tag. The new training set fully utilizes the connections between different

Hyperparameter	Value
Embedding dimension	256
Encoder layers	4
Decoder layers	4
Encoder hidden dimension	1024
Decoder hidden dimension	1024
Attention heads	4

Table 1: The hyperparameters used in our inflection models for both Task 0 and Task 2.

forms in the paradigm, and, in that way, provides more training instances to our model.

4.4 Hallucination Pretraining

Another effective tool to improve training in the low-resource setting is data hallucination (Anastasopoulos and Neubig, 2019). Using hallucination, new pseudo-instances are generated for training, based on suffixation and prefixation rules collected from the original dataset. For languages with less than 1000 training instances, we pretrain our models on a hallucinated training set consisting of 10,000 instances, before training on the multitask training set.

4.5 Submissions and Ensembling Strategies

We submit 4 different systems for Task 0. NYU-CUBoulder-2 consists of one pointer-generator transformer model, and, for NYU-CUBoulder-4, we train one vanilla transformer. Those two are our simplest systems and can be seen as baselines for our other submissions.

Because of the effects of random initialization in non-convex objective functions, we further use ensembling in combination with both architectures: NYU-CUBoulder-1 is an ensemble of three pointer-generator transformers, and NYU-CUBoulder-3 is an ensemble of five pointer-generator transformers. The final decision is made by majority voting. In case of a tie, the answer is chosen randomly among the most frequent predictions. Models participating in the ensembles are from different epochs during the same training run.

As previously stated, all systems are trained on the augmented multitask training sets, and systems trained on languages with less than 1000 training instances were pretrained on the hallucinated datasets.

4.6 Task 2: Model description

Our systems for Task 2 consist of a combination of the official baseline system (Jin et al., 2020) and our inflection systems for Task 0. The system is given raw text and a source file with lemmas, and generates the complete paradigm of each lemma. The baseline system finds inflected forms in the text, decides on the number of inflected forms per lemma, and produces pseudo training files for morphological inflection. Any inflections that the system has not found in the raw text are given as test instances. Our inflection model then learns from the files and, subsequently, generates all missing forms. We use the pointer-generator and vanilla transformers as our inflection models.

For Task 2, we use ensembling for all submissions. NYU-CUBoulder-1 is an ensemble of six pointer-generator transformers, NYU-CUBoulder-2 is an ensemble of six vanilla transformers, and NYU-CUBoulder-3 is an ensemble of all twelve models. For all models in both tasks, we use the hyperparameters described in Table 1.

5 Experiments

5.1 Task 0

Data. The dataset for Task 0 covers 90 languages in total: 45 development languages and 45 surprise languages. For details on the official dataset please refer to Vylomova et al. (2020).

Baselines. This year, several baselines are provided for the task. The first system has also been used as a baseline in previous shared tasks on morphological reinflection (Cotterell et al., 2017, 2018). It is a non-neural system which first scans the dataset to extract suffix- or prefix-based lemma-to-form transformations. Then, based on the morphological tag at inference time, it applies the most frequent suitable transformation to an input lemma to yield the output form (Cotterell et al., 2017). The other two baselines are neural models. One is a transformer (Vaswani et al., 2017; Wu et al., 2020), and the second one is a hard-attention model (Wu and Cotterell, 2019), which enforces strict monotonicity and learns a latent alignment while learning to transduce. To account for the low-resource settings for some languages, the organizers also employ two additional methods: constructing a multilingual model trained for all languages belonging to each language family (Kann et al., 2017), and data augmentation using halluci-

	Sub-1	Sub-2	Sub-3	Sub-4	Base
Development Set					
Low	**88.71**	88.02	84.90	84.07	-
Other	90.46	90.63	90.20	**90.94**	-
All	**90.06**	90.02	88.96	89.34	-
Test Set					
Low	84.8	84.8	85.5	83.9	**89.77**
Other	89.7	89.8	89.8	90.2	**92.43**
All	88.6	88.7	88.8	88.8	**91.81**

Table 2: Macro-averaged results over all languages on the official development and test sets for Task 0. Low=languages with less than 1000 train instances, Other=all other languages, All=all languages.

nation (Anastasopoulos and Neubig, 2019). Four model types are trained for each neural architecture: a plain model, a family-multilingual model, a data augmented model, and an augmented family-multilingual model. Overall, there are nine baseline systems for each language. We compare our models to an oracle baseline by choosing the best score over all baseline systems for each language.

Results. Our results for Task 0 are displayed in Table 2. All four systems produce relatively similar results. NYU-CUBoulder-3, our five-model ensemble, performs best overall with 88.8% accuracy on average. We further look at the results for low-resource ($<$ 1000 training examples) and high-resource ($>=$ 1000 training examples) languages separately. This way, we are able to see the advantage of the pointer-generator transformer in the low-resource setting, where all pointer-generator systems achieve an at least 0.9% higher accuracy than the vanilla transformer model. However, in the setting where training data is abundant, the effect of the copy mechanism vanishes, as NYU-CUBoulder-4 – our only vanilla transformer – achieved the best results for our high-resource languages.

5.2 Task 2

Data. For Task 2, a tokenized Bible in each language is given to the participants, along with a list of lemmas. Participants are required to construct the paradigms for all given lemmas.

The languages for Task 2 are again divided into development and test languages. Development languages are available for model development and hyperparameter tuning, but are not used during the final evaluation. The test languages are used for

System	Baseline 1		Baseline 2		Sub-1		Sub-2		Sub-3	
	Test Set									
	slots	macro	slots	macro	slots	macro	slots	macro	slots	macro
Basque	30	0.0006	27	0.0006	30	0.0005	30	0.0005	30	**0.0007**
Bulgarian	35	0.283	34	**0.3169**	35	0.2769	35	0.2894	35	0.2789
English	4	0.656	4	**0.662**	4	0.502	4	0.528	4	0.512
Finnish	21	0.0533	21	**0.055**	21	0.0536	21	0.0547	21	0.0535
German	9	0.2835	9	**0.29**	9	0.273	9	0.2735	9	0.2735
Kannada	172	0.1549	172	**0.1512**	172	0.111	172	0.1116	172	0.111
Navajo	3	0.0323	3	**0.0327**	3	0.004	3	0.0043	3	0.0043
Spanish	29	0.2296	29	**0.2367**	29	0.2039	29	0.2056	29	0.203
Turkish	104	0.1421	104	**0.1553**	104	0.1488	104	0.1539	104	0.1513
All		0.2039		**0.2112**		0.1749		0.1802		0.1765

Table 3: Results for all test languages on the official test sets for Task 2.

evaluation only, and do not have development sets. The development languages are: Maltese, Persian, Portuguese, Russian, Swedish. The test languages are: Basque, Bulgarian, English, Finnish, German, Kannada, Navajo, Spanish and Turkish.

Baselines. The baseline system for the task is composed of four components, eventually producing morphological paradigms (Jin et al., 2020). The first three modules perform edit tree (Chrupala, 2020) retrieval, additional lemma retrieval from the corpus, and paradigm size discovery, using distributional information. After the first three steps, pseudo training and test files for morphological inflection are produced. Finally, the non-neural Task 0 baseline system (Cotterell et al., 2017) or the neural transducer by Makarov and Clematide (2018) are used to create missing inflected forms.

Results. Systems for Task 2 are evaluated using macro-averaged best-match accuracy (Jin et al., 2020). Results are shown in in Table 3. All three systems produce relatively similar results. NYU-CUBoulder-2, our vanilla transformer ensemble, performed slightly better overall with an average best-match accuracy of 18.02%. Since our system is close to the baseline models, it performs similarly, achieving slightly worse results. For Basque, our all-round ensemble NYU-CUBoulder-2 outperformed both baselines with a best-match accuracy of 00.07%, achieving the highest result in the shared task.

5.3 Low-resource Setting

As most inflected forms derive their characters from the source lemma, the use of a mechanism for copying characters directly from the lemma has proven to be effective for morphological inflection generation, especially in the low-resource setting (Aharoni and Goldberg, 2017; Makarov et al., 2017). As all Task 0 datasets are fairly large, we further design a low-resource experiment to investigate the effectiveness of our model.

Data. We simulate a low-resource setting by sampling 100 instances from all languages that we already consider low-resource, i.e., all languages with less than 1000 training instances. We then keep their development and test sets unchanged. Overall, we perform this experiment on 21 languages.

Experimental setup. We train a pointer-generator transformer and a vanilla transformer on the modified datasets to examine the effects of the copy mechanism. We keep the hyperparameters unchanged, i.e., they are as mentioned in Table 1. We use a majority-vote ensemble consisting of 5 individual models for each architecture.

Baseline. We additionally train the neural transducer by Makarov and Clematide (2018), which has achieved the best results for the 2018 shared task in the low-resource setting (Cotterell et al.,

System	Trm	Trm-PG	Baseline
All	63.06	67.61	**70.06**

Table 4: Results on the official development data for our low-resource experiment. Trm=Vanilla transformer, Trm-PG=Pointer-generator transformer, Baseline=neural transducer by Makarov and Clematide (2018).

Model:	1	2	3	4	5
Copy	✓	✓			✓
Multitask Train	✓		✓		✓
Hallucination	✓	✓	✓	✓	

Table 5: System components for the ablation study for Task 0. Each model is a transformer which contains a combination of the following components: copy mechanism, multitask training and hallucination pretraining.

Model:	1	2	3	4	5
	Development Set				
Low	88.20	**90.00**	87.52	89.84	86.35
Other	90.63	**92.66**	90.93	92.60	90.63
All	90.02	**92.04**	90.13	91.96	89.63

Table 6: Ablation study for Task 0; development set results, averaged over all languages. Low=languages with less than 1000 train instances, Other=all other languages, All=all languages.

2018). The neural transducer uses hard monotonic attention (Aharoni and Goldberg, 2017) and transduces the lemma into the inflected form by a sequence of explicit edit operations. It is trained with an imitation learning method (Makarov and Clematide, 2018). We use this model as a reference for the state of the art in the low-resource setting.

Results. As seen in Table 4, for the low-resource dataset, the pointer-generator transformer clearly outperforms the vanilla transformer by an average accuracy of 4.46%. For some languages, such as Chichicapan Zapotec, the difference is up to 14%. While the neural transducer achieves a higher accuracy, our model performs only 2.45% worse than this state-of-the-art model.[2] We are also able to observe the use of the copy mechanism for copying of OOV characters in the test sets of some languages.

6 Ablation Studies

Our systems use three components on top of the vanilla transformer: a copy mechanism, multitask training and hallucination pretraining. We further perform an ablation study to measure the contribution of each component to the overall system performance. For this, we additionally train five different systems with different combinations of components. A description of which component is used in which system for this ablation study is shown in Table 5.

6.1 Results

Copy mechanism. Comparing models 2 and 4, which are both trained on the original dataset, pretrained with hallucination and differ only by the use of the copy mechanism, we are able to see that adding this component slightly improves performance by $0.06 - 0.16\%$. When comparing models 1 and 3, the copy mechanism decreases performance slightly by 0.3% for the high-resource languages

and 0.11% overall, but increases performance for low-resource languages by 0.68%.

Multitask training. Unlike the copy mechanism, multitask training actually consistently decreases the performance of the models. Looking at models 1 and 2, training the pointer-generator transformer on the multitask dataset decreases accuracy by $1.8 - 2.03\%$ for all three language groups. The same happens for the vanilla transformer with an accuracy decrease of $1.67 - 2.32\%$. A possible explanation are the relatively large training sets provided for the shared task, as this method is more suitable for the low-resource setting.

Hallucination pretraining. In order to examine the effect of hallucination pretraining on our submitted models, we now compare the pointer-generator transformers trained on the multitask data with and without hallucination pretraining (models 1 and 5). Hallucination pretraining shows to be helpful: it increases the accuracy on low-resource languages by 1.85%. The performance on the high-resource languages is necessarily the same, as only models for low-resource languages are actually pretrained.

7 Conclusion

We presented the NYU-CUBoulder submissions for SIGMORPHON 2020 Task 0 and Task 2.

We developed morphological inflection models, based on a transformer and a new model for the task, a pointer-generator transformer, which is a transformer-analogue of a pointer-generator model. For Task 0, we further added multitask training and hallucination pretraining. For Task 2, we combined our inflection models with additional components from the provided baseline to obtain a fully functional system for unsupervised morphological paradigm completion.

We performed an ablation study to examine the

---

[2]We could probably obtain better results with appropriate hyperparameter tuning.

effects of all components of our inflection system. Finally, we designed a low-resource experiment to show that using the copy mechanism on top of the vanilla transformer is beneficial if training sets are small, and achieved results close to a state-of-the-art model for low-resource morphological inflection.

Acknowledgments

We would like to thank the organizers of SIGMOR-PHON 2020 Task 0 and Task 2.

References

Roee Aharoni and Yoav Goldberg. 2017. Morphological inflection generation with hard monotonic attention. In *Proceedings of the 55th Annual Meeting of the Association for Computational Linguistics, ACL 2017, Vancouver, Canada, July 30 - August 4, Volume 1: Long Papers*, pages 2004–2015.

Rami Al-Rfou, Dokook Choe, Noah Constant, Mandy Guo, and Llion Jones. 2019. Character-level language modeling with deeper self-attention. In *The Thirty-Third AAAI Conference on Artificial Intelligence, AAAI 2019, The Thirty-First Innovative Applications of Artificial Intelligence Conference, IAAI 2019, The Ninth AAAI Symposium on Educational Advances in Artificial Intelligence, EAAI 2019, Honolulu, Hawaii, USA, January 27 - February 1, 2019.*, pages 3159–3166.

Antonios Anastasopoulos and Graham Neubig. 2019. Pushing the limits of low-resource morphological inflection. In *Proceedings of the 2019 Conference on Empirical Methods in Natural Language Processing and the 9th International Joint Conference on Natural Language Processing, EMNLP-IJCNLP 2019, Hong Kong, China, November 3-7, 2019*, pages 984–996. Association for Computational Linguistics.

Dzmitry Bahdanau, Kyunghyun Cho, and Yoshua Bengio. 2015. Neural machine translation by jointly learning to align and translate. In *3rd International Conference on Learning Representations, ICLR 2015, San Diego, CA, USA, May 7-9, 2015, Conference Track Proceedings*.

Grzegorz Chrupala. 2020. Towards a machine-learning architecture for lexical functional grammar parsing.

Ryan Cotterell, Christo Kirov, John Sylak-Glassman, Géraldine Walther, Ekaterina Vylomova, Arya D. McCarthy, Katharina Kann, S. J. Mielke, Garrett Nicolai, Miikka Silfverberg, David Yarowsky, Jason Eisner, and Mans Hulden. 2018. The conll-sigmorphon 2018 shared task: Universal morphological reinflection. In *Proceedings of the CoNLL SIGMORPHON 2018 Shared Task: Universal Morphological Reinflection, Brussels, October 31 - November 1, 2018*, pages 1–27. Association for Computational Linguistics.

Ryan Cotterell, Christo Kirov, John Sylak-Glassman, Géraldine Walther, Ekaterina Vylomova, Patrick Xia, Manaal Faruqui, Sandra Kübler, David Yarowsky, Jason Eisner, and Mans Hulden. 2017. Conll-sigmorphon 2017 shared task: Universal morphological reinflection in 52 languages. In *Proceedings of the CoNLL SIGMORPHON 2017 Shared Task: Universal Morphological Reinflection, Vancouver, BC, Canada, August 3-4, 2017*, pages 1–30. Association for Computational Linguistics.

Ryan Cotterell, Christo Kirov, John Sylak-Glassman, David Yarowsky, Jason Eisner, and Mans Hulden. 2016a. The SIGMORPHON 2016 shared task - morphological reinflection. In *Proceedings of the 14th SIGMORPHON Workshop on Computational Research in Phonetics, Phonology, and Morphology, Berlin, Germany, August 11, 2016*, pages 10–22. Association for Computational Linguistics.

Ryan Cotterell, Hinrich Schütze, and Jason Eisner. 2016b. Morphological smoothing and extrapolation of word embeddings. In *Proceedings of the 54th Annual Meeting of the Association for Computational Linguistics, ACL 2016, August 7-12, 2016, Berlin, Germany, Volume 1: Long Papers*. The Association for Computer Linguistics.

Jacob Devlin, Ming-Wei Chang, Kenton Lee, and Kristina Toutanova. 2019. BERT: pre-training of deep bidirectional transformers for language understanding. In *Proceedings of the 2019 Conference of the North American Chapter of the Association for Computational Linguistics: Human Language Technologies, NAACL-HLT 2019, Minneapolis, MN, USA, June 2-7, 2019, Volume 1 (Long and Short Papers)*, pages 4171–4186. Association for Computational Linguistics.

Alexander Erdmann, Micha Elsner, Shijie Wu, Ryan Cotterell, and Nizar Habash. 2020. The paradigm discovery problem. *CoRR*, abs/2005.01630.

Kyle Gorman, Lucas F.E. Ashby, Aaron Goyzueta, Arya D. McCarthy, Shijie Wu, and Daniel You. 2020. The sigmorphon 2020 shared task on multilingual grapheme-to-phoneme conversion. In *Proceedings of the 17th SIGMORPHON Workshop on Computational Research in Phonetics, Phonology, and Morphology*. Association for Computational Linguistics.

Sepp Hochreiter and Jürgen Schmidhuber. 1997. Long short-term memory. *Neural Computation*, 9(8):1735–1780.

Klara Janecki. 2000. 300 polish verbs. Barron's Educational Series.

Huiming Jin, Liwei Cai, Yihui Peng, Chen Xia, Arya D. McCarthy, and Katharina Kann. 2020. Unsupervised morphological paradigm completion. In *Proceedings of the 58th Annual Meeting of the Association for Computational Linguistics*. Association for Computational Linguistics.

Katharina Kann, Ryan Cotterell, and Hinrich Schütze. 2017. One-shot neural cross-lingual transfer for paradigm completion. In *Proceedings of the 55th Annual Meeting of the Association for Computational Linguistics (Volume 1: Long Papers)*, pages 1993–2003, Vancouver, Canada. Association for Computational Linguistics.

Katharina Kann, Arya D. McCarthy, Garrett Nicolai, and Mans Hulden. 2020. The SIGMORPHON 2020 shared task on unsupervised morphological paradigm completion. In *Proceedings of the 17th SIGMORPHON Workshop on Computational Research in Phonetics, Phonology, and Morphology*. Association for Computational Linguistics.

Katharina Kann and Hinrich Schütze. 2016a. MED: the LMU system for the SIGMORPHON 2016 shared task on morphological reinflection. In *Proceedings of the 14th SIGMORPHON Workshop on Computational Research in Phonetics, Phonology, and Morphology, Berlin, Germany, August 11, 2016*, pages 62–70.

Katharina Kann and Hinrich Schütze. 2016b. Single-model encoder-decoder with explicit morphological representation for reinflection. In *Proceedings of the 54th Annual Meeting of the Association for Computational Linguistics, ACL 2016, August 7-12, 2016, Berlin, Germany, Volume 2: Short Papers*.

Aleksandr E. Kibrik. 1998. The handbook of morphology. In *Andrew Spencer and Arnold M. Zwicky, editors*, pages 455–476. Oxford: Blackwell Publishers.

Peter Makarov and Simon Clematide. 2018. UZH at conll-sigmorphon 2018 shared task on universal morphological reinflection. In *Proceedings of the CoNLL SIGMORPHON 2018 Shared Task: Universal Morphological Reinflection, Brussels, October 31 - November 1, 2018*, pages 69–75. Association for Computational Linguistics.

Peter Makarov, Tatiana Ruzsics, and Simon Clematide. 2017. Align and copy: UZH at SIGMORPHON 2017 shared task for morphological reinflection. *CoRR*, abs/1707.01355.

Einat Minkov, Kristina Toutanova, and Hisami Suzuki. 2007. Generating complex morphology for machine translation. In *ACL 2007, Proceedings of the 45th Annual Meeting of the Association for Computational Linguistics, June 23-30, 2007, Prague, Czech Republic*. The Association for Computational Linguistics.

Abigail See, Peter J. Liu, and Christopher D. Manning. 2017. Get to the point: Summarization with pointer-generator networks. In *Proceedings of the 55th Annual Meeting of the Association for Computational Linguistics, ACL 2017, Vancouver, Canada, July 30 - August 4, Volume 1: Long Papers*, pages 1073–1083.

Wolfgang Seeker and Özlem Çetinoglu. 2015. A graph-based lattice dependency parser for joint morphological segmentation and syntactic analysis. *Trans. Assoc. Comput. Linguistics*, 3:359–373.

Abhishek Sharma, Ganesh Katrapati, and Dipti Misra Sharma. 2018. IIT(BHU)-IIITH at conll-sigmorphon 2018 shared task on universal morphological reinflection. In *Proceedings of the CoNLL SIGMORPHON 2018 Shared Task: Universal Morphological Reinflection, Brussels, October 31 - November 1, 2018*, pages 105–111.

Ashish Vaswani, Noam Shazeer, Niki Parmar, Jakob Uszkoreit, Llion Jones, Aidan N. Gomez, Lukasz Kaiser, and Illia Polosukhin. 2017. Attention is all you need. In *Advances in Neural Information Processing Systems 30: Annual Conference on Neural Information Processing Systems 2017, 4-9 December 2017, Long Beach, CA, USA*, pages 5998–6008.

Oriol Vinyals, Lukasz Kaiser, Terry Koo, Slav Petrov, Ilya Sutskever, and Geoffrey E. Hinton. 2015. Grammar as a foreign language. In *Advances in Neural Information Processing Systems 28: Annual Conference on Neural Information Processing Systems 2015, December 7-12, 2015, Montreal, Quebec, Canada*, pages 2773–2781.

Ekaterina Vylomova, Jennifer White, Elizabeth Salesky, Sabrina J. Mielke, Shijie Wu, Edoardo Ponti, Rowan Hall Maudslay, Ran Zmigrod, Joseph Valvoda, Svetlana Toldova, Francis Tyers, Elena Klyachko, Ilya Yegorov, Natalia Krizhanovsky, Paula Czarnowska, Irene Nikkarinen, Andrej Krizhanovsky, Tiago Pimentel, Lucas Torroba Hennigen, Christo Kirov, Garrett Nicolai, Adina Williams, Antonios Anastasopoulos, Hilaria Cruz, Eleanor Chodroff, Ryan Cotterell, Miikka Silfverberg, and Mans Hulden. 2020. The SIGMORPHON 2020 Shared Task 0: Typologically diverse morphological inflection. In *Proceedings of the 17th SIGMORPHON Workshop on Computational Research in Phonetics, Phonology, and Morphology*.

Shijie Wu and Ryan Cotterell. 2019. Exact hard monotonic attention for character-level transduction. In *Proceedings of the 57th Conference of the Association for Computational Linguistics, ACL 2019, Florence, Italy, July 28- August 2, 2019, Volume 1: Long Papers*, pages 1530–1537. Association for Computational Linguistics.

Shijie Wu, Ryan Cotterell, and Mans Hulden. 2020. Applying the transformer to character-level transduction.

Wei Zhao, Liang Wang, Kewei Shen, Ruoyu Jia, and Jingming Liu. 2019. Improving grammatical error correction via pre-training a copy-augmented architecture with unlabeled data. In *Proceedings of the 2019 Conference of the North American Chapter of the Association for Computational Linguistics: Human Language Technologies, NAACL-HLT 2019, Minneapolis, MN, USA, June 2-7, 2019, Volume 1 (Long and Short Papers)*, pages 156–165.

The IMS–CUBoulder System for the SIGMORPHON 2020 Shared Task on Unsupervised Morphological Paradigm Completion

Manuel Mager
Institute for Natural Language Processing
University of Stuttgart
manuel.mager@ims.uni-stuttgart.de

Katharina Kann
University of Colorado Boulder
katharina.kann@colorado.edu

Abstract

In this paper, we present the systems of the University of Stuttgart IMS and the University of Colorado Boulder (IMS–CUBoulder) for SIGMORPHON 2020 Task 2 on unsupervised morphological paradigm completion (Kann et al., 2020). The task consists of generating the morphological paradigms of a set of lemmas, given only the lemmas themselves and unlabeled text. Our proposed system is a modified version of the baseline introduced together with the task. In particular, we experiment with substituting the inflection generation component with an LSTM sequence-to-sequence model and an LSTM pointer-generator network. Our pointer-generator system obtains the best score of all seven submitted systems on average over all languages, and outperforms the official baseline, which was best overall, on Bulgarian and Kannada.

1 Introduction

In recent years, a lot of progress has been made on the task of morphological inflection, which consists of generating an inflected word, given a lemma and a list of morphological features (Kann and Schütze, 2017; Makarov and Clematide, 2018; Cotterell et al., 2016, 2017, 2018; McCarthy et al., 2019). The systems developed for this task learn to model inflection in morphologically complex languages in a supervised fashion.

However, not all languages have annotated data available. For the 2018 SIGMORPHON shared task (Cotterell et al., 2018), data for 103 unique languages has been provided. Even this highly multilingual dataset is just covering 1.61% of the 6359 languages[1] that exist in the world (Lewis, 2009). The unsupervised morphological paradigm completion task (Jin et al., 2020) aims at generating

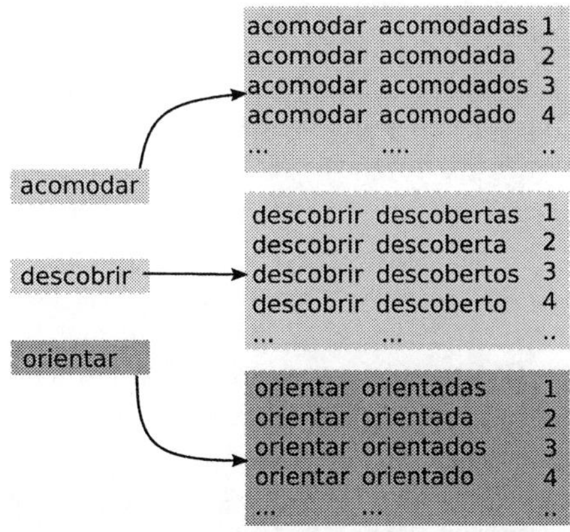

Figure 1: Partial Portuguese development examples. The input is a list of lemmas, and the output is a list of all inflected forms of each lemma. In this example, unnamed paradigm slots correspond to the following UniMorph features: 1=V.PTCP;FEM;PL;PST, 2=V.PTCP;FEM;SG;PST, 3=V.PTCP;MASC;PL;PST, 4=V.PTCP;MASC;SG;PST.

inflections – more specifically all inflected forms, i.e., the entire paradigms, of given lemmas – without any explicit morphological information during training. A system that is able to solve this problem can generate morphological resources for most of the world's languages easily. This motivates us to participate in the SIGMORPHON 2020 shared task on unsupervised morphological paradigm completion (Kann et al., 2020).

The task, however, is challenging: As the number of inflected forms per lemma is unknown a priori, an unsupervised morphological paradigm completion system needs to detect the paradigm size from raw text. Since the names of morphological features expressed in a language are not known if there is no supervision, a system should mark which inflections correspond to the same morphological features across lemmas, but needs to do so without using names, cf. Figure 1. For the shared

---

[1]The number of languages can vary depending on the classification schema used.

Proceedings of the Seventeenth SIGMORPHON Workshop on Computational Research in Phonetics, Phonology, and Morphology, pages 99–105
Online, July 10, 2020. ©2020 Association for Computational Linguistics
https://doi.org/10.18653/v1/P17

task, no external resources such as pretrained models, annotated data, or even additional monolingual text can be used. The same holds true for multilingual models.

We submit two systems, which are both modifications of the official shared task baseline. The latter is a pipeline system, which performs four steps: edit tree retrieval, additional lemma retrieval, paradigm size discovery, and inflection generation (Jin et al., 2020). We experiment with substituting the original generation component, which is either a simple non-neural system (Cotterell et al., 2017) or a transducer-based hard-attention model (Makarov and Clematide, 2018) with an LSTM encoder-decoder architecture with attention (Bahdanau et al., 2015) – IMS-CUB1– and a pointer-generator network (See et al., 2017) – IMS-CUB2. IMS-CUB2 achieves the best results of all submitted systems, outperforming the second best system by 2.07% macro-averaged best-match accuracy (BMAcc; Jin et al., 2020), when averaged over all languages. However, we underperform the baseline system, which performs 1.03% BMAcc better than IMS-CUB2. Looking at individual languages, IMS-CUB2 obtains the best results overall for Bulgarian and Kannada.

The findings from our work on the shared task are as follows: i) the copy capabilities of a pointer-generator network are useful in this setup; and ii) unsupervised morphological paradigm completion is a challenging task: no submitted system outperforms the baselines.

2   Related Work

Unsupervised methods have shown to be effective for morphological surface segmentation. LINGUISTICA (Goldsmith, 2001) and MORFESSOR (Creutz, 2003; Creutz and Lagus, 2007; Poon et al., 2009) are two unsupervised systems for the task.

In the realm of morphological generation, Yarowsky and Wicentowski (2000) worked on a task which was similar to unsupervised morphological paradigm completion, but required additional knowledge (e.g., a list of morphemes). Dreyer and Eisner (2011) used a set of seed paradigms to train a paradigm completion model. Ahlberg et al. (2015) and Hulden et al. (2014) also relied on information about the paradigms in the language. Erdmann et al. (2020) proposed a system for a task similar to this shared task.

Learning to generate morphological paradigms

Language	Training	Development	Test
Basque	85	16	499
Bulgarian	1609	441	2874
English	343	83	302
Finnish	2306	522	1789
German	3940	999	667
Kannada	832	211	2854
Navajo	17	4	279
Spanish	1940	494	2506
Turkish	3095	787	8502

Table 1: Number of instances retrieved by steps 1 to 3 in our pipeline, which are used for training and development of our inflection generation components. The test set contains the lemma and paradigm slot for forms that need to be generated.

in a fully supervised way is the more common approach. Methods include Durrett and DeNero (2013), Nicolai et al. (2015), and Kann and Schütze (2018). Supervised morphological inflection has further gained popularity through previous SIGMORPHON and CoNLL–SIGMORPHON shared tasks on the topic (Cotterell et al., 2016, 2017, 2018; McCarthy et al., 2019). The systems proposed for these shared tasks have a special relevance for our work, as we investigate the performance of morphological inflection components based on Kann and Schütze (2016a,b) and Sharma et al. (2018) within a pipeline for unsupervised morphological paradigm completion.

3   System Description

In this section, we introduce our pipeline system for unsupervised morphological paradigm completion. First, we describe the baseline system, since we rely on some of its components. Then, we describe our morphological inflection models.

3.1   The Shared Task Baseline

For the initial steps of our pipeline, we employ the first three components of the baseline (Jin et al., 2020), cf. Figure 2, which we describe in this subsection. We use the official implementation.[2]

Retrieval of relevant edit trees. This component (cf. Figure 2.1) identifies words in the monolingual corpus that could belong to a given lemma's paradigm by computing the longest common substring between the lemma and all words. Then, the

---

[2] https://github.com/cai-lw/
morpho-baseline

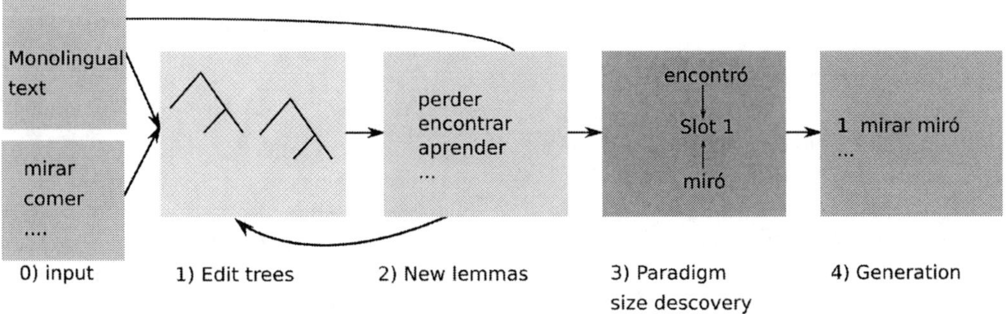

Figure 2: The baseline system. This paper experiments with modifying the generation module. All components are described in §3.1.

transformation from a lemma to each word potentially from its paradigm is represented by edit trees (Chrupała, 2008). Edit trees with frequencies are below a threshold are discarded.

Retrieval of additional lemmas. To increase the confidence that retrieved edit trees represent valid inflections, more lemmas are needed (cf. Figure 2.2). To find those, the second component of the system applies edit trees to potential lemmas in the corpus. If enough potential inflected forms are found in the corpus, a lemma is considered valid.

Paradigm size discovery. Now the system needs to find a mapping between edit trees and paradigms (cf. Figure 2.3). This is done based on two assumptions: that for each lemma a maximum of one edit tree per paradigm slot can be found, and that each edit tree only realizes one paradigm slot for all lemmas. In addition, the similarity of potential slots is measured. With these elements, similar potential slots are merged until the final paradigm size for a language is being determined.

Generation. Now, that the system has a set of lemmas and corresponding potential inflected forms, the baseline employs a morphological inflection component, which learns to generate inflections from lemmas and a slot indicator, and generates missing forms (cf. Figure 2.4). We experiment with substituting this final component.

In the remainder of this paper, we will refer to the original baselines with the non-neural system from Cotterell et al. (2017) and the inflection model from Makarov and Clematide (2018) as BL-1 and BL-2, respectively.

3.2   LSTM Encoder-Decoder

We use an LSTM encoder-decoder model with attention (Bahdanau et al., 2015) for our first system, IMS-CUB1, since it has been shown to obtain high performance on morphological inflection (Kann and Schütze, 2016a). This model takes two inputs: a sequence of characters and a sequence of morphological features. It then generates the sequence of characters of the inflected form. For the input, we simply concatenate the paradigm slot number and all characters.

3.3   Pointer-Generator Network

For IMS-CUB2, we use a pointer-generator network (See et al., 2017).[3] We expect this system to perform better than IMS-CUB1, given the pointer-generator's better performance on morphological inflection in the low-resource setting (Sharma et al., 2018). A pointer-generator network is a hybrid between an attention-based sequence-to-sequence model (Bahdanau et al., 2015) and a pointer network (Vinyals et al., 2015).

The standard pointer-generator network consists of a bidirectional LSTM (Hochreiter and Schmidhuber, 1997) encoder and a unidirectional LSTM decoder with a copy mechanism. Here, we follow (Sharma et al., 2018) and use two separate encoders: one for the lemma and one for the morphological tags. The decoder then computes the probability distribution of the output at each time step as a weighted sum of the probability distribution over the output vocabulary and the attention distribution over the input characters. The weights can be seen as the probability to generate or copy, respectively,

---

[3]We use the following implementation: https://github.com/abhishek0318/conll-sigmorphon-2018

Language	IMS-CUB		
	1	2-S	2-V
Basque	**25.00**	18.75	12.50
Bulgarian	97.73	**98.19**	97.28
English	96.39	**98.80**	**98.80**
Finnish	**99.04**	98.47	98.85
German	91.49	**93.39**	91.99
Kannada	91.47	**92.89**	91.00
Maltese	79.17	79.17	**85.42**
Navajo	0.00	75.00	**100.00**
Persian	95.56	94.81	**95.56**
Portuguese	93.81	**93.87**	93.74
Russian	92.15	93.02	**93.19**
Spanish	92.91	92.71	**93.52**
Swedish	93.48	**93.69**	93.27
Turkish	93.90	95.30	**95.68**

Table 2: Accuracy of our morphological inflection components on the development sets produced by the first three steps in our pipeline. We list both development and test languages.

and are computed by a feedforward network, given the last decoder hidden state. For details, we refer the reader to Sharma et al. (2018).

4 Experimental Setup

4.1 Data and Languages

The shared task organizers provide data for five development languages, for which development sets with gold solutions are given. Those languages – Maltese, Persian, Portuguese, Russian, Swedish – are not taken into account for the final evaluation.

The test languages, in contrast, are supposed to be only for system evaluation and do not come with developments sets. For those languages – Basque, Bulgarian, English, Finnish, German, Kannada, Navajo, Spanish, and Turkish – only a list of lemmas and a monolingual Bible (McCarthy et al., 2020) are given.

4.2 Evaluation Metric

The official evaluation metric of the shared task is BMAcc (Jin et al., 2020). Gold solutions are obtained from UniMorph (Kirov et al., 2018). Two versions of BMAcc exist: micro-averaged BMAcc and macro-averaged BMAcc. In this paper, we only report macro-averaged BMAcc, the official shared task metric.

During the development of our morphological generation systems, we use regular accuracy, the standard evaluation metric for morphological inflection (Cotterell et al., 2016).

4.3 Morphological Inflection Component

Morphological inflection data. We use the first three components of the baseline model, i.e., the ones performing edit tree retrieval, additional lemma retrieval, and paradigm size discovery, to create training and development data for our inflection models. Those datasets consist of lemma–inflection pairs found in the raw text, together with a number indicating the (predicted) paradigm slot, and are described in Table 1.

The test set for our morphological inflection systems consist of the lemma–paradigm slot pairs not found in the corpus.

Hyperparameters. For IMS-CUB1, we use an embedding size of 300, a hidden layer of size 100, a batch size of 20, Adadelta (Zeiler, 2012) for optimization, and a learning rate of 1. For each language, we train a system for 100 epochs, using early stopping with a patience of 10 epochs.

For IMS-CUB2, we follow two different approaches. The first is to use a single hyperparameter configuration for all languages (IMS-CUB2-S). The second consists of using a variable setup depending on the training set size (IMS-CUB2-V). For IMS-CUB2-S, we use an embedding size of 300, a hidden layer size of 100, a dropout rate of 0.3, and train for 60 epochs with an early-stopping patience of 10 epochs. We further use an Adam (Kingma and Ba, 2014) optimizer with an initial learning rate of 0.001.

For IMS-CUB2-V, we use the following hyperparameters for training set size T:

- $T < 101$: an embedding size of 100, a dropout coefficient of 0.5, 300 epochs of training, and an early-stopping patience of 100;

- $100 < T < 501$: an embedding size of 100, a dropout coefficient of 0.5, 80 training epochs, and an early-stopping patience of 20;

- $500 < T$: the same hyperparameters as for IMS-CUB2-S.

For IMS-CUB2, we select the best performing system (between IMS-CUB2-S and IMS-CUB2-V) as our final model. The models are evaluated on the morphological inflection task development set using accuracy. All scores are shown in Table 2.

| | BL | | KU-CST | | IMS-CUB | | NYU-CUB | | |
Language	1	2	1	2	1	2	1	2	3
Basque	0.06	0.06	0.02	0.01	0.04	00.06	0.05	0.05	**0.07**
Bulgarian	28.30	31.69	2.99	4.15	27.22	<u>**32.11**</u>	27.69	28.94	27.89
English	65.60	**66.20**	3.53	17.29	47.80	<u>61.00</u>	50.20	52.80	51.20
Finnish	05.33	**5.50**	0.39	2.08	04.90	<u>05.38</u>	5.36	5.47	05.35
German	28.35	**29.00**	0.70	4.98	24.60	<u>28.35</u>	27.30	27.35	27.35
Kannada	15.49	15.12	4.27	1.69	10.50	<u>**15.65**</u>	11.10	11.16	11.10
Navajo	3.23	**3.27**	0.13	0.20	0.33	<u>01.17</u>	0.40	0.43	0.43
Spanish	22.96	**23.67**	3.52	10.84	19.50	<u>22.34</u>	20.39	20.56	20.30
Turkish	14.21	**15.53**	0.11	0.71	13.54	14.73	14.88	<u>15.39</u>	15.13
Average	20.39	**21.12**	1.74	04.66	16.49	<u>20.09</u>	17.49	18.02	17.65

Table 3: Final performance (macro-average BMAcc in percentages) of all systems on all test languages. Best scores overall are in bold, and best scores of submitted systems are underlined.

4.4 Results

Table 3 shows the official test set results for IMS-CUB1 and IMS-CUB2, compared to the official baselines and all other submitted systems.

Our best system, IMS-CUB2, achieves the highest scores of all submitted systems (i.e., excluding the baselines), outperforming the second best submission by 2.07% BMAcc. However, BL-1 and BL-2 outperform IMS-CUB2 by 1.03% and 0.3%, respectively. Looking at the results for individual languages, IMS-CUB2 obtains the highest performance overall for Bulgarian (difference to the second best system 0.42%) and Kannada (difference to the second best system 0.53%). Comparing our two submissions, IMS-CUB1 underperforms IMS-CUB2 by 3.6%, showing that vanilla sequence-to-sequence models are not optimally suited for the task. We hypothesize that this could be due to the amount or the diversity of the generated morphological inflection training files.

As our systems rely on the output of the previous 3 steps of the baseline, only few training examples were available for Basque and Navajo: 85 and 17, respectively. Probably at least partially due to this fact, i.e., due to finding patterns in the raw text corpus being difficult, all systems obtain their lowest scores on these two languages. However, even though Finnish has 2306 training instances for morphological inflection, our best system surprisingly only reaches 5.38% BMAcc. The same happens in Kannada and Turkish: the inflection training set is relatively large, but the overall performance on unsupervised morphological paradigm completion is low. On the contrary, even though English has a relatively small training set (343 examples), the performance of IMS-CUB2 is highest for this language, with 66.20% BMAcc. We think that the quality of the generated inflection training set and the correctness of the predicted paradigm size of the languages are the main reasons behind these performance differences. Improving steps 1 to 3 in the overall pipeline thus seems important in order to achieve better results on the task of unsupervised morphological paradigm completion in the future.

5 Conclusion

In this paper, we described the IMS–CUBoulder submission to the SIGMORPHON 2020 shared task on unsupervised morphological paradigm completion. We explored two modifications of the official baseline system by substituting its inflection generation component with two alternative models. Thus, our final system performed 4 steps: edit tree retrieval, additional lemma retrieval, paradigm size discovery, and inflection generation. The last component was either an LSTM sequence-to-sequence model with attention (IMS-CUB1) or a pointer-generator network (IMS-CUB2). Although our systems could not outperform the official baselines on average, IMS-CUB2 was the best submitted system. It further obtained the overall highest performance for Bulgarian and Kannada.

Acknowledgments

Thanks to Arya McCarthy, Garrett Nicolai, and Mans Hulden for (co-)organizing this shared task, and to Huiming Jin, Liwei Cai, Chen Xia, and Yihui Peng for providing the baseline system! This project has benefited from financial support to MM by DAAD via a Doctoral Research Grant.

References

Malin Ahlberg, Markus Forsberg, and Mans Hulden. 2015. Paradigm classification in supervised learning of morphology. In *NAACL-HLT*, pages 1024–1029, Denver, Colorado. Association for Computational Linguistics.

Dzmitry Bahdanau, Kyunghyun Cho, and Yoshua Bengio. 2015. Neural machine translation by jointly learning to align and translate. In *International Conference on Learning Representations (ICLR)*.

Grzegorz Chrupała. 2008. *Towards a machine-learning architecture for lexical functional grammar parsing*. Ph.D. thesis, Dublin City University.

Ryan Cotterell, Christo Kirov, John Sylak-Glassman, Géraldine Walther, Ekaterina Vylomova, Arya D. McCarthy, Katharina Kann, Sebastian Mielke, Garrett Nicolai, Miikka Silfverberg, David Yarowsky, Jason Eisner, and Mans Hulden. 2018. The CoNLL–SIGMORPHON 2018 shared task: Universal morphological reinflection. In *Proceedings of the CoNLL–SIGMORPHON 2018 Shared Task: Universal Morphological Reinflection*, pages 1–27, Brussels. Association for Computational Linguistics.

Ryan Cotterell, Christo Kirov, John Sylak-Glassman, Géraldine Walther, Ekaterina Vylomova, Patrick Xia, Manaal Faruqui, Sandra Kübler, David Yarowsky, Jason Eisner, and Mans Hulden. 2017. CoNLL-SIGMORPHON 2017 shared task: Universal morphological reinflection in 52 languages. In *Proceedings of the CoNLL SIGMORPHON 2017 Shared Task: Universal Morphological Reinflection*, pages 1–30, Vancouver. Association for Computational Linguistics.

Ryan Cotterell, Christo Kirov, John Sylak-Glassman, David Yarowsky, Jason Eisner, and Mans Hulden. 2016. The SIGMORPHON 2016 shared Task—Morphological reinflection. In *Proceedings of the 14th SIGMORPHON Workshop on Computational Research in Phonetics, Phonology, and Morphology*, pages 10–22, Berlin, Germany. Association for Computational Linguistics.

Mathias Creutz. 2003. Unsupervised segmentation of words using prior distributions of morph length and frequency. In *ACL*, pages 280–287, Sapporo, Japan. Association for Computational Linguistics.

Mathias Creutz and Krista Lagus. 2007. Unsupervised models for morpheme segmentation and morphology learning. *ACM TSLP*, 4(1):3.

Markus Dreyer and Jason Eisner. 2011. Discovering morphological paradigms from plain text using a Dirichlet process mixture model. In *EMNLP*, pages 616–627, Edinburgh, Scotland, UK. Association for Computational Linguistics.

Greg Durrett and John DeNero. 2013. Supervised learning of complete morphological paradigms. In *NAACL-HLT*, pages 1185–1195, Atlanta, Georgia. Association for Computational Linguistics.

Alexander Erdmann, Micha Elsner, Shijie Wu, Ryan Cotterell, and Nizar Habash. 2020. The paradigm discovery problem. *arXiv preprint arXiv:2005.01630*.

John Goldsmith. 2001. Unsupervised learning of the morphology of a natural language. *Computational Linguistics*, 27(2):153–198.

Sepp Hochreiter and Jürgen Schmidhuber. 1997. Long short-term memory. *Neural computation*, 9(8):1735–1780.

Mans Hulden, Markus Forsberg, and Malin Ahlberg. 2014. Semi-supervised learning of morphological paradigms and lexicons. In *EACL*, pages 569–578, Gothenburg, Sweden. Association for Computational Linguistics.

Huiming Jin, Liwei Cai, Yihui Peng, Chen Xia, Arya D. McCarthy, and Katharina Kann. 2020. Unsupervised morphological paradigm completion. In *Proceedings of the 58th Annual Meeting of the Association for Computational Linguistics*. Association for Computational Linguistics.

Katharina Kann, Arya D. McCarthy, Garrett Nicolai, and Mans Hulden. 2020. The SIGMORPHON 2020 shared task on unsupervised morphological paradigm completion. In *Proceedings of the 17th SIGMORPHON Workshop on Computational Research in Phonetics, Phonology, and Morphology*. Association for Computational Linguistics.

Katharina Kann and Hinrich Schütze. 2016a. MED: The LMU system for the SIGMORPHON 2016 shared task on morphological reinflection. In *14th SIGMORPHON Workshop*, pages 62–70.

Katharina Kann and Hinrich Schütze. 2016b. Single-model encoder-decoder with explicit morphological representation for reinflection. In *Proceedings of the 54th Annual Meeting of the Association for Computational Linguistics (Volume 2: Short Papers)*, pages 555–560, Berlin, Germany. Association for Computational Linguistics.

Katharina Kann and Hinrich Schütze. 2017. The LMU system for the CoNLL-SIGMORPHON 2017 shared task on universal morphological reinflection. In *CoNLL SIGMORPHON 2017 Shared Task: Universal Morphological Reinflection*, pages 40–48, Vancouver. Association for Computational Linguistics.

Katharina Kann and Hinrich Schütze. 2018. Neural transductive learning and beyond: Morphological generation in the minimal-resource setting. In *Proceedings of the 2018 Conference on Empirical Methods in Natural Language Processing*, pages 3254–3264, Brussels, Belgium. Association for Computational Linguistics.

Diederik P Kingma and Jimmy Ba. 2014. Adam: A method for stochastic optimization. *arXiv preprint arXiv:1412.6980*.

Christo Kirov, Ryan Cotterell, John Sylak-Glassman, Géraldine Walther, Ekaterina Vylomova, Patrick Xia, Manaal Faruqui, Sabrina J. Mielke, Arya McCarthy, Sandra Kübler, David Yarowsky, Jason Eisner, and Mans Hulden. 2018. UniMorph 2.0: Universal morphology. In *Proceedings of the Eleventh International Conference on Language Resources and Evaluation (LREC 2018)*, Miyazaki, Japan. European Language Resources Association (ELRA).

M Paul Lewis. 2009. *Ethnologue: Languages of the world*. SIL international.

Peter Makarov and Simon Clematide. 2018. Imitation learning for neural morphological string transduction. In *Proceedings of the 2018 Conference on Empirical Methods in Natural Language Processing*, pages 2877–2882, Brussels, Belgium. Association for Computational Linguistics.

Arya D. McCarthy, Ekaterina Vylomova, Shijie Wu, Chaitanya Malaviya, Lawrence Wolf-Sonkin, Garrett Nicolai, Christo Kirov, Miikka Silfverberg, Sabrina J. Mielke, Jeffrey Heinz, Ryan Cotterell, and Mans Hulden. 2019. The SIGMORPHON 2019 shared task: Morphological analysis in context and cross-lingual transfer for inflection. In *Proceedings of the 16th Workshop on Computational Research in Phonetics, Phonology, and Morphology*, pages 229–244, Florence, Italy. Association for Computational Linguistics.

Arya D. McCarthy, Rachel Wicks, Dylan Lewis, Aaron Mueller, Winston Wu, Oliver Adams, Garrett Nicolai, Matt Post, and David Yarowsky. 2020. The johns hopkins university bible corpus: 1600+ tongues for typological exploration. In *Proceedings of The 12th Language Resources and Evaluation Conference*, pages 2884–2892, Marseille, France. European Language Resources Association.

Garrett Nicolai, Colin Cherry, and Grzegorz Kondrak. 2015. Inflection generation as discriminative string transduction. In *NAACL-HLT*, pages 922–931, Denver, Colorado. Association for Computational Linguistics.

Hoifung Poon, Colin Cherry, and Kristina Toutanova. 2009. Unsupervised morphological segmentation with log-linear models. In *NAACL-HLT*, pages 209–217. Association for Computational Linguistics.

Abigail See, Peter J. Liu, and Christopher D. Manning. 2017. Get to the point: Summarization with pointer-generator networks. In *ACL*, pages 1073–1083, Vancouver, Canada. Association for Computational Linguistics.

Abhishek Sharma, Ganesh Katrapati, and Dipti Misra Sharma. 2018. IIT(BHU)–IIITH at CoNLL–SIGMORPHON 2018 shared task on universal morphological reinflection. In *Proceedings of the CoNLL–SIGMORPHON 2018 Shared Task: Universal Morphological Reinflection*, pages 105–111, Brussels. Association for Computational Linguistics.

Oriol Vinyals, Meire Fortunato, and Navdeep Jaitly. 2015. Pointer networks. In *Advances in neural information processing systems*, pages 2692–2700.

David Yarowsky and Richard Wicentowski. 2000. Minimally supervised morphological analysis by multimodal alignment. In *ACL*, pages 207–216, Hong Kong. Association for Computational Linguistics.

Matthew D Zeiler. 2012. Adadelta: an adaptive learning rate method. *arXiv preprint arXiv:1212.5701*.

SIGMORPHON 2020 Task 0 System Description
ETH Zürich Team

Martina Forster[1] **Clara Meister**[1]
[1]ETH Zürich
`martfors@student.ethz.ch` `clara.meister@inf.ethz.ch`

Abstract

This paper presents our system for the SIG-MORPHON 2020 Shared Task. We build off of the baseline systems, performing exact inference on models trained on language family data. Our systems return the globally best solution under these models. Our two systems achieve 80.9% and 75.6% accuracy on the test set. We ultimately find that, in this setting, exact inference does not seem to help or hinder the performance of morphological inflection generators, which stands in contrast to its affect on Neural Machine Translation (NMT) models.

1 Introduction

Morphological inflection generation is the task of generating a specific word form given a lemma and a set of morphological tags. It has a wide range of applications—in particular, it can be useful for morphologically rich, but low-resource languages. If a language has complex morphology, but only scarce data are available, vocabulary coverage is often poor. In such cases, morphological inflection can be used to generate additional word forms for training data.

Typologically diverse morphological inflection is the focus of task 0 of the SIGMORPHON Shared Tasks (Vylomova et al., 2020), to which we submit this system. Specifically, the task requires the aforementioned transformation from lemma and morphological tags to inflected form. A main challenge of the task is that it covers a typologically diverse set of languages, i.e. languages have a wide range of structural patterns and features. Additionally, for a portion of these languages, only scant resources are available.

Our approach is to train models on language families rather than solely on individual languages. This strategy should help us overcome the problems frequently encountered for low-resource tasks, e.g.,

overfitting, by increasing the amount of training data used for each model. The strategy is viable due to the typological similarities between languages within the same family. We combine two of the neural baseline architectures provided by the task organizers, a multilingual Transformer (Wu et al., 2020) and a (neuralized) hidden Markov model with hard monotonic attention (Wu and Cotterell, 2019), albeit with a different decoding strategy: we perform exact inference, returning the globally optimal solution under the model.

2 Background

Neural character-to-character transducers (Faruqui et al., 2016; Kann and Schütze, 2016) define a probability distribution $p_\theta(\mathbf{y} \mid \mathbf{x})$, where θ is a set of weights learned by a neural network and $\mathbf{x}$ and $\mathbf{y}$ are inputs and (possible) outputs, respectively. In the case of morphological inflection, $\mathbf{x}$ represents the lemma we are trying to inflect and the morphosyntactic description (MSDs) indicating the inflection we desire; $\mathbf{y}$ is then a candidate inflected form of the lemma from the set of all valid character sequences $\mathcal{Y}$. Note that valid character sequences are padded with distinguished tokens, BOS and EOS, indicating the beginning and end of the sequence.

The neural character-to-character transducers we consider in this work are locally normalized. Specifically, the model p_θ is a probability distribution over the set of possible characters which models $p_\theta(\cdot \mid \mathbf{x}, \mathbf{y}_{<t})$ for any time step t. By the chain rule of probability, $p_\theta(\mathbf{y} \mid \mathbf{x})$ decomposes as

$$p_\theta(\mathbf{y} \mid \mathbf{x}) = \prod_{t=1}^{|\mathbf{y}|} p_\theta(y_t \mid \mathbf{x}, \mathbf{y}_{<t}) \qquad (1)$$

The decoding objective then aims to find the most probable sequence among all valid sequences:

Proceedings of the Seventeenth SIGMORPHON Workshop on Computational Research in Phonetics, Phonology, and Morphology, pages 106–110
Online, July 10, 2020. ©2020 Association for Computational Linguistics
https://doi.org/10.18653/v1/P17

$$\mathbf{y}^\star = \operatorname*{argmax}_{\mathbf{y} \in \mathcal{Y}} \log p_{\boldsymbol{\theta}}(\mathbf{y} \mid \mathbf{x}) \qquad (2)$$

This is known as maximum a posteriori (MAP) decoding. While the above optimization problem implies that we find the global optimum $\mathbf{y}^\star$, we often only perform a heuristic search, e.g., beam search, since performing exact search can be quite computationally expensive due to the size of $\mathcal{Y}$ and the dependency of $p_{\boldsymbol{\theta}}(\cdot \mid \mathbf{x}, \mathbf{y}_{<t})$ on all previous output tokens. For neural machine translation (NMT) specifically, while beam search often yields better results than greedy search, translation quality almost always decreases for beam sizes larger than 5. We refer the interested reader to the large number of works that have studied this phenomenon in detail (Koehn and Knowles, 2017; Murray and Chiang, 2018; Yang et al., 2018; Stahlberg and Byrne, 2019).

Exact decoding effectively stretches the beam size to infinity (i.e. does not limit it), finding the globally best solution. While the effects of exact decoding have been explored for neural machine translation (Stahlberg and Byrne, 2019), to the best of our knowledge, they have not yet been explored for morphological inflection generation. This is a natural research question as the architectures of morphological inflection generation systems are often based off of those for NMT.

3 Data

We use the data provided by the SIGMORPHON 2020 shared task, which features lemmas, inflections, and corresponding MSDs (following unimorph schema (Kirov et al., 2018)) for 90 languages in total. Data was released in two phases; the first phase included languages from five families: Austronesian, Niger-Congo, Uralic, Oto-Manguean, and Indo-European. Data from the second phase included languages belonging to Afro-Asiatic, Algic, Australian, Dravidian, Germanic, Indo-Aryan, Iranian, Niger-Congo, Nilo-Sahan, Romance, Sino-Tibetan, Siouan, Tungusic, Turkic, Uralic, and Uto-Aztecan families. The full list of languages can be found on the task website: `https://sigmorphon.github.io/sharedtasks/2020/task0/`.

Due to scarcity of resources available to the task organizers, many of the languages had only a few morphological forms annotated. For example, Zarma, a Songhay language, had only 56 available inflections in the training set and 9 in the development set.

4 System description

Our systems are built using two model architectures provided as baselines by the task organizers: a multilingual Transformer (Wu et al., 2020) and a (neuralized) hidden Markov model (HMM) with hard monotonic attention (Wu and Cotterell, 2019). We then perform exact inference on the models. The following subsections explain the two components separately.

4.1 Model Architectures

The architectures of both models exactly follow those of the Transformer and HMM proposed as baselines for the SIGMORPHON 2020 Task 0. We do this in part to create a clear comparison between morphological inflection generation systems that perform inference with exact vs. heuristic decoding strategies.

We trained HMMs for each language family for a maximum of 50 epochs and Transformers for a maximum of 20000 steps. Early stopping was performed if subsequent validation set losses differed by less than $1e-3$. Batch sizes of 30 and 100, respectively, were used. Other training configurations followed those of the baseline systems.

Due to the resource scarcity for many of the task's languages, we used entire language families to train models rather than individual languages. Specifically, we aggregated the data from all languages of a given family, using a cross-lingual learning approach. We did not subsequently fine-tune the models on individual languages. Specifically, we do not do any additional training on individual languages nor do we re-target the vocabulary during decoding. This means generation of invalid characters (i.e. invalid for a specific language) is possible.

4.2 Decoding

For decoding, we perform exact inference with a search strategy built on top of the SGNMT library (Stahlberg et al., 2017). Specifically, we use Dijkstra's search algorithm, which provably returns the optimal solution when path scores monotonically decrease with length. From equation 1, we can see that the scoring function for sequences $\mathbf{y}$ is monotonically decreasing in t, therefore meeting this criterion. Additionally, to prevent a large

	Greedy		Beam5	
	acc	dist	acc	dist
ang	0.720	0.52	0.726	0.48
azg	0.921	0.22	0.920	0.28
ceb	0.820	0.41	0.820	0.39
cly	0.764	0.44	0.762	0.50
cpa	0.846	0.22	0.845	0.23
czn	0.800	0.48	0.793	0.54
deu	0.977	0.03	0.976	0.03
dje	0.188	1.88	0.000	2.38

Table 1: Accuracy and Levenshtein distance on the test set for greedy and beam search with beam size 5 for HMMs.

	Greedy		Beam5	
	acc	dist	acc	dist
ang	0.574	0.76	0.578	0.75
azg	0.808	0.63	0.813	0.62
ceb	0.874	0.27	0.874	0.27
cly	0.653	0.72	0.657	0.71
cpa	0.651	0.52	0.653	0.52
czn	0.695	0.62	0.702	0.59
deu	0.883	0.19	0.882	0.19
dje	0.938	0.12	0.938	0.12

Table 2: Accuracy and Levenshtein distance on the test set for greedy and beam search with beam size 5 for Transformers.

memory footprint, we can lower bound the search by the score of the empty string, i.e. stop exploring solutions whose scores become less than the empty string at any point in time. We return the globally best inflection.

5 Results on the Shared Task test data

Results on the test data from SIGMORPHON 2020 Task 0 can be found in Table 3. For comparison purposes, Tables 1 and 2 show the performance of our models with greedy and beam search for a selection of languages.

5.1 Discussion

The results in Table 3 indicate that the HMM performed better in combination with exact decoding than the Transformer. On average over the 90 languages, the HMM achieved an accuracy of 80.9% in comparison to only 75.6% for the Transformer. Performance by Levenshtein distance looks similar: the average Levenshtein distances were 0.5 and 0.62 for the HMM and Transformer, respectively.

A particularly interesting language to study in this scenario is Zarma (dje), which only has 56 samples in the training set, 9 samples in the development set and 16 samples in the test set. Moreover, it is the only language in its family, Nilo-Sahan. The terrible performance of our system on this language compared with greedy search suggests that low-resource settings may lead to weak performance with exact decoding. Out of the other languages that performed poorly, many were from the Germanic and Uralic family. Poor performance on these languages may stem from the fact that they belong to a family with high-resource languages. As we trained on language family data and did not fine-tune the models, it is possible that lower-resource languages in a high-resource family, which are underrepresented in the training data, are not adequately modelled. In these setting, performance would likely be improve noticeably by fine-tuning on the individual languages.

6 Conclusion

We perform exact inference on two baseline neural architectures for morphological inflection, a Transformer and a (neuralized) hidden Markov model with hard monotonic attention, to find the inflections with the globally best score under the model. On test data, the hidden Markov model showed better results: on average, it achieved 80.9% accuracy and a Levenshtein distance of 0.5, while the Transformer performed worse with 75.6% and 0.62 respectively. Overall, exact decoding of morphological inflection generators does not appear to significantly affect model performance compared with greedy search. This is notable when compared with NMT systems, for which exact search often leads to performance degradation.

| | Our Systems | | | | Baselines | | | |
| | Transformer | | HMM | | Transformer | | HMM | |
language	acc	dist	acc	dist	acc	dist	acc	dist
aka	0.966	0.105	0.980	0.059	0.999	0.000	1.000	0.000
ang	0.569	0.770	0.715	0.512	0.683	0.540	0.719	0.640
ast	0.925	0.178	0.976	0.061	0.993	0.010	0.996	0.010
aze	0.833	0.342	0.786	0.410	0.813	0.340	0.727	0.880
azg	0.813	0.618	0.919	0.283	0.922	0.220	0.916	0.270
bak	0.961	0.080	0.921	0.133	0.993	0.010	0.960	0.290
ben	0.965	0.072	0.989	0.024	0.993	0.010	0.993	0.040
bod	0.828	0.235	0.838	0.213	0.844	0.200	0.832	0.220
cat	0.948	0.116	0.939	0.146	0.996	0.010	0.996	0.010
ceb	0.874	0.270	0.820	0.387	0.865	0.280	0.847	0.310
cly	0.657	0.713	0.762	0.487	0.800	0.390	0.799	0.500
cpa	0.650	0.526	0.841	0.232	0.776	0.320	0.864	0.200
cre	0.684	1.250	0.694	1.210	0.667	1.200	0.668	1.260
crh	0.963	0.045	0.971	0.042	0.977	0.030	0.969	0.060
ctp	0.339	1.523	0.525	1.167	0.441	1.310	0.527	1.970
czn	0.702	0.593	0.793	0.551	0.784	0.490	0.813	0.430
dak	0.955	0.097	0.933	0.145	0.956	0.080	0.929	0.160
dan	0.583	0.664	0.672	0.448	0.655	0.450	0.684	5.270
deu	0.882	0.188	0.976	0.033	0.935	0.100	0.984	0.040
dje	0.938	0.125	0.000	4.313	0.875	0.190	0.000	2.880
eng	0.943	0.128	0.958	0.083	0.954	0.090	0.963	0.080
est	0.604	0.996	0.872	0.432	0.880	0.270	0.882	0.480
evn	0.572	1.061	0.536	1.281	0.571	1.060	0.540	1.200
fas	0.999	0.001	0.999	0.001	1.000	0.000	0.999	0.000
fin	0.847	0.280	0.982	0.033	0.958	0.070	0.992	0.020
frm	0.963	0.102	0.986	0.092	0.995	0.010	0.995	0.010
frr	0.214	2.885	0.317	3.539	0.637	1.080	0.782	0.700
fur	0.951	0.075	0.614	0.829	0.994	0.010	0.974	0.120
gaa	0.793	0.746	0.828	0.426	1.000	0.000	1.000	0.000
glg	0.746	0.560	0.927	0.161	0.996	0.010	0.997	0.010
gmh	0.248	1.766	0.766	0.340	0.745	0.360	0.887	0.150
gml	0.106	2.447	0.494	1.267	0.502	1.150	0.537	2.070
gsw	0.722	0.766	0.873	0.244	0.803	0.370	0.888	0.550
hil	0.945	0.172	0.924	0.315	0.950	0.150	0.941	0.210
hin	1.000	0.001	1.000	0.000	1.000	0.000	1.000	0.000
isl	0.745	0.544	0.933	0.136	0.878	0.260	0.950	0.300
izh	0.107	2.357	0.223	1.616	0.563	0.830	0.683	0.790
kan	0.761	0.779	0.768	0.799	0.767	0.640	0.740	0.750
kaz	0.936	0.304	0.955	0.254	0.971	0.150	0.955	0.240
kir	0.953	0.073	0.970	0.064	0.976	0.040	0.976	0.040
kjh	0.875	0.229	0.900	0.138	0.992	0.010	0.921	0.100
kon	0.981	0.038	0.981	0.026	0.987	0.010	0.987	0.010
kpv	0.672	0.711	0.749	0.550	0.945	0.100	0.932	0.250
krl	0.831	0.309	0.964	0.072	0.948	0.080	0.971	0.050
lin	0.891	0.261	0.870	0.283	0.978	0.020	1.000	0.000
liv	0.286	1.893	0.646	0.721	0.603	0.880	0.713	2.230
lld	0.926	0.158	0.974	0.052	0.996	0.010	0.998	0.000
lud	0.220	2.207	0.390	1.573	0.415	1.230	0.512	1.050
lug	0.852	0.295	0.870	0.228	0.909	0.130	0.901	0.150
mao	0.667	0.667	0.524	1.071	0.619	0.710	0.548	0.930
mdf	0.578	1.094	0.692	0.781	0.910	0.200	0.891	0.310
mhr	0.616	1.135	0.724	0.833	0.866	0.250	0.838	0.350
mlg	0.984	0.024	0.984	0.016	1.000	0.000	0.984	0.020
mlt	0.935	0.093	0.890	0.170	0.935	0.090	0.873	0.250
mwf	0.887	0.279	0.779	0.500	0.896	0.270	0.608	0.920
myv	0.779	0.587	0.782	0.546	0.930	0.180	0.888	0.360
nld	0.880	0.210	0.971	0.054	0.961	0.070	0.980	0.040
nno	0.472	0.799	0.636	0.517	0.698	0.480	0.789	0.610
nob	0.661	0.659	0.674	0.630	0.752	0.470	0.748	0.680
nya	0.974	0.060	0.966	0.090	1.000	0.000	1.000	0.000
olo	0.795	0.372	0.896	0.185	0.876	0.200	0.930	0.130
ood	0.793	0.439	0.745	0.529	0.809	0.410	0.758	0.490
orm	0.990	0.020	0.978	0.049	0.990	0.010	0.975	0.040
ote	0.913	0.142	0.964	0.084	0.969	0.040	0.991	0.010
otm	0.793	0.592	0.955	0.130	0.915	0.240	0.981	0.050
pei	0.620	0.800	0.715	0.679	0.728	0.570	0.714	0.610
pus	0.888	0.280	0.878	0.315	0.898	0.260	0.886	0.380
san	0.906	0.185	0.915	0.183	0.931	0.140	0.910	0.210
sme	0.776	0.481	0.978	0.053	0.944	0.110	0.986	0.040
sna	0.965	0.094	0.961	0.103	1.000	0.000	1.000	0.000
sot	0.879	0.343	0.909	0.242	0.990	0.010	1.000	0.000
swa	1.000	0.000	1.000	0.000	1.000	0.000	1.000	0.000
swe	0.782	0.387	0.947	0.093	0.897	0.180	0.976	0.200
syc	0.916	0.084	0.901	0.099	0.900	0.100	0.898	0.100
tel	0.938	0.300	0.941	0.333	0.949	0.260	0.934	0.270
tgk	0.563	1.125	0.875	0.375	0.688	0.750	0.875	0.380
tgl	0.699	0.862	0.617	1.368	0.705	0.830	0.640	1.070
tuk	0.858	0.510	0.848	0.530	0.856	0.430	0.858	0.450
udm	0.796	0.525	0.840	0.400	0.970	0.060	0.959	0.110
uig	0.953	0.163	0.983	0.065	0.988	0.020	0.991	0.010
urd	0.987	0.023	0.991	0.016	0.991	0.020	0.991	0.080
uzb	0.991	0.028	0.991	0.067	0.995	0.020	0.995	0.020
vec	0.816	0.414	0.924	0.174	0.995	0.010	0.996	0.010
vep	0.666	0.636	0.800	0.357	0.781	0.330	0.805	0.340
vot	0.043	3.032	0.093	2.192	0.470	0.930	0.605	0.800
vro	0.175	2.583	0.233	1.689	0.233	1.640	0.388	1.320
xno	0.235	3.039	0.549	1.686	0.765	1.240	0.804	2.880
xty	0.842	0.360	0.875	0.360	0.868	0.330	0.882	0.470
zpv	0.724	0.750	0.789	0.535	0.816	0.410	0.803	1.500
zul	0.628	1.000	0.808	0.449	0.910	0.190	0.872	0.210
average	0.756	0.620	0.809	0.500	0.859	0.307	0.860	0.485
std.dev.	0.237	0.712	0.208	0.692	0.161	0.371	0.170	0.785

Table 3: Accuracy and Levenshtein distance for both of our systems, as well as for the baselines.

References

Manaal Faruqui, Yulia Tsvetkov, Graham Neubig, and Chris Dyer. 2016. Morphological inflection generation using character sequence to sequence learning. In *Proceedings of the 2016 Conference of the North American Chapter of the Association for Computational Linguistics: Human Language Technologies*, pages 634–643, San Diego, California. Association for Computational Linguistics.

Katharina Kann and Hinrich Schütze. 2016. Single-model encoder-decoder with explicit morphological representation for reinflection. In *Proceedings of the 54th Annual Meeting of the Association for Computational Linguistics (Volume 2: Short Papers)*, pages 555–560, Berlin, Germany. Association for Computational Linguistics.

Christo Kirov, Ryan Cotterell, John Sylak-Glassman, Géraldine Walther, Ekaterina Vylomova, Patrick Xia, Manaal Faruqui, Sabrina J. Mielke, Arya McCarthy, Sandra Kübler, David Yarowsky, Jason Eisner, and Mans Hulden. 2018. UniMorph 2.0: Universal morphology. In *Proceedings of the Eleventh International Conference on Language Resources and Evaluation (LREC 2018)*, Miyazaki, Japan. European Language Resources Association (ELRA).

Philipp Koehn and Rebecca Knowles. 2017. Six challenges for neural machine translation. In *Proceedings of the First Workshop on Neural Machine Translation*, pages 28–39, Vancouver. Association for Computational Linguistics.

Kenton Murray and David Chiang. 2018. Correcting length bias in neural machine translation. In *Proceedings of the Third Conference on Machine Translation: Research Papers*, pages 212–223, Brussels, Belgium. Association for Computational Linguistics.

Felix Stahlberg and Bill Byrne. 2019. On NMT search errors and model errors: Cat got your tongue? In *Proceedings of the 2019 Conference on Empirical Methods in Natural Language Processing and the 9th International Joint Conference on Natural Language Processing (EMNLP-IJCNLP)*, pages 3356–3362, Hong Kong, China. Association for Computational Linguistics.

Felix Stahlberg, Eva Hasler, Danielle Saunders, and Bill Byrne. 2017. SGNMT – a flexible NMT decoding platform for quick prototyping of new models and search strategies. In *Proceedings of the 2017 Conference on Empirical Methods in Natural Language Processing: System Demonstrations*, pages 25–30, Copenhagen, Denmark. Association for Computational Linguistics.

Ekaterina Vylomova, Jennifer White, Elizabeth Salesky, Sabrina J. Mielke, Shijie Wu, Edoardo Ponti, Rowan Hall Maudslay, Ran Zmigrod, Joseph Valvoda, Svetlana Toldova, Francis Tyers, Elena Klyachko, Ilya Yegorov, Natalia Krizhanovsky, Paula Czarnowska, Irene Nikkarinen, Andrej Krizhanovsky, Tiago Pimentel, Lucas Torroba Hennigen, Christo Kirov, Garrett Nicolai, Adina Williams, Antonios Anastasopoulos, Hilaria Cruz, Eleanor Chodroff, Ryan Cotterell, Miikka Silfverberg, and Mans Hulden. 2020. The SIGMORPHON 2020 Shared Task 0: Typologically diverse morphological inflection. In *Proceedings of the 17th SIGMORPHON Workshop on Computational Research in Phonetics, Phonology, and Morphology*.

Shijie Wu and Ryan Cotterell. 2019. Exact hard monotonic attention for character-level transduction. In *Proceedings of the 57th Annual Meeting of the Association for Computational Linguistics*, pages 1530–1537, Florence, Italy. Association for Computational Linguistics.

Shijie Wu, Ryan Cotterell, and Mans Hulden. 2020. Applying the transformer to character-level transduction. *CoRR*, abs/2005.10213.

Yilin Yang, Liang Huang, and Mingbo Ma. 2018. Breaking the beam search curse: A study of (re-)scoring methods and stopping criteria for neural machine translation. In *Proceedings of the 2018 Conference on Empirical Methods in Natural Language Processing*, pages 3054–3059, Brussels, Belgium. Association for Computational Linguistics.

KU-CST at the SIGMORPHON 2020 Task 2 on Unsupervised Morphological Paradigm Completion

Manex Agirrezabal and **Jürgen Wedekind**
Centre for Language Technology (CST)
University of Copenhagen
`manex.aguirrezabal@hum.ku.dk, jwedekind@hum.ku.dk`

Abstract

We present a model for the unsupervised discovery of morphological paradigms. The goal of this model is to induce morphological paradigms from the bible (raw text) and a list of lemmas. We have created a model that splits each lemma in a stem and a suffix, and then we try to create a plausible suffix list by considering lemma pairs. Our model was not able to outperform the official baseline, and there is still room for improvement, but we believe that the ideas presented here are worth considering.

1 Introduction

In this paper we describe our attempt to capture morphological paradigms totally from scratch (Kann et al., 2020) prepared for the task of morphological paradigm completion in the CoNLL–SIGMORPHON 2020 Shared Task. Computational morphology is not a new area and there is plenty of related work. Some years ago, this problem was commonly tackled using finite-state and two-level approaches, such as in Kaplan and Kay (1994), Beesley and Karttunen (2003), and Koskenniemi (1983). Recent works, on the other hand, rely mostly on statistical approaches, such as in Faruqui et al. (2016) and Kann and Schütze (2017).

There have been several Shared Tasks recently on morphological inflection (Cotterell et al., 2016, 2017, 2018; McCarthy et al., 2019). The task for this year is more complex, as we are asked to discover paradigms from scratch. This is an intriguing research area that could give us the chance of recovering dead languages that have only limited written resources. Several researchers have attempted to solve this task, such as Goldsmith et al. (2017), Jin et al. (2020), and Erdmann et al. (2020).

We present a pipeline that assumes that all morphological realizations in a paradigm (for each language) follow a fixed structure: `stem+suffix`.

Based on that logic, we look for the best candidates to compose the suffix inventory, we cluster them using K-means and after that, we join stems and suffixes. We employ language models to get the most natural outputs. The pipeline that we have developed does not contain any neural network component, but we contemplate it as a possibility to extend our work in the near future.

This paper is structured as follows: In the next section we introduce the task that we have worked on. We describe our approach in the third section. Afterwards, we show our results compared to the baseline model. To conclude, we discuss our results and provide possible future directions.

2 Task

In this competition there was one task that we had to perform. A computational system had to be built, which, given a raw text and a set of lemmas, it would return the complete list of paradigms for each verb. The computational model should be able to read a text like this,

The aircraft landed at the JFK airport. Other pilots decided to land in Philadelphia. As you may imagine, landing a plane is not an easy job, but imagination can help.

and extract morphological paradigms. In the shared task, a list of lemmas is also given as a starting point. This list of lemmas could include verbs like *land* and *imagine*.

In the case of the verb *land*, in the example above, it is pretty easy to get its inflections (*land*, *landed*, *landing*). This could, for example, be done with a Minimum Edit Distance based method and it is relatively easy, as there is no usage of *land* with the function of a noun. It gets slightly more complicated with the verb *imagine*, as a simple distance-based algorithm could fail, because it could find

Proceedings of the Seventeenth SIGMORPHON Workshop on Computational Research in Phonetics, Phonology, and Morphology, pages 111–116
Online, July 10, 2020. ©2020 Association for Computational Linguistics
https://doi.org/10.18653/v1/P17

imagination as a possible conjugation of the verb *imagine*.

2.1 Dataset

As one of the most widely extended resources is the bible, the organizers decided to consider it as the raw text input data. Together with the bible, a list of verbal lemmas was given. The languages for development were Maltese, Persian, Portuguese, Russian and Swedish. The languages for testing included the following: Basque, Bulgarian, English, Finnish, German, Kannada, Navajo, Spanish and Turkish.

3 Method

Our method has a very strong assumption, which oversimplifies the problem but it also gives the chance of recognizing some patterns. The assumption is that all lemmas and their inflections have the following form for all languages

$$STEM + SUFFIX \rightarrow STEM + SUFFIX'$$

as illustrated in the following examples for English and Spanish:

$play \rightarrow playing$	$play + \epsilon \rightarrow play + ing$
$jugar \rightarrow jugando$	$jug + ar \rightarrow jug + ando$

Pipeline

We use a pipeline that includes four different steps. These are described below.

3.1 Step 1

In the first step, for each lemma l in the lemma list L and each word w in the corpus/dictionary D, all possible splits $l_1^1 + l_2^{|l|}, l_1^2 + l_3^{|l|}, ..., l_1^{|l|} + \epsilon$, and $w_1^1 + w_2^{|w|}, w_1^2 + w_3^{|w|}, ..., w_1^{|w|} + \epsilon$ are generated. (We use v_i^j, with $0 \leq i \leq j \leq |v|$, to denote the substring $v_i..v_j$ of a string v.) We assume the stem (the hypothesized *STEM*) to be nonempty but allow the suffix to be empty. For the Spanish lemma *jugar* we thus get $j + ugar$, $ju + gar$, $jug + ar$, $juga + r$, and $jugar + \epsilon$.

3.2 Step 2

In the second step, we determine the inflections of the regular verbs of the language. These will be used for the estimation of the morphological richness r_m of the lemmas (verbs) in the third step. The morphological richness of the lemmas can be identified with the number of combinations of those tense, aspect, mood, and agreement features

that can be distinctively morphologically realized. Because the morphological richness of the lemmas (verbs) does not tend to vary much across the different lemmas (verbs), even if they inflect semi-irregularly or irregularly, we assume that each lemma has r_m different inflections. r_m thus provides an upper bound on the number of cells of the paradigms of the language/corpus.

For determining r_m we identify the inflections of the lemmas with regular inflection. First, we determine for each splitted lemma $l = r + s$ the number of potential inflections of the hypothesized stem r, that is $r + s'$, in D. This is the set $S_{r+s} = \{s' \mid r + s' \in D\}$. Then, for regularly inflecting lemmas, S_{r+s} will be large for the actual split but also for any split within the stem. This is illustrated for the German lemma *spielen* (play) with the actual split *spiel+en* below.

$$S_{spiele+n} = \{\epsilon, n\}$$
$$S_{spiel+en} = \{e, st, t, en, ...\}$$
$$S_{spie+len} = \{le, lst, lt, len, ...\}$$

To accommodate for this deficiency, we also consider pairs of splitted lemmas $l = r + s$, $l' = r' + s$ with distinct stem endings $r_{|r|} \neq r'_{|r'|}$ and we determine the split $\hat{i}$ of s that yields the maximum number of common inflections:

$$\hat{i} = \max_{i \in \{0,...,|s|\}} |S_{rs_0^i + s_{i+1}^{|s|}} \cap S_{r's_0^{i-1} + s_i^{|s|}}|$$

We choose for each lemma pair l, l' the splits $\hat{r} + \hat{s}$ and $\hat{r}' + \hat{s}$, with $\hat{r} = rs_0^{\hat{i}}$, $\hat{r}' = r's_0^{\hat{i}}$, and $\hat{s} = s_{i+1}^{|s|}$, and consider their common suffixes in D: $S_{\hat{r}+\hat{s}} \cap S_{\hat{r}'+\hat{s}}$.

Because regularly inflecting verbs tend to share their inflections, this lemma pairing allows us to reliably predict that, for example, the stems of *spielen* and *gehen* are *spiel* and *geh*.

$$S_{spiele+n} \cap S_{gehe+n} = \{\epsilon, n\}$$
$$S_{spiel+en} \cap S_{geh+en} = \{e, st, t, en, ...\}$$
$$S_{spie+len} \cap S_{ge+hen} = \emptyset$$

Finally, for all splitted lemmas $\hat{r} + \hat{s}$ we collect the suffixes in $S_{\hat{r}+\hat{s}}$ in one bag.

3.3 Step 3

The goal of this step is to group different realizations of the same suffix. The previous step captures relevant suffixes, but in some cases, some parts of the stem are also included in these suffixes, or there might be some slight differences, because of morphophonological changes. In order to group them, we employ K-Means.

When using K-means we need a function that calculates the distance between the elements, and based on this distance, the instances will be clustered. We decided to employ a modified version of Minimum Edit Distance. Our modified version tries to punish changes that are made at the end of the suffix. The assumption in this case, is that changes at the beginning of the suffix are more likely to be caused by the stem (and they could be the same suffix). On the other hand, if there are changes at the end, it would be a different suffix. Our edit distance algorithm allows insertion and deletion as possible changes. We also assume that it is worse to substitute a vowel with a consonant, than changing a vowel with a vowel. Therefore, this would happen:

Distance (*era*, *bra*) > Distance (*era*, *ara*)

	ntar	*ntaron*	*aron*	*ar*
ntar	0.000	0.939	0.778	0.094
ntaron	-	0.000	0.015	0.832
aron	-	-	0.000	0.656
ar	-	-	-	0.000

We estimate that the number of paradigms (r_m) in a language is approximately the third of the number of different suffixes found in the previous step. This number was estimated based on the behaviour of the model considering Swedish data. Therefore, K-means will reduce the number of possible suffixes to the third (this is a parameter that will be tuned in the future). For example, one of the clustered groups found in this step considering the Spanish data would be this: {*rá, erá, derá, ará, irá*}. This corresponds to the suffix of future simple, third person singular.

3.4 Step 4

In the previous steps we will have generated possible suffixes for each cell in a paradigm. Now, the goal is to make a guess of how a word form should be generated. For example, in Spanish, if we have the lemma *sanar*, and we want to build the first person singular of the future simple tense (*sanaré*), we could expect the lemma to be combined with suffixes like *é, ré, aré, iré*, and so on. These suffixes would be the output of the previous step.

First of all, for each lemma, the model needs to decide the position in which we will split the lemma, as following the previous assumption a word will have this shape: *STEM+SUFFIX*. In order make that decision, we check how often we associate each lemma with a specific stem in the

output of step 2, and use the most frequently occurring stem for all the suffixes. For example, for the verb *sanar*, in Spanish, we get these frequencies: `san:15`, `sana:21`, `sa:1`, and therefore, we would use the stem *sana*.

We, then, try to join that stem with the clustered suffixes. Each stem will be joined with one suffix from each cluster. In order to decide which is the best suffix, we use a bigram character-level language model to estimate the probability of the output sequences, trained on the input bible. These are the probabilities that we get if we consider the example of the stem *sana* (from *sanar*) and suffixes *é, ré, aré* and *iré* in Spanish.

Candidate output	Probability
sanaé	0.0
sanaré	$4.097e-07$
sanaaré	$1.272e-10$
sanairé	$2.201e-10$

Obviously, in this case, the conjugation *sanaré* would be returned.

3.5 Expansion of the lemma list

At this point, the model produced a little amount of suffixes. Then, we decided to extend the list of input lemmas, so that it can find new suffixes and increase, therefore, the recall of the model.

We obtain new lemmas by training a very simple verb classifier. We create a simple dataset with the input lemmas and some random words from the corpus. The input lemmas will be tagged as verbs and the random words will be tagged as non-verbs. We, then, train a simple Logistic Regression model, using character uni-, bi- and trigrams for representing each word. We also include word boundary symbols. For instance, in Spanish we would have cases like:

Word	Features (trigrams)	class
comer	`<co, com, ome, mer, me>`	V
plaza	`<pl, pla, laz, aza, za>`	NV

Using this approach we obtain new verbs that can be used in our Pipeline. The model that uses the extended list of lemmas for extracting suffixes is called the **Flexible model**, and on the other hand, the initial model (the one that uses only the initial lemmas as input) is called the **Non-flexible model**.

4 Results

Table 1 and table 2 show our models performance for the development languages and also the test

Language	Development languages						
	Gold	Baseline		Non-flexible model		Flexible model	
	no. of slots	no. of slots	macro	no. of slots	macro	no. of slots	macro
Maltese	32	17	0.2029	2	0.013	254	0.0022
Persian	136	31	0.0605	2	0.0074	11	0.0155
Portuguese	76	34	0.3964	70	0.1275	1104	0.0109
Russian	16	19	0.4132	10	0.0706	387	0.0035
Swedish	11	15	0.4167	17	0.2282	588	0.0093

Table 1: Macro average results and the number of predicted slots for the Baseline model together with our Non-flexible and Flexible models, tested on development languages.

Language	Test languages						
	Gold	Baseline		Non-flexible model		Flexible model	
	no. of slots	no. of slots	macro	no. of slots	macro	no. of slots	macro
Basque	1658	27	0.0006	2	0.0001	30	0.0002
Bulgarian	54	34	0.3169	13	0.0415	138	0.0299
English	5	4	0.662	7	0.1729	51	0.0353
Finnish	141	21	0.055	108	0.0208	1169	0.0039
German	20	9	0.29	40	0.0498	425	0.007
Kannada	57	172	0.1512	1	0.0169	44	0.0427
Navajo	30	3	0.0327	2	0.002	38	0.0013
Spanish	70	29	0.2367	40	0.1084	225	0.0352
Turkish	120	104	0.1553	502	0.0071	1772	0.0011

Table 2: Macro average results and the number of predicted slots for the Baseline model together with our Non-flexible and Flexible models, tested on test languages.

languages. Unfortunately, we could not surpass the baseline model in any of the languages. We can say that among the development language results, Portuguese and Swedish are the ones that are best captured by the Non-flexible model. Considering the test languages, Spanish and English are the ones that were best modeled by the Non-flexible model.

It also seems that while the flexible model might have a better recall, the obtained result is not good enough, and therefore, it still requires some filtering.

5 Discussion and Future Work

We have presented our approach for automatically discovering morphological paradigms, given a text and list of lemmas. As mentioned above, our results are behind the official baseline, and therefore, there is a wide range of possibilities for improvement. We discuss some of them below.

We assumed each inflected form to be decomposable into a stem and a suffix. This could be, for example, sufficient for English or Spanish, but not for languages such as German that follow a two splits pattern:

$$STEM + SUFFIX \rightarrow PREFIX + STEM + SUFFIX'$$

In German, for example, participles are formed by prefixing ge:

$$
\begin{array}{l|l}
play \rightarrow played & play + \epsilon \rightarrow play + ed \\
spielen \rightarrow gespielt & spiel + en \rightarrow ge + spiel + t
\end{array}
$$

Apart from that, a much more straightforward estimate of the morphological richness r_m could, for example, be obtained by just considering the triple $l^1 = \hat{r}^1 + s$, $l^2 = \hat{r}^2 + s$, $l^3 = \hat{r}^3 + s$ of optimally splitted distinct lemmas with the maximum number of common suffixes. Because these lemmas are most likely to be frequently used lemmas with regular inflection, the size of the union of their inflections would presumably yield a good estimate of r_m. Clustering of these triples could also help in identifying verb classes with distinct but regular inflection.

Moreover, splitting of compound verbs of the form X+V, with X typically a noun or verb, would certainly improve performance because the inflections of the verb V could be used for the typically less frequent compound verb X+V.

With respect to the writing system, the Basque bible follows old orthographical rules. On the other hand, the lemmas were written following more recent orthography rules. This lack of consistency makes the task a challenge, and we expect it to happen in other languages as well. This issue requires special attention, by maybe applying some preprocessing to the lemmas to accommodate to the old writing system (Etxeberria et al., 2019).

Also, we mentioned at the beginning of the article that we have not used any neural network based component, and these would be very useful for learning the morphophonological changes that commonly happen when inflecting words. Therefore, we would like to incorporate a Sequence-to-Sequence model at the end of our pipeline (Sutskever et al., 2014; Bahdanau et al., 2015; Vaswani et al., 2017).

Acknowledgments

We acknowledge the anonymous reviewers for their relevant comments and possible extra future directions, and also the organizers of the CoNLL–SIGMORPHON 2020 Shared Task for giving us the opportunity of participating in such a challenging task.

References

Dzmitry Bahdanau, Kyunghyun Cho, and Yoshua Bengio. 2015. Neural machine translation by jointly learning to align and translate. In *3rd International Conference on Learning Representations, ICLR 2015, San Diego, CA, USA, May 7-9, 2015*.

Kenneth R. Beesley and Lauri Karttunen. 2003. *Finite-state Morphology: Xerox Tools and Techniques*. CSLI, Stanford University.

Ryan Cotterell, Christo Kirov, John Sylak-Glassman, Géraldine Walther, Ekaterina Vylomova, Arya D. McCarthy, Katharina Kann, Sabrina J. Mielke, Garrett Nicolai, Miikka Silfverberg, David Yarowsky, Jason Eisner, and Mans Hulden. 2018. The CoNLL–SIGMORPHON 2018 shared task: Universal morphological reinflection. In *Proceedings of the CoNLL–SIGMORPHON 2018 Shared Task: Universal Morphological Reinflection*, pages 1–27, Brussels. Association for Computational Linguistics.

Ryan Cotterell, Christo Kirov, John Sylak-Glassman, Géraldine Walther, Ekaterina Vylomova, Patrick Xia, Manaal Faruqui, Sandra Kübler, David Yarowsky, Jason Eisner, and Mans Hulden. 2017. CoNLL-SIGMORPHON 2017 shared task: Universal morphological reinflection in 52 languages. In *Proceedings of the CoNLL SIGMORPHON 2017 Shared Task: Universal Morphological Reinflection*, pages 1–30, Vancouver. Association for Computational Linguistics.

Ryan Cotterell, Christo Kirov, John Sylak-Glassman, David Yarowsky, Jason Eisner, and Mans Hulden. 2016. The SIGMORPHON 2016 shared Task—Morphological reinflection. In *Proceedings of the 14th SIGMORPHON Workshop on Computational Research in Phonetics, Phonology, and Morphology*, pages 10–22, Berlin, Germany. Association for Computational Linguistics.

Alexander Erdmann, Micha Elsner, Shijie Wu, Ryan Cotterell, and Nizar Habash. 2020. The Paradigm Discovery Problem. *arXiv preprint arXiv:2005.01630*.

Izaskun Etxeberria, Iñaki Alegria, and Larraitz Uria. 2019. Weighted finite-state transducers for normalization of historical texts. *Natural Language Engineering*, 25(2):307–321.

Manaal Faruqui, Yulia Tsvetkov, Graham Neubig, and Chris Dyer. 2016. Morphological inflection generation using character sequence to sequence learning. In *Proceedings of the 2016 Conference of the North American Chapter of the Association for Computational Linguistics: Human Language Technologies*, pages 634–643, San Diego, California. Association for Computational Linguistics.

John A Goldsmith, Jackson L Lee, and Aris Xanthos. 2017. Computational learning of morphology. *Annual Review of Linguistics*, 3:85–106.

Huiming Jin, Liwei Cai, Yihui Peng, Chen Xia, Arya D. McCarthy, and Katharina Kann. 2020. Unsupervised morphological paradigm completion. In *Proceedings of the 58th Annual Meeting of the Association for Computational Linguistics*. Association for Computational Linguistics.

Katharina Kann, Arya D. McCarthy, Garrett Nicolai, and Mans Hulden. 2020. The SIGMORPHON 2020 shared task on unsupervised morphological paradigm completion. In *Proceedings of the 17th SIGMORPHON Workshop on Computational Research in Phonetics, Phonology, and Morphology*. Association for Computational Linguistics.

Katharina Kann and Hinrich Schütze. 2017. The LMU system for the CoNLL-SIGMORPHON 2017 Shared Task on Universal Morphological Reinflection. In *Proceedings of the CoNLL SIGMORPHON 2017 Shared Task: Universal Morphological Reinflection*, pages 40–48.

Ronald M. Kaplan and Martin Kay. 1994. Regular Models of Phonological Rule Systems. *Computational Linguistics*, 20(3):331–378.

Kimmo Koskenniemi. 1983. Two-level morphology: A general computational model for word-form production and generation. *Publications of the Department of General Linguistics, University of Helsinki.*

Arya D. McCarthy, Ekaterina Vylomova, Shijie Wu, Chaitanya Malaviya, Lawrence Wolf-Sonkin, Garrett Nicolai, Christo Kirov, Miikka Silfverberg, Sabrina J. Mielke, Jeffrey Heinz, Ryan Cotterell, and Mans Hulden. 2019. The SIGMORPHON 2019 shared task: Morphological analysis in context and cross-lingual transfer for inflection. In *Proceedings of the 16th Workshop on Computational Research in Phonetics, Phonology, and Morphology*, pages 229–244, Florence, Italy. Association for Computational Linguistics.

Ilya Sutskever, Oriol Vinyals, and Quoc V Le. 2014. Sequence to sequence learning with neural networks. In *Advances in Neural Information Processing Systems*, pages 3104–3112.

Ashish Vaswani, Noam Shazeer, Niki Parmar, Jakob Uszkoreit, Llion Jones, Aidan N Gomez, Lukasz Kaiser, and Illia Polosukhin. 2017. Attention is all you need. In *Advances in Neural Information Processing Systems*, pages 5998–6008.

Low-Resource G2P and P2G Conversion
with Synthetic Training Data

Bradley Hauer, Amir Ahmad Habibi, Yixing Luan, Arnob Mallik, Grzegorz Kondrak
Department of Computing Science
University of Alberta, Edmonton, Canada
{bmhauer,amirahmad,yixing1,amallik,gkondrak}@ualberta.ca

Abstract

This paper presents the University of Alberta systems and results in the SIGMORPHON 2020 Task 1: Multilingual Grapheme-to-Phoneme Conversion. Following previous SIGMORPHON shared tasks, we define a low-resource setting with 100 training instances. We experiment with three transduction approaches in both standard and low-resource settings, as well as on the related task of phoneme-to-grapheme conversion. We propose a method for synthesizing training data using a combination of diverse models.

1 Introduction

In this system paper, we discuss the participation of the University of Alberta team in the SIGMORPHON 2020 Task 1: Multilingual Grapheme-to-Phoneme Conversion (Gorman et al., 2020). This is a sequence-to-sequence transduction task, in which a word, represented by a sequence of graphemes, must be converted into the sequence of phonemes representing its pronunciation. For example, given the French word *connaissent* the correct output is the phoneme sequence [k ɔ n ɛ s].

Following previous SIGMORPHON shared tasks, in addition to the standard setting with 3600 training examples for each language (which we refer to as the high-resource setting), we define a low-resource setting in which training data is limited to 100 examples. This emulates a plausible scenario of working with a low-resource language for which only a small quantity of reliable phonological data is available. For example, a typical IPA description of the phonological inventory of a single language contains about a hundred phonetic transcriptions of individual words (IPA, 1999). We analyze the relative performance of different systems depending on the size of the training data.

The task of phoneme-to-grapheme (P2G) conversion is the inverse of grapheme-to-phoneme Con-

version (G2P), in which the goal is to predict the spelling of a word given its phonetic transcription (Rentzepopoulos and Kokkinakis, 1996). While G2P reflects the difficulty of reading, P2G may indicate the complexity of writing in a given language. Training instances for one of the two tasks can easily be applied to the other one by simply reversing the input and output. We use the shared task datasets to investigate how systems designed for G2P perform on P2G. We also leverage raw text corpora to improve the accuracy on P2G, which indirectly leads to improvements on G2P as well.

We develop a novel method of mitigating resource limitations by synthesizing additional training data using a combination of multiple G2P and P2G models. The underlying intuition is that a P2G model should be the inverse of the corresponding G2P model. Since models trained on a small number of instances tend to have limited accuracy, we attempt to distinguish between the correct and incorrect predictions by ensuring that P2G model output matches the corresponding G2P model input. The precision of this approach is further improved by comparing predictions of different systems. Figure 1 illustrates this idea.

The principal contributions of this paper include a novel G2P data augmentation method that leverages multiple systems and text corpora, as well as a thorough comparison of several G2P and P2G systems in both low-resource and high-resource settings.

2 Prior Work

Our methods build upon the prior work of the University of Alberta teams on string transduction. DirecTL, a feature-based discriminative transducer, was originally designed for the G2P task (Jiampojamarn et al., 2008). In DirecTL+ (Jiampojamarn et al., 2010), the feature set was augmented with

Proceedings of the Seventeenth SIGMORPHON Workshop on Computational Research
in Phonetics, Phonology, and Morphology, pages 117–122
Online, July 10, 2020. ©2020 Association for Computational Linguistics
https://doi.org/10.18653/v1/P17

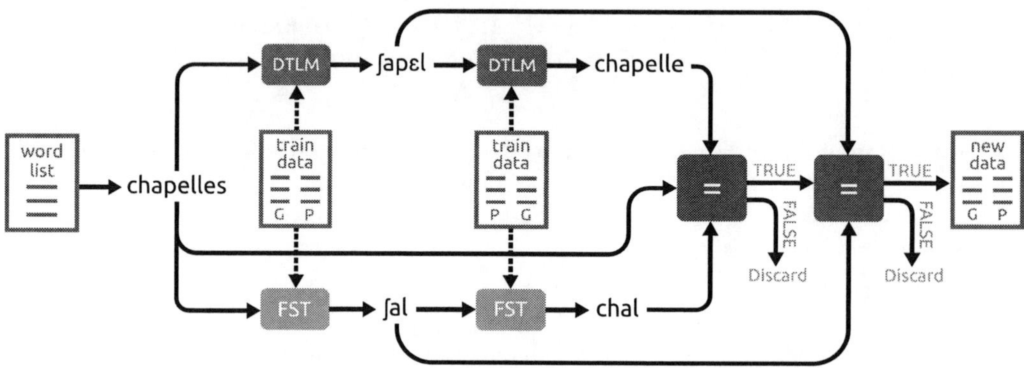

Figure 1: Our approach to synthesizing additional G2P training data.

joint n-grams defined on both source and target substrings. The system was applied to related tasks such as transliteration (Jiampojamarn et al., 2009), morphological inflection (Nicolai et al., 2015), stemming (Nicolai and Kondrak, 2016), and cognate projection (Hauer et al., 2019), proving to be particularly competitive in low-resource settings. DTLM (Nicolai et al., 2018), our principal tool in this work, is a successor of DirecTL+, which incorporates target-side language models and a high-precision alignment. DTLM achieved state-of-the-art results on several tasks in which plain word types constitute the transduction target strings. Finally, our data augmentation approach is inspired by the self-training approach of Hauer et al. (2017).

3 Methods

In this section, we first describe DTLM, a multi-purpose string discriminative transduction system which we apply to both G2P and P2G tasks. We then introduce our approach to synthesizing additional training data from unannotated texts.

3.1 Discriminative String Transduction

The core of DTLM, adapted from DirecTL+, is a dynamic programming algorithm which uses a set of feature templates to transduce multiple characters in a single operation. The feature set includes context features (n-grams on the source side), transition features (target side bigrams), linear-chain features (conjunction of context and transition features), and joint n-gram features (on both source and target).

The transduction quality of DTLM depends on a high precision one-to-many alignment, which is performed with M2M+ aligner (Jiampojamarn

et al., 2007) in a two-step process. In the first step, M2M+ induces a one-to-one alignment in which null symbols may be inserted on either side. In the second step, the null links on the source side are removed by merging adjacent target symbols.

The accuracy of DTLM can be enhanced by leveraging target character and word language models. A 4-gram character languages model, which is induced from a set of word types extracted from a text corpus, encourages the prediction of high-probability letter sequences. A unigram word language model (which we also refer to as *word counts*) biases DTLM toward the production of known word-forms, with more common words and prefixes being preferred. Thus, DTLM is able to take advantage of existing multi-lingual text corpora, such as Wikipedia, to improve its accuracy on P2G. Since we have no access to any corpora of phonetic transcriptions, the language model component is not used for G2P.

3.2 Data Augmentation

Inspired by the data hallucination technique for neural model training (Silfverberg et al., 2017; Anastasopoulos and Neubig, 2019), we introduce a method to synthesize additional training instances from unannotated texts. For each language under consideration, we train base transduction models on the available training data, and extract a list of words from a text corpus. A naive self-training approach would be to simply apply a base G2P model to the words in the list to produce new training instances. However, without some mechanism to filter out incorrect predictions, a model trained on the augmented data would learn to replicate many of the errors made by the base model. Instead, we reduce the noise by cross-checking the predictions of the independent base transduction systems applied in both directions.

Figure 1 illustrates the data augmentation process. For each word in the word list, we perform multiple sanity checks before accepting a new training instance. First, both G2P models (in this case, DTLM and FST) must agree on their phoneme predictions. Second, when applied to the common G2P prediction, the corresponding base P2G models must not only agree, but also output the original orthographic word. If both G2P models predict the same phoneme sequence, and both P2G models recover the original grapheme sequence, that grapheme–phoneme pair is added to the synthetic training data. The final augmented model is trained on the combined original and synthetic data.

4 Development

In this section, we describe our development experiments on both G2P and P2G with three different transduction systems and the synthetic training data.

4.1 Datasets

We created low-resource datasets of 100 instances from each standard (high-resource) training set of 3600 instances (Lee et al., 2020). We extracted every 36th instance, starting from the first instance, in a deterministic manner, to ensure replicability. The P2G datasets were created by swapping the grapheme and phoneme strings in the task datasets. The official development sets of 450 instances were used for model tuning only.

4.2 Task Baselines

The task organizers provided implementations of three baseline systems, which are referred to as FST, LSTM, and TRANSFORMER. These are not baselines in the traditional sense of "the simplest possible algorithm" (Manning and Schutze, 2001, page 234), but rather sophisticated systems capable of achieving state-of-the-art results on related tasks. Rather than develop a novel competitive approach, our goal was to combine the unmodified baselines and DTLM to achieve a relative improvement with respect to the individual systems.

As our neural base system, we selected TRANSFORMER, an encoder-decoder architecture with fully-connected layers and self-attention mechanism, which was originally developed for machine

Language	DTLM	-LM	-WC	-LM -WC
Dutch	21.6	25.6	25.1	29.8
French	28.2	28.4	48.4	52.2
Greek	33.1	40.9	52.0	59.6

Table 1: WER for variants of DTLM on P2G development sets in the standard (high-resource) setting.

translation (Vaswani et al., 2017). Our choice of TRANSFORMER over LSTM was based on initial development experiments.[1] The system is implemented using the Fairseq toolkit (Ott et al., 2019).

Unlike FST, which only needs to be tuned on the size of n-grams, TRANSFORMER requires extensive tuning which may take several days to complete. We attempted to follow the tuning guidelines as they became available. We kept the hyperparameters as specified in the source code, with the maximum number of training epochs set to 400. The tuning was performed separately for each language in terms of word error rate (WER). We trained the models on two Nvidia Titan RTX GPUs, using Adam optimizer. We varied dropout probability between 0.1, 0.2, and 0.3. and batch size between 256, 512, and 1024 in the high-resource setting, and 64 in the low-resource setting. Due to the underspecification in the guidelines, instead of tuning the number of epochs, we took the model checkpoint of the last epoch.

Unfortunately, we were ultimately unsuccessful in replicating the official results of TRANSFORMER. The implementation used for producing the official results was not available at the system submission time, and used different hyperparameter settings.[2]

4.3 DTLM and P2G

DTLM was our principal system for both G2P and P2G. The models were tuned on the official development sets separately for each task (G2P and P2G), language, and setting (high-resource and low-resource). The context size was varied from 1 to 3 in low-resource, and from 2 to 7 in high-resource settings. We also varied joint n-gram features from 1 to 6, and Markov order from 0 to 2, with and without linear chain features.

For P2G models, we extracted word frequency lists for each language from the first one million

---

[1]However, the official baseline results, show LSTM as more accurate than TRANSFORMER on most languages. The model results and predictions were not available at the system submission time.

[2]Unlike the earlier implementation that we used, it tuned the number of training epochs without a fixed maximum.

lines of Wikipedia[3], excluding words with frequency less than 10, shorter than 4 characters, or containing non-alphabetic characters. From the word lists, we generated 4-gram character language models using the CMU Toolkit[4]. Target language models are not used for the G2P task because of the lack of phonetic transcription corpora.

Table 1 demonstrates the impact of word counts (WC) and character language models (LM) on P2G accuracy. The results on three challenging languages suggest that most of the DTLM advantage comes from leveraging monolingual text corpora. Furthermore, word counts help more than character LMs. Without those two components, DTLM results on P2G in the standard (high-resource) setting were in the same range as FST and TRANSFORMER.

4.4 Synthetic Training Data

For our data augmentation approach outlined in Section 3.2, we required base G2P and P2G transduction systems. We preferred FST and DTLM over TRANSFORMER, as they performed better on small training datasets in terms of both accuracy and speed. Although data augmentation could also be applied to P2G, we used it exclusively for G2P, which is the primary focus of this shared task.

The starting point for generating the synthetic training data were the word lists extracted from Wikipedia, as described in Section 4.3. We applied the base models to the lists, and filtered out the instances on which the models disagreed or failed to recover the original spelling from their own phonetic predictions. We further limited the number of synthetic training instances to 20,000 per language. This process failed to produce a substantial number of new instances for Vietnamese and Korean, which we attribute to the unusual characteristics of the two scripts.

The data augmentation approach was successful in our development experiments on the standard high-resource datasets, reducing the average WER with respect to base TRANSFORMER from 17.0% to 16.0%, We obtained improvements on 13 out of 15 languages, with the exception of Bulgarian and Korean.[5]

---

[3] https://dumps.wikimedia.org

[4] http://www.speech.cs.cmu.edu/SLM

[5] Only 36% of the graphemes in the Korean test set are observed in the low-resource train set. The corresponding number in Japanese is 90%.

Language	High Resource			Low Resource		
	DTLM	FST	TF	DTLM	FST	TF
Adyghe	18.2	16.7	21.3	53.1	56.0	87.8
Armenian	4.9	5.1	8.0	14.0	27.3	80.7
Bulgarian	6.0	6.4	8.4	20.9	28.7	83.8
Dutch	23.8	27.3	21.1	34.0	66.7	90.4
French	28.7	50.4	51.3	51.6	72.4	94.0
Georgian	1.1	0.7	1.1	4.4	6.4	74.7
Greek	32.9	59.6	56.9	41.3	89.1	97.6
Hindi	3.8	12.0	15.1	18.0	45.8	86.9
Hungarian	4.0	6.9	8.0	14.9	28.7	81.8
Icelandic	13.6	12.0	15.6	28.0	45.6	82.4
Japanese	4.4	9.8	3.6	61.1	59.3	97.8
Korean	39.1	50.0	32.7	96.7	97.3	100
Lithuanian	4.0	3.6	3.3	15.1	25.8	75.1
Romanian	1.8	1.3	2.9	17.8	15.6	57.3
Vietnamese	16.2	18.4	16.2	71.8	85.6	96.9
Average	**13.5**	**18.7**	**17.7**	**36.2**	**50.0**	**85.8**

Table 2: WER on P2G test sets.

5 Test Results

Table 2 shows the P2G results on the test sets. All models are trained on the same training sets, without any synthesized instances. TRANSFORMER (TF) completely fails with only 100 training instances (low resource), but outperforms FST with 3600 training instances (high resource).[6] DTLM is substantially more accurate on average than the other two systems in both settings. Although DTLM benefits from information extracted from freely-available unannotated text corpora, the results of the three systems are directly comparable because they all use the same annotated training material. This further confirms the claim of Nicolai et al. (2018) that DTLM achieves state-of-the-art results on the task of phoneme-to-grapheme conversion.

Table 3 shows the G2P results on the test sets. The DTLM models were trained without any synthetic data or target language models. Although DTLM results are generally lower than on P2G, it outperforms FST in both settings.[7] TRANSFORMER again fails in the low resource setting, In the standard (high resource) setting, DTLM is about 6% worse on average than TRANSFORMER in terms of WER, but 10% better in terms of PER (3.9% vs 4.3% according to the official results). In addition, DTLM is much easier and faster to train.

The TRANSFORMER models trained on the data

---

[6] We note that the P2G accuracy is particularly high on Georgian, which, unlike French, seems to be easier to write than to read.

[7] FST, which is not included in Table 3, obtains 22.0% WER average in the standard setting according to the official results, and 58.1% WER average in the low-resource setting, as our submission with RunID=5.

Language	High Resource			Low Resource		
	DTLM	TF	TF+	DTLM	TF	TF+
RunID	1	2	3	4	6	-
Adyghe	29.8	28.9	28.2	54.4	92.9	58.4
Armenian	16.9	13.1	16.0	36.4	82.9	36.2
Bulgarian	35.8	30.0	36.7	67.6	93.3	66.4
Dutch	19.6	19.3	16.9	58.7	93.6	57.6
French	7.6	6.4	6.4	53.3	94.9	44.9
Georgian	28.2	25.8	27.1	39.6	84.4	42.2
Greek	15.8	17.1	17.3	39.1	88.0	44.0
Hindi	12.2	10.7	8.7	48.2	89.8	43.1
Hungarian	5.3	6.0	5.3	27.6	87.6	22.7
Icelandic	13.1	10.2	11.3	61.6	90.9	62.0
Japanese	8.7	6.7	6.7	57.8	98.0	53.1
Korean	45.3	45.1	45.1	95.1	100	100
Lithuanian	21.8	22.7	24.4	62.7	90.7	64.0
Romanian	11.3	12.7	10.7	30.2	69.3	28.9
Vietnamese	7.8	7.3	8.7	75.3	95.3	87.3
Average	**18.6**	**17.5**	**18.0**	**53.8**	**90.1**	**54.1**

Table 3: WER on G2P test sets.

augmented with synthesized instances (labeled as TF+ in Table 3) achieved consistently higher results in our development experiments in the standard (high resource) setting (Section 4.4). Unfortunately, a corresponding improvement is not seen in the official test results. Possible explanations include the limit of 400 on the number of epochs made by the task organizers, as well as the suboptimal tuning procedure, which might have accidentally resulted in the overfitting of the augmented model. This is also suggested by the fact that the results of our TRANSFORMER models are often better than the official results on the test datasets.

On the other hand, the data augmentation approach is remarkably successful in the low-resource setting, yielding an average WER improvement over 35% with respect to base TRANSFORMER. We interpret these results as a strong proof-of-concept of the validity of our data augmentation approach; when training data is limited, it can dramatically improve the accuracy of neural models, without any change to their architecture.

6 Conclusion

We have presented a novel data augmentation method that combines the strengths of multiple string transduction methods. We have also explored both G2P and P2G tasks in both the standard high-resource setting, and a low-resource setting of our own design. The results demonstrate that the weakness of neural systems in low-resource settings can be mitigated through the application of data augmentation.

Acknowledgements

We thank Garrett Nicolai for the assistance with DTLM. We thank the organizers of the shared task for their effort. In particular, we thank Kyle Gorman for promptly answering our questions during the pandemic lockout.

This research was supported by the Natural Sciences and Engineering Research Council of Canada, Alberta Innovates, and Alberta Advanced Education.

References

Antonios Anastasopoulos and Graham Neubig. 2019. Pushing the limits of low-resource morphological inflection. In *Proceedings of the 2019 Conference on Empirical Methods in Natural Language Processing and the 9th International Joint Conference on Natural Language Processing (EMNLP-IJCNLP)*, pages 984–996, Hong Kong, China. Association for Computational Linguistics.

Kyle Gorman, Lucas F.E. Ashby, Aaron Goyzueta, Arya D. McCarthy, Shijie Wu, and Daniel You. 2020. The SIGMORPHON 2020 shared task on multilingual grapheme-to-phoneme conversion. In *this volume*.

Bradley Hauer, Amir Ahmad Habibi, Yixing Luan, Rashed Rubby Riyadh, and Grzegorz Kondrak. 2019. Cognate projection for low-resource inflection generation. In *Proceedings of the 16th Workshop on Computational Research in Phonetics, Phonology, and Morphology*, pages 6–11, Florence, Italy. Association for Computational Linguistics.

Bradley Hauer, Garrett Nicolai, and Grzegorz Kondrak. 2017. Bootstrapping unsupervised bilingual lexicon induction. In *Proceedings of the 15th Conference of the European Chapter of the Association for Computational Linguistics: Volume 2, Short Papers*, pages 619–624.

IPA, 1999. *Handbook of the International Phonetic Association*. Cambridge University Press.

Sittichai Jiampojamarn, Aditya Bhargava, Qing Dou, Kenneth Dwyer, and Grzegorz Kondrak. 2009. DirecTL: a language independent approach to transliteration. In *Proceedings of the 2009 Named Entities Workshop: Shared Task on Transliteration (NEWS 2009)*, pages 28–31, Suntec, Singapore. Association for Computational Linguistics.

Sittichai Jiampojamarn, Colin Cherry, and Grzegorz Kondrak. 2008. Joint processing and discriminative training for letter-to-phoneme conversion. In *Proceedings of ACL-08: HLT*, pages 905–913.

Sittichai Jiampojamarn, Kenneth Dwyer, Shane Bergsma, Aditya Bhargava, Qing Dou, Mi-Young

Kim, and Grzegorz Kondrak. 2010. Transliteration generation and mining with limited training resources. In *Proceedings of the 2010 Named Entities Workshop*, pages 39–47, Uppsala, Sweden. Association for Computational Linguistics.

Sittichai Jiampojamarn, Grzegorz Kondrak, and Tarek Sherif. 2007. Applying many-to-many alignments and hidden Markov models to letter-to-phoneme conversion. In *Human Language Technologies 2007: The Conference of the North American Chapter of the Association for Computational Linguistics; Proceedings of the Main Conference*, pages 372–379, Rochester, New York. Association for Computational Linguistics.

Jackson L. Lee, Lucas F.E. Ashby, M. Elizabeth Garza, Yeonju Lee-Sikka, Sean Miller, Alan Wong, Arya D. McCarthy, and Kyle Gorman. 2020. Massively multilingual pronunciation mining with WikiPron. In *Proceedings of the 12th Language Resources and Evaluation Conference*, pages 4216–4221, Marseille.

Christopher D. Manning and Hinrich Schutze. 2001. *Foundations of Statistical Natural Language Processing*. The MIT Press.

Garrett Nicolai, Colin Cherry, and Grzegorz Kondrak. 2015. Inflection generation as discriminative string transduction. In *Proceedings of the 2015 conference of the North American chapter of the association for computational linguistics: human language technologies*, pages 922–931.

Garrett Nicolai and Grzegorz Kondrak. 2016. Leveraging inflection tables for stemming and lemmatization. In *Proceedings of the 54th Annual Meeting of the Association for Computational Linguistics (Volume 1: Long Papers)*, pages 1138–1147.

Garrett Nicolai, Saeed Najafi, and Grzegorz Kondrak. 2018. String transduction with target language models and insertion handling. In *Proceedings of the Fifteenth Workshop on Computational Research in Phonetics, Phonology, and Morphology*, pages 43–53.

Myle Ott, Sergey Edunov, Alexei Baevski, Angela Fan, Sam Gross, Nathan Ng, David Grangier, and Michael Auli. 2019. fairseq: A fast, extensible toolkit for sequence modeling. In *Proceedings of the 2019 Conference of the North American Chapter of the Association for Computational Linguistics (Demonstrations)*, pages 48–53, Minneapolis, Minnesota. Association for Computational Linguistics.

Panagiotis A. Rentzepopoulos and George K. Kokkinakis. 1996. Efficient multilingual phoneme-to-grapheme conversion based on HMM. *Computational Linguistics*, 22(3):351–376.

Miikka Silfverberg, Adam Wiemerslage, Ling Liu, and Lingshuang Jack Mao. 2017. Data augmentation for morphological reinflection. In *Proceedings of the*

CoNLL SIGMORPHON 2017 Shared Task: Universal Morphological Reinflection, pages 90–99, Vancouver. Association for Computational Linguistics.

Ashish Vaswani, Noam Shazeer, Niki Parmar, Jakob Uszkoreit, Llion Jones, Aidan N Gomez, Łukasz Kaiser, and Illia Polosukhin. 2017. Attention is all you need. In *Advances in neural information processing systems*, pages 5998–6008.

Frustratingly Easy Multilingual Grapheme-to-Phoneme Conversion

Nikhil Prabhu and **Katharina Kann**
University of Colorado Boulder
{nikhil.prabhu,katharina.kann}@colorado.edu

Abstract

In this paper, we describe two CU Boulder submissions to SIGMORPHON 2020 Task 1 on multilingual grapheme-to-phoneme conversion (G2P). Inspired by the high performance of a standard transformer model (Vaswani et al., 2017) on the task, we improve over this approach by adding two modifications: (i) Instead of training exclusively on G2P, we additionally create examples for the opposite direction, phoneme-to-grapheme conversion (P2G). We then perform multi-task training on both tasks. (ii) We produce ensembles of our models via majority voting. Our approaches, though being conceptually simple, result in systems that place 6th and 8th amongst 23 submitted systems, and obtain the best results out of all systems on Lithuanian and Modern Greek, respectively.

1 Introduction

This paper describes the CU Boulder submissions to the SIGMORPHON 2020 shared task on multilingual grapheme-to-phoneme conversion (G2P). G2P is an important task, due to its applications in text-to-speech and automatic speech recognition systems. It is explained by Jurafsky and Martin (2009) as:

> The process of converting a sequence of letters into a sequence of phones is called grapheme-to-phoneme conversion, sometimes shortened g2p. The job of a grapheme-to-phoneme algorithm is thus to convert a letter string like *cake* into a phone string like [K EY K].

While the earliest G2P algorithms have used handwritten parser-based rules in the format of Chomsky-Halle rewrite rules, often called letter-to-sound, or LTS, rules (Chomsky and Halle, 1968),

later techniques have moved on to generating semi-automatic alignment tables such as in Pagel et al. (1998). Today, a lot of work aims at using machine learning – in particular deep learning techniques – to solve sequence-to-sequence problems like this.

We explore using a transformer model (Vaswani et al., 2017) for this problem, since it has shown great promise in several areas of natural language processing (NLP), outperforming the previous state of the art on a large variety of tasks, including machine translation (Vaswani et al., 2017), summarization (Raffel et al., 2019), question-answering (Raffel et al., 2019), and sentiment-analysis (Munikar et al., 2019). While previous work has used transformers for G2P, experiments have only been performed on English, specifically on the CMUDict (Weide, 2005) and NetTalk[1] datasets (Yolchuyeva et al., 2020; Sun et al., 2019). Our approach builds upon the standard architecture by adding two straightforward modifications: multi-task training (Caruana, 1997) and ensembling. We find that these simple additions lead to performance improvements over the standard model, and our models place 6th and 8th among 23 submissions to the SIGMORPHON 2020 shared task on multilingual grapheme-to-phoneme conversion. Our two models further perform the best on the languages Lithuanian and Modern Greek, respectively.

2 Task and Background

2.1 Grapheme-to-Phoneme Conversion

G2P can be cast as a sequence-to-sequence task, where the input sequence is a sequence of graphemes, i.e., the spelling of a word, and the output sequence is a sequence of IPA-like symbols, representing the pronunciation of the same word.

---

[1] https://archive.ics.uci.edu/ml/datasets/Connectionist+Bench+(Nettalk+Corpus)

Proceedings of the Seventeenth SIGMORPHON Workshop on Computational Research in Phonetics, Phonology, and Morphology, pages 123–127
Online, July 10, 2020. ©2020 Association for Computational Linguistics
https://doi.org/10.18653/v1/P17

Formally, let Σ_G be an alphabet of graphemes and Σ_P be an alphabet of phonemes. For a word w in a language, G2P then refers to the mapping

$$g(w) \mapsto p(w), \tag{1}$$

with $g(w) \in \Sigma_G^*$ and $p(w) \in \Sigma_P^*$ being the grapheme and phoneme representations of w, respectively.

2.2 Related Work

Many different approaches to G2P exist in the literature, including rule-based systems (Black et al., 1998), LSTMs (Rao et al., 2015), joint-sequence models (Galescu and Allen, 2002), and encoder-decoder architectures, based on convolutional neural networks (Yolchuyeva et al., 2019), LSTMs (Yao and Zweig, 2015), or transformers (Yolchuyeva et al., 2020; Sun et al., 2019). In this paper, we improve over previous work by exploring two straightforward extensions of a standard transformer (Vaswani et al., 2017) model for the task: multi-task training (Caruana, 1997) and ensembling. Multi-task training has been explored previously for G2P (Milde et al., 2017), with the tasks being training on different languages and alphabet sets. Sun et al. (2019) successfully used token-level ensemble distillation for G2P to boost accuracy and reduce model-size, ensembling models based on multiple different architectures.

3 Proposed Approach

We submit two different systems to the shared task, which are based on the transformer architecture, multi-task learning, and ensembling. We describe all components individually in this section.

3.1 Model

Our model architecture is shown in Figure 1; the vanilla transformer proposed by Vaswani et al. (2017). In short, the transformer is an auto-regressive encoder-decoder architecture, which uses stacked self-attention and fully-connected layers for both the encoder and decoder. The decoder is connected to the encoder via multi-head attention over the encoder outputs. Details can be found in the original paper.

3.2 Multi-task Training

We propose to train our model jointly on two tasks: (i) G2P and (ii) phoneme-to-grapheme conversion

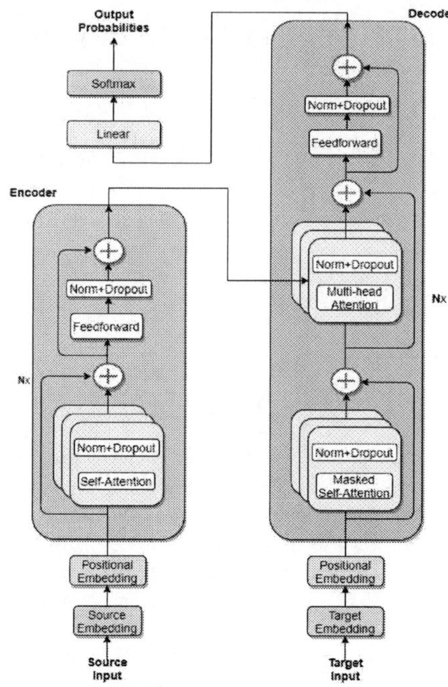

Figure 1: The transformer model architecture.

Hyperparameter	Value
Batch Size	128
Embedding Dimension	256
Hidden Dimension	1024
Dropout	0.3
Number of Encoder Layers	4
Number of Decoder Layers	4
Number of Attention Heads	4
Learning Rate	1e-3
β_1	0.9
β_2	0.998
Label Smoothing Coefficient	0.1
Max Norm (Gradient clipping)	1

Table 1: The hyperparameters used in our experiments.

(P2G). Using our formalization from before, given a word w, P2G corresponds to the mapping

$$p(w) \mapsto g(w). \tag{2}$$

We denote the set of our original G2P training examples as D_{g2p} and our P2G examples, which we obtain by inverting all examples in D_{g2p}, as D_{p2g}. We then aim to obtain model parameters θ that maximize the joint log-likelihood of both datasets:

$$\mathcal{L}(\theta) = \sum_{(w \in D_{g2p})} \log p_\theta(p[w] \mid g[w], \lambda_g) + \tag{3}$$

$$\sum_{(w \in D_{p2g})} \log p_\theta(g[w] \mid p[w], \lambda_p)$$

Grapheme	Phoneme	Phoneme	Grapheme
! a a n d a c h t	aː n d ɑ x t	? aː n d ɑ x t	a a n d a c h t
! b a s s o n	b ɑ s ɔ n	? b ɑ s ɔ n	b a s s o n
! b e g i n t	b ə ɣ ɪ n t	? b ə ɣ ɪ n t	b e g i n t
! g i e r s t	x iː r s t	? x iː r s t	g i e r s t
! h e u p	ɦ ø: p	? ɦ ø: p	h e u p

Table 2: G2P (left) and P2G (right).

$\lambda_g, \lambda_p \notin \Sigma_G \cup \Sigma_P$ are special symbols which we prepend to each input. These so-called *task-embeddings* indicate to our model which task each individual input belongs to. Examples for both tasks are shown in Table 2.

Intuition. By training our model jointly on G2P and P2G, we expect it to learn properties that both tasks have in common. First, both tasks require learning of a monotonic left-to-right mapping. Second, for some languages, $\Sigma_G \cap \Sigma_P \neq \emptyset$, cf. Table 2 for Dutch as an example. Symbols in $\Sigma_G \cap \Sigma_P$ are commonly mapped onto each other in both directions, such that we expect the model to learn this from both tasks.

3.3 Ensembling

Our second straightforward modification of the standard transformer model is that we create ensembles via majority voting. In particular, each of our two submitted systems is an ensemble of multiple different models for each language, which we generate using different random seeds. We then create predictions with all models participating in each ensemble, and choose the solution that occurs most frequently, with ties being broken randomly.

Our first submitted model – **CU-1** – is an ensemble of 5 standard G2P transformers and 5 multi-task transformers. Our second system – **CU-2** – is an ensemble of 5 multi-task transformers.

4 Experiments

4.1 Data

The datasets provided for the shared task spans 15 individual languages, with each training set consisting of 3600 pairs of graphemes and their associated phonemes. The datasets include an initial set of core languages – Armenian (arm), Bulgarian (bul), French (fre), Georgian (geo), Modern Greek (gre), Hindi (hin), Hungarian (hun), Icelandic (ice), Korean (kor), and Lithaunian (lit) –, and a set of surprise languages, which have been released shortly before the shared task deadline – Adyghe (ady), Dutch (dut), Japanese (hiragana) (jap), Romanian

	CU-1		CU-2		CU-TB	
	WER	PER	WER	PER	WER	PER
arm	13.56	2.75	14.22	2.94	16.10	3.37
bul	29.11	6.98	30.22	7.41	32.06	7.32
fre	8.00	2.00	8.00	1.84	10.29	2.65
geo	25.33	4.98	24.67	4.83	26.03	5.20
gre	17.56	3.05	17.78	3.14	17.92	3.40
hin	6.22	1.58	6.89	1.78	8.78	2.28
hun	2.89	0.66	3.11	0.60	4.52	1.03
ice	9.78	2.13	9.11	2.13	12.20	2.83
kor	23.11	6.83	24.22	6.61	26.61	7.43
lit	21.56	4.11	22.44	4.18	22.88	4.41
ady	22.89	5.68	23.11	5.68	24.66	6.33
dut	14.67	2.84	14.44	2.63	16.80	3.46
jap	6.67	2.14	6.67	2.18	7.23	2.42
rum	12.22	3.15	12.00	3.09	13.04	3.37
vie	2.89	1.07	2.89	0.99	4.70	1.60
avg.	**14.43**	**3.33**	**14.65**	**3.34**	**16.25**	**3.80**

Table 3: Development results in WER and PER; CU-1=standard and multi-task transformer ensemble, CU-2=multi-task transformer ensemble, CU-TB=standard transformer ensemble.

(rum), and Vietnamese (vie). The data is primarily extracted from Wiktionary using the wikipron library (Lee et al., 2020).

4.2 Hyperparameters

Following the official shared task baseline, we employ the hyperparameters shown in Table 1. All models are trained for 150 epochs. Starting from epoch 100, we evaluate every 5 epochs for early stopping. Encoder and decoder embeddings are tied, and the maximum sequence length is 24. Our system is built on the transformer implementation by Wu et al. (2020), and our final code is available on github.[2]

4.3 Metrics

Word error rate (WER). Word error rate is the percentage of words for which the model's prediction does not exactly match the gold transcription. **Phoneme error rate (PER).** Phoneme error rate is the percentage of wrong characters in the model's prediction as compared to the gold standard.

Both metrics are calculated using the official evaluation script[3] provided for the shared task.

4.4 Development Results

The results on the development sets are shown in Table 3. CU-TB represents a transformer baseline

---

[2] https://github.com/NikhilPr95/neural-transducer

[3] https://github.com/sigmorphon/2020/blob/master/task1/evaluation/evaluate.py

	CU-1		CU-2		SIG-TB		SIG-LSTM	
	WER	PER	WER	PER	WER	PER	WER	PER
arm	12.89	2.91	13.56	3.04	14.22	3.29	14.67	3.49
bul	26.89	5.65	29.78	6.30	34.00	7.89	31.11	5.94
fre	5.78	1.48	5.56	1.28	6.89	1.72	6.22	1.32
geo	25.78	4.83	27.11	5.08	28.00	5.43	26.44	5.14
gre	15.11	2.51	14.44	2.42	18.89	3.06	18.89	3.30
hin	6.67	1.58	6.44	1.55	9.56	2.40	6.67	1.47
hun	4.89	1.12	5.11	1.15	5.33	1.28	5.33	1.18
ice	9.56	2.11	9.78	2.14	10.22	2.21	10.00	2.36
kor	30.67	9.22	31.56	8.79	43.78	17.5	46.89	16.78
lit	18.67	3.53	20.00	3.93	20.67	3.65	19.11	3.55
ady	26.00	5.87	26.22	6.31	28.44	6.49	28.00	6.53
dut	16.00	2.92	15.78	2.86	15.78	2.89	16.44	2.94
jap	5.78	1.44	6.00	1.47	7.33	1.86	7.56	1.79
rum	10.44	2.35	10.89	2.41	12.00	2.62	10.67	2.53
vie	2.67	1.12	2.22	0.91	7.56	2.27	4.67	1.52
avg.	**14.52**	**3.24**	**14.96**	**3.31**	**17.51**	**4.30**	**16.84**	**3.99**

Table 4: Official Test results in WER and PER; CU-1=standard and multi-task transformer ensemble, CU-2=multi-task transformer ensemble, SIG-TB=SIGMORPHON transformer baseline, SIG-LSTM=SIGMORPHON LSTM baseline.

	T	T-E	MT	MT-E
arm	16.10	15.11	14.89	14.22
bul	32.06	28.22	31.82	30.22
fre	10.29	8.22	8.80	8.00
geo	26.03	25.78	25.29	24.67
gre	17.92	17.78	17.60	17.78
hin	8.78	6.67	7.20	6.89
hun	4.52	3.11	3.64	3.11
ice	12.20	10.00	10.53	9.11
kor	26.61	23.33	25.92	24.22
lit	22.88	21.56	23.02	22.44
ady	24.66	22.67	24.22	23.11
dut	16.80	15.33	15.11	14.44
jap	7.23	6.67	6.84	6.67
rum	13.04	12.89	12.31	12.00
vie	4.70	4.00	3.38	2.89
avg.	**16.25**	**14.76**	**15.37**	**14.65**

Table 5: Results of our ablation study in WER; T=standard transformer, T-E=standard transformer ensemble, MT=multi-task transformer, MT-E=multi-task transformer ensemble.

trained by us (an average of 5 models), while CU-1 and CU-2 are our submitted systems, which are described in Section 3.3. CU-1 performs best with an average performance of 14.43 WER and 3.33 PER, followed by CU-2 with 14.65 WER and 3.34 PER, respectively. Both CU-1 and CU-2 improve over the baseline for each of the 15 languages, with an average improvement of 1.82 WER and 1.6 WER, respectively. Both systems show an average improvement of 0.47 PER over the baseline, performing better on all languages, with the sole exception of Bulgarian, where the baseline slightly outperforms CU-2.

4.5 Official Shared Task Results

The results on the test set in Table 4 mirror our development set results. Our systems CU-1 and CU-2 are compared with the two best official baselines: a transformer (SIG-TB) and an LSTM sequence-to-sequence model (SIG-LSTM). CU-1 gives the best performance, with an average of 14.52 WER and 3.24 PER, followed by CU-2, with 14.96 WER and 3.31 PER. CU-1 shows an average improvement of 2.99 WER and 2.32 WER as well as 1.06 PER and 0.75 PER over SIG-TB and SIG-LSTM, respectively. CU-2 shows an average of 2.55 WER and 0.99 PER and, respectively, 1.88 WER and 0.68 PER improvement. Compared to all system submissions (Gorman et al.) CU-1 performs best on Lithuanian, with 18.67 WER and 3.53 PER. CU-2 performs best on Modern Greek, with 14.44 WER and 2.42 PER.

4.6 Ablation Study

We further perform an ablation study to explicitly investigate the impact of our two modifications – multi-task training and ensembling – with results shown in Table 5. T and MT are the standard and multi-task transformer, while T-E and MT-E are the ensembled versions of the same. The ensembles obtain better results: T-E shows an average improvement of 1.50 WER over T, and MT-E outperforms MT by 0.72 WER. Multi-task training also leads to performance gains, with MT improving over T by 0.88 WER and MT-E over T-E by 0.11 WER, showing that the effect of multi-task training is not as strong as that of ensembling. We conclude that both multi-task training and ensembling boost performance overall.

5 Conclusion

We described two CU Boulder submissions to SIGMORPHON 2020 Task 1. Our systems consisted of transformer models, some of which were trained in a multi-task fashion on G2P and P2G. We further created ensembles consisting of multiple individual models via majority voting.

Our internal experiments and the official results showed that these two straightforward extensions of the transformer model enabled our systems to improve over the official shared task baselines and a standard transformer model for G2P. Our final models, CU-1 and CU-2, placed 6th and 8th out of 23 submissions, and obtained the best results of all systems for Lithuanian and Modern Greek, respectively.

Acknowledgments

We would like to thank all organizers of SIGMOR-PHON 2020 Task 1!

References

Alan W Black, Kevin Lenzo, and Vincent Pagel. 1998. Issues in building general letter to sound rules. In *The Third ESCA Workshop in Speech Synthesis*. International Speech Communication Association.

Rich Caruana. 1997. Multitask learning. *Machine Learning*, 28:41–75.

Noam Chomsky and Morris Halle. 1968. *The sound pattern of English*. Harper & Row New York.

Lucian Galescu and James F Allen. 2002. Pronunciation of proper names with a joint n-gram model for bi-directional grapheme-to-phoneme conversion. In *Seventh International Conference on Spoken Language Processing*.

Kyle Gorman, Lucas F.E. Ashby, Aaron Goyzueta, Arya D. McCarthy, Shijie Wu, and Daniel You. The sigmorphon 2020 shared task on multilingual grapheme-to-phoneme conversion.

Daniel Jurafsky and James H. Martin. 2009. *Speech and Language Processing (2nd Edition)*. Prentice-Hall, Inc., USA.

Jackson L. Lee, Lucas F.E. Ashby, M. Elizabeth Garza, Yeonju Lee-Sikka, Sean Miller, Alan Wong, Arya D. McCarthy, and Kyle Gorman. 2020. Massively multilingual pronunciation mining with WikiPron. In *Proceedings of the 12th Language Resources and Evaluation Conference*, pages 4216–4221, Marseille.

Benjamin Milde, Christoph Schmidt, and Joachim Köhler. 2017. Multitask sequence-to-sequence models for grapheme-to-phoneme conversion. In *INTERSPEECH*, pages 2536–2540.

Manish Munikar, Sushil Shakya, and Aakash Shrestha. 2019. Fine-grained sentiment classification using BERT. In *2019 Artificial Intelligence for Transforming Business and Society (AITB)*, volume 1, pages 1–5. IEEE.

Vincent Pagel, Kevin Lenzo, and Alan Black. 1998. Letter to sound rules for accented lexicon compression. *arXiv preprint cmp-lg/9808010*.

Colin Raffel, Noam Shazeer, Adam Roberts, Katherine Lee, Sharan Narang, Michael Matena, Yanqi Zhou, Wei Li, and Peter J Liu. 2019. Exploring the limits of transfer learning with a unified text-to-text transformer. *arXiv preprint arXiv:1910.10683*.

Kanishka Rao, Fuchun Peng, Haşim Sak, and Françoise Beaufays. 2015. Grapheme-to-phoneme conversion using long short-term memory recurrent neural networks. In *2015 IEEE International Conference on Acoustics, Speech and Signal Processing (ICASSP)*, pages 4225–4229. IEEE.

Hao Sun, Xu Tan, Jun-Wei Gan, Hongzhi Liu, Sheng Zhao, Tao Qin, and Tie-Yan Liu. 2019. Token-level ensemble distillation for grapheme-to-phoneme conversion. *arXiv preprint arXiv:1904.03446*.

Ashish Vaswani, Noam Shazeer, Niki Parmar, Jakob Uszkoreit, Llion Jones, Aidan N Gomez, Łukasz Kaiser, and Illia Polosukhin. 2017. Attention is all you need. In *Advances in neural information processing systems*, pages 5998–6008.

Robert Weide. 2005. The carnegie mellon pronouncing dictionary [cmudict. 0.6]. *Pittsburgh, PA: Carnegie Mellon University*.

Shijie Wu, Ryan Cotterell, and Mans Hulden. 2020. Applying the transformer to character-level transduction. *arXiv preprint arXiv:2005.10213*.

Kaisheng Yao and Geoffrey Zweig. 2015. Sequence-to-sequence neural net models for grapheme-to-phoneme conversion. *arXiv preprint arXiv:1506.00196*.

Sevinj Yolchuyeva, Géza Németh, and Bálint Gyires-Tóth. 2019. Grapheme-to-phoneme conversion with convolutional neural networks. *Applied Sciences*, 9(6):1143.

Sevinj Yolchuyeva, Géza Németh, and Bálint Gyires-Tóth. 2020. Transformer based grapheme-to-phoneme conversion. *arXiv preprint arXiv:2004.06338*.

Exploring Neural Architectures And Techniques For Typologically Diverse Morphological Inflection

Pratik Jayarao, Siddhanth Pillay, Pranav Thombre, Aditi Chaudhary
{pjayarao,spillay,pthombre,aschaudh}@cs.cmu.edu

Abstract

Morphological inflection in low resource languages is critical to augment existing corpora in Low Resource Languages, which can help develop several applications in these languages with very good social impact. We describe our attention-based encoder-decoder approach that we implement using LSTMs and Transformers as the base units. We also describe the ancillary techniques that we experimented with, such as hallucination, language vector injection, sparsemax loss and adversarial language network alongside our approach to select the related language(s) for training. We present the results we generated on the constrained as well as unconstrained SIGMOR-PHON 2020 dataset (Vylomova et al., 2020). One of the primary goals of our paper was to study the contribution varied components described above towards the performance of our system and perform an analysis on the same.

1 Introduction

Morphological inflection is the process of generating varied representations of words based on several linguistic properties(gender, tense,etc). Inflections of words retain their core meanings, however they differ in their word structure. As mentioned by (Faruqui et al., 2015), morphological inflections can be generated from the root word through two primary methods: concatenative measures and non-concatenative measures. In the case of concatenative measures, suffixes and prefixes are added to the original word to generate various inflectional forms of the word. Non-concatenative inflectional forms are generated by changing the basic structure of the original word. The generation of inflectional forms of a word has proved to be an asset in a wide array of NLP tasks.

Prominent languages like English, Spanish, French, etc. have large corpora that can be utilised to train large scale machine learning applications. However there are several languages in today's world that are not as well documented. These languages are termed as "low resource" languages. Morphological inflection has proven to be an effective tool to augment the datasets of "low resource" languages, so that they corpora can be better modeled using NLP techniques.

To this end, several studies have been done on morphological inflection on monolingual high resource settings, such as in the SIGMORPHON 2016, 2017, 2018 challenges. However, the low resource setting has been extensively studied in the SIGMORPHON 2019 and 2020 shared task (Vylomova et al., 2020). The data in these tasks consists of the form of [I, O, T], where I, O, T stand for input lemma, inflected form and tags respectively. The inflected form is essentially the inflected form of the input lemma upon applying the tags specified by T.

In this paper, we present an overview of the various techniques that we implemented to perform the task of Morphological Inflection in both the constrained and unconstrained settings. We start by describing the different models that we experimented with to improve our performance on this dataset. Furthermore, we describe hallucination, sparsemax/sparseloss, adversarial language network and language vector injection techniques that we prototyped to improve the performance of our system. In order to understand the impact of each component on the performance of the system, we perform a detailed analysis on the influence of these techniques on varied set of languages.

2 Related Works

In recent years there has been an increase in work in the field of extremely low resource languages. The work recent work done in the field of mor-

Proceedings of the Seventeenth SIGMORPHON Workshop on Computational Research in Phonetics, Phonology, and Morphology, pages 128–136
Online, July 10, 2020. ©2020 Association for Computational Linguistics
https://doi.org/10.18653/v1/P17

phological inflection can be divided into two main categories: Non-neural approaches and Neural approaches.

The non-neural based approach proposed by (Cotterell et al., 2017) has two stages, alignment and rule generation. A prominent work that combines neural and non-neural approaches is that of (Wu and Cotterell, 2019), where they seek to incorporate monotonicity as an inductive bias in their approach and develop a cubic-time based dynamic programming approach with a greedy decoding scheme. The paper hypothesizes that the monotonic attention-based models perform worse off because they were not jointly trained to incorporate the alignments.

Neural based approaches have recently outperformed the non neural based approaches. (Faruqui et al., 2015) introduces a neural network based strategy, for the task of morphological inflection generation, for languages that are morphologically rich. The authors introduce an encoder decoder based architecture which makes use of character level embeddings. (Çöltekin, 2019) on the other hand adopts the idea from transition-based parsers where the aim is to predict the parsing actions (copy, replace(c), insert(c), delete) in a given state of parser. In the recent years attention based models have gained huge popularity in Natural Language Processing tasks. (Peters and Martins, 2019) introduce a model inspired by sparse sequence to sequence models with a two-headed attention mechanism. The attention and output distributions are computed with Sparsemax function and Sparsemax loss is optimized. (Anastasopoulos and Neubig, 2019) introduce yet another attention based model which is trained on multiple languages and tries to leverage the knowledge learnt on high resource languages for low resource languages. The authors propose a novel two-step attention decoder architecture. Moreover, (Anastasopoulos and Neubig, 2019) augment low resource datasets with data hallucination.

3   Methodology

We implemented four variants of Sequence to Sequence architectures to tackle the problem of morphological injection. We primarily utilize LSTM and Transformers (Vaswani et al., 2017) to construct our models. Additionally we experimented with four techniques Hallucination (Anastasopoulos and Neubig, 2019), Sparse Max-Loss (Peters

and Martins, 2019), Language Adversarial Network (Anastasopoulos and Neubig, 2019)(Chen et al., 2019) and Language Vector Injection (Littell et al., 2017).

3.1   LSTM Encoder Decoder (LSTM)

We prototyped an elementary LSTM sequence to sequence model. We incorporated two LSTM encoders with each individual encoder taking the input as the Lemma and Tags respectively. Furthermore, we implemented two separate attention heads one for the encoded representation of the input Lemma and one for the encoded representation Tags. The decoder was input the context vector and the LSTM representations with the inflected form being generated in an autoregressive manner. The architecture can be seen in Figure 1.

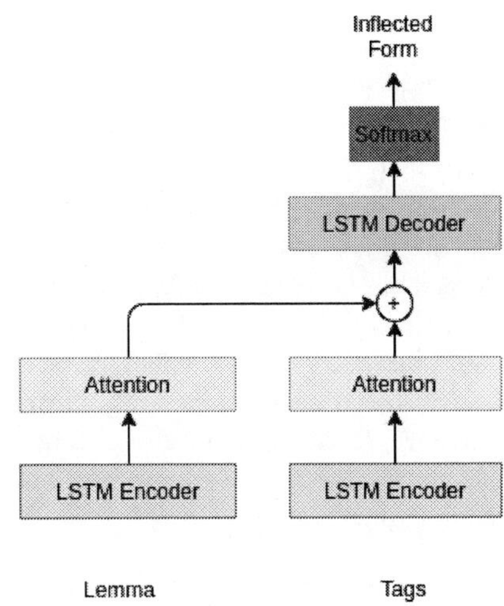

Figure 1: Lstm Encoders Decoder (LSTM)

3.2   Transformer Encoders LSTM Decoder (TELD)

Sequence Translation models such as Recurrent Neural Networks or Convolutions Neural Networks are typically trained in an encoder decoder configuration. Recently, the use of attention has shown improvement in the performance of such models. Thus we replace the LSTM encoders in the previous modules with Transformer encoder (Vaswani et al., 2017). The rest of the architecture is the same as presented in the LSTM model. We generate the output sequence using a LSTM Decoder. The structure of the architecture is shown in Figure 2.

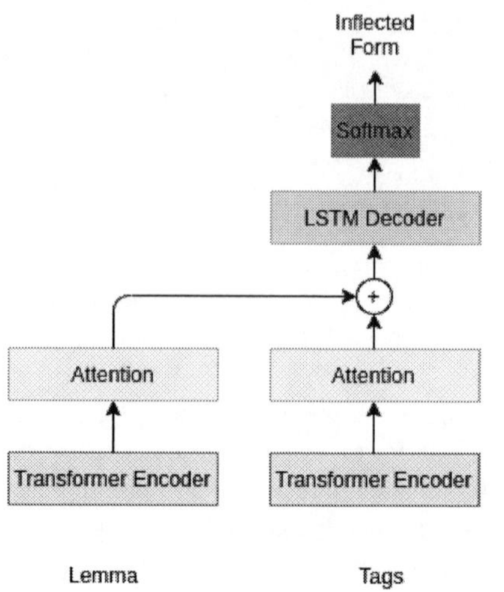

Figure 2: Transformer Encoders LSTM Decoder (TELD)

3.3 Transformer Encoders Transformer Decoder (TETD)

We further replace the LSTM Decoder with a Transformer Decoder. The two Transformer Encoders separate disparate encoder representations for the Lemma and Tags respectively. We concatenate the representations generated by the two Transformer Encoders and feed it to the output Decoder. Since the Transformer Decoder inherently has a multi-head attention layer, we remove the explicit attention over the encoders. An outline of the model can be seen in Figure 3.

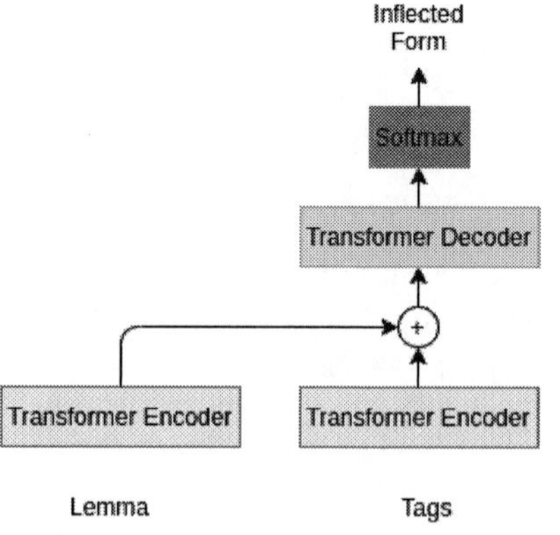

Figure 3: Transformer Encoders Transformer Decoder (TETD)

3.4 Joint Transformers (TJ)

The final architecture we implement is an end-to-end Transformer model. We concatenate the Lemma and the Tag and feed it to the Transformer. The Transformer encoder learns a joint representation for the Lemma and Tag. And the decoder generates the required output. A representation of the architecture can be seen in Figure 4.

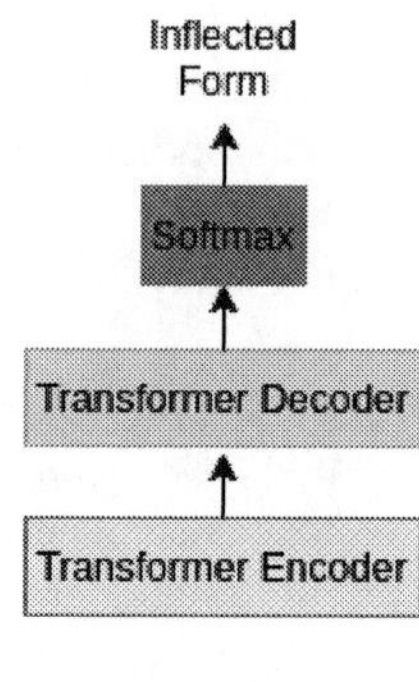

Figure 4: Joint Transformers (TJ)

3.5 Hallucination (HALL)

(Anastasopoulos and Neubig, 2019) incorporated Hallucination techniques and observed a performance boost in their system. Since the data for low resource language is scarce, the distribution learnt by the model for the language doesn't match the true distribution. To help alleviate this problem, we use this data augmentation technique. In this process each part is considered as a "stem", characters inside the region are randomly substituted with other characters without changing the overall length. A detailed explanation can be found in (Anastasopoulos and Neubig, 2019).

3.6 Sparse-Max and Sparse Loss (SPARSE)

Output vocabulary space can be potentially large with some of the characters not being used as frequently in the language. Sparsemax assigns exactly zero attention weight to irrelevant source tokens and implausible hypotheses and is shown to return sparse posterior distributions. This makes the model output more interpretable and can also help to filter out large output spaces. SparseLoss is the loss typically associated with Sparsemax and is known to be computationally very feasible. The incorporation of Sparse-max and Sparse loss in a manner similar to that of (Peters and Martins, 2019) can be seen in Figure 5.

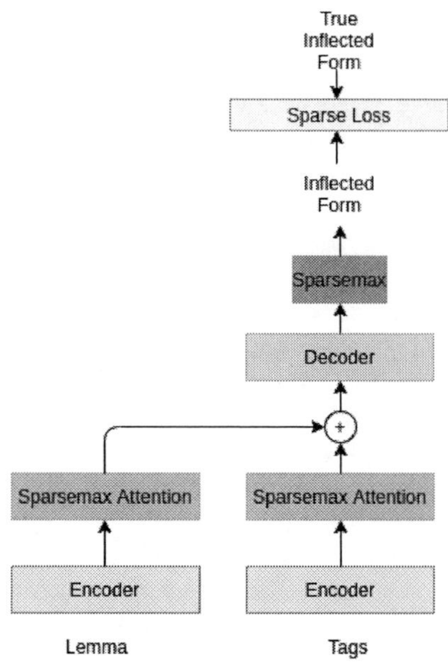

Figure 5: Sparse-Max and Sparse Loss

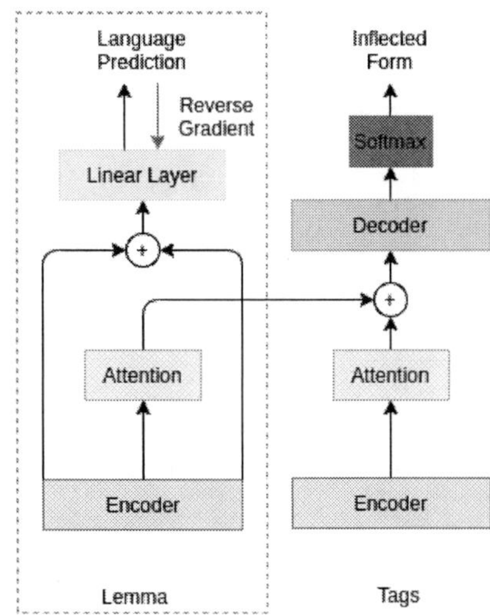

Figure 6: Adversarial Language Network

3.7 Adversarial Language Network (ADV-LANG)

In multilingual setting and in particular trying to transfer knowledge between related language(s) and a target language it is sometimes useful to learn language agnostic representations. Thus we implement a Language Adversarial Network which encourages the same. We extract the representations generated at the first time step and the last time step by the Lemma encoder and concatenate these representations. This representation is then passed through a linear layer and a softmax layer which produces a prediction for the Language. We then reverse the gradient while training. An illustration of the same can be seen in Figure 6.

3.8 Language Vector Injection (LVI)

(Tsvetkov et al., 2016) show that vectors which encode information about the genetics of language outperform simple one-hot representations. The lang2vec released by (Littell et al., 2017) represent languages using rich typological, geographical and phylogenetic vectors. These vectors mainly consist of binary language facts pertaining to the language such as if negation precedes a verb, is it represented as a suffix, if a language is part of Germanic family, etc. with the value of each of these facts represented between [0.0, 1.0]. We propose that the injection of these rich vectors into our model may increase the performance for low resource languages where training data is scarce and all round characteristics of a language cannot be learnt just from the training data.

To integrate language vectors we first extract the lang2vec vector for a particular language. We pass it through a two layer dense neural network. This provides us a compact representation for the vector. We then concatenate this representation with the output representation generated by the decoder. We then pass this through a softmax layer and the output character is evaluated. The integration can be seen in figure 7.

Furthermore we conducted a set of experiments by initializing the hidden and cell states of the (LSTM) model with language vectors but did not see promising results.

3.9 Selecting Related Language(s) for given Target Language

To select the related language(s) and target language pairs for training, we utilised the precomputed feature distance present in the Lang2Vec library(Littell et al., 2017). This distance is the cosine distance between the vectors obtained by combining the Geographical, Phonological, Syntactic, Inventory and Genetic features present in the Lang2Vec database. We assume that this distance accurately represents a metric to measure the similarity between language pairs.

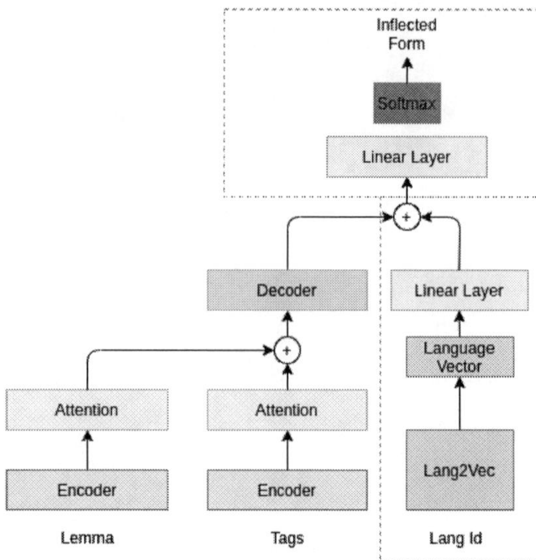

Figure 7: Language Vector Injection

4 Experimental Results

We performed our experiments on the data provided in the SIGMORPHON 2020 shared task. The dataset consists of 90 languages. The data for each language consisted of triplets in the {input, output, tags} format, where the 'output' was the output word generated after applying the morphological tags as specified by 'tags' on the 'input' word. The languages we split into two halves.The first half consisted of 45 languages development languages and the latter half consisted of 45 surprise languages.

We made submissions on all 90 languages for two different settings, unconstrained and constrained. For the unconstrained setting we trained our model in a cross-lingual manner. To complement the languages with a low number of training examples we included genetically close languages to augment the training process as explained above. For the constrained setting we restricted our training to only a single language.

As explained above we implemented various models such as (LSTM), (TELD), (TETD) and (TJ) augmented with techniques such as (HALL), (ADV-LANG), (SPARSE), (LVI). Since (HALL) has proven to perform better than the original setting we augment all languages with less then 10,000 training samples to a complete 10,000 training instances and thus all models and techniques presented below are built on top of hallucinated data. We present the results on a small subset of

languages (due to the space constraints) on the development set (since we have results on all the models we trained on the development set) for the unconstrained and constrained settings in table 2 and table 3 respectively.

We did not experiment with hyperparameters and had a constant set of hyperparameters for all languages. We trained our models with the following hyperparameters 1. A further fine-tuning per language basis might have provided us with a more competitive score. But since one of the primary goals of our study was to understand the influence of the various components on our system we did not pursue this avenue in great detail.

We made a total of 5 submissions to the shared task: 3 in the unconstrained settings and 2 in the constrained setting. The submissions made to the unconstrained section are the top 3 ranked results we obtained on the development set and top 2 results for the constrained section.

Hyperparameter	Value
Optimizer	Adam
Initial Learning Rate	0.001
State Size	1024
Embedding Size	256
Number of Heads	4
Dropout	0.3
Batch Size	32

Table 1: Hyperparameters used for training the 4 models

5 Analysis

Our approach of generating morphological inflections, encapsulates several models namely: LSTM Encoder Decoders, Transformer Encoder LSTM Decoder(TELD), Transformer Encoder and Transformer Decoder(TETD) and Joint Transformers(TJ). To supplement these models, we have utilised additional strategies namely Adversarial Language Networks, Language Vector Injection and Sparse Max and Sparse Loss.

5.1 Analysis of Models Used

In our experiments, we saw that the Transformer based models, usually outperformed LSTM based

Target Language	Related Language(s) (ISO 639-3)	Model	L1+L2	ADV-LANG	SPARSE	LVI
Zulu	gaa,lug,aka	LSTM	0.81	0.83	0.81	0.83
		TELD	0.83	0.84	0.83	**0.86**
		TETD	0.81	0.84	0.83	0.83
Chichicapan Zapotec	azg,cly	LSTM	0.84	0.83	0.87	0.84
		TELD	0.87	**0.88**	**0.88**	**0.88**
		TETD	0.85	0.86	0.85	**0.88**
Yoloxóchitl Mixtec	gmh,ang	LSTM	0.86	**0.89**	0.87	0.88
		TELD	0.84	0.84	0.84	0.83
		TETD	0.81	0.79	0.81	0.79
Sotho	nya,dan	LSTM	**1.0**	**1.0**	**1.0**	**1.0**
		TELD	0.98	**1.0**	0.96	**1.0**
		TETD	0.94	0.96	0.90	0.96
Luganda	lin,zul,ceb	LSTM	0.90	0.90	0.90	0.89
		TELD	0.91	0.90	**0.91**	0.90
		TETD	0.82	0.83	0.82	0.82
Livonian	gmh,ang,kon,swa	LSTM	0.91	0.91	0.92	0.91
		TELD	0.92	0.92	**0.94**	0.92
		TETD	0.67	0.71	0.71	0.70
Classical Syriac	ang	LSTM	**0.94**	0.92	0.83	**0.94**
		TELD	0.92	0.91	0.93	0.94
		TETD	0.93	0.92	**0.94**	0.93
Kannada	nob	LSTM	0.79	0.78	**0.83**	0.80
		TELD	0.79	0.79	0.79	0.80
		TETD	0.77	0.75	0.79	0.57
Swiss German	mlg,dan	LSTM	0.87	0.86	0.87	0.87
		TELD	0.85	**0.88**	0.86	0.85
		TETD	0.78	0.77	0.76	0.78

Table 2: Accuracy obtained on 6 languages from the SIGMORPHON 2020 dataset in the unconstrained setting, where the languages were trained in conjunction with related language(s). Related language(s) have been presented in their ISO 639-3 code format.

models in general for most language pairs. Specifically, the Transformer encoder and LSTM decoder model showed the most optimal performance across all the language pairs. The ability of Transformer based models to capture long-distance dependencies, makes them more adept at generating inflections for words that were longer in length. This ensures that these models have a higher accuracy at the morphological inflection task as compared to standard LSTM based models. We can also observe that the joint transformer method was the least optimal method for most language pairs. We assume this is primarily because this method encodes both the input lemma and tags together. By encoding the lemma and tags together, we cannot utilise the information present in the tags to determine the next character to be generated during the decoding process.

5.2 Utility of Adversarial Language Network

As mentioned in (Anastasopoulos and Neubig, 2019), in a multi-lingual setting it is essential to ensure that the output of the encoder should be independent of the input language. This is vital in the task of morphological inflection generation for low resource languages. The primary reason behind this, is that while training inflection generation systems, low resource languages are trained with related language(s) that has a similar structure, due to paucity of training data.

In the context of our experiments, the adversarial language network was applied with each model that we trained, to ensure that the output of the encoder was language invariant. For the SIGMORPHON 2020 dataset, the use of adversarial language net-

Language	Model	SPARSE + LVI
Zulu	LSTM	0.81
	TELD	**0.86**
	TETD	0.83
Chichipan Zapotec	LSTM	0.85
	TELD	**0.88**
	TETD	0.87
Yoloxóchitl Mixtec	LSTM	**0.87**
	TELD	0.84
	TETD	0.79
Sotho	LSTM	1.0
	TELD	**1.0**
	TETD	0.94
Luganda	LSTM	**0.91**
	TELD	0.90
	TETD	0.80
Livonian	LSTM	**0.91**
	TELD	0.91
	TETD	0.82
Classical Syriac	LSTM	**0.94**
	TELD	0.93
	TETD	0.93
Kannada	LSTM	**0.80**
	TELD	**0.80**
	TETD	**0.80**
Swiss German	LSTM	**0.90**
	TELD	0.89
	TETD	0.80

Table 3: Accuracy obtained on 6 languages from the SIGMORPHON 2020 dataset in the constrained setting, where the languages were trained without using any related language(s).

work was found to be beneficial for most of the language pairs that we tested. However for some of our models, performance remained unchanged after the introduction of the adversarial language network. We believe that the reason for this static performance lies in the fact that the related language(s) and target language we chose during training already possessed high structural similarity. We hypothesize that this particular method would be highly useful in cases where the related language(s) and the target language pair differ widely in their structure.

5.3 Use of SparseMax and Sparse Loss

In the SIGMORPHON 2020 challenge, this technique was useful for the Chichicapan Zapotec,Zulu and Livonian languages. We hypothesize that this improvement in performance due to the addition of SparseMax is primarily because of the large vocabularies of these language pairs. For all the other languages that we tested, we noticed that we achieved a similar level of performance after the incorporation of SparseMax. The addition of SparseMax and Sparse loss aided the LSTM encoder-decoder models to a greater extent as compared to the Transformer based models that we proposed.

5.4 Utility of Language Vector Injection

We seek to use language vectors to improve performance for low resource languages where we find a paucity of data. These vectors contain embedded information about the language that we hope will be useful while generating inflectional forms of input lemmas. For the SIGMORPHON 2020 dataset, the use of language vectors helped us improve performance in almost all the language pairs that we tested. We believe the structural information embedded in the language vectors helped our model efficiently generate morphological inflections.

6 Future Work

Due to the time constraints we were not able to search through all combinations of the techniques that were mentioned such as LVI+SPARSE+LANG-ADV+NO-HALL and various others. Moreover, further fine-tuning the model hyperparameters for each language could have yielded better results.

Additionally multiple approaches to language vector injection can be explored. The vectors can be fed to the model at every-time step of the encoder by concatenating the input with the vectors or the decoder by concatenating the language vector to the context vector. This form of early injection of the vectors may help the system perform better. Another approach can be feeding the language vector to the system in place of the <sos> token.

The limited availability of supervised data for low resource languages makes it difficult to train the various data hungry Neural Network models. It has been shown that incorporation of unlabelled data can help improve the performance of such models and thus we propose to integrate a semi-supervised approach by learning Language Models over these low resource languages.These language models inherently contain information about the appropriate character sequences in a given language and thus provide valuable information for predicting the next character in the decoding process. We propose to combine the probability generated by the language model with the with probability generated by the inflection model and learn the interpolation weights during training similar to the experimental setup of that of (Faruqui et al., 2016).The language model can be constructed using a basic recurrent model or even complex models such as BERT. (Devlin et al., 2018).

7 Conclusion

This paper presents a detailed description of the models that we implemented to undertake the "Typologically Diverse Morphological Inflection" shared task. We describe our encoder-decoder based approach using both LSTMs and Transformers. We also describe the different supporting techniques that we implemented, such as hallucination, language vector injection, adversarial language traning and sparsemax. We present a brief subset of the results for the SIGMORPHON 2020 dataset. We also delve deeper and try to present a detailed analysis of the different components of our model and their influence on the performance.

References

Antonios Anastasopoulos and Graham Neubig. 2019. Pushing the limits of low-resource morphological inflection. In *Proc. EMNLP*, Hong Kong.

Xilun Chen, Ahmed Hassan Awadallah, Hany Hassan, Wei Wang, and Claire Cardie. 2019. Multisource cross-lingual model transfer: Learning what to share. In *Proceedings of the 57th Annual Meeting of the Association for Computational Linguistics*, pages 3098–3112, Florence, Italy. Association for Computational Linguistics.

Çağrı Çöltekin. 2019. Cross-lingual morphological inflection with explicit alignment. In *Proceedings of the 16th Workshop on Computational Research in Phonetics, Phonology, and Morphology*, pages 71–79, Florence, Italy. Association for Computational Linguistics.

Ryan Cotterell, Christo Kirov, John Sylak-Glassman, Géraldine Walther, Ekaterina Vylomova, Patrick Xia, Manaal Faruqui, Sandra Kübler, David Yarowsky, Jason Eisner, et al. 2017. Conll-sigmorphon 2017 shared task: Universal morphological reinflection in 52 languages. *arXiv preprint arXiv:1706.09031*.

Jacob Devlin, Ming-Wei Chang, Kenton Lee, and Kristina Toutanova. 2018. BERT: pre-training of deep bidirectional transformers for language understanding. *CoRR*, abs/1810.04805.

Manaal Faruqui, Yulia Tsvetkov, Graham Neubig, and Chris Dyer. 2015. Morphological inflection generation using character sequence to sequence learning. *arXiv preprint arXiv:1512.06110*.

Manaal Faruqui, Yulia Tsvetkov, Graham Neubig, and Chris Dyer. 2016. Morphological inflection generation using character sequence to sequence learning. In *Proceedings of the 2016 Conference of the North American Chapter of the Association for Computational Linguistics: Human Language Technologies*, pages 634–643, San Diego, California. Association for Computational Linguistics.

Patrick Littell, David R. Mortensen, Ke Lin, Katherine Kairis, Carlisle Turner, and Lori Levin. 2017. URIEL and lang2vec: Representing languages as typological, geographical, and phylogenetic vectors. In *Proceedings of the 15th Conference of the European Chapter of the Association for Computational Linguistics: Volume 2, Short Papers*, pages 8–14, Valencia, Spain. Association for Computational Linguistics.

Ben Peters and André F. T. Martins. 2019. IT–IST at the SIGMORPHON 2019 shared task: Sparse two-headed models for inflection. In *Proceedings of the 16th Workshop on Computational Research in Phonetics, Phonology, and Morphology*, pages 50–56, Florence, Italy. Association for Computational Linguistics.

Yulia Tsvetkov, Sunayana Sitaram, Manaal Faruqui, Guillaume Lample, Patrick Littell, David Mortensen, Alan W Black, Lori Levin, and Chris Dyer. 2016. Polyglot neural language models: A case study in cross-lingual phonetic representation learning. In *Proceedings of the 2016 Conference of the North American Chapter of the Association for Computational Linguistics: Human Language Technologies*, pages 1357–1366, San Diego, California. Association for Computational Linguistics.

Ashish Vaswani, Noam Shazeer, Niki Parmar, Jakob Uszkoreit, Llion Jones, Aidan N Gomez, Ł ukasz Kaiser, and Illia Polosukhin. 2017. Attention is all you need. In I. Guyon, U. V. Luxburg, S. Bengio, H. Wallach, R. Fergus, S. Vishwanathan, and R. Garnett, editors, *Advances in Neural Information Processing Systems 30*, pages 5998–6008. Curran Associates, Inc.

Ekaterina Vylomova, Jennifer White, Elizabeth Salesky, Sabrina J. Mielke, Shijie Wu, Edoardo Ponti, Rowan Hall Maudslay, Ran Zmigrod, Joseph Valvoda, Svetlana Toldova, Francis Tyers, Elena Klyachko, Ilya Yegorov, Natalia Krizhanovsky, Paula Czarnowska, Irene Nikkarinen, Andrej Krizhanovsky, Tiago Pimentel, Lucas Torroba Hennigen, Christo Kirov, Garrett Nicolai, Adina Williams, Antonios Anastasopoulos, Hilaria Cruz, Eleanor Chodroff, Ryan Cotterell, Miikka Silfverberg, and Mans Hulden. 2020. The SIGMORPHON

2020 Shared Task 0: Typologically diverse morphological inflection. In *Proceedings of the 17th Workshop on Computational Research in Phonetics, Phonology, and Morphology.*

Shijie Wu and Ryan Cotterell. 2019. Exact hard monotonic attention for character-level transduction. *arXiv preprint arXiv:1905.06319.*

University of Illinois Submission to the SIGMORPHON 2020 Shared Task 0: Typologically Diverse Morphological Inflection

Marc E. Canby, Aidana Karipbayeva, Bryan J. Lunt,
Sahand Mozaffari, Charlotte R. Yoder, Julia Hockenmaier
University of Illinois at Urbana-Champaign
{marcec2,aidana2,bjlunt2,sahandm2,yoder6,juliahmr}@illinois.edu

Abstract

The objective of this shared task is to produce an inflected form of a word, given its lemma and a set of tags describing the attributes of the desired form. In this paper, we describe a transformer-based model that uses a bidirectional decoder to perform this task, and evaluate its performance on the 90 languages and 18 language families used in this task.

1 Introduction

The world's languages vary greatly in the richness and complexity of their morphological inflection systems. Indo-European languages such as Latin or German tend to inflect words by adding suffixes to a meaning-bearing root, while Austronesian languages like Malay or Tagalog use circumfixes to change the forms of nouns and verbs. It is important that Natural Language Processing (NLP) systems be able to generate inflected forms for a variety of languages, which can be used in downstream tasks such as language modeling or machine translation.

Task 0 of the SIGMORPHON 2020 Shared Task (Vylomova et al., 2020) encourages the development of morphological transduction models for a variety of the world's language families. Since the task features such a diverse set of languages, it is important to create a generalized model that is not overly biased toward certain language typologies.

In this paper, we present the University of Illinois submission to the task. We have modified the baseline transformer model (Wu et al., 2020) to use bidirectional decoding, following the work in Zhou et al. (2019). We believe the additional attention provided by the right-to-left decoding direction improves performance on many of the languages in the dataset. Our model outperforms the baseline transformer model on average rank and

is among the best performing submissions for this year's task.

2 Task

The objective of Task 0 of the SIGMORPHON 2020 Shared Task (Vylomova et al., 2020) is to build a system that learns to generate morphological inflections. The model takes a lemma and a group of morphosyntactic tags as input and outputs the word inflected in the desired form. The following example comes from the German dataset:

$$predigen + \text{V;IMP;SG;2}$$
$$\downarrow$$
$$predig$$

Here, we want to inflect *predigen* in the form specified by the tags V;IMP;SG;2, a 2nd person singular imperative verb. The desired output is *predig*.

2.1 Dataset

The organizers of the task provide datasets for 90 languages in total. 45 languages are treated as *development* languages — these languages span the Austronesian, Germanic, Niger-Congo, Oto-Manguean, and Uralic families, and were available for several months. The remaining 45 languages were released one week before the test sets and are considered *surprise* languages — they span 16 families, 13 of which are not represented by the development languages. The late release of these languages encourages the development of models that do not overly favor the development languages.

Each language has training and development files that consist of lemmata, morphosyntactic tags in the Unimorph Schema (Kirov et al., 2018), and inflected forms. A test set was released for each language one week before the deadline that contains only lemmata and morphosyntactic tags. The languages vary widely in the amount of data provided: for example, Finnish has approximately 100,000

Proceedings of the Seventeenth SIGMORPHON Workshop on Computational Research
in Phonetics, Phonology, and Morphology, pages 137–145
Online, July 10, 2020. ©2020 Association for Computational Linguistics
https://doi.org/10.18653/v1/P17

training examples, while the Iranian language Tajik has only 53 training examples. This large disparity underscores the need for models that are not biased toward certain datasets or languages.

3 Method

3.1 Motivation

Recent work on morphological inflection has shown that an encoder-decoder framework using transformers produces state-of-the-art results (Wu et al., 2020). In our study, we have modified the baseline transformer model to use bidirectional *decoding* – that is, the prediction of a character is conditioned not only on the characters preceding it but also on those following it.

This approach is linguistically motivated, because it is common for an inflectional affix to be phonetically conditioned on the phonemes in its environment. For example, the underlying morpheme $\bar{a}$ (a long a) marking the Latin present indicative can be expressed as the allomorph a (a short a) when followed by a stop consonant: *laudās* (2nd sg.) vs. *laudat* (3rd sg.). Kazakh exhibits regressive assimilation when adding the third person possessive suffix: the lemma *kitap* changes to *kitabı*. Here, the vowel in the suffix precipitates the voicing of the previous consonant.

It is standard to use bidirectional encoding to capture context in the source word (Wu and Cotterell, 2019; Wu et al., 2018), but we believe that a bidirectional decoder can better capture phonetic and orthographic dependencies in inflected forms. To our knowledge, no such method has been applied to a morphological transduction task before.

3.2 Previous Work

Neural models for morphological inflection have been studied extensively in previous SIGMORPHON Shared Tasks (Cotterell et al., 2017, 2018; McCarthy et al., 2019). Successful approaches include encoder-decoder frameworks using recurrent neural networks (RNN's) with attention (Cho et al., 2014; Wu and Cotterell, 2019; Wu et al., 2018). Hard monotonic attention has been particularly successful, due to the relatively rigid copy-like nature of inflection. Recent advances in the transformer architecture (Vaswani et al., 2017) have allowed transformer-based encoder-decoder models to become successful for inflection tasks as well (Wu et al., 2020). Indeed, the organizers provide us with two baselines: an RNN-based model with hard monotonic attention and a transformer baseline.

There has been some work on bidirectional decoding in the machine translation literature; however, we are unaware of any such work in morphological transduction tasks. Zhang et al. (2018) introduce an asynchronous bidirectional deocder based on RNN's; this approach first predicts the target sequence in reverse and then attends over this result to predict the target sequence left-to-right. Zhou et al. (2019) use a transformer model to predict both directions of the target sequence simultaneously, producing state-of-the-art results on translation tasks.

3.3 Model Architecture

Our model uses the technique of synchronous bidirectional decoding (Zhou et al., 2019). In this approach, the decoder pursues predictions of the inflected form in both the left-to-right (L2R) and right-to-left (R2L) directions simultaneously; that is, the first and last letters of the form are predicted first, then the second and second-to-last letters, and so on. At each step of decoding, each direction attends to the predictions of the other direction, so that an entire L2R prediction has been conditioned not only on itself but also on the R2L prediction. At inference time, the highest probability prediction in either direction is selected; it is reversed in the case that an R2L prediction has the highest probability.

In our implementation, the lemma and morphosyntactic tags are first embedded and encoded using the transformer-based encoder of the baseline. The decoder has been modified from the baseline in two ways. First, the decoder operates on previous L2R and R2L outputs in parallel at each time step. All weight matrices are shared between the two directions, and so this model has the same number of parameters as the baseline. Thus, the decoder makes both an L2R and an R2L prediction at each time step.

The second modification is the replacement of the multi-head intra-attention mechanism with a "Synchronous Bidirectional Attention" (SBAtt) mechanism, which allows each direction to attend to the opposite direction. The SBAtt mechanism is mostly the same as the standard intra-attention mechanism, except that the dot product attention has been replaced with "Synchronous Bidirectional Dot Product Attention". This can be summarized as follows:

$$\overrightarrow{H}^{history} = \text{Attention}\left(\overrightarrow{Q}, \overrightarrow{K}, \overrightarrow{V}\right)$$

$$\overrightarrow{H}^{future} = \text{Attention}\left(\overrightarrow{Q}, \overleftarrow{K}, \overleftarrow{V}\right)$$

$$\overrightarrow{H} = \text{Fusion}\left(\overrightarrow{H}^{history}, \overrightarrow{H}^{future}\right)$$

A similar equation holds for calculating $\overleftarrow{H}$. Here, Q, K, and V are the output hidden-state matrices of the previous layer, and the forward and backward arrows indicate the L2R and R2L matrices respectively. Zhou et al. (2019) provides three options for the Fusion function; given the empirical results of their study, we have used nonlinear interpolation in our implementation:

$$\overrightarrow{H} = (1 - \lambda)\overrightarrow{H}^{history} + \lambda \tanh\left(\overrightarrow{H}^{future}\right)$$

We perform inference with a modified beam search. The algorithm tracks the k best L2R hypotheses and the k best R2L hypotheses. At each time step, the ith best L2R hypothesis is paired with the ith best R2L hypothesis, and these are fed to the decoder, which makes an L2R prediction and an R2L prediction. In the end, we select the hypothesis with the highest probability to length ratio; if an R2L hypothesis is selected, it is reversed before returning it.

3.4 Training & Model Configuration

Given training examples $\{x^{(i)}, y^{(i)}\}_{i=1}^{N}$, the model is trained to maximize the likelihood of the training data, accounting for both L2R and R2L probabilities:

$$J(\theta) = \frac{1}{N}\sum_{i=1}^{N}\sum_{j=1}^{M}\left[\log p\left(\overrightarrow{y}_j^{(i)}\middle|x^{(i)}, \overrightarrow{y}_{<j}^{(i)}, \overleftarrow{y}_{<j}^{(i)};\theta\right)\right.$$

$$\left. + \log p\left(\overleftarrow{y}_j^{(i)}\middle|x^{(i)}, \overleftarrow{y}_{<j}^{(i)}, \overrightarrow{y}_{<j}^{(i)};\theta\right)\right]$$

We train the model to minimize the negative log-likelihood loss function with label smoothing (Szegedy et al., 2016). We use an Adam optimizer with $\beta_1 = 0.9$ and $\beta_2 = 0.98$. We employ a warmup-decay strategy for the learning rate as described in Vaswani et al. (2017) using 4000 warmup steps and initial learning rate of 0.001. Furthermore, special start-of-sentence tags $\langle l2r \rangle$ and $\langle r2l \rangle$ are used as the input to the decoder at the first step. A shared end-of-sentence token is used for both directions.

We keep most hyperparameters fixed for all languages in the dataset and train a separate model for each language. We use a batch size of 150, dropout of 0.3, embedding dimension of 256, maximum decoding length of 128, and gradient maximum ℓ_2 of 1.0. We tune the number of layers, the number of attention heads, the hidden dimension size, the label smoothing parameter λ_{smooth}, and the linear interpolation parameter for the Fusion function λ_{fusion}. The selection of these hyperparameters is described in Section 3.5.

Models were trained for 50,000 steps, or until accuracy on the development set flattened. In some cases, the accuracy curve was still rising, so some languages were trained to around 100,000 steps. We choose the model checkpoint with the highest development set accuracy to be used on the test data.

3.5 Hyperparameter Selection

We train a separate model for each language in the dataset and choose the hyperparameters by family. We perform a grid search for two languages in each family and select the best combination of hyperparameters based on accuracy on both of these languages. Where possible, we try to select two languages from different genera within a family, and in some families there is only one language present in the dataset. After selecting the optimal hyperparameters based on these results, we train individual models on each language in the family.

The hyperparameters we consider in our grid search are as follows:

- Num. Layers $\in \{4, 6\}$
- Num. Heads $\in \{4, 8\}$
- Hidden dimension $\in \{512, 1024\}$
- $\lambda_{smooth} \in \{0.0, 0.1\}$
- $\lambda_{fusion} \in \{0.1, 0.5\}$

We chose these hyperparameters because they appeared to cause variation in performance in our initial experiments. After tuning the development languages, it became clear that setting λ_{fusion} to 0.5 almost always degraded performance, and so this was left out of the hyperparameter search on the surprise languages. Setting $\lambda_{fusion} = 0.1$ is consistent with the experimental results in Zhou et al. (2019) on machine translation datasets. Table 3 in Appendix A.1 shows the hyperparameters chosen for each family.

There are some cases in which the languages used for hyperparameter tuning achieve better per-

Family	Accuracy			Edit-Distance		
	MONO	TRM	BI-TRM	MONO	TRM	BI-TRM
Afro-Asiatic	92.93	95.67	**96.37**	0.11	**0.05**	**0.05**
Algic	67.20	68.70	**70.30**	1.26	1.20	**1.16**
Australian	61.40	**90.00**	87.80	0.92	0.27	**0.26**
Austronesian	77.66	81.28	**82.30**	0.58	0.44	**0.41**
Dravidian	86.05	**87.10**	85.30	0.48	**0.46**	0.54
Germanic	86.88	**88.00**	87.38	0.30	**0.23**	0.25
Indo-Aryan	97.78	98.02	**98.18**	0.05	0.05	**0.04**
Iranian	63.00	82.50	**82.53**	1.04	**0.42**	0.46
Niger-Congo	97.72	97.72	**97.87**	0.04	0.04	**0.03**
Nilo-Sahan	0.00	87.50	**100.00**	2.88	0.19	**0.00**
Oto-Manguean	82.71	86.59	**87.49**	0.49	0.32	**0.28**
Romance	95.51	**99.25**	98.72	0.12	**0.02**	0.03
Sino-Tibetan	83.20	**84.40**	84.40	0.22	**0.20**	0.21
Siouan	92.90	**95.60**	94.90	0.16	**0.08**	0.10
Tungusic	55.30	**58.60**	58.30	1.20	**1.06**	1.09
Turkic	95.33	**95.96**	95.80	0.13	**0.10**	0.11
Uralic	83.21	**88.34**	88.18	0.39	0.29	**0.28**
Uto-Aztecan	76.30	80.80	**82.50**	0.49	0.41	**0.39**

Table 1: Macro-averages of accuracy and edit distance by language family. MONO refers to the hard monotonic baseline, TRM refers to the transformer baseline, and BI-TRM refers to our implementation using a bidirectional decoder.

formance with hyperparameters other than those selected for the family. In these cases, we used the best-performing hyperparameters found during the grid search. Table 4 in Appendix A.1 presents the hyperparameters used for these languages.

4 Experimental Results

Table 2 shows the number of languages on which our model is equal to or outperforms the baseline.

	Acc.		Avg. Edit Dist.	
	$\geq$	$>$	$\leq$	$<$
Development	27	18	30	14
Surprise	29	13	33	15

Table 2: The number of languages (out of 45) on which our model equals or outperforms ($\geq$ and $\leq$) or strictly outperforms ($>$ and $<$) the best of the two neural baseline models. It should be noted that on 5 of the development languages and 7 of the surprise languages, the baseline achieves perfect or near-perfect accuracy, making these languages impossible to outperform.

It is clear that by either metric, our model equals or outperforms the baseline on more than half of the languages, demonstrating that our model generally does not perform worse than the baseline.

Table 1 shows macro-averages of accuracy and edit distance by language family. For both metrics, our model outperforms the baseline transformer on 9 of the 18 language families and equals it on only one family. Interestingly, the two metrics do not

agree on which families our model is best; when considering either metric, our model outperforms the baseline on 12 of the families.

Tables 5 and 6 in Appendix A.2 present full results on every language in the dataset. It is interesting to consider the L2R column, which indicates the percentage of test examples on which an L2R hypothesis was selected over an R2L hypothesis. There is considerable spread in the values of this column; this demonstrates that some languages strongly prefer one direction over the other, while others do not favor one direction in particular. It is important to remember that even though the inference algorithm returns only the best L2R or R2L hypothesis, the chosen direction is conditioned on the opposite direction; therefore, a language that appears to strongly prefer one direction may still gain important insight from the opposite direction.

5 Conclusion & Future Work

The promising results of our experiments demonstrate that some languages may be amenable to bidirectional decoding; however, more investigation is required to fully understand the merits of such an approach. For example, our results show that some languages strongly favor L2R or R2L hypotheses while others are less preferential. We would like to determine if there are particular linguistic features that make one direction more valuable than the other — for example, do inflected forms with suffixes prefer L2R decoding while inflected forms with prefixes favor R2L decoding? We propose performing this analysis by exploring correlations with linguistic features in the WALS database (Dryer and Haspelmath, 2013).

We would also like to investigate how often each direction produces the correct form, as well as the percentage of examples on which the two directions agree with each other. A high disagreement could indicate a higher value in one direction with respect to the other for a particular language. It would also be informative to compare the bidirectional decoding approach with a purely R2L transformer baseline, in addition to the L2R baseline provided by the organizers.

We also suspect that the bidirectional beam search algorithm can be improved if the hypotheses in one direction are paired with each of the hypotheses in the opposite direction when fed to the decoder at each time step. Furthermore, once the halfway-point of the target form is passed in the decoding, we should expect lots of overlap between the L2R and R2L forms. We would like to see if this information can be used to join the L2R and R2L predictions to produce a better inflected form.

In initial experiments we noticed that on some languages the bidirectional decoding model converges in considerably fewer epochs than the baseline transformer model, despite the same number of parameters. We want to fully investigate this phenomenon because, if it holds for many languages, it means that the model can gain insight more quickly with both directions than with just one.

Finally, in this work our models were trained from scratch on each individual language. We would like to investigate multilingual approaches by training separate models on individual language families or a single model for every involved language. In these ways, we hope to demonstrate the merits of bidirectional decoding and its implications for a morphological transduction task.

Acknowledgments

This research is part of the Blue Waters sustained-petascale computing project, which is supported by the National Science Foundation (awards OCI-0725070 and ACI-1238993) the State of Illinois, and as of December, 2019, the National Geospatial-Intelligence Agency. Blue Waters is a joint effort of the University of Illinois at Urbana-Champaign and its National Center for Supercomputing Applications.

References

Kyunghyun Cho, Bart van Merriënboer, Caglar Gulcehre, Dzmitry Bahdanau, Fethi Bougares, Holger Schwenk, and Yoshua Bengio. 2014. Learning phrase representations using RNN encoder–decoder for statistical machine translation. In *Proceedings of the 2014 Conference on Empirical Methods in Natural Language Processing (EMNLP)*, pages 1724–1734, Doha, Qatar. Association for Computational Linguistics.

Ryan Cotterell, Christo Kirov, John Sylak-Glassman, Géraldine Walther, Ekaterina Vylomova, Arya D. McCarthy, Katharina Kann, Sebastian Mielke, Garrett Nicolai, Miikka Silfverberg, David Yarowsky, Jason Eisner, and Mans Hulden. 2018. The CoNLL–SIGMORPHON 2018 shared task: Universal morphological reinflection. In *Proceedings of the CoNLL–SIGMORPHON 2018 Shared Task: Universal Morphological Reinflection*, pages 1–27, Brussels. Association for Computational Linguistics.

Ryan Cotterell, Christo Kirov, John Sylak-Glassman, Géraldine Walther, Ekaterina Vylomova, Patrick Xia, Manaal Faruqui, Sandra Kübler, David Yarowsky, Jason Eisner, and Mans Hulden. 2017. CoNLL-SIGMORPHON 2017 shared task: Universal morphological reinflection in 52 languages. In *Proceedings of the CoNLL SIGMORPHON 2017 Shared Task: Universal Morphological Reinflection*, pages 1–30, Vancouver. Association for Computational Linguistics.

Matthew S. Dryer and Martin Haspelmath, editors. 2013. *WALS Online*. Max Planck Institute for Evolutionary Anthropology, Leipzig.

Christo Kirov, Ryan Cotterell, John Sylak-Glassman, Géraldine Walther, Ekaterina Vylomova, Patrick Xia, Manaal Faruqui, Sebastian Mielke, Arya McCarthy, Sandra Kübler, David Yarowsky, Jason Eisner, and Mans Hulden. 2018. UniMorph 2.0: Universal morphology. In *Proceedings of the Eleventh International Conference on Language Resources and Evaluation (LREC-2018)*, Miyazaki, Japan. European Languages Resources Association (ELRA).

Arya D. McCarthy, Ekaterina Vylomova, Shijie Wu, Chaitanya Malaviya, Lawrence Wolf-Sonkin, Garrett Nicolai, Christo Kirov, Miikka Silfverberg, Sebastian J. Mielke, Jeffrey Heinz, Ryan Cotterell, and Mans Hulden. 2019. The SIGMORPHON 2019 shared task: Morphological analysis in context and cross-lingual transfer for inflection. In *Proceedings of the 16th Workshop on Computational Research in Phonetics, Phonology, and Morphology*, pages 229–244, Florence, Italy. Association for Computational Linguistics.

Christian Szegedy, Vincent Vanhoucke, Sergey Ioffe, Jon Shlens, and Zbigniew Wojna. 2016. Rethinking the inception architecture for computer vision. *2016 IEEE Conference on Computer Vision and Pattern Recognition (CVPR)*.

Ashish Vaswani, Noam Shazeer, Niki Parmar, Jakob Uszkoreit, Llion Jones, Aidan N Gomez, Ł ukasz Kaiser, and Illia Polosukhin. 2017. Attention is all you need. In I. Guyon, U. V. Luxburg, S. Bengio, H. Wallach, R. Fergus, S. Vishwanathan, and R. Garnett, editors, *Advances in Neural Information Processing Systems 30*, pages 5998–6008. Curran Associates, Inc.

Ekaterina Vylomova, Jennifer White, Elizabeth Salesky, Sabrina J. Mielke, Shijie Wu, Edoardo Ponti, Rowan Hall Maudslay, Ran Zmigrod, Joseph Valvoda, Svetlana Toldova, Francis Tyers, Elena Klyachko, Ilya Yegorov, Natalia Krizhanovsky, Paula Czarnowska, Irene Nikkarinen, Andrej Krizhanovsky, Tiago Pimentel, Lucas Torroba Hennigen, Christo Kirov, Garrett Nicolai, Adina Williams, Antonios Anastasopoulos, Hilaria Cruz, Eleanor Chodroff, Ryan Cotterell, Miikka Silfverberg, and Mans Hulden. 2020. The SIGMORPHON 2020 Shared Task 0: Typologically diverse morphological inflection. In *Proceedings of the 17th SIGMORPHON Workshop on Computational Research in Phonetics, Phonology, and Morphology*.

Shijie Wu and Ryan Cotterell. 2019. Exact hard monotonic attention for character-level transduction. In *Proceedings of the 57th Annual Meeting of the Association for Computational Linguistics*, pages 1530–1537, Florence, Italy. Association for Computational Linguistics.

Shijie Wu, Ryan Cotterell, and Mans Hulden. 2020. Applying the transformer to character-level transduction.

Shijie Wu, Pamela Shapiro, and Ryan Cotterell. 2018. Hard non-monotonic attention for character-level transduction. In *Proceedings of the 2018 Conference on Empirical Methods in Natural Language Processing*, pages 4425–4438, Brussels, Belgium. Association for Computational Linguistics.

Xiangwen Zhang, Jinsong Su, Yue Qin, Yang Liu, Rongrong Ji, and Hongji Wang. 2018. Asynchronous bidirectional decoding for neural machine translation. In *AAAI Conference on Artificial Intelligence*.

Long Zhou, Jiajun Zhang, and Chengqing Zong. 2019. Synchronous bidirectional neural machine translation. *Transactions of the Association for Computational Linguistics*, 7:91–105.

A Appendices

A.1 Hyperparameter Selection

In this section we present the hyperparameters used for each language. Tables 3 and 4 contain information about specific hyperparameter configurations for each family and for specific languages.

Family	Languages	# Layers	Hidden Size	# Heads	λ_{smooth}
Afro-Asiatic	Oromo Syriac	6	512	4	0.0
Algic	Cree	4	1024	4	0.0
Australian	Murrinh-Patha	6	512	4	0.1
Austronesian	Maori Tagalog	6	1024	4	0.1
Germanic	Old English Norwegian Bokmål	4	1024	8	0.0
Indo-Ayran	Sanskrit Bengali	4	512	8	0.0
Iranian	Persian Pashto	4	1024	4	0.0
Niger-Congo	Luganda Zulu	4	1024	4	0.0
Nilo-Sahan	Zarma	4	1024	4	0.0
Oto-Manguean	Yaitepec Chatino Chichimeca-Jonaz	4	1024	4	0.1
Romance	Asturian Ladin	6	512	8	0.0
Sino-Tibetan	Tibetan	6	1024	8	0.1
Siouan	Dakota	4	1024	8	0.0
Tungusic	Evenki	4	1024	4	0.1
Turkic	Kazakh Uyghur	4	1024	4	0.0
Uralic	Moksha Votic	4	512	4	0.0
Uto-Aztecan	O'odham	6	1024	4	0.1

Table 3: Selected hyperparameters by family. The "Languages" column indicates the languages we used for selecting the hyperparameters. The Dravidian family is not present, since it has exactly two languages; the hyperparameters for these languages can be seen in Table 4.

Family	Languages	# Layers	Hidden Size	# Heads	λ_{smooth}
Afro-Asiatic	Oromo	4	512	4	0.0
Austronesian	Tagalog	6	1024	8	0.0
Dravidian	Kannada	4	1024	8	0.1
Dravidian	Telugu	4	1024	4	0.0
Germanic	Old English	4	512	8	0.0
Oto-Manguean	Chichimeca-Jonaz	6	1024	8	0.1
Uralic	Votic	6	512	8	0.0

Table 4: Selected hyperparameters for certain languages on which we performed a grid search. These languages use different hyperparameters than their corresponding families, shown in Table 3, due to the fact that a more optimal configuration was discovered.

A.2 Complete Results Tables

In this section we show full results on each language.

Family	Language	Accuracy			Edit Distance			L2R
		MONO	TRM	BI-TRM	MONO	TRM	BI-TRM	
Austronesian	Cebuano	83.80	83.80	**87.40**	0.31	0.33	**0.26**	57.66
	Hiligaynon	92.40	**97.90**	96.60	0.22	**0.09**	0.10	26.47
	Maori	47.60	**52.40**	**52.40**	1.10	1.02	**0.95**	52.38
	Malagasy	99.20	**100**	**100**	0.01	**0**	**0**	9.45
	Tagalog	65.30	72.30	**75.10**	1.27	0.78	**0.73**	33.89
Germanic	Old English	75.80	**79.10**	78.40	0.44	**0.37**	0.38	77.41
	Danish	74.60	**76.30**	73.00	0.60	**0.25**	0.29	93.92
	German	**98.50**	97.70	98.00	0.06	0.03	**0.02**	95.18
	English	96.60	**96.90**	**96.90**	0.10	**0.06**	**0.06**	89.91
	North Frisian	86.10	**87.90**	87.60	0.40	**0.39**	0.42	54.30
	Middle High German	90.80	91.50	**92.90**	0.17	**0.11**	**0.11**	82.98
	Icelandic	97.10	97.00	**97.60**	0.06	0.07	**0.04**	88.79
	Dutch	98.90	99.00	**99.50**	0.02	0.02	**0.01**	79.48
	Norwegian Bokmål	76.90	**77.30**	74.80	0.47	**0.46**	0.51	95.20
	Swedish	98.80	98.70	**99.00**	0.08	**0.02**	**0.02**	92.04
Niger-Congo	Akan	**100**	**100**	99.90	**0**	**0**	**0.00**	67.23
	Gã	**100**	97.60	97.00	**0**	0.04	0.05	52.66
	Kongo	**98.70**	98.10	**98.70**	**0.01**	0.03	**0.01**	78.85
	Lingala	**100**	**100**	**100**	**0**	**0**	**0**	67.39
	Luganda	90.00	91.20	**92.80**	0.17	0.13	**0.11**	46.47
	Chewa	**100**	**100**	**100**	**0**	**0**	**0**	98.01
	Sotho	**100**	98.00	98.00	**0**	0.03	0.03	91.92
	Swahili	**100**	**100**	**100**	**0**	**0**	**0**	72.64
	Zulu	88.50	**92.30**	**92.30**	0.19	**0.13**	**0.13**	43.59
Oto-Manguean	San Pedro Amuzgos Amuzgo	93.50	94.70	**95.20**	0.17	0.13	**0.12**	21.12
	Eastern Highland Chatino	78.70	91.40	**91.80**	0.39	**0.15**	0.16	22.14
	Tlatepuzco Chinantec	89.00	91.60	**92.30**	0.16	**0.12**	**0.12**	64.64
	Yaitepec Chatino	45.90	61.20	**62.50**	2.28	1.00	**0.97**	63.71
	Zenzontepec Chatino	79.30	79.70	**84.60**	0.44	0.49	**0.33**	60.33
	Mezquital Otomi	**99.10**	99.00	**99.10**	**0.01**	**0.01**	**0.01**	32.13
	Sierra Otomi	97.90	**98.20**	98.00	0.06	**0.05**	**0.05**	82.91
	Chichimeca-Jonaz	**74.60**	74.50	74.20	0.59	0.60	**0.57**	63.96
	Yoloxóchitl Mixtec	90.70	91.00	**91.70**	0.23	0.22	**0.16**	69.33
	Chichicapan Zapotec	78.40	84.60	**85.50**	0.55	0.39	**0.32**	75.44
Uralic	Estonian	95.10	**95.60**	95.20	0.19	**0.17**	0.18	68.04
	Finnish	99.60	99.60	**99.70**	0.02	**0.01**	**0.01**	62.97
	Ingrian	68.80	87.10	**87.50**	0.60	0.24	**0.23**	86.16
	Karelian	99.30	99.30	**99.50**	0.04	**0.01**	**0.01**	50.79
	Livonian	92.50	**96.40**	95.50	0.13	**0.06**	0.07	52.24
	Moksha	92.80	**93.90**	93.60	0.24	**0.18**	0.19	81.11
	Meadow Mari	**93.30**	92.90	92.60	0.19	**0.15**	0.16	85.81
	Erzya	93.60	**94.50**	94.10	0.21	**0.17**	0.18	90.65
	Northern Sami	99.60	99.60	**99.70**	**0.01**	**0.01**	**0.01**	69.86
	Veps	82.70	**84.80**	83.30	0.45	**0.25**	0.27	84.56
	Votic	69.40	**86.10**	84.30	0.49	**0.21**	0.24	51.25

Table 5: Results for individual languages in the development language set. MONO refers to the hard monotonic baseline, TRM refers to the transformer baseline, and BI-TRM refers to our implementation using a bidirectional decoder. The L2R column shows the percentage of words in each language for which our model selects a left-to-right hypothesis as its final result. It should be noted that this column really indicates a "forwardness" percentage, as languages with a right-to-left orthography are processed in a right-to-left manner.

Family	Language	Accuracy			Edit Distance			L2R
		MONO	TRM	BI-TRM	MONO	TRM	BI-TRM	
Afro-Asiatic	Maltese	88.70	**97.20**	96.60	0.22	**0.05**	**0.05**	67.99
	Oromo	98.30	**99.00**	98.00	0.03	**0.02**	0.04	30.86
	Syriac	91.80	90.80	**94.50**	0.08	0.09	**0.06**	70.07
Algic	Cree	67.20	68.70	**70.30**	1.26	1.20	**1.16**	69.34
Australian	Murrinh-Patha	61.40	**90.00**	87.80	0.92	0.27	**0.26**	63.06
Dravidian	Kannada	77.30	**78.30**	76.10	0.70	**0.67**	0.76	60.15
	Telugu	94.80	**95.90**	94.50	0.25	**0.24**	0.32	42.49
Germanic	Middle Low German	60.60	**63.50**	58.40	1.03	**0.84**	1.10	52.16
	Swiss German	90.10	92.70	**93.20**	0.18	0.11	**0.10**	68.83
	Norwegian Nynorsk	84.60	86.40	**86.60**	0.24	0.21	**0.20**	85.76
Indo-Aryan	Bengali	98.80	99.40	**99.90**	0.03	0.05	**0.00**	93.54
	Hindi	**100**	**100**	**100**	**0**	**0**	**0**	75.07
	Sanskrit	92.90	**93.40**	**93.40**	0.16	0.15	**0.14**	65.77
	Urdu	**99.40**	99.30	**99.40**	**0.01**	**0.01**	**0.01**	88.62
Iranian	Persian	**100**	**100**	99.90	**0**	**0**	0.00	45.26
	Pashto	89.00	91.20	**91.40**	0.30	**0.25**	**0.25**	62.85
	Tajik	0.00	**56.30**	**56.30**	2.81	**1.00**	1.12	75.00
Niger-Congo	Shona	**100**	**100**	**100**	**0**	**0**	**0**	85.31
Nilo-Sahan	Zarma	0.00	87.50	**100**	2.88	0.19	**0**	43.75
Romance	Asturian	98.50	**99.40**	99.30	0.03	**0.01**	**0.01**	46.88
	Catalan	99.60	**99.80**	**99.80**	0.01	**0.00**	**0.00**	84.35
	Middle French	99.50	**99.80**	**99.80**	0.01	**0.00**	**0.00**	83.48
	Friulian	97.70	**99.80**	99.70	0.03	**0.00**	**0.00**	66.11
	Galician	99.70	**99.80**	**99.80**	**0.01**	**0.01**	**0.01**	80.65
	Ladin	99.00	**99.50**	**99.50**	0.02	**0.01**	**0.01**	61.38
	Venetian	99.50	**99.80**	99.70	0.01	0.01	**0.00**	52.60
	Anglo-Norman	70.60	**96.10**	92.20	0.82	**0.10**	0.18	60.78
Sino-Tibetan	Tibetan	83.20	**84.40**	**84.40**	0.22	**0.20**	0.21	37.39
Siouan	Dakota	92.90	**95.60**	94.90	0.16	**0.08**	0.10	71.20
Tungusic	Evenki	55.30	**58.60**	58.30	1.20	**1.06**	1.09	65.55
Turkic	Azerbaijani	79.50	**82.20**	81.90	0.42	**0.34**	**0.34**	87.70
	Bashkir	99.60	**99.80**	**99.80**	0.01	**0.00**	**0.00**	69.80
	Crimean Tatar	98.80	99.10	**99.30**	0.10	**0.01**	**0.01**	78.05
	Kazakh	97.40	97.90	**98.00**	0.15	0.12	**0.11**	63.46
	Kyrgyz	97.90	98.30	**98.80**	0.04	0.03	**0.02**	67.95
	Khakas	99.20	**99.60**	**99.60**	0.01	**0.00**	0.01	81.67
	Turkmen	86.50	**87.40**	85.60	0.45	**0.42**	0.50	82.09
	Uyghur	99.50	99.50	**99.70**	0.01	0.01	**0.00**	48.17
	Uzbek	99.60	**99.80**	99.50	**0.01**	**0.01**	0.02	67.58
Uralic	Komi-Zyrian	96.30	**96.90**	**96.90**	0.11	**0.07**	**0.07**	75.61
	Ludic	24.10	**32.90**	**32.90**	2.14	2.35	**2.13**	68.29
	Livvi	**94.50**	94.30	**94.50**	0.14	**0.09**	**0.09**	82.53
	Udmurt	97.80	**98.40**	**98.40**	0.06	**0.03**	**0.03**	74.02
	Võro	32.00	61.20	**63.10**	1.27	0.66	**0.62**	63.11
Uto-Aztecan	O'odham	76.30	80.80	**82.50**	0.49	0.41	**0.39**	62.42

Table 6: Results for individual languages in the surprise language set. MONO refers to the hard monotonic baseline, TRM refers to the transformer baseline, and BI-TRM refers to our implementation using a bidirectional decoder. The L2R column shows the percentage of words in each language for which our model selects a left-to-right hypothesis as its final result. It should be noted that this column really indicates a "forwardness" percentage, as languages with a right-to-left orthography are processed in a right-to-left manner.

One Model to Pronounce Them All: Multilingual Grapheme-to-Phoneme Conversion With a Transformer Ensemble

Kaili Vesik[1,2], Muhammad Abdul-Mageed[1,2,3], Miikka Silfverberg[2]
[1] Natural Language Processing Lab
[2] Department of Linguistics
[3] School of Information
The University of British Columbia
[1] {kaili.vesik,muhammad.mageed,miikka.silfverberg}@ubc.ca

Abstract

The task of grapheme-to-phoneme (G2P) conversion is important for both speech recognition and synthesis. Similar to other speech and language processing tasks, in a scenario where only small-sized training data are available, learning G2P models is challenging. We describe a simple approach of exploiting model ensembles, based on multilingual Transformers and self-training, to develop a highly effective G2P solution for 15 languages. Our models are developed as part of our participation in the SIGMORPHON 2020 Shared Task 1 focused at G2P. Our best models achieve 14.99 word error rate (WER) and 3.30 phoneme error rate (PER), a sizeable improvement over the shared task competitive baselines.

1 Introduction

Speech technologies are becoming increasingly pervasive in our lives. The task of *grapheme-to-phoneme (G2P)* conversion is an important component of both speech recognition and synthesis. In G2P conversion, sequences of graphemes (the symbols used to write words) are mapped to corresponding phonemes (pronunciation symbols, e.g., symbols of the International Phonetic Alphabet). Members of the Special Interest Group on Computational Morphology and Phonology (SIGMORPHON) have proposed a G2P shared task (SIGMOR-PHON 2020 Shared Task 1) [1] involving multiple languages. In this paper, we describe our submissions to the shared task. Organizers provide an overview of the task and submitted systems in Gorman et al. (2020) (this volume).

The task was introduced with data from 10 languages, with an additional 5 'surprise' languages released during the task timeline. Our goal was to develop an effective system based on modern deep learning methods as a solution. However, deep learning technologies work best with sufficiently large training data. Hence, a clear challenge we came across is the limited size of the shared task training data for each of the 15 individual languages. To ease this bottleneck, we decided to view the task through a *multilingual machine translation lens* where we build a single model mapping from input to output across all the languages simultaneously. In this, we hypothesized that a multilingual model would allow for shared representations across the various languages that may be more powerful than individual representations of monolingual models. Abundant evidence now exists for approaching machine translation tasks from a multilingual perspective (Johnson et al., 2017a; Dong et al., 2015; Firat et al., 2016), which inspired our choice.

In order to make use of unlabeled data, we also explore a straightforward *self-training approach*. In particular, we employ our trained models to convert sequences of multilingual unlabeled graphemes, taken from Wikipedia data, into multilingual phonemes. We then select sequences of phonemes predicted with our models above a certain confidence threshold to augment the shared task training data, thus re-training our models with larger (gold and silver) training data from scratch. Our models are based on the Transformer architecture which exploits effective self-attention. We show that both our multilingual model and the self-trained variation outperform the results of the competitive baseline monolingual

---

[1]The shared task webpage is accessible at: `https://sigmorphon.github.io/sharedtasks/2020/task1`.

Proceedings of the Seventeenth SIGMORPHON Workshop on Computational Research in Phonetics, Phonology, and Morphology, pages 146–152
Online, July 10, 2020. ©2020 Association for Computational Linguistics
https://doi.org/10.18653/v1/P17

models provided by the task organizers. Ultimately, we demonstrate how our simple modeling choices enable us to provide an effective solution to the problem in spite of the low-resource challenge. Intrinsically, our approach also enjoys the simplicity of a single model rather than 15 different models.

The rest of the paper is organized as follows: Section 2 is a description of the shared task data, evaluation metrics, and baselines. Section 3 introduces both our fully supervised, multilingual models (Section 3.1) and self-trained model (Section 3.2). We present our results in Section 4. We provide an analysis of results and report on an ablation study in Section 5. We overview related work in Section 6, and conclude in Section 7.

2 Task Data, Evaluation, and Baselines

The data provided by the organizers of the shared task are extracted from Wiktionary [2] using the WikiPron library (Lee et al., 2020), and consist of 4,050 gold labeled grapheme-phoneme pairs for each of 15 languages, split into a **training** set (3,600 per language) and a **development** set (450 per language). The blind **test** data comprise 450 sources for each language. The data involves languages in the set *{Adyghe (ady), Armenian (arm), Bulgarian (bul), Dutch (dut), French (fre), Georgian (geo), Modern Greek (gre), Hindi (hin), Hungarian (hun), Icelandic (ice), Japanese hiragana (jpn), Korean (kor), Lithuanian (lit), Romanian (rum), Vietnamese (vie)}.* [3] This set of languages employ a variety of writing systems: *alphabets* (e.g. French), *alphasyllabary* (e.g. Hindi), and *syllabary* (e.g. Japanese hiragana), thus introducing enough diversity and modelling challenge. Table 1 shows sample pairs from training data across 5 languages.

Evaluation. For evaluation, the task organizers use both Word Error Rate (WER) and Phoneme Error Rate (PER). WER is the percentage of words whose predicted transcription does not match the gold transcription; PER is the micro-averaged edit distance between predicted and gold transcriptions. We follow this

Language	Source	Target (IPA)
Alphabet:		
arm	ɯհեղ	ɑ h ɛ ʁ
	լհɯɗեք	l j ɑ ɾ ʒ ɛ kʰ
fre	front	f ʁ ɔ̃
	vêtu	v ɛ t y
Alphasyllabary:		
hin	दिखावा	d ɪ kʰ ɑː ʋ ɑː
	हटना	ɦ ə ʈ n ɑː
kor	개벽	k e̞ b j ʌ k˺
	오빠	o̞ p a̠
Syllabary:		
jpn	いなり	i n a̠ ɾʲ i
	やせん	j a̠ s ẽ̞ ɴ

Table 1: Sample pairs from training data

set-up in evaluating our models on the development data as well, as reported in this paper.

Baselines. Organizers provide a number of monolingual baselines. The first is a pair n-gram model encoded as a weighted finite-state transducer (FST), implemented using the OpenGRMtoolkit [4]. The second is a bi-LSTM encoder-decoder sequence model implemented using the Fairseq toolkit [5]. The third is a Transformer model also implemented using the Fairseq toolkit. Organizer-provided shared task baselines are shown in Table 2 as WER and PER averages over the 15 languages. We now introduce our models.

Model	Avg over 15 langs	
	WER	PER
FST	22.00	4.92
Bi-LSTM	16.84	3.99
Transformer	17.51	4.30

Table 2: Baseline performance as avg. WER and PER over the 15 languages as provided by task organizers. Baselines exploit monolingual models.

3 Models

As explained, our models are based on Transformers and we offer two primary types of models, depending on how we supervise each. We first introduce *fully supervised* multilin-

---

[2] https://www.wiktionary.org/.
[3] We use three-character ISO-639-2 abbreviations as not all of the task languages have ISO-639-1 codes.
[4] http://www.opengrm.org/twiki/bin/view/GRM.
[5] https://github.com/pytorch/fairseq.

147

gual models, then we introduce our *semi-supervised* models (also multilingual). Our semi-supervised models follow a self-training set up. We now explain each of these models.

3.1 Supervised, Multilingual Models

We use a multilingual approach where we train a single model on data from all 15 languages. For this purpose, we prepend a token comprising a language code (e.g. `fre`) to each grapheme sequence source. For our implementation, we use the PyTorch Transformer architecture in the OpenNMT Neural Machine Translation Toolkit (Klein et al., 2017). We set the model hyper-parameters as shown in Table 3, which follows those adopted by Vaswani et al. (2017).

Hyper-Parameter	Value
Number of layers	6
Hidden state size	512
Word embedding size	512
Hidden feed-forward size	2,048
Number of self-attention heads	8
Optimizer	Adam
Dropout probability	0.1
Number of training steps	200K

Table 3: Multilingual Transformer hyper-parameters.

We train the model with 3 different random seeds, and at inference we employ an ensemble consisting of the models from 4 training checkpoints (at 50k, 100k, 150k, and 200k steps) for each of the 3 models generated by the random seeds. We note that OpenNMT averages individual models' prediction distributions, which is how we deploy our ensemble. We use beam search with the OpenNMT default beam width of 5. [6]

3.2 Self-Trained Model

3.2.1 Wikipedia Data Augmentation

One of the models we submitted to the task employs a self-training approach, as a way to augment training data. The additional data is sourced from Wikipedia articles from 12 of the 15 languages (excluding Adyghe,

Japanese, and Vietnamese) [7]. We download the Wikipedia dumps from the Wikimedia website [8] and use an off-the-shelf tool [9] for extracting text. Further pre-processing involved removing any remaining XML markup, discarding leading and trailing punctuation and numerals for each word, and ignoring any words with remaining word-internal punctuation or numerals.

Due to time constraints, only one million words from each language were used, and from those only unique entries were submitted to the model for translation and subsequent evaluation as potential candidates for augmenting training data. Table 4 summarizes the size of the Wikipedia data used for each available language. Selection methods and thresholds are discussed in Section 3.2.2.

Language	Translated	Selected
arm	9,947	4,723
bul	9,999	3,197
dut	2,275	860
fre	9,985	2,888
geo	5,038	3,043
gre	9,949	3,419
hin	1,450	727
hun	10,000	3,444
ice	9,839	3,719
kor	4,282	2,681
lit	7,033	3,615
rum	9,785	3,102
Total	89,582	35,418

Table 4: Number of Wikipedia words translated vs. number of words selected for self-training.

3.2.2 Procedure

As explained, self-training data is drawn from the translations of Wikipedia text in 12 languages as predicted by an ensemble model. In order to select pairs to augment the training set, we first calculate the mean per-class softmax value in the development set (which we

---

[6] We also experimented with beam size 10, but did not obtain improvements on the development set.

[7] We note that there is no Adyghe Wikipedia. Also, the Japenese Wikipedia is not strictly in Hiragana and so we exclude it. By mistake, we did not include Vietnamese either. Clearly, we average results from the self-training models only on the languages for which we augment the data.

[8] https://dumps.wikimedia.org/.

[9] https://github.com/attardi/wikiextractor

find to be at 0.11). [10] Comparatively, the average per-class softmax value for the predicted Wikipedia targets for each language ranges from 0.12 to 0.30. Based on this analysis, we select only those Wikipedia pairs whose predicted targets have a probability greater than 0.2. [11] The selected data are combined with the original (i.e., from official task) training set and the models are re-trained using the same hyper-parameters as the fully-supervised setting.

4   Results

	Multilingual		Self-trained	
Lang	WER	PER	WER	PER
ady	25.56	6.40	25.11	6.47
arm	16.67	3.37	16.89	3.37
bul	28.44	7.30	27.33	7.12
dut	16.00	2.84	15.33	2.84
fre	8.22	1.96	8.44	1.92
geo	24.44	4.92	26.22	5.22
gre	15.11	2.72	16.22	3.00
hin	6.44	1.66	6.89	1.89
hun	2.89	0.54	3.56	0.66
ice	9.56	1.88	10.89	2.23
jpn	7.33	2.18	7.11	2.11
kor	24.22	6.54	26.00	6.50
lit	20.00	4.11	21.11	3.96
rum	12.00	2.94	11.78	2.97
vie	5.56	1.77	5.56	1.91
avg	14.83	3.41	15.23	3.48

Table 5:   Development set results for *fully-supervised multilingual* and *self-trained multilingual* models.

Both models demonstrate lower word error rates (WER) and phoneme error rates (PER), averaged across languages, than the baseline monolingual models provided by the task organizers (see Table 2 in Section 2). Error rates per language are shown in Table 5 for the development set and Table 6 for the blind test set (results published by organizers). Table 7

	Multilingual		Self-trained	
Lang	WER	PER	WER	PER
ady	28.44	6.46	29.11	6.46
arm	13.11	2.98	12.89	3.07
bul	27.11	5.91	30.89	6.92
dut	15.78	2.98	16.89	3.07
fre	5.33	1.24	5.78	1.36
geo	26.00	5.25	26.67	5.23
gre	16.67	2.68	15.78	2.60
hin	6.44	1.58	6.67	1.66
hun	4.67	1.05	4.22	0.98
ice	9.56	2.11	9.11	1.83
jpn	6.00	1.44	6.00	1.40
kor	32.22	8.54	32.44	8.86
lit	19.33	3.63	20.00	3.68
rum	9.33	1.96	10.44	2.23
vie	4.89	1.66	4.00	1.28
avg	14.99	3.30	15.39	3.37

Table 6: Blind test set results for *fully-supervised multilingual* and *self-trained multilingual* models.

shows examples of prediction errors, which demonstrate some of the typical minor errors in phenomena such as voicing (e.g. k vs. g), epenthesis and elision (e.g. p ʁ u vs. p ʁ u l), and coarticulation (e.g. bʲ vs. b).

On average, the fully-supervised models performed slightly better than the self-trained model. We expected that the self-trained model would see (at least slightly) better performance than the fully supervised; however, due to time constraints, we were not able to augment the training data to such a degree that this hypothesized improvement would be tangible. We leave it as a question for the future whether, and if so to what extent, self-training can improve our models. We now provide an analysis of our findings and report on an ablation study under a number of settings.

5   Analysis & Ablation Study

We suspected that languages with shared writing systems (in our multilingual models) would benefit from the shared representation and hence see better results, posing a challenges to those languages with unique orthography (i.e., orthography not shared by o=any of the other languages considered). However, our results do not support this hypothesis; there did not

---

[10] As is known, the softmax function produces a probability distribution over the classes.

[11] There could be different ways to select predicted data for augmentation. For example, one can arbitrarily choose the top $n\%$ most confidently predicted points (with n being a hyper-parameter).

Lang	Source	Target	Prediction
arm	զուզարան	z u kʰ ɑ ɾ ɑ n	z u g ɑ ɾ ɑ n
	անխնա	ɑ ŋ χ ə n ɑ	ɑ ŋ χ n ɑ
fre	full	f u l	f y l
	proulx	p ʁ u	p ʁ u l
hin	धन्य	dʱ ə n j ə	dʱ ə n j
	मेहरबानी	m ɛːʱ r b ɑː n iː	m eː ɦ ə r b ɑː n iː
jpn	こたま	k o̞ d̪ a̠ m a̠	k o̞ t̪ a̠ m a̠
	ひぞう	ç i z oː	ç i z o̞ː
rum	ceri	t ʃ e rʲ	t͡ʃ e rʲ
	iubeau	j u bʲ æ u	j u b e̞ a w

Table 7: Sample prediction errors from development data.

appear to be a significant correlation between writing system and results on G2P conversion. For example, a total of 7 of the languages (i.e., dut, fre, hun, ice, lit, rum, vie) use the Roman alphabet, but the WERs for these languages cover a reasonably wide range (from first- to eleventh-best) of the results. It is worth noting, however, that the two languages that use the Cyrillic alphabet (ady, bul) were the two worst-performing languages of the set.

Both prior and subsequent to the task deadline, we performed several ablations in order to assess the effectiveness of our approach. First, we compare results based on single models vs. those based on the ensemble. Table 8 shows the error rates of development set translation by the four training checkpoints used in the ensemble, in this case trained with the default (random) seed. Given that each of these results is poorer than our ensemble results for the multilingual model (WER 14.83 / PER 3.41), it is clear that the ensemble approach is superior. Clearly, the ensemble has the advantage of exploiting multiple predictions for each word. This does result in reduced error rates as compared to individual models.

We also compare our multilingual model's error rates on a given language to those acquired by the respective monolingual models. We note that each of the monolingual models is otherwise initialized with the same parameters as the multilingual model described in Section 3.1. Results for the 15 monolingual models are shown in Table 9. The average WER across all languages is almost twice as big as that of our multilingual model (whether individual or ensemble), and the per-

	Avg over 15 langs	
Checkpoint	WER	PER
50k of 200k steps	16.70	3.93
100k of 200k steps	16.04	3.69
150k of 200k steps	16.25	3.78
200k of 200k steps	15.73	3.65
Ensemble	14.83	3.41

Table 8: Development set results for individual models vs. our ensemble

language results are worse across the board as well. The monolingual Georgian WER (25.33) was the only result to approach its multilingual counterpart (24.44). ***Our multilingual approach is clearly a significant improvement over otherwise equivalent monolingually-trained models***.

6 Related Work

Various data-driven models have been successfully applied to G2P conversion. In terms of English conversion, Bisani and Ney (2008) use co-segmentation and joint sequence models for early data-driven G2P. Novak et al. (2016) employ a joint multigram approach to generate weighted finite-state transducers for G2P. Recently, neural sequence-to-sequence models based on CNN and RNN architectures have been proposed for the G2P task delivering superior results compared to earlier non-neural approaches (Chae et al., 2018; Yolchuyeva et al., 2019a). Similar to our approach, Yolchuyeva et al. (2019b) use transformers (Vaswani et al., 2017) to perform English G2P conversion.

	Monolingual	
Lang	WER	PER
ady	33.56	9.31
arm	24.00	5.65
bul	41.33	12.07
dut	30.89	7.73
fre	34.89	12.69
geo	25.33	5.19
gre	24.00	5.13
hin	22.67	6.76
hun	20.89	5.30
ice	30.22	11.12
jpn	11.78	3.73
kor	30.67	9.17
lit	26.00	7.75
rum	20.00	5.52
vie	32.00	13.75
avg	27.22	8.06

Table 9: Development set results for monolingual models.

Multilingual training is a crucial component in our system. Our approach is closely related to multilingual neural machine translation (Johnson et al., 2017b), where a single model is trained to translate between multiple source and target languages. Others have also explored multilingual approaches to G2P. Deri and Knight (2016) use multilingual G2P conversion for the purpose of adapting models from high-resource languages to train weighted finite-state transducers for related low-resource languages. Ni et al. (2018) experiment with multilingual training for deep learning models. They use pretrained character embeddings with LSTM encoder-decoders in order to train multilingual G2P models for Chinese, Japanese, Korean and Thai. In contrast to Ni et al. (2018), we inspect multilingual training in the context of transformer models.

For our second model, whose training data is augmented from Wikipedia, we use a self-taining method. Sun et al. (2019) investigate self-training together with ensemble distillation for English G2P conversion, using transformer models. Their setting resembles ours: A teacher model is first trained using a gold standard labeled G2P training set. The teacher model is then used to label additional grapheme data, producing a silver standard training set. Subsequently, a model ensemble is trained on the combination of the gold and silver data. Sun et al. (2019) train on nearly 200k gold standard examples and 2M silver standard examples and report small improvements. In contrast, we do not observe improvements from self-training. This might be a consequence of the small size of the shared task datasets and our silver standard Wikipedia data.

7 Conclusion

We introduced a multilingual approach to G2P conversion, exploiting Transformers in a fully supervised multilingual setting. Strikingly, our choice to model all languages in a shared, nultilingual space reduces error rates (in WER and PER) by almost one half. We also showed how an ensemble of individually-trained multilingual Transformers, is an improvement over non-ensemble models. We also leveraged multilingual Wikipedia data via a self-training strategy, though due to time constraints we were not able to incorporate enough silver labeled data into training to see the results we had hoped for[12]. Nevertheless, the multilingual models successfully surpassed all organizer-provided baselines on the task and compared favorably to several other submitted models. Our future work includes scaling up our self-training with larger Wikipedia data and choosing fully-trained models (e.g., in our case ones at 200K steps) to include in the ensemble.

Acknowledgements

We acknowledge the support of the Natural Sciences and Engineering Research Council of Canada (NSERC), the Social Sciences Research Council of Canada (SSHRC), and Compute Canada (www.computecanada.ca).

References

Maximilian Bisani and Hermann Ney. 2008. Joint-sequence models for grapheme-to-phoneme conversion. *Speech communication*, 50(5):434–451.

---

[12]Training on all available Wikipedia data is in progress at the time of this paper's submission

Moon-jung Chae, Kyubyong Park, Jinhyun Bang, Soobin Suh, Jonghyuk Park, Namju Kim, and Longhun Park. 2018. Convolutional sequence to sequence model with non-sequential greedy decoding for grapheme to phoneme conversion. In *2018 IEEE International Conference on Acoustics, Speech and Signal Processing (ICASSP)*, pages 2486–2490. IEEE.

Aliya Deri and Kevin Knight. 2016. Grapheme-to-phoneme models for (almost) any language. In *Proceedings of the 54th Annual Meeting of the Association for Computational Linguistics (Volume 1: Long Papers)*, pages 399–408.

Daxiang Dong, Hua Wu, Wei He, Dianhai Yu, and Haifeng Wang. 2015. Multi-task learning for multiple language translation. In *Proceedings of the 53rd Annual Meeting of the Association for Computational Linguistics and the 7th International Joint Conference on Natural Language Processing (Volume 1: Long Papers)*, pages 1723–1732, Beijing, China. Association for Computational Linguistics.

Orhan Firat, Kyunghyun Cho, and Yoshua Bengio. 2016. Multi-way, multilingual neural machine translation with a shared attention mechanism. In *Proceedings of the 2016 Conference of the North American Chapter of the Association for Computational Linguistics: Human Language Technologies*, pages 866–875, San Diego, California. Association for Computational Linguistics.

Kyle Gorman, Lucas F.E. Ashby, Aaron Goyzueta, Arya D. McCarthy, Shijie Wu, and Daniel You. 2020. The SIGMORPHON 2020 shared task on multilingual grapheme-to-phoneme conversion. In *Proceedings of the 17th SIGMORPHON Workshop on Computational Research in Phonetics, Phonology, and Morphology.*

Melvin Johnson, Mike Schuster, Quoc V. Le, Maxim Krikun, Yonghui Wu, Zhifeng Chen, Nikhil Thorat, Fernanda Viégas, Martin Wattenberg, Greg Corrado, Macduff Hughes, and Jeffrey Dean. 2017a. Google's multilingual neural machine translation system: Enabling zero-shot translation. *Transactions of the Association for Computational Linguistics*, 5:339–351.

Melvin Johnson, Mike Schuster, Quoc V Le, Maxim Krikun, Yonghui Wu, Zhifeng Chen, Nikhil Thorat, Fernanda Viégas, Martin Wattenberg, Greg Corrado, et al. 2017b. Google's multilingual neural machine translation system: Enabling zero-shot translation. *Transactions of the Association for Computational Linguistics*, 5:339–351.

Guillaume Klein, Yoon Kim, Yuntian Deng, Jean Senellart, and Alexander M. Rush. 2017. OpenNMT: Open-source toolkit for neural machine translation. In *Proc. ACL*.

Jackson L. Lee, Lucas F.E. Ashby, M. Elizabeth Garza, Yeonju Lee-Sikka, Sean Miller, Alan Wong, Arya D. McCarthy, and Kyle Gorman. 2020. Massively multilingual pronunciation mining with WikiPron. In *Proceedings of the 12th Language Resources and Evaluation Conference*, pages 4216–4221, Marseille.

Jinfu Ni, Yoshinori Shiga, and Hisashi Kawai. 2018. Multilingual grapheme-to-phoneme conversion with global character vectors. In *Interspeech*, pages 2823–2827.

Josef Robert Novak, Nobuaki Minematsu, and Keikichi Hirose. 2016. Phonetisaurus: Exploring grapheme-to-phoneme conversion with joint n-gram models in the wfst framework. *Natural Language Engineering*, 22(6):907–938.

Hao Sun, Xu Tan, Jun-Wei Gan, Hongzhi Liu, Sheng Zhao, Tao Qin, and Tie-Yan Liu. 2019. Token-level ensemble distillation for grapheme-to-phoneme conversion. *arXiv preprint arXiv:1904.03446*.

Ashish Vaswani, Noam Shazeer, Niki Parmar, Jakob Uszkoreit, Llion Jones, Aidan N. Gomez, Lukasz Kaiser, and Illia Polosukhin. 2017. Attention is all you need.

Sevinj Yolchuyeva, Géza Németh, and Bálint Gyires-Tóth. 2019a. Grapheme-to-phoneme conversion with convolutional neural networks. *Applied Sciences*, 9(6):1143.

Sevinj Yolchuyeva, Géza Németh, and Bálint Gyires-Tóth. 2019b. Transformer based grapheme-to-phoneme conversion. *Interspeech 2019*.

Leveraging Principal Parts for Morphological Inflection

Ling Liu and **Mans Hulden**
Department of Linguistics
University of Colorado
`first.last@colorado.edu`

Abstract

This paper presents the submission by the CU Ling team from the University of Colorado to SIGMORPHON 2020 shared task 0 on morphological inflection. The task is to generate the target inflected word form given a lemma form and a target morphosyntactic description. Our system uses the Transformer architecture. Our overall approach is to treat the morphological inflection task as a paradigm cell filling problem and to design the system to leverage principal parts information indirectly for better morphological inflection when the training data is limited. We train one model for each language separately without external data. The overall average performance of our submission ranks the first in both average accuracy and Levenshtein distance from the gold inflection among all submissions including those using external resources.

1 Introduction

The task of morphological inflection is to generate a target inflected word form (henceforth *tgtform*) given a lemma form (henceforth *lemma*) and a target morphosyntactic description (henceforth *tgtmsd*). In the SIGMORPHON 2020 shared task 0 on morphological inflection (Vylomova et al., 2020) and previous years' SIGMORPHON shared tasks on morphological inflection (Cotterell et al., 2016, 2017a, 2018; McCarthy et al., 2019), the training data is provided in the format of tab-separated lemma-tgtmsd-tgtform triples, and participating systems are expected to predict the missing target forms in the test data released shortly before prediction submission.

The sequence-to-sequence (henceforth *seq2seq*) architecture has been very successful in dealing with morphological inflection, especially when there are abundant labeled data for training. The accuracies and Levenshtein distances on the devel-

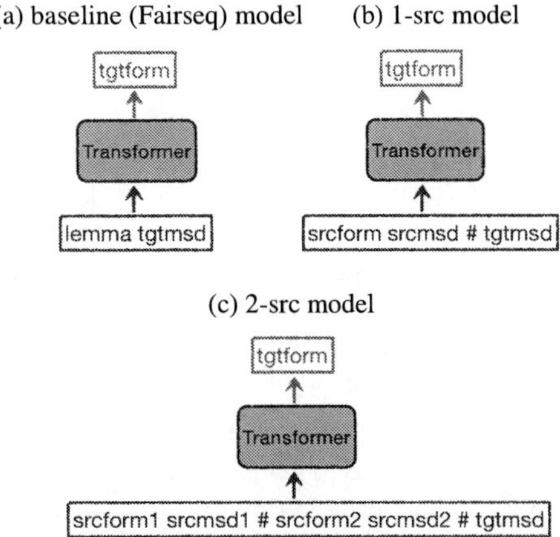

Figure 1: Illustration of general model architectures. All three of our models use the Transformer architecture for inflection. They are different from each other by the input to the Transformer model.

opment data inflected by 9 baseline models are provided for the 45 typologically and genealogically diversified development languages: a non-neural model based on lemma-tgtform alignment and transformation, a per-language Transformer model, a per-language-family Transformer model, a per-language Transformer model with data augmentation, a per-language-family Transformer model with data augmentation, LSTM seq2seq models with exact hard monotonic attention (Wu and Cotterell, 2019) trained per language, per language family, per language with data augmentation, and per language family with data augmentation respectively. The data augmentation method used by the baseline models is from Anastasopoulos and Neubig (2019). The baseline numbers indicate that the Transformer model for character-level transduction (Wu et al., 2020) is very competitive, achieving the highest average accuracy and lowest average edit distance and best performance on most lan-

*Proceedings of the Seventeenth SIGMORPHON Workshop on Computational Research
in Phonetics, Phonology, and Morphology*, pages 153–161
Online, July 10, 2020. ©2020 Association for Computational Linguistics
https://doi.org/10.18653/v1/P17

guages (33 out of 45) when the model is trained per language. Therefore, we adopt the Transformer architecture (Vaswani et al., 2017) for all three of our models (see Figure 1) which are different from each other by the input and output to the Transformer model, as will be presented in section 3.

Though not explicitly organized as a paradigm cell filling problem (PCFP) (Ackerman et al., 2009) task, the shared task is closely related to and can largely be seen as a computational instance of it (Malouf, 2016, 2017; Cotterell et al., 2017a; Silfverberg et al., 2018; Silfverberg and Hulden, 2018), where some slots are given in the paradigms as training data and others are to be inflected as development data or test data.[1] The data format of the shared task privileges the lemma as the source form (henceforth *srcform*) which all tgtforms are inflected from. However, the lemma form may not be the only and the most informative srcform to inflect all other slots from in the same paradigm. Morphologists refer to a lexeme's principal parts (Finkel and Stump, 2007) as the minimum subset of paradigm slots which, if known, provide all the information needed to generate the other slots in its paradigm. The principal parts which best predict an inflected form in a lexeme's paradigm do not necessarily include the lemma, and more than one of the principal parts may be needed to generate an inflected form reliably (see examples in Table 1 analyzed in section 3.2). Considering this, we convert the shared task of morphological inflection to the paradigm cell filling problem, and incorporate the principal part intuition into the inflection system. Our approaches achieve better or equally good performance compared to the official baselines for most (19 out of 24) relatively low-resource languages we experimented with.

To generate inflected forms for the test data for submission, our system uses the same input-output format as the baselines for high-resource languages, and includes two slightly different approaches of leveraging principal parts information for low-resource languages. The evaluation results indicate that the Transformer model augmented with principal parts information can handle morphological inflection very well for typologically and genealogically diverse languages, whether it

has been tuned on the language or not, even when the training data is limited.

2 Task and data description

The SIGMORPHON 2020 shared task 0 (Vylomova et al., 2020) is a typical morphological inflection task. Compared to previous years' SIGMORPHON shared tasks on morphological inflection, this year's task highlights the distinction between development languages and surprise languages and the inflection model's ability to generalize to new languages that may be genetically related or unrelated to the languages according to which it is developed. In the development phase, 45 languages from 5 language families were provided, and these languages are development languages. In the generalization phase, 45 surprise languages from 16 language families were released. In the evaluation phase, test data include both development languages and surprise languages.

Deviating from previous years' tasks, this year's task did not feature different (low/medium/high) data settings for the languages (Cotterell et al., 2017a, 2018) or manipulate the data size of genetically related language pairs (McCarthy et al., 2019). Instead, each language comes with different amount of training, development and test data, corresponding to the reality of data availability for the language. Of the total 90 languages from 18 language families, 44 have 5,000 or more lemma-tgtmsd-tgtform training triples and 46 have fewer than 5,000. Of the 45 development languages, 24 have fewer than 5,000 training examples. In this paper, we refer to languages with 5,000 or more training triples as high-resource and those with fewer than 5,000 training triples as low-resource.

3 System description

All our models use the self-attention Transformer architecture (Vaswani et al., 2017) as implemented in the Fairseq (Ott et al., 2019) tool, a PyTorch-based sequence modeling toolkit. Both the encoder and decoder have 4 layers with 4 attention heads, an embedding size of 256 and hidden layer size of 1024. Models are trained with the Adam algorithm (Kingma and Ba, 2014) for optimization with an initial learning rate of 0.001, a batch size of 400, 0.1 label smoothing, the gradient clip threshold as 1.0, and 4,000 warmup updates. The models are trained for a maximum of 20,000 or 30,000 optimizer updates depending on the amount of input-

---

[1]This does not hold perfectly—some languages have held-out data that come from paradigms where no form is ever witnessed in the training data, but these are a minority. We overcome this problem by adding an additional slot (tagged as *POS*;CANONICAL) for the lemma in the paradigm.

ID	MSD	Lexeme1	Lexeme2	Lexeme3	Lexeme4	Lexeme5
1	V;CANONICAL	pahinga	bayad	pukpok	linlang	gáling
2	V;AGFOC;LGSPEC1	–	magbabayad	manumukpok	lanlilinlang	gagáling
3	V;IPFV;AGFOC	?	nagbabayad	namumukpok	nanlilinlang	gumagáling
4	V;IPFV;PFOC	*	binabayaran	pinupukpok	nililinlang	iginagáling
5	V;NFIN	pahinga	bayad	pukpok	linlang	gáling
6	V;PFOC;LGSPEC1	*	babayaran	pupukpukin	?	igagáling
7	V;PFV;AGFOC	nagpahinga	nagbayad	namukpok	nanlinlang	gumáling
8	V;PFV;PFOC	*	binayaran	pinukpok	nilinlang	igináling

Table 1: Example of reconstructed paradigms from Tagalog data. – are slots in the development set, ? are slots in the test set, * are slots which didn't appear in the shared task data, and other slots which are filled with inflected forms are slots in the training set.

output tuples for training, with checkpoints saved every 10 epochs. The checkpoint with the smallest loss and the last checkpoint are also saved. The model with the best parameters was selected from all the saved checkpoints based on the accuracy on the development data. Beam search is used at decoding time with a beam width of 5.

Our submission is an ensemble of predictions from three types of models: baseline (Fairseq), 1-src, and 2-src. These three types of models have identical model architecture for inflection and are different from each other in the input and output. As the varied baseline results trained per language family provided by the organizers did not show consistent improvements compared to training languages separately, we train all the models per language without using external resources. We made our code publicly available.[2]

3.1 Baseline (Fairseq) model

The baseline (Fairseq) model (see Figure 1(a)) is very similar to the unaugmented per-language Transformer baseline (Wu et al., 2020) provided by the shared task organizers, except that the Fairseq implementation is used and that beam search rather than greedy search is used at decoding time. The inputs to this model are the individual characters of the lemma followed by the individual subtags of the tgtmsd. For example, for the English training triple `(look, looks, V;SG;3;PRS)`, the input to the model is `l o o k V SG 3 PRS` and the gold standard output is `l o o k s`. Our submissions for languages with 5,000 or more training triples are generated with this model. The model is trained for a maximum of 20,000 optimizer updates for languages with 5,000 to 20,000 training

triples, and for a maximum of 30,000 updates for languages with over 20,000 training triples.

3.2 Principal parts of a paradigm

The classical notion of "principal parts of a paradigm" is the minimal subset of paradigm slots that provides enough information according to which the inflection forms for other slots in the same paradigm can be correctly generated (Finkel and Stump, 2007). The principal part may be different for different slots in the same paradigm, and more than one principal part may be necessary in order to inflect for some slots correctly. For example, for each Tagalog lexeme in Table 1, slots 2 and 3 are very informative source forms for each other, which are different by the first consonant, or the presence or absence of um in the prefix. Slot 3 can predict slot 7 very well, and slot 8 can be easily generated from slot 4. Inflection of slot 6 is the most complex in the paradigms, for which slot 4 together with the lemma, i.e. slot 1, can be informative but not sufficient. Therefore, the lemma is not always a good choice as the source to generate all other slot forms from, and we can expect the morphological inflection system to be more effective and efficient if the principal parts information is incorporated.

The 1-src model (see Figure 1(b)) and the 2-src model (see Figure 1(c)) leverage the idea of paradigm principal parts. To do this, we first reconstruct the paradigm for each lexeme in the shared task data, from which we prepare input and output data for the inflection models.

We assume that each part-of-speech (henceforth *POS*) in a language has its own set of morphosyntactic descriptions (henceforth *MSD*s), which can be obtained by collecting the tgtmsd types in the training, development and test data for the language. Each slot in the paradigm of a lexeme locates an inflected word form, which can be considered a combination of a lexeme and an MSD. In this paper, slot is used to refer to both the inflected form and the corresponding MSD it locates, slot form refers to the inflected forms only, and slot MSD refers to the corresponding morphosyntactic description. If a slot contains both the MSD and the inflected form, it is a filled slot, while an empty slot needs to be filled with the corresponding inflected form. The slot MSD can be determined by the set of MSDs we collect for each POS, and we can fill in the slot if it appears in the training data and mark it if the inflected form is to be generated in the development or test data, or does not appear in the shared task data at all. In addition, the shared task data format has the first element in the triple as the lemma form, i.e. the canonical, or citation, form of the lexeme. We add an additional slot in the paradigm for the lemma form, and tag the slot as *POS;CANONICAL* where the *POS* in the tag is determined by the POS of the lemma. As a result, we create a paradigm for each lexeme in the shared task data and the reconstructed paradigm for each lexeme has at least one filled slot. Table 1 provides 5 example paradigms reconstructed from the Tagalog data, where – marks slots with tgtforms to be predicted in the development set, ? are slots in the test data and ∗ indicates slots which are not found in the shared task data,[3] and other slots which are filled with inflected word forms are data in the training set. In cases where slots have alternative forms in the data, only one form is kept. For example, there are two alternative forms for thanda V;SG;1;PRS in the Zulu training data: ngithanda and ngiyathanda, and our conversion only kept ngiyathanda.

1-src model In order to train the 1-src model, the reconstructed paradigm is organized so that each of the known slots is given as a srcform from which we predict every other known slot as the tgtform. The symbol # is inserted between the srcmsd and tgtmsd. For example, six input-output tuples (see Figure 2) are constructed from the Tagalog Lexeme1 paradigm example provided in Table 1. When only one slot is filled in the reconstructed paradigm, we make the slot predict

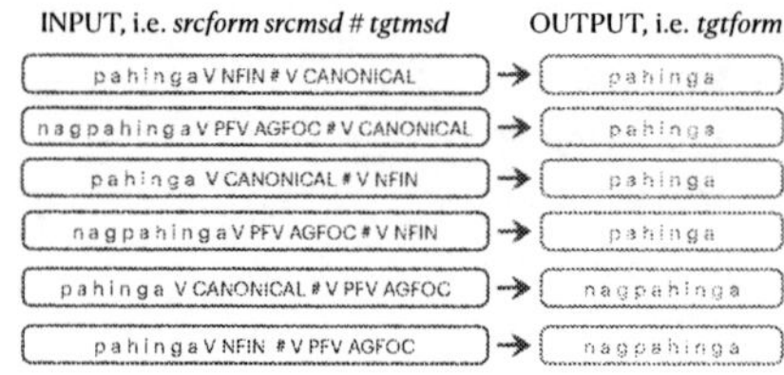

Figure 2: Input-output tuples for the 1-src model for Tagalog Lexeme1 (*pahinga* "rest") example paradigm

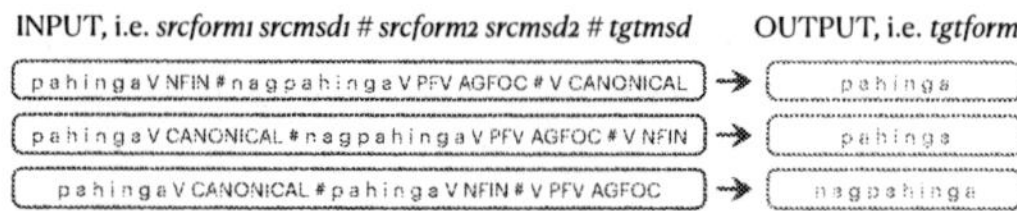

Figure 3: Input-output tuples for the 2-src model for Tagalog Lexeme1 (*pahinga* "rest") example paradigm

itself (i.e. input as *lemma POS;CANONICAL # POS;CANONICAL* and output as *lemma*) for training. All given srcform-srcmsd slots are used to predict the tgtform for each tgtmsd in the development and test data respectively. Consequently, for the Tagalog Lexeme1 example, each tgtsmd in the development and test sets will be predicted by three different source forms with the corresponding morphosyntactic description specified, rather than being predicted only by the lemma. This is the model we use to generate our submission predictions for 39 languages with fewer than 5,000 training triples. The languages aka, ben, cly, cre, kan, kir, kon, liv, lld, lug, nya, pus, sna, and swa are trained for 30,000 maximum updates, and other languages are trained for 20,000 maximum updates.

2-src model The 2-src model generates predictions for the remaining 7 low-resource languages (czn, frr, gsw, izh, mlt, mwf, zpv), because we only trained the 2-src model for languages with fewer than 2,000 training examples due to time constraints and because the 2-src model generates significantly better predictions for these 7 languages on the development data than the 1-src model. During training, the inputs to the 2-src model are all possible known two-slot combinations followed by the MSD for the slot to be filled; the output is the known inflected form for the target slot. The symbol # is inserted between the first srcmsd and the second srcform as well as between the second srcmsd and tgtmsd. For example, three input-output tuples (see Figure 3) are constructed from the Tagalog Lexeme1 example. When only one slot form is given in the paradigm, the given slot is made

---

[3]The ∗ slots may be invalid in the language. For example, the English noun cattle does not have a single form, and the single slot would be marked by ∗ in the paradigm for the lexeme cattle reconstructed by our method.

to predict itself by taking as input the *lemma* and *POS;CANONICAL* repeated twice together with the tgtmsd as *POS;CANONICAL*, and the output is the *lemma* form. When only two slots are filled in the paradigm, each slot form is treated as the tgtform and the other slot is repeated twice together with the MSD for the slot to be predicted as input to the model. For the development and test data, every two-slot combination of given slots is used as input to predict the tgtform corresponding to the tgtmsd. Therefore, each test and development tgtmsd in the Tagalog Lexeme1 example will be predicted by three different inputs, respectively.

Prediction selection   Because of the input and output construction for the 1-src and 2-src models, each tgtmsd may be predicted multiple times by different inputs which may generate more than one inflected form for the same tgtmsd. Two mechanisms are employed to pick the best prediction, both of which implicitly employ the principal parts intuition. The first mechanism is to select the prediction generated by most inputs, i.e. by majority vote for predictions by different inputs. The second mechanism is to select the prediction which gets the highest average log-likelihood, i.e. by averaging the scores for each prediction by different inputs. The intuition behind this mechanism is that the most informative source slots should be most confident about the inflection for the target slot. Unless the majority vote mechanism produces significantly higher accuracy on the development data for the language, the prediction with the highest average log-likelihood is selected as the final prediction for the target slot.

4   Experiments

Considering the time constraints and the already strong performance of the baseline models—especially when training data is abundant—we focused our experiments on the 24 low-resource development languages in the development phase, for which we attempted to augment the Transformer model for inflection by reorganizing the data into paradigms and making use of the principal parts morphology idea in different ways.

In addition to the 1-src and 2-src models described in section 3.2, other approaches we experimented with included 2-random-src, 3-random-src and 4-random-src models where we randomly pick two, three or four given slots as input which will be translated to the tgtform corresponding to the tgtmsd, as well as all-src-tgtform and all-src-all-form models, where the concatenation of all given slots followed by the tgtmsd are input to the inflection model which predicts the corresponding tgtform or all srcforms and the tgtform. Though these models produced better performance for one or two languages that we experimented with initially, we did not see consistent performance improvement proportional to the increasing model complexity over the 1-src and 2-src models. We also experimented with warming up the 1-src model with an additional copying task following the practice suggested by Anastasopoulos and Neubig (2019), but did not see improvements. Therefore, we focused exclusively on the 1-src and 2-src models after initial experiments.

Further experiments with the 1-src model were conducted on the 24 development languages with fewer than 5,000 training triples, and further experiments with the 2-src model were conducted on the 17 development languages, each of which has fewer than 2,000 training triples. The performance of the two selected models will be presented and discussed in the next section.

5   Results and discussion

The average inflection accuracy of development data for the 24 languages by the 1-src model is 91.72%, which is 1.3% higher than the unaugmented per-language Transformer baseline and 0.55% higher than the best performance of all baseline models. The 1-src model achieved higher or equal accuracy on 18 languages compared to the unaugmented per-language Transformer baseline and 17 languages compared to the best performance of all baselines. The 2-src models for the 17 languages we experimented with achieve an average accuracy of 91.63% and their performance on 7 languages (czn, frr, gsw, izh, mlt, mwf, zpv) is better than the 1-src model.

Figure 4 plots the difference in the accuracy on the development set for each language by the 1-src for 2-src model from that by the unaugmented per-language Transformer baseline. Figures 4(a) and 4(c) depict the relationship between this difference and the number of training triples. Figures 4(b) and 4(d) show the relationship between this difference and the completeness of the paradigms seen in training. The filled percentage of each paradigm is calculated by dividing the number of given slots by the number of all slots in the paradigm, and the

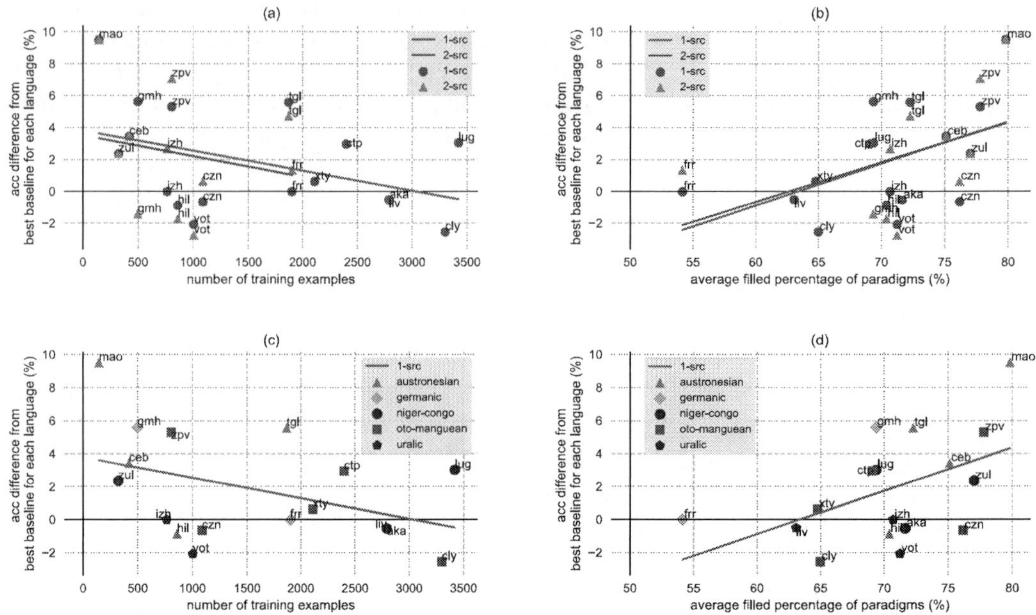

Figure 4: Scatter plots with trend lines for the difference in accuracy between the 1-src or 2-src model and the **per-language Transformer baseline without data augmentation** on low-resource dev languages: (a) 1-src vs 2-src: Size vs Δacc_1 or Δacc_2, (b) 1-src vs 2-src: Percentage vs Δacc_1 or Δacc_2, (c) 1-src and genealogy: Size vs Δacc_1, (d) 1-src and genealogy: Percentage vs Δacc_1. (Size: training data size, Percentage: average percentage of slots per paradigm in training data, $\Delta acc_1^i = acc_{1\text{-src}}^i - acc_{\text{per-lang-unaug-transformer-baseline}}^i$, $\Delta acc_2^j = acc_{2\text{-src}}^j - acc_{\text{per-lang-unaug-transformer-baseline}}^j$)

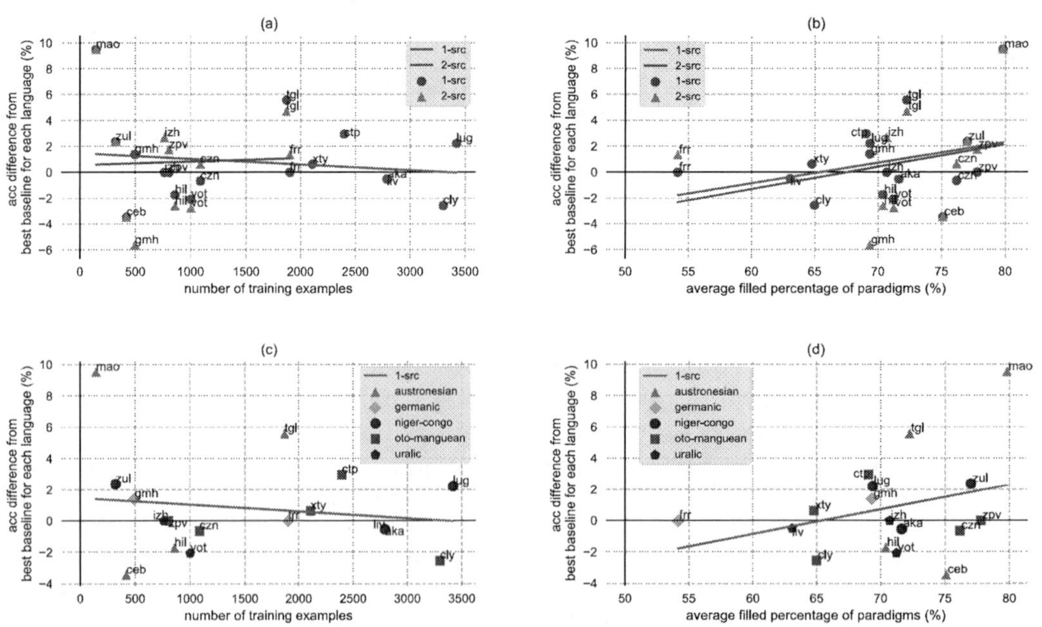

Figure 5: Scatter plots with trend lines for the difference in accuracy between the 1-src or 2-src model and the **best performance of all baselines** on low-resource dev languages: (a) 1-src vs 2-src: Size vs Δacc_3 or Δacc_4, (b) 1-src vs 2-src: Percentage vs Δacc_3 or Δacc_4, (c) 1-src and genealogy: Size vs Δacc_3, (d) 1-src and genealogy: Percentage vs Δacc_3. (Size: training data size, Percentage: average percentage of slots per paradigm in training data, $\Delta acc_3^i = acc_{1\text{-src}}^i - acc_{\text{best-baseline}}^i$, $\Delta acc_4^j = acc_{2\text{-src}}^j - acc_{\text{best-baseline}}^j$)

paradigm completion rate of a language is calculated by taking the average of the filled percentages of all the reconstructed paradigms. For instance, the completion rate of the Tagalog Lexeme1 paradigm is 37.5%, and the average completion rate of all the Tagalog example paradigms in Table 1 is 85%. The low-resource development languages have average completion rates between 54.16% (frr) and 79.81% (mao). Figure 5 plots the same relationships, but the difference is between the 1-src or 2-src model and the best performance of all baseline models. Languages for which both the baseline models and our models achieve 100% accuracy are excluded from the plots, because such languages have the potential to skew the performance comparison. Such languages include one Austronesian language: mlg and six Niger-Congo langauges: gaa, kon, lin, nya, sot and swa.

Model performance and training data size The improvements by the 1-src and 2-src models over the unaugmented Transformer baseline trained per language show the same tendency with relationship to the training data size: The more training data there is available, the less advantage our models have. This is shown in Figure 4(a). The baseline model begins to catch up with these improvements as is shown in Figure 5(a), where the 1-src model accuracy still has a decreasing trend as the training data increases while the 2-src model accuracies turn into a slightly increasing trend.

Model performance and paradigm completion rate The good performance of our models relies on the high completion rate of paradigms. The performance for both the 1-src and 2-src models tends to be better if the reconstructed paradigm contains a higher proportion of known slots. This is true whether our models are compared to the single unaugmented per-language Transformer baseline model or to the ensemble of all baseline models. This relationship is illustrated in Figure 4(b) and Figure 5(b). An extreme case of a low paradigm completion rate in the shared task languages is Ludic, where only 5.64% of the slots are known, and our best model for this language is the 1-src approach with average score selection, which generates an accuracy of 48.78% on the development data. This relationship supports the use of principal parts for morphological inflection, because given a random sampling, the more complete a paradigm is, the more likely it is that the principal parts are

included in the paradigm.

Model performance and genealogy Subplots (c) and (d) in Figure 4, and subplots (c) and (d) in Figure 5, show the performance of the 1-src model on languages with language family information. Uralic languages are challenging to our models. This is to be expected from the fact that Uralic languages usually have large inflection paradigms and therefore tend to have more incomplete slots on average given the same amount of data, and may hence be missing a principal part.

6 Related work

Morphological inflection is one of the natural language processing tasks which achieve great improvement by applying neural network models, especially sequence to sequence models, which initially outperformed other approaches by a large margin on high-resource languages (Cotterell et al., 2016; Kann and Schütze, 2016; Aharoni et al., 2016) and have been improved and augmented later to achieve state-of-the-art performance on low-resource languages as well (Aharoni and Goldberg, 2017; Cotterell et al., 2017a; Makarov and Clematide, 2018; Wu et al., 2018; Cotterell et al., 2018; Wu and Cotterell, 2019; McCarthy et al., 2019; Anastasopoulos and Neubig, 2019).

Subtask 2 of the CoNLL-SIGMORPHON 2017 shared task (Cotterell et al., 2017a) was about paradigm cell filling, and received submissions of neural network systems (Kann and Schütze, 2017; Silfverberg et al., 2017). There is also other work which targets the paradigm cell filling problem (Cotterell et al., 2017b; Silfverberg et al., 2018; Silfverberg and Hulden, 2018). Cotterell et al. (2017b) models the principal parts idea with graphical models to generate all the missing slots in paradigms. Our 1-src model has an input-output format similar to Silfverberg and Hulden (2018). Our work is also closely related to Kann et al. (2017) on multi-source inflection which is also motivated by a principal parts analysis. Cotterell et al. (2019) use an explicit neural model that organizes paradigm slots in their most predictable order to investigate measures of morphological complexity, an instantiation of the principal parts idea in another context.

7 Conclusion

We have presented the system for our submission to the SIGMORPHON 2020 shared task 0 on morphological inflection. It achieved the highest average accuracy and smallest average Levenshtein distance across all the 90 languages from 18 language families. The standard deviation of our submission is the lowest for accuracy and the second lowest (0.004 higher than the lowest) for edit distance.

Our work indicates that the self-attention Transformer architecture can perform well for the morphological inflection task for a genealogically and typologically diverse group of languages. The architecture has a strong generalization ability and can inflect new languages as effectively as the languages it is tuned on. We augment the Transformer model by converting the morphological inflection task to the paradigm cell filling problem and leveraging the principal parts of paradigms in indirect ways, which turns out to be helpful, especially when the training data is limited and the reconstructed paradigms have a high completion rate. Our primary strategy to incorporate principal parts information in this work is to use each given slot in the reconstructed paradigm to predict the target form and select the final prediction from predictions generated by different slots by highest average score or majority vote. Another strategy is to use all possible two-slot combinations to predict the target form.

According to principal parts morphology, the number of principal parts may vary between paradigms and languages, and different slots may require different numbers of principal parts to inflect correctly, indicating that uniformly using every slot individually or every two-slot combination may not always be the best choice. Future work is needed to explore how to use principal parts information more effectively, perhaps tuning the number and choice of forms on a per-language basis or developing strategies to explicitly determine principal parts for the paradigms.

References

Farrell Ackerman, James P. Blevins, and Robert Malouf. 2009. Parts and wholes: Implicative patterns in inflectional paradigms. In James P. Blevins and Juliette Blevins, editors, *Analogy in grammar: Form and acquisition*, pages 54–82. Oxford University Press.

Roee Aharoni and Yoav Goldberg. 2017. Morphological inflection generation with hard monotonic attention. In *Proceedings of the 55th Annual Meeting of the Association for Computational Linguistics (Volume 1: Long Papers)*, pages 2004–2015, Vancouver, Canada. Association for Computational Linguistics.

Roee Aharoni, Yoav Goldberg, and Yonatan Belinkov. 2016. Improving sequence to sequence learning for morphological inflection generation: The BIU-MIT systems for the SIGMORPHON 2016 shared task for morphological reinflection. In *Proceedings of the 14th SIGMORPHON Workshop on Computational Research in Phonetics, Phonology, and Morphology*, pages 41–48, Berlin, Germany. Association for Computational Linguistics.

Antonios Anastasopoulos and Graham Neubig. 2019. Pushing the limits of low-resource morphological inflection. In *Proceedings of the 2019 Conference on Empirical Methods in Natural Language Processing and the 9th International Joint Conference on Natural Language Processing (EMNLP-IJCNLP)*, pages 984–996, Hong Kong, China. Association for Computational Linguistics.

Ryan Cotterell, Christo Kirov, Mans Hulden, and Jason Eisner. 2019. On the complexity and typology of inflectional morphological systems. *Transactions of the Association for Computational Linguistics*, 7:327–342.

Ryan Cotterell, Christo Kirov, John Sylak-Glassman, Géraldine Walther, Ekaterina Vylomova, Arya D. McCarthy, Katharina Kann, Sebastian Mielke, Garrett Nicolai, Miikka Silfverberg, David Yarowsky, Jason Eisner, and Mans Hulden. 2018. The CoNLL–SIGMORPHON 2018 shared task: Universal morphological reinflection. In *Proceedings of the CoNLL–SIGMORPHON 2018 Shared Task: Universal Morphological Reinflection*, pages 1–27, Brussels. Association for Computational Linguistics.

Ryan Cotterell, Christo Kirov, John Sylak-Glassman, Géraldine Walther, Ekaterina Vylomova, Patrick Xia, Manaal Faruqui, Sandra Kübler, David Yarowsky, Jason Eisner, and Mans Hulden. 2017a. CoNLL-SIGMORPHON 2017 shared task: Universal morphological reinflection in 52 languages. In *Proceedings of the CoNLL SIGMORPHON 2017 Shared Task: Universal Morphological Reinflection*, pages 1–30, Vancouver. Association for Computational Linguistics.

Ryan Cotterell, Christo Kirov, John Sylak-Glassman, David Yarowsky, Jason Eisner, and Mans Hulden. 2016. The SIGMORPHON 2016 shared Task—Morphological reinflection. In *Proceedings of the 14th SIGMORPHON Workshop on Computational Research in Phonetics, Phonology, and Morphology*, pages 10–22, Berlin, Germany. Association for Computational Linguistics.

Ryan Cotterell, John Sylak-Glassman, and Christo Kirov. 2017b. Neural graphical models over strings for principal parts morphological paradigm completion. In *Proceedings of the 15th Conference of the European Chapter of the Association for Computational Linguistics: Volume 2, Short Papers*, pages

759–765, Valencia, Spain. Association for Computational Linguistics.

Raphael Finkel and Gregory Stump. 2007. Principal parts and morphological typology. *Morphology*, 17(1):39–75.

Katharina Kann, Ryan Cotterell, and Hinrich Schütze. 2017. Neural multi-source morphological reinflection. In *Proceedings of the 15th Conference of the European Chapter of the Association for Computational Linguistics: Volume 1, Long Papers*, pages 514–524, Valencia, Spain. Association for Computational Linguistics.

Katharina Kann and Hinrich Schütze. 2016. MED: The LMU system for the SIGMORPHON 2016 shared task on morphological reinflection. In *Proceedings of the 14th SIGMORPHON Workshop on Computational Research in Phonetics, Phonology, and Morphology*, pages 62–70, Berlin, Germany. Association for Computational Linguistics.

Katharina Kann and Hinrich Schütze. 2017. The LMU system for the CoNLL-SIGMORPHON 2017 shared task on universal morphological reinflection. In *Proceedings of the CoNLL SIGMORPHON 2017 Shared Task: Universal Morphological Reinflection*, pages 40–48, Vancouver. Association for Computational Linguistics.

Diederik P. Kingma and Jimmy Ba. 2014. Adam: A method for stochastic optimization. *arXiv preprint arXiv:1412.6980*.

Peter Makarov and Simon Clematide. 2018. Imitation learning for neural morphological string transduction. In *Proceedings of the 2018 Conference on Empirical Methods in Natural Language Processing*, pages 2877–2882, Brussels, Belgium. Association for Computational Linguistics.

Robert Malouf. 2016. Generating morphological paradigms with a recurrent neural network. *San Diego Linguistic Papers*.

Robert Malouf. 2017. Abstractive morphological learning with a recurrent neural network. *Morphology*, 27(4):431–458.

Arya D. McCarthy, Ekaterina Vylomova, Shijie Wu, Chaitanya Malaviya, Lawrence Wolf-Sonkin, Garrett Nicolai, Christo Kirov, Miikka Silfverberg, Sebastian J. Mielke, Jeffrey Heinz, Ryan Cotterell, and Mans Hulden. 2019. The SIGMORPHON 2019 shared task: Morphological analysis in context and cross-lingual transfer for inflection. In *Proceedings of the 16th Workshop on Computational Research in Phonetics, Phonology, and Morphology*, pages 229–244, Florence, Italy. Association for Computational Linguistics.

Myle Ott, Sergey Edunov, Alexei Baevski, Angela Fan, Sam Gross, Nathan Ng, David Grangier, and Michael Auli. 2019. fairseq: A fast, extensible toolkit for sequence modeling. In *Proceedings of the 2019 Conference of the North American Chapter of the Association for Computational Linguistics (Demonstrations)*, pages 48–53, Minneapolis, Minnesota. Association for Computational Linguistics.

Miikka Silfverberg and Mans Hulden. 2018. An encoder-decoder approach to the paradigm cell filling problem. In *Proceedings of the 2018 Conference on Empirical Methods in Natural Language Processing*, pages 2883–2889, Brussels, Belgium. Association for Computational Linguistics.

Miikka Silfverberg, Ling Liu, and Mans Hulden. 2018. A computational model for the linguistic notion of morphological paradigm. In *Proceedings of the 27th International Conference on Computational Linguistics*, pages 1615–1626, Santa Fe, New Mexico, USA. Association for Computational Linguistics.

Miikka Silfverberg, Adam Wiemerslage, Ling Liu, and Lingshuang Jack Mao. 2017. Data augmentation for morphological reinflection. In *Proceedings of the CoNLL SIGMORPHON 2017 Shared Task: Universal Morphological Reinflection*, pages 90–99, Vancouver. Association for Computational Linguistics.

Ashish Vaswani, Noam Shazeer, Niki Parmar, Jakob Uszkoreit, Llion Jones, Aidan N. Gomez, Łukasz Kaiser, and Illia Polosukhin. 2017. Attention is all you need. In *Advances in neural information processing systems*, pages 5998–6008.

Ekaterina Vylomova, Jennifer White, Elizabeth Salesky, Sabrina J. Mielke, Shijie Wu, Edoardo Ponti, Rowan Hall Maudslay, Ran Zmigrod, Joseph Valvoda, Svetlana Toldova, Francis Tyers, Elena Klyachko, Ilya Yegorov, Natalia Krizhanovsky, Paula Czarnowska, Irene Nikkarinen, Andrej Krizhanovsky, Tiago Pimentel, Lucas Torroba Hennigen, Christo Kirov, Garrett Nicolai, Adina Williams, Antonios Anastasopoulos, Hilaria Cruz, Eleanor Chodroff, Ryan Cotterell, Miikka Silfverberg, and Mans Hulden. 2020. The SIGMORPHON 2020 Shared Task 0: Typologically diverse morphological inflection. In *Proceedings of the 17th SIGMORPHON Workshop on Computational Research in Phonetics, Phonology, and Morphology*.

Shijie Wu and Ryan Cotterell. 2019. Exact hard monotonic attention for character-level transduction. In *Proceedings of the 57th Annual Meeting of the Association for Computational Linguistics*, pages 1530–1537, Florence, Italy. Association for Computational Linguistics.

Shijie Wu, Ryan Cotterell, and Mans Hulden. 2020. Applying the transformer to character-level transduction. *arXiv:2005.10213 [cs.CL]*.

Shijie Wu, Pamela Shapiro, and Ryan Cotterell. 2018. Hard non-monotonic attention for character-level transduction. In *Proceedings of the 2018 Conference on Empirical Methods in Natural Language Processing*, pages 4425–4438, Brussels, Belgium. Association for Computational Linguistics.

Linguist vs. Machine: Rapid Development of Finite-State Morphological Grammars

Sarah Beemer and **Zak Boston** and **April Bukoski** and **Daniel Chen** and
Princess Dickens and **Andrew Gerlach** and **Torin Hopkins** and
Parth Anand Jawale and **Chris Koski** and **Akanksha Malhotra** and **Piyush Mishra** and
Saliha Muradoğlu[☼] and **Lan Sang** and **Tyler Short** and **Sagarika Shreevastava** and
Elizabeth Spaulding and **Tetsumichi Umada** and **Beilei Xiang** and **Changbing Yang** and
Mans Hulden

University of Colorado
The Australian National University[☼]

Abstract

Sequence-to-sequence models have proven to be highly successful in learning morphological inflection from examples as the series of SIG-MORPHON/CoNLL shared tasks have shown. It is usually assumed, however, that a linguist working with inflectional examples could in principle develop a gold standard-level morphological analyzer and generator that would surpass a trained neural network model in accuracy of predictions, but that it may require significant amounts of human labor. In this paper, we discuss an experiment where a group of people with some linguistic training develop 25+ grammars as part of the shared task and weigh the cost/benefit ratio of developing grammars by hand. We also present tools that can help linguists triage difficult complex morphophonological phenomena within a language and hypothesize inflectional class membership. We conclude that a significant development effort by trained linguists to analyze and model morphophonological patterns are required in order to surpass the accuracy of neural models.

1 Introduction

Hand-written grammars for modeling derivational and inflectional morphology have long been seen as the gold standard for incorporating a word inflection aware component into NLP systems. However, the recent successes of sequence-to-sequence (seq2seq) models in learning morphological patterns, as seen in multiple shared tasks that address the topic (Cotterell et al., 2016, 2017, 2018; McCarthy et al., 2019), have raised the question whether there is any advantage in developing hand-written grammars for performance reasons. This question has special relevance with regard to low-resource languages when there is a desire to quickly develop fundamental NLP resources such as a morphological analyzer and generator with minimal

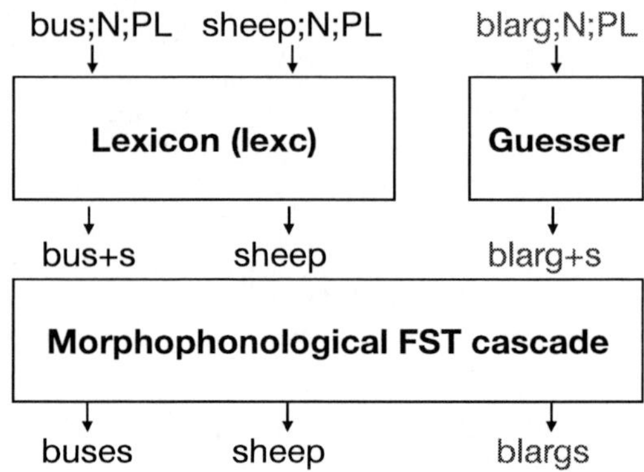

Figure 1: Basic FST grammar design used in this project which combines a lexicon-based model with a guesser to handle unseen lemmas.

resource expenditure (Maxwell and Hughes, 2006).

It is clear that there is a need for hand-written morphological grammars, even if neural network models approach the performance of carefully hand-crafted morphologies. Normative and pre-scriptive language models, such as those needed by language academies in many countries—e.g. RAE in Spain, Académie Française in France, or the Council of the Cherokee Nation in the U.S.—would need to rely on explicitly designed models for providing guidance in word inflection, spelling rules, and orthography if they were to be implemented computationally. Currently, neural models trained on examples provide no verifiable guarantees that certain prescriptive phenomena have been learned by a trained model and can be reliably used.

In this paper[1] we document an experiment where a number of morphological grammars were hand-written by a group of 19 students enrolled in the class "LING 7565—Computational Phonology & Morphology" at the University of Colorado, each

---

[1]All tools and grammars developed are available on `https://github.com/mhulden/7565tools`.

*Proceedings of the Seventeenth SIGMORPHON Workshop on Computational Research
in Phonetics, Phonology, and Morphology*, pages 162–170
Online, July 10, 2020. ©2020 Association for Computational Linguistics
https://doi.org/10.18653/v1/P17

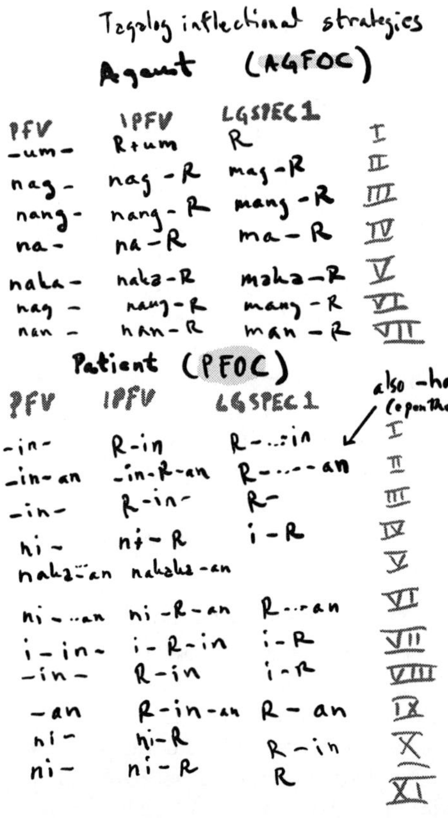

Figure 2: Old-school pencil-and-paper Linguistics: hypothesizing the possible inflectional patterns for Tagalog Actor Focus and Object Focus verb forms (from project notes). The symbol R represents reduplication of the first CV(V) in the stem.

student having training in either computer science or linguistics, and some previous training in writing finite-state morphological grammars. The languages were chosen from the 2020 SIGMOR-PHON shared task 0 (Vylomova et al., 2020), and the grammars were designed so as to be able to inflect unseen forms. The design was also such that the grammars were able to function as "guessers" and inflect lexemes never seen in the training data.

2 Finite-State Grammars

Finite-state Transducer (FST) solutions have long been the foremost paradigm in which to develop linguistically informed large-scale morphological grammars (Koskenniemi, 1983; Beesley and Karttunen, 2003; Hulden, 2009). The availability of a variety of tools (Hulden (2009); Riley et al. (2009); Beesley (2012) inter alia) has also supported this mode of development, and by now hundreds of languages have grammars developed by linguists in this paradigm.

The usual approach to developing morphological analyzers is to model the mapping from a lemma (citation form) and a morphosyntactic description (MSD) into an inflected form (target form) as a two-step process. The first step maps the lemma+MSD into an intermediate form that represents a combination of canonical morpheme representations, while the second step employs a cascade of transducers which handle morphophonological alternations. It is customary to handle inflectional classes by explicitly dividing lemmas into groups in the first step so that correct morphemes are chosen for each lemma. Analyzers built in such a way generally are not capable of inflecting lemmas that are not explicitly encoded in a lexicon. However, it is common to integrate an additional "guesser" component that can handle any valid lemma in a language, and pass it through the relevant morphophonological component only (Beesley and Karttunen, 2003). Basic finite-state calculus is then used to construct a single FST that "overrides" outputs from the guesser whenever a known lexeme is inflected, so conflicting outputs are avoided. The basic design is illustrated in Figure 1.

3 Approach

All of the grammars were built with the *foma* finite-state tool (Hulden, 2009). Before grammar writing commenced, the participants were urged to spend roughly 1 hour in groups of 3 to quickly analyze all the languages in the development and surprise groups as follows:

- Triage: the training sets for all languages in the shared task were rapidly analyzed for difficulty, and possible complex inflectional classes. Following this, a selection of languages were chosen by the participants to model. This was done once for the development languages, and through an additional round of triage for the surprise languages.

- Each language was scored for difficulty based on familiarity with the writing system, paradigm size, complexity, and the apparent number of inflectional classes; naturally the actual number was not known, and this represented an educated guess. Participants were asked to informally rate the difficulty of a language on a 1(easy)–5(very difficult) before choosing languages to work on. The participants were not explicitly instructed to pick an easy language, but rather, to choose one that would provide an interesting experience and would be feasible to complete.[2]

- Computational tools (discussed below) were used to reconstruct the partial paradigms given in the training data, to extract the alphabets used in the languages, to canonicalize the Uni-Morph tag order (Kirov et al., 2018) used in the data, and to provide a rapid development environment that could give instant feedback on accuracy on the training and dev sets after compilation of FSTs.

- A template grammar was used as a starting point; it provided both the possibility of developing a morphophonology-only grammar, or a grammar where all lemmas needed to be divided into inflectional classes.

Through the above process, a number of languages were selected as the primary targets, and development was launched for some 40 languages in total—roughly 20 for the development languages and a similar number for the surprise languages, as they were published. In the end, the output of 25 languages was submitted to the shared task. The criterion for actually submitting a language was that the grammar was mature enough, judged by examining whether accuracy on the development set was within 5% of the neural baseline models (Wu et al., 2020) provided by the organizers.

4   Tools

As mentioned above, a number of tools for the support of rapid grammar writing were also developed. These included the tools to reconstruct the partial inflection tables from the data and various analysis tools for accuracy and error reporting.

Apart from that, a separate tool for inflection table clustering and a non-neural tool for hypothesizing forms for missing slots in paradigms were also developed. This latter tools' output was also submitted as a second system (**CU-7565-02**) to the shared task for nearly all languages. These two tools were more involved and are discussed in detail below.

4.1   Inflection Table Clustering

Crucial in the development of a grammar from raw, partial inflection table data is the ability to hypothesize if lexemes fall into different inflectional classes quickly, and if so, how. This is non-trivial to determine, especially with large amounts of lexemes represented in the various data sets. It is also essential to disentangle phonological regularity from inflectional classes which may be significant red herrings in the analysis of a language. For example, while **cat** in English pluralizes as **cats**, **bus** pluralizes as **buses**—by an epenthetic **e** inserted between sibilants. A naive analysis would postulate that the two lexemes behave differently and place them in separate inflectional classes, although a properly designed phonological component could avoid this unnecessary complexity in the morphological component.

4.1.1   Lexeme similarity measure

To facilitate providing a linguist with a quick overview, we developed a model to perform rapid hierarchical clustering of all lexemes in a language's data set. To this end, we developed a metric for lexeme similarity with respect to inflectional behavior. This metric is calculated by a two-step process. First, all pairs of word forms for a lexeme (within a paradigm) are aligned using an out-of-the-box Monte Carlo aligner (Cotterell et al., 2016) written by the last author. This is shown in figure 3 (a). Following this alignment procedure, we automatically produce a crude approximation of the string transformation implied by the alignment as a regular expression, which is then compiled into an FST.

In the conversion process, matching input sequences in the alignment are modeled by ?+ (repeat one or more symbols[3]) and non-matching symbols are replaced by the symbol-pair found in the alignment: i:o. For example, the aligned pair **runs** ↔ **ran** in Figure 3 (b) is converted into the regular expression

$$?+ \quad u{:}a \quad ?+ \quad s{:}0 \qquad (1)$$

which can be compiled into a transducer in Figure 3 (c). This transducer generalizes over the matched elements in the input-output pair and can be applied to other third-person present forms, such as **outruns** to produce **outran**. Obviously, this example transformation only applies to this particular

---

[2]On average, the surprise languages were deemed considerably more difficult, largely because of paradigm size.

[3]We use foma regular expression notation.

inflectional class and will give incorrect transformations such as **pulls** → **pall** for words that do not have the same inflectional behavior. The purpose of calculating all-known-pairs mappings for each lexeme is to provide a *similarity measure* between lexemes. In particular, we use the following measure for two lexemes l_1 and l_2, which compares the overlap of all transformation rules found between the forms in l_1 with the transformation rules in l_2:

$$\text{sim}(l_1, l_2) = \frac{2 \times \#\text{shared}(l_1, l_2)}{\#\text{shared}(l_1, l_1) + \#\text{shared}(l_2, l_2)} \quad (2)$$

Here, $\#\text{shared}(l_1, l_2)$ is the simple count reflecting how many of the slot-to-slot transformation rules in l_1 are identical for l_2.

We subsequently convert this similarity score into a distance for the purposes of clustering:

$$\text{distance}(l_1, l_2) = 1 - \text{sim}(l_1, l_2) \quad (3)$$

Note that the denominator in the similarity calculation in effect expresses the maximum possible similarity scores for l_1 and l_2 by calculating the similarity with themselves, resulting in a range of $[0, 1]$ for the overall similarity and distance measures. Since many given paradigms contain missing forms and are therefore missing pair-transformations as well, this maximum score will vary from lexeme to lexeme.

With this similarity in hand between all lexemes, we can perform a (single-link) agglomerative hierarchical clustering of all lexemes in the training data of a language.

Example results of the clustering are shown in Figure 4 for Ingrian (the full training set which contained partial inflectional tables for 50 lexemes), and English (a small subset). Included in the Ingrian clustering are our final linguist-hypothesized inflectional class numbers for each lexeme for comparison.

4.2   Inflection with transformation FSTs

As a byproduct of the clustering distance measure that uses slot-to-slot transformation FSTs, we can also address the shared task itself. Since the development and test sets largely contain unknown inflections from lexemes where *some* forms have been seen, we can make use of the learned transformation rules from other lexemes that target an unknown form asked for in the development or

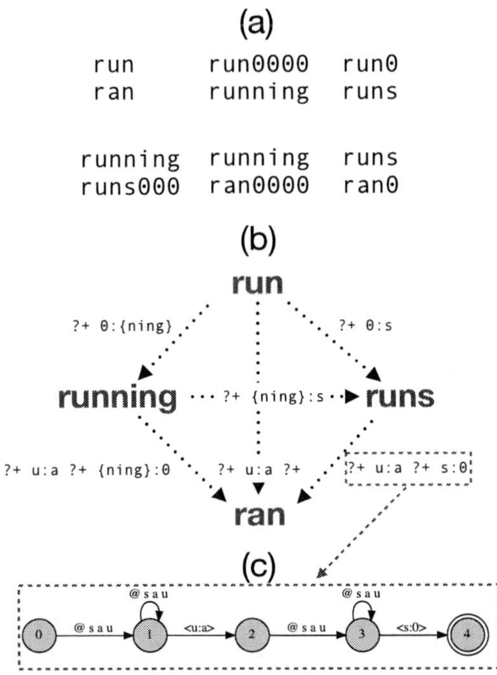

Figure 3: Generating transformation rules for each pairwise slot for a lexeme: (a) we perform alignment of all pairs, (b) a regular expression is issued to model the transformation which is compiled into an FST (c).

test sets. To this end, we collect all known *source → target* transformation rules from all other tables where the target form is the desired slot (MSD). We then apply all of these transformations, generating potentially hundreds of inflection candidates for the missing target slot of a lexeme. From among the candidates, we perform a majority vote. For all languages, we experimented with weighting the majority vote so that transformation rules that come from paradigms that share many transformation rules with the target lexeme's paradigm get a multiplier for the vote using the similarity measure in (2). This strategy produced slightly superior results throughout, as analyzed by performance on the development set, and was hence used in the final submission for our system **CU-7565-02**.

5   Results

The results for the hand-written grammars (**CU-7565-01**) and the non-neural paradigm completion model (**CU-7565-02**) are given in Table 1. We note that we were able to match or surpass the strongest neural participant in the task on 13 languages with the hand-written grammars. Several of these, how-

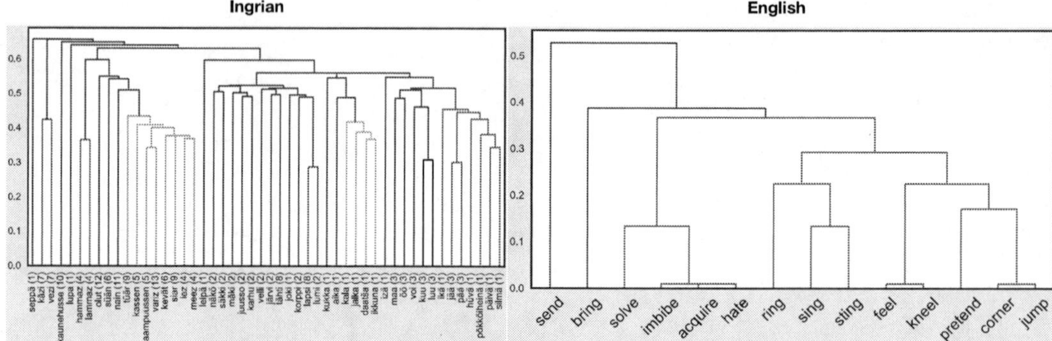

Figure 4: Hierarchical clustering of lexemes by apparent inflectional behavior based on string transformations between inflectional slots for Ingrian (left) and English (right). The numbers in parentheses in Ingrian refer to the Linguist-derived inflectional class number after developing a grammar. The Ingrian data is the output from the full training data while the English is a small selection of verbs to illustrate clustering behavior.

ever, were relatively "easy" languages and often did not contain any significant morphophonology at all. On two languages, Ingrian (izh) and Tagalog (tgl), we were able to significantly improve upon the other models participating in the task. These languages had a fairly large number of inflectional classes and very complex morphophonology. Ingrian features a large variety of consonant gradation patterns common in Uralic languages, and Tagalog features intricate reduplication patterns (see Figure 2).

We include results for train, dev, and test as we used tools to continuously evaluate our progress during development on the training set. It is worth noting that the linguist-driven development process does not seem to be prone to overfitting—accuracy for several languages on the test set was actually higher than on the training set.

The non-neural paradigm completion model (**CU-7565-02**), which was submitted for nearly all 90 languages performed reasonably well, and is to our knowledge the best-performing non-neural model available for morphological inflection. Never outperforming the strongest neural models; it nevertheless represents a strong improvement over the baseline non-neural model provided by the organizers. Additionally, it provides another tool to quickly see reasonable hypotheses for missing forms in inflection tables.

6 Discussion

6.1 Earlier work

To our knowledge, no extensive comparison between well-designed manual grammars and neural

Language	trn[1]	dev[1]	tst[1]	tst[2]
aka	100.0	100.0	**100.0**	89.8
ceb	85.2	86.2	86.5	84.7
crh	97.5	97.0	96.4	97.7
czn	79.0	76.0	72.5	76.1
dje	100.0	100.0	**100.0**	**100.0**
gaa	100.0	100.0	**100.0**	**100.0**
izh	93.4	91.1	**92.9**	77.2
kon	100.0	100.0	98.7	97.4
lin	100.0	100.0	**100.0**	**100.0**
mao	85.5	85.7	66.7	57.1
mlg	100.0	100.0	**100.0**	-
nya	100.0	100.0	**100.0**	**100.0**
ood	81.0	87.5	71.0	62.4
orm	99.6	100.0	**99.0**	93.6
ote	91.2	93.5	90.9	91.3
san	88.5	89.7	89.0	88.3
sna	100.0	100.0	**100.0**	99.3
sot	100.0	100.0	**100.0**	99.0
swa	100.0	100.0	**100.0**	**100.0**
syc	89.3	87.3	88.3	89.1
tgk	100.0	100.0	**93.8**	**93.8**
tgl	77.9	75.0	**77.8**	-
xty	81.1	80.0	81.7	70.3
zpv	84.3	77.9	78.9	81.1
zul	82.9	88.1	83.3	88.5

Table 1: Results for the train, dev, and test sets with our handwritten grammars ([1]) and our non-neural learner ([2]). The non-neural model also participated in additional languages not shown here. Languages with accuracies on par with or exceeding the best shared task participants are shown in boldface.

network models for morphology have been proposed. Pirinen (2019) reports on a small experiment that compares an earlier SIGMORPHON shared task winner's results to a Finnish hand-written morphological analyzer (Pirinen, 2015), with the seq2seq-based participant's model yielding higher precision than the rule-based FST analyzer. In another related experiment, Moeller et al. (2018) train neural seq2seq models from an existing hand-designed transducer acting as an oracle and note that the seq2seq model begins to converge to the FST with around 30,000 examples in a very complex language, Arapaho (arp).

The non-neural inflection model (**CU-7565-02**) builds upon paradigm generalization work by Forsberg and Hulden (2016), which in turn is an extension of Hulden et al. (2014) and Ahlberg et al. (2015). An earlier non-neural model for paradigm generalization is found in Dreyer and Eisner (2011).

6.2 Human Resources

We did not record the exact amounts of time spent on the project individually for each participant. However, we can estimate this based on previous years' class surveys in the same course (LING 7565—Computational Phonology and Morphology) as regards the number of hours per week students spend working on course projects. Each student on average in the course spends 6.6 hours per week; as the project ran for 5 weeks with 19 participants, we roughly estimate a total of 627 person-hours spent on the task of developing grammars. As reflected in the results, we considered 13–15 languages to have largely completed grammars, or very nearly completed. The remainder of the 25 languages submitted were known to require further work, but very little work to reach accuracies beyond or at the best-performing neural models for the task. These estimates do not include student training in morphology, finite-state machines, and grammar writing. Likewise, some languages with very large number of forms per lexeme—such as Erzya (myv) with 1,597 forms and Meadow Mari (mhr) with 1,597 forms—were deemed outside the realm of realistic analysis and linguist-driven grammar writing within a scope of 5 weeks that were allotted to the work.

6.3 Neural or Human?

Given the above estimates, we can provide a conservative estimate of at least 40 person-hours of work on average—not counting infrastructure development and strategizing—to develop a hand-written morphological analyzer and generator that is on par with a model learned by state-of-the-art neural approaches. There is large variance around this figure, however, as some very regular languages only required 30 minutes of work and a dozen-or-so lines of code to produce a model that captures all the morphology and morphophonology involved. Others required a much greater and more intense effort in analyzing the partial inflection tables given in the training data, classifying lemmas into inflectional classes and modeling morphophonological rules as FSTs. Additionally, we note that all the participants had already been trained in this kind of analysis and grammar writing, a factor that our estimate does not take into account.

6.4 Language Notes

In the course of the development of the grammars, we observed that many languages had a skewed selection of data, or inconsistencies that would not be fruitful to model in a hand-written grammar. This also meant that in such cases it was unlikely that the hand-written grammar would ever attain the performance of a neural model, which can better handle the inconsistencies described below. We hope to be able to clean up the data as the test data is released to re-evaluate our grammars for these languages, without this additional noise.

Maori (mao) is an example of a language where the given data set provides a hard ceiling on how much can be inferred either by a linguist or a machine learning model. The data provided contains only maximally two forms for each verb— the active and the passive. Some examples of active-passive alternations include: **neke $\sim$ neke-hia, nehu $\sim$ nehua, kati $\sim$ katia**. In this data set, the passive form is utterly unpredictable from the active form (but not vice versa). The standard phonological analysis of the data (Kiparsky, 1982; Harlow, 2007)—familiar to many from phonology textbooks—is that the underlying stem contains a consonant which is removed by a phonological rule that deletes word-final consonants in the language. The traditional phonological analysis is that the lemma listed as **neke**, for example, is underlyingly **/nekeh/**, and the passive suffix is regularly **-ia**, while the active suffix is the zero morpheme **-0**. The consonant-deletion rule applies to the active form, which surfaces as **neke**, but not to the

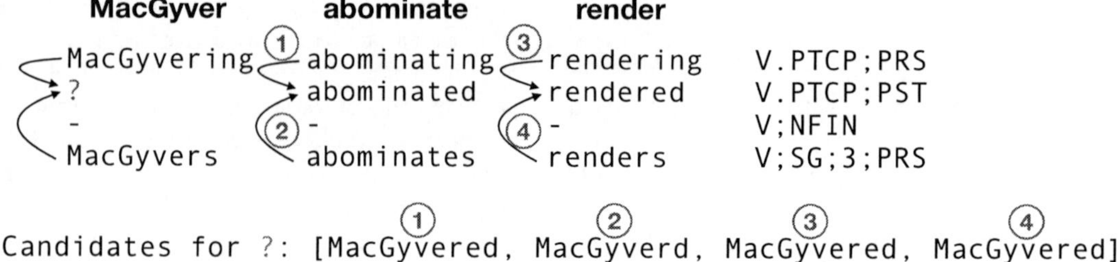

Figure 5: Generating candidate inflections for V.PTCP.PST for the verb "to **MacGyver**". We use all the candidates generated by known transformation rules from all other tables (only 2 other tables shown here). A list of candidate inflections is produced, where the final inflection is decided by majority vote.

passive form **nekehia**, where the added suffix prevents the consonant from deleting. There is also an additional hiatus-avoiding rule—deleting a vowel—seen in e.g. **/nehu/+/ia/** → **nehua**. Obviously, the consonant which is not seen in the active form given in the training data can not be used to predict the passive form. The best one can do is to guess the most likely consonant in the language as being present in the underlying stem. Had the training data contained a third form which maintains the consonant—e.g. the Maori gerundive suffix **/-aŋa/**—the missing consonant of the passive could be predicted from the gerundive and vice versa.[4]

Hiligaynon (hil) contained several lemmas listed with multiple alternate forms, such as:

```
bati/batian/pamatian ginpamantian V;PROG;PST
```

It is very challenging to account for the occasional lemma being listed in two or three parts in a standard FST design, and so this kind of transformation was not attempted.

Syriac, Sanskrit, Oromo, Tohono O'odham (syc,san,orm,ood) contained multiple lines where the lemma and MSD were identical, but the output was not. In some languages this was pervasive enough to cause us to exclude them (ctp,pei) from our selection of attempted languages.

Chichicapan Zapotec (zpv) contained several inflected forms where the target form actually contained two alternatives separated by a slash. Predicting and modeling when this happens was deemed to be irregular and was not attempted.

---

[4]"If we wanted an A on our [phonology] exam, we would of course say the underlying forms are [the ones with the consonant] …If someone were to say that the underlying forms are [consonantless] he'd flunk." (Kiparsky, 1982)

Zenzontepec Chatino (czn) contained a mixture of hyphens (-) and en-dashes (–) where presumably only one of them should have been used. Again, this was deemed hard to predict manually and no obvious pattern was found.

7 Conclusion

We have done a preliminary investigation in pitting neural inflection models against more traditional hand-written grammars, designed by non-naive grammar developers with some training in the field of linguistics and computational modeling. The results point to two main directions.

First, it is very difficult in many cases to outperform a state-of-the-art neural network model without significant development effort and attention to nuanced morphophonological patterns. Indeed, some data sets in the task were very simple, and in such cases, it is quite trivial to develop a high-accuracy grammar. This advantage is somewhat nullified by the apparent ability of neural seq2seq models to also model such morphologies with high accuracy, despite little data.

The second observation is the following: for languages where the group was able to significantly outperform neural models (such as Tagalog and Ingrian), success did not come cheaply. We estimate that for any language with high morphophonological complexity and a variety of inflectional classes, possibly hundreds of hours of development effort is required even by a trained linguist to surpass the performance of a current state-of-the-art seq2seq model. But it is also precisely in this latter case of high-complexity languages where linguists can still prevail with a margin.

References

Malin Ahlberg, Markus Forsberg, and Mans Hulden. 2015. Paradigm classification in supervised learning of morphology. In *Proceedings of the 2015 Conference of the North American Chapter of the Association for Computational Linguistics: Human Language Technologies*, pages 1024–1029, Denver, Colorado. Association for Computational Linguistics.

Kenneth R. Beesley. 2012. Kleene, a free and open-source language for finite-state programming. In *Proceedings of the 10th International Workshop on Finite State Methods and Natural Language Processing*, pages 50–54, Donostia–San Sebastián. Association for Computational Linguistics.

Kenneth R. Beesley and Lauri Karttunen. 2003. *Finite State Morphology*. CSLI Publications, Stanford, CA.

Ryan Cotterell, Christo Kirov, John Sylak-Glassman, Géraldine Walther, Ekaterina Vylomova, Arya D. McCarthy, Katharina Kann, Sebastian Mielke, Garrett Nicolai, Miikka Silfverberg, David Yarowsky, Jason Eisner, and Mans Hulden. 2018. The CoNLL–SIGMORPHON 2018 shared task: Universal morphological reinflection. In *Proceedings of the CoNLL–SIGMORPHON 2018 Shared Task: Universal Morphological Reinflection*, pages 1–27, Brussels. Association for Computational Linguistics.

Ryan Cotterell, Christo Kirov, John Sylak-Glassman, Géraldine Walther, Ekaterina Vylomova, Patrick Xia, Manaal Faruqui, Sandra Kübler, David Yarowsky, Jason Eisner, and Mans Hulden. 2017. CoNLL-SIGMORPHON 2017 shared task: Universal morphological reinflection in 52 languages. In *Proceedings of the CoNLL SIGMORPHON 2017 Shared Task: Universal Morphological Reinflection*, pages 1–30, Vancouver. Association for Computational Linguistics.

Ryan Cotterell, Christo Kirov, John Sylak-Glassman, David Yarowsky, Jason Eisner, and Mans Hulden. 2016. The SIGMORPHON 2016 shared Task—Morphological reinflection. In *Proceedings of the 14th SIGMORPHON Workshop on Computational Research in Phonetics, Phonology, and Morphology*, pages 10–22, Berlin, Germany. Association for Computational Linguistics.

Markus Dreyer and Jason Eisner. 2011. Discovering morphological paradigms from plain text using a Dirichlet process mixture model. In *Proceedings of the 2011 Conference on Empirical Methods in Natural Language Processing*, pages 616–627, Edinburgh, Scotland, UK. Association for Computational Linguistics.

Markus Forsberg and Mans Hulden. 2016. Learning transducer models for morphological analysis from example inflections. In *Proceedings of the SIGFSM Workshop on Statistical NLP and Weighted Automata*, pages 42–50, Berlin, Germany. Association for Computational Linguistics.

Ray Harlow. 2007. *Maori: A Linguistic Introduction*. Cambridge University Press.

Mans Hulden. 2009. Foma: a finite-state compiler and library. In *Proceedings of the Demonstrations Session at EACL 2009*, pages 29–32, Athens, Greece. Association for Computational Linguistics.

Mans Hulden, Markus Forsberg, and Malin Ahlberg. 2014. Semi-supervised learning of morphological paradigms and lexicons. In *Proceedings of the 14th Conference of the European Chapter of the Association for Computational Linguistics*, pages 569–578, Gothenburg, Sweden. Association for Computational Linguistics.

Paul Kiparsky. 1982. *Explanation in Phonology*, volume 4. Walter de Gruyter.

Christo Kirov, Ryan Cotterell, John Sylak-Glassman, Géraldine Walther, Ekaterina Vylomova, Patrick Xia, Manaal Faruqui, Sebastian Mielke, Arya McCarthy, Sandra Kübler, David Yarowsky, Jason Eisner, and Mans Hulden. 2018. UniMorph 2.0: Universal morphology. In *Proceedings of the Eleventh International Conference on Language Resources and Evaluation (LREC-2018)*, Miyazaki, Japan. European Languages Resources Association (ELRA).

Kimmo Koskenniemi. 1983. *Two-level morphology: A general computational model for word-form recognition and production*. Publication 11, University of Helsinki, Department of General Linguistics, Helsinki.

Mike Maxwell and Baden Hughes. 2006. Frontiers in linguistic annotation for lower-density languages. In *Proceedings of the Workshop on Frontiers in Linguistically Annotated Corpora 2006*, pages 29–37, Sydney, Australia. Association for Computational Linguistics.

Arya D. McCarthy, Ekaterina Vylomova, Shijie Wu, Chaitanya Malaviya, Lawrence Wolf-Sonkin, Garrett Nicolai, Christo Kirov, Miikka Silfverberg, Sebastian J. Mielke, Jeffrey Heinz, Ryan Cotterell, and Mans Hulden. 2019. The SIGMORPHON 2019 shared task: Morphological analysis in context and cross-lingual transfer for inflection. In *Proceedings of the 16th Workshop on Computational Research in Phonetics, Phonology, and Morphology*, pages 229–244, Florence, Italy. Association for Computational Linguistics.

Sarah Moeller, Ghazaleh Kazeminejad, Andrew Cowell, and Mans Hulden. 2018. A neural morphological analyzer for Arapaho verbs learned from a finite state transducer. In *Proceedings of the Workshop on Computational Modeling of Polysynthetic Languages*, pages 12–20, Santa Fe, New Mexico, USA. Association for Computational Linguistics.

Tommi A Pirinen. 2015. Omorfi — free and open source morphological lexical database for Finnish. In *Proceedings of the 20th Nordic Conference of Computational Linguistics (NODALIDA 2015)*, pages 313–315, Vilnius, Lithuania. Linköping University Electronic Press, Sweden.

Tommi A Pirinen. 2019. Neural and rule-based Finnish NLP models—expectations, experiments and experiences. In *Proceedings of the Fifth International Workshop on Computational Linguistics for Uralic Languages*, pages 104–114, Tartu, Estonia. Association for Computational Linguistics.

Michael Riley, Cyril Allauzen, and Martin Jansche. 2009. OpenFst: An open-source, weighted finite-state transducer library and its applications to speech and language. In *Proceedings of Human Language Technologies: The 2009 Annual Conference of the North American Chapter of the Association for Computational Linguistics, Companion Volume: Tutorial Abstracts*, pages 9–10, Boulder, Colorado. Association for Computational Linguistics.

Ekaterina Vylomova, Jennifer White, Elizabeth Salesky, Sabrina J. Mielke, Shijie Wu, Edoardo Ponti, Rowan Hall Maudslay, Ran Zmigrod, Joseph Valvoda, Svetlana Toldova, Francis Tyers, Elena Klyachko, Ilya Yegorov, Natalia Krizhanovsky, Paula Czarnowska, Irene Nikkarinen, Andrej Krizhanovsky, Tiago Pimentel, Lucas Torroba Hennigen, Christo Kirov, Garrett Nicolai, Adina Williams, Antonios Anastasopoulos, Hilaria Cruz, Eleanor Chodroff, Ryan Cotterell, Miikka Silfverberg, and Mans Hulden. 2020. The SIGMORPHON 2020 Shared Task 0: Typologically diverse morphological inflection. In *Proceedings of the 17th Workshop on Computational Research in Phonetics, Phonology, and Morphology*.

Shijie Wu, Ryan Cotterell, and Mans Hulden. 2020. Applying the transformer to character-level transduction. *arXiv:2005.10213 [cs.CL]*.

CLUZH at SIGMORPHON 2020 Shared Task on Multilingual Grapheme-to-Phoneme Conversion

Peter Makarov **Simon Clematide**
Institute of Computational Linguistics
University of Zurich, Switzerland
`makarov@cl.uzh.ch` `simon.clematide@cl.uzh.ch`

Abstract

This paper describes the submission by the team from the Institute of Computational Linguistics, Zurich University, to the Multilingual Grapheme-to-Phoneme Conversion (G2P) Task of the SIGMORPHON 2020 challenge. The submission adapts our system from the 2018 edition of the SIGMORPHON shared task. Our system is a neural transducer that operates over explicit edit actions and is trained with imitation learning. It is well-suited for morphological string transduction partly because it exploits the fact that the input and output character alphabets overlap. The challenge posed by G2P has been to adapt the model and the training procedure to work with disjoint alphabets. We adapt the model to use substitution edits and train it with a weighted finite-state transducer acting as the expert policy. An ensemble of such models produces competitive results on G2P. Our submission ranks second out of 23 submissions by a total of nine teams.

1 Introduction

G2P requires mapping a sequence of characters in some language into a sequence of International Phonetic Alphabet (IPA) symbols, which represent the pronunciation of this input character sequence in some abstract way (not necessarily phonemic, despite the name of the task) (Figure 1).

Multilingual G2P is Task I of this year's SIGMORPHON challenge. It features fifteen languages from various phylogenetic families and written in different scripts. We refer the reader to Gorman et al. (2020) for an overview of the language data. Each language comes with 3,600 training and 450 development set examples. It is permitted to use external resources as well as to build a single multilingual model.

We participate in this shared task with an adaptation of our SIGMORPHON 2018 system (Makarov

fathaigh $\mapsto$ /faː/ ("giants")
Irish of Cois Fhairrge (de Bhaldraithe, 1953)

Figure 1: Example of G2P.

and Clematide, 2018b), which was particularly successful in type-level morphological inflection generation. Our system is a neural transducer that operates over explicit edit actions and is trained with imitation learning (Daumé III et al., 2009; Ross et al., 2011; Chang et al., 2015, IL). It has a number of useful inductive biases, one of which is the familiar bias towards copying the input (implemented as the traditional copy edit). This is particularly useful for morphological string transduction problems, which typically involve small and local edits and where most of the input is preserved in the output. This contrasts with models that rely purely on generating characters such as generic encoder-decoder models, which as a result suffer, particularly on smaller-sized datasets.

Copying requires that the input and output character alphabets overlap, preferably substantially. This also allows our IL training to leverage a simple-to-implement expert policy (which during training provides demonstrations to the learner of how to optimally solve the task). The optimal completion of the target given the prediction generated so far during training requires finding edits that would extend the prediction so that the Levenshtein distance (Levenshtein, 1966) between the target and the partial prediction + the future suffix is minimized. Unfortunately, this objective alone would not discriminate between multiple edit action sequences that relate the input and the partial prediction + the future suffix. To address this spurious ambiguity, our IL training adds edit sequence scores, computed using traditional costs,[1] into the

---

[1] Copy costs zero, all other edits cost one.

Proceedings of the Seventeenth SIGMORPHON Workshop on Computational Research
in Phonetics, Phonology, and Morphology, pages 171–176
Online, July 10, 2020. ©2020 Association for Computational Linguistics
https://doi.org/10.18653/v1/P17

objective. This naturally encourages the system to copy, however this would fail on any editing problem with disjoint alphabets.

G2P poses an interesting challenge for a system like ours. On the one hand, G2P shares many similarities with morphological string transduction: The changes are mostly local, it would suffice to perform traditional left-to-right transduction, and a substantial part of the work is arguably applying equivalence rules (e.g. the German letter "g" most often converts to /g/, "a" to /a/ or /aː/), which is similar to copying. Yet, a general solution to G2P cannot rely on overlapping alphabets since many scripts do not share many symbols, if any at all, with IPA (e.g. Korean or Georgian).

Our solution adapts the model to use substitution edits and trains it with a weighted finite-state transducer acting as the expert policy.

2   Model description

The underlying model is a neural transducer introduced in Aharoni and Goldberg (2017). It defines a conditional distribution over traditional edits $p_\theta(\mathbf{y}, \mathbf{a} \mid \mathbf{x}) = \prod_{j=1}^{|\mathbf{a}|} p_\theta(a_j \mid a_{<j}, \mathbf{x})$, where $\mathbf{x}$ is an input sequence of graphemes and $\mathbf{a} = a_1 \ldots a_{|\mathbf{a}|}$ is an edit action sequence. (The output sequence of IPA symbols $\mathbf{y}$ is deterministically computed from $\mathbf{x}$ and $\mathbf{a}$.) The model is equipped with a long short-term memory (LSTM) decoder and a bidirectional LSTM encoder (Graves and Schmidhuber, 2005). The challenge is training this model: Due to the recurrent decoder, it cannot be trained with exact marginal likelihood unlike the more familiar weighted finite-state transducer (Mohri, 2004; Eisner, 2002, WFST) or its neuralizations (Yu et al., 2016). For a more detailed description of the model, we refer the reader to Makarov and Clematide (2018a).[2]

IL training   Makarov and Clematide (2018a) propose training the model using IL, a general model fitting framework for sequential problems over exponentially sized output spaces. IL has been applied successfully to natural language processing (NLP) problems, e.g. transition-based parsing (Goldberg and Nivre, 2012) and language generation (Welleck et al., 2019). IL relies on the availability of demonstrations of how the task can optimally

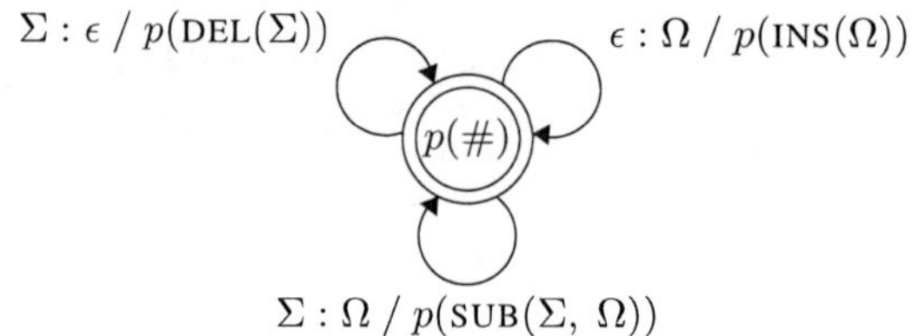

Figure 2: Stochastic edit distance (Ristad and Yianilos, 1998): A memoryless probabilistic FST. Σ and Ω stand for any input and output symbol, respectively.

be solved given any configuration. Due to the nature of many NLP problems, such demonstrations can often be provided by a rule-based program (known as expert policy).

Makarov and Clematide (2018a) use a combination of Levenshtein distance and edit sequence cost as the task objective ($\beta \, \textrm{ED}(\hat{\mathbf{y}}, \mathbf{y}) + \textrm{ED}(\mathbf{x}, \hat{\mathbf{y}}), \beta \geq 1$) and devise an expert policy for it. Given a target sequence $\mathbf{y}$, a partially completed prediction $\hat{\mathbf{y}}_{1:n}$, and the remaining input sequence $\mathbf{x}_{k:l}$, the expert needs to (1) identify the set of target suffixes $\mathbf{y}_{j:m}$ that when appended to $\hat{\mathbf{y}}_{1:n}$, lead to a prediction with minimum Levenshtein distance from the target, and (2) check which of the edit sequences producing those suffixes have the lowest cost, i.e. minimum Levenshtein distance from the remaining input.

The second part is crucial for training accurate models especially in the limited resource setting, as it reduces spurious ambiguity arising under the first part of the objective alone. It is also the second part of the training objective that hinges on the overlap of the input and output alphabets, as this permits minimization using the edit distance dynamic program with traditional costs.

2.1   Adaptation to G2P

The adaptation is two-fold: First, we introduce substitution edits, which have previously not been employed to keep the total number of edit actions to a minimum. For each output character c, there is now a substitution action $\textrm{SUBS}[c]$ which substitutes c for any input character x.

When the alphabets are disjoint, the completing edit sequences cannot be very informatively scored using traditional edit costs. For example, for the data sample кит $\mapsto$ /kʲit/ (Russian: "whale"), we would like the following most natural edit sequence to attain the lowest cost: $\textrm{SUBS}[k], \textrm{INS}[ʲ], \textrm{SUBS}[i], \textrm{SUBS}[t]$. Yet, it is clear

---

[2]The model uses shared input character / action embeddings of size 100 and one-layer LSTMs with hidden-state size 200.

that under traditional costs, this sequence attains the same cost as any other that consists of three substitutions and one insertion. Our solution to this is to learn costs from the training data to ensure an intuitive ranking of edit sequences.

SED policy Learning costs as well as computing string distance can be achieved with a very simple WFST: Stochastic Edit Distance (Ristad and Yianilos, 1998, SED), which is a probabilistic version of Levenshtein distance (Fig. 2). We use traditional multinomial parameterization.

Before starting training the neural transducer, we train a SED model using the Expectation–Maximization algorithm (Dempster et al., 1977). We use the following update in the M-step: $\theta^{(t+1)} \propto \max(0, \widetilde{\theta} + \alpha)$, where $\widetilde{\theta}$ is the unnormalized weight computed in the E-step and $0 < \alpha < 1$ is a sparse Dirichlet prior parameter associated with this edit. This corresponds to sparse regularization via Dirichlet prior (Johnson et al., 2007), which results in many edits having zero probability. We found this training to lead to more accurate SED models. Furthermore, it dramatically reduces the size of the edit action set that the neural transducer is defined over.

SED is integrated into the expert policy. During training, given a configuration consisting of a partial prediction, a remainder of the input, and the target, we query the expert policy for next optimal edits. We minimize the first part of the objective much like before, and we minimize the second part by decoding SED with the Viterbi algorithm.

Suppose we transduce the French word $\mathbf{x} = abject$ ("vile") into the target $\mathbf{y} = $ a b ʒ ɛ k t. Suppose also that the neural transducer currently attends to character $x_4 = e$ and the prediction built so far during training is $\hat{\mathbf{y}}_{1:7} = $ a b ʒ e (note the error). We query the SED policy to get the optimal edit action whose likelihood we will maximize. First, much like before, we find that the following edits are optimal with respect to the first term of the training objective (call them *permissible*) as they do not increase the Levenshtein distance of the prediction from the target (assuming all subsequent edits are permissible too): SUBS[ɛ], INS[ɛ], DEL, SUBS[ ], INS[ ]. (This can be verified by looking at the Levenshtein distance prefix matrix for strings $\hat{\mathbf{y}}_{1:7}$ and $\mathbf{y}$.) Each such edit starts a suffix that completes the target, e.g. it is "ɛ k t" for SUBS[ɛ] and " k t" for SUBS[ ]. Next, we use SED to rank the permissible edits by cost-to-go. For each of the edits and their corresponding suffixes, the expert needs to execute the edit (e.g. SUBS[ɛ] writes ɛ and moves the attention to $x_5 = c$) and then decode SED with Viterbi on the the remaining input and the suffix (both possibly modified by the edit). In this way, we obtain that SUBS[ ] is the optimal action with the lowest cost-to-go (=negative sum of the log probabilities of the edit and of the Viterbi path) of 15.28 (vs 17.65 for SUBS[ɛ], 21.09 for INS[ɛ], 17.31 for DEL, and 17.31 for INS[ ]).[3]

Exploration This time, we also train the transducer with an aggressive exploration schedule: $p_{\text{sampling}}(i) = \frac{1}{1+\exp(i)}$, where i is the training epoch number. After a couple of training epochs, training configurations are generated entirely by executing edit actions sampled from the model.

3 Submission details

We train separate models for each language on the official training data and use the development set for model selection.[4] Our submission does not use any additional lexical resources.

For most of the models, we employ Unicode decomposition normalization (NFKD)[5] as a data preprocessing step. Importantly, this helps decomposing Unicode syllable blocks used e.g. in Hangul.

The size of the development set is rather small (450 examples), and having examined the data, we suspect that overly relying on the development set for model selection might hurt generalization. For example, the French development set contains three exceptions to the "ill"–/j/ equivalence; thus, a single model that achieves a high score on the development set might, in fact, be overfitting. To counter this, we build an eleven-model–strong majority-vote ensemble. Fortunately, training a neural transducer is fast as one epoch takes just about four minutes on average on a single CPU, due to the relatively small number of model parameters.

---

[3] This particular SED is trained on the French training data for 3 EM epochs with Dirichlet prior $\alpha = $ 1e-05 for all edits.

[4] We train the SED model for 20 epochs of EM with $\alpha = $ 0.25 for insertions and 0.5 for all other edits. We train the neural transducer for a maximum of 60 epochs with a patience of 12 epochs. We use mini-batches of size 5. We decode using beam search with beam width 4.

[5] Using NFKD instead of NFD was a bit unfortunate because some superscript diacritics get normalized to their regular size. Luckily, as pointed out to us by Kyle Gorman, there is a unique mapping from NFKD to NFC for the spaced output format of this task. See http://www.unicode.org/reports/tr15/ for Unicode normalization forms.

LNG	CLUZH		ENS.		CLUZH WER AVG				LSTM	TF	BEST BY OTHERS			
	WER	PER	#C	#D	WER	±	Δ, %	$\perp$	WER	WER	WER	Δ, %	PER	Δ, %
ady	27.11	6.27	0	11	30.32	1.97	-12	16.89	28.00	28.44	**24.67**	9	**5.76**	8
arm	**12.22**	**2.82**	0	11	14.73	0.76	-21	8.89	14.67	14.22	12.67	-4	2.91	-3
bul	23.33	**4.70**	0	11	30.81	2.78	-32	13.78	31.11	34.00	**22.22**	5	**4.70**	0
dut	14.44	2.51	9	2	18.30	1.44	-27	9.33	16.44	15.78	**13.56**	6	**2.36**	6
fre	6.89	1.56	2	9	8.12	0.54	-18	3.56	6.22	6.89	**5.11**	26	**1.16**	26
geo	27.33	4.83	0	11	29.11	0.86	-7	8.89	26.44	28.00	**24.89**	9	**4.57**	5
gre	16.44	2.68	11	0	19.60	1.80	-19	7.33	18.89	18.89	**14.44**	12	**2.42**	10
hin	**5.11**	**1.20**	0	11	7.13	0.55	-40	2.67	6.67	9.56	**5.11**	0	**1.20**	0
hun	**4.00**	1.02	0	11	4.77	0.60	-19	2.89	5.33	5.33	**4.00**	0	**0.92**	10
ice	**9.11**	1.90	0	11	10.00	0.53	-10	5.78	10.00	10.22	**9.11**	0	**1.83**	4
jpn	6.00	1.58	0	11	7.19	0.30	-20	4.89	7.56	7.33	**4.89**	19	**1.16**	27
kor	28.44	4.88	0	11	28.26	1.39	1	11.78	46.89	43.78	**24.00**	16	**4.05**	17
lit	**18.67**	**3.27**	0	11	21.54	0.82	-15	14.22	19.11	20.67	**18.67**	0	3.38	-3
rum	11.33	2.68	0	11	13.66	1.11	-21	7.11	10.67	12.00	**9.78**	14	**2.23**	17
vie	1.56	0.35	0	11	1.60	0.21	-2	0.89	4.67	7.56	**0.89**	43	**0.27**	23
AVG	14.13	2.82	1.5	9.5	16.34	1.05	-16	7.93	16.84	17.51	**12.93**	8	**2.59**	8

Table 1: Overview of the test results. Δ gives relative error difference compared to our submission CLUZH. #C=number of NFC models in the ensemble. #D=number of NFKD models in the ensemble. CLUZH WER AVG=average WER, standard deviation, and relative error difference of the average computed over individual models. $\perp$=lower-bound on WER: correct if predicted by any individual model. LSTM=official seq2seq LSTM baseline. TF=official seq2seq Transformer baseline. BEST BY OTHERS=best results of other systems for each language.

4 Results and Discussion

Our system ranks second among 23 submissions by a total of nine teams (Table 1). It ties for first place on four languages (Hindi, Hungarian, Icelandic, Lithuanian) and outperforms every other submission for Armenian. It achieves strong gains over the neural baselines.

Ensembling gains us 16% in error reduction compared to test set averages—a substantial improvement. We leave it for future work to see whether dropout and a larger model size could be used instead as effectively as ensembling. Unicode decomposition normalization boosts the performance of our Korean models.[6] On average, at least one model predicts the output correctly for all but 7.93% of all the words ($\perp$)—Adyghe, Lithuanian, and Bulgarian being the most difficult languages. For some languages, WER standard deviation is high, likely confirming our hypothesis that model selection on the small-sized development set would lead to poor generalization.

Error analysis Table 2 shows the most frequent errors of our system for each language and helps to qualitatively assess their strongly varying error profiles. We take a closer look at the errors in French and Korean. Additional lexical information could improve our French models. E.g. the word's lexical category feature and/or morphological segmentation would probably help correctly transduce the word-final "-ent" (adverb "vraiement" (*truly*) /...ã/ vs verb "viennent" (*they come*), where the ending is silent). Many errors in French are in English borrowings.

We look in some detail at the errors on the Korean test data that all or almost all of the individual models of the ensemble make. As expected, lexicalized phenomena contribute most of the errors: vowel length (which is neither phonemic nor phonetically realized in the speech of all except elderly speakers (Sohn, 2001)) and tensification. Vowel length is not indicated in Korean orthography, and neither is tensification (with some exceptions). Knowing whether a word is an English borrowing (e.g. 섹스 seksŭ[7] (*sex*)) or whether a word is a compound and where the morpheme boundary lies (초승달 ch'osŭng-tal (*new moon*)) could help predict non-automatic tensification correctly in a small number of cases ([ṣekṣ̄ɯ] vs *[sʰ...] and [t͡ɕʰosʰɯŋ̍ta̠l] vs *[...da̠l]).

---

[6] In fact, in a post-submission analysis, we see a strong gain from decomposition only for Korean (17 percentage points on average). For the other languages, it has no impact on performance on average.

[7] This uses McCune-Reischauer transliteration of Korean.

ady	ʼ/ɛ/17	ǝ•/ɛ/9	ʃ/ʂ/8	ɛ/•ǝ/7	j•/ɛ/6	ɛ/ʼ/6	ɛ/ǝ•/5	ɭ/l/5	:/ɛ/5	a/ǝ/5
arm	ɔ/o/17	ɛ/ǝ•/12	o͡/•/12	ǝ•/ɛ/3	t/d/3	g/kʰ/2	ʃʰ/ʒ/2	ɛ/j/2	χ/ʁ/2	t͡ʃ/d•ʒ/1
bul	r/ɾ/26	o/ɔ/22	ǝ/a/14	a/ǝ/12	ọ/ɛ/9	ɛ/ọ/9	a/ɐ/7	ɫ/l/5	ɐ/ǝ/5	ɛ/ʲ/5
dut	ǝ/ɛ/9	ɛ/j•/4	aː/ɑ/4	eː/ǝ/4	ǝ/eː/3	t/d/3	:/ɛ/3	oː/ɔ/2	ɛ/ɛ•/2	n/m/2
fre	ɛ/•ã/2	ɛ/•s/2	a/ɑ/2	o/ɔ/2	w/ɔ/2	•j•ã/ɛ/1	ɛ/•k•s/1	ɔ•p/o/1	•ã/ɛ/1	e/ɛ•ʁ/1
geo	ɪ/i/103	i/ɪ/48	χ/x/5	ɣ/ʁ/4	ʁ/ɣ/3	x/χ/3	ɑ/a/2	•s/ɛ/1		
gre	ɾ/r/27	o/ɔ/19	r/ɾ/15	e/ɛ/9	ɟ/i/3	n•/ɛ/2	ç/i/2	m/ŋ/2	•m•e/ɛ/1	ɛ/s•/1
hin	ɛ/ǝ•/10	ǝ•/ɛ/5	ɛ/•ǝ/2	ɛː/ǝ/2	ɛ/ˌ•/2	ɑ/a/2	ɪ/iː/1	•fi/ɦ/1	ɪ/i/1	ǝ/j/1
hun	ʃ/ʒ/3	ɛ/ː/3	eː/i•n•t/1	ɛ/ɱ•v•/1	m/eːʲ/1	t͡s/xː/1	sː/ʃ•s/1	h•/ɛ/1	•h/o͡ʃ/1	o͡/•/1
ice	:/ɛ/11	ɛ/ː/9	t•/ɛ/4	v/f/3	ɛ/ọ/3	t/d/2	ʰ/ɛ/2	ɛ/ʰ/2	ɣ•ɣ/uː/1	cʰ/k/1
jpn	ɛ/o̥/8	ɛ/ọ/6	ɛ/ː/3	:/•ɯᵝ/2	:/•ọ/2	ɯᵝ/j•ọ/1	ɛ/•ẹ/1	ɯᵝ/ẹ/1	ọ:/ã̩/1	s•i/ɯ̃/1
kor	ɛ/ː/72	:/ɛ/18	ǝ:/ʌ/11	ʑ/ç/4	ʌ/ǝː/4	d/t/4	g/k̚/3	ɛ/ɲ•/3	d/t̚/2	ʎ/n/2
lit	ɛ/ọ/15	n/ŋ/14	ɐ/aː/12	:/ɛ/8	ʲ/ɛ/7	o/ɔ/7	ɛ/ː/6	ɛ/ʲ/5	ɛ/æː/3	aː/ɐ/3
rum	o͡/•/8	•/o͡/8	ẹ/j/6	r/ɾ/5	ʲ/•i/4	:/•j/3	i/j/3	ɛ/e•/2	o/e/2	j/i/2
vie	ɛ/ː/2	⊣•/ɛ/1	ɛ/e•/1	w•/ɛ/1	ˀ•/ɛ/1	o͡m/ɛ/1	ǝ/e/1	ʔ/n/1	⊥/ɛ/1	a/ɔ/1

Table 2: Ten most frequent errors per language. Notation: prediction / gold / error frequency. • denotes whitespace. Computed using the UTF-8 aware version of the ISRI Analytic Tools for OCR Evaluation.[8]

How good is SED policy? Somewhat surprisingly, using SED as part of the expert policy results in competitive performance. Yet, SED is a very crude model (e.g. because of the lack of context, when used as a conditional model, SED assigns less probability to any edit sequence containing insertions than the same sequence but with all the insertions removed; this e.g. makes it unusable as a standalone model for G2P). On top of this, we also do not use learned roll-out, which would be recommended when training with a sub-optimal expert (Chang et al., 2015). We leave it for future work to examine whether the neural transducer's performance on G2P would improve from replacing SED with a more powerful model.

5 Conclusion

This presents the approach taken by the CLUZH team to solving the SIGMORPHON 2020 Multilingual Grapheme-to-Morpheme Conversion challenge. Our submission is based on our successful SIGMORPHON 2018 system, which is a majority-vote ensemble of neural transducers trained with imitation learning. We adapt the 2018 system to work on transduction problems with disjoint input and output alphabets. We add substitution actions (not available in previous versions of the system) and employ a memoryless probabilistic finite-state transducer to define the expert policy for the imitation learning. We use majority-vote ensembling to counter the overfitting to the small development sets. These simple modifications result in a highly competitive performance even without the use of any exernal resources or learning a single multilingual model. Our ensemble ranks second out of 23 submissions by a total of nine teams. Our error analysis indicates that addressing many of the errors requires additional information such as knowing the word's lexical category, morphological segmentation, or etymology. We will make our code publicly available.

Acknowledgment

We would like to thank the organizers for their great effort in these turbulent times. We thank Kyle Gorman for taking the time to help us with our Unicode normalization problem. This work has been supported by the Swiss National Science Foundation under grant CR-SII5_173719.

References

Roee Aharoni and Yoav Goldberg. 2017. Morphological inflection generation with hard monotonic attention. In *ACL*.

Tomás de Bhaldraithe. 1953. *Gaeilge Chois Fhairrge: An Deilbhíocht*. Institiúid Ard-Léinn Bhaile Átha Cliath.

Kai-Wei Chang, Akshay Krishnamurthy, Alekh Agarwal, Hal Daume III, and John Langford. 2015. Learning to search better than your teacher. In *ICML*.

Hal Daumé III, John Langford, and Daniel Marcu. 2009. Search-based structured prediction. *Machine learning*.

---

[8]https://github.com/eddieantonio/ocreval

Arthur P Dempster, Nan M Laird, and Donald B Rubin. 1977. Maximum likelihood from incomplete data via the EM algorithm. *Journal of the Royal Statistical Society: Series B (Methodological)*, 39(1).

Jason Eisner. 2002. Parameter estimation for probabilistic finite-state transducers. In *ACL*.

Yoav Goldberg and Joakim Nivre. 2012. A dynamic oracle for arc-eager dependency parsing. In *COLING*.

Kyle Gorman, Lucas F.E. Ashby, Aaron Goyzueta, Arya D. McCarthy, Shijie Wu, and Daniel You. 2020. The SIGMORPHON 2020 shared task on multilingual grapheme-to-phoneme conversion. In *Proceedings of the 17th SIGMORPHON Workshop on Computational Research in Phonetics, Phonology, and Morphology*.

Alex Graves and Jürgen Schmidhuber. 2005. Framewise phoneme classification with bidirectional LSTM and other neural network architectures. *Neural Networks*, 18(5).

Mark Johnson, Thomas L Griffiths, and Sharon Goldwater. 2007. Bayesian inference for PCFGs via Markov Chain Monte Carlo. In *NAACL-HLT*.

Vladimir I Levenshtein. 1966. Binary codes capable of correcting deletions, insertions, and reversals. *Soviet physics doklady*, 10(8).

Peter Makarov and Simon Clematide. 2018a. Imitation learning for neural morphological string transduction. In *EMNLP*.

Peter Makarov and Simon Clematide. 2018b. UZH at CoNLL-SIGMORPHON 2018 shared task on universal morphological reinflection. *Proceedings of the CoNLL SIGMORPHON 2018 Shared Task: Universal Morphological Reinflection*.

Mehryar Mohri. 2004. Weighted finite-state transducer algorithms. An overview. In *Formal Languages and Applications*, volume 148 of *Studies in Fuzziness and Soft Computing*. Springer Berlin Heidelberg.

Eric Sven Ristad and Peter N Yianilos. 1998. Learning string-edit distance. *IEEE Transactions on Pattern Analysis and Machine Intelligence*.

Stéphane Ross, Geoffrey Gordon, and Drew Bagnell. 2011. A reduction of imitation learning and structured prediction to no-regret online learning. In *Proceedings of the fourteenth international conference on artificial intelligence and statistics*.

Ho-Min Sohn. 2001. *The Korean language*. Cambridge University Press.

Sean Welleck, Kianté Brantley, Hal Daumé III, and Kyunghyun Cho. 2019. Non-monotonic sequential text generation. In *ICML*.

Lei Yu, Jan Buys, and Phil Blunsom. 2016. Online segment to segment neural transduction. In *EMNLP*.

The UniMelb Submission to the SIGMORPHON 2020 Shared Task 0: Typologically Diverse Morphological Inflection

Andrei Shcherbakov
University of Melbourne, AU
`ultrasparc@yandex.ru`

Abstract

The paper describes the University of Melbourne's submission to the SIGMORPHON 2020 Shared Task 0: Typologically Diverse Morphological Inflection. Our team submitted three systems in total, two neural and one non-neural. Our analysis of systems' performance shows positive effects of newly introduced data hallucination technique that we employed in one of neural systems, especially in low-resource scenarios. A non-neural system based on observed inflection patterns shows optimistic results even in its simple implementation (>75% accuracy for 50% of languages). With possible improvement within the same modeling principle, accuracy might grow to values above 90%.

1 Introduction

According to WALS database 80% of the world's languages morphologically mark verb tense and 65% mark grammatical case (Dryer et al., 2005). Still, until recently most research in natural language processing was focused on a few well-documented languages with modest amount of morphological marking. A great variety of typologically diverse low-resource languages were left outside of NLP investigation and modeling. At the same time, neural systems outperformed non-neural ones on many benchmarks(cite) while being evaluated on a limited (and often not typologically representative) sample of languages. Nevertheless, some of such systems or architectures were stated as "universal". But are they universal? How well models trained a certain sample of language families can generalize outside of it? For instance, a model trained on Indo-European languages might be biased towards suffixing and will be working less well on languages that use infixing or prefixing. The SIGMORPHON 2020 Shared task 0 ("Typologically diverse morphological inflection"; Vy-

lomova et al. (2020)) aims at evaluation of the generalization ability of models. It continues recent trend of increasing linguistic diversity: starting with 10 well-documented languages in Cotterell et al. (2016) up to 103 in Cotterell et al. (2018). These shared tasks demonstrated that neural models outperform non-neural ones but generally struggle in low-resource settings. Therefore, the 2019 Shared Task focused on cross-lingual transfer (McCarthy et al., 2019) and explored transfer of morphological information from a high-resource to a low-resource language. In this paper, we describe three models submitted to the shared task 0. We investigate both generalization ability of models and their performance in low-resource languages. We propose a variation of data hallucination technique that significantly improves the results of neural models in low-resource settings.

2 Task Description

The task was organized in three stages: development, generalization and evaluation. In the development stage participants were provided with initial set of 45 development languages that were used to *develop* their systems. In the next stage, generalization, an extra and more diverse set of 45 languages was released, and participants were asked to fine-tune and optimize their systems on these languages. In both stages, only training and development datasets were released. Test splits for both development and generalization languages were provided in the final, evaluation, stage.

Systems were then evaluated and ranked based on the test set predictions.

3 Data

3.1 Data Format

All shared task data are in UTF-8 and follow UniMorph annotation schema (Sylak-Glassman,

Proceedings of the Seventeenth SIGMORPHON Workshop on Computational Research in Phonetics, Phonology, and Morphology, pages 177–183
Online, July 10, 2020. ©2020 Association for Computational Linguistics
https://doi.org/10.18653/v1/P17

2016). Training and developments samples consist of a lemma, an inflected (target) form, and its morphosyntactic description (tags). Test samples omit the target form.

3.2 Languages

Forty-five languages representing Austronesian, Niger-Congo, Oto-Manguean, Uralic and Indo-European language families were provided in the development stage. Another forty-five (surprise) languages from Afro-Asiatic, Algic, Altaic[1], Dravidian, Indo-European, Niger-Congo, Sino-Tibetan, Siouan, Songhay, Southern Daly, Uralic, and Uto-Aztecan families were provided in the generalization phase one week before the evaluation phase started. Importantly, the dataset sizes are highly imbalanced, ranging from tens of thousand of samples in some Uralic languages to a few hundreds in the Niger-Congo family.

4 Baseline Systems

Two types of baseline systems were provided: neural and non-neural. The **non-neural** baseline was essentially the same as in previous years' tasks (Cotterell et al., 2017, 2018). More specifically, it first extracts possible lemma–form alignments and associates them with corresponding target tags, then majority classifier chooses the most frequent transformation and applies it to a given lemma.

The **neural** baselines include a hard monotonic attention model (Wu and Cotterell, 2019) and a character level transformer (Wu et al., 2020). Both were trained in monolingual and multilingual modes. Organizers also provide a variation of the model that uses data hallucination technique from Anastasopoulos and Neubig (2019) to improve performance in low-resource languages.

5 Evaluation

The systems were evaluated in terms of test accuracy and Levenstein distance between predicted and gold forms. Unlike in earlier shared tasks where systems were ranked based on macro-averaging, here systems were ranked based on statistical significance of differences in their performance.

6 System Description

In terms of the shared task, we experimented with three systems, two neural and one non-neural. Sub-

sections below provide a short description of each.

6.1 A non-neural system based on differently refined alignment patterns

First, we implemented a non-neural system (`flexica01`) where possible patterns of lemma-to-inflected form transformation are generated directly by the following simple process:

1) We find all maximal continuous matches between lemma and inflected form; while doing this, we start with the longest possible match and then find matches across the remaining unmatched fragments, recursively. We replace the matches found with groups denoted as `\number`, like in regular expression syntax. Swapped order of groups in inflected forms is allowed. For the simplicity of implementation, we assumed that the number of group is increasing along the lemma word. If multiple matches of the same group lengths are possible for a given lemma - inflection pair, we produce all the respective transformations. However, for the vast majority of samples only a single variant is produced at this stage. For example, for the past tense of `"to understand"`:

`understand → understood`

we extract the following transformation rule:

`\0an\1 → \0oo\1,`

where `\0=underst` and `\1=d` are groups. Group substitutions are not stored leaving a transformation as abstract as possible. However, some statistics about group content is used to evaluate the confidence of substitution (see below).

2) Starting with previously generated transformation pattern(s) of maximal abstraction, we generate a set of patterns more specific to a given training word by treating a limited number $(0..ConcreteLetterLimit$, where $ConcreteLetterLimit$ is a hyperparameter) of characters as concrete (i.e. standing outside any group). For our previous example given $ConcreteLetterLimit = 1$ we would finally produce the following set of matching transformations: `\0an\1 → \0oo\1; u\0an\1 → u\0oo\1; \0n\1an\2 → \0n\1oo\2, ... (3 more), \0s\1an\2 → \0s\1oo\2, \0tan\1 → \0too\1, \0and → \0ood.`

All patterns generated for training samples are stored in a trie, which is separate for each combination of grammatical features. The resulting set of tries acts as a model.[2] At prediction phase, a multi-variant search against a given lemma is attempted over the trie for a respective grammatical tag combination. Here, multi-variance means that the search procedure both allows wildcards for possible groups and concrete characters to be matched against. After the search completes, all the candidate transformations found are then sorted by their associated score in order to find the best fit. In the version used to produce prediction submitted to the contest, the score was based on the following three components:

1. A (squashed) frequency f of transformation occurrence in a training set;

2. The diversity d of marginal (the first one and the last one) letters in groups as they occurred in different fits of a given transformation found in the training set. To grasp the underlying idea, take, for example, a $\backslash 0$ $\rightarrow \backslash 0 s$ transformation producing plural nouns in English that is considered as highly confident for any possible $\backslash 0$ value because $\backslash 0$ was observed to match various strings starting and ending with many different letters in a training set. In contrast, $\backslash 0 a \backslash 1$ $\rightarrow \backslash 0 o o \backslash 1$ matches a very limited set of examples such as $\mathtt{stand} \rightarrow \mathtt{stood}$, $\mathtt{understand} \rightarrow \mathtt{understood}$, where the last character of $\backslash 0$ is always $\mathtt{'d'}$ and the first character of $\backslash 1$ is $\mathtt{'n'}$. Such a poor diversity of characters should signal the predictor that the transformation pattern is not likely to be usable at different group values and it may be better to focus at more specific transformation patterns instead. Technically, we counted d as a product of the number of distinct characters over all start and end positions of groups. Still, if we have an exact match between currently considered substitution letter and one observed at the same position in a training sample, we consider this position exempt from scrutiny by assuming it as having a high "effective" diversity (currently, of 10).

3. Specificity s which here means the number

of concrete characters in the pattern (without counting characters falling into groups).

In the submitted version, the score was calculated by the following empirical formula:

$$G = \frac{1}{2} \log_2 f + 6 \log_2 d + 12s \qquad (1)$$

Note that in contrast to a conceptually similar approach proposed by Hulden et al. (2014), we didn't encourage the most general paradigms. Instead, we used a trade-off criterion that prefers better confidence but lower amount of abstraction in patterns. Also, we didn't attempt to build whole paradigms. We used an independent alignment process for each form.

Fig. 1 displays accuracy for the model measured across all 90 languages. We additionally show the accuracy that would be achieved in a case of ideal selection criteria (labelled as "+ Ideal Transform Choice" category) for every language. The accuracy equals to the proportion of test samples which succeeded in matching at least one transformation pattern that produces correct prediction. We also note that the proposed scoring formula (mostly inspired by Indo-European languages) does not fit well the Oto-Manguean family. If to speak about the potential ability to cover inflections by directly observable patterns, Finnic languages with their tricky morphology appear to be the most challenging ones.

We also roughly measured potential improvement that may arise from considering correlations between inflection patterns for different grammatical forms of a single lemma (in other words, from paradigm clustering). We trained embeddings for the generated transformations using lemmas as context markers. Then, we used cosine similarity between such embeddings as a candidate transformation selection criterion in cases when a lemma is both present in the train and in the test sets. The proportion of samples where application of such a criterion allowed to turn an incorrect prediction into a correct one, is labelled as "+ Paradigm Search" in Fig. 1.

Generally, the experiments with pattern-based inflection prediction were proposed to verify the following two hypotheses, (1) that it is sufficient to reuse observed substitution patterns for proper modeling of inflection in a wide range of languages, and (2) that candidate inflection pattern selection may be based on a simple statistical

---

[2]To simplify the implementation, a transformation pattern was stored as a mapping between two plain strings, one for the lemma and another one for the inflected form. Group references were represented by special characters added to the alphabet.

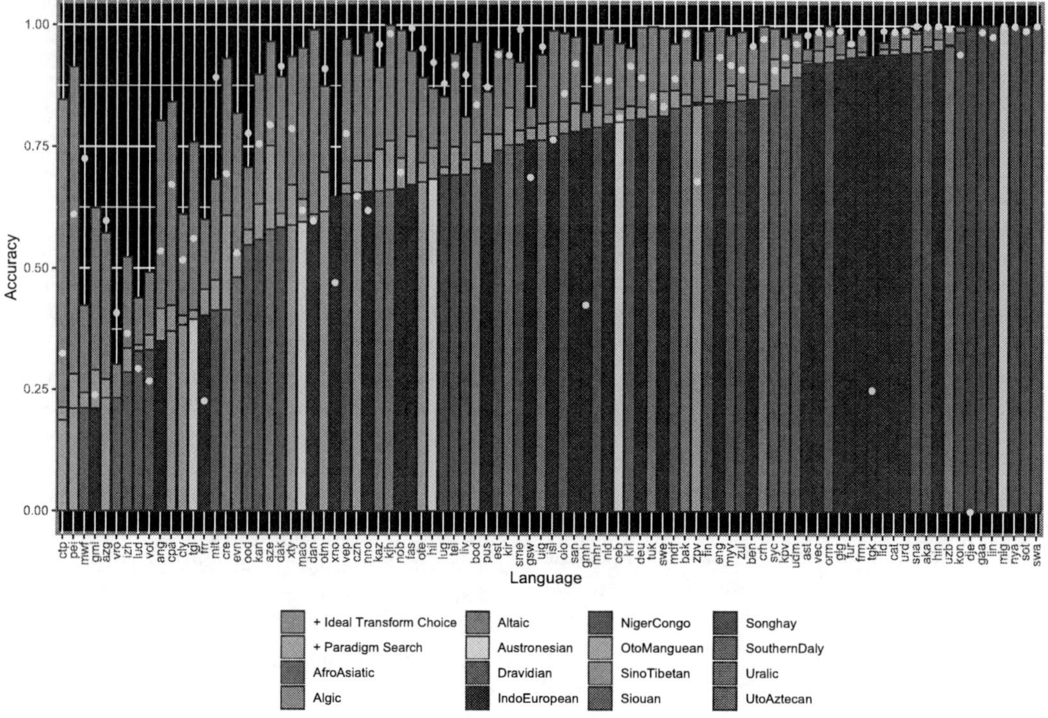

Figure 1: Accuracy for the non-neural `flexica01` solution based on immediately observed transform patterns. Accuracy for the `flexica02` hard attention neural system is also given for comparison (in white points).

criterion (frequency, entropy etc.) While a simple pattern selection rule hasn't yet been discovered, the experimental results largely support the first hypothesis. However, it should be noted that learnt patterns are often too sparse due to the lack of compositionality and abstraction in the initial system design. When an inflection involves complex, phonotactical transformations, it is unlikely to match a quite "similar" sample in a train set. It is especially true if the inflection is irregular which usually implies extreme sparsity of its domain. Another issue that limits pattern search capacity is related to the model size. The experiments have shown that greater values of $ConcreteLetterLimit$ enable greater accuracy figures. However, we had to stick with $ConcreteLetterLimit = 2$ because the choice of greater value led to unacceptably high memory consumption for most of training sets provided. Though, this issue is likely to be addressed by using of ongoing pruning procedures over learnt transformations.

6.2 Neural systems

Multilingual (family-based) learning The neural system (`flexica02`; multilingual) is based on hard monotonic attention model proposed in Aharoni and Goldberg (2017), with the same loss function, but with the following differences:

- We combined all the languages belonging to a given family[3] into a single dataset, having added two extra features such as language and genus. The idea was to let the model infer common cross-lingual inflection patterns when a resource for a particular language is low.

- We also made a minor modification of pre-processing. We used maximal continuous sub-string search to organize alignment between lemma and its inflected form in order to advance hard attention state during the learning phase. Compared to the original system,

---

[3] An exception was Uralic family. Due to excessively high volume of training data, we split this family into 5 subfamilies.

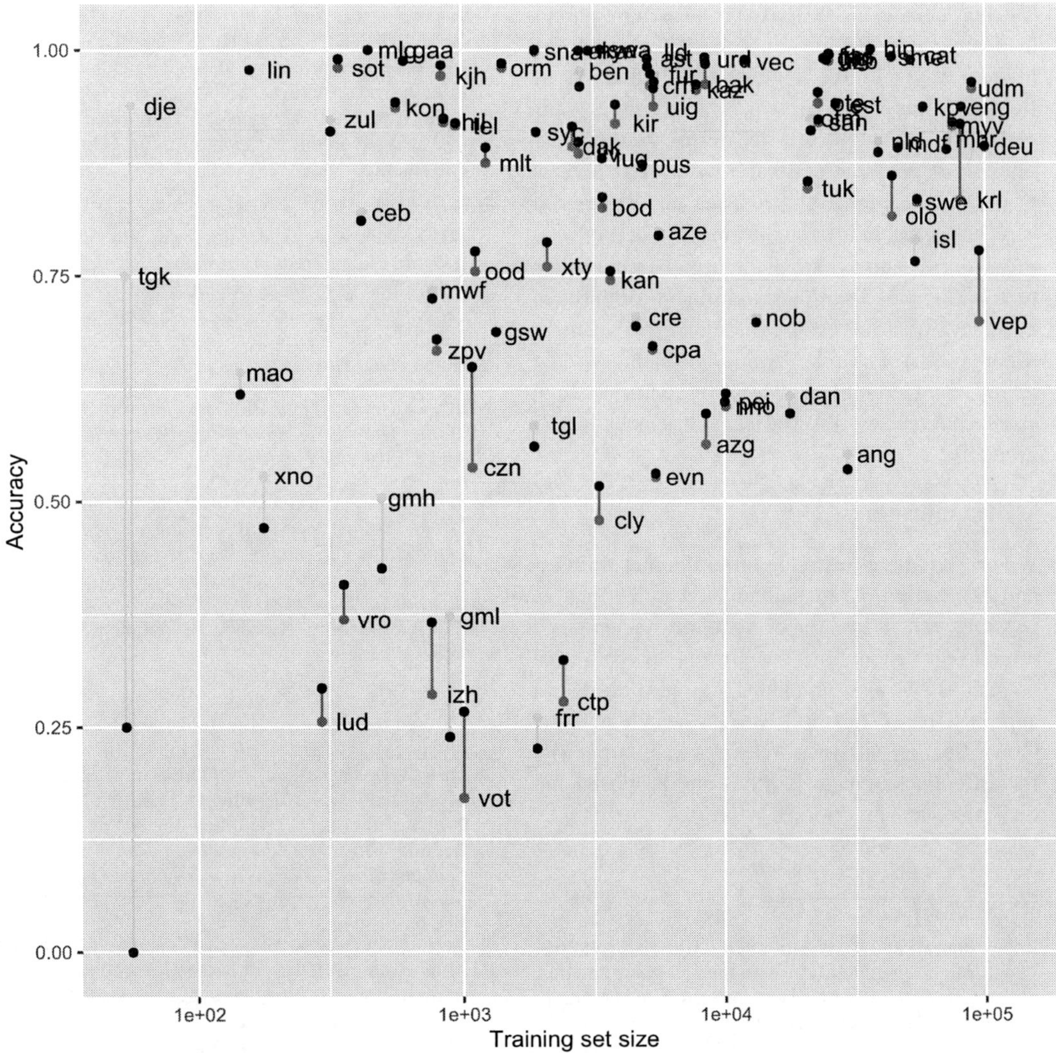

Figure 2: Comparison of accuracy for the proposed neural system with hallucinated data (green or red points for greater or lower accuracy, respectively) and one without hallucinated data (black points)

we abolished one-by-one alignment of mismatching characters, instead letting each mismatching segment to be put into correspondence to a single attention state as a whole.

Hyperparameters are set as follows: hidden and input dimensionality is set to 100, feature dimensionality is 20, the number of layers is 2. The model is trained with AdaDelta (Zeiler, 2012) for 100 and 20 epochs for small-sized and large-size families, respectively.

Adding Hallucinated Data Inspired by Anastasopoulos and Neubig (2019), our last model

(`flexica03`) is a variation of the above model that uses extra hallucinated samples. We added 200 samples[4] per language per part-of-speech (POS) in order to produce hallucinated inflection samples that look like real. We reused the predictor from `flexica01` (presented earlier) with the only difference that now it acts in the reverse direction predicting the best fitting tag–lemma combination for a given inflected form. We also enriched the model with word-generator

---

[4]We chose this number as an empirical approximation of minimum amount of training data required for the predictor to display stable convergence.

(Shcherbakov et al., 2016) to produce more phonotactically plausible forms. This works in the following way: 1) Word generator trained on inflected forms for a given POS produces samples of hallucinated inflected forms (without distinction of grammatical features); 2) The reverse `flexica01` predictor produces tag–lemma for each hallucinated inflected form.

As Fig. 2 shows, supplementing training data with hallucinated samples significantly improved accuracy in low-resource languages (such as Maori, Zarma, Tajik, Anglo-Norman, Middle High/Low German) while for medium to high sized resources we observe less consistency in positive effects.

7 Conclusion

We proposed and tested (1) multilingual training, and (2) pattern-based hallucinated inflections as possible enhancements of sequence-to-sequence morphology modeling for diverse low-resource languages. We also developed a simple non-neural approach based on multi-variant search of common inflection patterns. We explored its suitability for different language families and proposed further improvement options.

References

Roee Aharoni and Yoav Goldberg. 2017. Morphological inflection generation with hard monotonic attention. In *Proceedings of the 55th Annual Meeting of the Association for Computational Linguistics (Volume 1: Long Papers)*, pages 2004–2015, Vancouver, Canada. Association for Computational Linguistics.

Antonios Anastasopoulos and Graham Neubig. 2019. Pushing the limits of low-resource morphological inflection. In *Proceedings of the 2019 Conference on Empirical Methods in Natural Language Processing and the 9th International Joint Conference on Natural Language Processing (EMNLP-IJCNLP)*, pages 983–995.

Ryan Cotterell, Christo Kirov, John Sylak-Glassman, Géraldine Walther, Ekaterina Vylomova, Arya D McCarthy, Katharina Kann, Sebastian J Mielke, Garrett Nicolai, Miikka Silfverberg, et al. 2018. The CoNLL–SIGMORPHON 2018 Shared Task: Universal morphological reinflection. In *Proceedings of the CoNLL–SIGMORPHON 2018 Shared Task: Universal Morphological Reinflection*, pages 1–27.

Ryan Cotterell, Christo Kirov, John Sylak-Glassman, Géraldine Walther, Ekaterina Vylomova, Patrick Xia, Manaal Faruqui, Sandra Kübler, David Yarowsky, Jason Eisner, and Mans Hulden. 2017. CoNLL-SIGMORPHON 2017 shared task: Universal morphological reinflection in 52 languages. In *Proceedings of the CoNLL SIGMORPHON 2017 Shared Task: Universal Morphological Reinflection*, pages 1–30, Vancouver. Association for Computational Linguistics.

Ryan Cotterell, Hinrich Schütze, and Jason Eisner. 2016. Morphological smoothing and extrapolation of word embeddings. In *Proceedings of the 54th Annual Meeting of the Association for Computational Linguistics (Volume 1: Long Papers)*, pages 1651–1660, Berlin, Germany. Association for Computational Linguistics.

Matthew Dryer, David Gil, and Martin Haspelmath. 2005. *The world atlas of language structures*. Oxford University Press.

Mans Hulden, Markus Forsberg, and Malin Ahlberg. 2014. Semi-supervised learning of morphological paradigms and lexicons. In *Proceedings of the 14th Conference of the European Chapter of the Association for Computational Linguistics*, pages 569–578, Gothenburg, Sweden. Association for Computational Linguistics.

Arya D McCarthy, Ekaterina Vylomova, Shijie Wu, Chaitanya Malaviya, Lawrence Wolf-Sonkin, Garrett Nicolai, Christo Kirov, Miikka Silfverberg, Sebastian J Mielke, Jeffrey Heinz, et al. 2019. The SIGMORPHON 2019 Shared Task: Morphological analysis in context and cross-lingual transfer for inflection. In *Proceedings of the 16th Workshop on Computational Research in Phonetics, Phonology, and Morphology*, pages 229–244.

Andrei Shcherbakov, Ekaterina Vylomova, and Nick Thieberger. 2016. Phonotactic modeling of extremely low resource languages. In *Proceedings of the Australasian Language Technology Association Workshop 2016*, pages 84–93.

John Sylak-Glassman. 2016. The composition and use of the universal morphological feature schema (unimorph schema). *Johns Hopkins University*.

Ekaterina Vylomova, Jennifer White, Elizabeth Salesky, Sabrina J. Mielke, Shijie Wu, Edoardo Ponti, Rowan Hall Maudslay, Ran Zmigrod, Joseph Valvoda, Svetlana Toldova, Francis Tyers, Elena Klyachko, Ilya Yegorov, Natalia Krizhanovsky, Paula Czarnowska, Irene Nikkarinen, Andrej Krizhanovsky, Tiago Pimentel, Lucas Torroba Hennigen, Christo Kirov, Garrett Nicolai, Adina Williams, Antonios Anastasopoulos, Hilaria Cruz, Eleanor Chodroff, Ryan Cotterell, Miikka Silfverberg, and Mans Hulden. 2020. The SIGMORPHON 2020 Shared Task 0: Typologically diverse morphological inflection. In *Proceedings of the 17th Workshop on Computational Research in Phonetics, Phonology, and Morphology*.

Shijie Wu and Ryan Cotterell. 2019. Exact hard monotonic attention for character-level transduction. In

Proceedings of the 57th Annual Meeting of the Association for Computational Linguistics, pages 1530–1537.

Shijie Wu, Ryan Cotterell, and Mans Hulden. 2020. Applying the transformer to character-level transduction.

Matthew D Zeiler. 2012. Adadelta: an adaptive learning rate method. *arXiv preprint arXiv:1212.5701*.

Data Augmentation for Transformer-based G2P

Zach Ryan and **Mans Hulden**
University of Colorado
{zachary.j.ryan,mans.hulden}@colorado.edu

Abstract

The Transformer model has been shown to out-perform other neural seq2seq models in several character-level tasks. It is unclear, however, if the Transformer would benefit as much as other seq2seq models from data augmentation strategies in the low-resource setting. In this paper we explore methods for data augmentation in the g2p task together with the Transformer model. Our results show that a relatively simple alignment-based approach of identifying consistent input-output subsequences in grapheme-phoneme data combined with a subsequent splicing together of such pieces to generate hallucinated data works well in the low-resource setting, often delivering substantial performance improvement over a standard Transformer model.

1 Introduction

The Transformer model (Vaswani et al., 2017) has recently been shown to be robust for character-level translation tasks, outperforming other recurrent sequence-to-sequence (seq2seq) models in a wide range of tasks, including morphological inflection, grapheme-to-phoneme (g2p), and text normalization (Wu et al., 2020). A transformer-based model also served as the baseline system for both the SIGMORPHON 2020 shared tasks on grapheme-to-phoneme conversion (Gorman et al., 2020) and low-resource morphological inflection (Vylomova et al., 2020), delivering substantially better performance than other models.[1]

A common thread in research with character-level seq2seq has been that, for situations where few training examples are available, alternative strategies to produce more robust performance must be taken. For morphology tasks, this has included strategies such as instructing the model

---

[1]Our code is available at https://github.com/LonelyRider-cs/sig_shared_tasks.

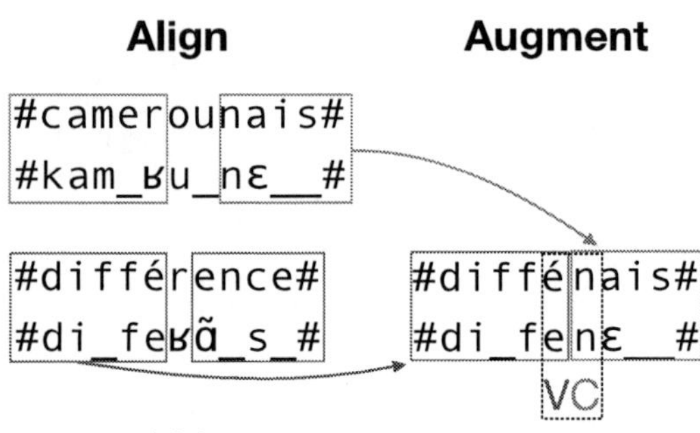

. . .

Figure 1: Augmentation strategy: after aligning all grapheme-phoneme pairs, we use input subsequences that are reliably mapped to the same output in the whole data set in creating an augmented data set from the pieces. We also enforce—using an unsupervised algorithm for detecting consonants and vowels—that only CV or VC is allowed at the boundary of the pieces spliced together.

to copy input symbols to the output (Makarov et al., 2017; Makarov and Clematide, 2018; Anastasopoulos and Neubig, 2019), which may require alignment of the input and output in the training. Another strategy is data augmentation (Bergmanis et al., 2017; Silfverberg et al., 2017), whereby some mechanism is employed to generate additional training examples from the few available ones. Pointer-generator networks (Vinyals et al., 2015), which facilitate copying of the input, have also been employed (Sharma et al., 2018). Perhaps since no low-resource g2p task has previously been organized, the performance of standard models of seq2seq in settings with limited training data have not been explored as much as in morphological inflection, where data augmentation has proven to be a successful strategy.

The Transformer model, as opposed to other seq2seq models such as bidirectional LSTM encoder-decoders, however, seems to be more ro-

Proceedings of the Seventeenth SIGMORPHON Workshop on Computational Research
in Phonetics, Phonology, and Morphology, pages 184–188
Online, July 10, 2020. ©2020 Association for Computational Linguistics
https://doi.org/10.18653/v1/P17

bust by itself in the low-resource setting, at least for morphology tasks. The multiple Transformer-based baselines in the SIGMORPHON 2020 morphological task did not provide any consistent improvement by data augmentation. Also, the best-performing systems did not seem to use this strategy, even in low-resource cases. For the grapheme-to-phoneme task, it is therefore unclear if the Transformer would also benefit from one of these strategies in low-resource scenarios. The SIGMORPHON g2p task (task 1) featured uniform amounts of training data of 3600 g/p word pairs, and so can not be considered a low-resource task.

The different strategies to fortify seq2seq models in the low-resource setting in other character-level tasks are not all applicable to the g2p task, however. The array of mechanisms for learning to copy the input—special copy symbols, pointer-generator networks— favored by many low-resource morphology systems do not naturally transfer to the g2p task since the input and output pairs use different alphabets. Data augmentation, however, remains a potentially viable strategy.

In this paper we discuss experiments on the SIGMORPHON 2020 task 1 data sets where we explored data augmentation strategies for the g2p setting. Our actual submission (team **CU-Z**) to the task was a bidirectional LSTM encoder-decoder which later turned out to perform much worse than the Transformer model described in this paper. We did not finish training the Transformer models before the submission deadline, and only submitted the BiLSTM. In this paper we only discuss data augmentation and the Transformer model.

2   Data Augmentation

We experimented with two strategies of data augmentation: our first strategy was to identify in the training data grapheme sequences in the beginning of words and at the ends of words that (almost) always map to the same phoneme sequence, such as a word-initial **c** consistently mapping to **k**. Subsequently we generated new training data by swapping such sequences across words, generating new words. This initial strategy failed to provide improvements on the development set, and we moved to a more refined version of this idea, discussed in more detail below.

procurions	p ʁ ɔ k y ʁ j ɔ̃
reconnaituer	ʁ ə k ɔ n ɛ t ɥ e
brancétude	b ʁ ɑ̃ ʃ e t y d
davasonnage	d a v ɑ̃ s ɔ n a ʒ
magazoulevard	m a g a z u l v a ʁ
oucoutume	w ɛ k u t y m
socendredi	s ɔ s ɑ̃ d ʁ ə d i
thapu	t a p y
sedi	s ə d i
sagementsier	s a ʒ m ɑ̃ z j e

Table 1: Example augmented French data from the original **min** data set that contains 100 examples. In total, 50,000 examples such as the ones shown here are created from each data set.

2.1   Slice-and-shuffle

In our main strategy, we first perform a 1-to-1 alignment of the input-output data, yielding alignments such as are shown in Figure 1. For the alignment, we use an MCMC-algorithm originally developed by the second author for the SIGMORPHON 2016 shared task baseline for morphological inflection (Cotterell et al., 2016), largely similar to Expectation-Maximization based models (Ristad and Yianilos, 1998; Novak et al., 2012), but using an MCMC sampler instead. After the alignment, we investigate how consistently some part of the word-initial substring graphemes $\#i_1, \ldots, i_m$ maps to the same phonemes $\#o_1, \ldots, o_n$, and likewise for the word-final parts $i_1, \ldots, i_m\#$ and $o_1, \ldots, o_n\#$. We use # here as a symbol to denote either beginning-of-word or end-of-word. Whichever is intended should be clear from the context.

For example, in French, the initial grapheme sequence #poin, whenever found in the data, is always aligned with #pwɛ̃, and the final grapheme sequence parer# is consistently aligned with the phoneme sequence paʁe#. Such pieces can then be used to create new grapheme/phoneme pairs in an augmented training data set, such as poinparer → pwɛ̃paʁe. See Figure 1 for another example.

In particular, for an input subsequence i, we estimate its reliability as being associated with an output subsequence o as the conditional probability of the output, given the input in the usual way as:

$$p(o|i) = \frac{\text{count}(i:o) + \alpha}{\sum\limits_{\text{ANY}} \text{count}(i:\text{ANY}) + \alpha|\text{ANY}|} \quad (1)$$

Here α is a smoothing parameter and ANY—through a slight notational abuse—represents all the witnessed different output alignments for a particular input subsequence i. For example, if we are calculating the conditional probability of some output sequence, conditioned on an initial #pho-sequence, and #pho has been aligned in the training data with #p, #f, and #fo, then ANY represents the set {#p, #f, #fo}.

To select which beginning and ending pieces can be reliably used for creation of augmented data, we declare a cutoff probability $c = 0.98$ and only use those pieces $i:o$ where $p(o|i) > c$. This yields a large number of usable pieces for each language, even in the lowest-resource setting of 100 training examples.[2] Note that the number of actual potential augmented input-output mappings corresponds to roughly the square of the number of discovered reliable beginning and ending pairings. We generate augmented words completely at random from all the pieces available to us, except we limit the output sequence length to 15 by excluding longer sequences, and put an additional restriction on the juncture where the splices come together regarding consonants and vowels, discussed below.

2.2 Consonants and Vowels

After estimating $p(o|i)$ for each seen subsequence in the training data the resulting "reliable" pieces can be spliced together to augment the data set, by combining word-initial and word-final pieces. Since phonological assimilations and coarticulations are very common in vowel-vowel and consonant-consonant sequences, and since we wish to avoid generating unnatural syllables, we do not splice together pieces where a slice ending in a phoneme-side consonant would be paired up with another one that begins with a vowel and vice versa. This is also shown in the example Figure 1. To determine which symbols on the phoneme side are consonants and vowels, we use the unsupervised

algorithm in Hulden (2017) to divide the set of phonemes seen in the training data for a language into consonants and vowels. Table 1 shows a selection of French "words" generated by this complete process of aligning, determining useful pieces, and splicing them together while avoiding CC or VV sequences at the juncture of splicing.

For each language and each original-size data set (100, 500, 3600) we generate 50,000 additional training examples from the original training data. To create the low-resource data training sets from the shared task training sets, we randomly select 100 (**min**), or 500 (**med**) examples from the original training data consisting of 3,600 examples. To determine the cutoff where the data-augmentation strategy stops paying dividends, we also create an augmented data set of 50,000 examples from the original data (we call the original task data the **full**) data set.

2.3 Training details

Following Wu et al. (2020), we use a relatively small transformer model (the Fairseq implementation; Ott et al. (2019)) with 4 encoder-decoder layers, and 4 attention heads. The embedding size is 256 and hidden layer size 1024. We use dropout (0.3) during training and a batch size of 400, a learning rate of 0.001. We train the models until no improvement is seen on the dev-set for 5 epochs.

3 Results

The main results are shown in Table 2 and Figure 2. As can be seen, there is a consistent pattern of diminishing returns as more training data becomes available, with word error rates being significantly lower for almost all the augmented cases where 100 or 500 examples were used.

4 Related Work

Recurrent neural networks in a variety of models have been applied to the g2p problem, including LSTMs and bidirectional LSTMs (Rao et al., 2015), as well as convolutional networks (Yolchuyeva et al., 2019). The Transformer for g2p is investigated in Wu et al. (2020) and Yolchuyeva et al. (2020), showing improvements over previous models, at least in high-resource settings. Low-resource settings for g2p in general are examined in Jyothi and Hasegawa-Johnson (2017), and a number of papers have experimented with high-resource to low-resource transfer learning (Schlippe et al., 2014;

---

[2] ady: 2933 (100), 11358 (500); arm: 2789 (100), 11840 (100), bul: 2862 (100), 10657 (500), dut: 4422 (100), 19058 (500); fre: 3005 (100), 11996 (500); 3089 (100), 13698 (500); gre: 3667 (100), 16341 (500); hin: 2073 (100), 8141 (500); hun: 3282 (100), 13748 (500); 2438 (100), 9556 (500); jpn: 725 (100), 3252 (500); kor: 331 (100), 1280 (500); lit: 4328 (100), 15414 (500); rum: 3330 (100) 12360 (500); vie: 2567 (100), 12309 (500).

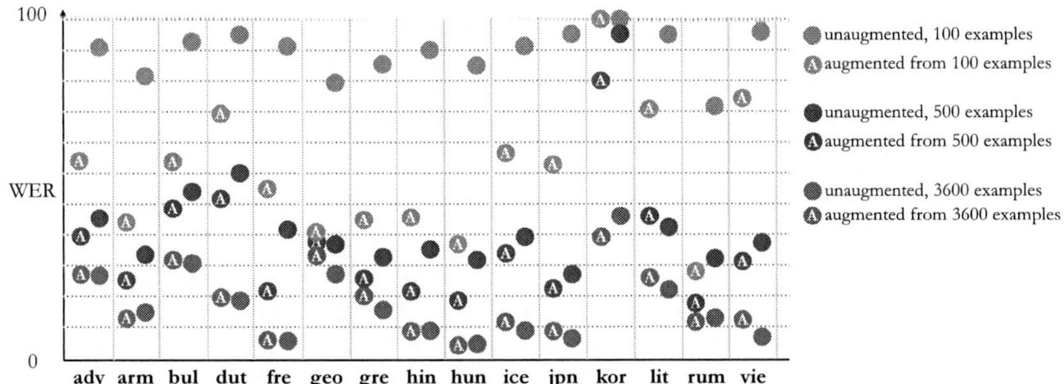

Figure 2: Main WER results on the SIGMORPHON test sets with augmented and unaugmented data.

Lang	100	100[aug]	500	500[aug]	full	full[aug]
ady	90.22	**64.67**	45.33	**39.78**	27.33	27.78
arm	82.89	**45.33**	33.11	**24.89**	14.89	**13.33**
bul	93.56	**64.89**	53.78	**48.44**	30.22	32.22
dut	95.33	**69.11**	50.67	**42.00**	18.22	19.11
fre	91.56	**56.22**	41.78	**22.00**	6.00	6.22
geo	79.78	**40.89**	37.33	38.89	27.78	33.33
gre	86.00	**44.89**	32.00	**26.67**	16.67	20.67
hin	90.44	**46.22**	34.44	**21.33**	9.56	**9.11**
hun	84.89	**37.33**	31.78	**17.11**	4.67	**4.44**
ice	91.11	**66.89**	39.33	**33.78**	9.56	10.67
jpn	95.56	**62.22**	28.22	**22.00**	6.67	8.67
kor	**100.0**	**100.0**	95.78	**79.78**	46.22	**39.78**
lit	94.89	**70.89**	**42.89**	46.44	21.78	26.22
rum	70.67	**28.67**	31.56	**17.11**	12.22	**11.33**
vie	96.44	**74.89**	37.33	**30.89**	7.11	11.78

Table 2: Word error rate (WER) results on the test set when trained with 100 examples, 500 examples, and the full data set, compared to augmentation ([aug]) for (100,500,3600) $\rightarrow$ 50,000 synthetic examples.

Deri and Knight, 2016), an avenue we did not explore in this work.

5 Conclusion

We have developed a method for data augmentation for the g2p task based on a 1-to-1 alignment of input/output strings together with a confidence calculation of what parts of the aligned strings can be used to splice together an augmented dataset. Used together with the popular Transformer seq2seq model, we see significant and consistent improvements on very small datasets of 100 examples, moderate improvements on medium-size datasets (500 examples), with the advantage tapering off and mostly disappearing completely with the shared tasks' datasets of 3,600 examples.

References

Antonios Anastasopoulos and Graham Neubig. 2019. Pushing the limits of low-resource morphological inflection. In *Proceedings of the 2019 Conference on Empirical Methods in Natural Language Processing and the 9th International Joint Conference on Natural Language Processing (EMNLP-IJCNLP)*, pages 984–996, Hong Kong, China. Association for Computational Linguistics.

Toms Bergmanis, Katharina Kann, Hinrich Schütze, and Sharon Goldwater. 2017. Training data augmentation for low-resource morphological inflection. In *Proceedings of the CoNLL SIGMORPHON 2017 Shared Task: Universal Morphological Reinflection*, pages 31–39, Vancouver. Association for Computational Linguistics.

Ryan Cotterell, Christo Kirov, John Sylak-Glassman, David Yarowsky, Jason Eisner, and Mans Hulden. 2016. The SIGMORPHON 2016 shared Task— Morphological reinflection. In *Proceedings of the 14th SIGMORPHON Workshop on Computational Research in Phonetics, Phonology, and Morphology*, pages 10–22, Berlin, Germany. Association for Computational Linguistics.

Aliya Deri and Kevin Knight. 2016. Grapheme-to-phoneme models for (almost) any language. In *Proceedings of the 54th Annual Meeting of the Association for Computational Linguistics (Volume 1: Long Papers)*, pages 399–408, Berlin, Germany. Association for Computational Linguistics.

Kyle Gorman, Lucas F. E. Ashby, Aaron Goyzueta, Arya D. McCarthy, Shijie Wu, and Daniel You. 2020. The SIGMORPHON 2020 shared task on multilingual grapheme-to-phoneme conversion. In *Proceedings of the 17th SIGMORPHON Workshop on Computational Research in Phonetics, Phonology, and Morphology*.

Mans Hulden. 2017. A phoneme clustering algorithm based on the obligatory contour principle. In *Proceedings of the 21st Conference on Computational*

Natural Language Learning (CoNLL 2017), pages 290–300, Vancouver, Canada. Association for Computational Linguistics.

Preethi Jyothi and Mark Hasegawa-Johnson. 2017. Low-resource grapheme-to-phoneme conversion using recurrent neural networks. In *2017 IEEE International Conference on Acoustics, Speech and Signal Processing (ICASSP)*, pages 5030–5034. IEEE.

Peter Makarov and Simon Clematide. 2018. Neural transition-based string transduction for limited-resource setting in morphology. In *Proceedings of the 27th International Conference on Computational Linguistics*, pages 83–93, Santa Fe, New Mexico, USA. Association for Computational Linguistics.

Peter Makarov, Tatiana Ruzsics, and Simon Clematide. 2017. Align and copy: UZH at SIGMORPHON 2017 shared task for morphological reinflection. In *Proceedings of the CoNLL SIGMORPHON 2017 Shared Task: Universal Morphological Reinflection*, pages 49–57, Vancouver. Association for Computational Linguistics.

Josef R. Novak, Paul R. Dixon, Nobuaki Minematsu, Keikichi Hirose, Chiori Hori, and Hideki Kashioka. 2012. Improving WFST-based G2P conversion with alignment constraints and RNNLM N-best rescoring. In *Thirteenth Annual Conference of the International Speech Communication Association*.

Myle Ott, Sergey Edunov, Alexei Baevski, Angela Fan, Sam Gross, Nathan Ng, David Grangier, and Michael Auli. 2019. fairseq: A fast, extensible toolkit for sequence modeling. In *Proceedings of the 2019 Conference of the North American Chapter of the Association for Computational Linguistics (Demonstrations)*, pages 48–53, Minneapolis, Minnesota. Association for Computational Linguistics.

Kanishka Rao, Fuchun Peng, Haşim Sak, and Françoise Beaufays. 2015. Grapheme-to-phoneme conversion using long short-term memory recurrent neural networks. In *2015 IEEE International Conference on Acoustics, Speech and Signal Processing (ICASSP)*, pages 4225–4229. IEEE.

Eric Sven Ristad and Peter N. Yianilos. 1998. Learning string-edit distance. *IEEE Transactions on Pattern Analysis and Machine Intelligence*, 20(5):522–532.

Tim Schlippe, Wolf Quaschningk, and Tanja Schultz. 2014. Combining grapheme-to-phoneme converter outputs for enhanced pronunciation generation in low-resource scenarios. In *Spoken Language Technologies for Under-Resourced Languages*.

Abhishek Sharma, Ganesh Katrapati, and Dipti Misra Sharma. 2018. IIT(BHU)–IIITH at CoNLL–SIGMORPHON 2018 shared task on universal morphological reinflection. In *Proceedings of the CoNLL–SIGMORPHON 2018 Shared Task: Universal Morphological Reinflection*, pages 105–111, Brussels. Association for Computational Linguistics.

Miikka Silfverberg, Adam Wiemerslage, Ling Liu, and Lingshuang Jack Mao. 2017. Data augmentation for morphological reinflection. In *Proceedings of the CoNLL SIGMORPHON 2017 Shared Task: Universal Morphological Reinflection*, pages 90–99, Vancouver. Association for Computational Linguistics.

Ashish Vaswani, Noam Shazeer, Niki Parmar, Jakob Uszkoreit, Llion Jones, Aidan N. Gomez, Łukasz Kaiser, and Illia Polosukhin. 2017. Attention is all you need. In *Advances in neural information processing systems*, pages 5998–6008.

Oriol Vinyals, Meire Fortunato, and Navdeep Jaitly. 2015. Pointer networks. In *Advances in neural information processing systems*, pages 2692–2700.

Ekaterina Vylomova, Jennifer White, Elizabeth Salesky, Sabrina J. Mielke, Shijie Wu, Edoardo Ponti, Rowan Hall Maudslay, Ran Zmigrod, Joseph Valvoda, Svetlana Toldova, Francis Tyers, Elena Klyachko, Ilya Yegorov, Natalia Krizhanovsky, Paula Czarnowska, Irene Nikkarinen, Andrej Krizhanovsky, Tiago Pimentel, Lucas Torroba Hennigen, Christo Kirov, Garrett Nicolai, Adina Williams, Antonios Anastasopoulos, Hilaria Cruz, Eleanor Chodroff, Ryan Cotterell, Miikka Silfverberg, and Mans Hulden. 2020. The SIGMORPHON 2020 Shared Task 0: Typologically diverse morphological inflection. In *Proceedings of the 17th SIGMORPHON Workshop on Computational Research in Phonetics, Phonology, and Morphology*.

Shijie Wu, Ryan Cotterell, and Mans Hulden. 2020. Applying the transformer to character-level transduction. *arXiv:2005.10213 [cs.CL]*.

Sevinj Yolchuyeva, Géza Németh, and Bálint Gyires-Tóth. 2019. Grapheme-to-phoneme conversion with convolutional neural networks. *Applied Sciences*, 9(6):1143.

Sevinj Yolchuyeva, Géza Németh, and Bálint Gyires-Tóth. 2020. Transformer based grapheme-to-phoneme conversion. *arXiv preprint arXiv:2004.06338*.

Transliteration for Cross-Lingual Morphological Inflection

Nikitha Murikinati, Antonios Anastasopoulos, and Graham Neubig
School of Computer Science
Carnegie Mellon University
nmurikin@andrew.cmu.edu {aanastas,gneubig}@cs.cmu.edu

Abstract

Cross-lingual transfer between typologically related languages has been proven successful for the task of morphological inflection. However, if the languages do not share the same script, current methods yield more modest improvements. We explore the use of transliteration between related languages, as well as grapheme-to-phoneme conversion, as data preprocessing methods in order to alleviate this issue. We experimented with several diverse language pairs, finding that in most cases transliterating the transfer language data into the target one leads to accuracy improvements, even up to 9 percentage points. Converting both languages into a shared space like the International Phonetic Alphabet or the Latin alphabet is also beneficial, leading to improvements of up to 16 percentage points.[1]

1 Introduction

The majority of the world's languages are synthetic, meaning they have rich morphology. As a result, modeling morphological inflection computationally can have a significant impact on downstream quality, not only in analysis tasks such as named entity recognition and morphological analysis (Zhu et al., 2019), but also for language generation systems for morphologically-rich languages.

In recent years, morphological inflection has been extensively studied in monolingual high resource settings, especially through the recent SIGMORPHON challenges (Cotterell et al., 2016, 2017, 2018). The latest SIGMOPRHON 2019 challenge (McCarthy et al., 2019) focused on low-resource settings and encouraged cross-lingual training, an approach that has been successfully applied in other low-resource tasks such as Machine

Transfer lang. (L$_1$)	(script)	Test lang. (L$_2$)	Acc.
Urdu	(Arabic)		42
Sanskrit	(Devanagari)	Bengali	44
Hindi	(Devanagari)	(Bengali)	49
Greek	(Greek)		42
Arabic	(Arabic)		18
Hebrew	(Hebrew)	Maltese	22
Italian	(Roman)	(Roman)	34

Table 1: The languages' script can affect the effectiveness of cross-lingual transfer (using L$_1$ data to train a L$_2$ inflection system). Bengali results display low variance, as all transfer languages differ in script. Maltese is typologically closer to Arabic and Hebrew than Italian, but accuracy is higher when transferring from a same-script language.

Translation (MT) or parsing. Cross-lingual learning is a particularly promising direction, due to its potential to utilize similarities across languages (often languages from the same linguistic family, which we will refer to as "related") in order to overcome the lack of training data. In fact, leveraging data from *several* related languages was crucial for the current state-of-the-art system over the SIGMORPHON 2019 dataset (Anastasopoulos and Neubig, 2019).

However, as Anastasopoulos and Neubig (2019) point out, cross-lingual learning even between closely related languages can be impeded if the languages do not use the same script. We present a few examples taken from Anastasopoulos and Neubig (2019) in Table 1. The first example presents cross-lingual transfer for Bengali, with the transfer languages varying from very related (Hindi, Sanskrit, Urdu) to only distantly related (Greek). Nevertheless, there is notably little variance in the performance of the systems. We believe that the culprit is the difference in writing systems between

---

[1] Our code and data are available at https://github.com/nikim99/Inflection-Transliteration.

Proceedings of the Seventeenth SIGMORPHON Workshop on Computational Research in Phonetics, Phonology, and Morphology, pages 189–197
Online, July 10, 2020. ©2020 Association for Computational Linguistics
https://doi.org/10.18653/v1/P17

all the transfer and test languages, which does not allow the system to easily leverage cross-lingual information: the Bengali data uses the Bengali script, the Urdu data uses the Nastaliq script (a derivative of the Arabic alphabet), the Hindi and Sanskrit data uses Devanagari, and the Greek data uses the Greek alphabet. In the second example, with transfer from Arabic, Hebrew, and Italian for morphological inflection in Maltese, we note that although Maltese is much closer typologically to Arabic and Hebrew (they are all Semitic languages), the test accuracy is higher when transferring from Italian, which despite only sharing a few typological elements with Maltese happens to also share the same script.

The aim of this work is to investigate this potential issue further. We first quantify the effect of script differences on the accuracy of morphological inflection systems through a series of controlled experiments (§2). Then, we attempt to remedy this problem by bringing the representations of the transfer and the test languages in the same, shared space *before* training the morphological inflection system. In one setting, we achieve this through transliteration of the transfer language into the test language's script as a preprocessing step. In another setting, we convert both languages into a shared space, using grapheme-to-phoneme (G2P) conversion into the International Phonetic Alphabet (IPA) as well as romanization. We discuss both settings and their effects on morphological inflection in low-resource settings (§3).

Our approach bears similarities to pseudo-corpus approaches that have been used in machine translation (MT), where low-resource language data are augmented with data generated from a related high-resource language. Among many, for instance, De Gispert and Marino (2006) built a Catalan-English MT by bridging through Spanish, while Xia et al. (2019) show that word-level substitutions can convert a high-resource (related) language corpus into a pseudo low-resource one leading to large improvements in MT quality. Such approaches typically operate at the word level, hence they do not need to handle script differences explicitly. NLP models that handle script differences do exist, but focus mostly on analysis tasks such as named entity recognition (Bharadwaj et al., 2016; Chaudhary et al., 2018; Rahimi et al., 2019) or entity linking (Rijhwani et al., 2019), whereas we focus in a *generation* task. Character-level transliteration was typically incorporated in phrase-based statistical

MT systems (Durrani et al., 2014), but was only used to handle named entity translation. Notably, there exist NLP approaches such as the document classification approach of Zhang et al. (2018) showing that indeed shared character-level information can facilitate cross-lingual transfer, but limit their analysis to same-script languages only. Specific to the the morphological inflection task, (Hauer et al., 2019) use cognate projection to augment low-resource data, while (Wiemerslage et al., 2018) explore the inflection task using inputs *in* phonological space as well as bundles of phonological features from PanPhon (Mortensen et al., 2016), showing improvements for both settings. Our work, in contrast, focuses on better cross-lingual transfer, attempting to combine the phonological and the orthographic space.

2   Quantifying the Issue

In Table 1 we offered a few examples from the literature to indicate that differences in script between the transfer and test language in a cross-lingual learning setting can be a potential issue. In this section, we provide additional evidence that this is indeed the case.

The intuition behind our analysis is that a model trained cross-lingually can only claim to indeed learn cross-lingually if it ends up sharing the representations of the different inputs, at least to some extent. This observation of a learned shared space has also been noted in massively multilingual models like the multilingual BERT (Pires et al., 2019), or for cross-lingual learning of word-level representations (Wang et al., 2020). For a character-level model, such as the ones typically used for neural morphological inflection, this implies a learned mapping between the characters of the two inputs. Our hypothesis is that such a learned character mapping, and in particular between related languages, should resemble a transliteration mapping, assuming that both languages use a phonographic writing system (such as the Latin or the Cyrillic alphabet and their variations), to use the notation of Faber (1992).[2]

To verify whether this intuition holds, we trained

---

[2]In contrast, one should not expect this to hold if one of the scripts is logographic, like the Chinese one, or if the two languages are coded differently, e.g. one script is syllabic and segmentally coded, like the Japanese kana, but the other is segmentally linear using a complete alphabet like the Latin script. If both scripts use the same level of coding, then the intuition holds (i.e. between Hebrew and Arabic).

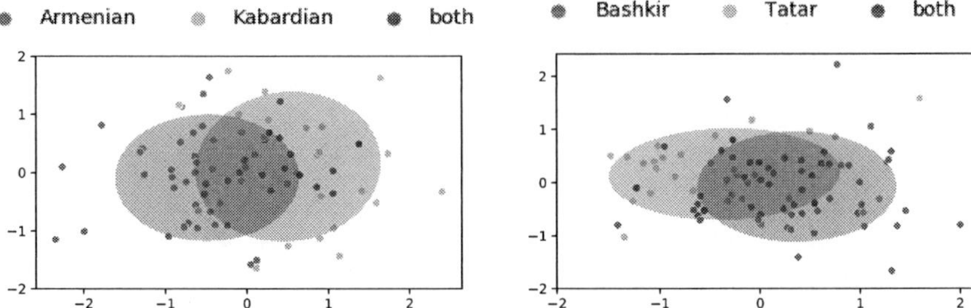

Figure 1: 2-D projection of the character embeddings learned after cross-lingual learning in two settings (Armenian–Kabardian and Bashkir–Tatar). The shaded area denotes the mean ± three standard deviations.

models on Armenian–Kabardian and Bashkir–Tatar (see details in Section §3). In the first setting, the transfer language (Armenian) uses the Armenian alphabet, while the test language (Kabardian) uses the Cyrillic one. In the second, we are transferring from Bashkir, which currently uses the Cyrillic alphabet, to Tatar, which is written with the Latin alphabet. We obtain the character representations from the final trained models, and we perform a simple search over the embedding space, returning for each of the transfer language characters the nearest neighbor from the test language alphabet. Our findings are that this type of mapping does not resemble a transliteration one, at all.

For example, one would expect that the Bashkir characters е, ә, or э would map to the Tatar e character, or at least to another vowel. Bashkir е indeed maps to Tatar e, but ә maps to Tatar i (which might be somewhat fine since they are both vowels), while Bashkir э maps to Tatar r. After a manual annotation of the mappings in both language pairs, we find that the absolute accuracy is less than 5% in both settings (2 of 54 are correct in Bashkir–Tatar, and 1 of 47 in Armenian–Kabardian). We also present a visualization (obtained through PCA (Wold et al., 1987)) of the character embeddings in Figure 1 for these two settings, which shows that the two languages are still, to an extent, separable.

In an attempt to also take into account potential slight differences in pronunciation, which are common across related languages, we also count mappings that agree in coarse phonetic categories as correct. We obtain rough grapheme-to-phoneme mappings from Omniglot[3] (Ager, 2008) which allows us to classify each character as mapping to a vowel, or a consonant category (we devise categories across both manner and place). For instance, the Bashkir characters с,ҫ,һ,з,ш map to sibilant

fricatives, so we count any mapping to Tatar characters that also map to sibilant fricatives (ç, z, s, ş) as correct. Overall, however, even this more flexible evaluation only leads to an accuracy of less than 30% (16 out of 54 characters for Bashkir–Tatar, 12 of 47 in Armenian–Kabardian).

3 Methodology

The previous section (§2) showcases that different scripts can inhibit the model's ability to represent both languages in a shared space, which can be damaging for downstream performance in cross-lingual learning scenarios. In order to bring the transfer and test languages into a shared space we explore two straightforward approaches:

1. We first transliterate the transfer language data into the script of the test language, and then use the data to train an inflection model. As our baseline or control experiment, we use the exact same data, model, and process, only removing the transliteration preprocessing step.

2. We convert both languages into a shared space, such as the International Phonetic Alphabet (IPA) or the Latin alphabet. In this case, we use both the converted and the original datasets during training. We note that this approach is perhaps the most viable one, for cases in which a transliteration tool between the transfer and the test scripts is not available.

The following sections provide details on transliteration, grapheme-to-phoneme conversion, the inflection model, and the data that we use for training and evaluation.

Transliteration In the absence of some sort of a universal transliteration approach, we rely on various libraries for our experiments. For transliterating between the Indic scripts (Devanagari, Bengali,

---

[3]https://omniglot.com/

Transfer L$_1$	Test L$_2$	Baseline L$_1$+L$_2$	with Transliteration L$_1$ Conversion	Tr(L$_1$)+L$_2$	Baseline L$_1$+L$_2$+$\mathcal{H}$	with Transliteration Tr(L$_1$)+L$_2$+$\mathcal{H}$
Hindi		33	Devanagari	**42**	47	**56**
Sanskrit	Bengali	27	$\rightarrow$	32	66	65
both		39	Bengali	41	58	63
Arabic		18	Arabic$\rightarrow$Roman	**27**	29	27
Hebrew	Maltese	22	Hebrew$\rightarrow$Roman	27	29	33
both		18		21	25	28
Kannada	Telugu	66	Kannada$\rightarrow$Telugu	66	70	62
Bashkir	Crimean Tatar	73	Cyrillic$\rightarrow$Roman	69	70	73
Bashkir	Tatar	**74**	Cyrillic$\rightarrow$Roman	59	73	74
Russian	Portuguese	34	Cyrillic$\rightarrow$Roman	**43**	61.5	**63.5**
(*) Adyghe		90	no conversion	–	96	–
(*)Armenian	Kabardian	80	Armenian$\rightarrow$Roman	78	86	86

Table 2: Transliteration of the transfer language (L$_1$) into the test language (L$_2$) improves accuracy in some cases (top), with and without hallucinated data ($\mathcal{H}$). In some language pairs (bottom) it can be harmful. We report exact match accuracy on the test set. We **highlight** statistically significant improvements ($p < 0.05$) over the baseline. "both" denotes that both L$_1$ languages are used for transfer. * marks an additional control experiment.

Kannada, and Telugu in our experiments) we rely on the IndicNLP library.[4] We also use the URo-man[5] library (Hermjakob et al., 2018) to transliterate into the Roman alphabet for the Arabic, Hebrew, Armenian, and Cyrillic scripts.

The lack of resources and transliteration tools for some directions severely limited the extent of the experiments that we could conduct. Notably, even though romanization is fairly well-studied and are easily attainable through tools like URoman, the opposite direction is fairly understudied. Most of the related work has focused on either to-English transliteration specifically (Lin et al., 2016; Durrani et al., 2014) or on *named entity* transliteration (Kundu et al., 2018; Grundkiewicz and Heafield, 2018). Even then, the state-of-the-art results on the recent NEWS named entity transliteration task (Chen et al., 2018) ranged from 10% to 80% in terms of accuracy across several scripts. The high variance in expected quality depending on the transliteration direction showcases the need for further work towards tackling hard transliteration problems.

Grapheme-to-Phoneme Conversion For G2P conversion, we used the Epitran[6] library (Mortensen et al., 2018) for transliteration into IPA. Since the library's script coverage is not extensive, it imposed another limitation on the amount of experiments we could conduct. Also, note that the library does not account for vowelization phenomena in Perso-Arabic scripts such as Arabic, Persian, and Urdu, which presents an avenue for further work.

Inflection Model We use the morphological inflection model of Anastasopoulos and Neubig (2019) which achieved the highest rank in terms of average accuracy in the SIGMORPHON 2019 shared task, using the publicly available code.[7] The neural character-level LSTM-based model uses decoupled representations of the morphological tags and the lemma learned from separate encoders. To generate the inflected form, the model first attends over tag sequence, before using the updated decoder state to attend over the character sequence of the lemma. In addition to standard cross-entropy loss, the model is trained with additional adversarial objectives and heavy regularization, in order to encourage attention monotonicity and cross-lingual learning. The authors also use a data hallucination technique similar to the one of Silfverberg et al.

---

[4]https://github.com/anoopkunchukuttan/indic_nlp_library

[5]https://github.com/isi-nlp/uroman

[6]https://github.com/dmort27/epitran

[7]https://github.com/antonisa/inflection

Grapheme-to-Phoneme Conversion					
Transfer L_1	Test L_2	Baseline L_1+L_2	with g2p +g2p(L_1) +g2p(L_2)	Baseline L_1+L_2+$\mathcal{H}$	with g2p +g2p(L_1)+ g2p(L_2) +$\mathcal{H}$
Hindi	Bengali	33	**47**	47	55
Arabic	Maltese	18	20	29	27
Russian	Portuguese	33.5	**53.9**	61.5	**66.2**
Romanization					
Transfer L_1	Test L_2	Baseline L_1+L_2	with Romanization +Rom(L_1)+Rom(L_2)	Baseline L_1+L_2+$\mathcal{H}$	with Romanization +Rom(L_1)+Rom(L_2)+$\mathcal{H}$
Hindi	Bengali	33	41	47	**59**
Kannada	Telugu	66	**84**	70	72
Portuguese	Russian	14.6	**23**	42.7	**45.9**

Table 3: G2P Conversion of both the transfer (L_1) and the test languages (L_2) into IPA improves accuracy in almost all cases, with and without hallucinated data ($\mathcal{H}$). Romanization of the both languages improves accuracy in all cases, with and without hallucinated data. We report exact match accuracy on the test set, and **highlight** statistically significant improvements ($p < 0.05$) over the baseline.

(2017), which we also use in ablation experiments.[8]

Data and Evaluation We use the data from the SIGMORPHON 2019 Shared Task on Morphological Inflection (McCarthy et al., 2019). We stick to the transfer learning cases that were studied in the shared task, but limit ourselves to the language pairs where (1) the two languages use different writing scripts, and (2) we have access to a transliteration model from the transfer to the test language. As a result, we evaluate our approach on the following language pairs: {Hindi,Sanskrit}–Bengali, Kannada–Telugu, {Arabic,Hebrew}–Maltese, Bashkir–Tatar, Bashkir–Crimean Tatar, Armenian–Kabardian, and Russian–Portuguese. We compare our systems' performance with the baselines using exact match accuracy over the test set. We also perform statistical significance testing using bootstrap resampling (Koehn, 2004).[9]

4 Experiments and Results

We perform experiments both with single-language transfer as well as transfer from multiple related languages, if available. We also perform ablations in two settings, with and without hallucinated data.

Transliterating the Transfer into the Test language We first focus on the setting where a transliteration tool between the transfer and the target language is available (in all cases, the target language data do not get converted – only the transfer language data are transliterated). Table 2 presents the exact match accuracy obtained on the test set for a total of 12 language settings. In 7 of them, we observe improvements due to our transliteration preprocessing step, some of them statistically significant.

Specifically, in the top two cases (for Bengali and Maltese as test languages) where the transfer and test languages are closely related, we see improvements across the board. In fact, for Hindi–Bengali and Arabic–Maltese the improvement is statistically significant with $p < 0.05$. Interestingly, the improvements are significant also when we use hallucinated data, which indicates that our transliteration preprocessing step is orthogonal to monolingual data augmentation through hallucination. For the case of Kannada–Telugu, despite the exact match accuracy being the same (66%) for the case without hallucinated data, we observed small improvements on the average Levenshtein distance between the produced and the gold forms.

On the other hand, when transferring from Bashkir to Tatar and Crimean Tatar, even though all three languages belong to the same branch (Kipchak) of the Turkic language family, transliterating Bashkir into the Roman alphabet that Tatar and Crimean Tatar use leads to performance degradation. In the case of Bashkir–Tatar, the degrada-

---

[8]We direct the reader to (Anastasopoulos and Neubig, 2019) for further details on the model.

[9]We use 10,000 bootstrap samples and a $\frac{1}{2}$ ratio of samples in each iteration.

Transliteration of Transfer Language (Russian to Latin)			
RUS–POR		RUS–POR $+\mathcal{H}$	
MASC	40.9	MASC	18.2
FUT	24.7	NFIN	14.8
V.PTCP	21.7	PFV	14.3
POS	19.2	COND	13.3
FEM	18.2	IPFV	8.7

Romanization of Test Language (Russian to Latin)			
POR–RUS		POR–RUS $+\mathcal{H}$	
ANIM	46.9	INAN	21.4
MASC	28.7	DAT	16.7
GEN	18.3	FUT	9.0
ADJ	16.7	PST	7.4
INS	14.6	V	6.5

Grapheme-to-Phoneme of both Languages			
RUS–POR		RUS–POR $+\mathcal{H}$	
MASC	63.6	PFV	14.3
FUT	54.8	MASC	13.6
V.PTCP	43.3	NFIN	12.5
COND	31.3	COND	10.8
POS	29.5	PST	9.4

Table 4: The top 5 tags on which performance was improved the most, compared to the simple cross-lingual transfer baseline, in our Portuguese–Russian experiments. The number reflects the proportion of forms that were improved in the Russian-Portuguese combinations using each of our techniques under each setting.

tion is statistically significant. It is of note, though, that hallucination also does not offer any improvements in these language pairs.

In a surprising result, transliterating Russian into the Roman alphabet, and using it for cross-lingual transfer to Portuguese also leads to statistically significant improvements. Both languages are Indo-European ones, but belong to different branches (Slavic and Romance). Nevertheless, both with and without hallucinated data the performance improves with transliteration, a finding that surely warrants further study.

Last, we discuss the control experiment of Armenian–Kabardian. Kabardian (and Adyghe, displayed for comparison) belong to the Circassian branch of the Northwest Caucasian languages, and are considered closely related, both using the Cyrillic alphabet; Armenian, in contrast, is an Indo-European language spoken in the same re-

gion. First, transferring from Adyghe leads to better performance compared to transfer from Armenian. Converting Armenian to the Roman script has no effect on downstream performance, as expected.

Converting both Transfer and Test Languages In the second exploratory thread, we focus on cases where the shared space is *not* the one of the test language. In the first set of experiments, we use a G2P model to transliterate both languages into IPA. The results in three language pairs are shown in Table 3 (top), where we observe statistically significant improvements in two cases (Hindi–Bengali and Russian–Portuguese). In fact, in the case of Russian–Portuguese, one can increase the performance by almost 60% (in the case without hallucinated data) from 33.5 to 53.9.

Similarly, using the Roman alphabet as the shared space is also beneficial in almost all cases. As the bottom part of Table 3 showcases, the increase can be significant. Our best Kannada–Telugu system, for example, is the one trained using additional romanized versions of both language data, improving even over the cases where hallucinated data are used (cf. accuracy of 84% to 72%).[10]

Last, we note that the trend of somewhat surprising results continues in these settings too, as we observe that transfer between Russian and Portuguese (and vice versa) is very beneficial. The improvement of 19.6 accuracy points that we observe in the G2P Russian–Portuguese experiment is in fact the largest we observe in our experiments.

Russian-Portuguese Investigation We further analyze the results of the Russian–Portuguese and Portuguese–Russian experiments, in the hopes of understanding where the improvements come from, when using cross-lingual transfer. For each of the experiments (transliteration into the test languages, G2P conversion, and romanization), we compute the percentage of times that an inflection with each morphological tag failed. Table 4 reports the tags with the highest difference in these ratios, between the baseline and our models for each method. The higher the number, the larger the improvements for this particular tag. For inflecting Portuguese (top and bottom sets of results), we find it hard to make any conclusions: both noun, adjective, and verb tags appear in the top lists. For inflecting Russian

---

[10]In fact, our submission to the SIGMORPHON 2020 Shared Task (Murikinati and Anastasopoulos, 2020) following this approach tied for first for Telugu (Vylomova et al., 2020).

(middle set), it is mostly noun/adjective tags pertaining to animacy (ANIM, INAN), gender (MASC) and case (GEN, DAT) that show the largest improvements. We still cannot explain the improvements we see in these language pairs, except for vague hypotheses that either the languages do share some similar inflection processes (besides, they are both Indo-European) or that the harder multi-task training setting regularizes the model leading to better accuracy overall.

5 Conclusion

With this work we study whether using transliteration as a preprocessing step can improve the accuracy of morphological inflection models under cross-lingual learning regimes. With a few exceptions, most cases indeed show accuracy improvements, some of them statistically significant. We also note that the improvements are orthogonal to those obtained by data augmentation through hallucination, even in typologically distant languages.

While this work represents a first step in the direction of understanding the effect of script differences in morphological inflection, it is still limited in scope, as the experiments were restricted by the lack of reliable transliteration tools for most scripts. The SIGMORPHON 2020 Shared Task on Morphological Inflection also provides more languages and better systems are being developed, so we plan to expand our analysis to the latest state-of-the-art models (Vylomova et al., 2020). Additionally, some of the transliteration models do not account for phenomena that could have an impact in downstream performance, such as vowelization for Abjad scripts like Arabic. As we aim to expand the scale of this study, a future direction will involve training transliteration models between most scripts of the world. This will allow more extensive experimentation, both by incorporating more language pairs and by allowing more control experiments across various scripts. We will also further explore the usage of more advanced G2P systems, such as those developed for the SIGMORPHON 2020 Shared Task on Grapheme-to-Phoneme conversion, or the models of Nicolai et al. (2018).

Acknowledgments

The authors extend their gratitude to the anonymous reviewers for their constructive remarks and suggestions. This work is supported by the National Science Foundation under grant 1761548.

References

Simon Ager. 2008. Omniglot writing systems and languages of the world. Retrieved March 30, 2020.

Antonios Anastasopoulos and Graham Neubig. 2019. Pushing the limits of low-resource morphological inflection. In *Proc. EMNLP*, Hong Kong.

Akash Bharadwaj, David R Mortensen, Chris Dyer, and Jaime G Carbonell. 2016. Phonologically aware neural model for named entity recognition in low resource transfer settings. In *Proceedings of the 2016 Conference on Empirical Methods in Natural Language Processing*, pages 1462–1472.

Aditi Chaudhary, Chunting Zhou, Lori Levin, Graham Neubig, David R. Mortensen, and Jaime Carbonell. 2018. Adapting word embeddings to new languages with morphological and phonological subword representations. In *Proceedings of the 2018 Conference on Empirical Methods in Natural Language Processing*, pages 3285–3295, Brussels, Belgium. Association for Computational Linguistics.

Nancy Chen, Rafael E. Banchs, Min Zhang, Xiangyu Duan, and Haizhou Li. 2018. Report of NEWS 2018 named entity transliteration shared task. In *Proceedings of the Seventh Named Entities Workshop*, pages 55–73, Melbourne, Australia. Association for Computational Linguistics.

Ryan Cotterell, Christo Kirov, John Sylak-Glassman, Géraldine Walther, Ekaterina Vylomova, Arya D. McCarthy, Katharina Kann, Sebastian Mielke, Garrett Nicolai, Miikka Silfverberg, David Yarowsky, Jason Eisner, and Mans Hulden. 2018. The CoNLL–SIGMORPHON 2018 shared task: Universal morphological reinflection. In *Proc. CoNLL–SIGMORPHON*.

Ryan Cotterell, Christo Kirov, John Sylak-Glassman, Géraldine Walther, Ekaterina Vylomova, Patrick Xia, Manaal Faruqui, Sandra Kübler, David Yarowsky, Jason Eisner, and Mans Hulden. 2017. CoNLL-SIGMORPHON 2017 shared task: Universal morphological reinflection in 52 languages. In *Proc. CoNLL SIGMORPHON*.

Ryan Cotterell, Christo Kirov, John Sylak-Glassman, David Yarowsky, Jason Eisner, and Mans Hulden. 2016. The SIGMORPHON 2016 shared task— morphological reinflection. In *Proc. SIGMORPHON*.

Adrià De Gispert and Jose B Marino. 2006. Catalan-english statistical machine translation without parallel corpus: bridging through spanish. In *Proc. of 5th International Conference on Language Resources and Evaluation (LREC)*, pages 65–68. Citeseer.

Nadir Durrani, Hassan Sajjad, Hieu Hoang, and Philipp Koehn. 2014. Integrating an unsupervised transliteration model into statistical machine translation. In *Proceedings of the 14th Conference of the European Chapter of the Association for Computational*

Linguistics, volume 2: Short Papers, pages 148–153, Gothenburg, Sweden. Association for Computational Linguistics.

Alice Faber. 1992. Phonemic segmentation as epiphenomenon. *The linguistics of literacy*, 21:111–134.

Roman Grundkiewicz and Kenneth Heafield. 2018. Neural machine translation techniques for named entity transliteration. In *Proceedings of the Seventh Named Entities Workshop*, pages 89–94, Melbourne, Australia. Association for Computational Linguistics.

Bradley Hauer, Amir Ahmad Habibi, Yixing Luan, Rashed Rubby Riyadh, and Grzegorz Kondrak. 2019. Cognate projection for low-resource inflection generation. In *Proceedings of the 16th Workshop on Computational Research in Phonetics, Phonology, and Morphology*, pages 6–11, Florence, Italy. Association for Computational Linguistics.

Ulf Hermjakob, Jonathan May, and Kevin Knight. 2018. Out-of-the-box universal Romanization tool uroman. In *Proceedings of ACL 2018, System Demonstrations*, pages 13–18, Melbourne, Australia. Association for Computational Linguistics.

Philipp Koehn. 2004. Statistical significance tests for machine translation evaluation. In *Proceedings of the 2004 Conference on Empirical Methods in Natural Language Processing*, pages 388–395, Barcelona, Spain. Association for Computational Linguistics.

Soumyadeep Kundu, Sayantan Paul, and Santanu Pal. 2018. A deep learning based approach to transliteration. In *Proceedings of the Seventh Named Entities Workshop*, pages 79–83, Melbourne, Australia. Association for Computational Linguistics.

Ying Lin, Xiaoman Pan, Aliya Deri, Heng Ji, and Kevin Knight. 2016. Leveraging entity linking and related language projection to improve name transliteration. In *Proceedings of the Sixth Named Entity Workshop*, pages 1–10, Berlin, Germany. Association for Computational Linguistics.

Arya D. McCarthy, Ekaterina Vylomova, Shijie Wu, Chaitanya Malaviya, Lawrence Wolf-Sonkin, Garrett Nicolai, Miikka Silfverberg, Sebastian J. Mielke, Jeffrey Heinz, Ryan Cotterell, and Mans Hulden. 2019. The SIGMORPHON 2019 shared task: Morphological analysis in context and cross-lingual transfer for inflection. In *Proceedings of the 16th Workshop on Computational Research in Phonetics, Phonology, and Morphology*, pages 229–244, Florence, Italy.

David R. Mortensen, Siddharth Dalmia, and Patrick Littell. 2018. Epitran: Precision G2P for many languages. In *Proceedings of the Eleventh International Conference on Language Resources and Evaluation (LREC 2018)*, Paris, France. European Language Resources Association (ELRA).

David R Mortensen, Patrick Littell, Akash Bharadwaj, Kartik Goyal, Chris Dyer, and Lori Levin. 2016. Panphon: A resource for mapping ipa segments to articulatory feature vectors. In *Proceedings of COLING 2016, the 26th International Conference on Computational Linguistics: Technical Papers*, pages 3475–3484.

Nikitha Murikinati and Antonios Anastasopoulos. 2020. The cmu-lti submission to the sigmorphon 2020 shared task 0: Language-specific cross-lingual transfer. In *Proceedings of the 17th Workshop on Computational Research in Phonetics, Phonology, and Morphology*.

Garrett Nicolai, Saeed Najafi, and Grzegorz Kondrak. 2018. String transduction with target language models and insertion handling. In *Proceedings of the Fifteenth Workshop on Computational Research in Phonetics, Phonology, and Morphology*, pages 43–53.

Telmo Pires, Eva Schlinger, and Dan Garrette. 2019. How multilingual is multilingual BERT? In *Proceedings of the 57th Annual Meeting of the Association for Computational Linguistics*, pages 4996–5001, Florence, Italy. Association for Computational Linguistics.

Afshin Rahimi, Yuan Li, and Trevor Cohn. 2019. Massively multilingual transfer for NER. In *Proceedings of the 57th Annual Meeting of the Association for Computational Linguistics*, pages 151–164, Florence, Italy. Association for Computational Linguistics.

Shruti Rijhwani, Jiateng Xie, Graham Neubig, and Jaime Carbonell. 2019. Zero-shot neural transfer for cross-lingual entity linking. In *Proceedings of the AAAI Conference on Artificial Intelligence*, volume 33, pages 6924–6931.

Miikka Silfverberg, Adam Wiemerslage, Ling Liu, and Lingshuang Jack Mao. 2017. Data augmentation for morphological reinflection. *Proc. SIGMORPHON*.

Ekaterina Vylomova, Jennifer White, Elizabeth Salesky, Sabrina J. Mielke, Shijie Wu, Edoardo Ponti, Rowan Hall Maudslay, Ran Zmigrod, Joseph Valvoda, Svetlana Toldova, Francis Tyers, Elena Klyachko, Ilya Yegorov, Natalia Krizhanovsky, Paula Czarnowska, Irene Nikkarinen, Andrej Krizhanovsky, Tiago Pimentel, Lucas Torroba Hennigen, Christo Kirov, Garrett Nicolai, Adina Williams, Antonios Anastasopoulos, Hilaria Cruz, Eleanor Chodroff, Ryan Cotterell, Miikka Silfverberg, and Mans Hulden. 2020. The SIGMORPHON 2020 Shared Task 0: Typologically diverse morphological inflection. In *Proceedings of the 17th Workshop on Computational Research in Phonetics, Phonology, and Morphology*.

Zirui Wang, Jiateng Xie, Ruochen Xu, Yiming Yang, Graham Neubig, and Jaime G. Carbonell. 2020. Cross-lingual alignment vs joint training: A comparative study and a simple unified framework. In

International Conference on Learning Representations (ICLR), Addis Ababa, Ethiopia.

Adam Wiemerslage, Miikka Silfverberg, and Mans Hulden. 2018. Phonological features for morphological inflection. In *Proceedings of the Fifteenth Workshop on Computational Research in Phonetics, Phonology, and Morphology*, pages 161–166.

Svante Wold, Kim Esbensen, and Paul Geladi. 1987. Principal component analysis. *Chemometrics and intelligent laboratory systems*, 2(1-3):37–52.

Mengzhou Xia, Xiang Kong, Antonios Anastasopoulos, and Graham Neubig. 2019. Generalized data augmentation for low-resource translation. In *Proceedings of the 57th Annual Meeting of the Association for Computational Linguistics*, pages 5786–5796, Florence, Italy. Association for Computational Linguistics.

Mozhi Zhang, Yoshinari Fujinuma, and Jordan Boyd-Graber. 2018. Exploiting cross-lingual subword similarities in low-resource document classification. *arXiv preprint arXiv:1812.09617*.

Yi Zhu, Benjamin Heinzerling, Ivan Vulić, Michael Strube, Roi Reichart, and Anna Korhonen. 2019. On the importance of subword information for morphological tasks in truly low-resource languages. In *Proceedings of the 23rd Conference on Computational Natural Language Learning (CoNLL)*, pages 216–226, Hong Kong, China. Association for Computational Linguistics.

Evaluating Neural Morphological Taggers for Sanskrit

Ashim Gupta[1], Amrith Krishna[2], Pawan Goyal[3], Oliver Hellwig[4]
[1]School of Computing, University of Utah
[2]ITU Copenhangen, [3]Dept. of Computer Science and Engineering, IIT Kharagpur
[4]University of Zürich, IVS
`ashim@cs.utah.edu, amrk@itu.dk,`
`pawang@cse.iitkgp.ac.in, oliver.hellwig@uzh.ch`

Abstract

Neural sequence labelling approaches have achieved state of the art results in morphological tagging. We evaluate the efficacy of four standard sequence labelling models on Sanskrit, a morphologically rich, fusional Indian language. As its label space can theoretically contain more than 40,000 labels, systems that explicitly model the internal structure of a label are more suited for the task, because of their ability to generalise to labels not seen during training. We find that although some neural models perform better than others, one of the common causes for error for all of these models is mispredictions due to syncretism.[1]

1 Introduction

Sanskrit is a fusional Indo-European language with rich morphology, both at the inflectional and derivational level. The language relies heavily on morphological markers to determine the syntactic, and to some extent the semantic roles, of words in a sentence. There exist limited and partly incompatible solutions (Hellwig, 2016; Goyal and Huet, 2016; Krishna et al., 2018) for morphological tagging of Sanskrit that heavily rely on lexicon driven shallow parsers and other linguistic knowledge. However recently, neural sequential labelling models have achieved competitive results in morphological tagging for multiple languages (Cotterell and Heigold, 2017; Tkachenko and Sirts, 2018; Malaviya et al., 2018). We therefore explore the efficacy of such models in performing morphological tagging for Sanskrit without access to extensive linguistic information.

Most recent research treats morphological tagging as a structured prediction problem where the morphological class of a word is either treated as a monolithic label or as a composite label with multiple features (Müller et al., 2013; Cotterell and Heigold, 2017). Schmid and Laws (2008); Hakkani-Tür et al. (2002) model the morphological tags as a sequence of individual morphological features. Recently, Tkachenko and Sirts (2018) proposed to generate this sequence of morphological features using a neural encoder-decoder architecture. Hellwig (2016) shows a significant improvement in performance for morphological tagging in Sanskrit by using a monolithic tagset with recurrent neural network based tagging model. In systems using monolithic labels, multiple feature values pertaining to a word are combined to form a single label (Müller et al., 2013; Heigold et al., 2017), which leads to data sparsity for morphologically rich languages such as Czech, Turkish and Sanskrit. The sparsity issue can be addressed by using composite labels which model the internal structure of a class as a set of individual features (Tkachenko and Sirts, 2018; Zalmout and Habash, 2017). Malaviya et al. (2018) use a neural factorial CRF to model inter-dependence between individual categories of the composite morphological label.

However, as the decision for monolithic vs. composite labels is one of the central design choices when tagging morphologically rich languages, we use Sanskrit as a test case for a systematic evaluation for this choice. For this evaluation, we consider several neural architectures with different modelling principles. For the monolithic tag model, the neural architecture is based on a bidirectional LSTM with a linear CRF layer stacked on top of it (Lample et al., 2016; Huang et al., 2015). For composite labels, we explored a neural generation model that generates a sequence of morphological features for each word in the input sequence. In order to explicitly capture the inter-dependencies between the morphological features, we use a model based on a factorial Conditional

---

[1]Code and data available at `https://github.com/ashim95/sanskrit-morphological-taggers`

Proceedings of the Seventeenth SIGMORPHON Workshop on Computational Research in Phonetics, Phonology, and Morphology, pages 198–203
Online, July 10, 2020. ©2020 Association for Computational Linguistics
https://doi.org/10.18653/v1/P17

Feature	Values	Noun	Fin. verb	Participle	Compound	Others
Tense	18		✓	✓		
Case	8	✓		✓		
Number	3	✓	✓	✓		
Gender	3	✓		✓		
Person	3		✓			
Last char.	31	✓		✓	✓	
Other	5					✓
Total	71	2232	162	40176	31	5

Table 1: Grammatical features and their distribution over inflectional classes. 'Others' include forms such as infinitives, absolutives, Indeclinables, etc.

Random Field (CRF) (Malaviya et al., 2018). Additionally, independent classifiers trained under a multi-task setting with sharing of parameters are also explored (Inoue et al., 2017; Søgaard and Goldberg, 2016). Our experiments specifically focus on the following problems and questions:

- **Syncretism:** We will show that syncretism, i.e., inflected forms of a lemma that share the same surface form for multiple morphological tags, is the major source of mispredictions. We evaluate if and how models with monolithic and composite labels deal with this phenomenon.

- **Performance on unseen tags:** For models with composite labels, it should be possible to predict morphological classes which were not seen in the training data. Our experiments show that the performance of the systems remains more or less the same irrespective of the neural architecture.

This raises an important point: Models that perform marginally better in terms of evaluation metrics are supposedly not superior, since we see similar performances on special test sets targeting particular statistical phenomenon (unseen tags) and linguistic phenomenon (syncretism).

2 Problem Formulation and Models

Tagset: Sanskrit, similar to Hungarian (Zsibrita et al., 2013) and Turkish (Çetinoğlu and Kuhn, 2013), relies on suffixes for marking inflectional information. As Sanskrit has a rich inflectional system, the size of the tagset plays a relevant role. Hellwig (2016) uses a tagset with 86 possible labels that merges some grammatical features based

on linguistic considerations. Krishna et al. (2018) use an extended tagset of 270 features, by adding the feature tense, but only to finite verbs. As the systems tested in this paper do not use external linguistic information that could restrict the range of applicable features, we choose a tagset consisting of the features shown in Table 1, which is in principle motivated by the traditional grammatical analysis of Sanskrit (Apte, 1885).[2] As the declensional type of a noun in Sanskrit is determined by the last character in the non-inflected stem of the word, we add the last character of the stem as a morphological feature in our predictions.

Notation: Given a sequence of tokens $\mathbf{x} = x_1, x_2..., x_T$, we aim at predicting a sequence of labels $\mathbf{y} = y_1, y_2, ...y_T$, one for each token. Each label y_i is a composite label $y_i = \{y_{i0}, y_{i1}, ...y_{it}\}$ and consists of a collection of grammatical features for x_i.

Encoder: All neural sequence labelling models tested in this paper (see below) use an encoder that generates the input representations of words as follows. Given a sequence of tokens as input, for each token $x_i \in \mathbf{x}$, its vector representation is obtained by concatenating its word embedding with a sub-word character embedding obtained from a bi-directional LSTM similar to Lample et al. (2016). These word representations are passed through a word level Bi-LSTM to obtain hidden state h_i for each token in the sequence.

Monolithic Sequence Model (MonSeq): This is a standard neural sequence labelling model with a neural-CRF tagger (Lample et al., 2016; Huang et al., 2015). A linear chain CRF is used as the output layer for the monolithic labels used.

Neural Factorial CRF (FCRF): The model proposed by Malaviya et al. (2018) is an end to end neural sequence labeling model with a factorial CRF (Sutton et al., 2007). The model is shown in Figure 1a. In order to model the inter-dependence between different morphological types, a pairwise potential between cotemporal variables and a transitional potential between variables of the same type of tags is used. As exact inference is computationally expensive, loopy belief propagation is

---

[2]Exhaustive list of inflectional tags used by three prevalent tagging schemes in Sanskrit computational linguistics: `https://sanskritlibrary.org/helpmorphids.html`

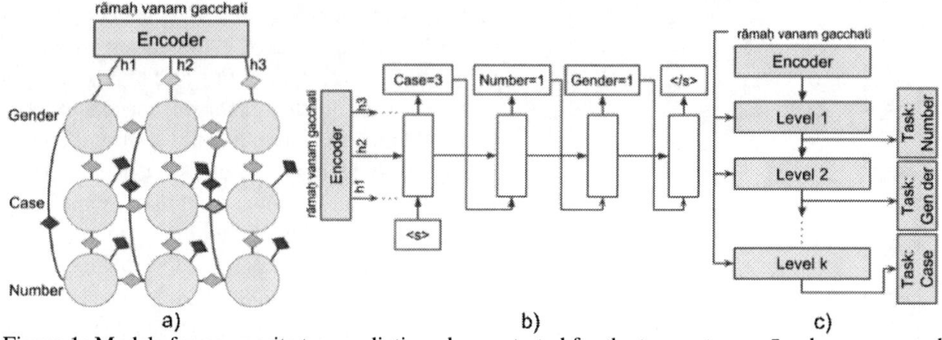

Figure 1: Models for composite tag prediction, demonstrated for the toy sentence *rāmaḥ vanaṃ gacchati* (English: 'Rāma goes to the forest'). a) FCRF b) Seq c) MTL-Hierarchy. For illustrative purposes, we consider a tagset consisting of only three categories.

used to compute approximate factor and variable marginals.

Sequence Generation Model (Seq): We use a sequence generation model (Tkachenko and Sirts, 2018) that predicts composite labels as sequences of feature values for every token in the sequence. For token x_i, the LSTM hidden state h_i is fed to an LSTM based decoder, which generates a sequence of feature values conditioned on the context vector h_i and the previous feature value. As shown in Figure 1b, the decoding is initiated with a special marker passed as input and terminates when the decoder predicts an end marker.

Multi task learning (MTL): Here, we consider each grammatical feature as shown in Table 1 as a separate task. We experiment with two settings for multi-task learning. In **MTL-Shared** the encoder parameters are shared across all the tasks, and supervision for all the tasks is performed at the same layer with each task having its own independent output CRF layer. In **MTL-Hierarchy**, as proposed by Søgaard and Goldberg (2016), we establish a hierarchy between the grammatical categories. A hierarchical inductive bias is introduced by supervising low-level tasks at the bottom layers and higher-level tasks at the higher layers (Sanh et al., 2019). Concretely, for a task k, only the parameters at the output CRF layer and those at the shallower layers are updated. The model is shown in Figure 1c. In order for the higher layers to have access to the inputs, we use shortcut connections as proposed in Hashimoto et al. (2017).

3 Experiments

Data: We use a training set of 50,000 and a test set of 11,000 sentences from the Digital Corpus of Sanskrit (DCS, Hellwig (2010–2020)). To prepare the training set, we sample sentences such that there exist at least 100 instances for each of the 71 features in Table 1. The training data still covers only 2,757 out of possible 42,606 labels, indicating that the true dimension of the target space is much lower than could be expected from Table 1. The test data we use contain only about 0.5 % of the tokens with labels not present in the training set. Additionally we use a separate **unseen** test set, where every sentence contains at least one word with a monolithic label not present in the training data.

3.1 Evaluation

We report the performance using average token-level accuracy and F1-scores (see Malaviya et al., 2018; Cotterell and Heigold, 2017; Buys and Botha, 2016). The average token-level accuracy is reported on the exact match of a morphological tag for a token, i.e., if it predicts all the morphological features correctly. The F1 measure is computed on a tag-by-tag basis, i.e. macro and micro averaged at the grammatical category level, which provides partial credit to partially correct tag sets.

3.2 Results

Table 2 shows the results for the five models studied in this paper. We find that three of the four models using composite labels obtain overall comparable results, with hierarchical Multi-task model obtaining the highest Macro and Micro F1-Scores, token accuracy as well as outperforming other models for category specific evaluation for 4 out of 5 categories. This highlights that there is some gains to be had by inducing a hierarchical bias among these morphological categories. As can be observed from

System	Token Accuracy	Macro F1* Score	Micro F1 Score	T	C	N	G	L
MonSeq	75.15	85.16	85.14	79.64	86.39	91.05	80.37	83.86
MTL-Shared	81.72	90.82	90.84	85.98	88.31	95.61	90.84	90.00
MTL-Hierarchy	**86.74**	**94.11**	**94.11**	**93.77**	**92.17**	**97.21**	**93.30**	94.01
FCRF	85.37	93.01	93.01	92.35	89.08	96.38	92.44	**94.03**
Seq	85.95	92.72	92.72	91.10	89.66	96.52	92.01	93.12

Table 2: Performance of different systems for the morphological tagging task. All the reported values for Macro-F1 are statistically significant ($p < 0.05$), based on pairwise t-tests between the systems. The features (refer Table 1) are marked using their first letter.

	Syncretism Macro F1	Unseen Macro F1
System		
Seq	70.44	55.98
MTL-Shared	70.26	55.02
MTL-Hierarchy	70.62	55.21
FCRF	68.80	55.62
MonSeq	52.55	–

Table 3: Macro-F1 score for the tokens which exhibit syncretism (top 25 pairs, based on reported mispredictions) and the unseen labels during training.

Hierarchy	Number	Tense
N-G-C-T-L	97.21	**93.77**
T-C-N-G-L	96.49	90.12
N-G-L-T-C	**97.24**	92.85

Table 4: Results for Number and Tense based on different configurations in MTL-Hierarchy. The shallow to deep levels are marked by first character of the features.

the results, all the composite models clearly outperform MonSeq in terms of Macro- and Micro F1-Score, indicating their better performance for rare morphological classes. Among the composite models, MTL-Shared clearly underperforms, which is probably due to the fact that most of its parameters are shared by all the tasks and no task specific adaptation was possible. We also perform pairwise t-tests and find that the gains reported are statistically significant ($p < 0.05$).

One of our key findings is that syncretism is a major source of error for all these systems. For the composite models, about 20 % to 25 % of all the mispredictions in nouns arise due to syncretism. As expected it is worse for MonSeq, where close to 37 % mispredictions are due to this linguistic phenomenon. For a more detailed analysis, we check the top 25 label-pairs of mis-predictions for each system. In Table 3, we report macro F1-Scores for the tokens which exhibit syncretism from this filtered set. The reported results are far below the overall F1-Macro scores, as shown in Table 2.

Composite-label models are also able to make partially correct predictions for more unusual forms. The 3rd person plural perfect form, *sasarjire* (English: 'they have created'), for example, is analysed as 3rd sg. perfect by Seq. This decision should be influenced by the last letter -e, which can indicate the 3rd singular of the perfect, while the correct, and relatively rare, affix is -ire. MonSeq predicts a locative singular of a non-existing noun *sasarjira* in this case. Again, this decision is probably based on the last letter -e, which in most cases derives the locative singular.

Table 3 (right half) shows how the models perform for tags unseen during training (on **unseen** test set). We consider 11 of such case, number and gender combinations, 14 tense, person and number combinations and two of the tenses additionally for the participles. Among four different composite models, the macro F1-Score for 'Seq' model is similar to what is observed in Tkachenko and Sirts (2018) for a fusional language like Czech. Moreover, the behaviour for all the composite models remains more or less same for unseen labels.

Next, we explore if there is a natural hierarchy for supervision of morphological categories in MTL-hierarchy model. For this, we train the system in different permutations of feature hierarchies as shown in Table 4. We observe that the feature *number* benefits from supervision at a shallower level, whereas *tense* always benefits from supervision at a deeper level. The trends for other features were not as conclusive, but these results show there might be an inherent hierarchy among some of the morphological features.

Krishna (2019), an extended version of the energy based model proposed in Krishna et al. (2018), report the state of the art results for morphological parsing in Sanskrit. They report a token level accuracy, macro averaged over sentences, of 95.33 % on a test set of 9,576 sentences. The FCRF and SeqGen models, when tested on their test dataset, achieve an average sentence level token accuracy of 80.26 % and 81.79 % respectively. Here, it needs to be noted that the morphological tagger used in Krishna (2019) relies on a lexicon driven shallow parser to obtain a smaller search space of candidates. However, this makes the model a closed vocabulary model as it would fail for cases where the words are not recognised by the lexicon-driven parser, as there will be no analyses for such words. On the contrary, none of the models presented in this work are constrained by the vocabulary of any lexicon.

4 Conclusion and Future Work

In this work, we evaluated various neural models for morphological tagging of Sanskrit, concentrating on models that are capable of using composite labels. We find that all the composite label models outperform MonSeq by significant margins. These models, with an exception to MTL-Shared, achieve overall competitive results when enough training data is available. A major problem for all the sequence labelling models studied in this paper is syncretism of morphological categories, which should constitute the main focus of future research.

References

Vaman Shivaram Apte. 1885. *The student's guide to Sanskrit composition: a treatise on Sanskrit syntax for the use of schools and colleges*. Chowkhamba Sanskrit Series Office.

Jan Buys and Jan A. Botha. 2016. Cross-lingual morphological tagging for low-resource languages. In *Proceedings of the 54th Annual Meeting of the Association for Computational Linguistics (Volume 1: Long Papers)*, pages 1954–1964. Association for Computational Linguistics.

Özlem Çetinoğlu and Jonas Kuhn. 2013. Towards joint morphological analysis and dependency parsing of Turkish. In *Proceedings of the Second International Conference on Dependency Linguistics (DepLing 2013)*, pages 23–32. Charles University in Prague, Matfyzpress, Prague, Czech Republic.

Ryan Cotterell and Georg Heigold. 2017. Cross-lingual character-level neural morphological tagging. In *Proceedings of the 2017 Conference on Empirical Methods in Natural Language Processing*, pages 748–759. Association for Computational Linguistics.

Pawan Goyal and Gérard Huet. 2016. Design and analysis of a lean interface for sanskrit corpus annotation. *Journal of Language Modelling*, 4(2):145–182.

Dilek Z Hakkani-Tür, Kemal Oflazer, and Gökhan Tür. 2002. Statistical morphological disambiguation for agglutinative languages. *Computers and the Humanities*, 36(4):381–410.

Kazuma Hashimoto, caiming xiong, Yoshimasa Tsuruoka, and Richard Socher. 2017. A joint many-task model: Growing a neural network for multiple NLP tasks. In *Proceedings of the 2017 Conference on Empirical Methods in Natural Language Processing*, pages 1923–1933. Association for Computational Linguistics.

Georg Heigold, Guenter Neumann, and Josef van Genabith. 2017. An extensive empirical evaluation of character-based morphological tagging for 14 languages. In *Proceedings of the 15th Conference of the European Chapter of the Association for Computational Linguistics: Volume 1, Long Papers*, volume 1, pages 505–513.

Oliver Hellwig. 2010–2020. DCS - The Digital Corpus of Sanskrit.

Oliver Hellwig. 2016. Improving the morphological analysis of classical Sanskrit. In *Proceedings of the 6th Workshop on South and Southeast Asian Natural Language Processing (WSSANLP2016)*, pages 142–151.

Zhiheng Huang, Wei Xu, and Kai Yu. 2015. Bidirectional LSTM-CRF models for sequence tagging. *arXiv preprint arXiv:1508.01991*.

Go Inoue, Hiroyuki Shindo, and Yuji Matsumoto. 2017. Joint prediction of morphosyntactic categories for fine-grained arabic part-of-speech tagging exploiting tag dictionary information. In *Proceedings of the 21st Conference on Computational Natural Language Learning (CoNLL 2017)*, pages 421–431.

Amrith Krishna. 2019. *Addressing Language Specific Characteristics for Data-Driven Modelling of Lexical, Syntactic and Prosodic Tasks in Sanskrit*. Ph.D. thesis, IIT Kharagpur, Kharagpur, West Bengal, India.

Amrith Krishna, Bishal Santra, Sasi Prasanth Bandaru, Gaurav Sahu, Vishnu Dutt Sharma, Pavankumar Satuluri, and Pawan Goyal. 2018. Free as in free word order: An energy based model for word segmentation and morphological tagging in Sanskrit. In *Proceedings of the 2018 Conference on Empirical Methods in Natural Language Processing*, pages 2550–2561. Association for Computational Linguistics.

Guillaume Lample, Miguel Ballesteros, Sandeep Subramanian, Kazuya Kawakami, and Chris Dyer. 2016. Neural architectures for named entity recognition. In *Proceedings of NAACL-HLT*, pages 260–270.

Chaitanya Malaviya, Matthew R. Gormley, and Graham Neubig. 2018. Neural factor graph models for cross-lingual morphological tagging. In *Proceedings of the 56th Annual Meeting of the Association for Computational Linguistics (Volume 1: Long Papers)*, pages 2653–2663. Association for Computational Linguistics.

Thomas Müller, Helmut Schmid, and Hinrich Schütze. 2013. Efficient higher-order CRFs for morphological tagging. In *Proceedings of the 2013 Conference on Empirical Methods in Natural Language Processing*, pages 322–332.

Victor Sanh, Thomas Wolf, and Sebastian Ruder. 2019. A hierarchical multi-task approach for learning embeddings from semantic tasks.

Helmut Schmid and Florian Laws. 2008. Estimation of conditional probabilities with decision trees and an application to fine-grained pos tagging. In *Proceedings of the 22Nd International Conference on Computational Linguistics - Volume 1*, COLING '08, pages 777–784, Stroudsburg, PA, USA. Association for Computational Linguistics.

Anders Søgaard and Yoav Goldberg. 2016. Deep multi-task learning with low level tasks supervised at lower layers. In *Proceedings of the 54th Annual Meeting of the Association for Computational Linguistics (Volume 2: Short Papers)*, pages 231–235. Association for Computational Linguistics.

Charles Sutton, Andrew McCallum, and Khashayar Rohanimanesh. 2007. Dynamic conditional random fields: Factorized probabilistic models for labeling and segmenting sequence data. *Journal of Machine Learning Research*, 8(Mar):693–723.

Alexander Tkachenko and Kairit Sirts. 2018. Modeling composite labels for neural morphological tagging. In *Proceedings of the 22nd Conference on Computational Natural Language Learning*, pages 368–379. Association for Computational Linguistics.

Nasser Zalmout and Nizar Habash. 2017. Don't throw those morphological analyzers away just yet: Neural morphological disambiguation for Arabic. In *Proceedings of the 2017 Conference on Empirical Methods in Natural Language Processing*, pages 704–713. Association for Computational Linguistics.

János Zsibrita, Veronika Vincze, and Richárd Farkas. 2013. magyarlanc: A tool for morphological and dependency parsing of hungarian. In *Proceedings of the International Conference Recent Advances in Natural Language Processing RANLP 2013*, pages 763–771. INCOMA Ltd. Shoumen, BULGARIA.

Stav Klein
Bar-Ilan University
klein.stav@gmail.com

Reut Tsarfaty
Bar-Ilan University
reut.tsarfaty@gmail.com

Abstract

This work investigates the most basic units that underlie contextualized word embeddings, such as BERT — the so-called *word pieces*. In Morphologically-Rich Languages (MRLs) which exhibit morphological *fusion* and *non-concatenative* morphology, the different units of meaning within a word may be fused, intertwined, and cannot be separated linearly. Therefore, when using word-pieces in MRLs, we must consider that: (1) a linear segmentation into sub-word units might not capture the full morphological complexity of words; and (2) representations that leave morphological knowledge on sub-word units inaccessible might negatively affect performance. Here we empirically examine the capacity of word-pieces to capture morphology by investigating the task of *multi-tagging* in Hebrew, as a proxy to evaluating the underlying segmentation. Our results show that, while models trained to predict multi-tags for complete words outperform models tuned to predict the distinct tags of WPs, we can improve the WPs tag prediction by purposefully constraining the word-pieces to reflect their internal functions. We conjecture that this is due to the naïve linear tokenization of words into word-pieces, and suggest that linguistically-informed word-pieces schemes, that make morphological knowledge explicit, might boost performance for MRLs.

1 Introduction

Contextualized word-embedding models, such as BERT (Devlin et al., 2019) and XLNet (Yang et al., 2019), rely on sub-word units called *word-pieces* (Johnson et al., 2017), that enable these models to generalize over frequent character-sequences and elegantly handle out-of-vocabulary items (with minimal resort to character-based models). This word-pieces architecture helps the models make better predictions for complete words without the need to keep a large dictionary for all the possible word-forms in a language.

Effectively analyzing the internal content of words is important for Morphologically-Rich Languages (MRLs) (Tsarfaty et al., 2010), that express multiple units of meaning at word level. Due to morphological ambiguity, the interpretation of the many functions of a complete word has to be determined in the context of the utterance, making explicit the contribution of each linguistic sub-word unit (a.k.a., *morpheme*) to the global meaning.

In this study we aim to investigate how well morphological information is captured by contextualized embedding models, or, more specifically, by their underlying *word-pieces*. We hypothesize that the word-pieces tokenization scheme in these models, which is not reflective of the actual morphology, will decrease the models ability to predict morphological functions on sub-word units.

In order to test this hypothesis we use Multilingual BERT (Devlin et al., 2019) on the task of *multi-tagging* raw words in a morphologically rich and ambiguous language, Modern Hebrew. Pre-neural studies on Hebrew found that explicitly modeling sub-word morphological information, substantially improves results on tagging and parsing down the NLP pipeline (More and Tsarfaty, 2016; More et al., 2019). Here our results show a significant drop in *multi-tagging* accuracy in word-level settings compared to settings where we aim to tag the distinct WPs. Nevertheless, when we purposefully incorporate morphological knowledge that reflect the internal functions of WPs, the tagging of WPs substantially improves.

We conjecture that current word-pieces architectures might be sub-optimal for capturing complex (e.g., fusional) morphology, and that more morphologically-informed schemes may yield better models, at least for MRLs.

*Proceedings of the Seventeenth SIGMORPHON Workshop on Computational Research
in Phonetics, Phonology, and Morphology*, pages 204–209
Online, July 10, 2020. ©2020 Association for Computational Linguistics
https://doi.org/10.18653/v1/P17

2 The Data: All Analytic Languages are Alike, Each MRL Is Rich In Its Own Way

Morphologically-Rich languages (MRLs) (Tsarfaty et al., 2010) are languages that express syntactic relations by inflection or agglutination at word level. In NLP, MRLs often require segmentation into sub-word units called *morphemes* as part of the pre-processing in the NLP pipelines. The term morphological fusion, or simply *fusion*, refers to the degree to which morphemes are connected to a word host or stem (Bickel and Nichols, 2013). There are three values for the degree of fusion: isolating (low), concatenative (mild) and non-concatenative (high). MRLs thus belong to the mild- and high-fusion language groups.

In concatenative MRLs like Turkish (Swift, 1963) and Russian (Wade, 1992; Shevelov, 1957) morphemes are linearly connected to the stem, and so a concatenated word-form can easily be segmented back into its composing morphemes. Segmenting highly fusional MRLs (henceforth fMRL), like Hebrew (Berman and Bolozky, 1978), is not as simple, since words can be affixed in such a way that makes the stem and/or affix undergo morpho-phonological changes resulting in ambiguous, syncretic word-forms. These changes cannot be restored without morphological disambiguation of the word in context of the whole sentence. Furthermore, word-forms may involve a combination of a root and a template which are intertwined via a non-concatenative process, and both contribute meaning to the word-form.

Let us consider two examples for high fusion morphological phenomena in Modern Hebrew. First, consider the word-form בצלם. It can either mean 'in their shadow' (ב-Preposition^צל-Noun^שלהם-Possessive), 'their onion' (בצל-Noun^שלהם-Possessive)), 'in the photographer' (ב-Preposition^ה-Definite^צלם-Noun) or 'Betselem' (בצלם-Proper Noun, a known organization). The differences between the actual word-form בצלם and the segments representing the composing morphemes in the different analyses, illustrate how complex morphological processes in Hebrew dictate the final word form — that is, the final form is no longer re-constructable by (simply concatenating) the morphological segments. Among the different analyses, no interpretation is a-priori more likely than others. Only in context the correct analysis can be determined.

Next, let us consider the following two verbs: שומר ('/somer', keep.PRES.MASC.SG, 'keeps') and נשמור ('ni-/smor', 1st.PL.FUT-keep.FUT, 'we will keep'). Here, although the affixes ו, נ can be separated from the root letters שמר, the analysis of the verb cannot be constructed by analyzing the mere character sequences, it must be understood from the unified form of the morphemes.

So, from the first example, we observe that morphological disambiguation is crucial, and that contextualized models may actually be good candidates for morphological disambiguation where the *external* context is crucial. But from the second example, we learn that the linear order and strict separation of words into word-pieces, as is done in current contextualized embeddings, may be too arbitrary and too strict, which may in turn undermine the performance of tasks down the NLP pipeline, particularly for fMRLs.

3 The Question: How Adequate are Word Pieces for Modeling Morphology

The Goal This paper aims to investigate whether word pieces capture sufficient morphological information about whole words. That is, we ask whether the information contained in such representations would allow to predict the multiple functions of an input, i.e. a space-delimited word-form. In particular, we empirically examine this capacity via the task of *multi-tag* assignment in Hebrew — where each *multi-tag* reflects the analyses of a single word-form bearing multiple POS tags — as illustrated in our Hebrew example in section 2. We conduct a series of experiments on multi POS-tag assignment to raw word forms in Hebrew texts, changing the granularity of the input and the output to reflect word-internal functions that are potentially captured by individual word-pieces.

The Task We define a *multitag* as a single label that consists of the multiple POS tags reflecting the categories of the (morphological) segments of a word-form. For example, we assign the word-form בבית, which means 'in the house', the *multitag* IN^DEF^NN. In all of our experiments, the model receives as input a sentence that underwent a tokenization into word pieces by the built-in tokenizer of mBERT (Wolf et al., 2019). We then output a multitag for each word as whole. Our models vary in how much (and what kind of) information is predicted for each of the word-pieces.

Experimental Setup We use the Hebrew section of the SPMRLs treebank, which consists of 6500 sentences from the daily newspaper Ha'aretz (Sima'an et al., 2001). This corpus was manually annotated for POS tags at morpheme-level by trained experts, and it is the accepted benchmark for all morphological processing tasks in Hebrew. We fine-tune the models using the Pytorch implementation of transformers by Wolf et al. (2019). We use its standard BertTokenizer and BertForTokenClassification, with multilingual BERT (cased) as our model for fine-tuning.

We use the standard train set as input for fine-tuning, and evaluate and report results on the dev set. We report on two measures. The first is *Exact Match (EM)*, that is, the percentage of correct multitag assignments from all multitag assignments to word-forms in the evaluation set.

$$EM = \frac{\text{\# correct multitags}}{\text{\# words}} \quad (1)$$

The second is *Existence F1*: precision and recall on the existence of correct POS tags in a (possible incorrect) multitag assignment. We compute *Existence F1* based on the precision and recall that follow. For calculating the precision and recall the predicted multitag is split into its composing simple POS tags. Note that *F1* gives partial credit on correctly identified POS in the case of partial identification or wrong order, while *EM* doesn't.

$$Precision = \frac{\text{\# correctly predicted individual POS tags}}{\text{\# individual POS tags in all } multitag \text{ assignments}} \quad (2)$$

$$Recall = \frac{\text{\# correctly predicted individual POS tags}}{\text{\# individual POS tags in all } multitags \text{ in the evaluation set}} \quad (3)$$

3.1 Models

3.1.1 Oracle

We begin with an Oracle scenario that emulates an English-like POS tagging scenario, where the input is a sequence of strings, in our case gold pre-segmented morphemes, and the output is a single POS tag per segment. For fine-tuning, we use pre-segmented words along with their corresponding POS tags, as it is gold-annotated in our training data. It should be noted that these segments undergo additional tokenization into *word pieces* by mBERT's tokenizer, based on its internal word-pieces lexicon, prior to fine-tuning.

For comparability with the other models, the evaluation is done on raw words i.e., we combine

	Before Tokenization:		After Tokenization:	
Nickname	Word	label	WP	label
Oracle	ל	IN	ל	IN
	ה	DEF	ה	DEF
	משטרה	NN	מש	NN
			טר##	NN
			ה##	NN
Word-Level	למשטרה	IN-DEF-NN	ל	IN-DEF-NN
			משטרה##	IN-DEF-NN
Word-Level Host	למשטרה	NN	ל	NN
			משטרה##	NN
Word-Level Prefix	למשטרה	IN-DEF	ל	IN-DEF
			משטרה##	IN-DEF
Decomposed	ל	IN	ל	IN
	ה	DEF	ה	DEF
	משטרה	NN	מש	NN
			טר##	NN
			ה##	NN
Decomposed Informed	למשטרה	IN-DEF-NN	ל	IN-DEF
			משטרה##	NN

Table 1: **The Labeled Data we crafted for Fine-Tuning the Models**. We illustrate it for the Hebrew form למשטרה (to-the-police, IN-DEF-NN), before and after the tokenization to WPs by BERT. At inference, the Oracle is given pre-segmented words to tag. All other models are given complete word-forms as input.

the predicted simple tags into a multitag and compare it to the original multitag per word. This scenario is of course not *realistic*, in the sense that gold segmented data at morpheme level are slow and costly to deliver. However, this setting provides an empirical upper-bound for the performance of BERT on a simple POS tagging in Hebrew. We hypothesize that, had BERT's tokenization into word pieces been morphologically informed, the model's accuracy in word-level settings could rise up to the level of performance on this pre-segmented Oracle scenario.

3.1.2 Word-Level Multi-tagging

Moving on to a *realistic* scenario, in our next task the input to the model is a sequence of raw word forms, and the output is a sequence of multi-tags, one multi-tag (i.e., multiple POS) per word. During fine-tuning, each word piece (WP) is assigned the multitag of the complete original word. Unlike the Oracle setting, where the input for fine-tuning reflected morphological phenomena, here no morphological knowledge is incorporated at all. During inference, the input is composed of raw words which undergo BERT's tokenization into word-pieces (WP), and each WP gets assigned one of the multi-tags encountered during fine-tuning.

The goal here is to examine the ability of the BERT-based representations to cope with a large space of complex labels (multi-tags) that re-

Model *Nickname*	Oracle	Word-Level	Word-Level Informed	Decomposed	Decomposed Informed
Model *Input*	Gold-Morph. Segment	Word	Word	Word	Word
Model *Output*	Tag	Multi-tag	{Prefix|Host} Multi-tag	WP-based Multi-tag	WP-based Multi-tag
Fine-Tuned on	Tagged Segments	Multi-tagged Words		{Single|Multi}-tagged Word-Pieces	
Exact Match	94.44	92.45	92.05	69.47	86.66
Existence F1	95.51	94.09	94.22	76.65	88.71

Table 2: **Empirical Results.** We report EM and F1 on raw-words' multi-tags, for all models and training regimes.

sult from different morphological (and morpho-phonological) processes that construct words in an MRL. This setting has several drawbacks; first, it is unable to generalize to an *unseen* composition of tagged-pieces into a new multitag, and second, throughout the process, the internal *morphological* segmentation of the tokens remains inaccessible.

3.1.3 Prefix/Host Multi-tagging

Retaining our *realistic* settings, where the input is composed of raw words, we split multi-tagging into two independent tasks. One predicts the multi-tag reflecting the prefix of that word, and the other predicts the multi-tag of its host (plus pronominal clitics).[1] The input for fine-tuning, in both cases, presents raw words having undergone BERT's tokenization, and each WP is assigned the multi-tag of the Prefix (/Host) of that word.

For the prefix task, we implemented a function that looks for all known tags that represent prefixes in Hebrew, and truncated the complete multitag of the word to include only them. For instance, a word that is assigned the multi-tag IN^DEF^NN will now get assigned the multi-tag IN^DEF. Words that don't contain a prefix get assigned the label '–'. Likewise for the host, words are assigned only the part of the multi-tag that doesn't contain prefix tags. For the above example, this would simply be NN. Fine-tuning is performed independently for each of the tasks. At inference time, the predictions for the prefix and host are combined into a single multi-tag, compared against the gold multi-tag for evaluation.

One technical advantage of this setting is that it substantially limits the label-space that needs to be learned per word. Also, unlike the previous scenario, the model is able to generate unseen multitags (to some extent) by creating previously unseen Prefix-Host compositions.

---

[1] Since Hebrew can stack prefixes before a host, the prefixes require a multi-tag. Similarly, hosts with pronominal clitics may also be assigned a multi-tag rather than one tag.

3.1.4 Decomposed Multi-tagging

In this scenario we aim to assign to each WP a single tag that corresponds to the actual function of that WP.

For *fine-tuning*, we use the same data as in the Oracle scenario. That is, we use pre-segmented morphemes that undergo BERT's tokenization, paired with their corresponding tags, a single tag per WP. Now, at inference time, *whole* words undergo BERT's tokenization into word-pieces. Since the model was trained (fine-tuned) to predict a single tag per word-piece, the hope is that we could predict the single tag that reflects the function of this specific WP. We then combine all the (unique) predictions for all the WPs in the word to concatenate them to a single multi-tag.

This setting tests whether the tokenization algorithm outputs WPs that are reflective of the actual morphemes the model was fine-tuned on. If this is the case, predicting a single POS tag per WP would perform similarly to the Oracle setting. Howvere, since the internal decomposition of the words at inference time is determined solely by BERT's WPs, any diversion between the WP tokenization and the gold morphological decomposition is expected to negatively affect performance.

3.1.5 Morphologically-Informed Decomposed Multi-tagging

Here again the input for the task consists of raw words, tokenized by BERT into word-pieces. As output we now aim to assign each word-piece a multi-tag that reflects *exactly* its own content.

The input to fine-tuning thus has to be modified. We use raw words having undergone BERT's tokenization into WPs, and each WP is assigned a multitag label that reflects *the actual POS tag(s) that this part of the word contains (an *informed* multi-tag). We obtain these *informed* multi-tags using a deterministic procedure that compares the WPs proposed by BERT to the gold morphological segmentation we have for the training data. During training, we can unambiguously detect which morphemes are relevant for the WP only, and the

WP gets assigned the multi-tag of the actual morphemes it contains. At inference time we provide BERT-tokenized words as input, and each WP gets assigned an *informed* multi-tag as observed during fine-tuning. For evaluation, we combine the prediction made on all WPs of a word to a single ordered multi-tag, and compare it to the gold multi-tag of that word. Interestingly, this setting can potentially generate previously unseen multi-tags, and it maximizes the extent to which we can access word-internal structure during fine-tuning.

4 Results

The input, output and training regimes for our models are illustrated in Table 1. Table 2 presents the results on multi-tagging for all of our models.

As expected, the Oracle scenario assigning single tags to gold segments outperformed all other models that aim to multi-tag complete words. For word-level multi-tagging, the word-level model performed at the same level as the Prefix/Host model — narrowing down the labels' space in this fashion does not seem to improve results or provide any further generalization capacity.

Purposefully fine-tuning our model to assign a single POS tag per WP (trained on our gold morphological data) did not help, in fact it dramatically hurts performance. This indicates that WPs in and of themselves do not coincide with the notion of morphemes. Curiously though, informing BERT's WPs as to *their own internal function* prior to fine-tuning significantly improves the results compared to the model trained to assign a POS-per-WP based on gold morphology.

This last result suggests that, while current WPs do not reflect morphological structure and lose morphological distinctions in their sub-word units, informing these word-units as to their own internal functions can provide a major performance boost. So far, we only incorporated such morphological information during *fine-tuning*. We conjecture that informing the WP algorithm earlier on, *prior* to pre-training, with a linguistically-informed decomposition into WPs, may greatly advance the performance of contextualized models for fMRLs.

5 Related Work

Although the term 'word pieces' was only coined in 2017, by Johnson et al. (2017), the idea that sub-word segmentation might be useful for downstream tasks was already well-known and studied, especially in the field on Neural Machine Translation. In 2010 Luong et al. (2010) explicitly showed that incorporating morphological knowledge in the translation process significantly improves translation. In 2017 Belinkov et al. (2017) found that for learning morphology it is better to use character based representation rather than word-based ones. They also found that neural networks encode morphology in the lower layers of the network, which might explain why mere fine-tuning is insufficient to capture morphological complexity. Later, Straka et al. (2019) achieved SoTA on POS tagging on 54 languages, including Heberew, but was using BERT embeddings along with character level embeddings and Fast-text (Bojanowski et al., 2017) word embeddings on gold morphology, which strengthen our claim that word pieces by themselves don't capture morphology well. This was also supported by Mielke and Eisner (2019), that explicitly mentioned the non-concatenativity of Hebrew and Arabic as the major drawback of sub word tokenization systems.

6 Conclusion

In this work we examined the adequacy of BERT's word-pieces as sub-word units for representing complex morphology. We chose to investigate *multi-tagging* in a high fusional language, as a proxy for assessing the underlying segmentation into distinct morphemes. We expected that if distinct word-pieces indeed reflect units of meaning, then tagging them would be as accurate as it is for languages that assign a single tag per word. Our results show that the current word pieces do not reflect actual morphology, resulting in decreased performance for tagging complex Hebrew words. Nonetheless, we found that imposing morphological knowledge during fine-tuning (an *Informed* setup) is indeed helpful, albeit a bit late. We conjecture that pre-training with a morphologically-informed word-pieces scheme that reflects a complex morphological reality, has the potential to improve multi-tagging, as well as other tasks down the pipeline, in Hebrew and other fMRLs.

Acknowledgements

We thank Yoav Goldberg, Noah Smith, Omer Levy and three reviewers for interesting discussions of an earlier draft. This research is funded by an ERC Grant #677352 and an ISF grant #1739/26, for which we are grateful.

References

Yonatan Belinkov, Nadir Durrani, Fahim Dalvi, Hassan Sajjad, and James Glass. 2017. What do neural machine translation models learn about morphology? In *Proceedings of the 55th Annual Meeting of the Association for Computational Linguistics (Volume 1: Long Papers)*, pages 861–872, Vancouver, Canada. Association for Computational Linguistics.

Ruth Aronson Berman and Shmuel Bolozky. 1978. *Modern Hebrew structure*. University Pub. Projects.

Balthasar Bickel and Johanna Nichols. 2013. Fusion of selected inflectional formatives. In Matthew S. Dryer and Martin Haspelmath, editors, *The World Atlas of Language Structures Online*. Max Planck Institute for Evolutionary Anthropology, Leipzig.

Piotr Bojanowski, Edouard Grave, Armand Joulin, and Tomas Mikolov. 2017. Enriching word vectors with subword information. *Transactions of the Association for Computational Linguistics*, 5:135–146.

Jacob Devlin, Ming-Wei Chang, Kenton Lee, and Kristina Toutanova. 2019. BERT: Pre-training of deep bidirectional transformers for language understanding. In *Proceedings of the 2019 Conference of the North American Chapter of the Association for Computational Linguistics: Human Language Technologies, Volume 1 (Long and Short Papers)*, pages 4171–4186, Minneapolis, Minnesota. Association for Computational Linguistics.

Melvin Johnson, Mike Schuster, Quoc V. Le, Maxim Krikun, Yonghui Wu, Zhifeng Chen, Nikhil Thorat, Fernanda Viégas, Martin Wattenberg, Greg Corrado, Macduff Hughes, and Jeffrey Dean. 2017. Google's multilingual neural machine translation system: Enabling zero-shot translation. *Transactions of the Association for Computational Linguistics*, 5:339–351.

Minh-Thang Luong, Preslav Nakov, and Min-Yen Kan. 2010. A hybrid morpheme-word representation for machine translation of morphologically rich languages. In *Proceedings of the 2010 Conference on Empirical Methods in Natural Language Processing*, pages 148–157. Association for Computational Linguistics.

Sabrina J. Mielke and Jason Eisner. 2019. Spell once, summon anywhere: A two-level open-vocabulary language model. In *AAAI*.

Amir More, Amit Seker, Victoria Basmova, and Reut Tsarfaty. 2019. Joint transition-based models for morpho-syntactic parsing: Parsing strategies for MRLs and a case study from modern Hebrew. *Transactions of the Association for Computational Linguistics*, 7:33–48.

Amir More and Reut Tsarfaty. 2016. Data-driven morphological analysis and disambiguation for morphologically rich languages and universal dependencies. In *Proceedings of COLING 2016, the 26th International Conference on Computational Linguistics: Technical Papers*, pages 337–348, Osaka, Japan. The COLING 2016 Organizing Committee.

George Y Shevelov. 1957. The structure of the root in modern russian. *The Slavic and East European Journal*, 1(2):106–124.

Khalil Sima'an, Alon Itai, Yoad Winter, Alon Altman, and Noa Nativ. 2001. Building a tree-bank of modern hebrew text. *Traitement Automatique des Langues*, 42(2):247–380.

Milan Straka, Jana Straková, and Jan Hajič. 2019. Evaluating contextualized embeddings on 54 languages in pos tagging, lemmatization and dependency parsing. *arXiv preprint arXiv:1908.07448*.

Lloyd B. Swift. 1963. *A Reference Grammar of Modern Turkish*. Indiana University Press, Bloomington.

Reut Tsarfaty, Djamé Seddah, Yoav Goldberg, Sandra Kübler, Marie Candito, Jennifer Foster, Yannick Versley, Ines Rehbein, and Lamia Tounsi. 2010. Statistical parsing of morphologically rich languages (spmrl): what, how and whither. In *Proceedings of the NAACL HLT 2010 First Workshop on Statistical Parsing of Morphologically-Rich Languages*, pages 1–12. Association for Computational Linguistics.

Terence L. B. Wade. 1992. *A Comprehensive Russian Grammar*. Blackwell, Oxford. Reprinted in 1995.

Thomas Wolf, Lysandre Debut, Victor Sanh, Julien Chaumond, Clement Delangue, Anthony Moi, Pierric Cistac, Tim Rault, R'emi Louf, Morgan Funtowicz, and Jamie Brew. 2019. Huggingface's transformers: State-of-the-art natural language processing. *ArXiv*, abs/1910.03771.

Zhilin Yang, Zihang Dai, Yiming Yang, Jaime Carbonell, Russ R Salakhutdinov, and Quoc V Le. 2019. Xlnet: Generalized autoregressive pretraining for language understanding. In *Advances in neural information processing systems*, pages 5754–5764.

Induced Inflection-Set Keyword Search in Speech

Oliver Adams,♡♠ Matthew Wiesner,♠ Jan Trmal,♠
Garrett Nicolai,◇♠ David Yarowsky♠
♠Center for Language and Speech Processing, Johns Hopkins University, USA
♡Atos zData, USA
◇Department of Linguistics, University of British Columbia, Canada
`oliver.adams@gmail.com, gnicolai@mail.ubc.ca,`
`{mwiesner,yenda,yarowsky}@jhu.edu`

Abstract

We investigate the problem of searching for a lexeme-set in speech by searching for its inflectional variants. Experimental results indicate how lexeme-set search performance changes with the number of hypothesized inflections, while ablation experiments highlight the relative importance of different components in the lexeme-set search pipeline and the value of using curated inflectional paradigms. We provide a recipe and evaluation set for the community to use as an extrinsic measure of the performance of inflection generation approaches.

1 Introduction

Keyword search (KWS) is the task of finding certain words or expressions of interest in a body of speech. KWS is relevant to incident-response situations such as those modeled by LORELEI (Strassel and Tracey, 2016) and was a focus of the IARPA Babel Program.[1] In the event of a humanitarian crisis, processing speech to determine mentions of certain keywords can inform better decision making when time is critical.

KWS is typically framed as searching for instances of a keyword in lattices that result from speech recognition decoding, as this means search is not restricted to a potentially incorrect one-best transcription. However, existing work on KWS assumes the relevant form of a keyword has been correctly specified. Many concepts to be searched for in speech take different forms through inflection as a result of the language's morphosyntax. In most cases, distinctions between such inflections (e.g. kill, kills, killing, killed) are irrelevant to the problem of searching for the underlying concept of interest.

Producing such inflection sets manually is arduous, even for native speakers, yet curators of

[1] www.iarpa.gov/index.php/research-programs/babel

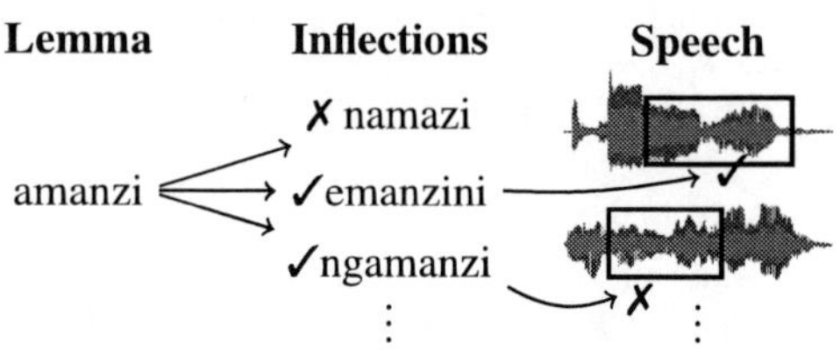

Figure 1: An example Zulu keyword lemma (left) is inflected (middle) and then searched for in a corpus of speech (right). ✓ and ✗ indicate correct/incorrect inflections, and correct/incorrect findings of the inflection in the corpus.

keyword lists may have to construct them cross-lingually using bilingual dictionaries, which typically only contain canonical forms. Compounding this issue are the limitations of existing language technology for most of the world's languages across the whole KWS pipeline, including inflection generation, the language model (LM), the pronunciation lexicon, and the acoustic model.

In this paper we explore the application of inflection generation to KWS by searching for instances of a lexeme (see Figure 1). To the best of our knowledge, this task has not been investigated before. Using Bengali and Turkish as evaluation languages, we scale the number of inflections generated per lexeme-set to examine how the trade-off between false positives and false negatives affects downstream KWS. We additionally perform experiments that assume varying quality of inflection generation. Our findings show that lexeme-set KWS yields promising results even when all inflections must be generated on the basis of a distantly supervised cross-lingual approach to training inflection tools, though we observe that having a curated set of inflectional paradigms is important for achieving good performance. These first results encourage future work for lexeme-set search in speech, and the use of KWS as an extrinsic eval-

Proceedings of the Seventeenth SIGMORPHON Workshop on Computational Research
in Phonetics, Phonology, and Morphology, pages 210–216
Online, July 10, 2020. ©2020 Association for Computational Linguistics
https://doi.org/10.18653/v1/P17

uation of inflection generation tools.

To this end, we make available to the community a lexeme-set KWS pipeline with baseline models for inflection generation, grapheme-to-phoneme conversion (G2P), multilingual acoustic modeling, and cross-lingual inflection generation, and a KWS evaluation set built on a suitable intersection of UniMorph inflection sets (Sylak-Glassman et al., 2015; Kirov et al., 2018) and the Babel speech (Andresen et al., 2016; Bills et al., 2016). The combination of these components serves as a novel downstream evaluation of inflection generation approaches, as well the other components in the pipeline. We make this recipe and evaluation set freely available online.[2]

2   The lexeme-set KWS Pipeline

The pipeline starts with a lexeme of interest from the evaluation set (§2.1). Inflections of the lexeme are generated using some generation tool or manual resource (§2.2). These inflections are then converted to a phonemic representation (§2.3) before being added to the lexicon used in speech recognition. KWS is then performed (§2.4) by decoding the speech and the model is scored on the how well it finds instanes of the lexeme.

2.1   Evaluation Set

We evaluate systems based on their ability to complete the following task: given a lemma, find all occurrences of its inflections in speech. To create an evaluation set for this task, we use UniMorph data, which provides ground truth inflection sets for a substantial number of languages. We use as our evaluation set instances of words in the Babel 10h development set that also are inflections in the UniMorph data. We remove from this set a small number of inflections that occur in more than one paradigm, as well as those that don't occur in the Babel pronunciation lexicon. This means that we can use the Babel lexicon as an oracle pronunciation lexicon with respect to our constructed evaluation sets to compare against our other methods. The result is an evaluation set tailored to morphologically salient word forms, with 1250 Turkish paradigms and 59 Bengali paradigms. The set of evaluation languages that can be extended to other languages in the Babel set for which we have ground truth paradigms.

2.2   Inflection Generation

Inflection generation is the task of producing an *inflection*, given a lemma and a *bundle* of morphosyntactic features. For example, run + {PRES;3;SG} $\mapsto$ "runs". The state of the art in inflection generation has arisen from the CoNLL–SIGMORPHON Shared Tasks (Cotterell et al., 2016, 2017, 2018; McCarthy et al., 2019), and typically consists of a modified sequence-to-sequence model with attention (Makarov and Clematide, 2018).

However, these systems are fully supervised, and hand-curated morphological dictionaries often do not exist. We instead turn to the methods of Nicolai and Yarowsky (2019), who use English annotation as distant supervision to induce target language morphology, using a widely-translated, verse-parallel text: the Bible. Starting from the inflection pairs extracted by their method, we ensemble generators trained using an RNN and DirecTL+ (Jiampojamarn et al., 2010). For each lemma in the respective UniMorph, we generate hypotheses for each feature bundle, ensembling via a linear combination of confidence scores. This gives us a set of inflections for each of the lexemes in the evaluation set which can then be searched for in the speech.

2.3   Grapheme-to-Phoneme Conversion

To include hypothesized inflections in the KWS pipeline, orthographic forms of inflections must be mapped to a phonemic form consistent with the units used by the acoustic model (Maskey et al., 2004; Chen et al., 2016; Mortensen et al., 2018; Schultz et al., 2007; Kominek and Black, 2006; Deri and Knight, 2016; Trmal et al., 2017). We use a finite-state transducer model trained with Phonetisaurus[3] on 5,000 word forms in the target language.

2.4   Keyword Search

After generating inflections of lemmas in the evaluation set, these inflections are then included in the lexicon used in KWS. The KWS involves decoding the speech into lattices, and assessing lattice's inclusion of the keyword of interest. Our pipeline builds on the Kaldi OpenKWS system (Trmal et al., 2017), which uses the standard lattice indexing approach of (Can and Saraclar, 2011). We

---

[2]https://github.com/oadams/inflection-kws

[3]github.com/AdolfVonKleist/
Phonetisaurus

use augmented pronunciation lexicons for KWS, which has been shown to outperform proxy KWS, a popular alternative (Chen et al., 2013).

The novel problem of lexeme-set KWS is related to work on out-of-vocabulary KWS, which has been approached by handling sub-word units such as syllables and morphemes (Trmal et al., 2014; Narasimhan et al., 2014; van Heerden et al., 2017; He et al., 2016). In contrast to KWS with sub-word granularity, our approach is to generate likely full-word inflections given a lemma.

For language modeling, we used a 4-gram modified Kneser-Ney baseline (Kneser and Ney, 1995). We compare using as training data the in-domain Babel text to the Bible, a resource available for many languages, and which was the resource used for cross-lingual distant supervision for inflection generation described in Section 2.2. Hypothesized inflections not seen in the training data receive some probability mass in language model smoothing as is default in SRILM (Stolcke, 2002), the language modeling tool used.

Though a monolingual acoustic model could have been used, we chose to use a "universal" phoneset acoustic model which can effectively be deployed on languages not seen in training and is motivated by work in multilingual acoustic modeling (Schultz and Waibel, 2001; Le and Besacier, 2005; Stolcke et al., 2006; Vesely et al., 2012; Vu et al., 2012; Heigold et al., 2013; Scharenborg et al., 2017; Karafiát et al., 2018). We train an acoustic model on 300 hours of data from 25 languages using a common phonemic representation across languages. The training data includes 10 hours for each of 21 different languages from the IARPA Babel corpus, a 20 hour subset of the Wall Street Journal,[4] Hub4 Spanish Broadcast news,[5] and the Russian and French portions of the Vox-forge[6] corpus.

3 KWS Evaluation Metrics

We evaluate KWS performance on a per lexeme-set basis, rewarding the system when it finds any form of an evaluation lexeme, regardless of how it is inflected, while also penalizing failure to find any inflection.

As an evaluation metric we use term weighted value (TWV), a standard metric in KWS developed for the NIST 2006 Spoken Term Detection evaluation (Fiscus et al., 2007), which rewards joint maximization of recall with minimization of false positives. TWV relies on a threshold parameter to determine what minimum level of confidence is required by the system in order to assert keyword findings. There are several variations of term weighted value (TWV) that are different in the way the threshold is handled: Actual (ATWV), Optimum (OTWV), and Supreme (STWV).

ATWV is the TWV of the system given some global threshold (provided by the system) of confidence common to all keywords, and is the most common metric used to compare systems.

OTWV determines a per-keyword (in our case, per lexeme-set) threshold. For our purposes this is the most informative metric because it gives a better sense of how the ATWV would be if system effectively normalized confidences across lexemes. Improvements to TWV may also potentially be made beyond what is represented by the OTWV. Some inflections are more likely than others, yet the thresholds for OTWV are made at a per lexeme-set basis, not a per-inflection basis. Improving how the system weights the likelihood of different inflections (either during inflection generation or in the LM probabilities) would likely substantially improve ATWV.

STWV is a recall-oriented version of TWV that disregards the confidence of the terms and does not penalize false positives. It is thus similar to lattice recall and serves as a useful metric in system analysis for determining whether low ATWV/OTWV is due to large number of false positives or issues in effective speech word lattice decoding.

4 Experiments

We conduct experiments to see how performance of KWS relates to the number of inflections hypothesized by the cross-lingual distantly-supervised method described in Section 2.2 (henceforth RNN+DTL), before comparing it to several alternative benchmark methods.

As evaluation languages we used Bengali and Turkish, a subset of languages for which we have Bibles and that also occur in UniMorph. We observed similar trends and relative performance of methods for both languages languages so in the subsequent results we present the arithmetic mean of the results of Bengali and Turkish.

---

[4]LDC94S13B
[5]LDC98T29
[6]http://voxforge.org

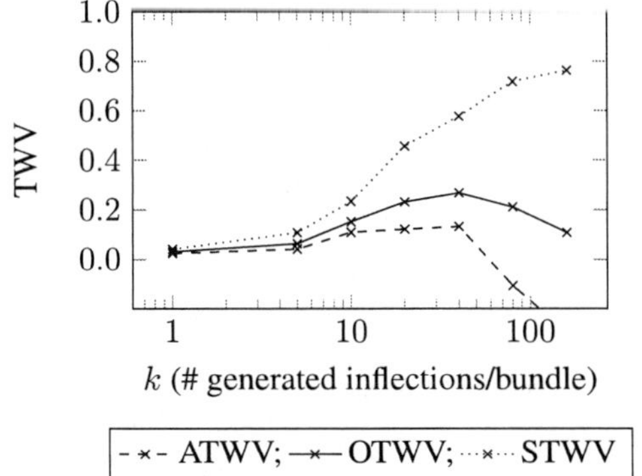

Figure 2: Variations on the term weighted value (TWV) metric for different numbers of generated inflections per morphosyntactic bundle (by RNN+DTL). Overgeneration of inflections improves recall, as captured by STWV, but leads to too many false positives when $k \geq 80$.

Inflections	LM	ATWV	OTWV	STWV
Oracle	Babel	0.315	0.463	0.866
UniMorph	Babel	0.392	0.513	0.864
RNN+DTL	Babel	0.133	0.269	0.577
Lemmas	Babel	0.169	0.219	0.281
RNN+DTL-NS	Babel	0.304	0.443	0.815
RNN+DTL	Bible	0.046	0.206	0.561

Table 1: Term weighted value (TWV) under varying conditions: Oracle inflections known to occur in the Babel speech; UniMorph inflections that additionally include true inflections not seen in speech; RNN+DTL-generated inflections via distant cross-lingual supervision; Lemmas-only search. Discounting spurious forms from RNN+DTL shows its high recall. Using an out-of-domain LM substantially decreases performance.

4.1 The Number of Generated Inflections

To gauge how over-generation of inflections affects KWS performance we scaled k, the number of inflections generated per morphosyntactic bundle. Figure 2 illustrates how TWV varies with respect to k for inflections generated by RNN+DTL in a KWS system that uses the in-domain Babel LM. At values of k beyond 40 the ATWV and OTWV began to decrease, as the number of false positives was too high. The recall-oriented STWV continued to increase, peaking at 0.764 when $k = 160$. It is noteworthy that OTWV only began to decrease at such a value of k. For Turkish nouns, with 23 bundles per lexeme-set, a value of $k = 40$ corresponds to 920 inflections, the vast majority of which are invalid inflections. This indicates that there is room for a substantial amount of inflection overgeneration in KWS, since the speech recognition can provide acoustic evidence against incorrect inflection candidates.

4.2 Comparison of Inflection Approaches

To get a comparative sense of the KWS performance of RNN+DTL at the best value of k, we compare it with three other approaches: Oracle, UniMorph, and Lemmas, as shown in Table 1.

Oracle includes exactly the set of inflections that occur in the evaluation set. UniMorph includes all the inflections that occur in the Uni-Morph data, which differs from Oracle in that it contains true inflections that don't happen to occur in the Babel speech. We included this to as-

sess how true inflections of the lexeme that are not found in the speech affect performance. It helps substantially for ATWV and OTWV, but not for STWV. This somewhat counterintuitive result suggests that including more inflectional variants of a lexeme may not improve recall (i.e. improve STWV) but can decrease the number of false positives.

Lemmas searches only for citation-form lemmas. It has a relatively decent ATWV (even outperforming RNN+DTL, though not by OTWV) despite low recall (as indicated by STWV) because it has few false positives and also because most inflections sound similar to the lemmas via the addition of an affix. As a result, searching for the lemma often catches inflectional variants too.

We consider two further points of comparison. Firstly, RNN+DTL with only a Bible-trained LM, which underperforms other systems substantially except in lattice recall as indicated by STWV. Secondly, RNN+DTL-NS, which removes from RNN+DTL spurious inflections that weren't found in Oracle. Comparison of RNN+DTL-NS and RNN+DTL demonstrates that while the system has some robustness to overgeneration of inflected forms (§4.1), it is also the case spurious inflections not only increase false positives, but can actually hurt recall too.

These results indicate that correctly generating inflected forms and properly weighting the hypothesized inflections (either via the inflection generation module, or in the language model) is the most critical bottleneck in the pipeline. The high relative performance of Unimorph indicates the value of making full use of available curated resources. Recent work has shown how effective inflection generation can be with limited resources in the target language (Cotterell et al., 2018). These results suggest that if such resources are not available, then in practice it is likely worth gathering training data with which train an inflection generator.

5 Conclusion

We have presented an evaluation of lexeme-set KWS. Our results shed light on the relative impact of undergenerating and overgenerating inflected forms on KWS, indicating that high recall can be achieved via an inflection method of cross-lingual distant supervision, but with the best all-round performance achieved by making use of Unimorph. We release our evaluation set along with scripts to reuse our pipeline so that the community can explore lexeme-set KWS as an extrinsic evaluation of inflection generation.

Acknowledgements

We would like to thank all reviewers for their constructive feedback.

References

Jess Andresen, Aric Bills, Eyal Dubinski, Jonathan G. Fiscus, Breanna Gillies, Mary Harper, T. J. Hazen, Amy Jarrett, Bergul Roomi, Jessica Ray, Anton Rytting, Wade Shen, and Evelyne Tzoukermann. 2016. IARPA Babel Turkish language pack IARPA-babel105b-v0.5. LDC2016S10.

Aric Bills, Anne David, Eyal Dubinski, Jonathan G. Fiscus, Breanna Gillies, Mary Harper, Amy Jarrett, Mara Encarnacin Prez Molina, Jessica Ray, Anton Rytting, Shelley Paget, Wade Shen, Ronnie Silber, Evelyne Tzoukermann, and Jamie Wong. 2016. IARPA Babel Bengali language pack IARPA-babel103b-v0.4b. LDC2016S08.

Doğan Can and Murat Saraclar. 2011. Lattice indexing for spoken term detection. *IEEE Transactions on Audio, Speech, and Language Processing*, 19(8):2338–2347.

Guoguo Chen, Daniel Povey, and Sanjeev Khudanpur. 2016. Acoustic data-driven pronunciation lexicon generation for logographic languages. In *Proc. ICASSP*.

Guoguo Chen, Oguz Yilmaz, Jan Trmal, Daniel Povey, and Sanjeev Khudanpur. 2013. Using proxies for OOV keywords in the keyword search task. In *2013 IEEE Workshop on Automatic Speech Recognition and Understanding*, pages 416–421. IEEE.

Ryan Cotterell, Christo Kirov, John Sylak-Glassman, Géraldine Walther, Ekaterina Vylomova, Arya D. McCarthy, Katharina Kann, Sebastian Mielke, Garrett Nicolai, Miikka Silfverberg, David Yarowsky, Jason Eisner, and Mans Hulden. 2018. The CoNLL–SIGMORPHON 2018 shared task: Universal morphological reinflection. In *Proceedings of the CoNLL–SIGMORPHON 2018 Shared Task: Universal Morphological Reinflection*, pages 1–27, Brussels. Association for Computational Linguistics.

Ryan Cotterell, Christo Kirov, John Sylak-Glassman, Géraldine Walther, Ekaterina Vylomova, Patrick Xia, Manaal Faruqui, Sandra Kübler, David Yarowsky, Jason Eisner, and Mans Hulden. 2017. CoNLL-SIGMORPHON 2017 shared task: Universal morphological reinflection in 52 languages. In *Proceedings of the CoNLL SIGMORPHON 2017 Shared Task: Universal Morphological Reinflection*, pages 1–30, Vancouver. Association for Computational Linguistics.

Ryan Cotterell, Christo Kirov, John Sylak-Glassman, David Yarowsky, Jason Eisner, and Mans Hulden. 2016. The SIGMORPHON 2016 shared Task—Morphological reinflection. In *Proceedings of the 14th SIGMORPHON Workshop on Computational Research in Phonetics, Phonology, and Morphology*, pages 10–22, Berlin, Germany. Association for Computational Linguistics.

Aliya Deri and Kevin Knight. 2016. Grapheme-to-phoneme models for (almost) any language. In *Proceedings of the 54th Annual Meeting of the Association for Computational Linguistics (Volume 1: Long Papers)*, pages 399–408, Berlin, Germany. Association for Computational Linguistics.

Jonathan G Fiscus, Jerome Ajot, John S Garofolo, and George Doddingtion. 2007. Results of the 2006 spoken term detection evaluation. In *Proc. SIGIR*, volume 7, pages 51–57.

Y. He, P. Baumann, H. Fang, B. Hutchinson, A. Jaech, M. Ostendorf, E. Fosler-Lussier, and J. Pierrehumbert. 2016. Using pronunciation-based morphological subword units to improve oov handling in keyword search. *IEEE/ACM Transactions on Audio, Speech, and Language Processing*, 24(1):79–92.

Georg Heigold, Vincent Vanhoucke, Alan Senior, Patrick Nguyen, Marc'Aurelio Ranzato, Matthieu Devin, and Jeffrey Dean. 2013. Multilingual acoustic models using distributed deep neural networks. In *ICASSP*.

Sittichai Jiampojamarn, Colin Cherry, and Grzegorz Kondrak. 2010. Integrating joint n-gram features into a discriminative training framework. In *Human Language Technologies: The 2010 Annual Conference of the North American Chapter of the Association for Computational Linguistics*, pages 697–700, Los Angeles, California. Association for Computational Linguistics.

Martin Karafiát, Murali Karthick Baskar, Shinji Watanabe, Takaaki Hori, Matthew Wiesner, and Jan "Honza" Černocký. 2018. Analysis of multilingual sequence-to-sequence speech recognition systems. *arXiv:1811.03451*.

Christo Kirov, Ryan Cotterell, John Sylak-Glassman, Géraldine Walther, Ekaterina Vylomova, Patrick Xia, Manaal Faruqui, Sebastian J. Mielke, Arya McCarthy, Sandra Kübler, David Yarowsky, Jason Eisner, and Mans Hulden. 2018. UniMorph 2.0: Universal morphology. In *Proceedings of the 11th Language Resources and Evaluation Conference*, Miyazaki, Japan. European Language Resource Association.

Reinhard Kneser and Hermann Ney. 1995. Improved backing-off for m-gram language modeling. In *1995 International Conference on Acoustics, Speech, and Signal Processing*, volume 1, pages 181–184. IEEE.

John Kominek and Alan W Black. 2006. Learning pronunciation dictionaries: Language complexity and word selection strategies. In *Proceedings of the Human Language Technology Conference of the NAACL, Main Conference*, pages 232–239, New York City, USA. Association for Computational Linguistics.

Viet Bac Le and Laurent Besacier. 2005. First steps in fast acoustic modeling for a new target language: application to Vietnamese. In *ICASSP*.

Peter Makarov and Simon Clematide. 2018. UZH at CoNLL–SIGMORPHON 2018 shared task on universal morphological reinflection. pages 69–75.

Sameer Maskey, Alan Black, and Laura Tomokiya. 2004. Boostrapping phonetic lexicons for new languages. In *Eighth International Conference on Spoken Language Processing*.

Arya D. McCarthy, Ekaterina Vylomova, Shijie Wu, Chaitanya Malaviya, Lawrence Wolf-Sonkin, Garrett Nicolai, Miikka Silfverberg, Sebastian J. Mielke, Jeffrey Heinz, Ryan Cotterell, and Mans Hulden. 2019. The SIGMORPHON 2019 shared task: Morphological analysis in context and crosslingual transfer for inflection. In *Proceedings of the 16th Workshop on Computational Research in Phonetics, Phonology, and Morphology*, pages 229–244, Florence, Italy. Association for Computational Linguistics.

David R. Mortensen, Siddharth Dalmia, and Patrick Littell. 2018. Epitran: Precision G2P for many languages. In *Proceedings of the Eleventh International Conference on Language Resources and Evaluation (LREC-2018)*, Miyazaki, Japan. European Languages Resources Association (ELRA).

Karthik Narasimhan, Damianos Karakos, Richard Schwartz, Stavros Tsakalidis, and Regina Barzilay. 2014. Morphological segmentation for keyword spotting. In *Proceedings of the 2014 Conference on Empirical Methods in Natural Language Processing (EMNLP)*, pages 880–885, Doha, Qatar. Association for Computational Linguistics.

Garrett Nicolai and David Yarowsky. 2019. Learning morphosyntactic analyzers from the Bible via iterative annotation projection across 26 languages. In *Proceedings of the 57th Annual Meeting of the Association for Computational Linguistics*, pages 1765–1774, Florence, Italy. Association for Computational Linguistics.

Odette Scharenborg, Francesco Ciannella, Shruti Palaskar, Alan Black, Florian Metze, Lucas Ondel, and Mark Hasegawa-Johnson. 2017. Building an ASR system for a low-research language through the adaptation of a high-resource language ASR system: preliminary results. In *International Conference on Natural Language, Signal and Speech Processing (ICNLSSP)*.

Tanja Schultz, Alan W Black, Sameer Badaskar, Matthew Hornyak, and John Kominek. 2007. Spice: Web-based tools for rapid language adaptation in speech processing systems. In *Eighth Annual Conference of the International Speech Communication Association*.

Tanja Schultz and Alex Waibel. 2001. Experiments on cross-language acoustic Modeling. *EUROSPEECH'01*, pages 2721–2724.

A. Stolcke, F. Grezl, Mei-Yuh Hwang, Xin Lei, N. Morgan, and D. Vergyri. 2006. Cross-domain and cross-language portability of acoustic features estimated by multilayer perceptrons. In *ICASSP*.

Andreas Stolcke. 2002. Srilm-an extensible language modeling toolkit. In *Seventh international conference on spoken language processing*.

Stephanie Strassel and Jennifer Tracey. 2016. LORELEI language packs: Data, tools, and resources for technology development in low resource languages. In *Proceedings of the Tenth International Conference on Language Resources and Evaluation (LREC 2016)*, pages 3273–3280, Portorož, Slovenia. European Language Resources Association (ELRA).

John Sylak-Glassman, Christo Kirov, David Yarowsky, and Roger Que. 2015. A language-independent feature schema for inflectional morphology. In *Proceedings of the 53rd Annual Meeting of the Association for Computational Linguistics and the 7th International Joint Conference on Natural Language Processing (Volume 2: Short Papers)*, pages 674–680, Beijing, China. Association for Computational Linguistics.

Jan Trmal, Guoguo Chen, Dan Povey, Sanjeev Khudanpur, Pegah Ghahremani, Xiaohui Zhang, Vimal Manohar, Chunxi Liu, Aren Jansen, Dietrich Klakow, et al. 2014. A keyword search system using open source software. In *2014 IEEE Spoken Language Technology Workshop (SLT)*, pages 530–535. IEEE.

Jan Trmal, Matthew Wiesner, Vijayaditya Peddinti, Xiaohui Zhang, Pegah Ghahremani, Yiming Wang, Vimal Manohar, Hainan Xu, Daniel Povey, and Sanjeev Khudanpur. 2017. The Kaldi OpenKWS System: Improving Low Resource Keyword Search. In *INTERSPEECH*, pages 3597–3601.

C. van Heerden, D. Karakos, K. Narasimhan, M. Davel, and R. Schwartz. 2017. Constructing sub-word units for spoken term detection. In *2017 IEEE International Conference on Acoustics, Speech and Signal Processing (ICASSP)*, pages 5780–5784.

Karel Vesely, Martin Karafiát, Frantisek Grezl, Marcel Janda, and Ekaterina Egorova. 2012. The language-independent bottleneck features. In *Spoken Language Technology Workshop (SLT), 2012 IEEE*.

Ngoc Thang Vu, Florian Metze, and Tanja Schultz. 2012. Multilingual bottle-neck features and its application for under-resourced languages. In *The third International Workshop on Spoken Language Technologies for Under-resourced languages*.

Representation Learning for Discovering Phonemic Tone Contours

Bai Li[1,2], Jing Yi Xie[1], Frank Rudzicz[1,2,3]
[1] University of Toronto, Toronto, Canada
[2] Vector Institute, Toronto, Canada
[3] St Michael's Hospital, Toronto, Canada
{bai, frank}@cs.toronto.edu, jingyi.xie@mail.utoronto.ca

Abstract

Tone is a prosodic feature used to distinguish words in many languages, some of which are endangered and scarcely documented. In this work, we use unsupervised representation learning to identify probable clusters of syllables that share the same phonemic tone. Our method extracts the pitch for each syllable, then trains a convolutional autoencoder to learn a low-dimensional representation for each contour. We then apply the mean shift algorithm to cluster tones in high-density regions of the latent space. Furthermore, by feeding the centers of each cluster into the decoder, we produce a prototypical contour that represents each cluster. We apply this method to spoken multi-syllable words in Mandarin Chinese and Cantonese and evaluate how closely our clusters match the ground truth tone categories. Finally, we discuss some difficulties with our approach, including contextual tone variation and allophony effects.

1 Introduction

Tonal languages use pitch to distinguish different words, for example, *yi* in Mandarin may mean 'one', 'to move', 'already', or 'art', depending on the pitch contour. Of over 6000 languages in the world, it is estimated that as many as 60-70% are tonal (Lewis, 2009; Yip, 2002). A few of these are national languages (e.g., Mandarin Chinese, Vietnamese, and Thai), but many tonal languages have a small number of speakers and are scarcely documented. There is a limited availability of trained linguists to perform language documentation before these languages become extinct, hence the need for better tools to assist linguists in these tasks.

One of the first tasks during the description of an unfamiliar language is determining its phonemic inventory: what are the consonants, vowels, and tones of the language, and which pairs of phonemes

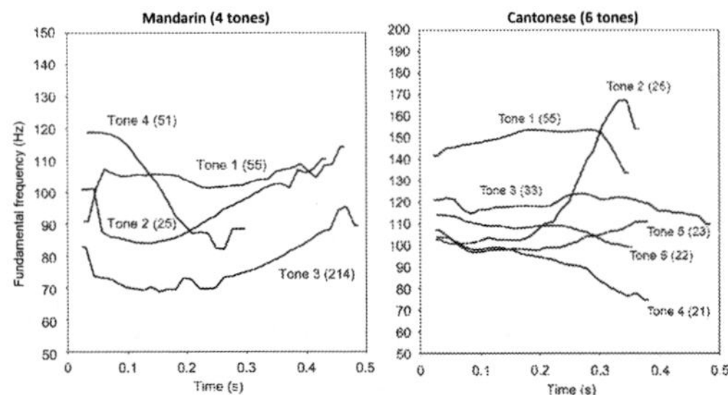

Figure 1: Fundamental frequency (F0) contours for the four Mandarin tones and six Cantonese tones in isolation, produced by native speakers. Figure adapted from (Francis et al., 2008).

are contrastive? Tone presents a unique challenge because unlike consonants and vowels, which can be identified in isolation, tones do not have a fixed pitch, and vary by speaker and situation. Since tone data is subject to interpretation, different linguists may produce different descriptions of the tone system of the same language (Yip, 2002).

In this work, we present a model to automatically infer phonemic tone categories of a tonal language. We use an unsupervised learning approach: a convolutional autoencoder learns a low-dimensional representation of each tone using only a set of spoken syllables in the target language. This is followed by mean shift clustering to identify clusters of syllables that probably have the same tone. We apply our method on Mandarin Chinese and Cantonese datasets, for which the ground truth annotation is used for evaluation. Our method does not make any language-specific assumptions, so it may be applied to low-resource languages whose phonemic inventories are not already established.

1.1 Tone in Mandarin and Cantonese

Mandarin Chinese (1.1 billion speakers) and Cantonese (74 million speakers) are two tonal lan-

217

Proceedings of the Seventeenth SIGMORPHON Workshop on Computational Research
in Phonetics, Phonology, and Morphology, pages 217–223
Online, July 10, 2020. ©2020 Association for Computational Linguistics
https://doi.org/10.18653/v1/P17

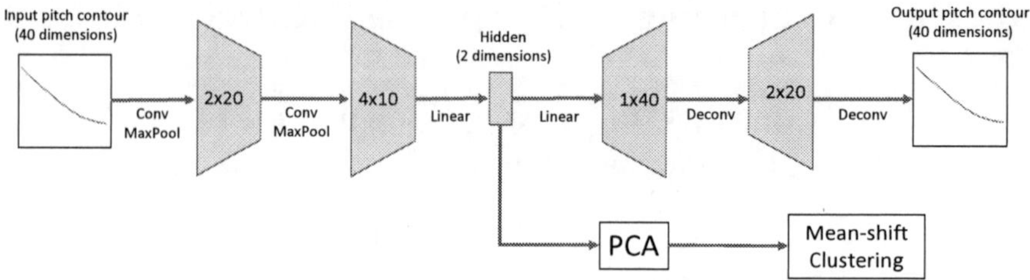

Figure 2: Diagram of our model architecture, consisting of a convolutional autoencoder to learn a latent representation for each pitch contour, and mean shift clustering to identify groups of similar tones.

guages in the Sinitic family (Lewis, 2009). Mandarin has four lexical tones: high (55), rising (25), low-dipping (214), and falling (51)[1]. The third tone sometimes undergoes sandhi, addressed in section 3. We exclude a fifth, neutral tone, which can only occur in word-final positions and has no fixed pitch.

Cantonese has six lexical tones: high-level (55), mid-rising (25), mid-level (33), low-falling (21), low-rising (23), and low-level (22). Some descriptions of Cantonese include nine tones, of which three are *checked* tones that are flat, shorter in duration, and only occur on syllables ending in /p/, /t/, or /k/. Since each one of the checked tones are in complementary distribution with an unchecked tone, we adopt the simpler six tone model that treats the checked tones as variants of the high, mid, and low level tones. Contours for the lexical tones in both languages are shown in Figure 1.

2   Related work

Many low-resource languages lack sufficient transcribed data for supervised speech processing, thus unsupervised models for speech processing is an emerging area of research. The Zerospeech 2015 and 2017 challenges featured unsupervised learning of contrasting phonemes in English and Xitsonga, evaluated by an ABX phoneme discrimination task (Versteegh et al., 2015). One successful approach used denoising and correspondence autoencoders to learn a representation that avoided capturing noise and irrelevant inter-speaker variation (Renshaw et al., 2015). Deep LSTMs for segmenting and clustering phonemes in speech have also been explored in (Müller et al., 2017b) and (Müller et al., 2017a).

In Mandarin Chinese, deep neural networks have been successful for tone classification in isolated

syllables (Chen et al., 2016) as well as in continuous speech (Ryant et al., 2014b,a). Both of these models found that Mel-frequency cepstral coefficients (MFCCs) outperformed pitch contour features, despite the fact that MFCC features do not contain pitch information. In Cantonese, support vector machines (SVMs) have been applied to classify tones in continuous speech, using pitch contours as input (Peng and Wang, 2005).

Unsupervised learning of tones remains largely unexplored. Levow (2006) performed unsupervised and semi-supervised tone clustering in Mandarin, using average pitch and slope as features, and k-means and asymmetric k-lines for clustering. Graph-based community detection techniques have been applied to group n-grams of contiguous contours into clusters in Mandarin (Zhang, 2019). In recent work concurrent to ours, Fry (2020) uses adversarial autoencoders and hierarchical clustering to identify tone inventories, and evaluate their method on Mandarin, Cantonese, Fungwa, and English data.

We further explore unsupervised deep neural networks for phonemic tone clustering. It should be noted that our unsupervised model is not given tone labels during training, and the number of tones is assumed to be unknown, so it cannot be directly compared to supervised tone classifiers in the literature.

3   Data and preprocessing

We use data from Mandarin Chinese and Cantonese. For each language, the data consists of a list of spoken words, recorded by the same speaker. The Mandarin dataset is from a female speaker and is provided by Shtooka[2], and the Cantonese dataset is from a male speaker and is downloaded from

---

[1] The numbers are Chao tone numerals, where 1 is the lowest and 5 is the highest pitch.

[2] `http://shtooka.net/`, specifically the cmn-caen-tan dataset.

Forvo[3], an online crowd-sourced pronunciation dictionary. We require all samples within each language to be from the same speaker to avoid the difficulties associated with channel effects and inter-speaker variation. We randomly sample 400 words from each language, which are mostly between 2 and 4 syllables; to reduce the prosody effects with longer utterances, we exclude words longer than 4 syllables.

We extract ground-truth tones for evaluation purposes. In Mandarin, the tones are extracted from the pinyin transcription; in Cantonese, we reference the character entries on Wiktionary[4] to retrieve the romanized pronunciation and tones. For Mandarin, we adjust for third-tone sandhi (a phonological rule where a pair of consecutive third-tones is always realized as a second-tone followed by a third-tone), and use the sandhi tone as the ground truth. We also exclude the neutral tone, which has no fixed pitch and is sometimes thought of as a lack of tone.

3.1 Pitch extraction and syllable segmentation

We use Praat's autocorrelation-based pitch estimation algorithm to extract the fundamental frequency (F0) contour for each sample, using a minimum frequency of 75Hz and a maximum frequency of 500Hz (Boersma, 1993). The interface between Python and Praat is handled using Parselmouth (Jadoul et al., 2018). We normalize the contour to be between 0 and 1, based on the speaker's pitch range.

Next, we manually segment each speech sample into syllables, necessary because syllable boundaries are not provided in our datasets. We sample the pitch at 40 equally spaced points, obtaining a constant length vector as input to our model. Note that by sampling a variable length contour to a constant length, the model does not have information about syllable length; we discuss this design choice in section 6.2.

4 Model

4.1 Convolutional autoencoder

We use a convolutional autoencoder (Figure 2) to learn a two-dimensional latent vector for each syllable. Convolutional layers are widely used in computer vision and speech processing to learn spatially local features that are invariant of position.

[3]https://forvo.com/
[4]https://en.wiktionary.org/

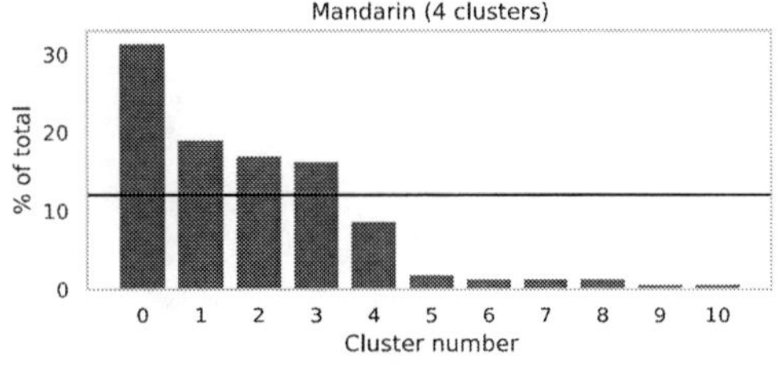

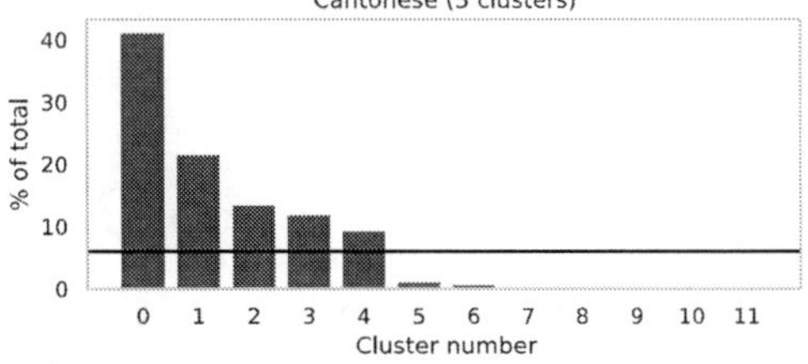

Figure 3: Clusters generated by the mean shift procedure. The black line shows the threshold: we discard clusters with size below this value and treat their points as unclustered.

We use a low dimensional latent space so that the model learns to generate a representation that only captures the most important aspects of the input contour, and also because clustering algorithms tend to perform poorly in high dimensional spaces.

Our encoder consists of three layers. The first layer applies 2 convolutional filters (kernel size 4, stride 1) followed by max pooling (kernel size 2) and a tanh activation. The second layer applies 4 convolutional filters (kernel size 4, stride 1), again with max pooling (kernel size 2) and a tanh activation. The third layer is a fully connected layer with two dimensional output. Our decoder is the encoder in reverse, consisting of one fully connected layer and two deconvolution layers, with the same layer shapes as the encoder.

We train the autoencoder using PyTorch (Paszke et al., 2017), for 500 epochs, with a batch size of 60. The model is optimized using Adam (Kingma and Ba, 2015) with a learning rate of 5e-4 to minimize the mean squared error between the input and output contours.

4.2 Mean shift clustering

We run the encoder on each syllable's pitch contour to get their latent representations; we apply principal component analysis (PCA) to remove any correlation between the two dimensions. Then, we run mean shift clustering (Comaniciu and Meer, 2002; Ghassabeh and Rudzicz, 2018), estimating

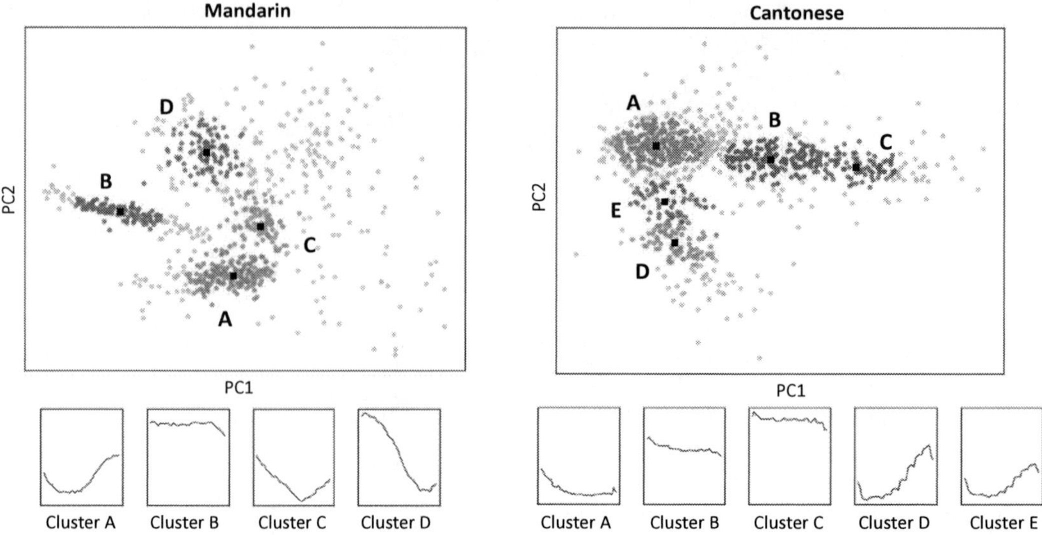

Figure 4: Latent space generated by autoencoder and the results of mean shift clustering for Mandarin and Cantonese. Each cluster center is fed through the decoder to generate the corresponding pitch contour. The clusters within each language are ordered by size, from largest to smallest.

a probability density function in the latent space. The procedure performs gradient ascent on all the points until they converge to a set of stationary points, which are local maxima of the density function. These stationary points are taken to be cluster centers, and points that converge to the same stationary point belong to the same cluster. We feed the cluster centers into the decoder to generate a prototype pitch contour for each cluster.

Unlike k-means clustering, the mean shift procedure does not require the number of clusters to be specified, only a bandwidth parameter (set to 0.6 for our experiments). The cluster centers are always in regions of high density, so they can be viewed as prototypes that represent their respective clusters. Another advantage is that unlike k-means, mean shift clustering is robust to outliers.

4.3 Selecting bandwidth and threshold

The bandwidth parameter controls the size of the clusters: a higher bandwidth value generates fewer and larger clusters. We tune the bandwidth parameter to produce linguistically plausible tone clusters: we expect between 3 to 8 different clusters, each clusters should have at least 1/10 of the points be assigned to it, and most points should belong to some cluster.

The mean shift procedure assigns every point to some cluster, even if the resulting cluster contains only a few points. Thus, we set a threshold: we treat clusters smaller than the threshold as spurious, and leave their points as unclustered. Figure 3 shows the effect of the threshold on both languages.

4.4 k-means baseline

We implement a simple k-means baseline similar to Levow (2006), using two engineered features. The first feature is the average pitch of all the points in the pitch contour; the second feature is the slope of an ordinary least squares regression fit on the pitch contour. After extracting these features for every syllable, we run k-means clustering, using the same number of clusters that is chosen by the mean shift algorithm.

5 Results

Figure 4 shows the latent space learned by the autoencoders and the clustering output. Our model found 4 tone clusters in Mandarin, matching the number of phonemic tones (Table 1) and 5 in Cantonese, which is one fewer than the number of phonemic tones (Table 2). In Mandarin, the 4 clusters correspond very well with the the 4 phonemic tone categories, and the generated contours closely match the ground truth in Figure 1. There is some overlap between tones 3 and 4; this is because tone 3 is sometimes realized a low-falling tone without the final rise, a process known as half T3 sandhi

Cluster	T1	T2	T3	T4
A	1	163	12	4
B	108	0	0	1
C	0	5	53	31
D	1	0	0	97
N/A	47	30	53	129

Table 1: Cluster and tone frequencies for Mandarin.

Cluster	T1	T2	T3	T4	T5	T6
A	5	5	59	109	7	105
B	102	3	36	2	2	7
C	93	0	0	2	0	0
D	0	64	4	3	2	11
E	0	28	2	4	30	2
N/A	70	39	51	45	15	49

Table 2: Cluster and tone frequencies for Cantonese.

(Chen, 2000), thus, it may overlap with tone 4 (falling tone).

In Cantonese, the 5 clusters A-E correspond to low-falling, mid-level, high-level, mid-rising, and low-rising tones. Tone clustering in Cantonese is expected to be more difficult than in Mandarin because of 6 contrastive tones, rather than 4. The model is more effective at clustering the higher tones (1, 2, 3), and less effective at clustering the lower tones (4, 5, 6), particularly tone 4 (low-falling) and tone 6 (low-level). This confirms the difficulties in prior work, which reported worse classification accuracy on the lower-pitched tones because the lower region of the Cantonese tone space is more crowded than the upper region (Peng and Wang, 2005).

To evaluate how much the clusters match the ground truth, we use normalized mutual information (NMI); this is preferable over accuracy because it does not require the number of detected clusters to be the same as the number of tones. In Table 3, we evaluate NMI for our autoencoder model and the k-means baseline. We consider two scenarios for each language: using all the syllables (All) and using only the first syllable of each word (First).

In all cases, the clusters from the autoencoder model have higher NMI than the k-means model. The improvement is due to the mean shift procedure identifying points that belong to a cluster with high confidence: it only only makes predictions for those points, whereas k-means assigns every point to a cluster. All models perform better on the

	Autoencoder	k-means
Mandarin (First)	0.846	0.829
Mandarin (All)	0.753	0.645
Cantonese (First)	0.575	0.493
Cantonese (All)	0.463	0.377

Table 3: Normalized mutual information (NMI) between cluster assignments and ground truth tones, considering only the first syllable of each word, or all syllables.

first syllable of each utterance than the rest of the syllables; we discuss the reasons for this in the next section.

6 Limitations

6.1 Contextual effects

One limitation of our model is it considers syllables in isolation, but in reality, pitch is affected by context. Two types of contextual effects are carry-over and declination. A carry-over effect is when the pitch contour of a tone undergoes contextual variation depending on the preceding tone; strong carry-over effects have been observed in Mandarin (Xu, 1997). Prior work (Levow, 2006) avoided carry-over effects by using only the second half of every syllable, but we do not consider language-specific heuristics in our model.

Declination is a phenomenon in which the pitch declines over an utterance (Yip, 2002; Peng and Wang, 2005). This is especially a problem in Cantonese, which has tones that differ only on pitch level and not contour: for example, a mid-level tone near the end of a phrase may have the same absolute pitch as a low-level tone at the start of a phrase.

Contextual effects are apparent in our results (Table 3). In both Mandarin and Cantonese, the clustering is more accurate when using only the first syllable (which is not affected by carry-over or declination), compared to using all the syllables.

6.2 Minimal pairs and allotones

Tone is not a purely phonetic property: it is impossible to determine, from phonetics alone, whether two pitch contours have the same or different tones. The same underlying tone may manifest as several different allotones depending on the phonetic context.

An example of this appears in Cantonese. Its tone system is sometimes analyzed as having nine tones instead of six, where six of the tones are only permitted in open syllables (e.g. *si*) and three are only permitted in checked syllables (e.g. *sik*). Other analyses use a six-tone system, treating the three checked tones as allotonic variants of the high, mid, and low tones. By taking this approach, one implies that length is a property of the syllable and cannot be solely responsible for contrasting two tones.

Length is not the only differentiating factor for allotones. Another example is in Wu Chinese, where syllables beginning with voiced consonants have lower pitch than those beginning with voiceless consonants (Yip, 2002). Thus the same language may have vastly different numbers of tones, depending on the analysis.

Linguistically, two phonemic tones are considered to be contrastive if there exists a minimal pair: two semantically different lexical items that are identical in every aspect except for tone. This definition is the most widely used because it clearly settles disagreements about whether two tones are same or different. However, it is problematic for unsupervised models that only have access to phonetic and not semantic information. This issue is not unique to tone: similar difficulties have been noted when attempting to identify consonant and vowel phonemes automatically (Kempton and Moore, 2014).

7 Conclusion

We propose a model for unsupervised clustering and discovery of phonemic tones in tonal languages, using spoken words as input. Our model extracts the F0 pitch contour, trains a convolutional autoencoder to learn a low-dimensional representation for each contour, and applies mean shift clustering to the resulting latent space. We obtain promising results with both Mandarin Chinese and Cantonese, using only 400 spoken words from each language. Cantonese presents more difficulties because of its larger number of tones, especially at the lower half of the pitch range, and also due to multiple contrastive level tones. Still, in both our languages, our method finds clusters of tones that better match the ground truth than the k-means baseline. Finally, we discuss the effects of contextual variation and the limitations of unsupervised learning for the tone induction problem.

8 Acknowledgments

We thank Prof Gerald Penn for his help suggestions during this project. Rudzicz is a CIFAR Chair in AI.

References

Paul Boersma. 1993. Accurate short-term analysis of the fundamental frequency and the harmonics-to-noise ratio of a sampled sound. In *Proceedings of the institute of phonetic sciences*, volume 17, pages 97–110. Amsterdam.

Charles Chen, Razvan C Bunescu, Li Xu, and Chang Liu. 2016. Tone classification in Mandarin Chinese using convolutional neural networks. In *INTERSPEECH*, pages 2150–2154.

Matthew Y Chen. 2000. *Tone sandhi: Patterns across Chinese dialects*, volume 92. Cambridge University Press.

Dorin Comaniciu and Peter Meer. 2002. Mean shift: A robust approach toward feature space analysis. *IEEE Transactions on Pattern Analysis & Machine Intelligence*, (5):603–619.

Alexander L Francis, Valter Ciocca, Lian Ma, and Kimberly Fenn. 2008. Perceptual learning of Cantonese lexical tones by tone and non-tone language speakers. *Journal of Phonetics*, 36(2):268–294.

Michael David Fry. 2020. *Grammaticus ex machina: tone inventories as hypothesized by machine*. Ph.D. thesis, University of British Columbia.

Y Aliyari Ghassabeh and F Rudzicz. 2018. Modified mean shift algorithm. *IET Image Processing*, 12(12):2172–2177.

Yannick Jadoul, Bill Thompson, and Bart De Boer. 2018. Introducing Parselmouth: A Python interface to Praat. *Journal of Phonetics*, 71:1–15.

Timothy Kempton and Roger K Moore. 2014. Discovering the phoneme inventory of an unwritten language: A machine-assisted approach. *Speech Communication*, 56:152–166.

Diederik P Kingma and Jimmy Ba. 2015. Adam: A method for stochastic optimization. *ICLR*.

Gina-Anne Levow. 2006. Unsupervised and semi-supervised learning of tone and pitch accent. In *Proceedings of the main conference on Human Language Technology Conference of the North American Chapter of the Association of Computational Linguistics*, pages 224–231. Association for Computational Linguistics.

M. Paul Lewis. 2009. *Ethnologue: Languages of the World*, 16th edition. SIL International, Dallas, Texas.

Markus Müller, Jörg Franke, Sebastian Stüker, and Alex Waibel. 2017a. Improving phoneme set discovery for documenting unwritten languages. *Elektronische Sprachsignalverarbeitung (ESSV)*, 2017.

Markus Müller, Jörg Franke, Alex Waibel, and Sebastian Stüker. 2017b. Towards phoneme inventory discovery for documentation of unwritten languages. In *2017 IEEE International Conference on Acoustics, Speech and Signal Processing (ICASSP)*, pages 5200–5204. IEEE.

Adam Paszke, Sam Gross, Soumith Chintala, Gregory Chanan, Edward Yang, Zachary DeVito, Zeming Lin, Alban Desmaison, Luca Antiga, and Adam Lerer. 2017. Automatic differentiation in PyTorch. In *NIPS Autodiff Workshop*.

Gang Peng and William S-Y Wang. 2005. Tone recognition of continuous Cantonese speech based on support vector machines. *Speech Communication*, 45(1):49–62.

Daniel Renshaw, Herman Kamper, Aren Jansen, and Sharon Goldwater. 2015. A comparison of neural network methods for unsupervised representation learning on the zero resource speech challenge. In *Sixteenth Annual Conference of the International Speech Communication Association*.

Neville Ryant, Malcolm Slaney, Mark Liberman, Elizabeth Shriberg, and Jiahong Yuan. 2014a. Highly accurate Mandarin tone classification in the absence of pitch information. In *Proceedings of Speech Prosody*, volume 7.

Neville Ryant, Jiahong Yuan, and Mark Liberman. 2014b. Mandarin tone classification without pitch tracking. In *2014 IEEE International Conference on Acoustics, Speech and Signal Processing (ICASSP)*, pages 4868–4872. IEEE.

Maarten Versteegh, Roland Thiolliere, Thomas Schatz, Xuan Nga Cao, Xavier Anguera, Aren Jansen, and Emmanuel Dupoux. 2015. The zero resource speech challenge 2015. In *Sixteenth Annual Conference of the International Speech Communication Association*.

Yi Xu. 1997. Contextual tonal variations in Mandarin. *Journal of phonetics*, 25(1):61–83.

Moira Yip. 2002. *Tone*. Cambridge University Press.

Shuo Zhang. 2019. Data mining Mandarin tone contour shapes. *SIGMORPHON 2019*, page 144.

Joint learning of constraint weights and gradient inputs in Gradient Symbolic Computation with constrained optimization

Max Nelson

University of Massachusetts, Amherst

Amherst, MA, USA

manelson@umass.edu

Abstract

This paper proposes a method for the joint optimization of constraint weights and symbol activations within the Gradient Symbolic Computation (GSC) framework. The set of grammars representable in GSC is proven to be a subset of those representable with lexically-scaled faithfulness constraints. This fact is then used to recast the problem of learning constraint weights and symbol activations in GSC as a quadratically-constrained version of learning lexically-scaled faithfulness grammars. This results in an optimization problem that can be solved using Sequential Quadratic Programming.

1 Introduction and background

This paper proposes a method for the joint optimization of constraint weights and symbol activations within the Gradient Symbolic Computation (GSC) framework. The set of grammars representable in GSC is proven to be a subset of those representable with lexically-scaled faithfulness constraints. This fact is then used to recast the problem of learning constraint weights and symbol activations in GSC as a quadratically-constrained version of learning lexically-scaled faithfulness grammars. This results in an optimization problem that can be solved using Sequential Quadratic Programming.

The remainder of this paper proceeds as follows. The rest of this section provides the relevant background on GSC, previous approaches to the same problem, and maximum entropy grammars which are used in the proposed model. §2 describes and proves the relationship between GSC grammars and lexically-scaled faithfulness constraints and then uses this proof to develop the proposed learning algorithm. §3 illustrates with a minimal test case of an example used through the GSC literature, French Liaison. §4 provides a brief discussion and concludes.

1.1 Phonological grammars in Gradient Symbolic Computation

Gradient Symbolic Computation is a general cognitive framework in which structures are represented as gradient blends of multiple symbolic representations. Smolensky and Goldrick (2016) adapt standard optimality-theoretic constraints and optimization procedures to allow for inputs which consist of blends of symbolic structures. They propose that each position in the input is associated with a blend of discrete units, each of which is associated with an activation. In phonological terms an input may be composed of a series of positions, each of which is associated with a set of phonemes with different degrees of activation. The evaluation of constraints that make reference to the input, traditionally only faithfulness constraints, is done with respect to the activations of individual segments in the gradient representation. So if this partially active /t/ is fully realized, then a constraint like Dep, which penalizes epenthesis, will be violated to the degree that reflects the extent of this epenthesis: in this example, a violation of strength 0.3. Phonological grammars that allow for gradient inputs will henceforth be referred to as gradient symbolic grammars (GS grammars).

GS grammars have been employed to capture phonological phenomena that are difficult for traditional representational theories, including opacity (Mai et al., 2018), and exceptionality (Zimmerman, 2018; Hsu, 2018)/subregularity (Rosen, 2016; Smolensky and Goldrick, 2016).

1.2 Learning gradient symbolic grammars

GS grammars present a unique learning problem. In standard constraint-based grammars a phonological learner must discover the discrete underlying forms of the target language as well as the ranking or weighting of the constraints. In GS gram-

Proceedings of the Seventeenth SIGMORPHON Workshop on Computational Research in Phonetics, Phonology, and Morphology, pages 224–232

Online, July 10, 2020. ©2020 Association for Computational Linguistics

https://doi.org/10.18653/v1/P17

mars the learner has to learn these things as well, while also learning the activations of all symbols at all positions in the underlying form. The complete GS grammar learning problem, discovering the discrete units, their activations, and the constraint ordering, has not been addressed in previous literature and will not be addressed here. Previous work has however looked at different subparts of this problem, including the learning of activations in isolation (Rosen, 2019) and the parallel learning of activations and constraint weights (Rosen, 2016; Smolensky et al., 2020). This parallel problem is the topic of the present work.

Rosen (2016) presents an approach to jointly optimizing constraint weights and input activations based on simulated annealing which is able to successfully learn a grammar capturing Japanese rendaku. As will be discussed below, the joint optimization of weights and activations is non-convex so simulated annealing is a promising approach. This work will not attempt to improve on the empirical performance of a simulated annealing model, but rather it will propose an alternative approach which is more closely related to gradient-based methods used elsewhere in the phonological learning literature (Goldwater and Johnson, 2003; Boersma and Pater, 2008; Hayes and Wilson, 2008).

Smolensky et al. (2020) apply the Gradual Learning Algorithm (GLA) for Harmonic Grammar (Boersma and Pater, 2008), which is based on the Perceptron Update Rule (Rosenblatt, 1958), to the problem of learning both constraint weights and input activations. They report promising results, however the convergence proof for the GLA does not necessarily apply to the case of GS grammars, where multiple interacting parameters are being simultaneously optimized. As will be discussed later, activations add quadratic terms to the Harmony function. This means that Harmonies are not linear in the parameters and consequently the relationship between Harmonic Grammar and the Perceptron does not hold between GS grammar and the Perceptron.

This work presents a third approach to jointly learning activations and constraint weights, based on the fact that blended inputs represent a scaling function on faithfulness violations and on previous work which has explored the learning of scaled faithfulness. The presented model is also not guaranteed to converge on a global optimum, so it does

not improve on the GLA approach in that respect. It does however have the benefit of casting the GS grammar learning problem as an explicit and well-understood optimization procedure while also relating it to a familiar problem, learning lexically-scaled constraint weights (Hughto et al., 2019).

1.3 Maximum entropy grammars

Unlike previous work in GSC, the learning algorithm in the present work will make use of Maximum Entropy (MaxEnt) Grammars (Goldwater and Johnson, 2003). A MaxEnt grammar is a log-linear model which allows for the probabilistic interpretation of a Harmonic Grammar (HG). In Harmonic Grammar the Harmony $\mathcal{H}$ of a candidate is the dot-product of its constraint violations and the constraint weights. Constraint violations are generally treated as strictly negative and weights as strictly positive, so given an input x a candidate y is optimal if it has the highest Harmony score in the set of all competing candidates $\mathcal{Y}(x)$.

$$\mathcal{H}_{(x,y)} = \sum_i w_i c_i(x, y) \qquad (1)$$

A MaxEnt probability distribution is computed by applying the softmax function to the set of Harmonies.

$$p(x) = \frac{e^{\mathcal{H}_{(x,y)}}}{\sum_{\gamma \in \mathcal{Y}(x)} e^{\mathcal{H}_{(x,\gamma)}}} \qquad (2)$$

MaxEnt grammars are used for the learning algorithm purely because it is intuitive to define an interpretable loss function when model outputs are a probability distribution, as will be discussed in §2.2. This is an expository choice: the learning algorithm presented below could be equivalently described as learning a Harmonic Grammar by minimizing a loss function that incorporates the softmax function. Because softmax is monotonic, a MaxEnt grammar makes the same prediction about the most well-formed candidate as its corresponding Harmonic Grammar.

2 Optimizing gradient symbolic grammars

2.1 Gradient symbolic computation as lexically scaled faithfulness

The observation driving the proposed learning algorithm for GS grammars is that GS grammars can be rewritten as a special case of lexically-scaled faithfulness (LSF) grammars. An LSF grammar (Linzen et al., 2013) is a grammar in which all morphemes come with a set of scales which combine additively with constraint weights. This section aims to prove that the set of expressible GS grammars is a subset of the expressible LSF grammars.

In this work I assume all outputs are discrete structures and consequently only faithfulness constraints are gradiently evaluated[1]. Within the faithfulness constraints, Smolensky and Goldrick (2016) describe two classes in terms of how gradient activations in the input influence evaluation. Constraints belonging to the PROPORTIONAL class are violated to a degree proportional to the activation level of a deleted feature or segment, for example MAX constraints in Smolensky and Goldrick. Constraints belonging to the COMPLEMENT class are violated to a degree proportional to one minus the activation level of a realized feature or segment, for example DEP constraints in Smolensky and Goldrick. Introducing gradient inputs to the grammar results in a rescaling of faithfulness constraint violations and in no effect on markedness constraint violations[2].

Consider the simple GS tableau in (1), where α is the activation of the input segment b, M is the weight of a PROPORTIONAL constraint, and Δ is the weight of some COMPLEMENT constraint. Two hypothetical candidates are competing on which of the two constraints is violated. Note that Harmony is a quadratic function of the weights and activations.

(1)

	M	Δ	
$/b_\alpha/$	PROP	COMP	$\mathcal{H}$
ϕ	0	$1-\alpha$	$\Delta - \alpha\Delta$
ψ	α	0	αM

Now consider the grammar in (2), which uses lexically scaled faithfulness (LSF) constraints. The scales are indexed to the input morpheme(s) and combine additively with constraint weights. So the functional weight of PROP when evaluated on the ith morpheme is the general weight of PROP, M, added with the scale brought by morpheme i, μ_i

(Linzen et al., 2013). In this case Harmony is a linear function of the weights and scales.

(2)

	μ_i	δ_i	
	M	Δ	
$/b/_i$	PROP	COMP	$\mathcal{H}$
[b]	0	1	$\Delta + \delta_i$
$\emptyset$	1	0	$M + \mu_i$

The tableaux in (1) and (2) make identical predictions as long as the equalities in Eq. (3) hold. In other words if these equalities are true then the two grammars assign the exact same Harmonies to the candidates.

$$\Delta - \alpha\Delta = \Delta + \delta_i$$
$$\alpha M = M + \mu_i \tag{3}$$

Given this fact, any GS grammar can be converted into an LSF grammar by replacing any morpheme's activation values with a set of scales. Scales for COMP and PROP constraints can be computed from activations by rearranging Eq. (3), as in Eq. (4).

$$\delta_i = -\alpha\Delta$$
$$\mu_i = \alpha M - M \tag{4}$$

Eq. (4) proves that any function representable with a GS grammar can be expressed with an equivalent LSF grammar. The converse however is not true – there are functions representable in LSF grammars that are not representable in GS grammars. This is be illustrated by considering how Eq. (3) would be used to convert an arbitrary LSF grammar into a GS grammar. Converting in this direction requires computing activations from the set of lexical scales. By rearranging Eq. (3), we see that there are two ways to compute activations from a given LSF grammar. Activations can be computed either from the MAX constraints or from the DEP constraints.

$$\alpha = \frac{\mu_i}{M} + 1$$
$$\alpha = -\frac{\delta_i}{\Delta} \tag{5}$$

It is not possible for a single segment or feature to have multiple distinct activation levels. An LSF grammar is a valid GS grammar only if both methods of computing a yield the same result. So while there is an LSF grammar for every GS grammar,

---

[1]In GSC this is expressed a strong quantization constraint, which pushes outputs into discrete states (Smolensky et al., 2014; Cho et al., 2017)

[2] Zimmerman (2018) advocates for gradient outputs, which will allow for gradiently evaluated markedness constraints. The approach outlined below can be extended to cover this by allowing for lexically scaled markedness constraints as well

there is not a GS grammar for every LSF grammar. Only the subset of LSF grammars that satisfy the equality in Eq. (6) are valid GS grammars.

$$\frac{\mu_i}{M} + 1 = -\frac{\delta_i}{\Delta} \quad (6)$$

For simplicity, Eq. (6) can be rearranged as in Eq. (7).

$$\mu_i\Delta + M\Delta + \delta_i M = 0 \quad (7)$$

This does not necessarily mean anything about the linguistic expressivity of GS and LSF grammars. The conversion from GS to LSF grammar assumes that there are no limits on the constraint set and consequently may require theoretically unwieldy constraints. For example in order to capture the fact that there are separate activations at all positions in the input, there must be separate constraints for every feature at every position in the input. This point is ultimately unimportant for the present work, which aims to address the relationship between the mathematical, rather than linguistic, functions that are representable in the two theories with the purpose of leveraging this relationship to construct a learning algorithm for GS grammars. The next section will outline exactly how this subset-superset relationship can be used to to formulate the problem of simultaneously learning input activations and constraint weights as a quadratically constrained optimization problem.

2.2 Learning gradient symbolic grammars with constrained optimization

The relationship between GS and LSF grammars described above is useful because it allows the problem of learning constraint weights and activations to be related to a well-understood problem, learning constraint weights and additive scales. Additive scales are themselves a special case of another formalism, lexically-indexed constraints. Because the scaled violations combine additively in the Harmony function, lexical scales can be represented as indexed versions of their general form which always incur the same number of violations as the general form. Moore-Cantwell and Pater (2016) show that the problem of learning lexically-indexed constraint weights is no different than the standard MaxEnt optimization problem and Hughto et al. (2019) show that similar approaches can be taken to learning additive lexical scales. So, like in standard MaxEnt (Goldwater and Johnson, 2003), the

task of learning an LSF grammar can be cast as optimizing the negative log-likelihood of the training data [3], which is convex in the constraint weights.

Unfortunately, because of the subset-superset relationship between GS and LSF grammars, the problem of learning GS grammars is not similarly reducible to the standard convex MaxEnt learning problem. Rather, the GS learning problem can be reduced to a constrained version of the LSF learning problem. Learning a GS grammar is equivalent to learning an LSF grammar subject to the hard constraint that the LSF grammar represents a possible GS grammar. This can be stated formally as the optimization problem in Eq. (8), where $p(x)$ is computed using the standard MaxEnt probability function in Eq. (2). The weight vector w includes: General PROP and COMP weights M and Δ, i lexically indexed scales on PROP $\mu_1, ..., \mu_i$, i lexically indexed scales on COMP $\delta_1, ..., \delta_i$, and n general markedness constraints $m^1, ..., m^n$. The rightmost term in the objective function is an L2 prior with strength λ.

$$w = [M, \Delta, \mu_1 ..., \mu_i, \delta_1 ..., \delta_i, m^1, ..., m^n]$$

$$\min_w \left[\left(-\sum_x log\, p(x) \right) + \lambda \parallel w \parallel_2 \right]$$

$$\text{Subject to: } \sum_i (\mu_i\Delta + M\Delta + \delta_i M)^2 = 0 \quad (8)$$

The constraint enforcing that the learned grammar is a viable GS grammar is the equality relationship in Eq. (7) summed over all input phonemes i. The constraint is squared within the sum to prevent positive and negative terms in the summation from canceling out. This ensures that activations computed for a given phoneme and morpheme index from both the PROP and COMP constraints will be guaranteed to return the same value.

There are a number of potential approaches to constrained optimization problems like that posed above. It is worth mentioning here why methods familiar in computational phonology will not work. Maximum Entropy and Harmonic Grammars are generally fit using projected gradient descent, which is itself a method of constrained optimization. This entails computing the weight update, independent of any constraints placed on the weights,

---

[3]Or other equivalent loss function, such as Kullback-Leibler divergence

and then projecting the updated weights onto the set defined by the constraint. The use familiar in phonology is in the enforcement non-negativity – a restriction against negative weights which maintains the theoretical tenant of Optimality Theory that constraints can penalize but not reward. In this case projected gradient descent is effective. Not only is the projection function simple to compute because the nearest non-negative number to any negative number is 0, but the space defined by the constraint is a convex set, meaning that projected gradient descent with this constraint has the same convergence guarantees as standard gradient descent (Levitin and Polyak, 1966). As defined in Eq. (8) the current problem is quadratically constrained, meaning that the set that satisfies the constraint is non-convex and a projection function onto the set is not easily computable. Consequently projected gradient descent is not only not guaranteed to converge, it is computationally intractable.

Another possible approach would be to treat the constraint as a prior. One simple issue with this is that priors are violable. Given that the goal is learn a GS grammar, the constraint on the solution space defined above cannot be violated. One possible workaround would be to set the strength of the prior arbitrarily high, making it functionally non-violable. However the intersection of the loss function and the space satisfying the constraint is non-convex and is not guaranteed to be connected. Consequently gradient descent and other widely applied optimization techniques are likely to fail.

The proposed solution is to use Sequential Quadratic Programming (SQP), an iterative generalization of Newton's method developed for minimizing a function under quadratic constraints. The general approach is to iteratively take the quadratic approximation of the constrained objective function at w, minimize this subproblem with quadratic programming, and then set w to the solution. This will yield increasingly better approximations and therefore increasingly better solutions. On a practical note, this requires computing the first three terms of the Taylor expansion of the objective function at a given point, meaning that it must be twice differentiable. For detailed derivation and discussion of the method see Boggs and Tolle (1995).

3 An example

To illustrate the promise of the proposed approach to learning GS grammars, this section applies it to a minimal example of the French liaison problem that Smolensky and Goldrick (2016) use to motivate the use of gradient representations in the phonological grammar. Liaison is a phenomenon in which, in certain syntactic contexts, a consonant surfaces between vowel-final and vowel-initial words when hiatus would otherwise occur. The identity of this consonant, the liaison consonant, is not phonologically predictable. There is a long literature on the phonological analysis on liaison and its interacting processes, including competing analyses that propose that the liaison consonant is specified by the first word (Tranel, 1996) and by the second word in the sequence (Morin, 2005).

There is a class of words which are phonologically vowel initial but exceptionally do not trigger the surfacing of a liaison consonant in environments where it is otherwise predicted to surface. These words are always the second word in the pair and are called the h-aspiré words, referencing the fact that they are orthographically h-initial.

Consider the following set of French surface forms. When *petit* comes together with *ami*, a vowel-initial word, the liaison consonant [t] surfaces.

[pøti] *petit*	+	[ami] *ami*
'small'		'friend'
[pøti<u>ta</u>mi]	*petit ami*	'boyfriend'

However, when *petit* is followed by *héros*, an h-aspiré word, no liaison consonant surfaces.

[pøti] *petit*	+	[eʁo] *héros*
'small'		'hero'
[pøt<u>ie</u>ʁo]	*petit héros*	'little hero'

The adjective [pøti] *petit* is associated with a liaison *t*. When it occurs in isolation the liaison consonant does not surface, however when it occurs before the vowel-initial [ami] *ami* the liaison consonant surfaces, preventing two adjacent vowels from surfacing. Despite being vowel-initial, the h-aspiré word [eʁo] *héros* does not trigger the surfacing of the liaison consonant when it surfaces after *peti*.

Smolensky and Goldrick (2016) offer an analysis of this phenomenon couched in Gradient Symbolic Computation, which suggests that the liaison consonant is specified by both the first and second word in the pair. In their analysis both words contain partially active edge consonants. When the words surface together the combined activation is enough to get cause the liaison consonant to surface. In this analysis h-aspiré words differ from their liaison-participating counterparts in that they have no or minimal activation on liaison consonants at their left edge, preventing them from contributing to the combined activation.

In terms of the minimal dataset above, they propose that there is a partially-activated /t/ in the input at both the right edge of *peti* and at the left edge of *ami*. When either word occurs in isolation there is not sufficient activation of the /t/ for it to surface. When the two words surface adjacent to one another the combined activation of /t/ in both words overcomes a threshold and liaison [t] surfaces. In the h-aspiré *héros* there is little to no activation on an input /t/ at the left edge. Despite the consequence of realizing a marked vowel-vowel sequence, the liaison [t] does not surface between [pøti] and [eʁo] because the combined activation of the input /t/s is not enough to justify its realization. They argue that this analysis overcomes empirical shortcomings of analyses which place the onus of specifying the liaison consonant on exclusively the first or second consonant, see Smolensky and Goldrick (2016) and Smolensky et al. (2020) for detailed discussion.

As proof of concept a GS grammar was fit to these data using the procedure described above. Model parameters include the weight of three constraints, HIATUS, MAX(t) and DEP(t), as well as the activation levels of liaison /t/ at the left edge of *petit* and at the right edge of *ami* and *héros*. MAX(t) is a PROP constraint and DEP(t) is a COMP constraint. In every tableau there are two competing candidates, one in which [t] surfaces and one in which it does not. Activations were constrained to being positive by adding the constraint in Eq. (9) to the optimization procedure.

$$\sum_i \min\left(\frac{\mu_i}{M} + 1, 0\right) = 0 \qquad (9)$$

In practice the Jacobian and Hessian of the objective function are estimated analytically, so the algorithm described above is non-deterministic. The quadratically-constrained optimization problem is also generally non-convex, so variation is expected across runs. Consequently 10 models were fit with weights randomly initialized in [-2,0). An L2 prior is included with $\lambda = 0.01$. Table (1) shows the average final probability of each candidate in the five tableaux across the 10 runs.

	Candidate	avg.	s.d.
▷	[pøti]	0.999	1e-4
	[pøtit]	0.001	
▷	[ami]	0.991	0.003
	[tami]	0.008	
▷	[eʁo]	0.999	2e-7
	[teʁo]	1e-6	
▷	[pøtit ami]	0.980	0.009
	[pøti ami]	0.020	
	[pøtit eʁo]	0.015	0.005
▷	[pøti eʁo]	0.985	

Table 1: Average final probability across 10 runs on all forms. ▷ indicates the target surface forms.

The average activations of input /t/s in all words are shown in Table (2). Recall that there are two possible ways to compute the activations, from the COMP or PROP constraints. To ensure that the model works correctly, both methods of computing activations are shown. Note that these are negligibly different, confirming that the final grammar is indeed a valid GS grammar.

	COMP	PROP
pøti(t)	0.296 (0.062)	0.296 (0.062)
(t)ami	0.614 (0.081)	0.614 (0.081)
(t)eʁo	-2e-5 (6e-5)	-1e-4 (2e-4)

Table 2: Average (s.d.) activation of liaison consonants in all words as computed from the Δ and M constraints.

The activations suggest that the model may be converging on a solution that resembles the analysis proposed by Smolensky and Goldrick. *Petit* and *ami* both have a partially-activated /t/ in the at the relevant edge, while the activation of liaison /t/ in *héros* is approximately 0. The individual tableaux confirm that the learned analysis resembles Smolensky and Goldrick's. For simplicity, and consistency with previous work, all tableaux will be presented without probabilities, as HG tableaux.

While *petit* and *ami* both have partially-activated underlying /t/s, the activation is low enough that when either of these words occur in isolation the /t/ is not realized. This is demonstrated in Tableaux (3) and (4).

$$(3) \quad \frac{/\text{pøtit}_{0.30}/}{\begin{array}{c}[\text{pøti}]\\[\text{pøtit}]\end{array}} \;\left|\; \begin{array}{ccc} -13.1 & -5.3 & -0.4 \\ \textsc{Dep}(t) & \textsc{Hiatus} & \textsc{Max}(t) \\ \hline 0 & 0 & 0.30 \\ 0.70 & 0 & 0 \end{array} \;\right|\; \begin{array}{c}\mathscr{H}\\ \hline -0.12 \\ -9.59\end{array}$$

(3) /pøtit$_{0.30}$/	−13.1 DEP(t)	−5.3 HIATUS	−0.4 MAX(t)	$\mathscr{H}$
[pøti]	0	0	0.30	-0.12
[pøtit]	0.70	0	0	-9.59

(4) /t$_{0.61}$ami/	−13.1 DEP(t)	−5.3 HIATUS	−0.4 MAX(t)	$\mathscr{H}$
[ami]	0	0	0.61	-0.24
[tami]	0.39	0	0	-5.12

In *héros* the underlying liaison /t/ has a 0 activation, so it trivially does not surface in isolation.

(5) /t$_{0.00}$eʁo/	−13.1 DEP(t)	−5.3 HIATUS	−0.4 MAX(t)	$\mathscr{H}$
[eʁo]	0	0	0.0	-0.0
[teʁo]	1.0	0	0	-13.1

When *petit* and *ami* are realized next to one another, their combined activation, as well as the threat of a HIATUS violation, are enough to make the liaison consonant surface.

(6) /pøti t$_{0.30+0.61}$ ami/	−13.1 DEP(t)	−5.3 HIATUS	−0.4 MAX(t)	$\mathscr{H}$
[pøtiami]	0	1	1.01	-5.70
[pøtitami]	0.01	0	0	-0.13

However this is not the case when *petit* and *héros* surface together. Because *héros* contributes 0 activation to /t/, the cost of epenthesizing the remaining activation needed for the /t/ to be realized does not outweigh the cost of incurring a HIATUS violation.

(7) /pøti t$_{0.30+0.00}$ eʁo/	−13.1 DEP(t)	−5.3 HIATUS	−0.4 MAX(t)	$\mathscr{H}$
[pøtieʁo]	0	1	0.30	-5.42
[pøtiteʁo]	0.70	0	0	-9.17

The presented learning algorithm for GS grammars reliably converges on the analysis of French liaison offered by Smolensky and Goldrick (2016) as a motivating pattern for the inclusion of gradient inputs in the phonological grammar. This serves to illustrate the fact that the proposed learning algorithm is capable of learning interpretable GS grammars and has promising application in future work, both in finding GSC analyses of linguistic phenomena and in evaluating the learnability of phenomena in the GSC framework.

4 Discussion and Conclusions

This paper has presented a method for the joint optimization of blended inputs and constraint weights in gradient symbolic grammars. The proposed method leverages the fact that the set of functions representable by GS grammars is a subset of those representable by lexically-scaled faithfulness grammars to cast the GS grammar learning problem as a constrained version of the LSF grammar learning problem. The primary aim of this work is to introduce and justify the method, rather than discuss its implications for linguistic theory, however points of interest to linguistic theory will be briefly addressed here.

The subset-superset relationship that was shown to hold between GS and LSF grammars does not make predictions regarding the expressivity of the two theories in terms of the linguistic phenomena they are capable of representing. It does, however, highlight differences between the two theories which may provide a starting point for comparing their linguistic expressivity. For example, representing GS grammars in the LSF framework requires a set of faithfulness constraints which make reference to every position in every input. This differs from standard approaches to positional faithfulness, where faithfulness constraints make reference to prosodic positions (Beckman, 1998), and may yield pathological predictions. Consequently, despite the fact that LSF grammars represent a greater range of functions, it is likely that there are phenomena that can be captured with GS grammars but not with LSF grammars given a limited constraint set. This is left to future work.

This work has also shown that the optimization problem for GS grammars is likely more difficult than the analogous problem in other frameworks designed to capture the same types of phonological phenomena. For example, grammars with lexically-scaled constraints like those mentioned throughout this paper have also been shown to capture lexical exceptionality and subregularity but, as described, they correspond to a convex optimization problem. Similarly, grammars with underlying representation constraints have also been shown to be a viable approach to capturing these phonological phenomena (Apoussidou, 2007; Smith, 2015) and, in learning problems like that described in this paper present a convex optimization problem. The critical difference between these approaches and GS grammars is that Harmony function for GS grammars is quadratic, consequently the optimization problem is not guaranteed to be convex. It is not necessarily the case that the complexity of the related optimization problems is a valid metric along which to compare linguistic theories. Previous work however, has made strong claims regarding the relationship between the numerical optimization of Max-Ent/HG grammars and the learning trajectories of human language learners (Boersma et al., 2000; Jäger, 2007; Jesney and Tessier, 2008, 2011), in which case there may be merit in comparing the optimization procedure for competing theories.

The broader GSC framework offers a novel theory of phonological grammars, the expressivity and restrictiveness of which has not been thoroughly explored. This work hopes to facilitate further research by introducing a method for simultaneously learning constraint weights and input activations of GS grammars which both relates GS grammars to an existing phonological framework and serves as a tool in finding GS analyses of phonological phenomena.

Acknowledgments

Thank you to Katherine Blake, Gaja Jarosz, Andrew Lamont, Joe Pater, Brandon Prickett and everyone at UMass Sound Workshop for productive discussion of the ideas presented above, as well as to four anonymous SIGMORPHON reviewers for specific comments on this paper. All remaining errors are my own.

References

Diana Apoussidou. 2007. *The learnability of metrical phonology*. Ph.D. thesis, University of Amsterdam.

Jill N. Beckman. 1998. *Positional faithfulness*. Ph.D. thesis.

Paul Boersma, Clara Levelt, et al. 2000. Gradual constraint-ranking learning algorithm predicts acquisition order. In *Proceedings of Child Language Research Forum*, volume 30, pages 229–237. CSLI Publications Stanford, CA.

Paul Boersma and Joe Pater. 2008. Convergence properties of a gradual learning algorithm for harmonic grammar.

Paul T. Boggs and Jon W. Tolle. 1995. Sequential quadratic programming. *Acta numerica*, 4:1–51.

Pyeong Whan Cho, Matthew Goldrick, and Paul Smolensky. 2017. Incremental parsing in a continuous dynamical system: Sentence processing in gradient symbolic computation. *Linguistics Vanguard*, 3(1).

Sharon Goldwater and Mark Johnson. 2003. Learning OT constraint rankings using a maximum entropy model. *Proceedings of the Stockholm Workshop on Variation in Optimality Theory*, pages 111–120.

Bruce Hayes and Colin Wilson. 2008. A maximum entropy model of phonotactic and phonotactic learning. *Linguistic Inquiry*, 39(3):379–440.

Brian Hsu. 2018. Scalar constraints and gradient symbolic representations generate exceptional prosodification effects without exceptional prosody. In *Handout, West Coast Conference on Formal Linguistics*, volume 36.

Coral Hughto, Andrew Lamont, Brandon Prickett, and Gaja Jarosz. 2019. Learning exceptionality and variation with lexically scaled maxent. In *Proceedings of the Second Annual Meeting of the Society for Computation in Linguistics (SCiL)*.

Gerhard Jäger. 2007. Maximum entropy models and stochastic optimality theory. *Architectures, rules, and preferences: variations on themes by Joan W. Bresnan. Stanford: CSLI*, pages 467–479.

Karen Jesney and Anne-Michelle Tessier. 2008. Gradual learning and faithfulness: consequences of ranked vs. weighted constraints.

Karen Jesney and Anne-Michelle Tessier. 2011. Biases in harmonic grammar: the road to restrictive learning. *Natural Language & Linguistic Theory*, 29(1):251–290.

Evgeny S. Levitin and Boris T. Polyak. 1966. Constrained minimization methods. *USSR Computational mathematics and mathematical physics*, 6(5):1–50.

Tal Linzen, Sofya Kasyanenko, and Maria Gouskova. 2013. Lexical and phonological variation in russian prepositions. *Phonology*, 30(3):453–515.

Anna Mai, Eric Bakovic, and Matt Goldrick. 2018. Phonological opacity as local optimization in gradient symbolic computation. *Proceedings of the Society for Computation in Linguistics*, 1(1):219–220.

Claire Moore-Cantwell and Joe Pater. 2016. Gradient exceptionality in maximum entropy grammar with lexically specific constraints. *Catalan Journal of Linguistics*, 15:53–66.

Yves Charles Morin. 2005. La liaison relève-t-elle d'une tendance à éviter les hiatus? réflexions sur son évolution historique. *Langages*, (2):8–23.

Eric R. Rosen. 2016. Predicting the unpredictable: Capturing the apparent semi-regularity of rendaku voicing in japanese through harmonic grammar. In *Proceedings of BLS*, volume 42, pages 235–249.

Eric R. Rosen. 2019. Learning complex inflectional paradigms through blended gradient inputs. In *Proceedings of the Society for Computation in Linguistics (SCiL) 2019*, pages 102–112.

Frank Rosenblatt. 1958. The perceptron: a probabilistic model for information storage and organization in the brain. *Psychological review*, 65(6):386.

Brian Smith. 2015. *Phonologically conditioned allomorphy and UR constraints*. Ph.D. thesis, University of Massachusetts Amherst.

Paul Smolensky and Matthew Goldrick. 2016. Gradient symbolic representations in grammar: The case of french liason. Technical report.

Paul Smolensky, Matthew Goldrick, and Donald Mathis. 2014. Optimization and quantization in gradient symbol systems: a framework for integrating the continuous and the discrete in cognition. *Cognitive science*, 38(6):1102–1138.

Paul Smolensky, Eric Rosen, and Matthew Goldrick. 2020. Learning a gradient grammar of French liaison. In *Proceedings of the 2019 Annual Meeting on Phonology, Stonybrook NY*.

Bernard Tranel. 1996. French liaison and elision revisited: A unified account within optimality theory. *Aspects of Romance linguistics*, pages 433–455.

Eva Zimmerman. 2018. Gradient Symbolic Representations in the output: A case study from Moses Columbian Salishan stress. In *Proceedings of the Forty-Eigth Annual Meeting of the North East Linguistic Society*.

In search of isoglosses: continuous and discrete language embeddings in Slavic historical phonology

Chundra A. Cathcart[1,2] **and Florian Wandl**[3]

[1]Department of Comparative Language Science, University of Zurich
[2]Center for the Interdisciplinary Study of Language Evolution, University of Zurich
[3]Slavisches Seminar, University of Zurich
`{chundra.cathcart,florian.wandl}@uzh.ch`

Abstract

This paper investigates the ability of neural network architectures to effectively learn diachronic phonological generalizations in a multilingual setting. We employ models using three different types of language embedding (dense, sigmoid, and straight-through). We find that the Straight-Through model outperforms the other two in terms of accuracy, but the Sigmoid model's language embeddings show the strongest agreement with the traditional subgrouping of the Slavic languages. We find that the Straight-Through model has learned coherent, semi-interpretable information about sound change, and outline directions for future research.

1 Introduction

Historical phonology is an important area of diachronic linguistics, allowing scholars to explore the space of possible sound change trajectories and resulting synchronic patterns, as well as posit degrees of relatedness between languages on the basis of sound changes shared across them. The latter practice traditionally involves the identification of innovations that are probative with respect to historical subgrouping. The internal genetic structure of many linguistic groups is uncontroversial. For others, scholars disagree in terms of which isoglosses are relevant to subgrouping, and whether the relevant features are indeed shared across groups of languages. The use of computational methods has aided in resolving a number of outstanding questions in diachronic linguistics, though little work has been done assessing the ability of computational models to learn meaningful patterns of sound change as well as capture language-level information that may bear on degrees of genetic relatedness.

This paper employs a neural encoder-decoder architecture to analyze patterns of sound change among Slavic languages, training a series of models on data from an etymological dictionary. Following the standard practice in multilingual NLP tasks, we make use of language embeddings concatenated to the model input. We make use of three different types of language embedding, comprising continuous real-valued DENSE, SIGMOID (defined on the $[0, 1]$ interval), and binary STRAIGHT-THROUGH embeddings. We assess the accuracy with which these encoder-decoder models predict held-out forms in contemporary Slavic languages from their corresponding Proto-Slavic input. We provide a detailed error analysis, observing differences across models in terms of the types of error introduced. We measure the extent to which the language embeddings learned by each model recapitulate the the most commonly accepted subgrouping of the Slavic languages. Finally, we assess the interpretability of the straight-through embedding, investigating the degree to which embeddings in binary latent space represent meaningful information regarding sound change.

We find that the model with straight-through language embeddings outperforms the Dense and Sigmoid models in terms of accuracy. At the same time, the language embeddings learned by the Sigmoid model display a signal that shows the highest agreement out of the three models with received wisdom regarding the dialect grouping of Slavic languages. We find that the latent binary representations learned capture meaningful and coherent information regarding sound patterns. We outline future directions for research using latent binary embeddings in neural historical phonology.

2 Background

The Slavic branch of Indo-European is traditionally divided into East, West, and South Slavic groups. Many of the oldest and most de-

Proceedings of the Seventeenth SIGMORPHON Workshop on Computational Research
in Phonetics, Phonology, and Morphology, pages 233–244
Online, July 10, 2020. ©2020 Association for Computational Linguistics
https://doi.org/10.18653/v1/P17

cisive isoglosses differentiating the Slavic languages are phonological in nature (cf. Shevelov 1964, Carlton 1991). For instance, tautosyllabic Proto-Slavic vowel+liquid sequences were subject to METATHESIS or re-ordering in West and South Slavic languages, whereas East Slavic languages underwent PLEOPHONY, inserting a vowel between the liquid and the following consonant. Variation between liquid metathesis and pleophony, accompanied by language-specific vowel changes, can be seen in the cognates Russian *górod*, Ukrainian *hórod*, Croatian *grâd*, Czech *hrad* (< *gôrdŭ 'city'); the *h-* found in Ukrainian (East Slavic) and Czech (West Slavic) shows also that certain shared features do not cleanly follow the taxonomy defined above.

It is traditionally assumed that the tripartite classification of Slavic either reflects the dialectal diversity of the so-called Slavic homeland, most probably situated on the outskirts of the Carpathian Mountains, or emerged as a result of the great Slavic expansion in the 6th century AD (Bräuer, 1961; Hock, 1998). The extensive study of loanwords, however, suggests that post-expansional Slavic was, despite the vast territory it occupied, still uniform. There seem to have been no significant differences between Slavic spoken in areas located as far away from each other as the Baltic sea and the Peloponnese, at least with regard to phonology. It has therefore been argued that it is this post-expansional Slavic that constitutes the ancestor of all Slavic languages and not the Slavic language spoken in the homeland (Holzer, 1995). One of the arguments put forward in support of this claim is the still largely reconstructible post-Proto-Slavic dialect continuum (Holzer, 1997). One objective of this paper to assess the degree to which neural models recapitulate the uncontroversial subgrouping of Slavic as an indicator of whether they are capable of resolving outstanding issues in the field.

3   Related Work

A growing body of research assesses the information captured by language embeddings trained on large data sets using neural models. There is some debate as to whether embeddings learned in these tasks can pick up on genetic signal (Östling and Tiedemann, 2017; Tiedemann, 2018), or whether the information learned represents structural similarity (Bjerva et al., 2019). The majority of work

of language embeddings involves models trained on large parallel corpora. Meloni et al. (2019) approach the issue of sound change using a GRU-based neural machine translation model with soft attention to reconstruct Latin forms from contemporary Romance reflexes; the authors employ language embeddings, but do not provide an analysis of the information captured by these embeddings. Phylogenetic approaches to sound change and the reconstruction of word forms incorporate a highly articulated genetic representation of language relatedness (Hruschka et al., 2013; Bouchard-Côté et al., 2013), but employ simplified representations of sound change in comparison to what can be captured by recurrent neural networks; at the same time, phylogenetic work explicitly models intermediate stages of change, a potential challenge for RNNs, which are better suited to learning patterns resulting from the telescoping of multiple changes. Related work seeks to disentangle genetic and areal pressures in shaping cross-linguistic patterns (Daumé III, 2009; Murawaki and Yamauchi, 2018; Cathcart, 2019, 2020b,a).

In general, while the signal learned by embeddings can be analyzed via visualization techniques (Maaten and Hinton, 2008), it is a challenge to link the behavior of embeddings to individual features in the data analyzed. This difficulty undoubtedly stems in part from the fact that embeddings are generally continuous, lacking the sparsity or discreteness needed to identify the behavior of the neural model when features are active or inactive. This issue has been addressed by the development of de-noising approaches designed to induce sparsity (Subramanian et al., 2018).

Binary latent variables are of key interest to linguistic questions, but pose many challenges for inference. Binary latent variable models such as the Indian Buffet Process (IBP, Ghahramani and Griffiths, 2006) have been used in some applications in computational phonology and typology (Doyle et al., 2014; Murawaki, 2017) using a combination of Gibbs Sampling and updates from the Metropolis-Hastings algorithm or Hamiltonian Monte Carlo, but it is not clear that these inference procedures are scalable to neural models. Discrete variables pose problems for differentiability in gradient-based optimization algorithms; marginalizing out all possible combinations of binary variables is generally unfeasible for binary latent variables. Variational approaches have attempted to circumvent this issue via the concrete (alternatively, Gumbel-Softmax) distribution (Maddison et al., 2017; Jang et al., 2017), which extends the reparameterization trick to categorical distributions and which produces gradient estimates that have lower variance than standard estimation techniques (Williams, 1992) but are still biased; subsequent approaches reduce bias but are less straightforward to implement (Grathwohl et al., 2018; Liu et al., 2019).

While concrete-distributed versions of the IBP have been used in neural models (Singh et al., 2017; Kessler et al., 2019), this work is limited to variational autoencoders, which use amortized variational inference to learn latent representations from the data via a global inference network; encoder-decoder mechanisms with attention like the one used in this paper cannot exploit this property of the data; training the latent variable with stochastic variational inference, while theoretically possible, is considerably more difficult (Kim et al., 2018). As an alternative, we use straight-through (ST) embeddings (Bengio et al., 2013; Courbariaux et al., 2016) in a maximum likelihood framework. Straight-through layers are discrete but have underlying continuous weights; model output is predicted on the basis of the discrete representation, while model loss is differentiated with respect to the continuous underlying weights. While this approach has the same problems with biased estimates as the concrete distribution, it is straightforward to implement. We compare the quality of straight-through embeddings to embeddings with no activation and embeddings with sigmoid activation.

4 Data

Our data set consists of Proto-Slavic etyma and corresponding reflexes in medieval and modern Slavic languages taken from a digitized version of a Slavic etymological dictionary (Derksen 2007; for alternative reconstructions see Holzer 1995; Andersen 1998). In order to minimize the chance of introducing morphologically non-congruent forms into our data set, we extracted the first form provided for each Slavic language in each entry, since these are most likely to agree morphologically with the Proto-Slavic headword.

We converted forms in modern Slavic languages to a narrow phonetic representation using IPA transcriptions from Wiktionary (`https://www.wiktionary.org`), which were used to train a neural encoder-decoder; these models were used to obtain IPA transcriptions for forms not in Wiktionary, and a portion was checked manually. In several cases we reconciled sources used in the etymological dictionary (e.g., Pleteršnik, 1894) with contemporary standardized orthographies, and made use of phonetic descriptions for languages where the training data were problematic (Schuster-Šewc, 1968; Lencek, 1982; Scatton, 1984; Comrie and Corbett, 1993; Ternes and Vladimirova-Buhtz, 1990; Landau et al., 1995; Šuštaršič et al., 1995; Dankovičová, 1997; Jassem, 2003; Gussmann, 2007; Stadnik-Holzer, 2009; Hanulíková and Hamann, 2010; Mojsijenko et al., 2010; Yanushevskaya and Bunčić, 2015; Howson, 2017, 2018; Pompino-Marschall et al., 2017). For the medieval languages Old Church Slavic and Church Slavic, orthographic forms were converted to a broad phonemic transcription based on Lunt (2001). Suprasegmental features were marked for all modern languages (pitch accent for Slovene and BCS and primary stress for the remainder; for consistency, we chose to mark primary stress on monosyllables in stress-timed languages). We excluded languages with fewer than 100 forms in the etymological dictionary (this resulted in the omission of Macedonian, Polabian and Slovincian).

We took additional steps to remove morphological mismatches in the data set. For Bulgarian verbs, which reflect the Proto-Slavic 1sg present in their citation form, we replaced the Proto-Slavic headword (the infinitive form by default) with a morphologically congruent form, and excluded a small number of forms based on athematic verbs. Additionally, Proto-Slavic adjectives are always given in the nominal or short form, although contemporary Slavic languages often reflect the so-called long form, which arose from the addition of an inflected element *-jĭ to the ending; we converted short Proto-Slavic adjectives to their long form in the appropriate contexts. We tried to ensure that Proto-Slavic verbs matched their reflexes according to the presence/absence of reflexive morphology and preverbs. Additionally, the original data source contains multiple gender inflections for certain Proto-Slavic etyma (e.g., *àblŭko n., *àblŭka f., and *àblŭkŭ m. for 'apple'), which are linked to the same reflexes irrespective of the reflexes' gender; for such forms, we discarded etymon-reflex pairs with mismatched

Language	Glottocode	# reflexes
Russian (Rus)	russ1263	1572
Slovene (Sln)	slov1268	1462
Serbo-Croatian (BCS[M])	sout1528	1434
Czech (Cze)	czec1258	1377
Polish (Pol)	poli1260	1282
Slovak (Slk)	slov1269	1091
Old Church Slavic (OCS)	chur1257	1097
Bulgarian (Bul)	bulg1262	950
Church Slavic (CS)	chur1257	392
Ukrainian (Ukr)	ukra1253	301
Upper Sorbian (USo)	uppe1395	243
Lower Sorbian (LSo)	lowe1385	120
Belarusian (Bel)	bela1254	79
Total		11400

Table 1: Number of forms in each language in data set, along with closest matching glottocodes.

gender. Ultimately, this process yielded 11400 forms in 13 languages (see Table 1), and allowed us to rid the data set of a large number (albeit not the entirety) of morphological mismatches.

5 Method

To learn mappings between Proto-Slavic etyma and the Slavic reflexes that descend from them, we use an LSTM Encoder-Decoder with 0th-order hard monotonic attention (Wu and Cotterell, 2019), trained on all languages in our data set. The basic model architecture used for the experiments in this study has the following structure (schematized in Figure 1): a trainable language-level embedding is concatenated to a one-hot representation of each input segment at each input time step; each concatenation is fed to a Dense layer (with no activation) to generate a embedding for each time step that encodes information about the input phoneme and language ID of the reflex; these embeddings subsequently are fed to the encoder-decoder in order to generate the output. The parameters of the encoder-decoder architecture are shared across languages in the data set; the sole language-specific variable employed is the language-level embedding fed to the model.

In all experiments, we set the dimension of the language-level embedding and the language/character embedding to 128, and the hidden layer dimension to 256. In our experiments, we employ different representations of the language-level embedding, including a dense layer with no activation (DENSE model), a dense layer with sigmoid activation, (SIGMOID model) and a dense layer with straight-through activation (ST model), which uses the Heaviside step function (negative

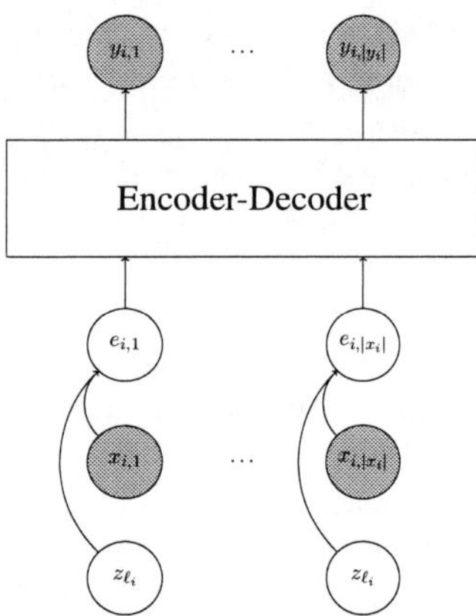

Figure 1: Basic schema of architecture used in this paper; for each input-output pair $\mathbf{x}_i, \mathbf{y}_i$, an embedding associated with the language ID for index i is concatenated to a one-hot representation of the input.

values map to 0, non-negative values to 1). We train our model for 200 epochs with a batch size of 256 using the Adam optimizer with a learning rate of .001 with the objective of minimizing the mean categorical cross-entropy between the predicted and observed distributions of the output. To evaluate model performance, we carry out K-fold cross-validation ($K = 10$), randomly holding out 10% of the forms in each language, and greedily decoding the held-out forms using the trained model. For additional analyses regarding the interpretability of the embeddings learned, we train the model on all forms in the data set. Models are implemented in Keras (Chollet, 2015) and Larq (Geiger and Team, 2020).[1]

6 Results

6.1 Accuracy

We assess the accuracy of each model by generating held-out forms on the basis of the language ID of the form and the Proto-Slavic etymon from which the form descends, greedily decoding on the basis of the trained model. We measure accuracy in terms of word error rate (WER), which gives the proportion of incorrectly generated forms, and the phoneme error rate (PER), which we define as the Levenshtein edit distance between generated and ground truth strings divided by the length of the longer form. Accuracy measures are found in Table 2. The ST model shows the best performance,

---

[1]Code accompanying this paper is available at `https://github.com/chundrac/slav-dial/tree/master/SIGMORPHON_2020`

	WER	PER
Dense	0.535	0.143
Sigmoid	0.559	0.151
ST	**0.530**	**0.140**

Table 2: Mean word error and phoneme error rate for each model

followed by the Dense and Sigmoid models. Figure 2 shows WER and PER for each model plotted by the log number of training examples for each language in our data set. There is at best a very weak negative correlation between error rates and training example frequencies; the worst performance seems to be restricted to four languages (Belarusian, Lower Sorbian, Ukrainian, and Upper Sorbian), which vary in training data frequency, but in our impression posed the most difficulties for phonetic conversion. Old Church Slavic and Church Slavic show the highest accuracy; forms in these languages tend to be close to their Proto-Slavic ancestral forms,[2] and were straightforward to convert to IPA.

6.2 Error analysis

6.2.1 Quantitative error analysis

We wish to obtain a fuller picture of the errors made by our models, and in particular, whether different models produce different types of errors. We analyze errors according to a taxonomy inspired by Gorman et al. (2019). At a high level, errors can be divided according to whether they stem from mistakes in the data or are a result of model idiosyncrasies. Errors in the data (target errors) largely consist of morphologically non-congruent etymon reflex pairs that we were unable to detect *a priori*: for instance, the Slavic etymon *dĭlti 'to hollow, chisel' is paired with reflexes such as Czech *dlbsti*, which contains the cluster -bs- due to analogical influence; similarly, the etymon *majati 'wave, beckon' (inf.) is paired with OCS *namaiaaxǫ* (3pl impf.). Additionally, there exists the possibility of doublet reflexes in contemporary Slavic languages due to dialect borrowing (free variation errors), e.g., Russian *óblako* from Church Slavic (Vasmer, 1953-1958). Incorrect phonetic conversion is another source of errors of this type.

In terms of linguistic errors that are not direct artifacts of our data set, we are interested in the degree to which the models' behavior results in a specific set of error pattern types. We wish to measure the extent to which models introduce errors when decoding forms in a given language due to overgeneralization on the basis of forms seen in the training data for the SAME LANGUAGE. For instance, all models fail to learn the Upper Sorbian development *pr > [pʃ], erroneously generalizing the change *r > [ʀ] to an incorrect environment (e.g., PSl *pręsti 'spin' > ['pʀʲast͡ʃ], expected ['pʃast͡ʃ]). Additionally, because our model leverages global information shared across languages along with language-specific information, errors in one language involving the application of a sound law from a DIFFERENT SLAVIC LANGUAGE are a potential concern. For example, the Sigmoid model generates the erroneous BCS reflex [lĕt͡ɕæti] 'to fly' (< PSl *letěti, expected [lĕtjeti]); [æ] is attested only in OCS, CS, Russian, and Slovak. Of additional interest are errors where the model produces a rule that is unattested across the data set, and hence UNMOTIVATED by the data. For instance, the Sigmoid model generates BCS [ppĕːta] (< PSl *pętà 'heel', expected [pĕːta]); word-initial [pp-] is unattested in our data set, and the origin of this error is unclear.

We quantitatively assess the issues enumerated above in the manner described below. To assess the prevalence of target errors, we measure the extent to which models agree in terms of the data points for which poor performance is exhibited. We take this agreement as a proxy for errors in the data; if the same data points cause problems across models, this poor performance may be an artifact of morphological mismatches in the data or fewer examples in the training data than needed to learn the patterns for the data points in question. The agreement matrix in Table 3 shows that agreement levels are quite high, indicating that some errors may be due to artifacts of the data used.

To gain an overview of the error types made by the model, we use the attention mechanism of the trained models to obtain alignments between all Proto-Slavic etyma and attested reflexes as well as between Proto-Slavic etyma and erroneously produced reflexes. We extract sound changes operating between Proto-Slavic and daughter languages from these alignments (e.g., PSl *o > Slovak ɔ), which indicate whether a given edit is attested in

---

[2]Note that according to the common practice in etymological dictionaries, OCS snd CS forms are given in a normalized form not reflecting regional differences.

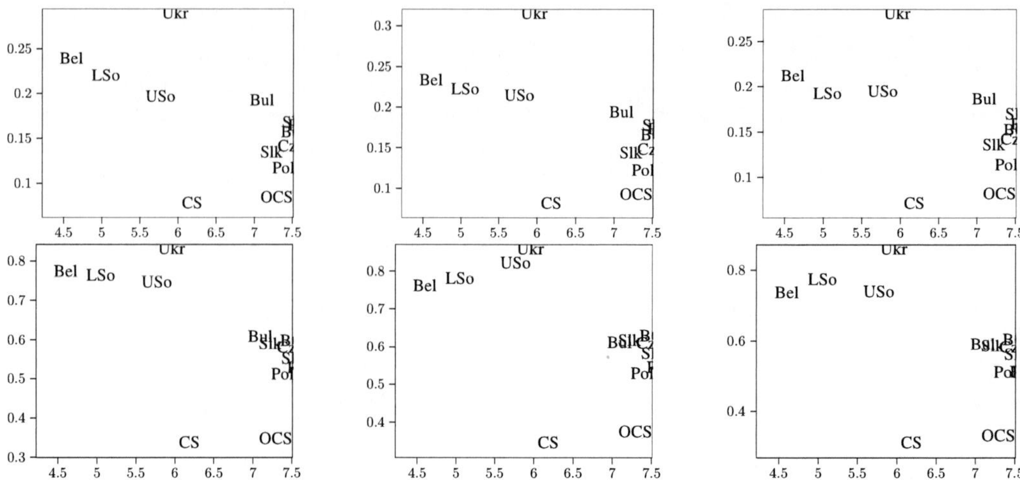

Figure 2: PER (top) and WER (top) values (y axis) plotted by the log number of training examples for each language (x axis), for Dense, Sigmoid and ST models (left to right)

Model	Dense	Sigmoid	ST
Dense	—	0.789	0.812
Sigmoid	0.824	—	0.827
ST	0.803	0.783	—

Table 3: Proportion of word errors produced by each model (rows) shared with other models (columns)

Model	SL	OL	U
Dense	0.551	0.105	0.342
Sigmoid	0.593	0.101	0.305
ST	0.617	0.101	0.281

Table 4: Proportion of errors produced by models that are present in the same language (SL), other languages (OL), or are unmotivated (U)

a language (irrespective of conditioning environment). We automatically annotate each erroneous edit according to whether it is attested in the same language as the decoded form in which it occurs (same language), if not, whether it is attested in another Slavic language (other language), or finally, if it is not attested in any Slavic language (unmotivated). Table 4 shows proportions of these error types produced by each model; the Sigmoid and ST models produce more other-language and unmotivated errors than the Dense model.

6.2.2 Qualitative error analysis

We present results of a detailed error analysis involving 422 forms spanning all languages in the data set where at least one of the three models produced an error. Roughly 15% of the forms surveyed contain some sort of morphological mismatch; many of these are trivial one-off analogical idiosyncrasies. In some cases, loanwords unmarked in the dictionary can be detected (cf. the example of Russian *óblako* mentioned above).

Annotated error types that occur more than once across all models include incorrect accent type (Dense: 18, Sigmoid: 12, ST: 10), accent misplacement (Dense: 40, Sigmoid: 40, ST: 32), consonant mismatches (Dense: 139, Sigmoid: 161, ST: 149), vowel quality mismatches (Dense: 192, Sigmoid: 219, ST: 195), vowel length mismatches (Dense: 35, Sigmoid: 47, ST: 31), and general segmental mismatches involving the erroneous substitution of a vowel for a consonant, or vice versa (Dense: 85, Sigmoid: 81, ST: 68). The ST model's overall higher performance bears out the larger-scale analysis of errors presented in the previous section.

Our manual error analysis was carried out by a single specialist; future research will involve more detailed error analyses carried out by multiple specialists in order to gauge inter-annotator reliability.

6.3 Genetic signal in embeddings

We wish to measure the degree to which the language-level embeddings learned by each model reflect received wisdom regarding the dialectal makeup of the Slavic languages. As stated previ-

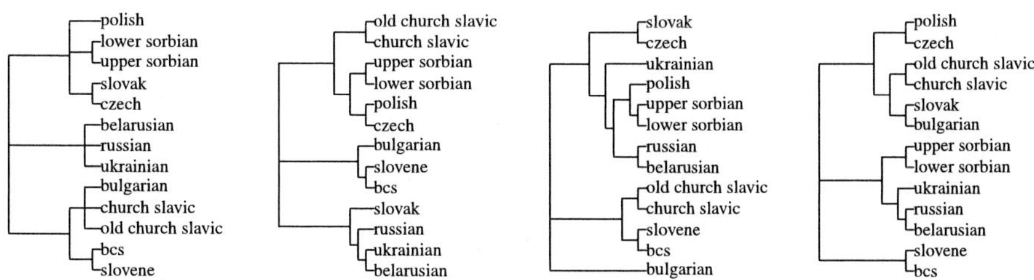

Figure 3: Reference phylogeny of Slavic languages and neighbor-joined trees from embeddings for Dense, Sigmoid, and Straight-Through models (left to right)

ously, languages employed in this paper are traditionally divided among East, South and West Slavic groups. To assess the signal contained by the embeddings, we generated trees from cosine distances between pairs of language embeddings learned by each model using neighbor joining (NJ, Saitou and Nei, 1987) as implemented in the R package `ape` (Paradis et al., 2019). These trees can be found in Figure 3 alongside a reference topology from Glottolog (Hammarström et al., 2017). The Sigmoid model's embeddings show the highest agreement with the Glottolog tree; the main discrepancies found are the placement of Bulgarian outside of South Slavic, as well as the placement of the Lechitic languages Polish, Upper Sorbian and Lower Sorbian within East Slavic. The ST embeddings show mixed performance; certain West and South Slavic languages are grouped correctly, but a large number of taxa are misplaced. We used the R package `Quartet` (Smith, 2019) to measure the generalized quartet distance (Pompei et al., 2011) between the reference tree and the trees constructed from the embeddings, equal to the number of four-taxon groups resolved differently across the two trees, divided by the number of resolved four-taxon groups found in the reference tree; lower values indicate greater agreement (Dense: 0.322, Sigmoid: **0.247**, ST: 0.368). It is possible that the ST model shows low agreement with the reference phylogeny but high accuracy because it has succeeded in detecting areal features that conflict with the traditional tripartite subgrouping. Further investigation into the treelikeness of each network (Wichmann et al., 2011) is needed in order to properly address this issue.

6.4 Interpretation of embeddings

A common goal of neural modeling with discrete latent variables is to learn sparse interpretable fea-

Figure 4: Active dimensions (white cells) in ST language embeddings

tures. Ideally, activating or deactivating a single binary latent variable should correlate with the presence or absence of a meaningful feature in the model's output. Inducing the level of sparsity needed to generate such latent variables is an ongoing issue in the deep learning literature (Singh et al., 2017). Our models have not learned meaningful features in the sense that turning a single variable "on" or "off" can produce a meaningful feature of Slavic dialectology (e.g., the presence of liquid metathesis/pleophony); these processes appear to be distributed across multiple latent binary variables.

As shown in Figure 4, language-level straight-through embeddings are far from sparse; of the 128 embedding dimensions, only 1 is inactive across languages. Individual language embeddings contain between 32 and 61 active dimensions. Preliminary attempts to turn individual dimensions "on" and feed the latent representation to the encoder-decoder along with a Proto-Slavic input do not produce interpretable or coherent results; it appears to be the case that it is not individual dimensions, but interactions between them, that influence the behavior of the decoder.

6.4.1 Nearest neighbors

Feeding all possible 2^{128} combinations of embedding values to the model is computationally infeasible, though it might allow us to discover which feature combinations are responsible for certain types of behavior of the encoder-decoder. In order to gain a better understanding of the behavior of these dimensions individually and as a group, we explore the NEAREST NEIGHBORS in embedding space of reflexes for languages in our data set by altering the values of each variable in our language embeddings, and feeding these altered embeddings to the model architecture along with a Proto-Slavic etymon and observing the set of resulting outputs. Specifically, we take language-level embeddings and alter each of the embedding's 128 dimensions.

By feeding these nearest neighbors to the encoder-decoder along with a Proto-Slavic etymon, it is possible to see how perturbations of an embedding result in different outputs from the expected contemporary Slavic reflex. In general, different perturbations often result in the same output form, indicating that the embedding space is perhaps less sparse than necessary, and more compact representations can be learned without losing information. To give a concrete example of this phenomenon, the nearest neighbors of Polish [ˈmidwɔ] 'soap, lather' (< PSl *mỳdlo) in embedding space yield only thirteen unique forms ([ˈmilo], [ˈmidlɔ], [mɪ̆ːdlɔ], [ˈmidwɔ], [miːlo], [ˈmidlɔ], [mɪllɐ], [mɪllɔ], [mɪ̆lɔ], [ˈmilɔ], [mɪ̆ːlɔ]); interestingly, there is no evidence for the otherwise naturalistic and plausible sound change *dl > [ll] in our data set.

Based on a qualitative appraisal of these nearest neighbors, it does not appear to be the case that the ST model has learned to entirely disentangle orthogonal developments in historical phonology. The unique nearest neighbors of Russian [məlɐˈko] 'milk' (< PSl *melkò), [mlɛkɔ], [ˈmlɛko], [mlĕːkɔ], [mlɪˈko], [mlĕːko], [ˈmlɛko], [məlɐˈko] and [mlɛˈkɔ], appear to show that our model learns patterns of pleophony/liquid metathesis and vowel change jointly, rather than learning disentangled abstractions (though interestingly, the same word in Polish has the neighbors [ˈmʲɪlkɔ] and [mlʲɪˈkɔ], showing metathesis independent of vowel quality). It is not clear, however, that this behavior goes against the received wisdom of Slavic linguistics; the operation of liquid metathesis or pleophony among Slavic languages is generally thought to be a change that has an early common origin but developed in different dialect-specific directions (Shevelov, 1964). Ultimately, this architecture shows the potential to generate typologically meaningful (i.e., naturalistic) but also novel representations of hypothetical Slavic reflexes.

6.4.2 Sampling from the latent space

An issue that arises in the use of latent variable models, particularly in the context of linguistic typology, concerns the coherence of the representations that they learn. If we randomly traverse our models' latent variable space or interpolate between representations, how likely are we to encounter a plausible unattested sister language of the languages attested in our data set? We briefly explore this question by randomly sampling 100 embeddings from variously parameterized distributions and feeding them to our models, along with a set of 100 randomly chosen Proto-Slavic etyma. For each etymon, we feed zero-mean Gaussian samples with standard deviation $\sigma \in \{.01, .1, 1, 10\}$ to the Dense model; symmetric Beta samples with shape parameters $\alpha = \beta \in \{.01, .1, 1, 10\}$ to the Sigmoid model; and Binomial samples with probability $p \in \{.2, .4, .6, .8\}$ to the ST model (all samples have the same dimension as our learned embeddings). Qualitatively speaking, output forms randomly generated by the ST model are consistently well formed and coherent across parameterization regimes. Conversely, when σ is greater than .01 (roughly equivalent to the empirical standard deviation of the learned embeddings), the Dense model often generates unrealistic strings (e.g., [bɬˈːɬə]), and when σ is very small, forms are coherent but there is virtually no variation; for the Sigmoid model, the strings become more realistic looking as $\alpha = \beta$ increases (the majority of values for the learned Sigmoid embeddings are close to .5). To highlight a related discrepancy, we observe the average number of unique outputs generated by each regime in each model (Dense: 3.21, 24.02, 93.08, 61.3; Sigmoid: 96.23, 94.14, 67.39 22.74; ST: 21.3, 24.3, 24.06, 20.1); the quantity of unique outputs stays constant across all regimes for the ST model, along with their quality.

Additionally, we wish to explore the extent to which samples from latent variable space generate realistic sound changes and plausible sound patterns. While certain diachronic trajectories can lead to the emergence of "crazy" rules (Bach and Harms, 1972; Buckley, 2000) and unnatural phonotactic restrictions (Beguš and Nazarov, 2017), we might expect the relatively infrequent nature of these phenomena to somehow be captured by the behavior of models like the ST model. To address this question, we feed sets of hypothetical well-formed Proto-Slavic phonological neighbors (generated by taking 12 etyma from our data set and generating echo-forms to create a cohort of forms differing according to initial *p-/t-/k-/b-/d-/g-; we exclude hypothetical forms with velar-front vowel sequences, which would have been affected by palatalization) to the ST model, randomly sampling binary latent embeddings from the binomial distribution with probabilities $\{.2, .4, .6, , 8\}$. For each probability regime, we attempt to evaulate the relative frequency of unnatural sound patterns displayed by these hypothetical forms' descendants; if our model embodies not only plausible but probable behavior, we predict that these etymological phonological neighbors, which differ only according to the word-initial consonant, should frequently yield similar echo-forms, and that other patterns may arise less frequently. For each pair of outputs within each cohort (with stress marking removed), we divide the number of agreeing final segments by the mean of the two strings' lengths, and report the proportion of pairs for which this value is greater than .5 (indicating greater agreement); these values are 0.427, 0.546, 0.574, and 0.526 for each respective probability regime, indicating that generated outputs tend not to be very echo-like. To exemplify, a representative sample output for *{p,t,b,d}ĭrtĭ comprises the forms ['pr̩t͡ɕ], ['tr̩t], ['br̩t͡s], ['dr̩t]. While long-distance assimilatory and dissimilatory processes operating between the left and right word edge are not unknown cross-linguistically, we believe that changes where differences in word-initial segments trigger divergent word-final reflexes should be rare, rather than typical. Further refinement of metrics designed to assess the validity of output patterns is much needed.[3]

From this small and rather premature investigation, it appears that the latent variable design space represented by the ST model generates coherent, realistic-looking output, but the frequency distributions of patterns in its output may not reflect cross-linguistic frequency distributions. A more in-depth analysis along these lines is outside the scope of this paper, and methods seeking to derive typological generalizations should include data from multiple families; at the same time, the issues raised here potentially bear on our understanding of the diachronic basis of synchronic patterns in phonology.

7 Discussion and outlook

This paper investigated the performance of multiple neural models in capturing patterns of sound change across Slavic languages. We found that a model with binarized straight-through language-level embeddings outperformed other models in terms of accuracy, and shows great potential for learning coherent and interpretable information regarding sound change. We found that the discrete features learned by our model appear for the most part to correspond to meaningful, realistic variation in sound patterns, though representations are not particularly sparse. Additionally, randomly sampling from discrete latent space tended to consistently generate coherent output; the preliminary attempts that we made to assess the likelihood of observing these samples in naturalistic contexts can be expanded considerably.

We used straight-through embeddings as a low-cost alternative to more involved means of training discrete latent variables. In the immediate future, we plan to extend our approach to make use of variational approaches, the flexibility of which may help in inducing sparsity in order to learn more meaningful, realistic representations (there is additionally room for exploration of simpler approaches that we did not make use of in this paper, such as dropout regularization); however, since our encoder-decoder model is different from the autoencoding models used in previous work, directly extending these methods presents a challenge that require considerable experimentation to overcome (an early attempt to adopt the IBP prior of Singh et al. 2017 was unsuccessful, as the monotonically decreasing prior probabilities rarely yielded non-zero values; thus far, attempts to weight the KL divergence term have not yielded success). Nevertheless, as low-variance, low-bias techniques for inferring discrete variables in neural models progress, we believe that they will be an increasingly valuable means of capturing meaningful, interpretable features in multilingual neural tasks like this paper's.

---

[3]Indeed, taking the proportion of agreeing final segments as a measure of naturalness would classify changes resulting from certain types of tonogenesis to be unnatural, e.g., *pa, *ba > Vietnamese *pa*, *pà* (Haudricourt, 1954), since dissimilarity in initial consonants often leads to dissimilarity at the right word edge.

References

Henning Andersen. 1998. Slavic. In Paolo Ramat and Anna G. Ramat, editors, *The Indo-European languages*, Routledge language family descriptions, page 415–453. Routledge, London and New York.

Emmon Bach and Robert T. Harms. 1972. How do languages get crazy rules? In *Linguistic Change and Generative Theory*, pages 1–21, Bloomington.

Gašper Beguš and Aleksei Nazarov. 2017. Lexicon against naturalness: Unnatural gradient phonotactic restrictions and their origins.

Yoshua Bengio, Nicholas Léonard, and Aaron Courville. 2013. Estimating or propagating gradients through stochastic neurons for conditional computation. *arXiv preprint arXiv:1308.3432*.

Johannes Bjerva, Robert Östling, Maria H. Veiga, Jörg Tiedemann, and Isabelle Augenstein. 2019. What do language representations really represent? *Computational Linguistics*, 45(2):381–389.

Alexandre Bouchard-Côté, David Hall, Thomas L. Griffiths, and Dan Klein. 2013. Automated reconstruction of ancient languages using probabilistic models of sound change. *Proceedings of the National Academy of Sciences*, 110:4224–4229.

Herbert Bräuer. 1961. *Slavische Sprachwissenschaft I. Einleitung, Lautlehre*. Walter de Gruyter Co., Berlin.

Eugene Buckley. 2000. On the naturalness of unnatural rules. In *Proceedings from the Second Workshop on American Indigenous Languages. UCSB working papers in linguistics*, volume 9, pages 1–14.

Terence R. Carlton. 1991. *Introduction to the phonological history of the Slavic languages*. Slavica Publishers, Columbus, Ohio.

Chundra A. Cathcart. 2019. Toward a deep dialectological representation of Indo-Aryan. In *Proceedings of the Sixth Workshop on NLP for Similar Languages, Varieties and Dialects*, pages 110–119.

Chundra A. Cathcart. 2020a. Dialectal layers in West Iranian: a Hierarchical Dirichlet Process approach to linguistic relationships. *arXiv preprint arXiv:2001.05297*.

Chundra A. Cathcart. 2020b. A probabilistic assessment of the Indo-Aryan Inner-Outer hypothesis. *Journal of Historical Linguistics*, 10:42–86.

François Chollet. 2015. Keras. https://github.com/fchollet/keras.

Bernard Comrie and Greville G. Corbett. 1993. *The Slavonic languages*. Routledge reference. Routledge, London.

Matthieu Courbariaux, Itay Hubara, Daniel Soudry, Ran El-Yaniv, and Yoshua Bengio. 2016. Binarized neural networks: Training deep neural networks with weights and activations constrained to $+1$ or -1. *arXiv preprint arXiv:1602.02830*.

Jana Dankovičová. 1997. Czech. *Journal of the International Phonetic Association*, 27(1-2):77–80.

Hal Daumé III. 2009. Non-parametric Bayesian areal linguistics. In *Human Language Technologies: The 2009 Annual Conference of the North American Chapter of the ACL*, pages 593–601, Boulder, CO. Association for Computational Linguistics.

Rick Derksen. 2007. *Etymological dictionary of the Slavic inherited lexicon*. Online version (https://ordbog.oesteuropastudier.dk/) accessed 1 February 2020. Brill, Leiden.

Gabriel Doyle, Klinton Bicknell, and Roger Levy. 2014. Nonparametric learning of phonological constraints in optimality theory. In *Proceedings of the 52nd Annual Meeting of the Association for Computational Linguistics (Volume 1: Long Papers)*, pages 1094–1103.

Lukas Geiger and Plumerai Team. 2020. Larq: An open-source library for training binarized neural networks. *Journal of Open Source Software*, 5(45):1746.

Zoubin Ghahramani and Thomas L Griffiths. 2006. Infinite latent feature models and the indian buffet process. In *Advances in neural information processing systems*, pages 475–482.

Kyle Gorman, Arya D. McCarthy, Ryan Cotterell, Ekaterina Vylomova, Miikka Silfverberg, and Magdalena Markowska. 2019. Weird inflects but ok: Making sense of morphological generation errors. In *Proceedings of the 23rd Conference on Computational Natural Language Learning (CoNLL)*, pages 140–151.

Will Grathwohl, Dami Choi, Yuhuai Wu, Geoffrey Roeder, and David Duvenaud. 2018. Backpropagation through the void: Optimizing control variates for black-box gradient estimation. *ICLR*.

Edmund Gussmann. 2007. *The phonology of Polish*. The phonology of the world's languages. Oxford University Press, New York.

Harald Hammarström, Robert Forkel, and Martin Haspelmath. 2017. Glottolog 3.3. Max Planck Institute for the Science of Human History.

Adriana Hanulíková and Silke Hamann. 2010. Slovak. *Journal of the International Phonetic Association*, 40(3):373–378.

André-Georges Haudricourt. 1954. De l'origine des tons en vietnamien. *Journal asiatique*, 242:69–82.

Wolfgang Hock. 1998. Das Urslavische. In Peter Rehder, editor, *Einfürung in die slavischen Sprachen*, pages 17–34. Wissenschaftliche Buchgesellschaft, Darmstadt.

Georg Holzer. 1995. Die Einheitlichkeit des Slavischen um 600 n. Chr. und ihr Zerfall. *Wiener Slavistisches Jahrbuch*, 41:55–89.

Georg Holzer. 1997. Zum gemeinslavischen Dialektkontinuum. *Wiener Slavistisches Jahrbuch*, 43:87–102.

Phil Howson. 2017. Upper Sorbian. *Journal of the International Phonetic Association*, 47(3):359–367.

Phil Howson. 2018. Upper Sorbian – CORRIGENDUM. *Journal of the International Phonetic Association*, 48(3):389–389.

Daniel J. Hruschka, Simon Branford, Eric D. Smith, Jon F. Wilkins, Andrew Meade, Mark Pagel, and Tanmoy Bhattacharya. 2013. Detecting regular sound changes in linguistics as events of concerted evolution. *Current Biology*, 25:1–9.

Eric Jang, Shixiang Gu, and Ben Poole. 2017. Categorical reparameterization with gumbel-softmax. *ICLR*.

Wiktor Jassem. 2003. Polish. *Journal of the International Phonetic Association*, 33(1):103–107.

Samuel Kessler, Vu Nguyen, Stefan Zohren, and Stephen Roberts. 2019. Indian buffet neural networks for continual learning. *4th workshop on Bayesian Deep Learning (NeurIPS 2019)*.

Yoon Kim, Sam Wiseman, and Alexander M Rush. 2018. A tutorial on deep latent variable models of natural language. *arXiv preprint arXiv:1812.06834*.

Ernestina Landau, Mijo Lončarić, Damir Horga, and Ivo Škarić. 1995. Croatian. *Journal of the International Phonetic Association*, 25(2):83–86.

Rado Ludovik Lencek. 1982. *The structure and history of the Slovene language*. Slavica Publishers, Columbus, Ohio.

Runjing Liu, Jeffrey Regier, Nilesh Tripuraneni, Michael Jordan, and Jon Mcauliffe. 2019. Rao-Blackwellized stochastic gradients for discrete distributions. pages 4023–4031.

Horace G. Lunt. 2001. *Old Church Slavonic Grammar*, seventh revised edition. Mouton de Gruyter, Berlin and New York.

Laurens van der Maaten and Geoffrey Hinton. 2008. Visualizing data using t-SNE. *Journal of machine learning research*, 9:2579–2605.

Chris J. Maddison, Andriy Mnih, and Yee Whye Teh. 2017. The concrete distribution: A continuous relaxation of discrete random variables. *ICLR*.

Carlo Meloni, Shauli Ravfogel, and Yoav Goldberg. 2019. Ab antiquo: Proto-language reconstruction with RNNs. *arXiv preprint arXiv:1908.02477*.

Aanatolij K. Mojsijenko et al. 2010. *Sučasna ukraïns'ka literaturna mova : pidručnyk*. Znannja, Kyïv.

Yugo Murawaki. 2017. Diachrony-aware induction of binary latent representations from typological features. In *Proceedings of the Eighth International Joint Conference on Natural Language Processing (Volume 1: Long Papers)*, pages 451–461.

Yugo Murawaki and Kenji Yamauchi. 2018. A statistical model for the joint inference of vertical stability and horizontal diffusibility of typological features. *Journal of Language Evolution*, 3(1):13–25.

Robert Östling and Jörg Tiedemann. 2017. Continuous multilinguality with language vectors. In *Proceedings of the 15th Conference of the European Chapter of the Association for Computational Linguistics: Volume 2, Short Papers*, pages 644–649.

Emmanuel Paradis, Simon Blomberg, Ben Bolker, Joseph Brown, Julien Claude, Hoa Sien Cuong, and Richard Desper. 2019. Package 'ape'. *Analyses of phylogenetics and evolution, version*, 2(4).

Maks Pleteršnik. 1894. *Slovensko-nemški slovar*. Knezoškofijstvo, Ljubljana.

Simone Pompei, Vittorio Loreto, and Francesca Tria. 2011. On the accuracy of language trees. *PloS one*, 6(6).

Bernd Pompino-Marschall, Elena Steriopolo, and Marzena Żygis. 2017. Ukrainian. *Journal of the International Phonetic Association*, 47(3):349–357.

Naruya Saitou and Masatoshi Nei. 1987. The neighbor-joining method: a new method for reconstructing phylogenetic trees. *Molecular Biology and Evolution*, 4(4):406–425.

Ernest A. Scatton. 1984. *A reference grammar of modern Bulgarian*. Slavica Publishers, Columbus, Ohio.

Heinz Schuster-Šewc. 1968. *Gramatika hornjoserbskeje rěče : 1 : Fonematika a morfologija*. Nakładnistwo Domowina, Budyśin.

George Y. Shevelov. 1964. *A prehistory of Slavic : the historical phonology of common Slavic*. Winter, Heidelberg.

Rachit Singh, Jeffrey Ling, and Finale Doshi-Velez. 2017. Structured variational autoencoders for the beta-bernoulli process. In *31st Conference on Neural Information Processing Systems*.

Martin R. Smith. 2019. Bayesian and parsimony approaches reconstruct informative trees from simulated morphological datasets. *Biology Letters*, 15(2):20180632.

Elena Stadnik-Holzer. 2009. Artikulatorische Phonetik. In Sebastian Kempgen, Peter Kosta, Tilman Berger, Karl Gutschmidt, and Sebastian Kempgen, editors, *Die slavischen Sprachen / The Slavic Languages*. De Gruyter Mouton, Berlin, Boston.

Anant Subramanian, Danish Pruthi, Harsh Jhamtani, Taylor Berg-Kirkpatrick, and Eduard Hovy. 2018. SPINE: Sparse interpretable neural embeddings. In *Thirty-Second AAAI Conference on Artificial Intelligence*.

Elmar Ternes and Tatjana Vladimirova-Buhtz. 1990. Bulgarian. *Journal of the International Phonetic Association*, 20(1):45–47.

Jörg Tiedemann. 2018. Emerging language spaces learned from massively multilingual corpora. In Eetu Mäkelä, Mikko Tolonen, and Jouni Tuominen, editors, *Proceedings of the Digital Humanities in the Nordic Countries 3rd Conference (DHN 2018)*, pages 188–197.

Max Vasmer. 1953-1958. *Russisches etymologisches Wörterbuch*, volume 1-3. Winter, Heidelberg.

Rastislav Šuštaršič, Smiljana Komar, and Bojan Petek. 1995. Slovene. *Journal of the International Phonetic Association*, 25(2):86–90.

Søren Wichmann, Eric W. Holman, Taraka Rama, and Robert S. Walker. 2011. Correlates of reticulation in linguistic phylogenies. *Language Dynamics and Change*, 1:205–240.

Ronald J. Williams. 1992. Simple statistical gradient-following algorithms for connectionist reinforcement learning. *Machine learning*, 8(3-4):229–256.

Shijie Wu and Ryan Cotterell. 2019. Exact hard monotonic attention for character-level transduction. In *Proceedings of the 57th Annual Meeting of the Association for Computational Linguistics*, pages 1530–1537, Florence, Italy. Association for Computational Linguistics.

Irena Yanushevskaya and Daniel Bunčić. 2015. Russian. *Journal of the International Phonetic Association*, 45(2):221–228.

Multi-Tiered Strictly Local Functions

Phillip Burness
University of Ottawa
pburn036@uottawa.ca

Kevin McMullin
University of Ottawa
kevin.mcmullin@uottawa.ca

Abstract

Tier-based Strictly Local functions, as they have so far been defined, are equipped with just a single tier. In light of this fact, they are currently incapable of modelling simultaneous phonological processes that would require different tiers. In this paper we consider whether and how we can allow a single function to operate over more than one tier. We conclude that multiple tiers can and should be permitted, but that the relationships between them must be restricted in some way to avoid overgeneration. The particular restriction that we propose comes in two parts. First, each input element is associated with a set of tiers that on their own can fully determine what the element is mapped to. Second, the set of tiers associated to a given input element must form a strict superset-subset hierarchy. In this way, we can track multiple, related sources of information when deciding how to process a particular input element. We demonstrate that doing so enables simple and intuitive analyses to otherwise challenging phonological phenomena.

1 Introduction

Many theoretical analyses of long-distance phonological patterns share the core intuition that a *tier* or *projection* of segments can allow for 'local' relationships to be established between non-adjacent elements by excluding material that is irrelevant from the implicated level of representation. For example, Samala (also known as Ineseño Chumash) has a long-distance process of sibilant harmony in which an underlying /s/ surfaces as [ʃ] if another [ʃ] appears anywhere later in the word, as in /ha-s-xintila-waʃ/ → [haʃxintilawaʃ] 'his former gentile name' (Applegate, 1972). The harmony target can be arbitrarily far from the harmony trigger in the full string of segments, but the trigger and target are rendered adjacent on a level

of representation containing all and only the sibilant consonants.

Within the subregular hierarchy of formal languages, the class of Strictly Local languages, which model local phonotactic restrictions (McNaughton and Papert, 1971; Rogers and Pullum, 2011; Rogers et al., 2013) have been extended to incorporate the notion of a tier, resulting in the class of *Tier-based Strictly Local* (TSL) languages (Heinz et al., 2011). Likewise, the Input Strictly Local (ISL) and Output Strictly Local (OSL) functions—which characterize locally-bounded phonological processes as subregular maps (Chandlee, 2014; Chandlee et al., 2014, 2015)—have been generalized to the classes of Input Tier-based Strictly Local (ITSL) and Output Tier-based Strictly Local (OTSL) functions in order to account for non-local phonological processes (Burness and McMullin, 2019; Hao and Andersson, 2019; Hao and Bowers, 2019).

These TSL formal languages and functions successfully model a wide range of long-distance phonological patterns (McMullin, 2016; McMullin and Hansson, 2016; Burness and McMullin, 2019; Hao and Bowers, 2019), and moreover have desirable properties for learnability (Jardine and Heinz, 2016; Jardine and McMullin, 2017; Burness and McMullin, 2019). However, they suffer from a major drawback in that they are restricted to a single tier, and as a consequence are ill-equipped to deal with multiple, simultaneous long-distance dependencies. For example, the Tamashek dialect of Tuareg exhibits regressive long-distance sibilant harmony and regressive long-distance labial dissimilation (Heath, 2005; McMullin, 2016). Each of the two processes can be modelled in isolation as a TSL function, but there is no single TSL function that can apply both rules simultaneously. The solution we pursue in this paper is to give functions access to more than

*Proceedings of the Seventeenth SIGMORPHON Workshop on Computational Research
in Phonetics, Phonology, and Morphology*, pages 245–255
Online, July 10, 2020. ©2020 Association for Computational Linguistics
https://doi.org/10.18653/v1/P17

one tier.

Incorporating multiple tiers into a single function is relatively straightforward; the difficulty lies in understanding the computational properties of such functions and establishing appropriate restrictions on the number of tiers and the relationships between tiers. Progress has been made with regards to properly restricting multi-tiered languages (Aksënova and Deskmukh, 2018; McMullin et al., 2019), and this paper considers the restrictions that need to be imposed onto the multiple tiers of a multi-tiered function. Our proposal is to associate each input element with a set of tiers that must fall into a strict subset-superset hierarchy (i.e., each tier in the set is a strict subset of the next largest tier in the set, if it exists). The output corresponding to an input element then depends on its dedicated set of tiers, and no others.

The rest of this paper is structured as follows. Section 2 introduces the notation that will be used throughout the paper. Section 3 presents the TSL functions as they are currently defined. Section 4 discusses some limitations of TSL functions that this paper aims to address. Section 5 formally defines the Multi-Tiered Strictly Local (MTSL) functions, and formalizes the restrictions that we propose must hold over the relationships among multiple tiers. Section 6 demonstrates how appropriately restricted MTSL functions overcome the limitations highlighted in Section 4. Finally, Section 7 concludes and provides directions for future research.

2 Preliminaries

To start, let Σ be an alphabet of symbols, which in the context of phonotactics represents a language's inventory of surface phones. A string w is a finite contiguous sequence of symbols from Σ, and $|w|$ denotes the length of w. We write λ for the unique string of length 0 (the empty string). We use Σ^* to denote the set of all strings of any length that can be made from elements in Σ. Note that Σ^* includes the empty string. Given two strings u and v, we write $u \cdot v$ to denote their concatenation, though we will often simply write uv when context permits. A k-factor of a string w is any contiguous substring of w with length k, though in the special case that $|w| \leq k$, w is its own and only k-factor. In what follows, $\mathtt{fac}_k(w)$ denotes all the k-factors contained in a string w.

A prefix of some string $w \in \Sigma^*$ is any string $u \in \Sigma^*$ such that $w = u \cdot x$ and $x \in \Sigma^*$. A suffix of some string $w \in \Sigma^*$ is any string $u \in \Sigma^*$ such that $w = x \cdot u$ and $x \in \Sigma^*$. Note that any string is a suffix of itself, and that λ is a suffix of every string. When $|w| \geq n$, $\mathtt{suff}^n(w)$ denotes the unique suffix of w with a length of n; when $|w| < n$, it simply denotes w itself. Given a string w and one of its prefixes u we write $u^{-1} \cdot w$ to denote w with u removed from its front. For example, $ab^{-1} \cdot abcde = cde$. Finally, given a set of strings S, we write $\mathtt{lcp}(S)$ to denote the *longest common prefix* of S, which is the string u such that u is a prefix of every $w \in S$, and there exists no other string v such that $|v| > |u|$ and v is also a prefix of every $w \in S$.

A string-to-string function pairs every $w \in \Sigma^*$ with one $y \in \Delta^*$, where Σ and Δ are the input alphabet and output alphabet respectively. Given a set of input strings $I \subseteq \Sigma^*$, $f(I) = \bigcup_{i \in I}\{f(i)\}$ is the set of all outputs associated to at least one of the inputs. An important concept is that of the *tails* of an input string w with respect to a function f.

Definition 1. Tails (Oncina and Garcia, 1991) *Given a function f and an input $w \in \Sigma^*$,*
$$\mathtt{tails}_f(w) = \{(y,v) \mid f(wy) = uv \wedge u = \mathtt{lcp}(f(w\Sigma^*))\}.$$

In words, $\mathtt{tails}_f(w)$ pairs every possible string $y \in \Sigma^*$ with the portion of $f(wy)$ that is *directly attributable* to y. Put another way, the tails of w are the effect that w has on the output of any subsequent string of input symbols. Consider a function f computing post-nasal voicing. The tails of w_1 = /tan/ relative to f will include pairs such as $\langle$t, d$\rangle$ since f(tant) = [tand] and $\langle$opu, opu$\rangle$ since f(tanopu) = [tanopu]. When $\mathtt{tails}_f(w_1)$ = $\mathtt{tails}_f(w_2)$, we say that w_1 and w_2 are *tail-equivalent* with respect to f. The string w_2 = /ken/ is tail-equivalent to w_1 with respect to f because they both end in a nasal consonant, and therefore both trigger post-nasal voicing. An example of a string that is not tail-equivalent to w_1 or w_2 would be w_3 = /sini/; its tail for /t/ is $\langle$t, t$\rangle$ since it does not end in a nasal consonant and so does not trigger post-nasal voicing.

Throughout the rest of this paper, we will need to be able to pick out the portion of the output that corresponds to actual input material. Viewed from another perspective, we need to be able to ignore the portion of the output that would correspond to a word-end symbol. To make this distinction,

Chandlee et al. (2015) defined the prefix function f^p associated with a function f such that $f^p(w)$ is equal to the longest common prefix of all strings $f(wx)$, where x is some member of Σ^*.

Definition 2. Prefix function
Given a function f, its associated prefix function f^p is such that $f^p(w) = \mathtt{lcp}(f(w\Sigma^*))$.

An example where $f(w)$ and $f^p(w)$ differ would be a function that appends a to the end of every input string. In this case, f^p is simply the identity map, so $f^p(abc) = abc$ whereas $f(abc) = abca$.

3 Background

Like their name suggests, the Input Strictly Local (ISL) and Output Strictly Local (OSL) functions take the Strictly Local (SL) languages as their base. Theorem 1 states the property of the SL languages that allowed for the jump to ISL and OSL functions. This property is known as Suffix Substitution Closure (SSC; Rogers and Pullum, 2011; Rogers et al., 2013). Informally, if two grammatical strings share a middle portion of at least length $k - 1$ (i.e., if $w_1 = axb$, $w_2 = cxd$, and $|x| \geq k - 1$), then we can substitute the suffixes that come after the overlap without causing ungrammaticality. A corollary of SSC is that any two grammatical strings from an SL_k language that end in the same $k-1$ (or more) symbols can be legally continued by the exact same set of strings (Chandlee et al., 2015).

Theorem 1. Suffix Substitution Closure (Rogers et al., 2013)
A stringset L is Strictly k-Local if and only if whenever there is a string x of length $k - 1$ and strings u_1, u_2, v_1, v_2, it is the case that:

$$[u_1xv_1 \in L \wedge u_2xv_2 \in L] \Rightarrow u_1xv_2 \in L$$

Corollary 1. Suffix-defined Residuals (Chandlee et al., 2015)
A stringset L is Strictly k-Local if and only if for all pairs $w_1, w_2 \in \Sigma^*$:

$$suff^{k-1}(w_1) = suff^{k-1}(w_2) \Rightarrow$$
$$\{v \mid w_1 \cdot v \in L\} = \{v \mid w_2 \cdot v \in L\}$$

The definitions of the ISL and OSL functions take the property in Corollary 1 and adapt it so that it applies to function tails. Informally, a function f is ISL if the tail-equivalence classes of f correspond to input suffixes, and a function f is OSL if

the tail-equivalence classes of f correspond to output suffixes (or more accurately, suffixes of f^p).

Definition 3. Input Strictly k-Local Functions
A function $f : \Sigma^* \to \Delta^*$ is ISL_k if for all w_1, w_2 in Σ^*:

$$suff^{k-1}(w_1) = suff^{k-1}(w_2) \Rightarrow$$
$$tails_f(w_1) = tails_f(w_2)$$

Definition 4. Output Strictly k-Local Functions
A function $f : \Sigma^* \to \Delta^*$ is OSL_k if for all w_1, w_2 in Σ^*:

$$suff^{k-1}(f^p(w_1)) = suff^{k-1}(f^p(w_2)) \Rightarrow$$
$$tails_f(w_1) = tails_f(w_2)$$

Chandlee (2014) and Chandlee et al. (2014, 2015) show that most iterative phonological processes can be modelled with an OSL function, with an important exception being long-distance iterative processes like consonant harmony. This is parallel to the fact that long-distance phonotactics cannot be represented with an SL stringset, which motivated Heinz et al. (2011) to define the Tier-based Strictly Local (TSL) languages— stringsets that are SL after an erasure function has applied, masking all symbols that are irrelevant to the restrictions that the language places on its strings. The erasure function takes a tier τ and a string w, returning w with all non-tier elements removed.

Definition 5. Erasure function
Given an alphabet Σ, a tier $\tau \subseteq \Sigma$, and a string $w = a_1...a_n$, $erase_\tau(w) = b_1...b_n$ where for all $i \leq n$, $b_i = a_i$ if $a_i \in \tau$, else $b_i = \lambda$.

Definition 6. Tier-based Strictly k-Local languages
A language L is TSL_k if there is a tier $\tau \subseteq \Sigma$ and a subset $S \subseteq fac_k(\rtimes\tau^*\ltimes)$ such that:

$$L = \{w \in \Sigma^* \mid fac_k(\rtimes erase_\tau(w)\ltimes) \subseteq S\}$$

As it turns out, the TSL languages also exhibit a form of Suffix Substitution Closure (Lambert and Rogers, 2020). In light of this fact, the legal continuations of any string w in a TSL_k language can be inferred simply by looking at the $k - 1$ suffix of $erase_\tau(w)$. Just as we did for the ISL and OSL functions, then, we can define the ITSL and OTSL functions according to how they partition Σ^* into tail-equivalence classes. For convenience, we will write $suff_\tau^n(w)$ to mean $suff^n(erase_\tau(w))$ in what follows.

Definition 7. Input Tier-based Strictly k-Local Functions

A function $f : \Sigma^* \to \Delta^*$ is $ITSL_k$ if there is a tier $\tau \subseteq \Sigma$ such that for all w_1, w_2 in Σ^*:

$$suff_\tau^{k-1}(w_1) = suff_\tau^{k-1}(w_2) \Rightarrow$$
$$tails_f(w_1) = tails_f(w_2)$$

Definition 8. Output Tier-based Strictly k-Local Functions

A function $f : \Sigma^* \to \Delta^*$ is $OTSL_k$ if there is a tier $\tau \subseteq \Delta$ such that for all w_1, w_2 in Σ^*:

$$suff_\tau^{k-1}(f^p(w_1)) = suff_\tau^{k-1}(f^p(w_2)) \Rightarrow$$
$$tails_f(w_1) = tails_f(w_2)$$

Informally, a function f is ITSL if the tail-equivalence classes of f correspond to input tier suffixes (where the tier is a subset of the input alphabet Σ), and a function f is OTSL if the tail-equivalence classes of f correspond to output tier suffixes (where the tier is a subset of the output alphabet Δ). Important to note is that the ITSL functions properly contain the ISL functions and that the OTSL functions properly contain the OSL functions. This is because anything SL is also TSL when the tier is simply the entire alphabet.

The above definitions of the ITSL and OTSL functions abstract away from reading direction, which divides each class into two overlapping but distinct classes. This is similar to how the subsequential functions can be divided into the left-subsequential functions which read the input from left to right and the right-subsequential functions which read the input from right to left (Heinz and Lai, 2013). We will also abstract away from reading direction when defining our multi-tiered functions, but will specify the directionality of individual functions.

4 Limitations of TSL functions

As discussed in Burness and McMullin (2019), the TSL functions are quite versatile, being able to model long-distance harmony and long-distance dissimilation, both with and without blocking effects. This is, however, only the case when we model each phonological process of a language in isolation.

Consider the Tamashek dialect of Tuareg, which contains a process of long-distance regressive sibilant harmony and a process of long-distance regressive labial dissimilation (Heath, 2005; McMullin, 2016). The sibilant harmony can be seen

in words where the causative prefix /s-/ is followed non-locally by another sibilant, whereupon it takes that other sibilant's values for anteriority, voicing, and pharyngealization as shown by the data in (1) from Heath (2005, p. 442). Note that the language has considerable vowel allophony, and we write 'V' where Heath (2005) does not provide the surface vowel quality. The labial dissimilation can be seen in words where a prefix /m/ (such as in the mediopassive) is followed non-locally by a labial consonant other than /w/, whereupon the prefix /m/ will dissimilate to [n]. Data for this process is shown in (2) from Heath (2005, p. 472). That both processes can occur simultaneously is demonstrated by the word in (3) from Heath (2005, p. 462), which contains the causative and mediopassive prefixes together.

(1)   Sibilant harmony: causative /s-/
        -s-VŋŋV-   'cook'
        -s-VsVfVr-   'treat (patient)'
        -sˤ-Vsˤuh V- 'strengthen'
        -ʃ-VluʃV-   'clean sand from'
        -z-VjVzzV   'scrutinize'

(2)   Labial dissimilation: mediopassive /m-/
        -m-VrtVj-   'become mixed'
        -n-VkmVm-   'be squeezed'

(3)   Both prefixes/processes
        ɑ-zˤ-ən:-ət-əlməzˤ   'spitting saliva'

The combination of sibilant harmony and labial dissimilation cannot, however, be computed by a single TSL function. To see why, consider what happens when we try with an $OTSL_2$ function whose tier consists of all sibilants and labial consonants. Producing a sibilant will push the most recent labial consonant (if any) out of the $k - 1$ window, and producing a labial consonant will push the most recent sibilant (if any) out of the $k - 1$ window. At any given point, then, we can only know how to correctly map an input /s/ or only know how to correctly map an input /m/. Increasing k does not eliminate the issue, since any number of sibilants can in principle occur between two labial consonants, and any number of labial consonants can in principle occur between two sibilants.

A further difficulty for TSL functions posed by Tamashek Tuareg is that long-distance regressive labial dissimilation interacts with a local process of regressive nasal place assimilation. The complication arises from the fact that the local process overrides the long-distance process: /m/ fails to dissimilate specifically when it is immediately followed by an oral labial stop, in order to avoid a heterorganic cluster. This can be seen in a word like (4) from Heath (2005, p. 476) where the reciprocal prefix /Vm-/ comes immediately before a /b/. We are faced with a paradox if we attempt to model this interaction as a single TSL function. In order to know when an input labial needs to dissimilate we need to ignore everything that is not a labial consonant, but in order to know when an input labial needs to obey place assimilation we cannot ignore anything.

(4)   Local blocking of dissimilation
        -æm-bæbbɑ-   'carried each other'

Whether these interactions are problematic depends on whether we conceive of a language's phonological system as a series of input-output maps or as a single "master" input-output map. The latter position is explored by Chandlee and Heinz (2018) and Chandlee et al. (2018) in the context of formal language theory and automata theory. They remark that the ISL functions are not closed under composition, but that certain opaque rule interactions (counterfeeding, counterbleeding, etc.) can nevertheless be modelled using a single ISL function when the component rules are also ISL functions.

5   Multi-Tiered Strictly Local functions

The main method that we will use to tackle the limitations presented in the previous Section is by allowing a single function to operate over multiple tiers. We call these the Multi-Tiered Strictly k-Local (MTSL$_k$) functions, for lack of a better name. Note that we use a large subscripted conjunction symbol to collapse a series of formulae that are identical aside from using different tiers.

Definition 9. Input Multi-Tiered Strictly k-Local functions

A function $f : \Sigma^* \to \Delta^*$ is IMTSL$_k$ if there is a finite set T of tiers $\tau \subseteq \Sigma$ such that for all $w_1, w_2 \in \Sigma^*$:

$$[\bigwedge_{\tau \in T} [suff_\tau^{k-1}(w_1) = suff_\tau^{k-1}(w_2)]]$$
$$\Rightarrow [tails_f(w_1) = tails_f(w_2)]$$

Definition 10. Output Multi-Tiered Strictly k-Local functions

A function $f : \Sigma^* \to \Delta^*$ is OMTSL$_k$ if there is a finite set T of tiers $\tau \subseteq \Delta$ such that for all $w_1, w_2 \in \Sigma^*$:

$$[\bigwedge_{\tau \in T} [suff_\tau^{k-1}(f^p(w_1)) = suff_\tau^{k-1}(f^p(w_2))]]$$
$$\Rightarrow [tails_f(w_1) = tails_f(w_2)]$$

In words, there is a finite set of tiers such that if two input strings share a $k-1$ suffix *on all tiers*, then they will have the same tails. Notice how this is a direct extension of the TSL$_k$ functions, since the singleton tier of a TSL$_k$ function will satisfy the above definition.

Of course, allowing any conceivable number of tiers and allowing any conceivable relationship between their contents is too powerful. One pathological behaviour that can arise from excessively free tier sets would be 'gang-up' effects. For example, given a collection of disjoint tiers that each contain a single element, we can describe processes where the output of some input element depends on the exact set of preceding elements regardless of their order. A similar behaviour can arise from overlapping but disjoint tiers. Given $\tau_1 = \{s, \int, t\}$ and $\tau_2 = \{s, \int, n\}$ we could describe a process of sibilant harmony that is blocked only when *both* 't' and 'n' intervene, regardless of their order. To the best of our knowledge, such processes are unattested and should be excluded.

In order to limit the "tier multiverse", we propose to reference the contribution of each $\sigma \in \Sigma$ separately, rather than referencing the entirety of $tails_f$. Informally, the contribution of a relative to w is the portion of $f(wa)$ uniquely and directly attributable to a (e.g., it is what we would append to the output upon reading a in a transducer after having read w). A more formal definition is provided below.

Definition 11. Contribution
Given a function f, some $a \in \Sigma$, and some $w \in \Sigma^*$, $cont_f(a, w) = lcp(f(w\Sigma^*))^{-1} \cdot lcp(f(wa\Sigma^*)) = f^p(w)^{-1} \cdot f^p(wa)$.

Using this notion of a contribution relative to w, which singles out a single element of $tails_f(w)$, we place the following condition on MTSL$_k$ functions, which we call *target specification*.

Definition 12. Target specification
An IMTSL$_k$ function $f : \Sigma^* \to \Delta^*$ is target specified if for each $\sigma \in \Sigma$ there is a finite set T_σ of tiers $\tau \subseteq \Sigma$ that form a strict superset-subset hierarchy,

and the following holds for all $w_1, w_2 \in \Sigma^*$

$$[\bigwedge_{\tau \in T_\sigma} [suff_\tau^{k-1}(w_1) = suff_\tau^{k-1}(w_2)]]$$

$$\Rightarrow [cont_f(\sigma, w_1) = cont_f(\sigma, w_2)]$$

An $OMTSL_k$ function $f : \Sigma^* \to \Delta^*$ is target speci-fied if for each $\sigma \in \Sigma$ there is a finite set T_σ of tiers $\tau \subseteq \Delta$ that form a strict superset-subset hierar-chy, and the following holds for all $w_1, w_2 \in \Sigma^*$:

$$[\bigwedge_{\tau \in T_\sigma} [suff_\tau^{k-1}(f^p(w_1)) = suff_\tau^{k-1}(f^p(w_2))]]$$

$$\Rightarrow [cont_f(\sigma, w_1) = cont_f(\sigma, w_2)]$$

In words, when an MTSL function is target specified, each $\sigma \in \Sigma$ (i.e., each potential target of one or more processes) can be associated with a group of tiers that together determine the contribution of σ. Viewed from another perspective, each input element specifies the tiers that it wants to track, and the contribution of an input element can always be determined by tracking only its specified set of tiers; tracking other tiers provides information that is either redundant or irrelevant. Importantly, each member of the tier group is a proper subset of the next largest member.

Requiring an input segment's multiple associated tiers to fall into a strict superset-subset hierarchy has two apparent positive consequences. First, this restriction will be beneficial for learning, since it drastically reduces the number of possible tier combinations that can influence a given input element. Aksënova and Deskmukh (2018) show that even with a small inventory of 10 elements, there are 1022 ways to create a superset-subset pair, 511 ways to create a pair of fully disjoint sets, and 27990 ways to create a pair of partially overlapping sets. This last number is already 95% larger than the other two combined, and the difference only increases as the size of the alphabet grows. Second, research into multi-tiered stringsets suggests that we never see a single restriction enforced on two partially overlapping tiers (Aksënova and Deskmukh, 2018; McMullin et al., 2019).

6 Multiple Tiers in Action

This section now considers a range of individual patterns and pattern interactions that standard TSL functions are incapable of capturing. We show that each of the considered patterns and interactions are simply and intuitively captured by the target-specified MTSL functions defined in the previous Section. In order, we consider interactions between independent processes (6.1), interactions between conflicting processes (6.2), cases where a single target is subject to multiple harmonies (6.3), and cases where some segments act as last-resort harmony triggers in the absence of canonical triggers (6.4).

6.1 Independent processes

Recall from Section 4 that Tamashek Tuareg contains simultaneous long-distance sibilant harmony and long-distance labial dissimilation. Postponing discussion of the complication that arises from local nasal place assimilation, we can describe the two processes with a single target-specified $OMTSL_2$ function as follows.

First, we associate input /s/ with the tier $\tau_s = \{s, s^\Omega, z, z^\Omega, \int, \mathbf{3}\}$ containing all and only the sibilant consonants. Doing so, we need only specify that if $suff_{\tau_s}^1(f^p(w)) \neq \lambda$ when reading from right to left, then $cont_f(s, w) = suff_{\tau_s}^1(f^p(w))$, else $cont_f(s, w) =$[s]. In other words, /s/ harmonizes with the closest sibilant to its right, if there is one, else it surfaces faithfully.

Second, we associate input /m/ with the tier $\tau_m = \{m, b, f\}$ containing all and only the labial obstruents. Doing so, we need only specify that if $suff_{\tau_m}^1(f^p(w)) \neq \lambda$ when reading from right to left, then $cont_f(m, w) = [n]$, else $cont_f(m, w) = [m]$. In other words, /m/ dissimilates to [n] if there is a labial obstruent somewhere to its right, else it surfaces faithfully.

Each of the input elements we are considering here is associated to a single tier, and so the definition of target specification is satisfied. By virtue of tracking separate tiers, the two processes do not interfere with each other and so can be computed in tandem, exactly as desired. The simultaneous computation of the two rules is shown pictorially in Figure 1 for the word [ɑ-z^ʕ-ən:-ət-əlməz^ʕ] 'act of spitting up saliva'. The string in the center of the figure is the output string. Solid lines represent projection to an output tier and dashed lines represent an output tier element's influence on an input element.

6.2 Conflicting processes

The previous Section abstracted away from the interaction between long-distance labial dissimilation and local nasal place assimilation, which we

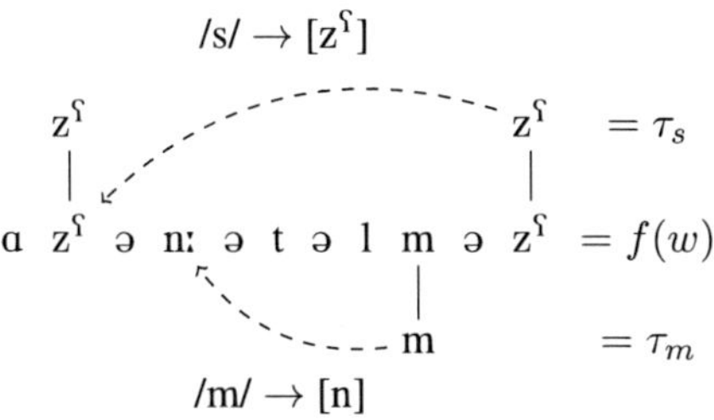

Figure 1: Simultaneous sibilant harmony and labial dissimilation in Tamashek Tuareg.

will now consider here. The interaction can be modelled with a target-specified OMTSL$_2$ functions as follows. First, we associate /m/ with a first tier $\tau_{m1} = \Delta$ containing all elements in the output alphabet. We furthermore associate /m/ with a second tier $\tau_{m2} = \{m, b, f\}$ containing all and only the labial obstruents. Assuming that the input is read from right to left, the full behaviour of /m/ can be described as follows. If $\mathrm{suff}^1_{\tau_{m1}}(f^p(w))$ is a labial obstruent, then $\mathrm{cont}_f(m, w) = [m]$ since /m/ is required to assimilate in place with the adjacent obstruent. If $\mathrm{suff}^1_{\tau_{m1}}(f^p(w)) \neq [b]$ and $\mathrm{suff}^1_{\tau_{m2}}(f^p(w)) \neq \lambda$, then $\mathrm{cont}_f(m, w) = [n]$ since /m/ is not immediately adjacent to a labial consonant, but nonetheless is preceded non-locally by a labial and must dissimilate. In all other cases, /m/ surfaces faithfully as [m]. Note especially how $\tau_{m2} \subset \tau_{m1}$, and so the function meets the definition of target specification.

This is not to say that local processes always override non-local processes. Indeed, the opposite is witnessed in Samala. The Samala language is well-known for its process of regressive sibilant harmony, whereby the anteriority of the rightmost sibilant overrides the anteriority of all sibilants to the left. As it turns out, the language contains an additional rule affecting the sibilant /s/. Namely, /s/ regressively palatalizes to [ʃ] when immediately followed by [t], [n], or [l] (Applegate, 1972; Poser, 1982, 1993; McCarthy, 2007; Hansson, 2010; McMullin, 2016). The long-distance process is given priority here, such that the local sequences [sn], [st] and [sl] are permitted precisely when palatalization would create a disharmonic sequence of non-local sibilants.[1] Data exempli-

fying the two processes and their interaction are provided in (5) through (7) taken from Applegate (1972, p. 117-120).

(5) Unbounded sibilant harmony
/s-xalam-ʃ/ → [ʃ-xalamʃ] 'it is wrapped'

(6) Local palatalization
/s-niʔ/ → [ʃ-niʔ] 'his neck'

(7) Harmony overrides palatalization
/s-net-us/ → [s-net-us] 'he does it to him'

We can also describe this with a target-specified OMTSL$_2$ function. In this case, the contribution of /s/ is dependent on two tiers: a tier $\tau_{s1} = \Delta$ relative to which local palatalization is considered, and a tier $\tau_{s2} = \{s, ʃ\}$ relative to which sibilant harmony is considered. Assuming that the input is read from right to left, the behaviour of /s/ can be described as follows. If $\mathrm{suff}^1_{\tau_{s2}}(f^p(w)) = \lambda$ and $\mathrm{suff}^1_{\tau_{s1}}(f^p(w))$ is one of [t], [n], or [l], then $\mathrm{cont}_f(s, w) = [ʃ]$ since it is adjacent to a palatalization trigger but not preceded non-locally by a [-anterior] sibilant. If $\mathrm{suff}^1_{\tau_{s2}}(f^p(w)) = [ʃ]$, then $\mathrm{cont}_f(s, w) = [ʃ]$ since /s/ is preceded non-locally by a [-anterior] sibilant and must harmonize. In all other contexts, /s/ surfaces faithfully as [s]. Once again, $\tau_{s2} \subset \tau_{s1}$ and so the function meets the definition of target specification.

6.3 Single target, multiple harmonies

The target-specified MTSL functions are not limited to describing interactions between a local and non-local process, they can equally describe cases where a single element is subject to two long-distance dependencies operating over different featural dimensions. An example of this comes from then Imdlawn dialect of Tashlhiyt. The language's causative prefix /s-/ agrees in both anteriority and voicing with a following sibilant, as shown in (8), although the voicing dimension of the harmony is blocked by an intervening voiceless obstruent (Elmedlaoui, 1995; Hansson, 2010; McMullin, 2016), as shown in (9).

(8) Anteriority and voicing harmony
/s-gruʒ:m/ → [ʒ-gruʒ:m]
'CAUS-be.extinguished'

(9) Voicing harmony blocked
/s-mħaraʒ/ → [ʃ-mħaraʒ]
'CAUS-get.angry.with.each.other'

We can describe this as a target-specified OMTSL$_2$ function wherein the contribution of /s/

---

[1]Some accounts of the data claim that the local process takes priority. See Heinz and Idsardi (2010) for a discussion and resolution of this inconsistency.

depends on one tier τ_{s1} for its voicing and another tier τ_{s2} for its anteriority. The voicing tier τ_{s1} contains all sibilants and all voiceless obstruents, while the anteriority tier τ_{s2} contains only the sibilants. Assuming that the input is read from right to left, the behaviour of /s/ can be described as follows. If $\mathtt{suff}^1_{\tau_{s1}}(f^p(w)) = \mathtt{suff}^1_{\tau_{s2}}(f^p(w))$, then an input /s/ harmonizes in both anteriority and voicing with that sibilant. Note that both tiers contain all sibilants and so the two tier suffixes can never be different sibilants. If $\mathtt{suff}^1_{\tau_{s2}}(f^p(w))$ is a sibilant and $\mathtt{suff}^1_{\tau_{s1}}(f^p(w))$ is a voiceless obstruent, then /s/ harmonizes in anteriority but not voicing with $\mathtt{suff}^1_{\tau_{s2}}(f^p(w))$. The voicing dimension of the harmony is blocked because $\tau_{s2} \subset \tau_{s1}$, and so the voiceless obstruent necessarily intervenes between the triggering sibilant and the target sibilant. In all other cases, /s/ surfaces faithfully as [s].

In this Imdlawn Tashlhiyt case, the harmony target agrees with the harmony source along two dimensions, but there are cases where a single target can agree with multiple sources in specific configurations. Suffixal high vowels in Turkish typically agree in backness and rounding with the next vowel to the left, as shown in (10) from Nevins (2010, p. 27). An interesting exception, however, concerns the consonants /k/, /g/, and /l/ which are contrastively [+back] and have the [-back] counterparts /kʲ/, /gʲ/, and /lʲ/ (Clements and Sezer, 1982). If one of these consonants intervenes between the suffixal high vowel and the next vowel to the left, the suffixal high vowel takes its backness value from the consonant and its rounding feature from the vowel, as shown in (11) from Nevins (2010, p. 54).

(10)   Two harmonies, same source
     son-un   'end-GEN
     sap-ɯn   'stalk-GEN'

(11)   Two harmonies, two sources
     usulʲ-y   'system-Acc.SG'
     sualʲ-i   'question-ACC.SG'

Let us assume that the harmonizing suffixal high vowels are underlyingly /U/, which lacks values for [back] and [round]. The potentially split harmony can be analyzed with the following target-specified OMTSL$_2$ function. We have a backness tier τ_{U1} containing all the vowels and the abovementioned consonants. We also also have a rounding tier τ_{U2} containing all and only the vowels. Assuming that the input is read from left to

right, the behaviour of /U/ can be described as follows. If $\mathtt{suff}^1_{\tau_{U1}}(f^p(w)) = \mathtt{suff}^1_{\tau_{U2}}(f^p(w))$, then the nearest source of backness and the nearest source of rounding are both the nearest leftward vowel. If, however, $\mathtt{suff}^1_{\tau_{U1}}(f^p(w)) \neq \mathtt{suff}^1_{\tau_{U2}}(f^p(w))$, then one of the relevant consonants must intervene between the suffixal vowel and the nearest leftward vowel. In this case, the suffixal vowel will take on the backness value of the consonant; the source of rounding will, however, always be the nearest leftward vowel.

6.4   Last-resort triggers

The final type of behaviour we will consider comes from a case of harmony that is triggered by a special class of segments in the absence of a more "preferred" trigger. Uyghur vowels are subject to a progressive backness harmony for which the non-low front vowels [i] and [e] are transparent (Lindblad, 1990; Vaux, 2000; Mayer and Major, 2018). The language's locative suffix shows that the harmony is an active process; its vowel alternates between front [æ] and back [a] as shown in (12) taken from Mayer and Major (2018).

(12)   Uyghur vowel harmony
     aʁinæ-dæ   'friend-LOC'
     qoichi-da   'shepherd-LOC'

Interestingly, dorsal consonants can trigger harmony in the absence of a harmonic vowel, with velar consonants causing front allomorphs of suffixes and uvulars causing back allomorphs (Lindblad, 1990; Vaux, 2000; Mayer and Major, 2018), as shown in (13). The harmony "prefers" to be triggered by vowels, however, which is witnessed by the fact that a back vowel can trigger back allormorphs across a velar consonant (Lindblad, 1990; Vaux, 2000; Mayer and Major, 2018), as shown in (14). Dorsal consonants only decide the front/back status of a suffix when the base lacks non-transparent vowels altogether, in a sense acting as a "last-resort trigger" (Lindblad, 1990; Vaux, 2000; Mayer and Major, 2018).

(13)   Harmony with a dorsal
     gezit-tæ   'newspaper-LOC'
     qiʁiz-da   'Kyrgyz-LOC'

(14)   Harmony across a dorsal
     rak-ta 'exercise-LOC'

This pattern too can be generated by a target-specified OMTSL$_2$ function. The suffixal low vowel /A/ is associated to one tier τ_{A1} containing all non-transparent vowels and dorsal consonants, and is also associated to a second tier τ_{A2} containing only the non-transparent vowels. Assuming that the input is read from left to right, the harmony can be described as follows. If $\text{suff}^1_{\tau_{A2}}(f^p(w)) \neq \lambda$, then there is a non-transparent vowel in the stem that triggers harmony. If, however, $\text{suff}^1_{\tau_{A2}}(f^p(w)) = \lambda$ and $\text{suff}^1_{\tau_{A1}}(f^p(w)) \neq \lambda$, then all stem vowels are transparent, but there is a dorsal consonant available to trigger harmony as a last resort.

7 Conclusion

This paper defined an extension of the Tier-based Strictly Local functions, allowing them to track multiple tiers so long as the inter-tier relationships obey certain restrictions. Rather than having the entirety of the functional tails depending on just one tier, we allow the contribution of each input element to separately depend on its own set of tiers, provided that the set falls into a strict superset-subset hierarchy.

Our strategy of dividing the work amongst several independent sets of tiers greatly resembles the search procedure of Nevins (2010), see also Andersson et al. (2020). In this search procedure, specific input elements initiate a search for the nearest item relevant to them in some specified direction, and their output fate depends on the identity of the first relevant element found. Our approach is in many ways the mirror of the search procedure: by tracking the tiers specified by σ, we preemptively remember the most recent element(s) that would be relevant to the output fate of σ, and we therefore always know what to do when σ is encountered. We demonstrated that a wide variety of otherwise challenging phonological processes receive simple and intuitive analyses from this perspective.

A reviewer asks about the closure of the TSL functions under composition, pointing out that the MTSL languages are the closure of the TSL languages under intersection. While we have not yet formally proven so, it is likely that the left-reading MTSL functions are indeed the closure of the left-reading TSL functions under composition (*mutatis mutandis* for right-reading functions). At the very least, all of the language patterns analyzed in Section 6 can be described as the composition of two same-direction TSL functions. Similar to how

Aksënova and Deskmukh (2018) and McMullin et al. (2019) argue that the full class of MTSL languages is too powerful, though, we believe that our proposal of target specification is necessary since free composition of TSL functions can lead to processes with bizarre properties (see Section 5).

One noteworthy behaviour not covered by the proposed class is bidirectional application. Research into bidirectional patterns has established that they can be modelled by *weakly deterministic functions* (Heinz and Lai, 2013). These are those functions from Σ^* to Δ^* that can be modelled as a pair of subsequential functions that apply in sequence and meet the following criteria: (i) the two functions read in opposite directions, (ii) the first function is from Σ^* to Σ^*, and (iii) the first function is not permitted to increase the length of the string. Since the function class considered in this paper is a proper subclass of the subsequential functions, it would be interesting to see whether we can lower the complexity bound of these bidirectional processes. Namely, can we instead model them as a pair of MTSL functions running in opposite directions?

Finally, future work will consider the learnability of MTSL functions. Burness and McMullin (2019) showed that any OTSL function is efficiently learnable from positive data if the tier is known in advance. This result can likely be carried over to MTSL functions once they receive a suitable automata characterization. When the tier is not known in advance, however, Burness and McMullin (2019) show that only total OTSL_2 functions are learnable from positive data. The induction of multiple tiers, necessary for the learning of MTSL functions, will thus likely be a significant challenge. That being said, McMullin et al. (2019) developed a method for learning the Multi-Tiered Strictly 2-Local languages, and their methods may perhaps be fruitfully applied to the function case.

Acknowledgements

We thank reviewers of this paper for their helpful comments. This research was supported by the Social Sciences and Humanities Research Council of Canada.

References

Aksënova, A. and Deskmukh, S. (2018). Formal restrictions on multiple tiers. In *Proceedings of the*

Society for Computation in Linguistics (SCiL) 2018, pages 64–73.

Andersson, S., Dolatian, H., and Hao, Y. (2020). Computing vowel harmony: The generative capacity of search and copy. In Baek, H., Takahashi, C., and Hong-Lun Yeung, A., editors, *Proceedings of the 2019 Annual Meeting on Phonology*.

Applegate, R. B. (1972). *Ineseño Chumash Grammar*. Doctoral Dissertation, University of California, Berkeley.

Burness, P. and McMullin, K. (2019). Efficient learning of Output Tier-based Strictly 2-Local functions. In *Proceedings of the 16th Meeting on the Mathematics of Language*, pages 78–90. Association for Computational Linguistics.

Chandlee, J. (2014). *Strictly Local Phonological Processes*. Doctoral Dissertation, University of Delaware.

Chandlee, J., Eyraud, R., and Heinz, J. (2014). Learning strictly local subsequential functions. *Transactions of the Association for Computational Linguistics*, 2:491–503.

Chandlee, J., Eyraud, R., and Heinz, J. (2015). Output strictly local functions. In *Proceedings of the 14th Meeting on the Mathematics of Language (MOL 2015)*, pages 112–125.

Chandlee, J. and Heinz, J. (2018). Strict Locality and Phonological Maps. *Linguistic Inquiry*, 49(1):23–59.

Chandlee, J., Heinz, J., and Jardine, A. (2018). Input Strictly Local opaque maps. *Phonology*, 35(2):171–205.

Clements, G. N. and Sezer, E. (1982). Vowel and consonant disharmony in Turkish. In van der Hulst, H. and Smith, N., editors, *The Structure of Phonological Representations (Part II)*, pages 213–255. Foris, Dordrecht.

Elmedlaoui, M. (1995). *Aspects de Représentations Phonolgiques Dans Certains Langues Chamito-Sémitiques [Aspects of Phonological Representations in Certain Chamito-Semitic Languages]*. Doctoral Dissertation, Université Mohammed V, Rabat, Morocco.

Hansson, G. Ó. (2010). *Consonant Harmony: Long-Distance Interaction in Phonology*. Number 145 in University of California Publications in Linguistics. University of California Press, Berkeley, CA.

Hao, Y. and Andersson, S. (2019). Action-Sensitive Phonological Dependencies. In *Proceedings of the 16th SIGMORPHON Workshop on Computational Research in Phonetics, Phonology and Morphology*, pages 135–143, Florence, Italy. Association for Computational Linguistics.

Hao, Y. and Bowers, D. (2019). Action-Sensitive Phonological Dependencies. In *Proceedings of the 16th SIGMORPHON Workshop on Computational Research in Phonetics, Phonology and Morphology*, pages 218–228, Florence, Italy. Association for Computational Linguistics.

Heath, J. (2005). *A Grammar of Tamashek (Tuareg of Mali)*. Mouton de Gruyter, Berlin.

Heinz, J. and Idsardi, W. J. (2010). Learning opaque generalizations: the case of Samala. Unpublished Manuscript.

Heinz, J. and Lai, R. (2013). Vowel harmony and subsequentiality. In Kornai, A. and Kuhlmann, M., editors, *Proceedings of the 13th Meeting on the Mathematics of Language (MoL13)*, pages 52–63, Sofia, Bulgaria. Association for Computational Linguistics.

Heinz, J., Rawal, C., and Tanner, H. G. (2011). Tier-based strictly local constraints for phonology. In *Proceedings of the 49th Annual Meeting of the Association for Computational Linguistics*, pages 58–64, Portland, OR. Association for Computational Linguistics.

Jardine, A. and Heinz, J. (2016). Learning Tier-based Strictly 2-Local languages. *Transactions of the Association for Computational Linguistics*, 4:87–98.

Jardine, A. and McMullin, K. (2017). Efficient Learning of Tier-Based Strictly k-Local Languages. In *International Conference on Language and Automata Theory and Applications (LATA 2017)*, pages 64–76.

Lambert, D. and Rogers, J. (2020). Tier-Based Strictly Local Stringsets: Perspectives from Model and Automata Theory. In *Proceedings of the Society for Computation in Linguistics (SCiL) 2020*, pages 330–337, New Orleans, Louisianna.

Lindblad, V. M. (1990). *Neutralization in Uyghur*. Master's Thesis, University of Washington.

Mayer, C. and Major, T. (2018). A challenge for tier-based strict locality from Uyghur backness harmony. In *Formal Grammar 2018*, number 10950 in Lecture Notes in Computer Science, pages 62–83. Springer, Berlin.

McCarthy, J. (2007). Consonant harmony via correspondence: Evidence from Chumash. In Bateman, L., O'Keefe, M., Reilly, E., and Werle, A., editors, *Papers in Optimality Theory III*, pages 223–237. University of Massachusetts Occasional Papers in Linguistics.

McMullin, K. (2016). *Tier-Based Locality in Long-Distance Phonotactics: Learnability and Typology*. Doctoral Dissertation, University of British Columbia, Vancouver, BC.

McMullin, K., Aksënova, A., and De Santo, A. (2019). Learning phonotactic restrictions on multiple tiers. In *Proceedings of the Society for Computation in Linguistics (SCiL) 2019*, volume 2, pages 377–378.

McMullin, K. and Hansson, G. Ó. (2016). Long-distance phonotactics as Tier-based Strictly 2-Local Languages. In Albright, A. and Fullwood, M. A., editors, *Proceedings of the 2014 Annual Meeting on Phonology*, Washington, DC. Linguistic Society of America.

McNaughton, R. and Papert, S. A. (1971). *Counter-Free Automata*. MIT Press, Cambridge, MA.

Nevins, A. (2010). *Locality in Vowel Harmony*. Number 55 in Linguistic Inquiry Monographs. MIT Press.

Oncina, J. and Garcia, P. (1991). Inductive learning of subsequential functions. Technical Report DSIC II-34, University Politecnia de Valencia.

Poser, W. (1982). Phonological representations and action-at-a-distance. In van der Hulst, H. and Smith, N., editors, *The Structure of Phonological Representations*, volume 2, pages 121–158. Foris, Dordrecht.

Poser, W. (1993). Are strict cycle effects derivable? In Hargus, S. and Kaisse, E., editors, *Studies in Lexical Phonology*, pages 315–321. Academic Press, New York.

Rogers, J., Heinz, J., Fero, M., Hurst, J., Lambert, D., and Wibel, S. (2013). Cognitive and sub-regular complexity. In *Formal Grammar*, number 8036 in Lecture Notes in Artificial Intelligence, pages 90–108. Springer.

Rogers, J. and Pullum, G. K. (2011). Aural pattern recognition experiments and the subregular hierarchy. *Journal of Logic, Language and Information*, 20:329–342.

Vaux, B. (2000). Disharmony and derived transparency in Uyghur vowel harmony. In *Proceedings of NELS 30*, pages 671–698.

Association for Computational Linguistics
209 N. Eighth Street
Stroudsburg, Pennsylvania 18360

ISBN 978-1-7138-1390-3